A
Garland
from the
Golden Age

A Garland from the Golden Age

AN ANTHOLOGY OF
CHILDREN'S LITERATURE FROM 1850 TO 1900

Edited by Patricia Demers

Toronto Oxford University Press 1983

FOR MY MOTHER AND FATHER

CANADIAN CATALOGUING IN PUBLICATION DATA
Main entry under title:
A Garland from the golden age
Includes index.
Bibliography: p.
ISBN 0-19-540414-9
1. Children's literature, English. I. Demers,
Patricia, 1946-
PR1145.G37   820'.8'09282   C83-098218-3

CONTENTS

ERRATA

Page 216: *The heading* Mary Louisa Stewart Charlesworth *should read* MARY LOUISA STEWART MOLESWORTH. *All references to Mary Louisa Stewart Charlesworth*—in the Table of Contents, on pages 219, 221, and in the Index— *should read* MARY LOUISA STEWART MOLESWORTH.

ILLUSTRATIONS

ACKNOWLEDGEMENTS

HILAIRE BELLOC. "The Hippopotamus" and "The Frog" from *The Bad Child's Book of Beasts*. Reprinted by permission of Gerald Duckworth & Co. Ltd. LUCY LANE CLIFFORD. "The New Mother" from *Anyhow Stories Moral and Otherwise* (Macmillan, 1882). WALTER DE LA MARE. All poems from *Songs of Childhood* by Walter de la Mare. Reprinted by permission of The Literary Trustees of Walter de la Mare and The Society of Authors as their representative. CHARLES LUTWIDGE DODGSON. "The Crocodile Song", "Twinkle, Twinkle, Little Bat", and "You are Old, Father William" from *Alice's Adventures in Wonderland* (Macmillan, 1865); "Jabberwocky" from *Through the Looking Glass and What Alice Found There* (Macmillan, 1872). NORMAN DUNCAN. "Delivering Her Majesty's Mail" from *The Adventures of Billy Topsail* by Norman Duncan. Reprinted by permission of Fleming H. Revell Company. EUGENE FIELD. All poems from *Poems of Childhood*. Reprinted courtesy Charles Scribner's Sons. KENNETH GRAHAME. "Exit Tyrannis" from *The Golden Age* by Kenneth Grahame is reproduced by permission of The Bodley Head. RUDYARD KIPLING. *Stalky & Co.* reprinted by permission of Jonathan Cape Ltd. HOWARD PYLE. *Pepper & Salt; or, Seasoning for Young Folk* (Harper & Row, Publishers, Inc.). JAMES WHITCOMB RILEY. All poems from *The Book of Joyous Children*. Reprinted courtesy Charles Scribner's Sons. CHRISTINA GEORGINA ROSSETTI. All poems from *Sing-Song. A Nursery Rhyme Book* (Macmillan, 1872); and "A Party in the Land of Nowhere" from *Speaking Likenesses* (Macmillan, 1874). *St. Nicholas; An Illustrated Magazine for Young Folk*, reprinted courtesy Charles Scribner's Sons. ERNEST THOMPSON SETON. "Silverspot: The Story of a Crow" from *Wild Animals I Have Known*. Copyright under the Berne Convention. Reprinted by permission of Charles Scribner's Sons. ROBERT LOUIS STEVENSON. All poems from A Child's Garden of Verse. Reprinted courtesy Charles Scribner's Sons.

PREFACE

When I was a sprig and my standards were low,
Uncritical, unautocratic,
I used to delight in Jack London and Poe,
Which I read in bed, bathroom, and attic.
Alas, that's the truth of my terrible youth,
Such the books I thought away above par.
Gee, I thought they were great in my juvenile state . . .
And I still am convinced that they are!
—*William Rose Benét, "Books et Veritas"*

Children are the true democrats among readers. Enthusiastic, venturesome, and, as Benét remembered, "uncritical", they welcome all kinds of books—not only delighting in those written specially for them but annexing some from adult shelves. They ask only that their books make claims on the imagination strong enough to transport them to another world.

In the second half of the nineteenth century—the richest short period in the history of children's literature—these readers had more varied and superb new books from which to choose than ever before. Stories and poems for the young, which had long been considered mainly as vehicles of moral instruction, underwent vast changes in style and subject, appearing as rich fantasies, intense and dramatic novels, thrilling adventures, lyric poetry of beguiling simplicity, and wonderfully outrageous nonsense verse. More often than not the writers of these books had one purpose: enjoyment. The half-century that produced such entertainment can properly be called the "Golden Age" of children's literature.

This anthology presents for modern readers some of the rich literary heritage that includes such masterpieces as Ruskin's *The King of the Golden River*, Hughes' *Tom Brown's Schooldays*, Dickens' *The Magic Fishbone*, Wilde's *The Happy Prince*, Grahame's *The Golden Age*, Rossetti's *Sing-Song*, and Stevenson's *A Child's Garden of Verses*, as well as many once-popular works by writers who are now largely forgotten and unjustly neglected: among them Frances Browne, Jean Ingelow, Flora Shaw, Hesba Stretton, Lucy Clifford, and Annie Keary. (Considerations of space have led to a decision to exclude readily available texts—like Carroll's *Alice* books, MacDonald's *Curdie* stories, and Kipling's *Jungle Books*—and concentrate instead on the lesser-known works.) Awaiting rediscovery are the jewelled descriptions of Browne's *Granny's Wonderful Chair*, the terrors of Clifford's *Anyhow Stories*, and the perils of Stretton's destitute orphan, "Little Meg", along with several selections revealing that all was not sweetness and light in the Golden Age. Shaw's *Castle Blair* describes youngsters planning to murder a hated adult, while

Keary's *Father Phim* places a heroic six-year-old girl in the midst of bloody sectarian violence. Though the miniature Victorians delineated in many of these books often strain credibility—they tend to be loquacious, knowledgeable, and for the most part supremely good—they are not mere idealizations but reflections of the rigorously high standards and prevailing middle-class expectations of another age.

To satisfy a widening readership for children's books during the Golden Age, more accessible genres—such as school and adventure stories—became highly popular, as did a less "respectable" form of publishing: lurid "penny dreadfuls" and "shilling shockers" that were churned out in weekly instalments by various hacks and money grubbers, and were devoured just as comic books are in our day. Since they were a prominent feature of the Victorian literary climate, they too have been represented here.

Quite apart from matters like literary quality and enjoyment, the writing that was taken up by young readers late in the nineteenth century reflects major social changes, the most noticeable of which was the role of women. While there were numerous women authors in the Golden Age and they employed female characters in fairy tales, evangelical tracts, domestic novels, and nursery fiction, women had been largely excluded from the male preserve of adventure stories and the more sensational "penny dreadfuls". In Edwardian England, however, the social climate encouraged the writing of stories about adventurous women, and this development is represented here by one of Bessie Marchant's many stories involving plucky girls. Not only did such books answer a felt need, and address a growing agitation for women's rights, but they were enjoyed by both adult women and young girls. Two genres that were especially affected by this trend were the murder mystery and the love story. (Very popular were Baroness Orczy's *Lady Molly of Scotland Yard* (1910) and H.G. Wells's *Ann Veronica: A Modern Love Story* (1909). Orczy—in twelve stories that combine some of the improbable ingredients of the dreadfuls with genuine suspense and skilled narration—writes about a member of the "Female Department of Scotland Yard", a mistress of disguises. The partly autobiographical Wells novel—about a young woman's affair with a married man who becomes a writer—enjoyed a *succès de scandale* and was very appealing to adolescent girls: the heroine, Ann Veronica, stood up to her father, took a room on her own in London, was imprisoned as a suffragette, and finally ran off to Switzerland with her lover.) And in the hands of Angela Brazil and Jean Webster the school story began to open its doors to female characters. The *Garland*'s closing date has been extended to include these writers.

Selections in this anthology have also been chosen to show that gifted writers for children were at work in North America as well as Britain in the Golden Age. They offer fresh glimpses of the stories and poems of such American writers as Helen Hunt Jackson, Thomas Bailey Aldrich, Joel Chandler Harris, Howard Pyle, and James Whitcomb Riley. I have a particular interest in early Canadian children's literature, much of which was esteemed in its day, and rightly so. The inclusion of formerly prominent Canadian authors—James De Mille, Margaret Murray Robertson, Norman Duncan, W.A. Fraser, and Catharine Parr Traill—should dispel the notion that praiseworthy and internationally recognized stories for children did not originate (or were not set) in Canada until the first decades of the twentieth century.

The cornucopia of Golden Age literature exerted a long and lasting influence—on reading tastes and publishing trends as well as on artistic endeavours. The legacy of the best Golden Age books is still evident in outstanding literature for children today.

One of the most pleasant and humbling features of bringing a project to completion is acknowledging the many debts of gratitude incurred. A travel grant from the Faculty of Arts, University of Alberta, enabled me to continue research at the Osborne Collection, Toronto Public Library; another from the Social Sciences and Humanities Research Committee of the University allowed me to do further work in London and also defrayed the cost of photographic reproductions. Librarians in many institutions have been helpful. For their co-operation I am particularly grateful to Angie Renville, Curator of the Library Science Collection at the University of Alberta; to Margaret Maloney, Dana Tenny, and Jill Shefrin of the Osborne Collection; and to Robert Howell of the Victoria and Albert Museum Library. The typists in the Department of English of the University of Alberta have been consistently patient and cheerful with my almost endless requests. I wish to thank Sheila Egoff for the benefit of her comments during a long and informative summer conversation. As in the earlier volume, I am especially thankful to my editor, William Toye, for his support and guidance.

PATRICIA DEMERS

University of Alberta
November 1982

A
Garland
from the
Golden Age

1. BEAUTY, HUMOUR, AND TERROR: THE FAIRY TALE

In an utilitarian age, of all other times, it is a matter of grave importance that Fairy tales should be respected. . . . They must be as much preserved in their simplicity, and purity, and innocent extravagance, as if they were actual fact.—Charles Dickens, "Frauds on the Fairies", Household Words *(1 October 1853).*

At mid-century fairy tales available to English readers were mainly translations: Perrault had been translated as far back as 1729, the Grimm Brothers in 1823, and Hans Christian Andersen in 1846. Children appreciated their storytelling qualities, and God-fearing parents approved of their succinct moral teaching. The invented English fairy tale, before 1850, had made only a tentative appearance—embedded in Catherine Sinclair's *Holiday House* (1839) and providing the narrative scheme for Francis Paget's *The Hope of the Katzekopfs: A Fairy Tale* (1844): both novels have malicious giants and an abundance of magical happenings that delighted young readers, and both used the fairy-tale form to teach some daunting lessons—an ingredient that pleased their elders. The genre rose in general esteem when it attracted the interest of some of the leading literary artists of the day. John Ruskin's *The King of the Golden River* was published in 1851, William Make-

peace Thackeray's *The Rose and the Ring* in 1855. In his weekly, *Household Words*, Dickens lamented the bowdlerizing of fairy stories—those "nurseries of fancy"—in the retold *Fairy Library* of the brilliant illustrator but misguided editor, George Cruikshank: "Whosoever alters them to suit his own opinions, whatever they are, is guilty, to our thinking, of an act of presumption, and appropriates to himself what does not belong to him." Dickens himself published *A Holiday Romance*, containing "The Magic Fishbone", in 1868. And Ruskin, in his Introduction to a reissue of Edgar Taylor's translation of Grimm in *German Popular Stories* (1868), composed an eloquent tribute to his "favorite old stories", praising fairy tales as a means of "exercising [the] power of grasping realities". Jean Ingelow's *Mopsa the Fairy* (1869), Christina Rossetti's *Speaking Likenesses* (1874), and Oscar Wilde's *The Happy Prince* (1888) are among the scores of highly popular invented fairy tales that were published until the close of the century (and a little beyond). The last decade of the Golden Age was crowned by the numerous volumes of Andrew Lang's retellings of classic fairy tales and by Joseph Jacob's works on British folklore.

Whether celebrated or obscure, all the writers featured in this section wrote stories that had many common elements: magic objects and agents, a journey to another world either dreamed or realized, and frequent transformations. (Two of them are open imitations of *Alice in Wonderland*.) They created more subtle characterizations than were usually found in European fairy tales, and had a fondness for highly coloured descriptions. The stories normally begin with a formulaic opening, sometimes explaining the entry into the fairy realm: Jean Ingelow has her boy-hero climb inside the hollow of a massive thorn tree, and George Farrow whisks his young adventurers out of a flooded cottage into a "marvellous journey". Other stories start with the conventional "Once upon a time" (Browne) or "In old time" (Ruskin). Many plunge into the action by introducing the main characters immediately: "A little boy named Ernest was once playing at ball" (Knatchbull-Hugessen) or "The children were always called Blue Eyes and the Turkey" (Clifford). As in the classic European fairy tales, the moral and didactic components of the themes are conveyed by simple yet incisive contrasts: against an easily acquired reward stands the enduring value of an everlasting one; next to the gaudy parade of riches are set the humble virtues of poverty; selfishness has its foil in quiet dutifulness. Tables are often turned, true identities discovered, and fitting prizes and punishments meted out.

Fairies do not always appear in these stories. When they do they rarely wear the satin gowns and lamé capes we might expect—Mrs Calkill, in Annie Keary's *Little Wanderlin** (1865), wears a grey pelisse and high frilled cap, and Dickens' grandmotherly Fairy Grandmarina is dressed in shot-silk "of the richest quality"—nor do they simply spread their wands over passive and insipid characters. The ferocious Mrs Calkill, a governess, threatens the title character with a dreadful nutcracker if he does not keep busy, and can bring about alarming transformations. Fairy Grandmarina gives her magic fishbone to a resourceful child who must decide for herself when to use it.

Considerations of space have meant that the most topical form of Victorian fairy tale, the court satire, is not represented in this anthology. Best exemplified in Thackeray's *The Rose and the Ring* and Tom Hood's *Petsetilla's Posy* (1870), these witty but lengthy narratives poke gentle fun at the whole traditional cast of noble monarchs, gracious princesses, and stalwart princes.

The finest of these Golden Age tales do not limit themselves to topical satire; nor do they indulge in tedious moralizing. Instead of dinning instructional points, the narratives of Ruskin, Browne, and Wilde especially make effective use of lush descriptions and symbolism drawn from nature: they pave the way for de la Mare, Sandburg, and Ransome. A special bonus for modern readers is the elegance of all these tales; this is apparent not only in their simplicity but in their blending of lyricism, humour, and terror. Finally they are good stories: their inventions, characters, emotional appeal, and compelling action can be enjoyed today just as they were enjoyed in the Golden Age.

---

* This has not been included, for reasons of space; however, Annie Keary's *Father Phim* is presented on pp. 233-49.

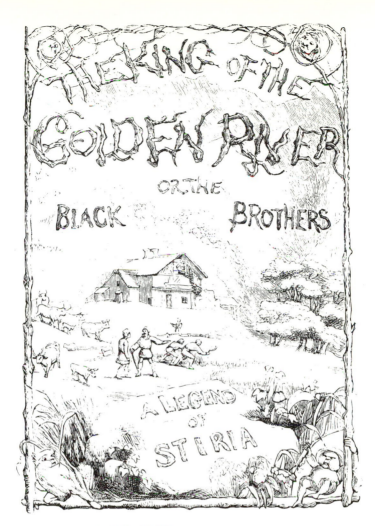

JOHN RUSKIN (1819-1900)
The King of the Golden River; or, The Black Brothers:
A Legend of Styria (1851)

Ruskin wrote *The King of the Golden River*—a decade before it was published—for a twelve-year-old girl who later became his wife. Since he was a life-long devotee of the works of the Brothers Grimm, it is fitting that he based his only fairy story on their tale "The Water of Life", which relates the search of an ageing king for his youth. *The King of the Golden River* is another quest story; but it opposes virtue and greed, stressing rewards and punishments, as the selfless Gluck and his two wicked brothers go in search of a golden river that is offered by the South West Wind to the most virtuous of the three. Nature—always described with eloquence by Ruskin—is a dominant force in this story, whether it is presented in the form of the powerful South West Wind, in the descriptions of the majestic valley through which the brothers journey, or in the transformations that are inflicted on two of the brothers.

In his defence of fairy stories in *German Popular Stories*, written seventeen years after *The King of the Golden River*, Ruskin praised "the simplicity of [their] sense of beauty" and "the simplicity of their conception of love". These two features also distinguish his own classic fairy tale.

CHAPTER 1

How the Agricultural System of the Black Brothers Was
Interfered with by Southwest Wind, Esquire

In a secluded and mountainous part of Stiria there was, in old time, a valley of the most surprising and luxuriant fertility. It was surrounded, on all sides, by steep and rocky mountains, rising into peaks which were always covered with snow, and from which a number of torrents descended in constant cataracts. One of these fell westward over the face of a crag so high, that, when the sun had set to everything else, and all below was darkness, his beams still shone full upon this waterfall, so that it looked like a shower of gold. It was, therefore, called by the people of the neighborhood, the Golden River. It was strange that none of these streams fell into the valley itself. They all descended on the other side of the mountains, and wound away through broad plains and past populous cities. But the clouds were drawn so constantly to the snowy hills, and rested so softly in the circular hollow, that in time of drought and heat, when all the country round was burnt up, there was still rain in the little valley; and its crops were so heavy, and its hay so high, and its apples so red, and its grapes so blue, and its wine so rich, and its honey so sweet, that it was a marvel to every one who beheld it, and was commonly called the Treasure Valley.

The whole of this little valley belonged to three brothers called Schwartz, Hans, and Gluck. Schwartz and Hans, the two elder brothers, were very ugly men, with overhanging eyebrows and small dull eyes, which were always half shut, so that you could not see into them, and always fancied they saw very far into you. They lived by farming the Treasure Valley, and very good farmers they were. They killed everything that did not pay for its eating. They shot the blackbirds, because they pecked the fruit; and killed the hedgehogs, lest they should suck the cows; they poisoned the crickets for eating the crumbs in the kitchen; and smothered the cicadas, which used to sing all summer in the lime trees. They worked their servants without any wages, till they would not work any more, and then quarrelled with them, and turned them out of doors without paying them. It would have been very odd if with such a farm and such a system of farming they hadn't got very rich; and very rich they did get. They generally contrived to keep their corn by them till it was very dear, and then sell it for twice its value; they had heaps of gold lying about on their floors, yet it was never known that they had given so much as a penny or a crust in charity; they never went to mass; grumbled perpetually at paying tithes; and were, in a word, of so cruel and grinding a temper, as to receive from all those with whom they had any dealings, the nickname of the "Black Brothers."

The youngest brother, Gluck, was as completely opposed, in both appearance and character, to his seniors as could possibly be imagined or desired. He was not above twelve years old, fair, blue-eyed, and kind in temper to every living thing. He did not, of course, agree particularly well with his brothers, or rather, they did not agree with him. He was usually appointed to the honorable office of turnspit, when there was anything to roast, which was not often; for, to do the brothers justice, they were hardly less sparing upon themselves than upon other people. At other times he used to clean the shoes, floors, and sometimes the plates, occasionally getting what was left on them, by way of encouragement, and a wholesome quantity of dry blows, by way of education.

Things went on in this manner for a long time. At last came a very wet summer, and everything went wrong in the country around. The hay had hardly been got in when the haystacks were floated bodily down to the sea by an inundation; the vines were cut to pieces with the hail; the corn was all killed by a black blight; only in the Treasure Valley, as usual, all was safe. As it had rain when there was rain nowhere else, so it had sun when there was sun nowhere else. Everybody came to buy corn at the farm, and went away pouring maledictions on the Black Brothers. They asked what they liked, and got it, except from the poor people, who could only beg, and several of whom were starved at their very door without the slightest regard.

It was drawing towards winter, and very cold weather, when one day the two elder brothers had gone out, with their usual warning to little Gluck, who was left to mind the roast, that he was to let nobody in and give nothing out. Gluck sat down quite close to the fire, for it was raining very hard, and the kitchen walls were by no means dry or comfortable looking. He turned and turned, and the roast got nice and brown. "What a pity," thought Gluck, "my brothers never ask anybody to dinner. I'm sure when they have such a nice piece of mutton as this, and nobody else has so much as a piece of dry bread, it would do their hearts good to have somebody to eat it with them."

Just as he spoke there came a double knock at the house door, yet heavy and dull, as though the knocker had been tied up—more like a puff than a knock.

"It must be the wind," said Gluck; "nobody else would venture to knock double knocks at our door."

No; it wasn't the wind: there it came again very hard; and what was particularly astounding, the knocker seemed to be in a hurry, and not to be in the least afraid of the consequences. Gluck went to the window, opened it, and put his head out to see who it was.

It was the most extraordinary-looking little gentleman he had ever seen in his life. He had a very large nose, slightly brass-colored; his cheeks were very round, and very red, and might have warranted a supposition that he had been blowing a refractory fire for the last eight-and-forty hours; his eyes twinkled merrily through long silky eyelashes, his moustaches curled twice round like a corkscrew on each side of his mouth, and his hair, of a curious mixed pepper-and-salt color, descended far over his shoulders. He was about four-feet-six in height,

and wore a conical pointed cap of nearly the same altitude, decorated with a black feather some three feet long. His doublet was prolonged behind into something resembling a violent exaggeration of what is now termed a "swallow tail," but was much obscured by the swelling folds of an enormous black, glossy-looking cloak, which must have been very much too long in calm weather, as the wind, whistling round the old house, carried it clear out from the wearer's shoulders to about four times his own length.

Gluck was so perfectly paralyzed by the singular appearance of his visitor that he remained fixed without uttering a word, until the old gentleman, having performed another and a more energetic concerto on the knocker, turned round to look after his fly-away cloak. In so doing he caught sight of Gluck's little yellow head jammed in the window, with his mouth and eyes very wide open indeed.

"Hollo!" said the little gentleman, "that's not the way to answer the door: I'm wet, let me in."

To do the little gentleman justice, he was wet. His feather hung down between his legs like a beaten puppy's tail, dripping like an umbrella; and from the ends of his moustaches the water was running into his waistcoat pockets, and out again like a mill stream.

"I beg pardon, sir," said Gluck, "I'm very sorry, but I really can't."

"Can't what?" said the old gentleman.

"I can't let you in, sir—I can't indeed; my brothers would beat me to death, sir, if I thought of such a thing. What do you want, sir?"

"Want?" said the old gentleman, petulantly. "I want fire and shelter; and there's your great fire there, blazing, crackling, and dancing on the walls, with nobody to feel it. Let me in, I say; I only want to warm myself."

Gluck had had his head so long out of the window by this time that he began to feel it was really unpleasantly cold, and when he turned and saw the beautiful fire rustling and roaring, and throwing long bright tongues up the chimney, as if it were licking its chops at the savory smell of the leg of mutton, his heart melted within him that it should be burning away for nothing. "He does look very wet," said little Gluck; "I'll just let him in for a quarter of an hour." Round he went to the door and opened it; and as the little gentleman walked in there came a gust of wind through the house that made the old chimneys totter.

"That's a good boy," said the little gentleman. "Never mind your brothers. I'll talk to them."

"Pray, sir, don't do any such thing," said Gluck. "I can't let you stay till they come; they'd be the death of me."

"Dear me," said the old gentleman, "I'm very sorry to hear that. How long may I stay?"

"Only till the mutton's done, sir," replied Gluck, "and it's very brown."

Then the old gentleman walked into the kitchen, and sat himself down on the hob, with the top of his cap accommodated up the chimney, for it was a great deal too high for the roof.

"You'll soon dry there, sir," said Gluck, and sat down again to turn the mutton. But the old gentleman did not dry there, but went on drip, drip, dripping among the cinders, and the fire fizzed, and sputtered, and began to look very black and uncomfortable. Never was such a cloak; every fold in it ran like a gutter.

"I beg pardon, sir," said Gluck at length, after watching for a quarter of an hour the water spreading in long, quicksilver-like streams over the floor; "may I take your cloak?"

"No, thank you," said the old gentleman.

"Your cap, sir?"

"I am all right, thank you," said the old gentleman, rather gruffly.

"But,—sir,—I'm very sorry," said Gluck, hesitatingly; "but—really, sir,—you're—putting the fire out."

"It'll take longer to do the mutton, then," replied his visitor, dryly.

Gluck was very much puzzled by the behavior of his guest; it was such a strange mixture of coolness and humility. He turned away at the string meditatively for another five minutes.

"That mutton looks very nice," said the old gentleman at length. "Can't you give me a little bit."

"Impossible, sir," said Gluck.

"I'm very hungry," continued the old gentleman; "I've had nothing to eat yesterday nor to-day. They surely couldn't miss a bit from the knuckle!"

He spoke in so very melancholy a tone that it quite melted Gluck's heart. "They promised me one slice to-day, sir," said he; "I can give you that, but not a bit more."

"That's a good boy," said the old gentleman again.

Then Gluck warmed a plate, and sharpened a knife. "I don't care if I do get beaten for it," thought he. Just as he had cut a large slice out of the mutton, there came a tremendous rap at the door. The old gentleman jumped off the hob, as if it had suddenly become inconveniently warm. Gluck fitted the slice into the mutton again, with desperate efforts at exactitude, and ran to open the door.

"What did you keep us waiting in the rain for?" said Schwartz, as he walked in, throwing his umbrella in Gluck's face. "Ay! what for, indeed, you little vagabond?" said Hans, administering an educational box on the ear, as he followed his brother into the kitchen.

"Bless my soul!" said Schwartz when he opened the door.

"Amen," said the little gentleman, who had taken his cap off, and was standing in the middle of the kitchen, bowing with the utmost possible velocity.

"Who's that?" said Schwartz, catching up a rolling-pin, and turning to Gluck with a fierce frown.

"I don't know, indeed, brother," said Gluck in great terror.

"How did he get in?" roared Schwartz.

"My dear brother," said Gluck, deprecatingly, "he was so very wet!"

The rolling-pin was descending on Gluck's head; but at the instant the old gentleman interposed his conical cap, on which it crashed with a shock that shook the water out of it all over the room. What was very odd, the rolling-pin no sooner touched the cap than it flew out of Schwartz's hand, spinning like a straw in a high wind, and fell into the corner at the further end of the room.

"Who are you, sir?" demanded Schwartz, turning upon him.

"What's your business?" snarled Hans.

"I'm a poor old man, sir," the little gentleman began very modestly, "and I saw your fire through the window, and begged shelter for a quarter of an hour."

"Have the goodness to walk out again, then," said Schwartz. "We've quite enough water in our kitchen without making it a drying-house."

"It is a cold day to turn an old man out in, sir; look at my gray hairs." They hung down to his shoulders, as I told you before.

"Ay!" said Hans, "there are enough of them to keep you warm. Walk!"

"I'm very, very hungry, sir; couldn't you spare me a bit of bread before I go?"

"Bread, indeed!" said Schwartz; "do you suppose we've nothing to do with our bread but to give it to such red-nosed fellows as you?"

"Why don't you sell your feather?" said Hans; sneeringly. "Out with you!"

"A little bit," said the old gentleman.

"Be off!" said Schwartz.

"Pray, gentlemen—"

"Off, and be hanged!" cried Hans, seizing him by the collar. But he had no sooner touched the old gentleman's collar, than away he went after the rolling-pin, spinning round and round, till he fell into the corner on the top of it. Then Schwartz was very angry, and ran at the old gentleman to turn him out; but he also had hardly touched him, when away he went after Hans and the rolling-pin, and hit his head against the wall as he tumbled into the corner. And so there they lay, all three.

Then the old gentleman spun himself round with velocity in the opposite direction; continued to spin until his long cloak was all wound neatly about him; clapped his cap on his head, very much on one side (for it could not stand upright without going through the ceiling), gave an additional twist to his corkscrew moustaches, and replied with perfect coolness: "Gentlemen, I wish you a very good morning. At twelve o'clock to-night I'll call again; after such a refusal of hospitality as I have just experienced, you will not be surprised if that visit is the last I ever pay you."

"If ever I catch you here again," muttered Schwartz, coming, half frightened, out of the corner—but, before he could finish his sentence, the old gentleman had shut the house door behind him with a great bang: and there drove past the window, at the same instant, a wreath of ragged cloud, that whirled and rolled away down the valley in all manner of shapes; turning over and over in the air, and melting away at last in a gush of rain.

"A very pretty business, indeed, Mr. Gluck!" said Schwartz. "Dish the mutton, sir. If ever I catch you at such a trick again—bless me, why the mutton's been cut!"

"You promised me one slice, brother, you know," said Gluck.

"Oh! and you were cutting it hot, I suppose, and going to catch all the gravy. It'll be long before I promise you such a thing again. Leave the room, sir; and have the kindness to wait in the coal-cellar till I call you."

Gluck left the room melancholy enough. The brothers ate as much mutton as they could, locked the rest into the cupboard, and proceeded to get very drunk after dinner.

Such a night as it was! Howling wind, and rushing rain, without intermission. The brothers had just sense enough left to put up all the shutters, and double bar the door, before they went to bed. They usually slept in the same room. As the clock struck twelve, they were both awakened by a tremendous crash. Their door burst open with a violence that shook the house from top to bottom.

"What's that?" cried Schwartz, starting up in his bed.

"Only I," said the little gentleman.

The two brothers sat up on their bolster, and stared into the darkness. The room was full of water; and by a misty moonbeam, which found its way through a hole in the shutter, they could see in the midst of it an enormous foam globe, spinning round, and bobbing up and down like a cork, on which, as on a most luxurious cushion, reclined the little old gentleman, cap and all. There was plenty of room for it now, for the roof was off.

"Sorry to incommode you," said their visitor, ironically. "I'm afraid your beds are dampish; perhaps you had better go to your brother's room: I've left the ceiling on there."

They required no second admonition, but rushed into Gluck's room, wet through, and in an agony of terror.

"You'll find my card on the kitchen table," the old gentleman called after them. "Remember, the last visit."

"Pray Heaven it may!" said Schwartz, shuddering. And the foam globe disappeared.

Dawn came at last, and the two brothers looked out of Gluck's little window in the morning. The Treasure Valley was one mass of ruin and desolation. The inundation had swept away trees, crops, and cattle, and left in their stead a waste of red sand and gray mud. The two brothers crept shivering and horror-struck into the kitchen. The water had gutted the whole first floor; corn, money, almost every movable thing had been swept away, and there was left only a small white card on the kitchen table. On it, in large, breezy, long-legged letters, were engraved the words:—

CHAPTER 2

Of the Proceedings of the Three Brothers After the Visit of Southwest Wind,
Esquire; and How Little Gluck Had an Interview with the
King of the Golden River

Southwest Wind, Esquire, was as good as his word. After the momentous visit above related, he entered the Treasure Valley no more; and what was worse, he had so much influence with his relations, the West Winds in general, and used it so effectually, that they all adopted a similar line of conduct. So no rain fell in the valley from one year's end to another. Though everything remained green and flourishing in the plains below, the inheritance of the Three Brothers was a desert. What had once been the richest soil in the kingdom became a shifting heap of red sand; and the brothers, unable longer to contend with the adverse skies, abandoned their valueless patrimony in despair, to seek some means of gaining a livelihood among the cities and people of the plains. All their money was gone, and they had nothing left but some curious, old-fashioned pieces of gold plate, the last remnants of their ill-gotten wealth.

"Suppose we turn goldsmiths?" said Schwartz to Hans, as they entered the large city. "It is a good knave's trade; we can put a great deal of copper into the gold without any one's finding it out."

The thought was agreed to be a very good one; they hired a furnace, and turned goldsmiths. But two slight circumstances affected their trade: the first, that people did not approve of the coppered gold; the second, that the two elder brothers whenever they had sold anything used to leave little Gluck to mind the furnace, and go and drink out the money in the ale-house next door. So they melted all their gold, without making money enough to buy more, and were at last reduced to one large drinking mug, which an uncle of his had given to little Gluck, and which he was very fond of, and would not have parted with for the world; though he never drank anything out of it but milk and water. The mug was a very odd mug to look at. The handle was formed of two wreaths of flowing golden hair, so finely spun that it looked more like silk than metal, and these wreaths descended into and mixed with a beard and whiskers of the same exquisite workmanship, which surrounded and decorated a very fierce little face, of the reddest gold imaginable, right in the front of the mug, with a pair of eyes in it which seemed to command its whole circumference. It was impossible to drink from the mug without being subjected to an intense gaze out of the side of these eyes; and Schwartz positively averred that once after emptying it full of Rhenish seventeen times he had seen them wink! When it came to the mug's turn to be made into spoons, it half broke poor little Gluck's heart; but the brothers only laughed at him, tossed the mug into the melting-pot, and staggered out to the ale-house, leaving him, as usual, to pour the gold into bars, when it was all ready.

When they were gone, Gluck took a farewell look at his old friend in the melting-pot. The flowing hair was all gone; nothing remained but the red nose and the sparkling eyes, which looked more malicious than ever. "And no wonder," thought Gluck, "after being treated in that way." He sauntered disconsolately to the window, and sat himself down to catch the fresh evening air, and escape the hot breath of the furnace. Now this window commanded a direct view of the range of mountains, which, as I told you before, overhung the Treasure Valley, and more especially of the peak from which fell the Golden River. It was just at the close of the day; and when Gluck sat down at the window, he saw the rocks of the mountain tops all crimson and purple with the sunset. There were bright tongues of fiery cloud burning and quivering about them; and the river, brighter than all, fell in a waving column of pure gold from precipice to precipice, with the double arch of a broad purple rainbow stretched across it, flushing and fading alternately in the wreaths of spray.

"Ah!" said Gluck aloud, after he had looked at it for a while, "if that river were really all gold, what a nice thing it would be."

"No, it wouldn't, Gluck," said a clear metallic voice, close at his ear.

"Bless me! what's that?" exclaimed Gluck, jumping up. There was nobody there. He looked round the room, and under the table, and a great many times behind him, but there was certainly nobody there, and he sat down again at the window. This time he did not speak, but he could not help thinking again that it would be very convenient if the river were really all gold.

"Not at all, my boy," said the same voice, louder than before.

"Bless me!" said Gluck again, "what is that?" He looked again into all the corners and cupboards, and then began turning round and round as fast as he could in the middle of the room, thinking there was somebody behind him, when the same voice struck again on his ear. It was singing now very merrily, "Lala-lira-la"; no words, only a soft, running, effervescent melody, something like that of a kettle on the boil. Gluck looked out of the window. No, it was certainly in the house. Upstairs, and downstairs. No, it was certainly in that very room, coming in quicker time and clearer notes every moment. "Lala-lira-la." All at once it struck Gluck that it sounded louder near the furnace. He ran to the opening, and looked in: it seemed to be coming not only out of the furnace, but out of the pot. He uncovered it, and ran back in a great fright, for the pot was certainly singing! He stood in the farthest corner of the room for a minute or two with his hands up and his mouth open, when the singing stopped, and the voice became clear and distinct.

"Hullo!" said the voice.

Gluck made no answer

"Hullo! Gluck, my boy," said the pot again.

Gluck summoned all his energies, walked straight up to the crucible, drew it out of the furnace and looked in. The gold was all melted, and its surface as smooth and polished as a river; but instead of reflecting little Gluck's head as he looked in, he saw meeting his glance from beneath the gold the red nose and sharp eyes of his old friend of the mug, a thousand times redder and sharper than ever he had seen them in his life.

"Come, Gluck, my boy," said the voice out of the pot again, "I'm all right; pour me out."

But Gluck was too much astonished to do anything of the kind.

"Pour me out, I say," said the voice, rather gruffly.

Still Gluck couldn't move.

"Will you pour me out?" said the voice, passionately, "I'm too hot."

By a violent effort Gluck recovered the use of his limbs, took hold of the crucible, and sloped it so as to pour out the gold. But instead of a liquid stream there came out, first, a pair of pretty little yellow legs, then some coat tails, then a pair of arms stuck a-kimbo, and, finally, the well-known head of his friend the mug; all which articles, uniting as they rolled out, stood up energetically on the floor, in the shape of a little golden dwarf about a foot and a half high.

"That's right!" said the dwarf, stretching out first his legs, and then his arms, and then shaking his head up and down, and as far round as it

would go, for five minutes without stopping, apparently with the view of ascertaining if he were quite correctly put together, while Gluck stood contemplating him in speechless amazement. He was dressed in a slashed doublet of spun gold, so fine in its texture that the prismatic colors gleamed over it, as if on a surface of mother of pearl; and over this brilliant doublet his hair and beard fell full halfway to the ground in waving curls, so exquisitely delicate, that Gluck could hardly tell where they ended; they seemed to melt into air. The features of the face, however, were by no means finished with the same delicacy; they were rather coarse, slightly inclining to coppery in complexion, and indicative, in expression, of a very pertinacious and intractable disposition in their small proprietor. When the dwarf had finished his self-examination, he turned his small sharp eyes full on Gluck, and stared at him deliberately for a minute or two. "No, it wouldn't, Gluck, my boy," said the little man.

This was certainly rather an abrupt way of commencing conversation. It might indeed be supposed to refer to the course of Gluck's thoughts, which had first produced the dwarf's observations out of the pot; but whatever it referred to, Gluck had no inclination to dispute what he said.

"Wouldn't it, sir?" said Gluck, very mildly and submissively indeed.

"No," said the dwarf, conclusively. "No, it wouldn't." And with that the dwarf pulled his cap hard over his brows, and took two turns, of three feet long, up and down the room, lifting his legs up very high and setting them down very hard. This pause gave time for Gluck to collect his thoughts a little, and seeing no great reason to view his diminutive visitor with dread, and feeling his curiosity overcome his amazement, he ventured a question of peculiar delicacy.

"Pray, sir," said Gluck, rather hesitatingly, "were you my mug?"

On which the little man turned sharp round, walked straight up to Gluck, and drew himself up to his full height. "I," said the little man, "am the King of the Golden River." Whereupon he turned about again, and took two more turns some six feet long in order to allow time for the consternation which this announcement produced in his auditor to evaporate. After which he again walked up to Gluck and stood still, as if expecting some comment on his communication.

Gluck determined to say something at all events. "I hope your Majesty is very well," said Gluck.

"Listen!" said the little man, deigning no reply to this polite inquiry. "I am the King of what you mortals call the Golden River. The shape you saw me in was owing to the malice of a stronger king, from whose enchantments you have this instant freed me. What I have seen of you, and your conduct toward your wicked brothers, renders me willing to serve you; therefore, attend to what I tell you. Whoever shall climb to the top of that mountain from which you see the Golden River issue, and shall cast into the stream at its source three drops of holy water, for him, and for him only, the river shall turn to gold. But no one failing in his first can succeed in a second attempt; and if any one shall cast unholy water into the river it will overwhelm him, and he will become a black stone." So saying, the King of the Golden River turned away and deliberately walked into the centre of the hottest flame of the furnace. His figure became red, white, transparent, dazzling,—a blaze of intense light—rose, trembled, and disappeared. The King of the Golden River had evaporated.

"Oh!" cried poor Gluck, running to look up the chimney after him; "oh dear, dear, dear me! My mug! my mug! my mug!"

CHAPTER 3

How Mr. Hans Set Off on an Expedition to the Golden River
and How He Prospered Therein

The King of the Golden River had hardly made the extraordinary exit related in the last chapter, before Hans and Schwartz came roaring into the house very savagely drunk. The discovery of the total loss of their last piece of plate had the effect of sobering them just enough to enable them to stand over Gluck, beating him very steadily for a quarter of an hour; at the expiration of which period they dropped into a couple of chairs, and requested to know what he had got to say for himself. Gluck told them his story, of which, of course, they did not believe a word. They beat him again, till their arms were tired, and staggered to bed. In the morning, however, the steadiness with which he adhered to his story obtained him some degree of credence; the immediate consequence of which was that the two brothers, after wrangling a long time on the knotty question, which of them should try his fortune first, drew their swords and began fighting. The noise of the fray alarmed the neighbors, who, finding they could not pacify the combatants, sent for the constable.

On hearing this, Hans contrived to escape, and hid himself; but Schwartz was taken before the magistrate, fined for breaking the peace, and having drunk out his last penny the evening before, was thrown into prison till he should pay.

When Hans heard this, he was much delighted, and determined to set out immediately for the Golden River. How to get the holy water was the question. He went to the priest, but the priest could not give any holy water to so abandoned a character. So Hans went to vespers in the evening for the first time in his life, and, under pretence of crossing himself, stole a cupful and returned home in triumph.

Next morning he got up before the sun rose, put the holy water into a strong flask, and two bottles of wine and some meat in a basket, slung them over his back, took his alpine staff in his hand, and set off for the mountains.

On his way out of the town he had to pass the prison, and as he looked in at the windows, whom should he see but Schwartz himself peeping out of the bars, and looking very disconsolate.

"Good morning, brother," said Hans; "have you any message for the King of the Golden River?"

Schwartz gnashed his teeth with rage, and shook the bars with all his strength; but Hans only laughed at him, and advising him to make himself comfortable till he came back again, shouldered his basket, shook the bottle of his holy water in Schwartz's face till it frothed again, and marched off in the highest spirits in the world.

It was indeed a morning that might have made any one happy, even with no Golden River to seek for. Level lines of dewy mist lay stretched along the valley, out of which rose the massy mountains—their lower cliffs in pale gray shadows, hardly distinguishable from the floating vapor, but gradually ascending till they caught the sunlight, which ran in sharp touches of ruddy color along the angular crags, and pierced, in long level rays, through their fringes of spear-like pine. Far above, shot up red splintered masses of castellated rock, jagged and shivered into myriads of fantastic forms, with here and there a streak of sunlit snow, traced down their chasms like a line of forked lightning; and far beyond and above all these, fainter than the morning cloud, but purer and changeless, slept in the blue sky the utmost peaks of the eternal snow.

The Golden River, which sprang from one of the lower and snowless elevations, was now nearly in shadow; all but the uppermost jets of spray, which rose like slow smoke above the undulating line of the cataract, and floated away in feeble wreaths upon the morning wind.

On this object, and on this alone, Hans' eyes and thoughts were fixed. Forgetting the distance he had to traverse, he set off at an imprudent rate of walking, which greatly exhausted him before he had scaled the first range of the green and low hills. He was, moreover, surprised, on surmounting them, to find that a large glacier, of whose existence, notwithstanding his previous knowledge of the mountains, he had been absolutely ignorant, lay between him and the source of the Golden River. He mounted it though, with the boldness of a practiced mountaineer; yet he thought he had never in his life traversed so strange or so dangerous a glacier. The ice was excessively slippery, and out of all its chasms came wild sounds of gushing water; not monotonous or low, but changeful and loud, rising occasionally into drifting passages of wild melody, then breaking off into short melancholy tones, or sudden shrieks, resembling those of human voices in distress or pain. The ice was broken into thousands of confused shapes, but none, Hans thought, like the ordinary forms of splintered ice. There seemed a curious expression about all their outlines—a perpetual resemblance to living features, distorted and scornful. Myriads of deceitful shadows, and lurid lights, played and floated about the through the pale blue pinnacles, dazzling and confusing the sight of the traveller; while his ears grew dull and his head giddy with the constant gush and roar of the concealed waters. These painful circumstances increased upon him as he advanced; the ice crashed and yawned into fresh chasms at his feet, tottering spires nodded around him, and fell thundering across his path; and though he had repeatedly faced these dangers on the most terrific glaciers, and in the wildest weather, it was with a new and oppressive feeling of panic terror that he leaped the last chasm, and flung himself, exhausted and shuddering, on the firm turf of the mountain.

He had been compelled to abandon his basket of food, which became a perilous incumbrance on the glacier, and had now no means of refreshing himself but by breaking off and eating some of the pieces of ice. This, however, relieved his thirst; an hour's repose recruited his hardy frame, and with the indomitable spirit of avarice, he resumed his laborious journey.

His way now lay straight up a ridge of bare red rocks, without a blade of grass to ease the foot, or a projecting angle to afford an inch of shade from the south sun. It was past noon, and the rays beat intensely upon the steep path, while the whole atmosphere was motionless and penetrated with heat. Intense thirst was soon added to the bodily fatigue with which Hans was now afflicted; glance after glance he cast on the flask of water which hung at his belt. "Three drops are enough," at last thought he; "I may at least cool my lips with it."

He opened the flask, and was raising it to his lips, when his eye fell on an object lying on the rock beside him; he thought it moved. It was a small dog, apparently in the last agony of death from thirst. Its tongue was out, its jaws dry, its limbs extended lifelessly, and a swarm of black ants were crawling about its lips and throat. Its eye moved to the bottle which Hans held in his hand. He raised it, drank, spurned the animal with his foot and passed on. And he did not know how it was, but he thought that a strange shadow had suddenly come across the blue sky.

The path became steeper and more rugged every moment; and the

high hill air, instead of refreshing him, seemed to throw his blood into a fever. The noise of the hill cataracts sounded like mockery in his ears; they were all distant and his thirst increased every moment. Another hour passed, and he again looked down to the flask at his side; and it was half empty, but there was much more than three drops in it. He stopped to open it and again, as he did so, something moved in the path above him. It was a fair child, stretched nearly lifeless on the rock, its breast heaving with thirst, its eyes closed, and its lips parched and burning. Hans eyed it deliberately, drank, and passed on. And a dark gray cloud came over the sun, and long, snake-like shadows crept up along the mountain-sides. Hans struggled on. The sun was sinking, but its descent seemed to bring no coolness; the leaden weight of the dead air pressed upon his brow and heart, but the goal was near. He saw the cataract of the Golden River springing from the hill-side, scarcely five hundred feet above him. He paused for a moment to breathe, and sprang on to complete his task.

At this instant a faint cry fell on his ear. He turned, and saw a gray-haired old man extended on the rocks. His eyes were sunk, his features deadly pale, and gathered into an expression of despair. "Water!" he stretched his arms to Hans, and cried feebly, "Water! I am dying."

"I have none," replied Hans; "thou hast had thy share of life." He strode over the prostrate body, and darted on. And a flash of blue lightning rose out of the East, shaped like a sword; it shook thrice over the whole heaven, and left it dark with one heavy impenetrable shade. The sun was setting; it plunged towards the horizon like a red-hot ball.

The roar of the Golden River rose on Hans' ear. He stood at the brink of the chasm through which it ran. Its waves were filled with the red glory of the sunset: they shook their crests like tongues of fire, and flashes of bloody light gleamed along their foam. Their sound came mightier and mightier on his senses; his brain grew giddy with the prolonged thunder. Shuddering, he drew the flask from his girdle and hurled it into the centre of the torrent. As he did so, an icy chill shot through his limbs: he staggered, shrieked, and fell. The waters closed over his cry. And the moaning of the river rose wildly into the night, as it gushed over

THE BLACK STONE.

CHAPTER 4

How Mr Schwartz Set Off on an Expedition to the Golden River,
and How He Prospered Therein

Poor little Gluck waited very anxiously alone in the house for Hans' return. Finding he did not come back, he was terribly frightened, and
went and told Schwartz in the prison all that had happened. Then
Schwartz was very much pleased, and said that Hans must certainly
have been turned into a black stone, and he should have all the gold to
himself. But Gluck was very sorry, and cried all night. When he got up
in the morning there was no bread in the house, nor any money; so
Gluck went and hired himself to another goldsmith, and he worked so
hard and so neatly and so long every day, that he soon got money
enough together to pay his brother's fine. He went then and gave it all to
Schwartz, and Schwartz got out of prison. Then Schwartz was quite
pleased, and said he should have some of the gold of the river. But
Gluck only begged he would go and see what had become of Hans.

Now when Schwartz had heard that Hans had stolen the holy water,
he thought to himself that such a proceeding might not be considered altogether correct by the King of the Golden River, and he determined to
manage matters better. So he took some more of Gluck's money, and
went to a bad priest, who gave him some holy water very readily for it.
Then Schwartz was sure it was all quite right. He got up early in the
morning before the sun rose, took some bread and wine in a basket, put
his holy water in a flask, and set off for the mountains. Like his brother,
he was much surprised at the sight of the glacier, and had great difficulty in crossing it, even after leaving his basket behind him. The day
was cloudless, but not bright: there was a heavy purple haze hanging
over the sky, and the hills looked lowering and gloomy. And as
Schwartz climbed the steep rock path the thirst came upon him, as it
had upon his brother, until he lifted his flask to his lips to drink. Then he
saw the fair child lying near him on the rocks, and it cried to him, and
moaned for water.

"Water, indeed," said Schwartz; "I haven't half enough for myself,"
and passed on. As he went he thought the sunbeams grew more dim,
and he saw a lower bank of black cloud rising out of the West. When he
had climbed for another hour the thirst overcame him again, and he
would have drunk. Then he saw the old man lying before him on the
path, and heard him cry out for water. "Water, indeed," said Schwartz;
"I haven't half enough for myself," and on he went.

Then again the light seemed to fade from before his eyes, and he
looked up, and, behold, a mist, of the color of blood, had come over the
sun. The bank of black cloud too had risen very high, and its edges were
tossing and tumbling like the waves of the angry sea. And they cast long
shadows, which flickered over Schwartz's path.

Then Schwartz climbed for another hour, and again his thirst returned. As he lifted his flask to his lips, he thought he saw his brother Hans lying exhausted on the path before him, and, as he gazed, the figure stretched its arms to him, and cried for water. "Ha, ha," laughed Schwartz, "are you there? remember the prison bars, my boy. Water, indeed! do you suppose I carried it all the way up here for you!" And he strode over the figure; yet, as he passed, he thought he saw a strange expression of mockery about its lips. When he had gone a few yards farther he looked back; but the figure was not there.

A sudden horror came over Schwartz, he knew not why; but the thirst for gold prevailed over his fear, and he rushed on. The bank of black cloud rose to the zenith, and out of it came bursts of spiry lightning, and waves of darkness seemed to heave and float between their flashes over the whole heavens. The sky where the sun was setting was all level, like a lake of blood; and a strong wind came out of that sky, tearing its crimson clouds into fragments, and scattering them far into the darkness. And when Schwartz stood by the brink of the Golden River, its waves were black, like thunder clouds, but their foam was like fire; and the roar of the waters below, and the thunder above, met as he cast the flask into the stream. As he did so the lightning glared into his eyes, the earth gave way beneath him, and the waters closed over his cry. And the moaning of the river rose wildly into the night, as it gushed over the TWO BLACK STONES.

CHAPTER 5

How Little Gluck Set Off on an Expedition to the Golden River, and How He Prospered Therein; with Other Matters of Interest

When Gluck found that Schwartz did not come back he was very sorry, and did not know what to do. He had no money, so he was obliged to go and hire himself again to the goldsmith, who worked him very hard and gave him very little money. After a month or two, Gluck grew tired, and made up his mind to go and try his fortune with the Golden River. "The little king looked very kind," thought he. "I don't think he will turn me into a black stone." So he went to the priest, and the priest gave him some holy water as soon as he asked for it. Then Gluck took some bread in his basket, and the bottle of water, and set off very early for the mountains.

If the glacier had occasioned a great deal of fatigue to his brothers, it was twenty times worse for him, who was neither so strong nor so practiced on the mountains. He had several bad falls, lost his basket and bread, and was very much frightened at the strange noises under the ice. He lay a long time to rest on the grass, after he had crossed over, and began to climb the hill just in the hottest part of the day. When he had climbed for an hour, he became dreadfully thirsty, and was going to

drink as his brothers had done, when he saw an old man coming down
the path above him, looking very feeble, and leaning on a staff. "My
son," said the old man, "I am faint with thirst; give me some of that
water." Then Gluck looked at him, and when he saw that he was pale
and weary, he gave him the water; "Only pray don't drink it all," said
Gluck. But the old man drank a great deal, and gave him back the bottle
two-thirds empty. Then he bade him good speed, and Gluck went on
again merrily. The path became easier to his feet, and two or three
blades of grass appeared upon it; some grasshoppers began singing on
the bank beside it, and Gluck thought he had never heard such merry
singing.

Then he went on for another hour, and the thirst increased on him so
that he thought he should be forced to drink. But as he raised the flask
he saw a little child lying panting by the roadside, and it cried out
piteously for water. Gluck struggled with himself, and determined to
bear the thirst a little longer; and he put the bottle to the child's lips, and
it drank it all but a few drops. Having done this it smiled on him, and
got up, and ran down the hill; and Gluck looked after it, till it became as
small as a little star. He then turned and began climbing again. And behold there were all kinds of sweet flowers growing on the rocks, bright
green moss, with pale pink starry flowers, and soft belled gentians more
blue than the sky at its deepest, and pure white transparent lilies. Crimson and purple butterflies darted hither and thither, and the sky sent

down such pure light that Gluck had never felt so happy in his life.

Yet after he had climbed for another hour, his thirst became intolerable again; and when he looked at his bottle he saw that there were only five or six drops left in it, and he could not venture to drink. But just as he was hanging the flask to his belt again, he saw a little dog lying on the rocks, gasping for breath—precisely as Hans had seen it on the day of his ascent. Gluck stopped and looked at it, and then at the Golden River, not five hundred yards above him; and he thought of the dwarf's words, "that no one could succeed, except in his first attempt." He tried to pass the dog, but it whined piteously, and he stopped again. "Poor beastie," said Gluck, "it'll be dead when I come down again, if I don't help it." Then he looked closer and closer at it, and its eye turned on him so mournfully, that he could not stand it. "Confound the King and his gold too," said Gluck; and he opened the flask, and poured all the water into the dog's mouth.

The dog sprang up and stood on its hind legs. Its tail disappeared, its ears became long, longer, silky, golden; its nose became very red, its eyes became very twinkling; in three seconds the dog was gone, and before Gluck stood his old acquaintance, the King of the Golden River.

"Thank you," said the monarch; "but don't be frightened, it's all right"; for Gluck showed manifest symptoms of consternation at this unlooked-for reply to his last observation. "Why didn't you come before," continued the dwarf, "instead of sending me those rascally brothers of yours, for me to have the trouble of turning into stones? Very hard stones they make, too."

"Oh dear me!" said Gluck, "have you really been so cruel?"

"Cruel!" said the dwarf; "they poured unholy water into my stream: do you suppose I'm going to allow that?"

"Why," said Gluck, "I am sure, sir—your Majesty, I mean—they got the water out of the church font."

"Very probably," replied the dwarf; "but", and his countenance grew stern as he spoke, "the water which has been refused to the cry of the weary and dying, is unholy, though it had been blessed by every saint in heaven; and the water which is found in the vessel of mercy is holy, though it had been defiled with corpses."

So saying, the dwarf stopped and plucked a lily that grew at his feet. On its white leaves there hung three drops of clear dew. And the dwarf shook them into the flask which Gluck held in his hand. "Cast these into the river," he said, "and descend on the other side of the mountains into the Treasure Valley. And so good speed."

As he spoke, the figure of the dwarf became indistinct. The playing colors of his robe formed themselves into a prismatic mist of dewy light; he stood for an instant veiled with them as with the belt of a broad rainbow. The colors grew faint, the mist rose into the air; the monarch had evaporated.

And Gluck climbed to the brink of the Golden River; its waves were as clear as crystal, and as brilliant as the sun. When he cast the three drops of dew into the stream, there opened where they fell a small circular whirlpool, into which the waters descended with a musical noise.

Gluck stood watching it for some time, very much disappointed, because not only the river was not turned into gold, but its waters seemed much diminished in quantity. Yet he obeyed his friend the dwarf, and descended the other side of the mountains towards the Treasure Valley; and, as he went, he thought he heard the noise of water working its way under the ground. Now, when he came in sight of the Treasure Valley, behold, a river, like the Golden River, was springing from a new cleft of the rocks above it, and was flowing in innumerable streams among the dry heaps of red sand.

As Gluck gazed, fresh grass sprang beside the new streams, and creeping plants grew and climbed among the moistening soil. Young flowers opened suddenly along the river sides, as stars leap out when twilight is deepening, and thickets of myrtle and tendrils of vine cast lengthening shadows over the valley as they grew. And thus the Treasure Valley became a garden again, and the inheritance which had been lost by cruelty was regained by love.

And Gluck went and dwelt in the valley, and the poor were never driven from his door; so that his barns became full of corn, and his house of treasure. For him the river had, according to the dwarf's promise, become a River of Gold.

And to this day the inhabitants of the valley point out the place where the three drops of holy dew were cast into the stream, and trace the course of the Golden River under the ground, until it emerges in the Treasure Valley. And at the top of the cataract of the Golden River are still to be seen two black stones, round which the waters howl mournfully every day at sunset; and these stones are still called by the people of the valley

THE BLACK BROTHERS.

FRANCES BROWNE (1816-1880)
"Sour and Civil" from *Granny's Wonderful Chair* (1857)

The seventh in a poor Irish family of twelve children, Miss Browne was blind from infancy. She relied on her siblings as readers and companions, and was an entertaining raconteur for them. When, in 1847, she and a sister travelled to Edinburgh, and then later to London, Frances's express intention was to support herself by writing. She was amazingly productive, composing poems, historical romances, and a three-volume autobiography (*My Share of the World*), as well as a long list of stories for children. *Granny's Wonderful Chair*, a collection of seven stories, established, and has maintained—through more than fifteen editions—her revered place in children's literature. The tales, framed by an introductory and closing chapter, are set "in an old time, long ago, when the fairies were in the world", and recount the adventures of the child Snowflower whose grandmother, Dame Frostyface, has left her a wonderful chair that on certain commands is able to transport Snowflower and, once a day, to tell her a story. Aided and protected by her magical chair, the little orphan journeys to the country of King Winwealth and his consort, Queen Wantall, where great entertainments are being mounted for the seven-day celebration of the birthday of the King's stepdaughter, Princess Greedalind. Snowflower's chair regales the court with a different story each day.

The rewards and punishments of "Sour and Civil", as in the other stories, have equivalents in the frame story, in which Snowflower's humility and the wonderful tales cause her fortunes to improve, and the avarice of Wantall and Greedalind forces them to leave the court and burrow further and further into the ground in an abortive search for gold. Snowflower is reunited with her grandmother; King Winwealth's long lost brother, Prince Wisewit, returns; and together they rule the land—with Snowflower as their heiress.

For the Irish Miss Browne there was an unfortunate absence of fairies in the England of her time. In the closing chapter of *Granny's Wonderful Chair* she speculates on this, and alludes to the model that inspired the jewelled palaces and remarkably vivid word-pictures of her stories:

Kings make no seven-day feasts now. . . . Chairs tell no tales. . . . For the fairies dance no more. Some say it was the din of factories that frightened them; but nobody has been known to have seen them for many a year, except, it is said, one Hans Christian Andersen, in Denmark, whose tales of the fairies are so good that they must have been heard from themselves.

"Sour and Civil", the *Chair's* sixth story, recalls the setting, theme, and descriptions of Andersen's "The Little Mermaid".

SOUR AND CIVIL

"Once upon a time there stood upon the sea-coast of the west country a certain hamlet of low cottages, where no one lived but fishermen. All round it was a broad beach of snow-white sand, where nothing was to be seen but gulls and cormorants, and long tangled seaweeds cast up by the tide that came and went night and day, summer and winter. There was no harbour nor port on all that shore. Ships passed by at a distance, with their white sails set, and on the land-side there lay wide grassy downs, where peasants lived and shepherds fed their flocks. The fishermen thought themselves as well off as any people in that country. Their families never wanted for plenty of herrings and mackerel; and what they had to spare the landsmen bought from them at certain village markets on the downs, giving them in exchange butter, cheese, and corn.

"The two best fishermen in that village were the sons of two old

widows, who had no other children, and happened to be near neighbours. Their family names were short, for they called the one Sour, and
the other Civil. There was no relationship between them that ever I
heard of; but they had only one boat, and always fished together,
though their names expressed the difference of their humours—for Civil
never used a hard word where a soft one would do, and when Sour was
not snarling at somebody, he was sure to be grumbling at everything.

Nevertheless they agreed wonderfully, and were lucky fishers. Both
were strong, active, and of good courage. On winter's night or summer's morning they would steer out to sea far beyond the boats of their
neighbours, and never came home without some fish to cook and some
to spare. Their mothers were proud of them, each in her own fashion—
for the saying held good, 'Like mother, like son.' Dame Civil thought
the whole world didn't hold a better than her son; and her boy was the
only creature at whom Dame Sour didn't scold and frown. The hamlet
was divided in opinion concerning the young fishermen. Some thought
Civil was the best; some said, without Sour he would catch nothing. So
things went on, till one day about the fall of winter, when mists were
gathering darkly on sea and sky, and the air was chill and frosty, all the
boatmen of the hamlet went out to fish, and so did Sour and Civil.

"That day they had not their usual luck. Cast their net where they
would, not a single fish came in. Their neighbours caught boatsful, and
went home, Sour said, laughing at them. But when the sea was growing
crimson with the sunset their nets were empty, and they were tired.
Civil himself did not like to go home without fish—it would damage the
high repute they had gained in the village. Besides, the sea was calm
and the evening fair, and, as a last attempt, they steered still further out,
and cast their nets beside a rock which rose rough and grey above the
water, and was called the Merman's Seat—from an old report that the
fishermen's fathers had seen the mermen, or sea-people, sitting there
on moonlight nights. Nobody believed that rumour now, but the villagers did not like to fish there. The water was said to be deep beyond
measure, and sudden squalls were apt to trouble it; but Sour and Civil
were right glad to see by the moving of their lines that there was something in their net, and gladder still when they found it so heavy that all
their strength was required to draw it up. Scarcely had they landed it on
the Merman's Seat, when their joy was changed to disappointment, for
besides a few starved mackerel, the net contained nothing but a monstrous ugly fish as long as Civil (who was taller than Sour), with a huge
snout, a long beard, and a skin covered with prickles.

" 'Such a horrid ugly creature!' said Sour, as they shook it out of the
net on the rough rock, and gathered up the mackerel. 'We needn't fish
here any more. How they will mock us in the village for staying out so
late, and bringing home so little!'

" 'Let us try again,' said Civil, as he set his creel of mackerel in the
boat.

" 'Not another cast will I make to-night;' and what more Sour would have said, was cut short by the great fish, for, looking round at them, it spoke out—

" 'I suppose you don't think me worth taking home in your dirty boat; but I can tell you that if you were down in my country, neither of you would be thought fit to keep me company.'

"Sour and Civil were terribly astonished to hear the fish speak. The first could not think of a cross word to say, but Civil made answer in his accustomed manner.

" 'Indeed, my lord, we beg your pardon, but our boat is too light to carry such a fish as you.'

" 'You do well to call me lord,' said the fish, 'for so I am, though it was hard to expect you could have known my quality in this dress. However, help me off the rock, for I must go home; and for your civility I will give you my daughter in marriage, if you will come and see me this day twelvemonth.'

"Civil helped the great fish off the rock as respectfully as his fear would allow him. Sour was so terrified at the whole transaction, that he said not a word till they got safe home; but from that day forward, when he wanted to put Civil down, it was his custom to tell him and his mother that he would get no wife but the ugly fish's daughter.

"Old Dame Sour heard this story from her son, and told it over the whole village. Some people wondered, but the most part laughed at it as a good joke; and Civil and his mother were never known to be angry but on that occasion. Dame Civil advised her son never to fish with Sour again; and as the boat happened to be his, Civil got an old skiff which one of the fishermen was going to break up for firewood, and cobbled it up for himself.

"In that skiff he went to sea alone all the winter, and all the summer; but though Civil was brave and skilful, he could catch little, because his boat was bad—and everybody but his mother began to think him of no value. Sour having the good boat got a new comrade, and had the praise of being the best fishermen.

"Poor Civil's heart was getting low as the summer wore away. The fish had grown scarce on that coast, and the fishermen had to steer further out to sea. One evening when he had toiled all day and caught nothing, Civil thought he would go further too, and try his fortune beside the Merman's rock. The sea was calm, and the evening fair; Civil did not remember that it was the very day on which his troubles began by the great fish talking to him twelve months before. As he neared the rock the sun was setting, and much astonished was the fisherman to see upon it three fair ladies, with sea-green gowns and strings of great pearls wound round their long fair hair; two of them were waving their hands to him. They were the tallest and stateliest ladies he had ever seen; but Civil could perceive as he came nearer that there was no colour in their cheeks, that their hair had a strange bluish shade, like that of deep sea-water, and there was a fiery light in their eyes that frightened him. The third, who was less of stature, did not notice him at all, but kept her eyes fixed on the setting sun. Though her look was mournful, Civil could see that there was a faint rosy bloom on her cheek—that her hair was a golden yellow, and her eyes were mild and clear like those of his mother.

" 'Welcome! welcome! noble fisherman!' cried the two ladies. 'Our father has sent us for you to visit him,' and with one bound they leaped into his boat, bringing with them the smaller lady, who said—

" 'Oh! bright sun and brave sky that I see so seldom!' But Civil heard no more, for his boat went down miles deep in the sea, and he thought himself drowning; but one lady had caught him by the right arm, and the other by the left, and pulled him into the mouth of a rocky cave, where there was no water. On they went, still down and down, as if on a steep hill-side. The cave was very long, but it grew wider as they came to the bottom. Then Civil saw a faint light, and walked out with his fair company into the country of the sea-people. In that land there grew neither grass nor flowers, bushes nor trees, but the ground was covered with bright-coloured shells and pebbles. There were hills of marble, and rocks of spar; and over all a cold blue sky with no sun, but a light clear and silvery as that of the harvest moon. The fisherman could see no smoking chimneys, but there were grottoes in the sparry rocks, and halls in the marble hills, where lived the sea-people—with whom, as old stories say, fishermen and mariners used to meet on lonely capes and headlands in the simple times of the world.

"Forth they came in all directions to see the stranger. Mermen with long white beards, and mermaids such as walk with the fishermen, all clad in sea-green, and decorated with strings of pearls; but every one with the same colourless face, and the same wild light in their eyes. The mermaids led Civil up one of the marble hills to a great cavern with halls and chambers like a palace. Their floors were of alabaster, their walls of porphyry, and their ceilings inlaid with coral. Thousands of crystal lamps lit the palace. There were seats and tables hewn out of shining spar, and a great company sat feasting; but what most amazed Civil was the quantity of cups, flagons, and goblets, made of gold and silver, of such different shapes and patterns that they seemed to have been gathered from all the countries in the world. In the chief hall there sat a merman on a stately chair, with more jewels than all the rest about him. Before him the mermaids brought Civil, saying—

" 'Father, here is our guest.'

" 'Welcome, noble fisherman!' cried the merman, in a voice which Civil remembered with terror, for it was that of the great ugly fish; 'welcome to our halls! Sit down and feast with us, and then choose which of my daughters you will have for a bride.'

"Civil had never felt himself so thoroughly frightened in all his life. How was he to get home to his mother? and what would the old dame think when the dark night came without bringing him home? There was no use in talking—Civil had wisdom enough to see that: he therefore tried to take things quietly; and, having thanked the merman for his invitation, took the seat assigned him on his right hand. Civil was hungry with the long day at sea, but there was no want of fare on that table: meats and wines, such as he had never tasted, were set before him in the richest of golden dishes: but, hungry as he was, the fisherman perceived that everything there had the taste and smell of the sea.

"If the fisherman had been the lord of lands and castles he would not have been treated with more respect. The two mermaids sat by him— one filled his plate, another filled his goblet; but the third only looked at him in a stealthy, warning way when nobody perceived her. Civil soon finished his share of the feast, and then the merman showed him all the splendours of his cavern. The halls were full of company, some feasting, some dancing, and some playing all manner of games, and in every hall was the same abundance of gold and silver vessels; but Civil was most astonished when the merman brought him to a marble chamber full of heaps of precious stones. There were diamonds there whose value the fisherman knew not—pearls larger than ever a diver had gathered— emeralds, sapphires, and rubies, that would have made the jewellers of the world wonder; the merman then said—

" 'This is my eldest daughter's dowry.'

" 'Good luck attend her!' said Civil. 'It is the dowry of a queen.' But the merman led him on to another chamber: it was filled with heaps of gold coin, which seemed gathered from all times and nations. The images and inscriptions of all the kings that ever reigned were there; and the merman said:

" 'This is my second daughter's dowry.'

" 'Good luck attend her!' said Civil. 'It is a dowry for a princess.'

" 'So you may say,' replied the merman. 'But make up your mind which of the maidens you will marry, for the third has no portion at all, because she is not my daughter; but only, as you may see, a poor silly girl taken into my family for charity.'

" 'Truly, my lord,' said Civil, whose mind was already made up, 'both your daughters are too rich and far too noble for me; therefore I choose the third. Her poverty will best become my estate of a poor fisherman.'

" 'If you choose her,' said the merman, 'you must wait long for a wedding. I cannot allow an inferior girl to be married before my own daughters.' And he said a great deal more to persuade him; but Civil would not change his mind, and they returned to the hall.

"There was no more attention for the fisherman, but everybody watched him well. Turn where he would, master or guest had their eyes upon him, though he made them the best speeches he could remember, and praised all their splendours. One thing, however, was strange— there was no end to the fun and the feasting; nobody seemed tired, and nobody thought of sleep. When Civil's very eyes closed with weariness, and he slept on one of the marble benches—no matter how many hours—there were the company feasting and dancing away; there were the thousand lamps within, and the cold moonlight without. Civil wished himself back with his mother, his net, and his cobbled skiff.

Fishing would have been easier than those everlasting feasts; but there was nothing else among the sea-people—no night of rest, no working day.

"Civil knew not how time went on, till, waking up from a long sleep, he saw, for the first time, that the feast was over, and the company gone. The lamps still burned, and the tables, with all their riches, stood in the empty halls; but there was no face to be seen, no sound to be heard, only a low voice singing beside the outer door; and there, sitting all alone, he found the mild-eyed maiden.

" 'Fair lady,' said Civil, 'tell me what means this quietness, and where are all the merry company?'

" 'You are a man of the land,' said the lady, 'and know not the sea-people. They never sleep but once a year, and that is at Christmas time. Then they go into the deep caverns, where there is always darkness, and sleep till the new year comes.'

" 'It is a strange fashion,' said Civil; 'but all folks have their way. Fair lady, as you and I are to be good friends, tell me, whence come all the wines and meats, and gold and silver vessels, seeing there are neither cornfields nor flocks here, workmen nor artificers?'

" 'The sea-people are heirs of the sea,' replied the maiden; 'to them come all the stores and riches that are lost in it. I know not the ways by which they come; but the lord of these halls keeps the keys of seven gates, where they go out and in; but one of the gates, which has not been open for thrice seven years, leads to a path under the sea, by which I heard the merman say in his cups, one might reach the land. Good fisherman, if by chance you gain his favour, and ever open that gate, let me bear you company; for I was born where the sun shines and the grass grows, though my country and my parents are unknown to me. All I remember is sailing in a great ship, when a storm arose, and it was wrecked, and not one soul escaped drowning but me. I was then a little child, and a brave sailor had bound me to a floating plank before he was washed away. Here the sea-people came round me like great fishes, and I went down with them to this rich and weary country. Sometimes, as a great favour, they take me up with them to see the sun; but that is seldom, for they never like to part with one who has seen their country; and, fisherman, if you ever leave them, remember to take nothing with you that belongs to them, for if it were but a shell or a pebble, that will give them power over you and yours.'

" 'Thanks for your news, fair lady,' said Civil. 'A lord's daughter, doubtless, you must have been, while I am but a poor fisherman; yet, as we have fallen into the same misfortune, let us be friends, and it may be we shall find means to get back to the sunshine together.'

" 'You are a man of good manners,' said the lady, 'therefore, I accept your friendship; but my fear is that we shall never see the sunshine again.'

" 'Fair speeches brought me here,' said Civil, 'and fair speeches may help me back; but be sure I will not go without you.' "

"This promise cheered the lady's heart, and she and Civil spent that Christmas time seeing the wonders of the sea country. They wandered through caves like that of the great merman. The unfinished feast was spread in every hall; the tables were covered with most costly vessels; and heaps of jewels lay on the floors of unlocked chambers. But for the lady's warning, Civil would fain have put away some of them for his mother.

"The poor woman was sad of heart by this time, believing her son to be drowned. On the first night when he did not come home, she had gone down to the sea and watched till morning. Then the fishermen steered out again, and Sour having found his skiff floating about, brought it home, saying the foolish young man was doubtless lost; but what better could be expected when he had no discreet person to take care of him?

"This grieved Dame Civil sore. She never expected to see her son again; but, feeling lonely in her cottage at the evening hour when he used to come home, the good woman accustomed herself to go down at sunset and sit beside the sea. That winter happened to be mild on the coast of the west country, and one evening when the Christmas time was near, and the rest of the village preparing to make merry, Dame Civil sat, as usual, on the sands. The tide was ebbing and the sun going down, when from the eastward came a lady clad in black, mounted on a black palfrey, and followed by a squire in the same sad clothing; as the lady came near, she said—

" 'Woe is me for my daughter, and for all that have lost by the sea!'

" 'You say well, noble lady,' said Dame Civil. 'Woe is me also for my son, for I have none beside him.'

"When the lady heard that, she alighted from her palfrey, and sat down by the fisherman's mother, saying—

" 'Listen to my story. I was the widow of a great lord in the heart of the east country. He left me a fair castle, and an only daughter, who was the joy of my heart. Her name was Faith Feignless; but, while she was yet a child, a great fortune-teller told me that my daughter would marry a fisherman. I thought this would be a great disgrace to my noble family, and, therefore, sent my daughter with her nurse in a good ship, bound for a certain city where my relations live, intending to follow myself as soon as I could get my lands and castles sold. But the ship was wrecked, and my daughter drowned; and I have wandered over the world with my good Squire Trusty, mourning on every shore with those who have lost friends by the sea. Some with whom I have mourned grew to forget their sorrow, and would lament with me no more; others being sour and selfish, mocked me, saying, my grief was nothing to them: but you have good manners, and I will remain with you, however humble be your dwelling. My squire carries gold enough to pay all our charges.' So the mourning lady and her good Squire Trusty went home with Dame Civil, and she was no longer lonely in her sorrow, for when the dame said—

" 'Oh! if my son were alive, I should never let him go to sea in a cobbled skiff!' the lady answered—

" 'Oh! if my daughter were but living, I should never think it a disgrace though she married a fisherman!'

"The Christmas passed as it always does in the west country—shepherds made merry on the downs, and fishermen on the shore; but when the merrymakings and ringing of bells were over in all the land, the sea-people woke up to their continual feasts and dances. Like one that had forgotten all that was past, the merman again showed Civil the chamber of gold and the chamber of jewels, advising him to choose between his two daughters; but the fisherman still answered that the ladies were too noble, and far too rich for him. Yet as he looked at the glittering heap, Civil could not help recollecting the poverty of the west country, and the thought slipped out—

" 'How happy my old neighbours would be to find themselves here!'

" 'Say you so?' said the merman, who always wanted visitors.

" 'Yes,' said Civil, 'I have neighbours up yonder in the west country whom it would be hard to send home again if they got sight of half this wealth;' and the honest fisherman thought of Dame Sour and her son.

"The merman was greatly delighted with these speeches—he thought there was a probability of getting many land-people down, and by and by said to Civil—

" 'Suppose you took up a few jewels, and went up to tell your poor neighbours how welcome we might make them?'

"The prospect of getting back to his country rejoiced Civil's heart, but he had promised not to go without the lady, and therefore, answered prudently what was indeed true—

" 'Many thanks, my lord, for choosing such a humble man as I am to bear your message; but the people of the west country never believe anything without two witnesses at the least; yet if the poor maid whom I have chosen could be permitted to accompany me, I think they would believe us both.'

"The merman said nothing in reply, but his people, who had heard Civil's speech, talked it over among themselves till they grew sure that the whole west country would come down, if they only had news of the riches, and petitioned their lord to send up Civil and the poor maid by way of letting them know.

"As it seemed for the public good, the great merman consented; but, being determined to have them back, he gathered out of his treasure chamber some of the largest pearls and diamonds that lay covenient, and said—

" 'Take these as a present from me, to let the west country people see what I can do for my visitors.'

"Civil and the lady took the presents, saying—

" 'Oh, my lord, you are too generous. We want nothing but the pleasure of telling of your marvellous riches up yonder.'

" 'Tell everybody to come down, and they will get the like,' said the merman; 'and follow my eldest daughter, for she carries the key of the land gate.'

"Civil and the lady followed the mermaid through a winding gallery, which led from the chief banquet hall far into the marble hill. All was dark, and they had neither lamp nor torch, but at the end of the gallery they came to a great stone gate, which creaked like thunder on its hinges. Beyond that there was a narrow cave, sloping up and up like a steep hill-side. Civil and the lady thought they would never reach the top; but at last they saw a gleam of daylight; then a strip of blue sky, and the mermaid bade them stoop and creep through what seemed a crevice in the ground, and both stood up on the broad sea-beach as the day was breaking and the tide ebbing fast away.

" 'Good times to you among your west country people,' said the mermaid. 'Tell any of them that would like to come down to visit us, that they must come here midway between the high and low water-mark, when the tide is going out at morning or evening. Call thrice on the sea-people, and we will show them the way.'

"Before they could make answer, she had sunk down from their sight, and there was no track or passage there, but all was covered by the loose sand and sea-shells.

" 'Now,' said the lady to Civil, 'we have seen the heavens once more, and we will not go back. Cast in the merman's present quickly before the sun rises;' and taking the bag of pearls and diamonds, she flung it as far as she could into the sea.

"Civil never was so unwilling to part with anything as that bag, but he thought it better to follow a good example, and tossed his into the sea also. They thought they heard a long moan come up from the waters; but Civil saw his mother's chimney beginning to smoke, and with the fair lady in her sea-green gown he hastened to the good dame's cottage.

"The whole village were woke up that morning with cries of 'Welcome back, my son!' 'Welcome back, my daughter!' for the mournful lady knew it was her lost daughter, Faith Feignless, whom the fisherman had brought back, and all the neighbours assembled to hear their story. When it was told, everybody praised Civil for the prudence he had shown in his difficulties, except Sour and his mother: they did nothing but rail upon him for losing such great chances of making himself and the whole country rich. At last, when they heard over and over again of the merman's treasures, neither mother nor son would consent to stay any longer in the west country, and as nobody persuaded them, and they would not take Civil's direction, Sour got out his boat and steered away with his mother toward the Merman's Rock. From that voyage they never came back to the hamlet. Some say they went down and lived among the sea-people; others say—I know not how they learned it—that Sour and his mother grumbled and growled so much that even the sea-people grew weary of them, and turned them and their boat out on the open sea. What part of the world they chose to land on nobody is certain: by all accounts they have been seen everywhere, and I should not be surprised if they were in this good company. As for Civil, he married Faith Feignless, and became a great lord."

Here the voice ceased, and two that were clad in sea-green silk, with coronets of pearls, rose up, and said—

"That's our story."

"Oh, mamma, if we could get down to that country!" said Princess Greedalind.

"And bring all the treasures back with us!" answered Queen Wantall.

"Except the tale of yesterday, and the four that went before it, I have not heard such a story since my brother Wisewit went from me, and was lost in the forest," said King Winwealth. "Readyrein, the second of my pages, rise, and bring this maiden a purple velvet mantle."

The mantle was brought, and Snowflower having thanked the king, went down upon her grandmother's chair; but that night the little girl went no further than the lowest banquet hall, where she was bidden to stay and share the feast, and sleep hard by in a wainscot chamber. That she was well entertained there is no doubt, for King Winwealth had been heard to say that it was not clear to him how he could have got through the seven days' feast without her grandmother's chair and its stories; but next day being the last of the seven, things were gayer than ever in the palace. The music had never been so merry, the dishes so rich, or the wines so rare; neither had the clamours at the gate ever been so loud, nor the disputes and envies so many in the halls.

Perhaps it was these doings that brought the low spirits earlier than usual on King Winwealth, for after dinner his majesty fell into them so deeply that a message came down from the highest banquet hall, and the cupbearer told Snowflower to go up with her chair, for King Winwealth wished to hear another story.

THE MAGIC FISH-BONE

CHARLES DICKENS (1812-1870)
"The Magic Fish-bone" from *A Holiday Romance* (1868)

The four stories in *A Holiday Romance*—of which "The Magic Fish-bone" was the second—were commissioned by the American magazine *Our Young Folks* and published there in 1868. Dickens, at the height of his popularity just two years before his death, took the commission seriously enough to turn away from the sombre world of his novels and concoct for the pleasure of children four whimsical entertainments. He prepares a festive atmosphere by having the child-storytellers proclaim their resolve to "throw our thoughts into something educational for the grown-up people, hinting to them how things ought to be."

The title page of "The Magic Fish-bone" announces that it is a "romance from the pen of Miss Alice Rainbird Aged Seven"; accordingly the heroine is a seven-year-old girl. To the courtly manners, derring-do, and magical charms associated with the romance, Dickens adds a touch of humorous absurdity. The impecunious King Watkins is dependent on a pay-cheque, the ailing queen is ineffectual, and their daughter Princess Alicia takes care of her eighteen younger siblings. (There were presumably many multiple births in the royal household!) While the humour of the romance depends on Dickens' lighthearted exaggerations, these become a little unnerving when he describes the child marriage of Princess Alicia and Prince Certainpersonio, and the choking death of "the dreadful little snapping pug-dog". Nurse, cook, governess, and rescuer, Alicia is a veritable paragon. She easily finds favour with the omnipotent Fairy Grandmarina, who gives her a fishbone that can work its magic only when the self-reliant little girl asks help of others.

The gaiety of the story, in which all cares are wonderfully relieved, makes it a continuing favourite—and also demonstrates the power of Dickens' imagination to create a world that was the antithesis of the one he endured.

THE MAGIC FISH-BONE

There was once a king, and he had a queen; and he was the manliest of his sex, and she was the loveliest of hers. The king was, in his private profession, under government. The queen's father had been a medical man out of town.

They had nineteen children, and were always having more. Seventeen of these children took care of the baby; and Alicia, the eldest, took care of them all. Their ages varied from seven years to seven months.

Let us now resume our story.

One day the king was going to the office, when he stopped at the fishmonger's to buy a pound and a half of salmon not too near the tail, which the queen (who was a careful housekeeper) had requested him to send home. Mr Pickles, the fishmonger, said, "Certainly, sir; is there any other article? Good-morning."

The king went on towards the office in a melancholy mood; for quarter-day was such a long way off, and several of the dear children were growing out of their clothes. He had not proceeded far, when Mr Pickles's errand-boy came running after him, and said, "Sir, you didn't notice the old lady in our shop."

"What old lady?" inquired the king. "I saw none."

Now the king had not seen any old lady, because this old lady had been invisible to him, though visible to Mr Pickles's boy. Probably because he messed and splashed the water about to that degree, and flopped the pairs of soles down in that violent manner, that, if she had not been visible to him, he would have spoilt her clothes.

Just then the old lady came trotting up. She was dressed in shot-silk of the richest quality, smelling of dried lavender.

"King Watkins the First, I believe?" said the old lady.

"Watkins," replied the king, "is my name."

"Papa, if I am not mistaken, of the beautiful Princess Alicia?" said the old lady.

"And of eighteen other darlings," replied the king.

"Listen. You are going to the office," said the old lady.

It instantly flashed upon the king that she must be a fairy, or how could she know that?

"You are right," said the old lady, answering his thoughts. "I am the good Fairy Grandmarina. Attend! When you return home to dinner, politely invite the Princess Alicia to have some of the salmon you bought just now."

"It may disagree with her," said the king.

The old lady became so very angry at this absurd idea, that the king was quite alarmed, and humbly begged her pardon.

"We hear a great deal too much about this thing disagreeing, and that thing disagreeing," said the old lady, with the greatest contempt it was possible to express. "Don't be greedy. I think you want it all yourself."

The king hung his head under this reproof, and said he wouldn't talk about things disagreeing any more.

"Be good, then," said the Fairy Grandmarina, "and don't! When the beautiful Princess Alicia consents to partake of the salmon—as I think she will—you will find she will leave a fish-bone on her plate. Tell her to dry it, and to rub it, and to polish it, till it shines like mother-of-pearl, and to take care of it as a present from me."

"Is that all?" asked the king.

"Don't be impatient, sir," returned the Fairy Grandmarina, scolding him severely. "Don't catch people short, before they have done speaking. Just the way with you grown-up persons. You are always doing it."

The king again hung his head, and said he wouldn't do so any more.

"Be good, then," said the Fairy Grandmarina, "and don't! Tell the Princess Alicia, with my love, that the fish-bone is a magic present which can only be used once; but that it will bring her, that once, whatever she wishes for, *provided she wishes for it at the right time*. That is the message. Take care of it." The king was beginning, "Might I ask the reason?" when the fairy became absolutely furious.

"*Will* you be good, sir?" she exclaimed, stamping her foot on the ground. "The reason for this, and the reason for that, indeed! You are always wanting the reason. No reason. There! Hoity toity me! I am sick of your grown-up reasons."

The king was extremely frightened by the old lady's flying into such a passion, and said he was very sorry to have offended her, and he wouldn't ask for reasons any more.

"Be good, then," said the old lady, "and don't!"

With those words, Grandmarina vanished, and the king went on and on and on, till he came to the office. There he wrote and wrote and wrote, till it was time to go home again. Then he politely invited the Princess Alicia, as the fairy had directed him, to partake of the salmon. And when she had enjoyed it very much, he saw the fish-bone on her plate, as the fairy had told him he would, and he delivered the Fairy's message, and the Princess Alicia took care to DRY the bone, and to RUB it and to POLISH it, till it shone like mother-of-pearl.

And so, when the queen was going to get up in the morning, she said, "Oh, dear me, dear me; my head, my head!" and then she fainted away.

The Princess Alicia, who happened to be looking in at the chamber door, asked about breakfast, was very much alarmed when she saw her royal mamma in this state, and she rang the bell for Peggy, which was the name of the lord chamberlain. But remembering where the smelling-bottle was, she climbed on a chair and got it; and after that she climbed on another chair by the bedside, and held the smelling-bottle to the queen's nose; and after that she jumped down and got some water; and after that she jumped up again and wetted the queen's forehead; and, in short, when the lord chamberlain came in, that dear old woman said to the little princess, "What a trot you are! I couldn't have done it better myself!"

"HE DELIVERED THE FAIRY'S MESSAGE"

But that was not the worst of the good queen's illness. Oh, no! She was very ill indeed, for a long time. The Princess Alicia kept the seventeen young princes and princesses quiet, and dressed and undressed and danced the baby, and made the kettle boil, and heated the soup, and swept the hearth, and poured out the medicine, and nursed the queen, and did all that ever she could, and was as busy, busy, busy as busy could be; for there were not many servants at that palace for three reasons: because the king was short of money, because a rise in his office never seemed to come, and because quarter-day was so far off that it looked almost as far off and as little as one of the stars.

But on the morning when the queen fainted away, where was the magic fish-bone? Why, there it was in the Princess Alicia's pocket! She had almost taken it out to bring the queen to life again, when she put it back, and looked for the smelling-bottle.

After the queen had come out of her swoon that morning, and was dozing, the Princess Alicia hurried upstairs to tell a most particular secret to a most particularly confidential friend of hers, who was a duchess. People did suppose her to be a doll; but she was really a duchess, though nobody knew it except the princess.

This most particular secret was the secret about the magic fish-bone, the history of which was well-known to the duchess, because the princess told her everything. The princess kneeled down by the bed on which the duchess was lying, full-dressed and wide-awake, and whispered the secret to her. The duchess smiled and nodded. People might have supposed that she never smiled and nodded; but she often did, though nobody knew it except the princess.

Then the Princess Alicia hurried downstairs again to keep watch in the queen's room. She often kept watch by herself in the queen's room; but every evening, while the illness lasted, she sat there watching with the king. And every evening the king sat looking at her with a cross look, wondering why she never brought out the magic fish-bone. As often as she noticed this, she ran upstairs, whispered the secret to the duchess over again, and said to the duchess besides, "They think we children never have a reason or a meaning!" And the duchess, though the most fashionable duchess that ever was heard of, winked her eye.

"Alicia," said the king, one evening, when she wished him good-night.

"Yes, papa."

"What is become of the magic fish-bone?"

"In my pocket, papa."

"I thought you had lost it?"

"Oh, no, papa!"

"Or forgotten it?"

"No, indeed, papa."

And so another time the dreadful little snapping pug-dog, next door, made a rush at one of the young princes as he stood on the steps coming home from school, and terrified him out of his wits; and he put his hand through a pane of glass, and bled, bled, bled. When the seventeen other young princes and princesses saw him bleed, bleed, bleed, they were terrified out of their wits too, and screamed themselves black in their seventeen faces all at once. But the Princess Alicia put her hands over all their seventeen mouths, one after another, and persuaded them to be quiet because of the sick queen. And then she put the wounded prince's hand in a basin of fresh cold water, while they stared with their twice seventeen are thirty-four, put down four and carry three, eyes, and then she looked in the hand for bits of glass, and there were fortunately no bits of glass there. And then she said to two chubby-legged princes, who were sturdy though small, "Bring me in the royal rag-bag: I must snip and stitch and cut and contrive." So these two young princes tugged at the royal rag-bag, and lugged it in; and the Princess Alicia sat down on the floor, with a large pair of scissors and a needle and thread, and snipped and stitched and cut and contrived, and made a bandage, and put it on, and it fitted beautifully; and so when it was all done, she saw the king her papa looking on by the door.

"Alicia."

"Yes, papa."

"What have you been doing?"

"Snipping, stitching, cutting, and contriving, papa."

"Where is the magic fish-bone?"

"In my pocket, papa."

"I thought you had lost it?"

"Oh, no, papa!"

"Or forgotten it?"

"SNIPPING, STITCHING, CUTTING, AND CONTRIVING, PAPA."

"No, indeed papa."

After that, she ran upstairs to the duchess, and told her what had passed, and told her the secret over again; and the duchess shook her flaxen curls, and laughed with her rosy lips.

Well! and so another time the baby fell under the grate. The seventeen young princes and princesses were used to it; for they were almost always falling under the grate or down the stairs; but the baby was not used to it yet, and it gave him a swelled face and a black eye. The way the poor little darling came to tumble was, that he was out of the Princess Alicia's lap just as she was sitting, in a great coarse apron that quite smothered her, in front of the kitchen fire, beginning to peel the turnips for the broth for dinner; and the way she came to be doing that was, that the king's cook had run away that morning with her own true love, who was very tall but very tipsy soldier. Then the seventeen young princes and princesses, who cried at everything that happened, cried and roared. But the Princess Alicia (who couldn't help crying a little herself) quietly called to them to be still, on account of not throwing back the queen upstairs, who was fast getting well, and said, "Hold your tongues, you wicked little monkeys, every one of you, while I examine baby." Then she examined baby, and found that he hadn't broken anything; and she held cold iron to his poor dear eye, and smoothed his poor dear face, and he presently fell asleep in her arms. Then she said to the seventeen princes and princesses, "I am afraid to let him down yet, lest he should wake and feel pain; be good, and you shall all be cooks." They jumped for joy when they heard that, and began making themselves cooks' caps out of old newspapers. So to one she gave the salt-box, and to one she gave the barley, and to one she gave the herbs, and to one she gave the turnips, and to one she gave the carrots, and to one she gave the onions, and to one she gave the spice-box, till they were all cooks, and all running about at work, she sitting in the middle, smothered in the great coarse apron, nursing baby.

By and by the broth was done; and the baby woke up, smiling like an angel, and was trusted to the sedatest princess to hold, while the other princes and princesses were squeezed into a far-off corner to look at the Princess Alicia turning out the saucepanful of broth, for fear (as they were always getting into trouble) they should get splashed and scalded. When the broth came tumbling out, steaming beautifully, and smelling like a nosegay good to eat, they clapped their hands. That made the baby clap his hands; and that, and his looking as if he had a comic toothache, made all the princes and princesses laugh. So the Princess Alicia said, ''Laugh and be good; and after dinner we will make him a nest on the floor in a corner, and he shall sit in his nest and see a dance of eighteen cooks.'' That delighted the young princes and princesses, and they ate up all the broth, and washed up all the plates and dishes, and cleared away, and pushed the table into a corner; and then they in their cooks' caps, and the Princess Alicia in the smothering coarse apron that belonged to the cook that had run away with her own true love that was the very tall but very tipsy soldier, danced a dance of eighteen cooks before the angelic baby, who forgot his swelled face and his black eye, and crowed with joy.

''A DANCE OF EIGHTEEN COOKS BEFORE THE ANGELIC BABY''

And so then, once more the Princess Alicia saw King Watkins the First, her father, standing in the doorway looking on, and he said, "What have you been doing, Alicia?"

"Cooking and contriving, papa."

"What else have you been doing, Alicia?"

"Keeping the children light-hearted, papa."

"Where is the magic fish-bone, Alicia?"

"In my pocket, papa."

"I thought you had lost it?"

"Oh, no, papa!"

"Or forgotten it?"

"No, indeed, papa."

The king then sighed so heavily, and seemed so low-spirited, and sat down so miserably, leaning his head upon his hand, and his elbow upon the kitchen table pushed away in the corner, that the seventeen princes and princesses crept softly out of the kitchen, and left him alone with the Princess Alicia and the angelic baby.

"What is the matter, papa?"

"I am dreadfully poor, my child."

"Have you no money at all, papa?"

"None, my child."

"Is there no way of getting any, papa?"

"No way," said the king. "I have tried very hard, and I have tried all ways."

When she heard those last words, the Princess Alicia began to put her hand into the pocket where she kept the magic fish-bone.

"Papa," she said, "when we have tried very hard, and tried all ways, we must have done our very, very best?"

"No doubt, Alicia."

"When we have done our very, very best, papa, and that is not enough, then I think the right time must have come for asking help of others." This was the very secret connected with the magic fish-bone, which she had found out for herself from the good Fairy Grandmarina's words, and which she had so often whispered to her beautiful and fashionable friend, the duchess.

So she took out of her pocket the magic fish-bone, that had been dried and rubbed and polished till it shone like mother-of-pearl; and she gave it one little kiss, and wished it was quarter-day. And immediately it *was* quarter-day; and the king's quarter's salary came rattling down the chimney, and bounced into the middle of the floor.

But this was not half of what happened—no, not a quarter; for immediately afterwards the good Fairy Grandmarina came riding in, in a carriage and four (peacocks), with Mr Pickles's boy up behind, dressed in silver and gold, with a cocked hat, powdered hair, pink silk stockings, a jewelled cane, and a nosegay. Down jumped Mr Pickles's boy, with his cocked hat in his hand, and wonderfully polite (being entirely changed by enchantment), and handed Grandmarina out; and there she stood, in

THE KING'S QUARTER'S SALARY CAME RATTLING DOWN THE CHIMNEY

her rich shot-silk smelling of dried lavender, fanning herself with a sparkling fan.

"Alicia, my dear," said this charming old fairy, "how do you do? I hope I see you pretty well? Give me a kiss."

The Princess Alicia embraced her; and then Grandmarina turned to the king, and said rather sharply, "Are you good?"

The king said he hoped so.

"I suppose you know the reason *now*, why my god-daughter here," kissing the princess again, "did not apply to the fish-bone sooner?" said the fairy.

The king made a shy bow.

"Ah! but you didn't *then*?" said the fairy.

The king made a shyer bow.

"Any more reasons to ask for?" said the fairy.

The king said, No, and he was very sorry.

"Be good, then," said the fairy, "and live happy ever afterwards."

Then Grandmarina waved her fan, and the queen came in most splendidly dressed; and the seventeen young princes and princesses, no longer grown out of their clothes, came in, newly fitted out from top to toe, with tucks in everything to admit of its being let out. After that, the fairy tapped the Princess Alicia with her fan; and the smothering coarse apron flew away, and she appeared exquisitely dressed, like a little bride, with a wreath of orangeflowers and a silver veil. After that, the kitchen dresser changed of itself into a wardrobe, made of beautiful woods and gold and looking-glass, which was full of dresses of all sorts, all for her and all exactly fitting her. After that, the angelic baby came in running alone, with his face and eye not a bit the worse, but much the better. Then Grandmarina begged to be introduced to the duchess; and, when the duchess was brought down, many compliments passed between them.

A little whispering took place between the fairy and the duchess; and then the fairy said out loud, "Yes, I thought she would have told you." Grandmarina then turned to the king and queen, and said, 'We are going in search of Prince Certainpersonio. The pleasure of your company is requested at church in half an hour precisely." So she and the Princess Alicia got into the carriage; and Mr Pickles's boy handed in the duchess, who sat by herself on the opposite seat; and then Mr Pickles's boy put up the steps and got up behind, and the peacocks flew away with their tails behind.

Prince Certainpersonio was sitting by himself, eating barley-sugar, and waiting to be ninety. When he saw the peacocks, followed by the carriage, coming in at the window, it immediately occurred to him that something uncommon was going to happen.

"Prince," said Grandmarina, "I bring you your bride."

The moment the fairy said those words, Prince Certainpersonio's face left off being sticky, and his jacket and corduroys changed to peach-bloom velvet, and his hair curled, and a cap and feather flew in like a bird and settled on his head. He got into the carriage by the fairy's invitation; and there he renewed his acquaintance with the duchess, whom he had seen before.

In the church were the prince's relations and friends, and the Princess Alicia's relations and friends, and the seventeen princes and princesses, and the baby, and a crowd of neighbours. The marriage was beautiful beyond expression. The duchess was bridesmaid, and beheld the ceremony from the pulpit, where she was supported by the cushion of the desk.

Grandmarina gave a magnificent wedding-feast afterwards, in which there was everything and more to eat, and everything and more to drink. The wedding cake was delicately ornamented with white satin ribbons, frosted silver, and white lilies, and was forty-two yards round.

When Grandmarina had drunk her love to the young couple, and Prince Certainpersonio had made a speech, and everybody had cried, Hip, hip, hip, hurrah! Grandmarina announced to the king and queen that in future there would be eight quarter-days in every year, except in leap-year, when there would be ten. She then turned to Certainpersonio and Alicia, and said, "My dears, you will have thirty-five children, and they will all be good and beautiful. Seventeen of your children will be boys, and eighteen will be girls. The hair of the whole of your children will curl naturally. They will never have the measles, and will have recovered from the whooping-cough before being born."

On hearing such good news, everybody cried out "Hip, hip, hip, hurrah!" again.

THE MARRIAGE WAS BEAUTIFUL BEYOND EXPRESSION

"It only remains," said Grandmarina in conclusion, "to make an end of the fish-bone."

So she took it from the hand of the Princess Alicia, and it instantly flew down the throat of the dreadful little snapping pug-dog, next door, and choked him, and he expired in convulsions.

JEAN INGELOW (1820-1897)
"Melon Seeds" from *Mopsa the Fairy* (1869)

Jean Ingelow was widely respected in mid-Victorian England as a narrative poet before she wrote the quest romance *Mopsa the Fairy*. Many aspects of this children's novel show the deep influence of poetry on her writing: the language is metaphorical and songs are frequent. Even though incidents in the plot spring forth arbitrarily and characters appear at the whim of the author, *Mopsa* is the work of a skilled storyteller. It possesses a delicately arranged circularity in which a human boy, Jack, journeys to a fully realized domain called Fairyland and back again, and his fairy comrade, Mopsa, flees her queenly duties only to resume them at the end. Having been flown to and from Fairyland by an albatross called Jenny—who informs Jack that "when boys go to Fairyland, their parents never are uneasy about them"—the lad returns to his unperturbed family in the evening, just in

time for bed. Although, in the interval, Jack and Mopsa have travelled through a region whose machine-like inhabitants are wound up each day by the Fairy Queen, lost one fairy companion to an attacking raven, and met an untrustworthy gipsy woman and the Stone People (petrified on account of their heartlessness), their exploits are neither dreadful nor frightening. A series of charming adventures, *Mopsa the Fairy* is a romantic dream in which a generous, protective boy comes to love a fairy girl but consents to leave her behind in the capable hands of his fairy double, appropriately named Jack. The story also contains some moral lessons, but Ingelow teaches with amiable gentleness.

"Melon Seeds", one of the middle chapters of *Mopsa the Fairy*, relates the continuing adventures of Jack and Mopsa as they journey deeper into Fairyland.

MELON SEEDS

ROSALIND. Well, this is the forest of Arden.
TOUCHSTONE. Ay, now am I in Arden: the more fool I: when I was
at home I was in a better place; but travellers must be content.
                                    —As You Like It.

"Where is it now?" said the stone-woman; and when Jack heard that he ran down to the river, and looked right and looked left. At last he saw his boat—a mere speck in the distance, it had floated so far.

He called it, but it was far beyond the reach of his voice; and Mopsa, who had followed him, said:

"It does not signify, Jack, for I feel that no place is the right place for me but that country beyond the purple mountains, and I shall never be happy unless we go there."

So they walked back towards the stone-people hand in hand, and the apple-woman presently joined them. She was crying gently, for she knew that she must soon pass over the little stream and part with these whom she called her dear children. Jack had often spoken to her that day about going home to her own country, but she said it was too late to think of that now, and she must end her days in the land of Faery.

The kind stone-people asked them to come and sit by their little fire; and in the dusk the woman whose baby had slept in a stone cradle took it up and began to sing to it. She seemed astonished when she heard

that the apple-woman had power to go home if she could make up her
mind to do it; and as she sang she looked at her with wonder and pity.

> Little babe, while burns the west,
> Warm thee, warm thee in my breast;
> While the moon doth shine her best,
>   And the dews distil not.
>
> All the land so sad, so fair—
> Sweet its toils are, blest its care.
> Child, we may not enter there!
>   Some there are that will not.
>
> Fain would I thy margins know,
> Land of work, and land of snow;
> Land of life, whose rivers flow
>   On, and on, and stay not.
>
> Fain would I thy small limbs fold,
> While the weary hours are told,
> Little babe in cradle cold.
>   Some there are that may not.

"You are not exactly fairies, I suppose?" said Jack. "If you were, you
could go to our country when you please."

"No," said the woman; "we are not exactly fairies; but we shall be
more like them when our punishment is over."

"I am sorry you are punished," answered Jack, "for you seem very
nice, kind people."

"We were not always kind," answered the woman; "and perhaps we
are only kind now because we have no time and no chance of being
otherwise. I'm sure I don't know about that. We were powerful once,
and we did a cruel deed. I must not tell you what it was. We were told
that our hearts were all as cold as stones—and I suppose they were—
and we were doomed to be stones all our lives, excepting for the two
hours of twilight. There was no one to sow the crops, or water the grass,
so it all failed, and the trees died, and our houses fell, and our possessions were stolen from us."

"It is a very sad thing," observed the apple-woman; and then she said
that she must go, for she had a long way to walk before she should reach
the little brook that led to the country of her own queen; so she kissed
the two children, Jack and Mopsa, and they begged her again to think
better of it, and return to her own land. But she said No; she had no
heart for work now, and could not bear either cold or poverty.

Then the woman who was hugging her little baby, and keeping it cosy
and warm, began to tell Jack and Mopsa that it was time they should
begin to run away to the country over the purple mountains, or else the
Queen would overtake them and be very angry with them; so, with
many promises that they would mind her directions, they set off hand in

hand to run; but before they left her they could see plainly that she was beginning to turn again into stone. However, she had given them a slice of melon with the seeds in it. It had been growing on the edge of the river, and was stone in the daytime, like everything else. "When you are tired," she said, "eat the seeds, and they will enable you to go running on. You can put the slice into this little red pot, which has string handles to it, and you can hang it on your arm. While you have it with you it will not turn to stone, but if you lay it down it will, and then it will be useless."

So, as I said before, Jack and Mopsa set off hand in hand to run; and as they ran all the things and people gradually and softly settled themselves to turn into stone again. Their cloaks and gowns left off fluttering, and hung stiffly; and then they left off their occupations, and sat down, or laid down themselves; and the sheep and cattle turned stiff and stonelike too, so that in a very little while all that country was nothing but red stones and red sands, just as it had been in the morning.

Presently the full moon, which had been hiding behind a cloud, came out, and they saw their shadows, which fell straight before them; so they ran on hand in hand very merrily till the half-moon came up, and the shadows she made them cast fell sideways. This was rather awkward, because as long as only the full moon gave them shadows they had but to follow them in order to go straight towards the purple mountains. Now they were not always sure which were her shadows; and presently a crescent moon came, and still further confused them; also the sand began to have tufts of grass in it; and then, when they had gone a little farther, there were beautiful patches of anemones, and hyacinths, and jonquils, and crown imperials, and they stopped to gather them; and they got among some trees, and then, as they had nothing to guide them but the shadows, and these went all sorts of ways, they lost a great deal of time, and the trees became of taller growth; but they still ran on and on till they got into a thick forest where it was quite dark, and here Mopsa began to cry, for she was tired.

"If I could only begin to be a queen," she said to Jack, "I could go wherever I pleased. I am not a fairy, and yet I am not a proper queen. Oh, what shall I do? I cannot go any farther."

So Jack gave her some of the seeds of the melon, though it was so dark that he could scarcely find the way to her mouth, and then he took some himself, and they both felt they were rested, and Jack comforted Mopsa.

"If you are not a queen yet," he said, "you will be by to-morrow morning; for when our shadows danced on before us yours was so very nearly the same height as mine that I could hardly see any difference."

When they reached the end of that great forest, and found themselves out in all sorts of moonlight, the first thing they did was to laugh—the shadows looked so odd, sticking out in every direction; and the next thing they did was to stand back to back, and put their heels together, and touch their heads together, to see by the shadow which was the taller; and Jack was still the least bit in the world taller than Mopsa; so they knew she was not a queen yet, and they ate some more melon seeds, and began to climb up the mountain.

They climbed till the trees of the forest looked no bigger than gooseberry bushes, and then they climbed till the whole forest looked only like a patch of moss; and then, when they got a little higher, they saw the wonderful river, a long way off, and the snow glittering on the peaks overhead; and while they were looking and wondering how they should find a pass, the moons all went down, one after the other, and, if Mopsa had not found some glow-worms, they would have been quite in the dark again. However, she took a dozen of them, and put them round Jack's ankles, so that when he walked he could see where he was going; and he found a little sheep-path, and she followed him.

Now they had noticed during the night how many shooting-stars kept darting about from time to time, and at last one shot close by them, and fell in the soft moss on before. There it lay shining; and Jack, though he began to feel very tired again, made haste to it, for he wanted to see what it was like.

It was not what you would have supposed. It was soft and round, and about the colour of a ripe apricot, it was covered with fur, and in fact it was evidently alive, and had curled itself up into a round ball.

"The dear little thing!" said Jack, as he held it in his hand, and showed it to Mopsa; "how its heart beats! Is it frightened?"

"Who are you?" said Mopsa to the thing. "What is your name?"

The little creature made a sound that seemed like "Wisp."

"Uncurl yourself, Wisp," said Mopsa. "Jack and I want to look at you."

So Wisp unfolded himself, and showed two little black eyes, and spread out two long filmy wings. He was like a most beautiful bat, and the light he shed out illuminated their faces.

"It is only one of the air fairies," said Mopsa. "Pretty creature! It never did any harm, and would like to do us good if it knew how, for it knows that I shall be a queen very soon. Wisp, if you like, you may go and tell your friends and relations that we want to cross over the mountains, and if they can they may help us."

Upon this Wisp spread out his wings, and shot off again; and Jack's feet were so tired that he sat down, and pulled off one of his shoes, for he thought there was a stone in it. So he set the little red jar beside him, and quite forgot what the stone woman had said, but went on shaking his shoe, and buckling it, and admiring the glowworms round his ankle, till Mopsa said, "Darling Jack, I am so dreadfully tired! Give me some more melon seeds." Then he lifted up the jar, and thought it felt very heavy; and when he put in his hand, jar, and melon, and seeds were all turned to stone together.

They were both very sorry, and they sat still for a minute or two, for they were much too tired to stir; and then shooting-stars began to appear in all directions. The fairy bat had told his friends and relations,

and they were coming. One fell at Mopsa's feet, another in her lap; more, more, all about, behind, before, and over them. And they spread out long filmy wings, some of them a yard long, till Jack and Mopsa seemed to be enclosed in a perfect network of the rays of shooting-stars, and they were both a good deal frightened. Fifty or sixty shooting-stars, with black eyes that could stare, were enough, they thought, to frighten anybody.

"If we had anything to sit upon," said Mopsa, "they could carry us over the pass." She had no sooner spoken than the largest of the bats bit off one of his own long wings, and laid it at Mopsa's feet. It did not seem to matter much to him that he had parted with it, for he shot out another wing directly, just as a comet shoots out a ray of light sometimes, when it approaches the sun.

Mopsa thanked the shooting fairy, and, taking the wing, began to stretch it, till it was large enough for her and Jack to sit upon. Then all the shooting fairies came round it, took its edges in their mouths, and began to fly away with it over the mountains. They went slowly, for Jack and Mopsa were heavy, and they flew very low, resting now and then; but in the course of time they carried the wing over the pass, and half-way down the other side. Then the sun came up; and the moment he appeared all their lovely apricot-coloured light was gone, and they only looked like common bats, such as you can see every evening.

They set down Jack and Mopsa, folded up their long wings, and hung down their heads.

Mopsa thanked them, and said they had been useful; but still they looked ashamed, and crept into little corners and crevices of the rock, to hide.

EDWARD KNATCHBULL-HUGESSEN (1829-1893)
"Ernest" from *Puss-Cat Mew and Other Stories for My Children* (1869)

While serving as a Liberal member of Parliament, Knatchbull-Hugessen (Baron Brabourne) evidently found time to entertain his four children with evening stories. He, and presumably his children, favoured horrific tales, and Knatchbull-Hugessen published at least ten collections of them. *Stories for My Children* (1869) elicited "unfavourable criticism" for the cruelty in the tales, and in his next volume, *Crackers for Christmas* (1870), he promised "certain tender-hearted people" more moderate fare. However, in his later and best-known collection, *Queer Folk* (1874), he positively exulted in accounts of warlocks, witches, barn elves, and a society of pig-faced ladies, calling the work "as queer a collection of creatures as ever came together in a story-book".

"Ernest" is not one of his exceptionally cruel tales. Knatchbull-Hugessen, though, gives it special mention in his preface because he was pleased to claim for it "a family resemblance to 'Alice in Wonderland' ", while hastening to exonerate himself from the "suspicion . . . of plagiarism". Ernest is certainly as polite as Alice, as confused by Toad-land as Alice was by Wonderland, and as hectored by the Toad as Alice was by the March Hare. The parody songs of the Toadstools recall—but are inferior to—Carroll's brilliant lyrics, and the problems that beset Ernest, like devising the proper etiquette for dancing with "a delicate White Mouse", are comparable to—but less witty than—the topsy-turvy logic and conundrums of Wonderland. Nonetheless, Knatchbull-Hugessen's tale is both highly inventive and enjoyable.

ERNEST

A little boy named Ernest was once playing at ball by himself in the garden, when his ball suddenly bounded into the well, and fell down with a loud splash. Many boys would have bitten their thumbs with vexation, and given the matter up as a bad job; some might even have cried; and hardly a boy but what would have been more or less put out at losing a new ball in so stupid a manner.

Ernest, however, not being a common boy, and having a particular liking for this ball, immediately splashed in head foremost after it. He knocked himself a little against the sides of the well, but he didn't care for that a bit; and though the water felt rather cold, it only freshened him up, and made him all the more determined to find his ball. Down he went for some distance, and at last got to what he supposed to be the bottom of the well. He wasn't far wrong, either; but the well was much larger at the bottom than the top, and all the water in it seemed to come up like a wall from the ground, leaving a large dry space all round it, into which Ernest crept out of the water, and began to look about him. It wasn't so *very* dry, either, but rather moist, and he could see no ball anywhere; but all round the sides of the kind of cave in which he was there was a bright substance like crystal, which lighted up the place, and on the floor sat an enormous Toad, smoking a very bad cigar, and evidently thinking himself every body. He turned upon Ernest directly, and cried out to him in an angry tone,

"You presumptuous fool, how dare you come down here?"

Now Ernest, having been carefully brought up, was well aware that no one loses any thing by politeness. Far from being angry, therefore, he replied, with the lowest bow which circumstances enabled him to make,

"Presumptuous, sir, I may possibly be, but it can hardly be the act of a fool which has brought me into the presence of so noble and handsome a Toad as yourself."

"Not so bad," replied the Toad; "I see you have been taught manners. But what do you want?"

"My ball, sir," said Ernest; when instantly a low silvery laugh echoed through the cave, and the Toad, after swelling till Ernest thought he must certainly burst, went into a fit of laughter which rather puzzled the boy.

"Your ball!" at length shouted the Toad. "If you mean that india rubber affair that came crashing down here some time ago, I should hope it was long since cut up into gaiters for the tame Mice; for it was fit for nothing else, and they were beginning to want new leggings. But as for balls, you shall see such a ball as you've never seen up above Toadland, if you only wait for a moment."

With that the Toad spat in the air, which was his way of ringing the bell, and immediately a door was thrown open behind him, and several hundred Toadstools came rushing in and stood on their heads all round him.

The Toad then marched solemnly through the door, and the Toadstools after him, two and two, till Ernest had counted about four hundred. Then he got tired of counting, and thought he might as well follow and see what they were all going to do. So he kicked aside several Toadstools that came in his way, and passed on through the door after the procession.

Presently they came to quite a large room, entirely lighted by Glowworms; and here were assembled a great number of Mice, some of whom had gaiters on, which appeared to Ernest to be made of some stuff suspiciously like india rubber. He had no time, however, to think about it, for as they entered the room the band was striking up a merry tune, and the Mice were asking each other to dance, and forming sets of Lancers just as people do in the world above.

"Will you dance in a sixteen set?" said the Toad to Ernest; but he was so confused that he hardly knew what to say: at last he stammered out,

"If you please, sir, shan't I stamp on somebody? I'm very much afraid I shall never be able to help it."

"That's *their* look-out," replied the Toad. "Now don't be a fool, but get a partner at once."

Ernest was dreadfully puzzled, for he didn't know whether he ought to ask a Mouse, a Toadstool or the Toad itself to dance; but while he was doubting what to do, a delicate White Mouse came softly up to him, and murmured in a soft but somewhat shrill voice,

"If you would please to dance with me, sir, in a quiet set of eight, I shall be *so* delighted!"

So Ernest bowed civilly, and, as he could not give his arm to the Mouse, he offered her his hand, upon which she sat till the set was formed and they began to dance. Ernest took great care, and all went well until the last figure, when the music went quick, and he was so terribly afraid of hurting somebody that he came to a dead stop, and sat down, as ill-luck would have it, right on the top of a Toadstool, who squashed instantly.

His companions began to abuse Ernest violently, telling him that he was an awkward Fungus, and, in fact, no better than a mere Mushroom. But the White Mouse took his part, and explained that it was all a mistake; and as the squashed Toadstool was not by any means a popular person, he was soon forgotten.

Ernest now asked his partner if he should fetch her some lemonade or a glass of sherry, to which she mildly responded that she felt inclined for a crumb or two of toasted cheese, if he knew where it was to be found. He looked right and left, and seeing a number of the Mice crowding up into one corner, justly guessed that the supper was there: so pushing his way along, with his partner in his hand, he soon discovered a table, on which toasted cheese formed a large part of the eatables. Having placed his partner on this table, he soon saw that she was so fully occupied that he might just as well amuse himself by looking about him. Accordingly he walked back to the middle of the room, and perceived the Toad seated upon a Toadstool, and making facetious remarks upon every body about him.

As soon as he saw Ernest, "Halloo, you upper-world boy!" he cried; "how do you like the ball?"

"Very much sir," replied Ernest, respectfully; upon which the Toad rejoined,

"But you must have had enough of it now—at least I know *I* have; so come and feed the gold and silver Fish;" and beckoning Ernest to follow him, he hopped off to a passage in one side of the room, down which he went for some little way, when there appeared more and more light; and Ernest presently found himself in a pleasant garden, in which was a large round pond, full of gold and silver Fish. The Toad knew all these by their names, and they came at his call like dogs to their master. He then began to feed them, his method of doing which was rather peculiar: the Toadstools put crumbs on his back, and then he leaped into the water, and the Fish came swimming round, and took the crumbs off as he told them.

"Come," said he to Ernest, "do as I do, young Worlding."

But Ernest said he was afraid of catching cold, and had rather stay where he was.

"Why *didn't* you stay where you were, then—up above?" said the Toad; "if you come to Toad-land, you ought to do as Toads do: and as to catching cold, you can't do that here; *our* colds run so fast that nobody ever catches them, and if they do, they are not such fools as to keep them, as you human beings sometimes do, for weeks together."

Ernest bowed silently, for he feared to continue the argument, lest he might be obliged to feed the Fish in the very unpleasant manner adopted by the Toad. The latter, however, soon got tired of his amusement, and, leaping from the pond, told Ernest to come along with him and hear the Toadstools sing. To this Ernest willingly consented; and the first Toadstool who was in attendance upon the Royal Toad immediately began, in a voice hoarse with emotion,

> "Abroad in the morning to see the bold Toads
> Squat silently down by the side of the roads,
>   With speckles so yellow and bright,
> With their servants behind them, the marsh-loving Frogs,
> Who hurry to follow, from ponds and from bogs,
>   And croak till the coming of night."

"There!" said the Toad, triumphantly, "you won't hear such a singer as *that* every day. What would you do with him, if you had him up above?"

"I think," quietly observed Ernest, "that as he seems so hoarse, I should give him a lozenge."

"Fool!" answered the Toad, angrily, "what would be the use of *that*, when he has got no mouth?"

"No more he has," said Ernest; "I quite forgot that."

"Think before you speak, then," said the Toad. And Ernest began wondering how a creature without a mouth could sing at all, and whether a Toadstool could properly be called a creature; and then he began to say, half aloud, some verses which he remembered to have heard his nurse sing to him:

> " 'Tis the voice of the Toadstool, I heard him complain,
> I came up in the night from a smart shower of rain;
> As a worthless old Fungus, so he in his bed
> Is left, while the people pick Mushrooms instead."

But these unlucky words were hardly out of his mouth, when a chorus of Toadstool voices began abusing him in the most furious language, and the Toad himself flew into a violent passion.

"Frogs' legs and heads!" exclaimed he; "was ever person so insulted? A common Mushroom, that folks eat upon toast with ketchup, preferred to an elegant and ornamental Toadstool! Out upon you, Worldling!—you tasteless monster!"

Ernest was rather confused at this, and could think of nothing better to say than that he had meant no harm, and that it was from love and admiration for Toadstools that people in the upper world forbore to eat them. This statement somewhat calmed the offended followers of the Toad; but a sulkiness seemed to pervade the party, until the Toad, who had cooled down quite suddenly, and appeared as friendly as ever, asked Ernest what he would like to do next. Wishing to make himself as pleasant as possible, the boy suggested a game of "leap-frog."

"Leap-toad, I suppose you mean," grumbled the Toad; "but you seem determined to call every thing by its wrong name to-day: but you shall have what you want." And ringing the bell again in his usual manner, he directed the Toadstools to fetch in the leapers; upon which several of them vanished, and soon returned, ushering in a large number of small Toads, who began dancing and leaping about in every direction.

"But that isn't what I meant," said Ernest; "don't you know how to play the real game of leap-frog—I mean leap-toad—down here? One of you stands still and bends forward, and another jumps over him—like this." And Ernest imitated the manner in which one boy makes a back and another jumps over it at leap-frog.

"Don't come down here to teach your betters," shouted the Toad; "that may be upper-world leap-toad, but this is Toad-land leap-toad. We ought to know best, being regular toads; and if you don't like it, you may lump it;" and so saying, he sat down again and didn't speak another word for several minutes, during which time Ernest watched the

Toads skipping about as fast as they could, till, at a signal from the old Toad, they suddenly ranged themselves in a line against the side of the room, and remained perfectly silent and motionless.

"Now," said the Toad, "you shall see an illumination;" and at the word of command each of the leaping Toads drew from his pocket a lucifer-match, lighted it by striking it against the wall, and stuck it into his mouth. This produced a curious effect, and the Toad appeared highly delighted at it, keeping the leapers there until the matches had burnt so low that their eyes began to wink, and they trembled visibly; then, at a wave of his cigar, they all got rid of their matches as quickly as they could, and at a second signal disappeared down the passage out of which they had come.

Ernest now began to recollect that, with all these amusements, he was no nearer getting his ball, and therefore he politely remarked to the Toad that he should be much obliged if he would tell him where it was to be found.

"Drat your ball!" angrily answered the Toad; "it's dead—it's burst—it's changed into a mouse—any thing you please, only don't bother, but be contented."

"But I would go to the end of the world to get my ball," said Ernest, mournfully.

"Yes, you stupid world-child," remarked the Toad, "and tumble off when you'd got there, as a friend of mine once did, and fell down, and down, till he turned into a star, poor fool, and has stuck there, shining like an idiot of a Glow-worm ever since. I should have thought you had had enough of tumbling by this time; but if you really want your ball, you must tumble again."

So saying, the Toad fiercely stamped his foot upon the ground, at the same time taking his eyes out of his head, throwing them up to the ceiling, and catching them again as cleverly as an Indian juggler; after which he replaced them carefully, but took care to put the right eye where the left one was before, and the left in the place of the right. As soon as he had done this, he winked in the most frightful manner, and stamped upon the ground again. Immediately Ernest felt the floor giving way beneath him, and down he sunk, so quickly that he could not even try to save himself, and all he heard was the voice of the Toad croaking, more and more faintly as he got farther and farther off,

"*Go* to the end of the world, then, and see how you like it!"

Somehow or other Ernest found this kind of sinking a remarkably easy way of travelling; he went so softly and smoothly that he did not feel the least uncomfortable or giddy; and though he seemed to be passing now through clay, now chalk, and now through something so black that he thought it must be coal, nothing seemed to come off on his jacket, and when he was brought up with a sudden jerk, he was as clean and comfortable, and just as self-composed, as if he had been all the time in his father's garden at home.

He shook himself thoroughly, to be sure that he was awake, and then looked around. Where in the world—or out of the world—was he? On the brink of an enormous precipice, to look over which made him giddy at once; and he felt sure, without being told, that he had really got to the end of the world.

Giddy as he was, he still determined that he must and would peep over to see what there was to be seen; and accordingly he lay down flat on his stomach and looked over. He saw lights at different distances from each other, which he took to be stars; some so large and glaring that they made him wink and shut his eyes when he tried to look at them, others paler and more dim, as if farther off. And then he saw, floating all round him in every direction, a quantity of clouds—at least they looked like clouds at first; but each one had a face, and an uncomfortable sort of anxious expression seemed to rest on every countenance, as it blew first one way and then another, like leaves at the corner of the street which the wind whirls about and catches up and drives in different directions. Still, each Cloud-face seemed to be trying to go its own way, and never to be quite satisfied whichever way it was going.

"What on earth are these?" said Ernest to himself.

"On earth, my child," said a voice near him, "they were undecided people, who spent their time in making and unmaking all their plans, small and great, and could never settle what was best to be done. So now, having left the earth, they are doomed to pursue the same course which they did in life, and are making up their minds—or trying to do it—as you see. The end of the world makes no difference to them, and it will probably be centuries before their minds are finally made up, until which event they blow about here as undecided as ever."

Ernest started at the sound of this voice, and turning round his head as well as he could, saw to his surprise a venerable Oyster close to him, whose large beard betokened his extreme age. He was open, or else of course Ernest could not have seen his beard; and the sight of him would have reminded the boy at once of vinegar and thin slices of brown bread and butter, had not his voice so surprised him that he could think of nothing else. It was a soft, low voice, sweet to the ear, and not unlike the gentle pattering of the rain against the window when the wind blows it up from the south-west. And Ernest, in spite of his surprise at hearing the Oyster speak, felt a great respect for him at once, and addressed him with the reverence due from youth to age.

"Pray, sir," asked he in a humble tone, "is this the end of the world?"

"Shut me tight if I know!" replied the Oyster; "but by all accounts I believe it is, and I wouldn't go too near the edge, if I was you."

"Thank you, sir," replied Ernest; and then, after a moment's hesitation, "How long have you been here, and how did you come?"

"I was born here," said the Oyster, "about a thousand years ago, more or less; but it is very impertinent to ask questions. I thought that nobody did *that*, except the commoner sort of Mussels, or the discarded shell of an old Crab. Pray don't get into such habits."

"But," remarked Ernest, "I am very anxious to find my ball, and I want to know all about the strange places I come to in looking for it."

"Then," solemnly replied the Oyster, "you had better ask somebody else."

"But there *is* nobody else," said Ernest.

"Ah!" sighed the Oyster, "no more there is. I had never thought of *that*; but you know, one can't go on talking forever." And without another word he suddenly shut, nor would he open again for any thing that Ernest could say.

This was decidedly unpleasant; the more especially as the place on which Ernest was lying was a kind of ledge, with the precipice in front and a wall of chalk behind, and on this ledge he could see nothing but the Oyster. However, he was determined not to be annoyed by trifles: so he crept along the ledge a little way, and presently came to a turning which led away from the precipice right into the chalk. He went down this a few yards, when he suddenly heard a laugh, and, looking up, saw a little old Man sitting on a shelf above his head. He couldn't have been more than two feet high, and he had a hooked nose, rather like Punch, and a merry eye, and a clay pipe in his mouth, which he had taken out to laugh.

"I hope I don't intrude, sir," said Ernest.

"By no means," answered the little Man; "I am very glad to see you. I am the Man in the Moon, and of course I have come down before my time; and as to asking my way to Norwich, it is quite useless, for I find the people there are frightened at my very name just now; so I have sauntered down here to be out of the way for a time."

"And can you get back again when you please, sir?" said Ernest.

"To be sure I can," replied the little Man, "but I don't want to go just yet. I like to be on the shelf for a little while, now and then; it rests me. And there is a good look-out up here, too. Come up and try!" So saying, he held out his hand to Ernest, and helped him up to the shelf.

There, indeed, was the strangest sight you ever saw. A number of windows, cut in the chalk, enabled you to look out over the whole country around the end of the world, and out of each window you had quite a different view.

Ernest looked through the first one, and saw a number of people pushing and panting with exertion, trying to get through a door which was shut, and which no effort of theirs could force open. They seemed dreadfully disappointed, and their faces were yards long with vexation.

"Who are those?" asked Ernest.

"Oh!" said the man in the Moon, "those are the people who always declared there was no other world than the one they lived in: so now that they have got to the end of it, they have been taken at their word. They have done with one world, and no other will have any thing to say to them; so there they are, pushing and struggling on, unable to go backward or forward."

Ernest looked, and looked again; and then, as it was rather a sad sight, he moved a little way along the shelf and looked through another window. There he saw a number of things like very large leaves of trees, tossing up and down in inextricable confusion, sometimes blown up high as if by the wind, and sometimes sinking down again, each with a curious face to it, on which appeared a restless and unhappy expression.

"Whatever are these?" said Ernest.

"These are Senses," said his companion. "When people up above have lost their senses, they generally blow down here, where they perhaps do less harm than if they had remained with their former owners. They are always, however, trying to get back again; but there is so much nonsense in the world that they hardly ever do so, and not one person out of a hundred in the world gets his senses back when he once loses them, as his brain is instantly stuffed full of nonsense, so that there would be no room for them if they *did* get back."

Ernest turned away and looked through another window, and saw a quantity of birds, of every sort and description, flying about all over the place.

"Ah!" said his friend, "these are the rotten eggs. Don't suppose that a rotten egg in a nest means that there was no bird belonging to it. Only, instead of hatching like a common bird, the rotten-egg birds fly off here to the end of the world, and there, you see, is a regular comfortable place provided for them."

Ernest thought this a very fair arrangement; for why should one egg fare better than another?

He moved on, however, and, looking through another window, saw a number of men walking up and down on a platform, from which they could not move, while opposite them were placed a number of large boards, with various inscriptions in large blue and gold and red letters.

"What does this mean?" asked the boy.

"These," said the Man in the Moon, "are railway directors, who have bored people so terribly, when waiting for their trains, by having great staring advertisements put up at their railway stations, that now, while *they* are waiting at the end of the world, they are condemned to stay on a platform and have nothing to read but these same advertisements. Look at that stout old gentleman with 'Thorley's Food for Cattle' before him, and that one next him looking up at 'Horniman's Tea.' I warrant they'll never allow such things again if they should ever be directors of an underground railway, or an atmospheric company."

Ernest thought this was all very curious, and rather puzzling: so he didn't look through any more of the windows; but, turning to his pleasant friend, told him the reason why he had come to the end of the world, and asked him where he thought the ball was to be found.

"Found!" said the Man in the Moon; "why, don't you know that india-rubber balls always rebound? Of course, as soon as your ball got to the bottom of the well and struck the ground, it bounded up again as fast as it could, and the wonder is that it didn't strike you in the face as you came down. Your ball is probably waiting for you at the place where you were playing with it when you lost it."

"Dear me!" said Ernest, "I never thought of that. But how am *I* to get up again? *I* can't rebound, you know."

"Of course not," replied his friend; "but there is nothing easier in the world than to do what you wish. I am going back myself directly, and will show you all about it in a minute."

Accordingly, he took his pipe in his left hand, and with the stem of it touched a spring in the chalk rock, when a door immediately opened and disclosed a large cupboard, in which were several enormous tumblers.

"Now," said the Man in the Moon, "have you ever taken a saline draught?"

"Yes," replied Ernest; "you mean the thing that fizzes up when you put water on the powder?"

"Exactly so," rejoined his friend; "but I dare say you never *were* a saline draught, were you?"

Ernest stared, and said he certainly never had been yet; but having long ceased to be surprised at any thing, he was quite ready to believe that he might become a draught, or a pill, or even a dose of rhubarb and magnesia, at any moment. The Man in the Moon told him that he must do exactly as he saw *him* do; and he then took two small powders, wrapped in blue paper, out of his waistcoat pocket, and shook one of them into each of two tumblers, which he took out and placed upon the shelf. He then deliberately got into one of the tumblers, and told Ernest to get into the other; after which he took a bottle from the cupboard, which was labelled Double X, meaning, no doubt, that it was a very extraordinary mixture. And so it was; for the Man in the Moon had no sooner poured half of it into Ernest's tumbler and half of it into his own, than they both began bubbling and fizzing like soda-water very much "up." Very much "up" they soon were; for the mixture, carrying them with it, fizzed right up out of the tumblers and through the earth. Every thing seemed to give way before them, or else they had hit upon the same passage as that down which Ernest had come, or one very like it. Up, up they went, past coal, and clay, and chalk, as comfortably and as easily as possible; and the last thing Ernest remembered was seeing the Man in the Moon nodding, and smiling, and kissing his hand to him, as he mounted far above him. Then Ernest lifted up his head, opened his eyes wide, and looked around. Where was he? Why, under the mulberry-trees that grew near the well in his own father's garden! The cool air was blowing on his face, and the pleasant sunlight was shining down upon him, and there was a gentle rustling of the mulberry-leaves above his head, and he sat up and rubbed his eyes in astonishment. Close to him, on the ground, uncut and unhurt, dry and safe, was his india-rubber ball.

"Then the Toad told a story," cried he, "and the tame Mice have *not* got new leggings!"

"New leggings, indeed!" said a voice near him. "What's all that nonsense about mice and leggings? I think we poor maids shall be wanting new legs soon if we have to run about after you children so long. Why, Master Ernest, I've been hunting for you this half-hour. There have your sisters gone in to tea, and Miss Jones has been asking after you, and here you are fast asleep under the mulberry-trees!—I declare it's enough to worrit one to death; and all because of that apple-pie and custard you ate such a lot of at dinner, I'll be bound! *Do* come along, there's a good boy!

So Ernest got up and looked the maid straight in the face, and said, "Jane, were you ever down a well?"

"Down a well, Master Ernest!—no, to be sure not; who ever heard of such a thing? But I shall be up a tree if I don't bring you in to Miss Jones pretty soon!"

Ernest said no more, but went quietly with the maid, who told his sisters and their governess that he had been asleep under the mulberry-trees all the afternoon. You and I know better, but it does not always do to tell all one knows out loud. But, as the Toad, and the Oyster, and the Man in the Moon all knew too, it is no wonder that the real truth came out in spite of Ernest's silence; and in fact, if one of them hadn't told me, *I* should never have known all the wonderful things that I have been telling you, for I don't believe the india-rubber ball would ever have said a word about it!

CHRISTINA GEORGINA ROSSETTI (1830-1894)
"A Party in the Land of Nowhere" from *Speaking Likenesses* (1874)

Sister of the Pre-Raphaelite poet Dante Gabriel Rossetti, Christina, a celebrated poet herself, had already written *Goblin Market* (1862) and *Sing-Song: A Nursery Rhyme Book* (1872) before the three stories that make up *Speaking Likenesses* were published. Her working title for this collection was "Nowhere", the name of the land where the adventures take place. "Speaking Likenesses", however, is a more precise description of these tales in which thought, speech, and action all convey symbolic messages. In sending off this "Christmas trifle, would-be in the Alice style" to her London publisher, Macmillan, Miss Rossetti admitted the influence of her friend Lewis Carroll.

The first of these untitled stories—reproduced below—is told by a loving yet instructive Aunt to several little girls. The petty bickering of the young guests at eight-year-old Flora's birthday party supplies the pretext for a second party, which is a grotesque exaggeration of the first—an anti-masque during which Flora is jostled and poked. The mode of entry to Nowhere, the changes in size that occur there, and the chaotic arbitrariness that prevails—along with the unfriendly treatment of Flora—all suggest a strong Carrollean influence. But the magic of Wonderland is absent from this basically didactic fantasy.

The return to the first party is shatteringly abrupt: it would seem that Rossetti tired of the story after she had finished with the second party. It is in this nightmarish Land of Nowhere sequence, however, that her considerable strength and interest as a storyteller are most evident.

A PARTY IN THE LAND OF NOWHERE

Come sit round me, my dear little girls, and I will tell you a story. Now I start my knitting and my story together.

Whoever saw Flora on her birthday morning, at half-past seven o'clock on that morning, saw a very pretty sight. Eight years old to a minute, and not awake yet. Her cheeks were plump and pink, her light hair was all tumbled, her little red lips were held together as if to kiss some one; her eyes also, if you could have seen them, were blue and merry, but for the moment they had gone fast asleep and out of sight under fat little eyelids. Wagga the dog was up and about, Muff the cat was up and about, chirping birds were up and about; or if they were mere nestlings and so could not go about (supposing, that is, that there were still a few nestlings so far on in summer), at least they sat together wide awake in the nest, with wide open eyes and most of them with wide open beaks, which was all they could do: only sleepy Flora slept on, and dreamed on, and never stirred.

Her mother stooping over the child's soft bed woke her with a kiss. "Good morning, my darling, I wish you many and many happy returns of the day," said the kind, dear mother: and Flora woke up to a sense of sunshine, and of pleasure full of hope. To be eight years old when last night one was merely seven, this is pleasure: to hope for birthday presents without any doubt of receiving some, this also is pleasure. And doubtless you now think so, my children, and it is quite right that so you should think: yet I tell you, from the sad knowledge of my older experience, that to every one of you a day will most likely come when sunshine, hope, presents and pleasure will be worth nothing to you in comparison with the unattainable gift of your mother's kiss.

On the breakfast table lay presents for Flora: a story-book full of pictures from her father, a writing-case from her mother, a gilt pincushion like a hedgehog from nurse, a box of sugar-plums and a doll from Alfred her brother and Susan her sister; the most tempting of sugar-plums, the most beautiful of curly-pated dolls, they appeared in her eyes.

A further treat was in store. "Flora," said her mother, when admiration was at last silent and breakfast over: "Flora, I have asked Richard, George, Anne and Emily to spend the day with you and with Susan and Alfred. You are to be queen of the feast, because it is your birthday; and I trust you will all be very good and happy together."

Flora loved her brother and sister, her friend Emily, and her cousins Richard, George and Anne: indeed I think that with all their faults these children did really love each other. They had often played together before; and now if ever, surely on this so special occasion they would play pleasantly together. Well, we shall see.

Anne with her brothers arrived first: and Emily having sent to ask permission, made her appearance soon after accompanied by a young friend, who was spending the holidays with her, and whom she introduced as Serena.

Emily brought Flora a sweet-smelling nosegay; and Serena protested that Flora was the most charming girl she had ever met, except of course dearest Emily.

"Love me," said Serena, throwing her arms round her small hostess and giving her a clinging kiss: "I will love you so much if you will only let me love you."

The house was a most elegant house, the lawn was a perfect park, the elder brother and sister frightened her by their cleverness: so exclaimed Serena: and for the moment silly little Flora felt quite tall and superior, and allowed herself to be loved very graciously.

After the arrivals and the settling down, there remained half-an-hour before dinner, during which to cultivate acquaintance and exhibit presents. Flora displayed her doll and handed round her sugar-plum box. "You took more than I did and it isn't fair," grumbled George at Richard: but Richard retorted, "Why, I saw you picking out the big ones." "Oh," whined Anne, "I'm sure there were no big ones left when they came to me." And Emily put in with a smile of superiority: "Stuff, Anne: you got the box before Serena and I did, and *we* don't complain." "But there wasn't one," persisted Anne. "But there were dozens and dozens," mimicked George, "only you're such a greedy little baby." "Not one," whimpered Anne. Then Serena remarked soothingly: "The sugar-plums were most delicious, and now let us admire the lovely doll. Why, Flora, she must have cost pounds and pounds."

Flora, who had begun to look rueful, brightened up: "I don't know

what she cost, but her name is Flora, and she has red boots with soles. Look at me opening and shutting her eyes, and I can make her say Mamma. Is she not a beauty?" "I never saw half such a beauty," replied smooth Serena. Then the party sat down to dinner.

Was it fact? Was it fancy? Each dish in turn was only fit to be found fault with. Meat underdone, potatoes overdone, beans splashy, jam tart not sweet enough, fruit all stone; covers clattering, glasses reeling, a fork or two dropping on the floor. Were these things really so? or would even finest strawberries and richest cream have been found fault with, thanks to the children's mood that day?

Sad to say, what followed was a wrangle. An hour after dinner blindman's buff in the garden began well and promised well: why could it not go on well? Ah, why indeed? for surely before now in that game toes have been trodden on, hair pulled, and small children overthrown. Flora fell down and accused Alfred of tripping her up, Richard bawled out that George broke away when fairly caught, Anne when held tight muttered that Susan could see in spite of bandaged eyes. Susan let go, Alfred picked up his little sister, George volunteered to play blindman in Susan's stead: but still pouting and grumbling showed their ugly faces, and tossed the apple of discord to and fro as if it had been a pretty plaything.

Would you like, any of you, a game at hide-and-seek in a garden, where there are plenty of capital hiding-places and all sorts of gay flowers to glance at while one goes seeking? I should have liked such a game, I assure you, forty years ago. But these children on this particular day could not find it in their hearts to like it. Oh dear no. Serena affected to be afraid of searching along the dusky yew alley unless Alfred went with her; and at the very same moment Flora was bent on having him lift her up to look down into a hollow tree in which it was quite obvious Susan could not possibly have hidden. "It's my birthday," cried Flora; "it's my birthday". George and Richard pushed each other roughly about till one slipped on the gravel walk and grazed his hands, when both turned cross and left off playing. At last in sheer despair Susan stepped out of her hiding-place behind the summer-house: but even then she did her best to please everybody, for she brought in her hand a basket full of ripe mulberries which she had picked up off the grass as she stood in hiding.

Then they all set to running races across the smooth sloping lawn: till Anne tumbled down and cried, though she was not a bit hurt; and Flora, who was winning the race against Anne, thought herself ill-used and so sat and sulked. Then Emily smiled, but not good-naturedly, George and Richard thrust each a finger into one eye and made faces at the two cross girls. Serena fanned herself, and Alfred looked at Susan, and Susan at Alfred, fairly at their wits' end.

Poor little Flora: was this the end of her birthday? was she eight years old at last only for this? Her sugar-plums almost all gone and not cared for, her chosen tart not a nice one, herself so cross and miserable: is it really worth while to be eight years old and have a birthday, if this is what comes of it? She lagged and dropped behind not noticed by any one, but creeping along slowly and sadly by herself.

Down the yew alley she turned, and it looked dark and very gloomy as she passed out of the sunshine into the shadow. There were twenty yew trees on each side of the path, as she had counted over and over again a great many years ago when she was learning to count; but now at her right hand there stood twenty-one: and if the last tree was really a yew tree at all, it was at least a very odd one, for a lamp grew on its topmost branch. Never before either had the yew walk led to a door: but now at its further end stood a door with bell and knocker, and "Ring also" printed in black letters on a brass plate; all as plain as possible in the lamplight.

Flora stretched up her hand, and knocked and rang also.

She was surprised to feel the knocker shake hands with her, and to see the bell handle twist round and open the door. "Dear me," thought she, "why could not the door open itself instead of troubling the bell?" But she only said, "Thank you," and walked in.

The door opened into a large and lofty apartment, very handsomely furnished. All the chairs were stuffed arm-chairs, and moved their arms and shifted their shoulders to accommodate sitters. All the sofas arranged and rearranged their pillows as convenience dictated. Footstools glided about, and rose or sank to meet every length of leg. Tables were

no less obliging, but ran on noiseless castors here or there when wanted. Tea-trays ready set out, saucers of strawberries, jugs of cream, and plates of cake, floated in, settled down, and floated out again empty, with considerable tact and good taste: they came and went through a square hole high up in one wall, beyond which I presume lay the kitchen. Two harmoniums, an accordion, a pair of kettledrums and a peal of bells played concerted pieces behind a screen, but kept silence during conversation. Photographs and pictures made the tour of the apartment, standing still when glanced at and going on when done with. In case of need the furniture flattened itself against the wall, and cleared the floor for a game, or I dare say for a dance. Of these remarkable details some struck Flora in the first few minutes after her arrival, some came to light as time went by. The only uncomfortable point in the room, that is, as to furniture, was that both ceiling and walls were lined throughout with looking-glasses: but at first this did not strike Flora as any disadvantage; indeed she thought it quite delightful, and took a long look at her little self full length.

The room was full of boys and girls, older and younger, big and little. They all sat drinking tea at a great number of different tables; here half a dozen children sitting together, here more or fewer; here one child would preside all alone at a table just the size for one comfortably. I should tell you that the tables were like telescope tables; only they expanded and contracted of themselves without extra pieces, and seemed to study everybody's convenience.

Every single boy and every single girl stared hard at Flora and went on staring: but not one of them offered her a chair, or a cup of tea, or anything else whatever. She grew very red and uncomfortable under so many staring pairs of eyes: when a chair did what it could to relieve her embarrassment by pressing gently against her till she sat down. It then bulged out its own back comfortably into hers, and drew in its arms to suit her small size. A footstool grew somewhat taller beneath her feet. A table ran up with tea for one; a cream-jug toppled over upon a saucerful of strawberries, and then righted itself again; the due quantity of sifted sugar sprinkled itself over the whole.

Flora could not help thinking everyone very rude and ill-natured to go on staring without speaking, and she felt shy at having to eat with so many eyes upon her: still she was hot and thirsty, and the feast looked most tempting. She took up in a spoon one large, very large strawberry with plenty of cream; and was just putting it into her mouth when a voice called out crossly: "You shan't, they're mine." The spoon dropped from her startled hand, but without any clatter: and Flora looked round to see the speaker. The speaker was a girl enthroned in an extra high armchair; with a stool as high as an ottoman under her feet, and a table as high as a chest of drawers in front of her. I suppose as she had it so she liked it so, for I am sure all the furniture laid itself out to be obliging. Perched upon her hair she wore a coronet made of tinsel; her face was a red face with a scowl: sometimes perhaps she looked nice and pretty, this time she looked ugly. "You shan't, they're mine," she repeated in a cross grumbling voice: "it's my birthday, and everything is mine."

Flora was too honest a little girl to eat strawberries that were not given her: nor could she, after this, take even a cup of tea without leave. Not to tantalize her, I suppose, the table glided away with its delicious untasted load; whilst the armchair gave her a very gentle hug as if to console her.

If she could only have discovered the door Flora would have fled through it back into the gloomy yew-tree walk, and there have moped in solitude, rather than remain where she was not made welcome: but either the door was gone, or else it was shut to and lost amongst the multitude of mirrors. The birthday Queen, reflected over and over again in five hundred mirrors, looked frightful, I do assure you: and for one minute I am sorry to say that Flora's fifty million-fold face appeared flushed and angry too; but she soon tried to smile good-humouredly and succeeded, though she could not manage to feel very merry.

The meal was ended at last: most of the children had eaten and stuffed quite greedily; poor Flora alone had not tasted a morsel. Then with a word and I think a kick from the Queen, her high footstool scudded away into a corner: and all the furniture taking the hint arranged itself as flat as possible round the room, close up against the walls.

All the children now clustered together in the middle of the empty

floor; elbowing and jostling each other, and disputing about what game should first be played at. Flora, elbowed and jostled in their midst, noticed points of appearance that quite surprised her. Was it themselves, or was it their clothes? (only who indeed would wear such clothes, so long as there was another suit in the world to put on?) One boy bristled with prickly quills like a porcupine, and raised or depressed them at pleasure; but he usually kept them pointed outwards. Another instead of being rounded like most people was facetted at very sharp angles. A third caught in everything he came near, for he was hung round with hooks like fishhooks. One girl exuded a sticky fluid and came off on the fingers; another, rather smaller, was slimy and slipped through the hands. Such exceptional features could not but prove inconvenient, yet patience and forbearance might still have done something towards keeping matters smooth: but these unhappy children seemed not to know what forbearance was; and as to patience, they might have answered me nearly in the words of a celebrated man—"Madam, I never saw patience."

"Tell us some new game," growled Hooks threateningly, catching in Flora's hair and tugging to get loose.

Flora did not at all like being spoken to in such a tone, and the hook hurt her very much. Still, though she could not think of anything new, she tried to do her best, and in a timid voice suggested "Les Grâces."

"That's a girl's game," said Hooks contemptuously.

"It's as good any day as a boy's game," retorted Sticky.

"I wouldn't give *that* for your girl's games," snarled Hooks, endeavouring to snap his fingers, but entangling two hooks and stamping.

"Poor dear fellow!" drawled Slime, affecting sympathy.

"It's quite as good," harped on Sticky: "It's as good or better."

Angles caught and would have shaken Slime, but she slipped through his fingers demurely.

"Think of something else, and let it be new," yawned Quills, with quills laid for a wonder.

"I really don't know anything new," answered Flora half crying: and she was going to add, "But I will play with you at any game you like, if you will teach me;" when they all burst forth into a yell of "Cry, baby, cry!—Cry, baby, cry!"—They shouted it, screamed it, sang it: they pointed fingers, made grimaces, nodded heads at her. The wonder was she did not cry outright.

At length the Queen interfered: "Let her alone;—who's she? It's *my* birthday, and we'll play at Hunt the Pincushion."

So Hunt the Pincushion it was. This game is simple and demands only a moderate amount of skill. Select the smallest and weakest player (if possible let her be fat: a hump is best of all), chase her round and round the room, overtaking her at short intervals, and sticking pins into her here or there as it happens: repeat, till you choose to catch and swing her; which concludes the game. Short cuts, yells, and sudden leaps give spirit to the hunt.

The pincushion was poor little Flora. How she strained and ducked and swerved to this side or that, in the vain effort to escape her tormentors! Quills with every quill erect tilted against her, and needed not a pin: but Angles whose corners almost cut her, Hooks who caught and slit her frock, Slime who slid against and passed her, Sticky who rubbed off on her neck and plump bare arms, the scowling Queen, and the whole laughing scolding pushing troop, all wielded longest sharpest pins, and all by turns overtook her. Finally the Queen caught her, swung her violently round, let go suddenly,—and Flora losing her balance dropped upon the floor. But at least that game was over.

Do you fancy the fall jarred her? Not at all: for the carpet grew to such a depth of velvet pile below her, that she fell quite lightly.

Indeed I am inclined to believe that even in that dreadful sport of Hunt the Pincushion, Flora was still better off than her stickers: who in the thick of the throng exasperated each other and fairly maddened themselves by a free use of cutting corners, pricking quills, catching hooks, glue, slime, and I know not what else. Slime, perhaps, would seem not so much amiss for its owner: but then if a slimy person cannot be held, neither can she hold fast. As to Hooks and Sticky they often in wrenching themselves loose got worse damage than they inflicted: Angles many times cut his own fingers with his edges: and I don't envy the individual whose sharp quills are flexible enough to be bent point inwards in a crush or a scuffle. The Queen must perhaps be reckoned exempt from particular personal pangs: but then, you see, it was her birthday! And she must still have suffered a good deal from the eccentricities of her subjects.

The next game called for was Self Help. In this no adventitious aids were tolerated, but each boy depended exclusively on his own resources. Thus pins were forbidden: but every natural advantage, as a quill or fishhok, might be utilized to the utmost.

[Don't look shocked, dear Ella, at my choice of words; but remember that my birthday party is being held in the Land of Nowhere. Yet who knows whether something not altogether unlike it has not ere now taken place in the Land of Somewhere? Look at home, children.]

The boys were players, the girls were played (if I may be allowed such a phrase): all except the Queen, who, being Queen, looked on, and merely administered a slap or box on the ear now and then to some one coming handy. Hooks, as a Heavy Porter, shone in this sport; and dragged about with him a load of attached captives, all vainly struggling to unhook themselves. Angles, as an Ironer, goffered or fluted several children by sustained pressure. Quills, an Engraver, could do little more than prick and scratch with some permanence of result. Flora falling to the share of Angles had her torn frock pressed and plaited after quite a novel fashion: but this was at any rate preferable to her experience as Pincushion, and she bore it like a philosopher.

Yet not to speak of the girls, even the boys did not as a body extract unmixed pleasure from Self Help; but much wrangling and some blows allayed their exuberant enjoyment. The Queen as befitted her lofty lot did, perhaps, taste of mirth unalloyed; but if so, she stood alone in satisfaction as in dignity. In any case, pleasure palls in the long run.

The Queen yawned a very wide loud yawn: and as everyone yawned in sympathy the game died out.

A supper table now advanced from the wall to the middle of the floor, and armchairs enough gathered round it to seat the whole party. Through the square hold,—not, alas! through the door of poor Flora's recollection,—floated in the requisite number of plates, glasses, knives, forks, and spoons; and so many dishes and decanters filled with nice things as I certainly never saw in all my lifetime, and I don't imagine any of you ever did.

[How many children were there at supper?—Well, I have not the least idea, Laura, but they made quite a large party: suppose we say a hundred thousand.]

This time Flora would not take so much as a fork without leave: wherefore as the Queen paid not the slightest attention to her, she was reduced to look hungrily on while the rest of the company feasted, and while successive dainties placed themselves before her and retired untasted. Cold turkey, lobster salad, stewed muchrooms, raspberry tart, cream cheese, a bumper of champagne, a méringue, a strawberry ice, sugared pine apple, some greengages: it may have been quite as well for her that she did not feel at liberty to eat such a mixture: yet it was none the less tantalizing to watch so many good things come and go without taking even one taste, and to see all her companions stuffing without limit. Several of the boys seemed to think nothing of a whole turkey at a time: and the Queen consumed with her own mouth and of sweets alone one quart of strawberry ice, three pine apples, two melons, a score of méringues, and about four dozen sticks of angelica, as Flora counted.

After supper there was no need for the furniture to withdraw: for the whole birthday party trooped out through a door (but still not through Flora's door) into a spacious playground. What they may usually have played at I cannot tell you; but on this occasion a great number of bricks happened to be lying about on all sides mixed up with many neat piles of stones, so the children began building houses: only instead of building from without as most bricklayers do, they built from within, taking care to have at hand plenty of bricks as well as good heaps of stones, and inclosing both themselves and the heaps as they built; one child with one heap of stones inside each house.

[Had they window panes at hand as well?—No, Jane, and you will soon see why none were wanted.]

I called the building material bricks: but strictly speaking there were no bricks at all in the playground, only brick-shaped pieces of glass instead. Each of these had the sides brilliantly polished; whilst the edges, which were meant to touch and join, were ground, and thus appeared to acquire a certain tenacity. There were bricks (so to call them) of all colours and many different shapes and sizes. Some were fancy bricks wrought in open work, some were engraved in running patterns, others were cut into facets or blown into bubbles. A single house might have its blocks all uniform, or of twenty different fashions.

Yet, despite this amount of variety, every house built bore a marked resemblance to its neighbour: colours varied, architecture agreed. Four walls, no roof, no upper floor; such was each house: and it needed neither window nor staircase.

All this building occupied a long long time, and by little and little a very gay effect indeed was produced. Not merely were the glass blocks of beautiful tints; so that whilst some houses glowed like masses of ruby, and others shone like enormous chrysolites or sapphires, others again showed the milkiness and fiery spark of a hundred opals, or glimmered like moonstone: but the playground was lighted up, high, low, and on all sides, with coloured lamps. Picture to yourselves golden twinkling lamps like stars overhead, bluish twinkling lamps like glowworms down almost on the ground; lamps like illuminated peaches, apples, apricots, plums, hung about with the profusion of a most fruitful orchard. Should we not all have liked to be there with Flora, even if supper was the forfeit?

Ah no, not with Flora: for to her utter dismay she found that she was being built in with the Queen. She was not called upon to build: but gradually the walls rose and rose around her, till they towered clear above her head; and being all slippery with smoothness, left no hope of her ever being able to clamber over them back into the road home, if indeed there was any longer such a road anywhere outside. Her heart sank within her, and she could scarcely hold up her head. To crown all, a glass house which contained no vestige even of a cupboard did clearly not contain a larder: and Flora began to feel sick with hunger and thirst, and to look forward in despair to no breakfast to-morrow.

Acoustics must have been most accurately studied,—

[But, Aunt, what are acoustics?—The science of sounds, Maude: pray now exercise your acoustical faculty.]

As I say, they must have been most accurately studied, and to practical purpose, in the laying out of this particular playground; if, that is, to hear distinctly everywhere whatever might be uttered anywhere within its limits, was the object aimed at. At any rate, such was the result.

Their residences at length erected, and their toils over, the youthful architects found leisure to gaze around them and bandy compliments.

First: "Look," cried Angles, pointing exultantly: "just look at Quills, as red as fire. Red doesn't become Quills. Quill's house would look a deal better without Quills."

"Talk of becomingness," laughed Quills, angrily, "you're just the colour of a sour gooseberry, Angles, and a greater fright than we've seen you yet. Look at him, Sticky, look whilst you have the chance:" for Angles was turning his green back on the speaker.

But Sticky—no wonder, the blocks *she* had fingered stuck together!—Sticky was far too busy to glance around; she was engrossed in making faces at Slime, whilst Slime returned grimace for grimace. Sticky's house was blue, and turned her livid: Slime's house—a very shaky one, ready to fall to pieces at any moment, and without one moment's warning:—Slime's house, I say, was amber-hued, and gave her the jaundice. These advantages were not lost on the belligerents, who stood working each other up into a state of frenzy, and having got long past variety, now did nothing but screech over and over again: Slime: "You're a sweet beauty,"—and Sticky (incautious Sticky!): "You're another!"

Quarrels raged throughout the playground. The only silent tongue was Flora's.

Suddenly, Hooks, who had built an engraved house opposite the Queen's bubbled palace (both edifices were pale amethyst coloured, and trying to the complexion), caught sight of his fair neighbour, and, clapping his hands, burst out into an insulting laugh.

"You're another!' shrieked the Queen (the girls all alike seemed wellnigh destitute of invention). Her words were weak, but as she spoke she stooped: and clutched—shook—hurled—the first stone.

"Oh don't, don't, don't," sobbed Flora, clinging in a paroxysm of terror, and with all her weight, to the royal arm.

That first stone was, as it were, the first hailstone of the storm: and soon stones flew in every direction and at every elevation. The very atmosphere seemed petrified. Stones clattered, glass shivered, moans and groans resounded on every side. It was as a battle of giants: who would excel each emulous peer, and be champion among giants?

The Queen. All that had hitherto whistled through mid-air were mere pebbles and chips compared with one massive slab which she now heaved up—poised—prepared to launch—

"Oh don't, don't, don't," cried out Flora again, almost choking with sobs. But it was useless. The ponderous stone spun on, widening an outlet through the palace wall on its way to crush Hooks. Half mad with fear, Flora flung herself after it through the breach—

And in one moment the scene was changed. Silence from human voices and a pleasant coolness of approaching twilight surrounded her. High overhead a fleet of rosy grey clouds went sailing away from the west, and outstripping these, rooks on flapping black wings flew home to their nests in the lofty elm trees, and cawed as they flew. A few heat-drops pattered down on a laurel hedge hard by, and a sudden gust of wind ran rustling through the laurel leaves. Such dear familiar sights and sounds told Flora that she was sitting safe within the home precincts: yes, in the very yew-tree alley, with its forty trees in all, not one more, and with no mysterious door leading out of it into a hall of misery.

She hastened indoors. Her parents, with Alfred, Susan, and the five visitors, were just sitting down round the tea-table, and nurse was leaving the drawing-room in some apparent perturbation.

Wagga wagged his tail, Muff came forward purring, and a laugh greeted Flora. "Do you know," cried George, "that you have been fast asleep ever so long in the yew walk, for I found you there? And now nurse was on her way to fetch you in, if you hadn't turned up."

Flora said not a word in answer, but sat down just as she was, with tumbled frock and hair, and a conscious look in her little face that made it very sweet and winning. Before tea was over, she had nestled close up to Anne, and whispered how sorry she was to have been so cross.

And I think if she lives to be nine years old and give another birthday party, she is likely on that occasion to be even less like the birthday Queen of her troubled dream than was the Flora of eight years old: who, with dear friends and playmates and pretty presents, yet scarcely knew how to bear a few trifling disappointments, or how to be obliging and good-humoured under slight annoyances.

LUCY LANE CLIFFORD (d. 1929)
"The New Mother" from *Anyhow Stories Moral and Otherwise* (1882)

Although Mrs Clifford enjoyed fame as a novelist and dramatist in late-Victorian England (George Eliot was instrumental in procuring a pension for her), her name is not widely known today. She was the recently widowed mother of two young daughters, nicknamed "the Turkey" and "Blue Eyes", when she wrote the thirteen *Anyhow Stories*, dedicated to her "Dear Ones". The quality of the stories is uneven: many attempt to probe the meaning of life in terms that seem too ponderous for any child to understand; the young often speak beyond their years and resort to a curious archive of folk wisdom or racial memory to explain difficult concepts to each other. "The New Mother", however, is both riveting and unsettling. It is about two sisters who are persuaded by a strange girl to be "naughty". Their gentle mother leaves them, having previously threatened that misbehaving would bring a "new mother". This sinister person, with flashing glass eyes and a wooden tail, does indeed enter the house and the children flee to the woods, where they are abandoned. The tension between the girls' conflicting de-

sires—to be naughty and to retain the love of their unhappy mother—is maintained by Clifford with chilling exactitude. Told through scenes inside and outside the snug cottage-home, the story is an allegory of innocence, here equated with goodness and docility, betrayed by the temptations of experience. Because it is so powerfully suggestive, "The New Mother" has had numerous interpretations. For some it dramatizes the conflicts of a rebellious, preadolescent state. Others see the new mother as a frightening incarnation of the "old" mother and the mysterious girl as the purveyor of forbidden (sexual) knowledge.

The thought of Mrs Clifford's dedicating, and likely reading, such a bizarre story to her "dear ones" arouses speculation about her views of discipline and motherhood. But assuming that she felt her children were in need of a horrifying cautionary tale, it is easy to imagine that Mrs Clifford let herself be carried away by her genuine and original creativity. A black and eerie children's story that carries with it a heavy freight of symbolism, "The New Mother" is unforgettable.

THE NEW MOTHER

I

The children were always called Blue-Eyes and the Turkey, and they came by the names in this manner. The elder one was like her dear father who was far away at sea, and when the mother looked up she would often say, "Child, you have taken the pattern of your father's eyes;" for the father had the bluest of blue eyes, and so gradually his little girl came to be called after them. The younger one had once, while she was still almost a baby, cried bitterly because a turkey that lived near to the cottage, and sometimes wandered into the forest, suddenly vanished in the middle of the winter; and to console her she had been called by its name.

Now the mother and Blue-Eyes and the Turkey and the baby all lived in a lonely cottage on the edge of the forest. The forest was so near that the garden at the back seemed a part of it, and the tall fir-trees were so close that their big black arms stretched over the little thatched roof, and when the moon shone upon them their tangled shadows were all over the white-washed walls.

It was a long way to the village, nearly a mile and a half, and the mother had to work hard and had not time to go often herself to see if there was a letter at the post-office from the dear father, and so very often in the afternoon she used to send the two children. They were very proud of being able to go alone, and often ran half the way to the post-office. When they came back tired with the long walk, there would be the mother waiting and watching for them, and the tea would be ready, and the baby crowing with delight; and if by any chance there was a letter from the sea, then they were happy indeed. The cottage room was so cosy: the walls were as white as snow inside as well as out, and against them hung the cake-tin and the baking-dish, and the lid of a large saucepan that had been worn out long before the children could remember, and the fish-slice, all polished and shining as bright as silver. On one side of the fireplace, above the bellows hung the almanac, and on the other the clock that always struck the wrong hour and was always running down too soon, but it was a good clock, with a little picture on its face and sometimes ticked away for nearly a week without stopping. The baby's high chair stood in one corner, and in another there was a cupboard hung up high against the wall, in which the mother kept all manner of little surprises. The children often wondered how the things that came out of that cupboard had got into it, for they seldom saw them put there.

"Dear children," the mother said one afternoon late in the autumn, "it is very chilly for you to go to the village, but you must walk quickly, and who knows but what you may bring back a letter saying that dear father is already on his way to England." Then Blue-Eyes and the Turkey made haste and were soon ready to go. "Don't be long," the mother said, as she always did before they started. "Go the nearest way and don't look at any strangers you meet, and be sure you do not talk with them."

"No, mother," they answered; and then she kissed them and called them dear good children, and they joyfully started on their way.

The village was gayer than usual, for there had been a fair the day before, and the people who had made merry still hung about the street as if reluctant to own that their holiday was over.

"I wish we had come yesterday," Blue-Eyes said to the Turkey; "then we might have seen something."

"Look there," said the Turkey, and she pointed to a stall covered with gingerbread; but the children had no money. At the end of the street, close to the Blue Lion where the coaches stopped, an old man sat on the ground with his back resting against the wall of a house, and by him, with smart collars round their necks, were two dogs. Evidently they were dancing dogs, the children thought, and longed to see them perform, but they seemed as tired as their master, and sat quite still beside him, looking as if they had not even a single wag left in their tails.

"Oh, I do wish we had been here yesterday," Blue-Eyes said again as they went on to the grocer's, which was also the post-office. The postmistress was very busy weighing out half-pounds of coffee, and when

she had time to attend to the children she only just said "No letter for you to-day," and went on with what she was doing. Then Blue-Eyes and the Turkey turned away to go home. They went back slowly down the village street, past the man with the dogs again. One dog had roused himself and sat up rather crookedly with his head a good deal on one side, looking very melancholy and rather ridiculous; but on the children went towards the bridge and the fields that led to the forest.

They had left the village and walked some way, and then, just before they reached the bridge, they noticed, resting against a pile of stones by the wayside, a strange dark figure. At first they thought it was some one asleep, then they thought it was a poor woman ill and hungry, and then they saw that it was a strange wild-looking girl, who seemed very un-happy, and they felt sure that something was the matter. So they went and looked at her, and thought they would ask her if they could do any-thing to help her, for they were kind children and sorry indeed for any one in distress.

The girl seemed to be tall, and was about fifteen years old. She was dressed in very ragged clothes. Round her shoulders there was an old brown shawl, which was torn at the corner that hung down the middle of her back. She wore no bonnet, and an old yellow handkerchief which she had tied round her head had fallen backwards and was all huddled up round her neck. Her hair was coal black and hung down uncombed and unfastened, just anyhow. It was not very long, but it was very

shiny, and it seemed to match her bright black eyes and dark freckled skin. On her feet were coarse gray stockings and thick shabby boots, which she had evidently forgotten to lace up. She had something hidden away under her shawl, but the children did not know what it was. At first they thought it was a baby, but when, on seeing them coming towards her, she carefully put it under her and sat upon it, they thought they must be mistaken. She sat watching the children approach, and did not move or stir till they were within a yard of her; then she wiped her eyes just as if she had been crying bitterly, and looked up.

The children stood still in front of her for a moment, staring at her and wondering what they ought to do.

"Are you crying?" they asked shyly.

To their surprise she said in a most cheerful voice, "Oh dear, no! quite the contrary. Are you?"

They thought it rather rude of her to reply in this way, for any one could see that they were not crying. They felt half in mind to walk away; but the girl looked at them so hard with her big black eyes they did not like to do so till they had said something else.

"Perhaps you have lost yourself?" they said gently.

But the girl answered promptly, "Certainly not. Why, you have just found me. "Besides," she added, "I live in the village."

The children were surprised at this, for they had never seen her before, and yet they thought they knew all the village folk by sight.

"We often go to the village," they said, thinking it might interest her.

"Indeed," she answered. That was all; and again they wondered what to do.

Then the Turkey, who had an inquiring mind, put a good straightforward question. "What are you sitting on?" she asked.

"On a peardrum," the girl answered, still speaking in a most cheerful voice, at which the children wondered, for she looked very cold and uncomfortable.

"What is a peardrum?" they asked.

"I am surprised at your not knowing," the girl answered. "Most people in good society have one." And then she pulled it out and showed it to them. It was a curious instrument, a good deal like a guitar in shape; it had three strings, but only two pegs by which to tune them. The third string was never tuned at all, and thus added to the singular effect produced by the village girl's music. And yet, oddly, the peardrum was not played by touching its strings, but by turning a little handle cunningly hidden on one side.

But the strange thing about the peardrum was not the music it made, or the strings, or the handle, but a little square box attached to one side. The box had a little flat lid that appeared to open by a spring. That was all the children could make out at first. They were most anxious to see inside the box, or to know what it contained, but they thought it might look curious to say so.

"It really is a most beautiful thing, is a peardrum," the girl said, looking at it, and speaking in a voice that was almost affectionate.

"Where did you get it?" the children asked.

"I bought it," the girl answered.

"Didn't it cost a great deal of money?" they asked.

"Yes," answered the girl slowly, nodding her head, "it cost a great deal of money. I am very rich," she added.

And this the children thought a really remarkable statement, for they had not supposed that rich people dressed in old clothes, or went about without bonnets. She might at least have done her hair, they thought; but they did not like to say so.

"You don't look rich," they said slowly, and in as polite a voice as possible.

"Perhaps not," the girl answered cheerfully.

At this the children gathered courage, and ventured to remark, "You look rather shabby"—they did not like to say ragged.

"Indeed?" said the girl in the voice of one who had heard a pleasant but surprising statement. "A little shabbiness is very respectable," she added in a satisfied voice. "I must really tell them this," she continued. And the children wondered what she meant. She opened the little box by the side of the peardrum, and said, just as if she were speaking to some one who could hear her, "They say I look rather shabby; it is quite lucky, isn't it?"

"Why, you are not speaking to any one!" they said, more surprised than ever.

"Oh dear, yes! I am speaking to them both."

"Yes. I have here a little man dressed as a peasant, and wearing a wide slouch hat with a large feather, and a little woman to match, dressed in a red petticoat, and a white handkerchief pinned across her bosom. I put them on the lid of the box, and when I play they dance most beautifully. The little man takes off his hat and waves it in the air, and the little woman holds up her petticoat a little bit on one side with one hand, and with the other sends forward a kiss."

"Oh! let us see; do let us see!" the children cried, both at once.

Then the village girl looked at them doubtfully.

"Let you see!" she said slowly. "Well, I am not sure that I can. Tell me, are you good?"

"Yes, yes," they answered eagerly, "we are very good!"

"Then it's quite impossible," she answered, and resolutely closed the lid of the box.

They stared at her in astonishment.

"But we are good," they cried, thinking she must have misunderstood them. "we are very good. Mother always says we are."

"So you remarked before," the girl said, speaking in a tone of decision.

Still the children did not understand.

"Then can't you let us see the little man and woman?" they asked.

"Oh dear, no!" the girl answered. "I only show them to naughty children."

"To naughty children!" they exclaimed.

"Yes, to naughty children," she answered; "and the worse the children the better do the man and woman dance."

She put the peardrum carefully under her ragged cloak, and prepared to go on her way.

"I really could not have believed that you were good," she said, reproachfully, as if they had accused themselves of some great crime. "Well, good day."

"Oh, but do show us the little man and woman," they cried.

"Certainly not. Good day." she said again.

"Oh, but we will be naughty," they said in despair.

"I am afraid you couldn't," she answered, shaking her head. "It requires a great deal of skill, especially to be naughty well. Good day," she said for the third time. "Perhaps I shall see you in the village tomorrow."

And swiftly she walked away, while the children felt their eyes fill with tears, and their hearts ache with disappointment.

"If we had only been naughty," they said, "we should have seen them dance; we should have seen the little woman holding her red petticoat in her hand, and the little man waving his hat. Oh, what shall we do to make her let us see them?"

"Suppose," said the Turkey, "we try to be naughty to-day; perhaps she would let us see them to-morrow."

"But, oh!" said Blue-Eyes, "I don't know how to be naughty; no one ever taught me."

The Turkey thought for a few minutes in silence. "I think I can be naughty if I try," she said. "I'll try to-night."

And then poor Blue-Eyes burst into tears.

"Oh, don't be naughty without me!" she cried. "It would be so unkind of you. You know I want to see the little man and woman just as much as you do. You are very, very unkind." And she sobbed bitterly.

And so, quarrelling and crying, they reached their home.

Now, when their mother saw them, she was greatly astonished, and, fearing they were hurt, ran to meet them.

"Oh, my children, oh, my dear, dear children," she said; "what is the matter?"

But they did not dare tell their mother about the village girl and the little man and woman, so they answered, "Nothing is the matter; nothing at all is the matter," and cried all the more.

"But why are you crying?" she asked in surprise.

"Surely we can cry if we like," they sobbed. "We are very fond of crying."

"Poor children!" the mother said to herself. "They are tired, and perhaps they are hungry; after tea they will be better." And she went back to the cottage, and made the fire blaze, until its reflection danced about on the tin lids upon the wall; and she put the kettle on to boil, and set the tea-things on the table, and opened the window to let in the sweet fresh air, and made all things look bright. Then she went to the little cupboard, hung up high against the wall, and took out some bread and put it on the table, and said in a loving voice, "Dear little children, come and have your tea; it is all quite ready for you. And see, there is the baby waking up from her sleep; we will put her in the high chair, and she will crow at us while we eat."

But the children made no answer to the dear mother; they only stood by the window and said nothing.

"Come, children," the mother said again. "Come, Blue-Eyes, and come, my Turkey; here is nice sweet bread for tea."

Then Blue-Eyes and the Turkey looked round, and when they saw the tall loaf, baked crisp and brown, and the cups all in a row, and the jug of milk, all waiting for them, they went to the table and sat down and felt a little happier; and the mother did not put the baby in the high chair after all, but took it on her knee, and danced it up and down, and sang little snatches of songs to it, and laughed, and looked content, and thought of the father far away at sea, and wondered what he would say to them all when he came home again. Then suddenly she looked up and saw that the Turkey's eyes were full of tears.

"Turkey!" she exclaimed, "my dear little Turkey! what is the matter? Come to mother, my sweet; come to own mother." And putting the baby down on the rug, she held out her arms, and the Turkey, getting up from her chair, ran swiftly into them.

"Oh, mother," she sobbed, "Oh, dear mother! I do so want to be naughty."

"My dear child!" the mother exclaimed.

"Yes, mother," the child sobbed, more and more bitterly. "I do so want to be very, very naughty."

And then Blue-Eyes left her chair also, and, rubbing her face against the mother's shoulder, cried sadly. "And so do I, mother. Oh, I'd give anything to be very, very naughty."

"But, my dear children," said the mother, in astonishment, "why do you want to be naughty?"

"Because we do; oh, what shall we do?" they cried together.

"I should be very angry if you were naughty. But you could not be, for you love me," the mother answered.

"Why couldn't we be naughty because we love you?" they asked.

"Because it would make me very unhappy; and if you love me you couldn't make me unhappy."

"Why couldn't we?" they asked.

Then the mother thought a while before she answered; and when she did so they hardly understood, perhaps because she seemed to be speaking rather to herself than to them.

"Because if one loves well," she said gently, "one's love is stronger than all bad feelings in one, and conquers them. And this is the test whether love be real or false, unkindness and wickedness have no power over it."

"We don't know what you mean," they cried; "and we do love you; but we want to be naughty."

"Then I should know you did not love me," the mother said.

"And what should you do?" asked Blue-Eyes.

"I cannot tell. I should try to make you better."

"But if you couldn't? If we were very, very, very naughty, and wouldn't be good, what then?"

"Then," said the mother sadly—and while she spoke her eyes filled with tears, and a sob almost choked her—"then," she said, "I should have to go away and leave you, and to send home a new mother, with glass eyes and wooden tail."

"You couldn't," they cried.

"Yes, I could," she answered in a low voice; "but it would make me very unhappy, and I will never do it unless you are very, very naughty, and I am obliged."

"We won't be naughty," they cried; "we will be good. We should hate a new mother; and she shall never come here." And they clung to their own mother, and kissed her fondly.

But when they went to bed they sobbed bitterly, for they remembered the little man and woman, and longed more than ever to see them; but how could they bear to let their own mother go away, and a new one take her place?

II

"Good-day," said the village girl, when she saw Blue-Eyes and the Turkey approach. She was again sitting by the heap of stones, and under her shawl the peardrum was hidden. She looked just as if she had not moved since the day before. "Good day," she said, in the same cheerful voice in which she had spoken yesterday; "the weather is really charming."

"Are the little man and woman there?" the children asked, taking no notice of her remark.

"Yes; thank you for inquiring after them," the girl answered; "they are both here and quite well. The little man is learning how to rattle the money in his pocket, and the little woman has heard a secret—she tells it while she dances."

"Oh, do let us see," they entreated.

"Quite impossible, I assure you," the girl answered promptly. "You see, you are good."

"Oh!" said Blue-Eyes, sadly; "but mother says if we are naughty she will go away and send home a new mother, with glass eyes and a wooden tail."

"Indeed," said the girl, still speaking in the same unconcerned voice, "that is what they all say."

"What do you mean?" asked the Turkey.

"They all threaten that kind of thing. Of course really there are no mothers with glass eyes and wooden tails; they would be much too expensive to make." And the common sense of this remark the children, especially the Turkey, saw at once, but they merely said, half crying—

"We think you might let us see the little man and woman dance."

"The kind of thing you would think," remarked the village girl.

"But will you if we are naughty?" they asked in despair.

"I fear you could not be naughty—that is, really—even if you tried," she said scornfully.

"Oh, but we will try; we will indeed," they cried; "so do show them to us."

"Certainly not beforehand," answered the girl, getting up and preparing to walk away.

"But if we are very naughty to-night, will you let us see them to-morrow?"

"Questions asked to-day are always best answered to-morrow," the girl said, and turned round as if to walk on. "Good day," she said blithely; "I must really go and play a little to myself; good day," she repeated, and then suddenly she began to sing—

"Oh, sweet and fair's the lady-bird,
    And so's the bumble-bee,
But I myself have long preferred
    The gentle chimpanzee,
    The gentle chimpanzee-e-e,
    The gentle chim----"

"I beg your pardon," she said, stopping, and looking over her shoulder; "it's very rude to sing without leave before company. I won't do it again."

"Oh, do go on," the children said.

"I'm going," she said, and walked away.

"No, we meant to go on singing," they explained, "and do let us just hear you play," they entreated, remembering that as yet they had not heard a single sound from the peardrum.

"Quite impossible," she called out as she went along. "You are good, as I remarked before. The pleasure of goodness centres in itself; the pleasures of naughtiness are many and varied. Good day," she shouted, for she was almost out of hearing.

For a few minutes the children stood still looking after her, then they broke down and cried.

"She might have let us see them," they sobbed.

The Turkey was the first to wipe away her tears.

"Let us go home and be very naughty," she said; "then perhaps she will let us see them to-morrow."

"But what shall we do?" asked Blue-Eyes, looking up. Then together all the way home they planned how to begin being naughty. And that afternoon the dear mother was sorely distressed, for, instead of sitting at their tea as usual with smiling happy faces, and then helping her to clear away and doing all she told them, they broke their mugs and threw their bread and butter on the floor, and when the mother told them to do one thing they carefully went and did another, and as for helping her to put away, they left her to do it all by herself, and only stamped their feet with rage when she told them to go upstairs until they were good.

"We won't be good," they cried. "We hate being good, and we always mean to be naughty. We like being naughty very much."

"Do you remember what I told you I should do if you were very very naughty?" she asked sadly.

"Yes, we know, but it isn't true," they cried. "There is no mother with a wooden tail and glass eyes, and if there were we should just stick pins into her and send her away; but there is none."

Then the mother became really angry at last, and sent them off to bed, but instead of crying and being sorry at her anger they laughed for joy, and when they were in bed they sat up and sang merry songs at the top of their voices.

The next morning quite early, without asking leave from the mother, the children got up and ran off as fast as they could over the fields towards the bridge to look for the village girl. She was sitting as usual by the heap of stones with the peardrum under her shawl.

"Now please show us the little man and woman," they cried, "and let us hear the peardrum. We were very naughty last night." But the girl kept the peardrum carefully hidden. "We were very naughty," the children cried again.

"Indeed," she said in precisely the same tone in which she had spoken yesterday.

"But we were," they repeated; "we were indeed."

"So you say," she answered. "You were not half naughty enough."

"Why, we were sent to bed!"

"Just so," said the girl, putting the other corner of the shawl over the peardrum. "If you had been really naughty you wouldn't have gone; but you can't help it, you see. As I remarked before, it requires a great deal of skill to be naughty well."

"But we broke our mugs, we threw our bread and butter on the floor, we did everything we could to be tiresome."

"Mere trifles," answered the village girl scornfully. "Did you throw cold water on the fire, did you break the clock, did you pull all the tins down from the walls, and throw them on the floor?"

"No!" exclaimed the children, aghast, "we did not do that."

"I thought not," the girl answered. "So many people mistake a little noise and foolishness for real naughtiness; but, as I remarked before, it wants skill to do the thing properly. Well, good day," and before they could say another word she had vanished.

"We'll be much worse," the children cried, in despair. "We'll go and do all the things she says;" and then they went home and did all these things. They threw water on the fire; they pulled down the baking-dish and the cake-tin, the fish-slice and the lid of the saucepan they had never seen, and banged them on the floor; they broke the clock and danced on the butter; they turned everything upside down; and then they sat still and wondered if they were naughty enough. And when the mother saw all that they had done she did not scold them as she had the day before or send them to bed, but she just broke down and cried, and then she looked at the children and said sadly—

"Unless you are good to-morrow, my poor Blue-Eyes and Turkey, I shall indeed have to go away and come back no more, and the new mother I told you of will come to you."

They did not believe her; yet their hearts ached when they saw how unhappy she looked, and they thought within themselves that when they once had seen the little man and woman dance, they would be good to the dear mother for ever afterwards; but they could not be good now till they had heard the sound of the peardrum, seen the little man and woman dance, and heard the secret told—then they would be satisfied.

The next morning, before the birds were stirring, before the sun had climbed high enough to look in at their bedroom window, or the flowers had wiped their eyes ready for the day, the children got up and crept out of the cottage and ran across the fields. They did not think the village girl would be up so very early, but their hearts had ached so much at the sight of the mother's sad face that they had not been able to sleep, and they longed to know if they had been naughty enough, and if they might just once hear the peardrum and see the little man and woman, and then go home and be good for ever.

To their surprise they found the village girl sitting by the heap of stones, just as if it were her natural home. They ran fast when they saw her, and they noticed that the box containing the little man and woman was open, but she closed it quickly when she saw them, and they heard the clicking of the spring that kept it fast.

"We have been very naughty," they cried. "We have done all the things you told us; now will you show us the little man and woman?" The girl looked at them curiously, then drew the yellow silk handkerchief she sometimes wore round her head out of her pocket, and began to smooth out the creases in it with her hands.

"You really seem quite excited," she said in her usual voice. "You should be calm; calmness gathers in and hides things like a big cloak, or like my shawl does here, for instance;" and she looked down at the ragged covering that hid the peardrum.

"We have done all the things you told us," the children cried again, "and we do so long to hear the secret;" but the girl only went on smoothing out her handkerchief.

"I am so very particular about my dress," she said. They could hardly listen to her in their excitement.

"But do tell if we may see the little man and woman," they entreated again. "We have been so very naughty, and mother says she will go away to-day and send home a new mother if we are not good."

"Indeed," said the girl, beginning to be interested and amused. "The things that people say are most singular and amusing. There is an endless variety in language." But the children did not understand, only entreated once more to see the little man and woman.

"Well, let me see," the girl said at last, just as if she were relenting. "When did your mother say she would go?"

"But if she goes what shall we do?" they cried in despair. "We don't want her to go; we love her very much. Oh! what shall we do if she goes?"

"People go and people come; first they go and then they come. Perhaps she will go before she comes; she couldn't come before she goes. You had better go back and be good," the girl added suddenly; "you are really not clever enough to be anything else; and the little woman's secret is very important; she never tells it for make-believe naughtiness."

"But we did do all the things you told us," the children cried, despairingly.

"You didn't throw the looking-glass out of window, or stand the baby on its head."

"No, we didn't do that," the children gasped.

"I thought not," the girl said triumphantly. "Well, good-day. I shall not be here to-morrow. Good-day."

"Oh, but don't go away," they cried. "We are so unhappy; do let us see them just once."

"Well, I shall go past your cottage at eleven o'clock this morning," the girl said. "Perhaps I shall play the peardrum as I go by."

"And will you show us the man and woman?" they asked.

"Quite impossible, unless you have really deserved it; make-believe naughtiness is only spoilt goodness. Now if you break the looking-glass and do the things that are desired——"

"Oh, we will," they cried. "We will be very naughty till we hear you coming."

"It's waste of time, I fear," the girl said politely; "but of course I should not like to interfere with you. You see the little man and woman, being used to the best society, are very particular. Good-day." she said, just as she always said, and then quickly turned away, but she looked back and called out, "Eleven o'clock, I shall be quite punctual; I am very particular about my engagements."

Then again the children went home, and were naughty, oh, so very very naughty that the dear mother's heart ached, and her eyes filled with tears, and at last she went upstairs and slowly put on her best gown and her new sun-bonnet, and she dressed the baby all in its Sunday clothes, and then she came down and stood before Blue-Eyes and the Turkey, and just as she did so the Turkey threw the looking-glass out of window, and it fell with a loud crash upon the ground.

"Good-bye, my children," the mother said sadly, kissing them. "Good-bye, my Blue-Eyes; good-bye, my Turkey; the new mother will be home presently. Oh, my poor children!" and then weeping bitterly the mother took the baby in her arms and turned to leave the house.

"But, mother," the children cried, "we are——" and then suddenly the broken clock struck half-past ten, and they knew that in half an hour the village girl would come by playing on the peardrum. "But, mother, we will be good at half-past eleven, come back at half-past eleven," they cried, "and we'll both be good, we will indeed; we must be naughty till eleven o'clock." But the mother only picked up the little bundle in which she had tied up her cotton apron and a pair of old shoes, and went slowly out at the door. It seemed as if the children were spellbound, and they could not follow her. They opened the window wide, and called after her—

"Mother! mother! oh, dear mother, come back again! We will be good, we will be good now, we will be good for evermore if you will come back." But the mother only looked round and shook her head, and they could see the tears falling down her cheeks.

"Come back, dear mother!" cried Blue-Eyes; but still the mother went on across the fields.

"Come back, come back!" cried the Turkey; but still the mother went on. Just by the corner of the field she stopped and turned, and waved her handkerchief, all wet with tears, to the children at the window; she made the baby kiss its hand; and in a moment mother and baby had vanished from their sight.

Then the children felt their hearts ache with sorrow, and they cried bitterly just as the mother had done, and yet they could not believe that she had gone. Surely she would come back, they thought; she would not leave them altogether; but, oh, if she did—if she did—if she did. And then the broken clock struck eleven, and suddenly there was a sound—a quick, clanging, jangling sound, with a strange discordant one at intervals; and they looked at each other, while their hearts stood still, for they knew it was the peardrum. They rushed to the open window, and there they saw the village girl coming towards them from the fields, dancing along and playing as she did so. Behind her, walking slowly, and yet ever keeping the same distance from her, was the man with the dogs whom they had seen asleep by the Blue Lion, on the day they first saw the girl with the peardrum. He was playing a flute that had a strange shrill sound; they could hear it plainly above the jangling of the peardrum. After the man followed the two dogs, slowly waltzing round and round on their hind legs.

"We have done all you told us," the children called, when they had recovered from their astonishment. "Come and see; and now show us the little man and woman."

The girl did not cease her playing or her dancing, but she called out in a voice that was half speaking half singing, and seemed to keep time to the strange music of the peardrum.

"You did it all badly. You threw the water on the wrong side of the fire, the tin things were not quite in the middle of the room, the clock was not broken enough, you did not stand the baby on its head."

Then the children, still standing spellbound by the window, cried out, entreating and wringing their hands, "Oh, but we have done everything you told us, and mother has gone away. Show us the little man and woman now, and let us hear the secret."

As they said this the girl was just in front of the cottage, but she did not stop playing. The sound of the strings seemed to go through their hearts. She did not stop dancing; she was already passing the cottage by. She did not stop singing, and all she said sounded like part of a terrible song. And still the man followed her, always at the same distance, playing shrilly on his flute; and still the two dogs waltzed round and round after him—their tails motionless, their legs straight, their collars clear and white and stiff. On they went, all of them together.

"Oh, stop!" the children cried, "and show us the little man and woman now."

But the girl sang out loud and clear, while the string that was out of tune twanged above her voice.

"The little man and woman are far away. See, their box is empty."

And then for the first time the children saw that the lid of the box was raised and hanging back, and that no little man and woman were in it.

"I am going to my own land," the girl sang, "to the land where I was born." And she went on towards the long straight road that led to the city many many miles away.

"But our mother is gone," the children cried; "our dear mother, will she ever come back?"

"No," sang the girl; "she'll never come back, she'll never come back. I saw her by the bridge; she took a boat upon the river; she is sailing to the sea; she will meet your father once again, and they will go sailing on, sailing on to the countries far away."

And when they heard this, the children cried out, but could say no more, for their hearts seemed to be breaking.

Then the girl, her voice getting fainter and fainter in the distance, called out once more to them. But for the dread that sharpened their ears they would hardly have heard her, so far was she away, and so discordant was the music.

"Your new mother is coming. She is already on her way; but she only walks slowly, for her tail is rather long, and her spectacles are left behind; but she is coming, she is coming—coming—coming."

The last word died away; it was the last one they ever heard the village girl utter. On she went, dancing on; and on followed the man, they could see that he was still playing, but they could no longer hear the sound of his flute; and on went the dogs round and round and round. On they all went, farther and farther away, till they were separate things no more, till they were just a confused mass of faded colour, till they were a dark misty object that nothing could define, till they had vanished altogether,—altogether and for ever.

Then the children turned, and looked at each other and at the little cottage home, that only a week before had been so bright and happy, so cosy and so spotless. The fire was out, and the water was still among the cinders; the baking-dish and cake-tin, the fish-slice and the saucepan lid, which the dear mother used to spend so much time in rubbing, were all pulled down from the nails on which they had hung so long, and were lying on the floor. And there was the clock all broken and spoilt, the little picture upon its face could be seen no more; and though it sometimes struck a stray hour, it was with the tone of a clock whose hours are numbered. And there was the baby's high chair, but no little baby to sit in it; there was the cupboard on the wall, and never a sweet loaf on its shelf; and there were the broken mugs, and the bits of bread tossed about, and the greasy boards which the mother had knelt down to scrub until they were white as snow. In the midst of all stood the children, looking at the wreck they had made, their hearts aching, their eyes blinded with tears, and their poor little hands clasped together in their misery.

"Oh, what shall we do?" cried Blue-Eyes. "I wish we had never seen the village girl and the nasty, nasty peardrum."

"Surely mother will come back," sobbed the Turkey. "I am sure we shall die if she doesn't come back."

"I don't know what we shall do if the new mother comes," cried Blue-Eyes. "I shall never, never like any other mother. I don't know what we shall do if that dreadful mother comes."

"We won't let her in," said the Turkey.

"But perhaps she'll walk in," sobbed Blue-Eyes.

Then Turkey stopped crying for a minute, to think what should be done.

"We will bolt the door," she said, "and shut the window; and we won't take any notice when she knocks."

So they bolted the door, and shut the window, and fastened it. And then, in spite of all they had said, they felt naughty again, and longed after the little man and woman they had never seen, far more than after the mother who had loved them all their lives. But then they did not really believe that their own mother would not come back, or that any new mother would take her place.

When it was dinner-time, they were very hungry, but they could only find some stale bread, and they had to be content with it.

"Oh, I wish we had heard the little woman's secret," cried the Turkey; "I wouldn't have cared then."

All through the afternoon they sat watching and listening for fear of the new mother; but they saw and heard nothing of her, and gradually they became less and less afraid lest she should come. Then they thought that perhaps when it was dark their own dear mother would come home; and perhaps if they asked her to forgive them she would. And then Blue-Eyes thought that if their mother did come she would be very cold, so they crept out at the back door and gathered in some wood, and at last, for the grate was wet, and it was a great deal of trouble to manage it, they made a fire. When they saw the bright fire burning, and the little flames leaping and playing among the wood and coal, they began to be happy again, and to feel certain that their own mother would return; and the sight of the pleasant fire reminded them of all the times she had waited for them to come from the post-office, and of how she had welcomed them, and comforted them, and given them nice warm tea and sweet bread, and talked to them. Oh, how sorry they were they had been naughty, and all for that nasty village girl! They did not care a bit about the little man and woman now, or want to hear the secret.

They fetched a pail of water and washed the floor; they found some rag, and rubbed the tins till they looked bright again, and, putting a footstool on a chair, they got up on it very carefully and hung up the things in their places; and then they picked up the broken mugs and made the room as neat as they could, till it looked more and more as if the dear mother's hands had been busy about it. They felt more and more certain she would return, she and the dear little baby together, and they thought they would set the tea-things for her, just as she had so often set them for her naughty children. They took down the tea-tray, and got out the cups, and put the kettle on the fire to boil, and made everything look as home-like as they could. There was no sweet loaf to put on the table, but perhaps the mother would bring something from the village, they thought. At last all was ready, and Blue-Eyes and the

Turkey washed their faces and their hands, and then sat and waited, for of course they did not believe what the village girl had said about their mother sailing away.

Suddenly, while they were sitting by the fire, they heard a sound as of something heavy being dragged along the ground outside, and then there was a loud and terrible knocking at the door. The children felt their hearts stand still. They knew it could not be their own mother, for she would have turned the handle and tried to come in without any knocking at all.

"Oh, Turkey!" whispered Blue-Eyes, "if it should be the new mother, what shall we do?"

"We won't let her in," whispered the Turkey, for she was afraid to speak aloud, and again there came a long and loud and terrible knocking at the door.

"What shall we do? oh, what shall we do?" cried the children, in despair. "Oh, go away!" they called out. "Go away; we won't let you in; we will never be naughty any more; go away, go away!"

But again there came a loud and terrible knocking.

"She'll break the door if she knocks so hard," cried Blue-Eyes.

"Go and put your back to it," whispered the Turkey, "and I'll peep out of the window and try to see if it is really the new mother."

So in fear and trembling Blue-Eyes put her back against the door, and the Turkey went to the window, and, pressing her face against one side of the frame, peeped out. She could just see a black satin poke bonnet with a frill round the edge, and a long bony arm carrying a black leather bag. From beneath the bonnet there flashed a strange bright light, and Turkey's heart sank and her cheeks turned pale, for she knew it was the flashing of two glass eyes. She crept up to Blue-Eyes. "It is—it is!" she whispered, her voice shaking with fear, "it is the new mother! She has come, and brought her luggage in a black leather bag that is hanging on her arm!"

"Oh, what shall we do?" wept Blue-Eyes; and again there was the terrible knocking.

"Come and put your back against the door too, Turkey," cried Blue-Eyes; "I am afraid it will break."

So together they stood with their two little backs against the door. There was a long pause. They thought perhaps the new mother had made up her mind that there was no one at home to let her in, and would go away, but presently the two children heard through the thin wooden door the new mother move a little, and then say to herself—"I must break open the door with my tail."

For one terrible moment all was still, but in it the children could almost hear her lift up her tail, and then, with a fearful blow, the little painted door was cracked and splintered.

With a shriek the children darted from the spot and fled through the cottage, and out at the back door into the forest beyond. All night long they stayed in the darkness and the cold, and all the next day and the next, and all through the cold, dreary days and the long dark nights that followed.

They are there still, my children. All through the long weeks and months have they been there, with only green rushes for their pillows and only the brown dead leaves to cover them, feeding on the wild strawberries in the summer, or on the nuts when they hang green; on the blackberries when they are no longer sour in the autumn, and in the winter on the little red berries that ripen in the snow. They wander about among the tall dark firs or beneath the great trees beyond. Sometimes they stay to rest beside the little pool near the copse where the ferns grow thickest, and they long and long, with a longing that is greater than words can say, to see their own dear mother again, just once again, to tell her that they'll be good for evermore—just once again.

And still the new mother stays in the little cottage, but the windows are closed and the doors are shut, and no one knows what the inside looks like. Now and then, when the darkness has fallen and the night is still, hand in hand Blue-Eyes and the Turkey creep up near to the home in which they once were so happy, and with beating hearts they watch and listen; sometimes a blinding flash comes through the window, and they know it is the light from the new mother's glass eyes, or they hear a strange muffled noise, and they know it is the sound of her wooden tail as she drags it along the floor.

OSCAR WILDE (1854-1900)
"The Happy Prince" from *The Happy Prince and Other Tales* (1888)

Playwright, novelist, poet, critic, and aesthete, Oscar Wilde was also the author of exquisite fairy tales. He described them as "an attempt to mirror modern life in a form remote from reality—to deal with modern problems in a mode that is ideal and not imitative." There is nothing escapist or merely whimsical in these stories. His most famous tale, "The Happy Prince", is a stirring literary reminder of the dictum, "Where your treasure lies, there also will your heart be" (Luke, 12.34). The Prince, who has left behind the Palace of Sans-Souci, "where sorrow is not allowed to enter", is a statue standing in the real world, where he becomes ruefully aware of the self-serving councillors and "all the ugliness and all the misery of my city". He pledges himself to alleviate the misfortune he sees around him. Wilde's themes of sacrifice and exposure of silly pretense were probably familiar from the works of Hans Andersen, yet his tales are anything but derivative. The poignant expression and careful narrative pattern of "The Happy Prince" are distinctly Wildean.

THE HAPPY PRINCE

High above the city, on a tall column, stood the statue of the Happy Prince. He was gilded all over with thin leaves of fine gold, for eyes he had two bright sapphires, and a large red ruby glowed on his sword-hilt.

He was very much admired indeed. "He is as beautiful as a weather-cock," remarked one of the Town Councillors who wished to gain a reputation for having artistic tastes; "only not quite so useful," he added, fearing lest people should think him unpractical, which he really was not.

"Why can't you be like the Happy Prince?" asked a sensible mother of her little boy who was crying for the moon. "The Happy Prince never dreams of crying for anything."

"I am glad there is some one in the world who is quite happy," muttered a disappointed man as he gazed at the wonderful statue.

"He looks just like an angel," said the Charity Children as they came out of the cathedral in their bright scarlet cloaks, and their clean white pinafores.

"How do you know?" said the Mathematical Master, "you have never seen one."

"Ah! but we have, in our dreams," answered the children; and the Mathematical Master frowned and looked very severe, for he did not approve of children dreaming.

One night there flew over the city a little Swallow. His friends had gone away to Egypt six weeks before, but he had stayed behind, for he was in love with the most beautiful Reed. He had met her early in the spring as he was flying down the river after a big yellow moth, and had been so attracted by her slender waist that he had stopped to talk to her.

"Shall I love you?" said the Swallow, who liked to come to the point at once, and the Reed made him a low bow. So he flew round and round her, touching the water with his wings, and making silver ripples. This was his courtship, and it lasted all through the summer.

"It is a ridiculous attachment," twittered the other Swallows, "she has no money, and far too many relations;" and indeed the river was quite full of Reeds. Then, when the autumn came, they all flew away.

After they had gone he felt lonely, and began to tire of his lady-love. "She has no conversation," he said, "and I am afraid that she is a coquette, for she is always flirting with the wind." And certainly, whenever the wind blew, the Reed made the most graceful curtsies. "I admit that she is domestic," he continued, "but I love travelling, and my wife, consequently, should love travelling also."

"Will you come away with me?" he said finally to her; but the Reed shook her head, she was so attached to her home.

"You have been trifling with me," he cried, "I am off to the Pyramids. Good-bye!" and he flew away.

All day long he flew, and at night-time he arrived at the city. "Where shall I put up?" he said; "I hope the town has made preparations."

Then he saw the statue on the tall column. "I will put up there," he cried; "it is a fine position with plenty of fresh air." So he alighted just between the feet of the Happy Prince.

"I have a golden bedroom," he said softly to himself as he looked round, and he prepared to go to sleep; but just as he was putting his head under his wing a large drop of water fell on him. "What a curious thing!" he cried, "there is not a single cloud in the sky, the stars are quite clear and bright, and yet it is raining. The climate in the north of Europe is really dreadful. The Reed used to like the rain, but that was merely her selfishness."

Then another drop fell.

"What is the use of a statue if it cannot keep the rain off?" he said; "I must look for a good chimney-pot," and he determined to fly away.

But before he had opened his wings, a third drop fell, and he looked up, and saw—Ah! what did he see?

The eyes of the Happy Prince were filled with tears, and tears were running down his golden cheeks. His face was so beautiful in the moonlight that the little Swallow was filled with pity.

"Who are you?" he said.

"I am the Happy Prince."

"Why are you weeping then?" asked the Swallow; "you have quite drenched me."

"When I was alive and had a human heart," answered the statue, "I did not know what tears were, for I lived in the Palace of Sans-Souci, where sorrow is not allowed to enter. In the daytime I played with my companions in the garden, and in the evening I led the dance in the Great Hall. Round the garden ran a very lofty wall, but I never cared to ask what lay beyond it, everything about me was so beautiful. My courtiers called me the Happy Prince, and happy indeed I was, if pleasure be happiness. So I lived, and so I died. And now that I am dead they have set me up here so high that I can see all the ugliness and all the misery of my city, and though my heart is made of lead yet I cannot choose but weep."

"What, is he not solid gold?" said the Swallow to himself. He was too polite to make any personal remarks out loud.

"Far away," continued the statue in a low musical voice, "far away in a little street there is a poor house. One of the windows is open, and through it I can see a woman seated at a table. Her face is thin and worn, and she has coarse, red hands, all pricked by the needle, for she is a seamstress. She is embroidering passion-flowers on a satin gown for the loveliest of the Queen's maids-of-honour to wear at the next Court-ball. In a bed in the corner of the room her little boy is lying ill. He has a fever, and is asking for oranges. His mother has nothing to give him but river water, so he is crying. Swallow, Swallow, little Swallow, will you not bring her the ruby out of my sword-hilt? My feet are fastened to this pedestal and I cannot move."

"I am waited for in Egypt," said the Swallow. "My friends are flying up and down the Nile, and talking to the large lotus-flowers. Soon they will go to sleep in the tomb of the great King. The King is there himself in his painted coffin. He is wrapped in yellow linen, and embalmed with spices. Round his neck is a chain of pale green jade, and his hands are like withered leaves."

"Swallow, Swallow, little Swallow," said the Prince, "will you not stay with me for one night, and be my messenger? The boy is so thirsty, and the mother so sad."

"I don't think I like boys," answered the Swallow. "Last summer, when I was staying on the river, there were two rude boys, the miller's sons, who were always throwing stones at me. They never hit me, of course; we swallows fly far too well for that, and besides, I come of a family famous for its agility; but still, it was a mark of disrespect."

But the Happy Prince looked so sad that the little Swallow was sorry. "It is very cold here," he said; "but I will stay with you for one night, and be your messenger."

"Thank you, little Swallow," said the Prince.

So the Swallow picked out the great ruby from the Prince's sword, and flew away with it in his beak over the roofs of the town.

He passed by the cathedral tower, where the white marble angels were sculptured. He passed by the palace and heard the sound of dancing. A beautiful girl came out on the balcony with her lover. "How wonderful the stars are," he said to her, "and how wonderful is the power of love!" "I hope my dress will be ready in time for the State-ball," she answered; "I have ordered passion-flowers to be embroidered on it; but the seamstresses are so lazy."

He passed over the river, and saw the lanterns hanging to the masts of the ships. He passed over the Ghetto, and saw the old Jews bargaining with each other, and weighing out money in copper scales. At last he came to the poor house and looked in. The boy was tossing feverishly on his bed, and the mother had fallen asleep, she was so tired. In he hopped, and laid the great ruby on the table beside the woman's thimble. Then he flew gently around the bed, fanning the boy's forehead with his wings. "How cool I feel," said the boy, "I must be getting better;" and he sank into a delicious slumber.

Then the Swallow flew back to the Happy Prince, and told him what he had done. "It is curious," he remarked, "but I feel quite warm now, although it is so cold."

"That is because you have done a good action," said the Prince. And the little Swallow began to think, and then he fell asleep. Thinking always made him sleepy.

When day broke he flew down to the river and had a bath. "What a remarkable phenomenon," said the Professor of Ornithology as he was passing over the bridge. "A swallow in winter!" And he wrote a long letter about it to the local newspaper. Every one quoted it, it was full of so many words that they could not understand.

"To-night I go to Egypt," said the Swallow, and he was in high spirits at the prospect. He visited all the public monuments, and sat a long time on top of the church steeple. Wherever he went the Sparrows chirruped, and said to each other, "What a distinguished stranger!" so he enjoyed himself very much.

When the moon rose he flew back to the Happy Prince. "Have you any commissions for Egypt?" he cried; "I am just starting."

"Swallow, Swallow, little Swallow," said the Prince, "will you not stay with me one night longer?"

"I am waited for in Egypt," answered the Swallow. "Tomorrow my friends will fly up to the Second Cataract. The river-horse couches there among the bulrushes, and on a great granite throne sits the God Memnon. All night long he watches the stars, and when the morning star shines he utters one cry of joy, and then he is silent. At noon the yellow lions come down to the water's edge to drink. They have eyes like green beryls, and their roar is louder than the roar of the cataract."

"Swallow, Swallow, little Swallow," said the Prince, "far away across the city I see a young man in a garret. He is leaning over a desk covered with papers, and in a tumbler by his side there is a bunch of withered violets. His hair is brown and crisp, and his lips are red as a pomegranate, and he has large and dreamy eyes. He is trying to finish a play for the Director of the Theatre, but he is too cold to write any more. There is no fire in the grate, and hunger has made him faint."

"I will wait with you one night longer," said the Swallow, who really had a good heart. "Shall I take him another ruby?"

"Alas! I have no ruby now," said the Prince; "my eyes are all that I have left. They are made of rare sapphires, which were brought out of India a thousand years ago. Pluck out one of them and take it to him. He will sell it to the jeweller, and buy food and firewood, and finish his play."

"Dear Prince," said the Swallow, "I cannot do that;" and he began to weep.

"Swallow, Swallow, little Swallow," said the Prince, "do as I command you."

So the Swallow plucked out the Prince's eye, and flew away to the student's garret. It was easy enough to get in, as there was a hole in the roof. Through this he darted, and came into the room. The young man had his head buried in his hands, so he did not hear the flutter of the bird's wings, and when he looked up he found the beautiful sapphire lying on the withered violets.

"I am beginning to be appreciated," he cried; "this is from some great admirer. Now I can finish my play," and he looked quite happy.

The next day the Swallow flew down to the harbour. He sat on the mast of a large vessel and watched the sailors hauling big chests out of the hold with ropes. "Heave a-hoy!" they shouted as each chest came up. "I am going to Egypt!" cried the Swallow, but nobody minded, and when the moon rose he flew back to the Happy Prince.

"I am come to bid you good-bye," he cried.

"Swallow, Swallow, little Swallow," said the Prince, "will you not stay with me one night longer?"

"It is winter," answered the Swallow, "and the chill snow will soon be here. In Egypt the sun is warm on the green palmtrees, and the crocodiles lie in the mud and look lazily about them. My companions are building a nest in the Temple of Baalbec, and the pink and white doves are watching them, and cooing to each other. Dear Prince, I must leave you, but I will never forget you, and next spring I will bring you back two beautiful jewels in place of those you have given away. The ruby shall be redder than a red rose, and the sapphire shall be as blue as the great sea."

"In the square below," said the Happy Prince, "there stands a little match-girl. She has let her matches fall in the gutter, and they are all spoiled. Her father will beat her if she does not bring home some money, and she is crying. She has no shoes or stockings, and her little head is bare. Pluck out my other eye, and give it to her, and her father will not beat her."

"I will stay with you one night longer," said the Swallow, "but I cannot pluck out your eye. You would be quite blind then."

"Swallow, Swallow, little Swallow," said the Prince, "do as I command you."

So he plucked out the Prince's other eye, and darted down with it. He swooped past the match-girl, and slipped the jewel into the palm of her hand. "What a lovely bit of glass," cried the little girl; and she ran home, laughing.

Then the Swallow came back to the Prince. "You are blind now," he said. "so I will stay with you always."

"No, little Swallow," said the poor Prince, "you must go away to Egypt."

"I will stay with you always," said the Swallow, and he slept at the Prince's feet.

All the next day he sat on the Prince's shoulder, and told him stories of what he had seen in strange lands. He told him of the red ibises, who stand in long rows on the banks of the Nile, and catch gold fish in their beaks; of the Sphinx, who is as old as the world itself, and lives in the desert, and knows everything; of the merchants, who walk slowly by the side of their camels, and carry amber beads in their hands; of the King of the Mountains of the Moon, who is as black as ebony, and worships a large crystal; of the great green snake that sleeps in a palm-tree, and has twenty priests to feed it with honey-cakes; and of the pygmies who sail over a big lake on large flat leaves, and are always at war with the butterflies.

"Dear little Swallow," said the Prince, "you tell me of marvellous things, but more marvellous than anything is the suffering of men and of women. There is no Mystery so great as Misery. Fly over my city, little Swallow, and tell me what you see there."

So the Swallow flew over the great city, and saw the rich making merry in their beautiful houses, while the beggars were sitting at the gates. He flew into dark lanes, and saw the white faces of starving children looking out listlessly at the black streets. Under the archway of a bridge two little boys were lying in one another's arms to try and keep themselves warm. "How hungry we are!" they said. "You must not lie here," shouted the Watchman, and they wandered out into the rain.

Then he flew back and told the Prince what he had seen.

"I am covered with fine gold," said the Prince, "you must take it off, leaf by leaf, and give it to my poor; the living always think that gold can make them happy."

Leaf after leaf of the fine gold the Swallow picked off, till the Happy Prince looked quite dull and grey. Leaf after leaf of the fine gold he brought to the poor, and the children's faces grew rosier, and they laughed and played games in the street. "We have bread now!" they cried.

Then the snow came, and after the snow came the frost. The streets looked as if they were made of silver, they were so bright and glistening; long icicles like crystal daggers hung down from the eaves of the houses, everybody went about in furs, and the little boys wore scarlet caps and skated on the ice.

The poor little Swallow grew colder and colder, but he would not leave the Prince, he loved him too well. He picked up crumbs outside the baker's door when the baker was not looking, and tried to keep himself warm by flapping his wings.

But at last he knew that he was going to die. He had just strength to fly up to the Prince's shoulder once more. "Good-bye, dear Prince!" he murmured, "will you let me kiss your hand?"

"I am glad that you are going to Egypt at last, little Swallow," said the Prince, "you have stayed too long here; but you must kiss me on the lips, for I love you."

"It is not to Egypt that I am going," said the Swallow. "I am going to the House of Death. Death is the brother of Sleep, is he not?"

And he kissed the Happy Prince on the lips, and fell down dead at his feet.

At that moment a curious crack sounded inside the statue, as if something had broken. The fact is that the leaden heart had snapped right in two. It certainly was a dreadfully hard frost.

Early the next morning the Mayor was walking in the square below in company with the Town Councillors. As they passed the column he looked up at the statue: "Dear me! how shabby the Happy Prince looks!" he said.

"How shabby indeed!" cried the Town Councillors, who always agreed with the Mayor, and they went up to look at it.

"The ruby has fallen out of his sword, his eyes are gone, and he is golden no longer," said the Mayor; "in fact, he is little better than a beggar!"

"Little better than a beggar," said the Town Councillors.

"And here is actually a dead bird at his feet!" continued the Mayor. "We must really issue a proclamation that birds are not to be allowed to die here." And the Town Clerk made a note of the suggestion.

So they pulled down the statue of the Happy Prince. "As he is no longer beautiful he is no longer useful," said the Art Professor at the University.

Then they melted the statue in a furnace, and the Mayor held a meeting of the Corporation to decide what was to be done with the metal. "We must have another statue, of course," he said, "and it shall be a statue of myself."

"Of myself," said each of the Town Councillors, and they quarrelled. When I last heard of them they were quarrelling still.

"What a strange thing!" said the overseer of the workmen at the foundry. "This broken lead heart will not melt in the furnace. We must throw it away." So they threw it on the dustheap where the dead Swallow was also lying.

"Bring me the two most precious things in the city," said God to one of His Angels; and the Angel brought Him the leaden heart and the dead bird.

"You have rightly chosen," said God, "for in my garden of Paradise this little bird shall sing for evermore, and in my city of gold the Happy Prince shall praise me."

GEORGE EDWARD FARROW (1866-1920)
"At the North Pole" from *The Little Panjandrum's Dodo* (1899)

Already popular with children for creating a meek and preposterous mannikin, "The Wallypug of Why", in a book of that name (1895), Farrow addressed the preface of *The Little Panjandrum's Dodo* to his "dear little friends", hoping the work would please them, and encouraged them to write him. He certainly knew how to concoct a marvellous adventure—with lively "extinct" characters, manufactured words, irrepressible puns, gently mocking caricatures, and liberal borrowings from Lewis Carroll. A paleontological romp through time and space, *The Little Panjandrum's Dodo* opens on a world in crisis. Three holidaying children—Richard, Marjorie, and Harold ("Fidge") Verrinder—wake one morning to discover a torrential flood and, claiming an overturned table as their boat, begin their "marvellous journey". The secondary world of imagination and fantasy then takes over. "I think you will believe in fairies before we have done with you," says a gnome to the children.

In exchange for the privilege of becoming whatever size they wish, the children are charged with the responsibility of apprehending the Dodo, who stands accused of the "dreadful offence", "contempt of Panjandrumosity". The Panjandrum character, "a little fat man in Oriental costume" who babbles imperiously in gibberish, turns out to be a disappointment; the Dodo, however, who has stolen his master's gloves, is remarkably self-possessed. He is always the centre of attention as he accompanies the children to the North Pole and to the Equator, introduces them to his "antediluvian friends", outwits the dim Panjan-

drum, and decides to apply for a secretarial position in London. He and the children are able to breathe underwater and drift through the air. A series of extemporaneous adventures, interlarded with nonsensical stories told to the children by people they meet, *The Dodo* is always good fun.

The comment of one of the raconteurs, the Sage of the Onion Field, about his jumbled story—"I'm making it up as I go along" (borrowed verbatim from Carroll)—might apply to the whole book. Farrow relishes inventing word-plays—a skipper jumps ropes and his sailors sit at spinning wheels with yarns—and coining words. The children must arrest the pilfering Dodo or else risk being "subtransexdistricated"—a "perfectly horrible treatment", the Dodo explains: "you are mygrylaled in pslmsms till you saukle, and then you are taken out and gopheled on both sides for a fortnight." Humorously depicted realities of late-Victorian life intrude into Farrow's imaginary world—whether in the form of the Aryan supremacist Herr Walrus, or of the snappish waitress in the railway refreshment room who sells stale seventeen-year-old buns and evaporated ginger beer. With its witty bravura and its juggling of primary and secondary worlds, *The Dodo* is not unworthy of standing between *Alice* and T.H. White's *The Sword in the Stone*.

Farrow's name is often neglected in the study of children's literature. The creator of characters like "the mysterious Shin Shira", Pixene and Pixette, and Professor Marmaduke Philanderpan ("un-teacher of proverbs, politics, and punctuation") is due for reconsideration.

AT THE NORTH POLE

The country looked very bleak and bare, but a little hut was visible a short distance from the shore, and the children, having fastened up the Dolphins to one of the wooden piles, assisted the Dodo to alight, and made their way towards it.

At the entrance they saw a large Walrus with a pipe in his mouth, and on the ground beside him an Esquimaux dog, also smoking.

Dick and the others hurried forward, and bowed politely.

"*Wie geths?*" said the Walrus, taking the pipe from his mouth, and immediately putting it back again, while the little dog glanced at them inquisitively out of the corners of his eyes.

"What does he mean?" asked Marjorie, staring blankly at her brother.

"I don't know," confessed Dick. "I beg your pardon," he went on, addressing the Walrus, "but I didn't quite hear what you said."

"*Sprechen sie Deutsch?*" enquired the Walrus, with an encouraging smile.

"I can't tell what the chap is talking about," said Dick, turning to the others in dismay.

"Dond't you undershtandt German, eh?" said the Walrus. "Ach! dat vos verry bad," and he shook his head reproachfully.

"I don't know," argued Dick. "I can't see that it matters much. We are not likely to go there, you know."

"Not?" said the Walrus, lifting his eyebrows. "Vell, dere vos some funny peoples in der world. Perhaps you dond't *vant* to go dere?"

"Not much," admitted Dick.

The Walrus shrugged his shoulders, and looked commiseratingly at the dog, who gave a sniff, and shrugged his shoulders too.

"What we want to know," said Dick, in a businesslike way, "is, Where are we now, and how are we to get back to England?"

"Vell, you vas in Germany now," said the Walrus.

"Germany!" exclaimed the children, in surprise. "Why, we're quite near to England, then."

"No," said the Walrus, shaking his head.

"But we must be," persisted Dick.

"No," repeated the Walrus. "Dis is not der Germany you mean, but id is Germany all der same—most of der vorld is Germany."

"What nonsense!" laughed Dick. "I'm sure it isn't. Why, there's heaps of places besides Germany. There's—er—Africa, for instance—"

"Thadt's Germany!" said the Walrus, nodding violently.

"Africa is?" cried Dick

"Yah! das is so," said the Walrus. "Africa, und China, und alle der blaces—dey is all Germany."

"The chap is evidently a little wrong in the head," explained Dick to the others in a whisper. "Never mind; don't take any notice. Well, to come to the point, *can* you direct us home again, that is the question?" he asked, aloud.

"No," said the Walrus, shaking his head.

"Or to the Equator?" suggested the Dodo, smoothing out his gloves.

The Walrus stared for a moment, and then, pointed to the Dodo with the stem of his pipe, enquired, "Vat is tat ting?"

The Dodo drew himself up to his full height, and gave him a withering look. "How dare you?" he cried.

"Vell, vat *is* id, anyhow?" chuckled the Walrus. "I never saw somethings like id before, never!"

"Of course not," said the Dodo, with dignity. "Our family have been extinct for some time."

"Vell, und vy didn't you keep so?" asked the Walrus. "It vas der best ting vat you could do. Dere is no goot for such things like you to be aboudt."

"Come along," said the Dodo, turning to the others; "let's go. I was never so insulted in all my life."

"Ach! dond't ged in a demper," said the Walrus, complacently. "Dat is no goot also. Come, I show you der vay to der Equador—dat is Germany, too," he added, in parenthesis. "Bud you must haf some glothes first to vare," he cried, looking at the children's scanty garments. "Id is so gold dere."

"Cold at the Equator?" laughed Marjorie. "Why, I always thought that is was very hot."

"Ach! dat is so," said the Walrus. "Bud id is der gedding dere dat is so gold. Come, I gif you some oudtfids," and he led the way into the little hut, which was hung all around with clumsy-looking fur garments, which, however, when they had got into them, the children found to be exceedingly comfortable.

Besides the clothes, there were all kinds of stores piled up around the inside of the hut, and a quantity of snow-shoes of various shapes, and little sleds, like those which Dick remembered having seen in pictures of Polar expeditions.

When the children had been accommodated with some garments, the Walrus turned to the Dodo, and said, "Vell, now, I egspecdt dat you vant some glothes, too, dond't id?"

"No, thank you," said the Dodo, proudly, settling his necktie and folding his wings primly. "I have my gloves; they are quite sufficient."

"Bud you haven't anyting on your body," said the Walrus. "You bedder haf some glothes, eh?" and he kindly brought forth some very large leather breeches, which the Dodo, after some hesitation, consented to put on.

Next the Walrus took down a rough, hairy coat, with mittens attached to the sleeves.

"Gom, put your arms in dis," he said, "and trow avay dose gloves you got on."

"What!" cried the Dodo, "take off my gloves? Never!"

And he wouldn't either; but put his wings (such as he had) into the coat sleeves with the gloves still on the end of them.

"' WHAT ! ' CRIED THE
DODO, ' TAKE OFF
MY GLOVES ?
NEVER ! ' "

"Now you musdt haf some stores," said the Walrus, going to a cupboard, and bringing out some tins of sardines, some jam, and other things, which he carefully tied on to the sled.

"Now ve are ready to stardt," he said, when these preparations were completed; and after harnessing the little dog to the sled the party made a move.

"I haven't the least idea where we are going to," said Dick, as they walked along; "have you?"

"Not the slightest," said the Dodo. "I don't suppose it matters much, though, as long as we get somewhere or another."

The old Walrus was trudging along in front, leading Fidge (who seemed to have taken a violent fancy to him) by the hand; presently he stopped in front of a big round hole, and waited for the others to catch up to him.

"Here ve are," he said, pointing to the enormous hole, which looked like the crater of an extinct volcano lined with ice.

"Whatever is that?" asked Marjorie, peering over the edge curiously.

"Der North Bole," said the Walrus. "Id vas German, too," he added, emphatically.

"The North Pole!" exclaimed the children. "Why, there isn't any pole at all!"

"No," said the Walrus, "das is so, id vas meldted all avay."

"Good gracious!" cried Dick.

"Yah! id vas mit der lightning struck, und meldted all avay, und made a big hole in der ground all der vay trough der earth to der Equador. Id vas made in Germany, dat pole," he added.

The children gazed with wondering eyes into the deep, dark hold, and Marjorie clung to Dick's arm nervously. "How wonderful!" she exclaimed; "but I'm glad we've seen where it was, aren't you, Dick?"

But Dick was thinking deeply.

"Are you sure it went right through to the Equator?" he asked of the Walrus.

"Yah!" said the worthy, "for sure."

"Then if we slid through, we should come out at the other end?" said Dick.

"Yah' das is so," said the Walrus, nodding violently.

"Well, then, I think we'll do it," said Dick, boldly.

"Oh, Dick!" cried Marjorie, in alarm.

"Well, why not?" said Dick, for, really, so many strange things had happened that nothing seemed impossible to him now. "it would be rather jolly to see what it's like at the other end, and it's no use stopping here. Do you know your way from the Equator?" he added, turning to the Dodo.

"Yes," said the bird, who was quite ready to start on the perilous voyage, and, grasping Fidge by the hand, he gave a loud whoop, and began to slide down the steep incline.

"Well, good-bye," cried Dick, hurriedly shaking hands with the Walrus. "Thanks for all your kindness." And, jumping on the sled behind Marjorie, he pushed off, and they shot over the edge after the others.

They just caught a glimpse of the little dog throwing up his arms in surprise, and as they disappeared into space they heard the Old Walrus crying, in an anxious voice—

"Gom back! gom back! I forgot to tell you somedings."

That was all very well for the Walrus to shout "Come back!" but *that* was a matter of utter impossibility, for down—and down—and down the children sped at a terrific rate, so quickly indeed that after a moment or two they must have lost their senses completely, for not one of them could remember anything about the marvellous journey through the centre of the earth.

2. ENCHANTMENT AND INSTRUCTION: THE ALLEGORICAL NARRATIVE

*He must be an artist indeed who can, in any mode, produce a strict
allegory that is not weariness to the spirit.—George MacDonald,
"The Fantastic Imagination", A Dish of Orts (1893).*

In his imaginative writing, George Mac-
Donald applied rigorous and absolute standards to the allegory, but he was also an artist. He most certainly did not weary the
spirit, as many contemporary writers of allegories did. MacDonald called some of his
allegorical stories fairy tales, acknowledging the undeniable resemblance between
these two kinds of narrative. Both frequently describe an adventure to a fairy
world of dream and wonder; and in both
forms the imagined worlds operate in accordance with fundamental rules of order
and justice. What distinguishes allegory,
however, is its built-in other meaning—its
capacity to signify a second, correlated
story. Writing in this symbolic mode, the
allegorist invents a powerfully suggestive
and allusive narrative that half conceals another, often didactic, story.

Allegorical writing was highly esteemed
during the Golden Age, especially by
preachers, for whom it was an ideal medium to inculcate moral lessons. In its de-

votional explicitness, *The Gold Thread*
(1861) by the Reverend Norman Macleod
is the most "naive" of the allegories, to
use Northrop Frye's term in *Anatomy of
Criticism*. For Macleod his "gold thread"
clearly symbolizes "duty to God"; consequently the wandering of young Eric (who
has temporarily lost this thread) in the vast
forest depicts the temptations and threats
to the soul in the search for a heavenly
home. The arrival of the frail human spirit
at its eternal home is also the theme of two
other preacher-allegorists, Charles Kingsley and George MacDonald. Kingsley's
poor chimney sweep, in *The Water Babies*
(1863), gains salvation by entering the sac-
ramentally cleansing water and becoming
a water baby. In *At the Back of the North
Wind* (1871) MacDonald's Diamond, a
sickly boy whose strength wanes throughout the story, is under the protection of
the motherly North Wind, who assists him
in alleviating the poverty around him and,
at the end, translates him to another exis-

tence. The image of transcendence that Mrs Craik uses in her more secular "parable", *The Little Lame Prince* (1875), is the travelling cloak given to Prince Dolor by his fairy godmother; it permits the lonely boy-hero, both literally and imaginatively, to rise above his unhappy situation. Relying on central images such as thread, river, wind, and cloak, these stories all relate real and allegorical journeys to some form of salvation.

Like Golden Age fairy tales, these allegories or parables have exerted a recognizable influence on fine—though less theological—classics for children written in this century. Frances Hodgson Burnett's *The Secret Garden* (1911) uses the controlling image of the garden as a reflection of curative growth; Mary and Colin, disagreeable ten-year-olds, not only find the garden and cultivate its beauty but in the process discover the goodness that has been locked inside them. Burnett constantly alludes to the connections between place and people, making her most pointed comment in the last chapter: "While the secret garden was coming alive . . . two children were coming alive with it." James Barrie's stage play and story, *Peter Pan* (1904; 1911), is another classic shaped by a tested Golden Age formula. In this allegory of maturing, the flight of the Darling children to and from the island of Neverland pictures the gradual acceptance of adulthood by all the characters, with the notable exception of the illiterate boy-hero—the cynic who steadfastly refuses "to be a man . . . to wake up and feel there was a beard". Through his witty art Barrie made the magic shores of Neverland live for generations of readers, while at the same time exposing the foibles of both adults and children.

Parables, from the Golden Age and beyond, have continued to appeal to readers whom MacDonald once characterized as "the childlike, whether of five, or fifty, or seventy-five". While critics may marvel at the adroit interlacing of primary and secondary stories—at what Frye calls allegory's "contrapuntal technique"—the childlike reader revels in the whole narrative entity, attracted as much by the enchantment of the story as by the intimation that something deeper is stirring.

NORMAN MACLEOD (1812-1872)
"The Journey Home—The Bird with the Gold Eggs—Trials and Difficulties" from *The Gold Thread: A Story for the Young* (1861)

When he published this allegory in his magazine *Good Words for the Young*, the Reverend Macleod spelled out its lesson with unflinching clarity: "We should always trust God and do what is right and thus hold fast our gold thread in spite of every temptation and danger." In five chapters he recounts the adventures and triumphs of Prince Eric, who wanders through a vast forest because he has lost the gold thread that belongs to his father, King Magnus. After this initial carelessness, however, Eric finds the thread and uses it to make his way to his father's palace—a symbol of heavenly bliss. He is a formidably stalwart journeyer: he befriends a young swineherd called Wolf; escapes from the robbers' den of Wolf's master, Ralph; avoids the ferocious jaws of a lion; saves Wolf's life; and remains untouched by the "smiles, flattery, and fair promises" of a beguiling (and, alas, deceitful) girl. The moral analogues of this young pilgrim's progress to his father's kingdom show Macleod's tireless zeal as a preacher. Unfortunately his touch is leaden; imaginative nuance is constantly sacrificed for the sake of dinning an instructional point. But Macleod's story has one ingenious feature: the gold thread becomes increasingly significant until, in the last two chapters, it virtually becomes a character. Assisted by this precious filament, Eric arrives at his "heavenly home",

where he is greeted, fittingly, by the beautiful lady, who helps him in the passage reproduced below, and by a chorus singing this benediction, neatly restating Macleod's message:

Oh, bless'd is the true one who follows the road,
Holding fast to his GOLD THREAD OF DUTY TO GOD,
Who, when tempted is firm, who in danger is brave,
Who, forgetting himself, will a lost brother save.
Then be joyful, be joyful, for Eric is come,
Little Eric, our darling, we welcome thee home.

In his *Journal* Macleod justified the "serious, solemn purpose" of his writing for the young: "I cannot write stories merely as a literary man, to give amusement, or as works of art only, but must always keep before me the one end of leading souls to know and love God." Despite its naïveté, *The Gold Thread* is historically interesting as an example of the way in which non-literary Victorian preachers fastened on the allegorical mode—which was as important for them as for John Bunyan—to teach moral precepts. We have to look to Charles Kingsley's *The Water Babies* (pp. 110-21), published two years later, to see an allegory handled by a clergyman who was also a literary artist.

THE JOURNEY HOME—THE BIRD WITH THE GOLD EGGS—TRIALS AND DIFFICULTIES

Eric knew not how long he slept, but, as in a dream, he heard a sweet voice singing these words:—

> "Rest thee, boy, rest thee, boy, lonely and dreary,
> Thy little heart breaking from losing the way;
> Thy father has not left thee friendless, though weary,
> When learning through suffering to fear and obey."

Eric opened his eyes, but moved not a limb, as if under some strange fascination. It was early morning. High over head a lark was "singing like an angel in the clouds." The mysterious voice went on in the same beautiful and soothing strain—

> "Oh, sweet is the lark as she sings o'er her nest,
> And warbles unseen in the clear morning light;
> But sweeter by far is the song in the breast
> When in life's early morning we do what is right!"

Eric could neither move nor speak; but in his heart he confessed with sorrow that he had done what was wrong. And again the voice sang—

> "Now, darling, awaken, thou art not forsaken!
> The old night is past and a new day begun;
> Let thy journey with love to thy father be taken,
> And at evening thy father will welcome thee home."

"I will arise and go to my father!" said Eric, springing to his feet. He saw beside him a beautiful lady, who looked like a picture he once saw of his mother, or like one of those angels from heaven about whom he had often read. And the lady said, "Fear not! I know you, Eric, and how it came to pass that you are here. Your father sent you for a wise and good purpose through the forest, and gave you hold of a gold thread to guide you, and told you never to let it go. It was your duty to him to have held it fast; but instead of doing your duty, trusting and obeying your father, and keeping hold of the thread, you let it go to chase butterflies, and gather wild-berries, and to amuse yourself. This you did more than once. You neglected your father's counsels and warnings, and because of your self-confidence and self-pleasing, you lost your thread, and then you lost your way. What dangers and troubles have you thus got into through disobedience to your father's commands, and want of trust in his love and wisdom! For had you only followed your father's directions, the gold thread would have brought you to his beautiful castle, where there is to be a happy meeting of your friends, with all your brothers and sisters." Poor little Eric began to weep! "Listen to me, child," said the lady, kindly, "for *you cannot have peace but by doing what is right*. Know, then, that all your brothers and sisters made this very journey by help of the gold thread, and they are at home with great joy." "Oh, save me! save me!" cried Eric, and caught the lady's hand. "Yes, I will save you," said she, "if you will learn obedience. I know and love you, dear boy. I know and love your father, and have been sent by him to deliver you. I heard what you said, and know all you did, last night, and I was very glad that you proved, in trial, your love to your father, your love of truth, and your love of others, and this makes me hope all good of you for the future. Come now with me!" And so the beautiful

women took him by the hand. The storm had passed away, and the sun was shining on the green leaves of the trees, and every drop of dew sparkled like a diamond. The birds were all warbling their morning hymns, and feeding their young ones in their nests. The streams were dancing down the rocks and through the glens. "The mountains broke forth into singing, and all the trees clapped their hands with joy." Everything thus seemed beautiful and happy to Eric, for he himself was happy at the thought of doing what was right, and of going home. The lady led him to a sunny glade in the wood, covered with wild-flowers, from which the bees were busy gathering their honey, and she said, "Now, child, you are willing to do your father's will?" "Oh, yes!" "Will you do it, whatever dangers may await you?" "Yes!" "Well, then, I must tell you that your father has given me the gold thread which you lost; and he bids me again tell you, with his warm love, that if you keep hold of it, and follow it wherever it leads, you are sure to come to him at sunset; but if you let it go, you may wander on in this dark forest till you die, or are again taken prisoner by robbers. Know, also, that there is no other possible way of saving you, but by your following the gold thread." "I am resolved to do my duty, come what may," said Eric. "May you be helped to do it!" said the lady. She then gave him a cake, to support him in his journey. "And now, child," she said, "one advice more I will give you, and it was given you by your father, though you forgot it; it is this—if ever you feel the thread slipping from your hands, or are yourself tempted to let it go, pray immediately, and you will get wisdom and strength to find it, to lay hold of it, and to follow it. Before we part, kneel down and ask assistance to be good and obedient, brave and patient, until you meet your father." The little boy knelt down and repeated the Lord's Prayer; and as he said, "Thy will be done on earth, as it is done in heaven," he felt calm and happy as he used to do when he knelt at his mother's knee, and he thought her hand was waving over him, as if to bless him. When he lifted up his head there was no one there but himself; but he saw an old gray cross, and a GOLD THREAD was tied to it, and passed away, away, shining through the woods.

With a firm hold of his gold thread, the boy began his journey home. He passed along pathways on which the brown leaves of last year's growth were thickly strewn, and from among which flowers of every colour were springing. He crossed little brooks that ran like silver threads, and tinkled like silver bells. He passed under trees with great trunks, and huge branches that swept down to the ground, and waved far up in the blue sky. The birds hopped about him, and looked down upon him from among the green leaves, and they sang him songs, and some of them seemed to speak to him. He thought one large bird like a crow cried, "Good boy! good boy!" and another whistled, "Cheer up! cheer up!" and so he went merrily on, and very often he gave the robins and blackbirds that came near him bits of his cake. After awhile, he came to a green spot in the middle of the wood, without trees, and a footpath went direct across it, to the place where the gold thread was leading him, and there he saw a sight that made him wonder and pause. It was a bird about the size of a pigeon, with feathers like gold and a crown like silver, and it was slowly walking near him, and he saw gold eggs glittering in a nest among the grass a few yards off. Now, he thought, it would be such a nice thing to bring home a nest with gold eggs! The bird did not seem afraid of him, but stopped and looked at him with a calm blue eye, as if she said, "Surely you would not rob me?" He could not, however, reach the nest with his hand, and though he pulled and pulled the thread, it would not yield one inch, but seemed as stiff as a wire. "I see the thread quite plain," said the boy to himself, "and the very place where it enters the dark wood on the other side. I will just leap to the nest, and in a moment I shall have the eggs in my pocket, and then spring back and catch the thread again. I cannot lose it here, with the sun shining; and, besides, I see it a long way before me." So he took one step to seize the eggs; but he was in such haste that he fell and crushed the nest, breaking the eggs to pieces, and the little bird screamed and flew away, and then suddenly the birds in the trees began to fly about, and a large owl swept out of a dark glade, and cried, "Whoo-whoo—whoo-oo-oo;" and a cloud came over the sun! Eric's heart beat quick, and he made a grasp at his gold thread, but it was not there! Another, and another grasp, but it was not there! and soon he saw it waving far above his head, like a gossamer thread in the breeze. You would have pitied him, while you could not have helped being angry with him for having been so silly and disobedient when thus tried, had you only seen his pale face, as he looked above him for his thread, and about him for the road, but could see neither! And he became so confused with his fall, that he did not know which side of the open glade he had entered, nor to which point he was travelling. But at last he thought he heard a bird chirping, "Seek—seek—seek!" and another repeating, "Try again—try again—try—try!" and then he remembered what the lady had said to him, and he fell on his knees and told all his grief, and cried, "Oh, give me back my thread! and help me never, never, to let it go again!" As he lifted up his eyes, he saw the thread come slowly, slowly down; and when it came near, he sprang to it and caught it, and he did not know whether to laugh, or cry, or sing, he was so thankful and happy! "Ah!" said he, "I hope I shall never forget this fall!" That part of the Lord's Prayer came into his mind which says, "Lead us not into temptation, but deliver us from evil." "Who would have thought," said he to himself, "that I was in any danger in such a beautiful, green, sunny place as this, and so very early, too, in my journey! Oh! shame upon me!" As he proceeded with much more thought and caution, a large crow up a tree was hoarsely croaking, and seemed to say, "Beware, beware!" "Thank you, Mr Crow," said the boy, "I shall;" and he threw him a bit of bread for his good advice. But now the thread led him through the strangest places. One was a very dark, deep ravine, with a stream that roared and rushed far down, and overhead the rocks seemed to meet, and thick bushes concealed the light, and nothing could Eric see but the gold thread, that looked like a thread of fire, though even that grew dim sometimes, until he could only feel it in his hand. And whither he was going he knew not. At one time he seemed to be on the edge of a precipice, until it seemed as if the next step *must* lead him over, and plunge him down; but when he came to the very edge, the thread led him quite safely along it. At another, a rock which looked like a wall rose before him, and he said to himself, "Well, I must be stopped here! I shall never be able to climb up!" But just as he touched it, he found steps cut in it, and up, up, the thread guided him to the top! Then it would bring him down, down, until he once stood beside a raging stream, and the water foamed and dashed. "Now," he thought, "I must be drowned; but come what may, I will not let my thread go." And so it was, that when he came so near the stream as to feel the spray upon his cheek, and was sure that he must leap in if he followed his thread, what did he see but a little bridge that passed from bank to bank, and by which he crossed in perfect safety; until at last he began to lose fear, and to believe more and more that he would always be in the right road, so long as he did not trust mere appearances, but kept hold of his thread!

CHARLES KINGSLEY (1819-1875)
"Tom's Life as a Water Baby" from *The Water Babies: A Fairy Tale for a Land Baby* (1863)

Novelist, poet, essayist, and clergyman, Kingsley was a vigorous spokesman for the tenets of his age: the robust manliness of his beliefs—best described in his own phrase "Muscular Christianity"—influenced his whole work. A clergyman's son, he took holy orders himself, and through association with Frederic Maurice became a leader in the Christian Socialist movement. He was appointed Chaplain to Queen Victoria in 1859 and was Professor of Modern History at Cambridge University (1860-9). For his own children he retold the stories of Perseus, Jason, and Theseus in *The Heroes; or, Greek Fairy Tales* (1856), and for them he also assumed the role of instructive parent-narrator in *The Water Babies*.

It is the story of the adventures of a chimney sweep who runs away, falls into a river, and enters an underwater world where—thanks to the tutelage of the controlling fairies, Mrs Bedonebyasyoudid and Mrs Doasyouwouldbedoneby—he is cleansed and saved. Kingsley's story is an allegory of redemption. Tom even assists in the salvation of his old master, the drunken and abusive Mr Grimes, who has fallen into the lake and drowned while poaching. Though often prolix and digressive, *The Water Babies* remains an enthusiastic statement of Kingsley's belief in the Christian's duty to realize his own sinfulness and participate actively in his own salvation.

TOM'S LIFE AS A WATER-BABY

> *"He prayeth well who loveth well,*
> *Both men and bird and beast;*
> *He prayeth best who loveth best,*
> *All things both great and small:*
> *For the dear God who loveth us,*
> *He made and loveth all."*
>
> —Coleridge

Tom was now quite amphibious. You do not know what that means? You had better, then, ask the nearest Government pupil teacher, who may possibly answer you smartly enough, thus—

"Amphibious. Adjective, derived from two Greek words, *amphi*, a fish, and *bios*, a beast. An animal supposed by our ignorant ancestors to be compounded of a fish and a beast; which therefore, like the hippopotamus, can't live on the land, and dies in the water."

However that may be, Tom was amphibious; and what is better still, he was clean. For the first time in his life, he felt how comfortable it was to have nothing on him but himself. But he only enjoyed it: he did not know it, or think about it; just as you enjoy life and health, and yet never think about being alive and healthy: and may it be long before you have to think about it!

He did not remember having ever been dirty. Indeed, he did not remember any of his old troubles, being tired, or hungry, or beaten, or sent up dark chimneys. Since that sweet sleep, he had forgotten all about his master, and Harthover Place, and the little white girl, and, in a word, all that had happened to him when he lived before; and what was best of all, he had forgotten all the bad words which he had learnt from Grimes, and the rude boys with whom he used to play.

That is not strange; for you know, when you came into this world, and became a land-baby, you remembered nothing. So why should he, when he became a water-baby?

Then have you lived before?

My dear child, who can tell? One can only tell that by remembering something which happened where we lived before; and as we remember nothing, we know nothing about it; and no book, and no man, can ever tell us certainly.

There was a wise man once, a very wise man, and a very good man, who wrote a poem about the feelings which some children have about having lived before; and this is what he said—

> "Our birth is but a sleep and a forgetting;
> The soul that rises with us, our life's star,
>   Hath elsewhere had its setting
>   And cometh from afar:
>   Not in entire forgetfulness,
>   And not in utter nakedness,
> But trailing clouds of glory, do we come
>   From God, who is our home."

There, you can know no more than that. But if I was you, I would believe that. For then the great fairy Science, who is likely to be queen of all the fairies for many a year to come, can only do you good, and never do you harm; and instead of fancying, with some people, that your body makes your soul, as if a steam engine could make its own coke; or, with some other people, that your soul has nothing to do with your body, but is only stuck into it like a pin into a pin cushion, to fall out with the first shake;—you will believe the one true,

orthodox,	inductive,
rational,	deductive,
philosophical,	seductive,
logical,	productive,
irrefragable,	salutary,
nominalistic,	comfortable,
realistic,	

and on-all-accounts-to-be-received

doctrine of this wonderful fairy tale; which is, that your soul makes your body, just as a snail makes his shell. For the rest, it is enough for us to be sure that whether or not we lived before, we shall live again; though not, I hope, as poor little heathen Tom did. For he went downward into the water; but we, I hope, shall go upward to a very different place.

But Tom was very happy in the water. He had been sadly overworked in the land-world; and so now, to make up for that, he had nothing but holidays in the water-world for a long, long time to come. He had nothing to do now but enjoy himself, and look at all the pretty things which are to be seen in the cool, clear water-world, where the sun is never too hot, and the frost is never too cold.

And what did he live on? Water-cresses, perhaps; or perhaps water-gruel, and water-milk: too many land-babies do so likewise. But we do not know what one-tenth of the water things eat; so we are not answerable for the water-babies.

*

Now you must know that all the things under the water talk, only not such a language as ours, but such as horses, and dogs, and cows, and birds talk to each other; and Tom soon learned to understand them and talk to them; so that he might have had very pleasant company if he had only been a good boy. But I am sorry to say he was too like some other little boys, very fond of hunting and tormenting creatures for mere sport. Some people say that boys cannot help it; that is is nature, and only a proof that we are all originally descended from beasts of prey. But whether it is nature or not, little boys can help it, and must help it. For if they have naughty, low, mischievous tricks in their nature, as monkeys have, that is no reason why they should give way to those tricks like monkeys, who know no better. And therefore they must not torment dumb creatures; for if they do, a certain old lady who is coming will surely give them exactly what they deserve.

But Tom did not know that; and he pecked and howked the poor water things about sadly, till they were all afraid of him, and got out of his way, or crept into their shells; so he had no one to speak to or play with.

The water-fairies, of course, were very sorry to see him so unhappy, and longed to take him, and tell him how naughty he was, and teach him to be good, and to play and romp with him too; but they had been forbidden to do that. Tom had to learn his lesson for himself by sound and sharp experience, as many another foolish person has to do, though there may be many a kind heart yearning over them all the while, and longing to teach them what they can only teach themselves.

At last one day he found a caddis, and wanted it to peep out of its house; but its house door was shut. He had never seen a caddis with a house door before; so what must he do, the meddlesome little fellow, but pull it open to see what the poor lady was doing inside. What a shame! How should you like to have anyone breaking your bedroom door in to see how you looked when you were in bed? So Tom broke to pieces the door, which was the prettiest little grating of silk, stuck all over with shining bits of crystal; and when he looked in the caddis poked out her head, and it had turned into just the shape of a bird's. But when Tom spoke to her she could not answer; for her mouth and face were tight tied up in a new nightcap of neat pink skin. However, if she didn't answer, all the other caddises did; for they held up their hands and shrieked like the cats in Struwwelpeter: "Oh, you nasty, horrid boy, there you are at it again! And she had just laid herself up for a fortnight's sleep, and then she would have come out with such beautiful wings and flown about, and laid such lots of eggs: and now you have broken her door, and she can't mend it because her mouth is tied up for a fortnight, and she will die. Who sent you here to worry us out of our lives?"

So Tom swam away. He was very much ashamed of himself, and felt all the naughtier; as little boys do when they have done wrong, and won't say so.

Then he came to a pool full of little trout, and began tormenting them, and trying to catch them; but they slipt through his fingers, and jumped clean out of water in their fright. But as Tom chased them, he came close to a great dark hover under an alder root, and out flushed a huge old brown trout ten times as big as he was, and ran right against him, and knocked all the breath out of his body; and I don't know which was the more frightened of the two.

Then he went on sulky and lonely, as he deserved to be; and under a bank he saw a very ugly dirty creature sitting, about half as big as himself, which had six legs, and a big stomach, and a most ridiculous head with two great eyes and a face just like a donkey's.

"Oh," said Tom, "you are an ugly fellow, to be sure!" and he began making faces at him; and put his nose close to him, and halloed at him, like a very rude boy.

When, hey presto! all the thing's donkey-face came off in a moment, and out popped a long arm with a pair of pincers at the end of it, and caught Tom by the nose. It did not hurt him much; but it held him quite tight.

"Yah, ah! Oh, let me go!" cried Tom.

"Then let me go," said the creature. "I want to be quiet. I want to split."

Tom promised to let him alone, and he let go. "Why do you want to split?" said Tom.

"Because my brothers and sisters have all split, and turned into beautiful creatures with wings; and I want to split too. Don't speak to me. I am sure I shall split. I will split!"

Tom stood still and watched him. And he swelled himself, and puffed, and stretched himself out stiff, and at last—crack, puff, bang— he opened all down his back, and then up to the top of his head.

And out of his inside came the most slender, elegant, soft creature, as soft and smooth as Tom; but very pale and weak, like a little child who has been ill a long time in a dark room. It moved its legs very feebly; and looked about it half ashamed, like a girl when she goes for the first time into a ballroom; and then it began walking slowly up a grass stem to the top of the water.

Tom was so astonished that he never said a word; but he stared with all his eyes. And he went up to the top of the water too, and peeped out to see what would happen.

And as the creature sat in the warm bright sun, a wonderful change came over it. It grew strong and firm; the most lovely colours began to show on its body, blue and yellow and black, spots and bars and rings; out of its back rose four great wings of bright brown gauze; and its eyes grew so large that they filled all its head, and shone like ten thousand diamonds.

"Oh, you beautiful creature!" said Tom; and he put out his hand to catch it.

But the thing whirred up into the air, and hung poised on its wings a moment, and then settled down again by Tom quite fearless.

"No!" it said, "you cannot catch me. I am a dragon-fly now, the king of all the flies; and I shall dance in the sunshine, and hawk over the river, and catch gnats, and have a beautiful wife like myself. I know what I shall do. Hurrah!" And he flew away into the air, and began catching gnats.

"Oh! come back, come back," cried Tom, "you beautiful creature. I have no one to play with and I am so lonely here. If you will but come back I will never try to catch you."

"I don't care whether you do or not," said the dragon-fly; "for you can't. But when I have had my dinner, and looked a little about this pretty place, I will come back; and have a little chat about all I have seen on my travels. Why, what a huge tree this is! and what huge leaves on it!"

It was only a big dock: but you know the dragon-fly had never seen any but little water-trees; starwort, and milfoil, and water-crowfoot, and such like; so it did look very big to him. Besides, he was very short-sighted, as all dragon-flies are; and never could see a yard before his nose; any more than a great many other folks, who are not half as handsome as he.

The dragon-fly did come back, and chatted away with Tom. He was a little conceited about his fine colours and his large wings; but you know, he had been a poor dirty creature all his life before; so there were great excuses for him. He was very fond of talking about all the wonderful things he saw in the trees and the meadows; and Tom liked to listen to him, for he had forgotten all about them. So in a little while they became great friends.

And I am very glad to say, that Tom learnt such a lesson that day, that he did not torment creatures for a long time after. And then the caddises grew quite tame, and used to tell him strange stories about the way they built their houses, and changed their skins, and turned at last into winged flies; till Tom began to long to change his skin, and have wings like them some day.

*

The other children warned him, and said, "Take care what you are at. Mrs Bedonebyasyoudid is coming." But Tom never heeded them, being quite riotous with high spirits and good luck, till, one Friday morning early, Mrs Bedonebyasyoudid came indeed.

A very tremendous lady she was; and when the children saw her, they all stood in a row, very upright indeed, and smoothed down their bathing dresses, and put their hands behind them, just as if they were going to be examined by the inspector.

And she had on a black bonnet, and a black shawl, and no crinoline at all; and a pair of large green spectacles, and a great hooked nose, hooked so much that the bridge of it stood quite up above her eyebrows; and under her arm she carried a great birch rod. Indeed, she was so ugly, that Tom was tempted to make faces at her: but did not; for he did not admire the look of the birch rod under her arm.

And she looked at the children one by one, and seemed very much pleased with them, though she never asked them one question about how they were behaving; and then began giving them all sorts of nice sea-things—sea-cakes, sea-apples, sea-oranges, sea-bulls'-eyes, sea-toffee; and to the very best of all she gave sea-ices, made out of sea-cows' cream, which never melt under water.

And, if you don't quite believe me, then just think—What is more cheap and plentiful than sea-rock? Then why should there not be sea-toffee as well? And everyone can find sea-lemons (ready quartered too) if they will look for them at low tide; and sea-grapes too sometimes, hanging in bunches; and, if you will go to Nice, you will find the fish-market full of sea-fruit, which they call "frutta di mare": though I suppose they call them "fruits de mer" now, out of compliment to that most successful, and therefore most immaculate, potentate who is seemingly desirous of inheriting the blessing pronounced on those who remove their neighbours' landmark. And, perhaps, that is the very reason why the place is called Nice, because there are so many nice things in the sea there: at least, if it is not, it ought to be.

Now little Tom watched all these sweet things given away, till his mouth watered, and his eyes grew as round as an owl's. For he hoped that his turn would come at last; and so it did. For the lady called him up, and held out her fingers with something in them, and popped it into his mouth; and, lo and behold, it was a nasty, cold, hard pebble.

"You are a very cruel woman," said he, and began to whimper.

"And you are a very cruel boy; who puts pebbles into the sea-anemones' mouths, to take them in, and make them fancy that they had caught a good dinner. As you did to them, so I must do to you."

"Who told you that?" said Tom.

"You did yourself, this very minute."

Tom had never opened his lips; so he was very much taken aback indeed.

"Yes; everyone tells me exactly what they have done wrong; and that without knowing it themselves. So there is no use trying to hide anything from me. Now go, and be a good boy, and I will put no more pebbles in your mouth, if you put none in other creatures'."

"I did not know there was any harm in it," said Tom.

"Then you know now. People continually say that to me: but I tell them, if you don't know that fire burns, that is no reason that it should not burn you; and if you don't know that dirt breeds fever, that is no reason why the fevers should not kill you. The lobster did not know that there was any harm in getting into the lobster pot; but it caught him all the same."

"Dear me," thought Tom, "she knows everything!" And so she did, indeed.

"And so, if you do not know that things are wrong, that is no reason why you should not be punished for them; though not as much, not as much, my little man" (and the lady looked very kindly after all), "as if you did know."

"Well, you are a little hard on a poor lad," said Tom.

"Not at all; I am the best friend you ever had in all your life. But I will tell you; I cannot help punishing people when they do wrong. I like it no more than they do; I am often very, very sorry for them, poor things: but I cannot help it. If I tried not to do it, I should do it all the same. For I work by machinery, just like an engine; and am full of wheels and springs inside; and am wound up very carefully, so that I cannot help going."

"Was it long ago since they wound you up?" asked Tom. For he thought, the cunning little fellow, "She will run down some day: or they may forget to wind her up, as old Grimes used to forget to wind up his watch when he came in from the public-house: and then I shall be safe."

"I was wound up once and for all, so long ago that I forget all about it."

"Dear me," said Tom, "you must have been made a long time!"

"I never was made, my child: and I shall go for ever and ever; for I am as old as Eternity, and yet as young as Time."

And there came over the lady's face a very curious expression—very solemn, and very sad; and yet very, very sweet. And she looked up and away, as if she were gazing through the sea, and through the sky, at something far, far off; and as she did so, there came such a quiet, tender, patient, hopeful smile over her face, that Tom thought for the moment that she did not look ugly at all. And no more she did; for she was like a great many people who have not a pretty feature in their faces, and yet are lovely to behold, and draw little children's hearts to them at once; because, though the house is plain enough, yet from the windows a beautiful and good spirit is looking forth.

And Tom smiled in her face, she looked so pleasant for the moment. And the strange fairy smiled too, and said:

"Yes. You thought me very ugly just now, did you not?"

Tom hung down his head, and got very red about the ears.

"And I am very ugly. I am the ugliest fairy in the world; and I shall be, till people behave themselves as they ought to do. And then I shall grow as handsome as my sister, who is the loveliest fairy in the world; and her name is Mrs Doasyouwouldbedoneby. So she begins where I end, and I begin where she ends; and those who will not listen to her must listen to me, as you will see. Now, all of you run away, except Tom; and he may stay and see what I am going to do. It will be a very good warning for him to begin with, before he goes to school.

"Now, Tom, every Friday I come down here and call up all who have ill-used little children, and serve them as they serve the children."

And at that Tom was frightened, and crept under a stone; which made the two crabs who lived there very angry, and frightened their friend the butter-fish into flapping hysterics; but he would not move for them.

And first she called up all the doctors who give little children so much physic (they were most of them old ones; for the young ones have learnt better, all but a few army surgeons, who still fancy that a baby's inside is much like a Scotch grenadier's), and she set them all in a row; and very rueful they looked; for they knew what was coming.

And first she pulled all their teeth out; and then she bled them all round; and then she dosed them with calomel, and jalap, and salts and senna, and brimstone and treacle; and horrible faces they made; and then she gave them a great emetic of mustard and water, and no basins; and began all over again; and that was the way she spent the morning.

And then she called up a whole troop of foolish ladies, who pinch up their children's waists and toes; and she laced them all up in tight stays, so that they were choked and sick, and their noses grew red, and their hands and feet swelled; and then she crammed their poor feet into the most dreadfully tight boots, and made them all dance, which they did most clumsily indeed; and then she asked them how they liked it; and when they said not at all, she let them go: because they had only done it out of foolish fashion, fancying it was for their children's good, as if wasps' waists and pigs' toes could be pretty, or wholesome, or of any use to anybody.

Then she called up all the careless nurserymaids, and stuck pins into them all over, and wheeled them about in perambulators with tight straps across their stomachs and their heads and arms hanging over the side, till they were quite sick and stupid, and would have had sun-strokes: but, being under the water, they could only have water-strokes; which, I assure you, are nearly as bad, as you will find if you try to sit under a mill wheel. And mind—when you hear a rumbling at the bottom of the sea, sailors will tell you that it is a groundswell: but now you know better. It is the old lady wheeling the maids about in perambulators.

And by that time she was so tired, she had to go to luncheon.

And after luncheon she set to work again, and called up all the cruel schoolmasters—whole regiments and brigades of them; and, when she saw them, she frowned most terribly, and set to work in earnest, as if the best part of the day's work was to come. More than half of them were nasty, dirty, frowzy, grubby, smelly old monks, who, because they dare not hit a man of their own size, amused themselves with beating little children instead; as you may see in the picture of old Pope Gregory (good man and true though he was, when he meddled with things which he did understand), teaching children to sing their fa-fa-mi-fa, with a cat-o'-nine tails under his chair: but, because they never had any children of their own, they took into their heads (as some folks do still) that they were the only people in the world who knew how to manage children; and they first brought into England, in the old Anglo-Saxon times, the fashion of treating free boys, and girls too, worse than you would treat a dog or a horse: but Mrs Bedonebyasyoudid has caught them all long ago; and given them many a taste of their own rods; and much good may it do them.

And she boxed their ears, and thumped them over the head with rulers, and pandied their hands with canes, and told them that they told stories, and were this and that bad sort of people; and the more they were very indignant, and stood upon their honour, and declared they told the truth, the more she declared they were not, and that they were only telling lies; and at last she birched them all round soundly with her great birch rod, and set them each an imposition of three hundred thousand lines of Hebrew to learn by heart before she came back next Friday. And at that they all cried and howled so, that their breaths came all up through the sea like bubbles out of soda-water; and that is one reason of the bubbles in the sea. There are others: but that is the one which principally concerns little boys. And by that time she was so tired that she was glad to stop; and, indeed, she had done a very good day's work.

Tom did not quite dislike the old lady: but he could not help thinking her a little spiteful—and no wonder if she was, poor old soul; for, if she has to wait to grow handsome till people do as they would be done by, she will have to wait a very long time.

Poor old Mrs Bedonebyasyoudid! she has a great deal of hard work before her, and had better have been born a washerwoman, and stood over a tub all day: but, you see, people cannot always choose their own profession.

*

And as for the pretty lady, I cannot tell you what the colour of her hair was, or of her eyes; no more could Tom; for when anyone looks at her, all they can think of is, that she has the sweetest, kindest, tenderest, funniest, merriest face they ever saw, or want to see. But Tom saw that she was a very tall woman, as tall as her sister; but instead of being gnarly, and horny, and scaly, and prickly, like her, she was the most nice, soft, fat, smooth, pussy, cuddly, delicious creature who ever nursed a baby; and she understood babies thoroughly, for she had plenty of her own, whole rows and regiments of them, and has to this day. And all her delight was, whenever she had a spare moment, to play with babies, in which she showed herself a woman of sense; for babies are the best company, and the pleasantest playfellows, in the world; at least, so all the wise people in the world think. And therefore when the

children saw her, they naturally all caught hold of her, and pulled her till she sat down on a stone, and climbed into her lap, and clung round her neck, and caught hold of her hands; and then they all put their thumbs into their mouths, and began cuddling and purring like so many kittens, as they ought to have done. While those who could get nowhere else sat down on the sand, and cuddled her feet—for no one, you know, wears shoes in the water, except horrid old bathing-women, who are afraid of the water-babies pinching their horny toes. And Tom stood staring at them; for he could not understand what it was all about.

"And who are you, my little darling?" she said.

"Oh, that is the new baby!" they cried, pulling their thumbs out of their mouths; "and he never had any mother," and they all put their thumbs back again, for they did not wish to lose any time.

"Then I will be his mother, and he shall have the very best place; so get out all of you, this moment."

And she took up two great armfuls of babies—nine hundred under one arm, and thirteen hundred under the other—and threw them away, right and left, into the water. But they minded it no more than the naughty boys in Struwwelpeter minded when St Nicholas dipped them in his inkstand; and did not even take their thumbs out of their mouths, but came paddling and wriggling back to her like so many tadpoles, till you could see nothing of her from head to foot for the swarm of little babies.

But she took Tom in her arms and laid him in the softest place of all, and kissed him, and patted him, and talked to him, tenderly and low, such things as he had never heard before in his life; and Tom looked up into her eyes, and loved her, and loved, till he fell fast asleep from pure love.

And when he woke she was telling the children a story. And what story did she tell them? One story she told them, which begins every Christmas Eve, and yet never ends at all for ever and ever; and, as she went on, the children took their thumbs out of their mouths, and listened quite seriously; but not sadly at all: for she never told them anything sad; and Tom listened too, and never grew tired of listening. And he listened so long that he fell fast asleep again, and when he woke the lady was nursing him still.

"Don't go away," said little Tom. "This is so nice. I never had anyone to cuddle me before."

"Don't go away," said all the children; "you have not sung us one song."

"Well, I have time for only one. So what shall it be?"

"The doll you lost! The doll you lost!" cried all the babies at once.

So the strange fairy sang:—

> I once had a sweet little doll, dears,
>   The prettiest doll in the world;
> Her cheeks were so red and so white, dears,
>   And her hair was so charmingly curled.
> But I lost my poor little doll, dears,
>   As I played in the heath one day;
> And I cried for her more than a week, dears;
>   But I never could find where she lay.
>
> I found my poor little doll, dears,
>   As I played in the heath one day:
> Folks say she is terribly changed, dears,
>   For her paint is all washed away,
> And her arm trodden off by the cows, dears,
>   And her hair not the least bit curled:
> Yet for old sakes' sake she is still, dears,
>   The prettiest doll in the world.

What a silly song for a fairy to sing!

And what silly water-babies to be quite delighted at it!

Well, but you see they have not the advantage of Aunt Agitate's Arguments in the sea-land down below.

"Now," said the fairy to Tom, "will you be a good boy for my sake, and torment no more sea-beasts, till I come back?"

"And you will cuddle me again?" said poor little Tom.

"Of course I will, you little duck. I should like to take you with me, and cuddle you all the way, only I must not;" and away she went.

So Tom really tried to be a good boy, and tormented no sea-beasts after that, as long as he lived; and he is quite alive, I assure you, still.

Oh, how good little boys ought to be, who have kind pussy mammas to cuddle them and tell them stories; and how afraid they ought to be of growing naughty, and bringing tears into their mammas' pretty eyes.

MORAL

And now, my dear little man, what should we learn from this parable?

We should learn thirty-seven or thirty-nine things, I am not exactly sure which: but one thing, at least, we may learn, and that is this—when we see efts in the ponds, never to throw stones at them, or catch them with crooked pins, or put them into vivariums with sticklebacks, that the sticklebacks may prick them in their poor little stomachs, and make them jump out of the glass into somebody's workbox, and so come to a bad end. For these efts are nothing else but the water-babies who are stupid and dirty, and will not learn their lessons and keep themselves clean; and, therefore (as comparative anatomists will tell you fifty years hence, though they are not learned enough to tell you now), their skulls grow flat, their jaws grow out, and their brains grow small, and their tails grow long, and they lose all their ribs (which I am sure you would not like to do), and their skins grow dirty and spotted, and they never get into the clear rivers, much less into the great wide sea, but hang about in dirty ponds, and live in the mud, and eat worms, as they deserve to do.

But that is no reason why you should ill-use them: but only why you should pity them, and be kind to them, and hope that some day they will wake up, and be ashamed of their nasty, dirty, lazy, stupid life, and try to amend, and become something better once more. For, perhaps, if they do so, then after 379,423 years, nine months, thirteen days, two hours, and twenty-one minutes (for aught that appears to the contrary), if they work very hard and wash very hard all that time, their brains may grow bigger, and their jaws grow smaller, and their ribs come back, and their tails wither off, and they will turn into water-babies again, and, perhaps, after that into land-babies; and after that, perhaps into grown men.

You know they won't? Very well, I dare say you know best. But, you see, some folks have a great liking for those poor efts. They never did anybody any harm, or could if they tried; and their only fault is, that they do no good—any more than some thousands of their betters. But what with ducks, and what with pike, and what with sticklebacks, and what with water-beetles, and what with naughty boys, they are "sae sair haddened doun", as the Scotsmen say, that it is a wonder how they live; and some folks can't help hoping with good Bishop Butler, that they may have another chance to make things fair and even, somewhere, somewhen, somehow.

Meanwhile, do you learn your lessons, and thank God that you have plenty of cold water to wash in; and wash in it too, like a true English man. And then, if my story is not true, something better is; and if I am not quite right, still you will be, as long as you stick to hard work and cold water.

But remember always, as I told you at first, that this is all a fairy tale, and only fun and pretence; and, therefore, you are not to believe a word of it, even if it is true.

GEORGE MAC DONALD (1824-1905)
"Once More" and "At the Back of the North Wind" from *At the Back of the North Wind* (1871)

Born at Huntly, Aberdeenshire, MacDonald was for a short period a Congregational minister. Charged with heresy by his chapel's deacons, he resigned from the active ministry in 1853 and spent the rest of his life in London, supporting his ever-growing family through his writing. His work has undeniable traces of a strong Calvinist pulpit tradition, yet MacDonald's finest tales are luminous fantasies that, in C.S. Lewis's words, "hover between the allegorical and the mythopoeic". In his first adult romance, *Phantastes* (1858), MacDonald described the ideal traveller to fairyland as one who "soon learns to forget the very idea of doing so, and takes everything as it comes; like a child, who, being in a chronic condition of wonder, is surprised at nothing" (Chapter 4). He refused to provide a code of interpretation for his tales, maintaining that readers would "find what they are capable of finding" ("The Fantastic Imagination").

Among MacDonald's long and short stories for children—the most memorable of which enshrine Christian principles in mystical experiences that are compelling for readers of all ages—the best known are *At the Back of the North Wind* (1871), *The Princess and the Goblin* (1872), and *The Princess and Curdie* (1882). First published serially in *Good Words for the Young*, a magazine that MacDonald briefly edited (1872-

3), *At the Back of the North Wind* relates the nocturnal journeys of seven-year-old Diamond, named after his cab-driving father's favourite horse. Transcending his poverty and sickness, Diamond travels under the protection—and literally in the hair—of the motherly North Wind, who conveys him high above the city and far out to sea, to a realm of peace, security, and enchantment. On a literal level the story is about the dying and death of this child; but as an allegory it describes his going home "to the back of the north wind". Diamond is preternaturally good; his angelic qualities are not only essential to the story, but they are believable. He assists an orphan girl, reunites long-separated lovers, drives the hansom during his father's illness, and is instrumental in his family's move to the healthy Kent countryside and in the improvement of their fortunes. This ingenuous illiterate is truly "God's Baby".

On his first visit to the back of the North Wind, Diamond is "not very happy"—for, as MacDonald explains, "he had neither his father nor mother with him—but he felt so still and quiet and patient and contented, that, as far as the mere feeling went, it was something better than . . . happiness" (Chap. 10). By the time of his second and last visit ("Once More"), the child is ready and eager "to go home".

ONCE MORE

The next night Diamond was seated by his open window, with his head on his hand, rather tired, but so eagerly waiting for the promised visit that he was afraid he could not sleep. But he started suddenly, and found that he had been already asleep. He rose, and looking out of the window saw something white against his beech-tree. It was North Wind. She was holding by one hand to a top branch. Her hair and her garments went floating away behind her over the tree, whose top was swaying about while the others were still.

"Are you ready, Diamond?" she asked.

"Yes," answered Diamond, "quite ready."

In a moment she was at the window, and her arms came in and took

him. She sailed away so swiftly that he could at first mark nothing but the speed with which the clouds above and the dim earth below went rushing past. But soon he began to see that the sky was very lovely, with mottled clouds all about the moon, on which she threw faint colours like those of mother-of-pearl, or an opal. The night was warm, and in the lady's arms he did not feel the wind which down below was making waves in the ripe corn, and ripples on the rivers and lakes. At length they descended on the side of an open earthy hill, just where, from beneath a stone, a spring came bubbling out.

"I am going to take you along this little brook," said North Wind. "I am not wanted for anything else to-night, so I can give you a treat."

She stooped over the stream, and holding Diamond down close to the surface of it, glided along level with its flow as it ran down the hill. And the song of the brook came up into Diamond's ears, and grew and grew and changed with every turn. It seemed to Diamond to be singing the story of its life to him. And so it was. It began with a musical tinkle which changed to a babble and then to a gentle rushing. Sometimes its song would almost cease, and then break out again, tinkle, babble, and rush, all at once. At the bottom of the hill they came to a small river, into which the brook flowed with a muffled but merry sound. Along the surface of the river, darkly clear below them in the moonlight, they floated; now, where it widened out into a little lake, they would hover for a moment over a bed of water-lilies, and watch them swing about, folded in sleep, as the water on which they leaned swayed in the presence of North Wind; and now they would watch the fishes asleep among their roots below. Sometimes she would hold Diamond over a deep hollow curving into the bank, that he might look far into the cool stillness. Sometimes she would leave the river and sweep across a clover-field.

The bees were all at home, and the clover was asleep. Then she would return and follow the river. It grew wider and wider as it went. Now the armies of wheat and of oats would hang over its rush from the opposite banks; now the willows would dip low branches in its still waters; and now it would lead them through stately trees and grassy banks into a lovely garden, where the roses and lilies were asleep, the tender flowers quite folded up, and only a few wide awake and sending out their life in sweet odours. Wider and wider grew the stream, until they came upon boats lying along its banks, which rocked a little in the flutter of North Wind's garments. Then came houses on the banks, each standing in a lovely lawn, with grand trees; and in parts the river was so high that some of the grass and the roots of some of the trees were under water, and Diamond, as they glided through between the stems, could see the grass at the bottom of the water. Then they would leave the river and float about and over the houses, one after another—beautiful rich houses, which, like fine trees, had taken centuries to grow. There was scarcely a light to be seen, and not a movement to be heard: all the people in them lay fast asleep.

"What a lot of dreams they must be dreaming!" said Diamond.

"Yes," returned North Wind. "They can't surely be all lies—can they?"

"I should think it depends a little on who dreams them," suggested Diamond.

"Yes," said North Wind. "The people who think lies, and do lies, are very likely to dream lies. But the people who love what is true will surely now and then dream true things. But then something depends on whether the dreams are home-grown, or whether the seed of them is blown over somebody else's garden wall. Ah! there's someone awake in this house!"

They were floating past a window in which a light was burning. Diamond heard a moan, and looked up anxiously in North Wind's face.

"It's a lady," said North Wind. "She can't sleep for pain."

"Couldn't you do something for her?" said Diamond.

"No, I can't. But you could."

"What could I do?"

"Sing a little song to her."

"She wouldn't hear me."

"I will take you in, and then she will hear you."

"But that would be rude, wouldn't it? You can go where you please, of course, but I should have no business in her room."

"You may trust me, Diamond. I shall take as good care of the lady as of you. The window is open. Come."

By a shaded lamp, a lady was seated in a white wrapper, trying to read, but moaning every minute. North Wind floated behind her chair, set Diamond down, and told him to sing something. He was a little frightened, but he thought a while, and then sang:

The sun is gone down,
   And the moon's in the sky;
But the sun will come up,
   And the moon be laid by.

The flower is asleep
   But it is not dead,
When the morning shines,
   It will lift its head.

When winter comes,
   It will die—no, no;
It will only hide
   From the frost and the snow.

Sure is the summer,
   Sure is the sun;
The night and the winter
   Are shadows that run.

The lady never lifted her eyes from her book, or her head from her hand.

As soon as Diamond had finished, North Wind lifted him and carried him away.

"Didn't the lady hear me?" asked Diamond, when they were once more floating down with the river.

"Oh yes, she heard you," answered North Wind.

"Was she frightened then?"

"Oh no."

"Why didn't she look to see who it was?"

"She didn't know you were there."

"How could she hear me then?"

"She didn't hear you with her ears."

"What did she hear me with?"

"With her heart."

"Where did she think the words came from?"

"She thought they came out of the book she was reading. She will search all through it to-morrow to find them, and won't be able to understand it at all."

"Oh, what fun!" said Diamond. "What *will* she do?"

"I can tell you what she won't do: she'll never forget the meaning of them; and she'll never be able to remember the words of them."

"If she sees them in Mr Raymond's book, it will puzzle her, won't it?"

"Yes, that it will. She will never be able to understand it."

"Until she gets to the back of the north wind," suggested Diamond.

"Until she gets to the back of the north wind," assented the lady.

"Oh!" cried Diamond, "I know now where we are. Oh! do let me go into the old garden, and into Mother's room, and Diamond's stall. I wonder if the hole is at the back of my bed still. I should like to stay there all the rest of the night. It won't take you long to get home from here, will it, North Wind?"

"No," she answered. "You shall stay as long as you like."

"Oh, how jolly!" cried Diamond, as North Wind sailed over the house with him, and set him down on the lawn at the back.

Diamond ran about the lawn for a little while in the moonlight. He found part of it cut up into flower-beds, and the little summerhouse with the coloured glass and the great elm-tree gone. He did not like this, and ran into the stable. There were no horses there at all. He ran upstairs. The rooms were empty. The only thing left that he cared about was the hole in the wall where his little bed had stood; and that was not enough to make him wish to stop. He ran down the stair again, and out upon the lawn. There he threw himself down and began to cry. It was all so dreary and lost!

"I thought I liked the place so much," said Diamond to himself, "but I find I don't care about it. I suppose it's only the people in it that make you like a place, and when they're gone, it's dead, and you don't care a bit about it. North Wind told me I might stop as long as I liked, and I've stopped longer already. North Wind!" he cried aloud, turning his face towards the sky.

The moon was under a cloud, and all was looking dull and dismal. A star shot from the sky, and fell in the grass beside him. The moment it lighted, there stood North Wind.

"Oh!" cried Diamond joyfully, "were you the shooting star?"

"Yes, my child."

"Did you hear me call you then?"

"Yes."

"So high up as that?"

"Yes; I heard you quite well."

"Do take me home."

"Have you had enough of your old home already?"

"Yes, more than enough. It isn't a home at all now."

"I thought that would be it," said North Wind. "Everything, dreaming and all, has got a soul in it, or else it's worth nothing, and we don't care a bit about it. Some of our thoughts are worth nothing, because they've got no soul in them. The brain puts them into the mind, not the mind into the brain."

"But how can you know about that, North Wind? You haven't got a body."

"If I hadn't, you wouldn't know anything about me. No creature can know another without the help of a body. But I don't care to talk about that. It is time for you to go home."

So saying, North Wind lifted Diamond and bore him away.

AT THE BACK OF THE NORTH WIND

I did not see Diamond for a week or so after this, and then he told me what I have told you. I should have been astonished at his being able even to report such conversations as he said he had had with North Wind, had I not known already that some children are profound in metaphysics. But a fear crosses me, lest, by telling so much about my friend, I should lead people to mistake him for one of those consequential, priggish little monsters, who are always trying to say clever things, and looking to see whether people appreciate them. When a child like that dies, instead of having a silly book written about him, he should be stuffed like one of those awful big-headed fishes you see in museums. But Diamond never troubled his head about what people thought of him. He never set up for knowing better than others. The wisest things he said came out when he wanted one to help him with some difficulty he was in. He was not even offended with Nanny and Jim for calling him a silly. He supposed there was something in it, although he could not quite understand what. I suspect, however, that the other name they gave him, "God's Baby," had some share in reconciling him to it.

Happily for me, I was as much interested in metaphysics as Diamond himself, and therefore, while he recounted his conversations with North Wind, I did not find myself at all in a strange sea, although certainly I could not always feel the bottom, being indeed convinced that the bottom was miles away.

"*Could* it be all dreaming, do you think, sir?" he asked anxiously.

"I daren't say, Diamond," I answered. "But at least there is one thing you may be sure of, that there is still better love than that of the wonderful being you call North Wind. Even if she be a dream, the dream of such a beautiful creature could not come to you by chance."

"Yes, I know," returned Diamond. "I know."

Then he was silent, but, I confess, appeared more thoughtful than satisfied.

The next time I saw him, he looked paler than usual.

"Have you seen your friend again?" I asked him.

"Yes," he answered solemnly.

"Did she take you out with her?"

"No. She did not speak to me. I woke all at once, as I generally do when I am going to see her, and there she was against the door into the big room, sitting just as I saw her sit on her own doorstep as white as snow, and her eyes as blue as the heart of an iceberg. She looked at me, but never moved or spoke."

"Weren't you afraid?" I asked.

"No. Why should I?" he answered. "I only felt a little cold."

"Did she stay long?"

"I don't know. I fell asleep again. I think I have been rather cold ever since though," he added with a smile.

I did not quite like this, but I said nothing.

Four days after, I called again at The Mound. The maid who opened the door looked grave, but I suspected nothing. When I reached the the drawing-room, I saw Mrs Raymond had been crying.

"Haven't you heard?" she said, seeing my questioning looks.

"I've heard nothing," I answered.

"This morning we found our dear little Diamond lying on the floor of the big attic-room, just outside his own door—fast alseep, as we thought. But when we took him up, we did not think he was alseep. We saw that—"

Here the kind-hearted lady broke out crying afresh.

"May I go and see him?" I asked.

"Yes," she sobbed. "You know your way to the top of the tower."

I walked up the winding stair, and entered his room. A lovely figure, as white and almost as clear as alabaster, was lying on the bed. I saw at once how it was. They thought he was dead. I knew that he had gone to the back of the north wind.

DINAH MARIA (MULOCK) CRAIK (1826-1887)
"The Travelling Cloak" from *The Little Lame Prince and His Travelling Cloak: A Parable for Old and Young* (1875)

By the time Mrs Craik wrote *The Little Lame Prince* she was a widely known children's author, with such well-liked books to her credit as *A Hero* (1853), a collection of tales called *The Fairy Book* (1865), and *The Adventures of a Brownie* (1872). With good reason Charlotte Yonge praised the "parable" of the lame prince as being "too beautiful and too earnest not to be worth reading". Set in the kingdom of Nomansland, the story begins as a conventional fairy tale—with the christening procession of the long-awaited royal baby interrupted by the ominous tidings of "a little old woman dressed all in gray". The first chapter hints at the serious turn this tale will take: the child is dropped by an "elegant and fashionable nursemaid" (hence his lameness), and he is christened Prince Dolor in memory of his recently deceased mother, Dolorez. These names might imply that Mrs Craik's parable is about the patient—if not passive—acceptance of pain. But *The Little Lame Prince* is an aesthetic tribute to imagination and beauty and their power to transcend loneli-

ness and deprivation. Dolor's sly uncle usurps the throne after his brother's death by circulating the story that the weak young prince has succumbed to sickness, and the boy spends a lonely childhood safely hidden in Hopeless Tower, where he is served only by a gruff nurse. Relief comes through the agency of the little grey fairy godmother, who introduces herself as "Stuff-and-Nonsense". She presents the lonely boy with a most unprepossessing gift, a shabby piece of dark green cloth, that she promises will be his "travelling cloak". As the chapter below shows, the cloak becomes Dolor's airborne passport to the undiscovered world outside his tower.

The nurse finally tells the orphan of his royal lineage and, following his uncle's death, Dolor is welcomed as monarch. His attachment to the wonderful cloak does not lessen. After a long reign, a tired King Dolor leaves his subjects in the hands of a fitting Prince Regent while, "with a joyful countenance", he floats away "on his travelling cloak to the Beautiful Mountains".

THE TRAVELLING CLOAK

If any reader, big or little, should wonder whether there is a meaning in this story deeper than that of an ordinary fairy tale, I will own that there is. But I have hidden it so carefully that the smaller people, and many larger folk, will never find it out, and meantime the book may be read straight on, like "Cinderella," or "Blue-Beard" or "Hop-o'-my-Thumb," for what interest it has, or what amusement it may bring.

Having said this, I return to Prince Dolor, that little lame boy whom many may think so exceedingly to be pitied. But if you had seen him as he sat patiently untying his wonderful cloak, which was done up in a very tight and perplexing parcel, using skillfully his deft little hands, and knitting his brows with firm determination, while his eyes glistened with pleasure and energy and eager anticipation—if you had beheld him thus, you might have changed your opinion.

When we see people suffering or unfortunate, we feel very sorry for them; but when we see them bravely bearing their sufferings and making the best of their misfortunes, it is quite a different feeling. We respect, we admire them. One can respect and admire even a little child.

When Prince Dolor had patiently untied all the knots, a remarkable thing happened. The cloak began to undo itself. Slowly unfolding it laid itself down on the carpet, as flat as if it had been ironed; the split joined with a little sharp crick-crack, and the rim turned up all round till it was breast-high; for meantime the cloak had grown and grown, and become quite large enough for one person to sit in it as comfortable as if in a boat.

The Prince watched it rather anxiously; it was such an extraordinary, not to say a frightening, thing. However, he was no coward, but a thorough boy, who, if he had been like other boys, would doubtless have grown up daring and adventurous—a soldier, a sailor, or the like. As it was, he could only show his courage morally, not physically, by being afraid of nothing, and by doing boldly all that it was in his narrow powers to do. And I am not sure but that in this way he showed more real valor than if he had had six pairs of proper legs.

He said to himself: "What a goose I am! As if my dear godmother would ever have given me anything to hurt me. Here goes!"

So, with one of his active leaps, he sprang right into the middle of the cloak, where he squatted down, wrapping his arms tight round his knees, for they shook a little and his heart beat fast. But there he sat, steady and silent, waiting for what might happen next.

Nothing did happen, and he began to think nothing would, and to feel rather disappointed, when he recollected the words he had been told to repeat—"Abracadabra, dum dum dum!"

He repeated them, laughing all the while, they seemed such nonsense. And then—and then—

Now I don't expect anybody to believe what I am going to relate, though a good many wise people have believed a good many sillier things. And as seeing's believing, and I never saw it, I cannot be ex-

pected implicitly to believe it myself, except in a sort of a way; and yet there is truth in it—for some people.

The cloak rose, slowly and steadily, at first only a few inches, then gradually higher and higher, till it nearly touched the skylight. Prince Dolor's head actually bumped against the glass, or would have done so had he not crouched down, crying "Oh, please don't hurt me!" in a most melancholy voice.

Then he suddenly remembered his godmother's express command— "Open the skylight!"

Regaining his courage at once, without a moment's delay he lifted up his head and began searching for the bolt—the cloak meanwhile remaining perfectly still, balanced in the air. But the minute the window was opened, out it sailed—right out into the clear, fresh air, with nothing between it and the cloudless blue.

Prince Dolor had never felt any such delicious sensation before. I can understand it. Cannot you? Did you never think, in watching the rooks going home singly or in pairs, soaring their way across the calm evening sky till they vanish like black dots in the misty gray, how pleasant it must feel to be up there, quite out of the noise and din of the world, able to hear and see everything down below, yet troubled by nothing and teased by no one—all alone, but perfectly content?

Something like this was the happiness of the little lame prince when he got out of Hopeless Tower, and found himself for the first time in the pure open air, with the sky above him and the earth below.

True, there was nothing but earth and sky; no houses, no trees, no rivers, mountains, seas—not a beast on the ground, or a bird in the air.

But to him even the level plain looked beautiful; and then there was the glorious arch of the sky, with a little young moon sitting in the west like a baby queen. And the evening breeze was so sweet and fresh—it kissed him like his godmother's kisses; and by and by a few stars came out—first two or three, and then quantities—quantities! so that when he began to count them he was utterly bewildered.

By this time, however, the cool breeze had become cold; the mist gathered; and as he had, as he said, no outdoor clothes, poor Prince Dolor was not very comfortable. The dews fell damp on his curls—he began to shiver.

"Perhaps I had better go home," thought he.

But how? For in his excitement the other words which his godmother had told him to use had slipped his memory. They were only a little different from the first, but in that slight difference all the importance lay. As he repeated his "Abracadabra," trying ever so many other syllables after it, the cloak only went faster and faster, skimming on through the dusky, empty air.

The poor little Prince began to feel frightened. What if his wonderful traveling-cloak should keep on thus traveling, perhaps to the world's end, carrying with it a poor, tired, hungry boy, who, after all, was beginning to think there was something very pleasant in supper and bed!

"Dear godmother," he cried pitifully, "do help me! Tell me just this once and I'll never forget again."

Instantly the words came rushing into his head—"Abracadabra, tum tum ti!" Was that it? Ah! yes—for the cloak began to turn slowly. He repeated the charm again, more ditinctly and firmly, when it gave a gentle dip, like a nod of satisfaction, and immediately started back, as fast as ever, in the direction of the tower.

He reached the skylight, which he found exactly as he had left it, and slipped in, cloak and all, as easily as he had got out. He had scarcely reached the floor, and was still sitting in the middle of his traveling-cloak,—like a frog on a water-lily leaf, as his godmother had expressed it,—when he heard his nurse's voice outside.

"Bless us! what has become of your Royal Highness all this time? To sit stupidly here at the window till it is quite dark, and leave the skylight open, too. Prince! what can you be thinking of? You are the silliest boy I ever knew."

"Am I?" said he absently, and never heeding her crossness; for his only anxiety was lest she might find out anything.

She would have been a very clever person to have done so. The instant Prince Dolor got off it, the cloak folded itself up into the tiniest possible parcel, tied all its own knots, and rolled itself of its own accord into the farthest and darkest corner of the room. If the nurse had seen it, which she didn't, she would have taken it for a mere bundle of rubbish not worth noticing.

Shutting the skylight with an angry bang, she brought in the supper and lit the candles with her usual unhappy expression of countenance.

But Prince Dolor hardly saw it; he only saw, hid in the corner where nobody else would see it, his wonderful traveling-cloak. And though his supper was not particularly nice, he ate it heartily, scarcely hearing a word of his nurse's grumbling, which to-night seemed to have taken the place of her sullen silence.

"Poor woman!" he thought, when he paused a minute to listen and look at her with those quiet, happy eyes, so like his mother's. "Poor woman! she hasn't got a traveling-cloak!"

And when he was left alone at last, and crept into his little bed, where he lay awake a good while, watching what he called his "sky-garden," all planted with stars, like flowers, his chief thought was—"I must be up very early to-morrow morning, and get my lessons done, and then I'll go travelling all over the world on my beautiful cloak."

So next day he opened his eyes with the sun, and went with a good heart to his lessons. They had hitherto been the chief amusement of his dull life; now, I am afraid, he found them also a little dull. But he tried to be good,—I don't say Prince Dolor always was good, but he generally tried to be,—and when his mind went wandering after the dark, dusty corner where lay his precious treasure, he resolutely called it back again.

"For," he said, "how ashamed my godmother would be of me if I grew up a stupid boy!"

But the instant lessons were done, and he was alone in the empty room, he crept across the floor, undid the shabby little bundle, his fingers trembling with eagerness, climbed on the chair, and thence to the table, so as to unbar the skylight,—he forgot nothing now,—said his magic charm, and was away out of the window, as children say, "in a few minutes less than no time."

Nobody missed him. He was accustomed to sit so quietly always that his nurse, though only in the next room, perceived no difference. And besides, she might have gone in and out a dozen times, and it would have been just the same; she never could have found out his absence.

For what do you think the clever godmother did? She took a quantity of moonshine, or some equally convenient material, and made an image, which she set on the window-sill reading, or by the table drawing, where it looked so like Prince Dolor that any common observer would never have guessed the deception; and even the boy would have been puzzled to know which was the image and which was himself.

And all this while the happy little fellow was away, floating in the air on his magic cloak, and seeing all sorts of wonderful things—or they seemed wonderful to him, who had hitherto seen nothing at all.

First, there were the flowers that grew on the plain, which, whenever the cloak came near enough, he strained his eyes to look at; they were very tiny, but very beautiful—white saxifrage, and yellow lotus, and ground-thistles, purple and bright, with many others the names of which I do not know. No more did Prince Dolor, though he tried to find them out by recalling any pictures he had seen of them. But he was too far off; and though it was pleasant enough to admire them as brilliant patches of color, still he would have liked to examine them all. He was, as a little girl I know once said of a playfellow, "a very examining boy."

"I wonder," he thought, "whether I could see better through a pair of glasses like those my nurse reads with, and takes such care of. How I would take care of them, too, if I only had a pair!"

Immediately he felt something queer and hard fixing itself to the bridge of his nose. It was a pair of the prettiest gold spectacles ever seen; and looking downward, he found that, though ever so high above the ground, he could see every minute blade of grass, every tiny bud and flower—nay, even the insects that walked over them.

"Thank you, thank you!" he cried, in a gush of gratitude—to anybody or everybody, but especially to his dear godmother, who he felt sure had given him this new present. He amused himself with it for ever so long, with his chin pressed on the rim of the cloak, gazing down upon the grass, every square foot of which was a mine of wonders.

Then, just to rest his eyes, he turned them up to the sky—the blue, bright, empty sky, which he had looked at so often and seen nothing.

Now surely there was something. A long, black, wavy line, moving on in the distance, not by chance, as the clouds move apparently, but deliberately, as if it were alive. He might have seen it before—he almost thought he had; but then he could not tell what it was. Looking at it through his spectacles, he discovered that it really was alive; being a long string of birds, flying one after the other, their wings moving steadily and their heads pointed in one direction, as steadily as if each were a little ship, guided invisibly by an unerring helm.

"They must be the passage-birds flying seaward!" cried the boy, who had read a little about them, and had a great talent for putting two and two together and finding out all he could. "Oh, how I should like to see them quite close, and to know where they come from and whither they are going! How I wish I knew everything in all the world!"

A silly speech for even an "examining" little boy to make; because, as we grow older, the more we know the more we find out there is to know. And Prince Dolor blushed when he had said it, and hoped nobody had heard him.

Apparently somebody had, however; for the cloak gave a sudden bound forward, and presently he found himself high up in air, in the very middle of that band of aerial travelers, who had no magic cloak to travel on—nothing except their wings. Yet there they were, making their fearless way through the sky.

Prince Dolor looked at them as one after the other they glided past him; and they looked at him—those pretty swallows, with their changing necks and bright eyes—as if wondering to meet in mid-air such an extraordinary sort of bird.

"Oh, I wish I were going with you, you lovely creatures! I'm getting so tired of this dull plain, and the dreary and lonely tower. I do so want to see the world! Pretty swallows, dear swallows! tell me what it looks like—the beautiful, wonderful world!"

But the swallows flew past him—steadily, slowly pursuing their course as if inside each little head had been a mariner's compass, to guide them safe over land and sea, direct to the place where they wished to go.

The boy looked after them with envy. For a long time he followed with his eyes the faint, wavy black line as it floated away, sometimes changing its curves a little, but never deviating from its settled course, till it vanished entirely out of sight.

Then he settled himself down in the center of the cloak, feeling quite sad and lonely.

"I think I'll go home," said he, and repeated his "Abracadabra, tum tum ti!" with a rather heavy heart. The more he had, the more he wanted; and it is not always one can have everything one wants—at least, at the exact minute one craves for it; not even though one is a prince, and has a powerful and beneficent godmother.

He did not like to vex her by calling for her and telling her how unhappy he was, in spite of all her goodness; so he just kept his trouble to himself, went back to his lonely tower, and spent three days in silent melancholy, without even attempting another journey on his traveling-cloak.

3. "TRAINING THE SYMPATHIES OF CHILDREN": EVANGELICAL WRITING

Doctrines are the pillars of a discourse. . . . Illustrations are the windows that let in the light.
—*Epigraph*, Ministering Children *(1854)*

Translating faith into action was the paramount concern of every staunch Evangelical. This social principle was the keystone of the fiction written by four women Evangelicals—Maria Louisa Charlesworth, Charlotte Tucker, Hesba Stretton, and Catherine Augusta Walton—whose work contributed substantially to nineteenth-century tract literature for children. Fairy tales contained moral precepts, and allegories doctrinal messages; but the tracts of these Evangelical writers stood apart in providing explicit and topical preaching. Set in the slums and workhouses of industrial cities, and portraying bony waifs shivering in a tenement close or a bare attic, gin-sodden parents, and a host of frail consumptives of all ages, they were intended

to reveal how the biblical tenets about love could be put into practice.

In each of the works included in this chapter poor children are not merely objects of pity. They are usually the "teachers" who show through example how the middle-class reader can perform acts of charity. Children like Charlesworth's orphaned Mercy Jones, Stretton's motherless Little Meg, and Walton's homeless Christie have learned from their rough experiences and from their unflagging trust in the promises of the New Testament. Though suffering from malnutrition, Mercy Jones is secure in her knowledge of the Bible and is even able to comfort the young daughter of prosperous Farmer Smith. While caring for her dying mother, and later when feeding and tending her younger brother and sister, Little Meg frequently summons courage through her prayers. By attending mission meetings, Walton's little organ grinder finds out about a heavenly "home sweet home". Their creators repeatedly insist that the lessons these children teach are more grave and necessary than any school exercise.

To extol the basic theme of caring, these writers made no bones about appealing to their readers' emotions. Miss Charlesworth's "The Story of Little Patience" is about an orphan, who, after a horrendous experience in service, is relegated to the workhouse, where she ministers to the other waifs by reading to them from the Bible. Miss Stretton, by far the most accomplished storyteller of the group, makes the reader feel the terrible earnestness of Meg, whom duties and fears have moulded into an "anxious little woman". Mrs Walton's story of a dying old pauper befriending an orphan boy has a readymade emotional appeal, but this writer insists on adding the burdensome and obsessive message of being washed in the blood of the Lamb to ensure that Old Treffy will arrive safely at his "home sweet home".

Contrived, riddled with clichés, often condescending, grossly sentimental, sometimes even lurid, the tracts wallowed in literary sins—while exposing more flagrant ones in Victorian England and promoting the efficacy of loving acts to counter them. On readers, however, the "message" risked being lost or ignored in the enjoyment of the literary excesses—especially the sentimentality—which were irresistible not only to children of all classes but to recently literate factory workers. Many of these books became extremely popular and made their authors financially independent.

More than any other form of Golden Age literature, Evangelical-tract fiction was a product of its time. In the first half of the nineteenth century Hannah More, Mrs Trimmer, and Mrs Sherwood wrote to further the twin causes of religious education and missionary activity. Only in the second half of the century did the locale for Evangelical fiction change from an idyllic countryside or exotic jungle to the teeming industrial centres of Manchester, Liverpool, and London. Certainly claims for the influence of tract writers as social reformers can be exaggerated. While these women were producing their sentimentally charged stories, activists like Dr Barnardo were reclaiming orphans from the London slums, and dedicated Evangelicals like William, Catherine, and Charles Booth of the Salvation Army* were marching to gain souls and minister to the downtrodden in England and on the Continent. But the most proficient tract writers did expose social abuses by recording the real life around them with sympathetic fidelity, and their tracts prompted later reforms to labour laws, public health, and education acts.

The vogue of tract fiction did not extend beyond the nineteenth century. Several of the abuses exposed in the tracts were gradually legislated out of existence. In addition, other forms of literature for the young—full-length novels and school, adventure, and animal stories—borrowed religious themes from the tracts and succeeded in incorporating them with appealing charm and subtlety into their narrative entertainments, thereby unseating the tract as the prime dispenser of moral precepts.

---

* As M.N. Cutt interestingly points out in her expert study of nineteenth-century Evangelical fiction, *Ministering Angels* (1979), Charlesworth's niece, Maud Ballington Booth, and Tucker's nephew, Frederick Booth-Tucker, led the vanguard of Salvation Army efforts in North America during the last decade of the nineteenth century.

MARIA LOUISA CHARLESWORTH (1819-1880)
"The Story of Little Patience" from *Ministering Children: A Tale* (1854)

The daughter of an Evangelical clergyman, and a ministering child herself who accompanied her father on the pastoral rounds of his living near Ipswich, Miss Charlesworth conducted her whole life in strict accordance with the fundamental principles of Evangelicalism. The earliest of her over twenty stories, *The Female Visitor to the Poor; or, Records of Female Parochial Visiting* (1846) announced these guiding tenets with absolute clarity. Her *Ministering Children*—425 pages of small type!—was the first Evangelical novel for the young. Appearing in at least eight editions and inspiring different sequels, it set a standard for later fiction of this genre in its rich, if unrestrained, treatment of character, emotion, and social abuses. Miss Charlesworth offered this Sunday School "tale" as a means of "training the sympathies of children by personal intercourse with want and sorrow".

Probably drawing on her recollection of village life in Suffolk and her first-hand knowledge of parish work in London, Miss Charlesworth designed *Ministering Children* as a series of affecting pictures to promote the theme "that the heart of Love is the only spring that can effectually govern and direct the hand of Charity". Set in an unnamed "large old town" and the surrounding countryside, Charlesworth's story mixes the lives of many characters representing all social strata. Two poor frail schoolgirls, Ruth and Patience, first claim our attention—the former because of her angelic generosity and the latter, neglected by her father and uncomforted by her teacher, because of her joyless life.

One actively charitable group in the town is the grocer's family, the Mansfields. Young Jane Mansfield resolves to donate her weekly penny to a poor orphaned child called Mercy Jones, who lives with her grandmother and her uncle Jem, a shepherd. Little Mercy also enjoys the friend-ship of saintly Mary Clifford, the Squire's daughter, who teaches at the Sunday School. The Cliffords have a second child, Herbert, who is likeably carefree and thoughtless. Having assessed himself as "passionate, selfish, sinful" (Chap. 7), Herbert learns how to be truly helpful from Jem Jones, a natural philosopher. Farmer Smith's family of five children completes the expansive catalogue of central characters. Little Rose Smith is actually taught prayers and Bible stories by the destitute but cheerful Mercy Jones. Adults who lack the charity that the children so amply display are uniformly disagreeable. In addition to Patience's narrowsighted teacher, Miss Wilson, Old Willy's stiffnecked and irresponsible landlord, Mr Sturgeon, and a neglectful old clergyman—who is replaced, significantly, by an eager young Evangelical curate—there is the intransigent Mrs Smith. She refuses to let Rose join Miss Clifford's Sunday School class, rebuffs an old widow whose son has been accused of poaching, dislikes the new curate, and alienates her invaluable maid Molly. But Charlesworth's huge novel illustrates how charity spreads, eventually softening the heart of people like Mrs Smith, and how the sterling children—like Little Patience in the story that follows—will endure. Not all the good people survive, however: the deaths of characters like poor Ruth, Miss Clifford, little Tim Smith, and Old Willy demonstrate the exemplary and pious endings of good lives. It was a convention of tracts to provide conclusions that, if not happy, were at least satisfying. The marriages of Patience to Jem Jones and of Herbert Clifford to Lady Gertrude, Patience's early benefactress, bring a nicely balanced sentimental close to Charlesworth's account of lives that have become intertwined through acts of benevolence.

THE STORY OF LITTLE PATIENCE

*"Now the end of the commandment is CHARITY out of a pure
heart, and a good conscience, and faith unfeigned."*—1 Tim. i. 5.

Christmas had passed away, New Year's Day was over and gone, and
the cold snowy month of January slowly drawing to a close. Rose had
returned for her last half year, to school. And poor little Patience had
taken her place again in the second class, among her companions; the
mistress said it was a disgrace for her to be still only in the second class,
when many younger than she had been months in the first; but no one
else took notice of it, for the poor child was so small and thin, so silent
and shrinking, that a stranger might have supposed her one of the
youngest, as well as the lowest which she generally was, in the second
class of healthy, happy children. It was at this same time that a travelling
carriage arrived at the Hall. Mr and Mrs Clifford were at the door to receive their guests; a rather elderly gentleman stepped out of the carriage, and then handed from it a young slight girl, whom Mrs Clifford
received with a mother's welcome. The hall-door was shut, and the carriage drove round to the stables. This young visitor was the only child of
Mrs Clifford's earliest friend; that friend had died some years before in
England, and the father had gone to reside with this his only child
abroad—more for change of scene than from any necessity of health. A
mother's sheltering tenderness has passed away from her, just when
she began to realize the power and blessing of it. But that mother had
led her from her earliest years to her God and Saviour, whose love is
more than a mother's love, and whose presence can never be taken
away; and the motherless child knew where to turn in her heart's desolation; she had been led so constantly to her Saviour's feet, that it was no
strange place to her, she had learned to tell the wishes of her infant life
to Him, to carry to Him her childhood's hopes and fears, and now when
bereft on Earth she turned with her aching heart to Heaven; and the love
of God, that filled the blank in life for her, filled also her life with sympathy for others. After her mother's death she had little intercourse with
any but her father, and this older companionship, with her mother's
loss, had made her grave beyond her years: her face was full of thought;
and when she smiled, it seemed rather the expression of her tenderness
for those she loved, or pleasure in others' mirth, than the bright gleam
of personal merriment. On the glee of those, like herself in childhood,
she seemed to look with distant pleasure: but wherever sorrow rested,
she drew near—as if she felt her call on Earth lay there. Young as she
was, she had drunk deep of the cup of grief; death and separation were
words, the reality of which her hourly life still learned; but she had
tasted also the love that can sweeten the bitterest trial, and her sense of
joy was still deeper than her feeling of sadness. She herself was comforted in all things—how could she then but long to comfort others!
There was no gloom in her sweet gravity, but a depth of tenderness, an

assurance of sympathy, that made her very presence soothe. Those who shrank most from the thought of intrusion in their grief, would welcome her, nor wish to turn from meeting her calm expressive eye, which seemed rather to take in the object on which it looked, than to search into that object with penetrating enquiry.

Miss Clifford had been like an elder sister to her; no place was like Miss Clifford's side, and no one else had so much power to waken in her the silent gladness of feeling, and the graceful play of thought—that had slept because there had been none to call them forth, or give responsive tones; but even when with her sister friend, her words were more often the earnest words that told of earnest thought. She looked upon the world around her, not as on a picture, as childhood for the most part beholds it—searching no deeper than its surface hues of light and shadow, but as one who had already learned the deep realities that live beneath the pictured scene. When her eye rested on sorrow's aspect, she instantly estimated the depth of suffering by her own sense of grief; and when she had tried to comfort or relieve, she still retained the feeling of the sorrow being like her own—not to be forgotten!—yet sometimes it was her's to sow the seeds of purest joy in the heart that grief had filled. Her friend, Miss Clifford, had known sorrow and want only as she had sought them out to relieve them; the feeling they called forth in her was—how best to aid and comfort; and when want was replenished, and sadness smiled on her, she passed away and felt only the joy of relieving. The one seemed to soothe by receiving the sorrows of others into her own deep sympathy: the other to brighten by shedding her own light of peace on the troubled. It was one of Earth's loveliest sights to see the two so young in years, with all the world could offer of attraction spread around them, intent in converse how best to use the blessed power entrusted to them—to brighten the sorrowful, and guide them to the holy Heaven to which their own youthful steps were bound!

The young guest at the Hall was anxious to lose no time in taking a drive to the neighbouring town, to see her old nurse, from whom she had been never separated till she left England with her father—when her mother's faithful maid became her attendant. The first suitable day was chosen, and as Patience was creeping back over the snow from school, a few minutes after four o'clock, Mr Clifford's carriage drove up and stopped beside her at the door of the house where she lived, No. 9, Ivy-lane, from which the old nurse's last letters had been dated. "Does Mrs Brame live here?" asked the footman of the child. "Yes," said Patience, looking up. The man went in, and Patience slowly followed.

"How unhappy that poor little girl looked!" said Mrs Clifford's young guest.

"Do you mean that neatly-dressed child now gone in?" asked Mrs Clifford.

"Yes, she looked as if she could not smile!"

"You don't say so! I was thinking how clean and comfortable she appeared."

Mrs Brame lived at the top of the large old house; and though aged now, and, for the most part, slow of movement, she descended the stairs almost as quickly as the footman had run up; and tears, and smiles, and words of astonishment and gladness, were the old woman's welcome to the child—whose infancy had been cradled in her arms, whose opening life had been her one object of interest, and who through years of absence had still retained the entire possession of her nurse's heart, which had never glowed with affection towards any other object through life.

For one whole hour the devoted nurse was to be allowed the sole possession of the child so precious to her! But as the time drew near its close, the youthful Lady Gertrude asked her nurse about the little girl whom she had seen enter the same house. Nurse Brame told the sad story of the poor child, and her young listener sighing, said, "I thought she looked as if her heart were empty."

"Ah, it's worse than that!" replied nurse Brame. "I doubt if she has a heart! Why, let happen what will, I have never seen her shed a tear! and if I have given to her once, I have twenty times, just because I could not bear to see such a miserable-looking child—but I don't believe she cares a bit more about me than if I had never shown her a kindness!"

"I wish I could see her again!" said the young Lady Gertrude.

"It's not the least use," replied the old nurse. "I have tried it fifty times, there's no getting anything out of her!"

"Oh, I must see her again if she is here!" said the Lady Gertrude, "I will go to her room and see her there!"

The old nurse went reluctantly to inquire, in the hope of finding that Patience was not within. But she returned, saying, the child was there and alone; adding in a tone of remonstrance, "If you won't be pacified without going, why then I must stand outside her door, for if I were to let you see that child's father I should never forgive myself!"

The Lady Gertrude made no answer, but followed her nurse down the first flight of stairs to the room where poor Patience dwelt; there was not much evidence of any "pacifying" being needed in her light step of youthful dignity, and her calm earnest eye—but her nurse had always been wont to suppose the necessity of "pacifying," as a reason for yielding to her young Lady's gentle yet decided will. The old nurse stood to listen and watch at the top of the stairs, and the Lady Gertrude entered the room. One glance round the apartment was sufficient to show that no mother's care, no mother's presence was known there; and a rush of almost sisterly feeling passed through the heart of the motherless child of rank and fortune, as she looked on the motherless child of want and sorrow. Patience was standing with her usual expression of dull and hopeless wretchedness. The young Lady Gertrude went up to her, and said, in a low tone of tenderness, "Dear little girl, I am sure you are not happy!" She asked no question, she called for no reply, but she gave expression to her own sense of a fact, a simple fact, that none had seemed to notice before. Patience took up her little white linen apron, and hid

her face in it, and wept. "Do not cry!" said the Lady Gertrude. "I want
to make you happy! Are you not cold without a fire?" and she laid her
hand on the chilblained hands of the child—"Yes, you are very cold! If
you have half-a-crown from my purse, then you could get some coal
and some wood, and make a fire when I am gone, could you not?" But
Patience still only hid her face and wept—Warm tears they were, melting the child's young heart, so early frozen, and preparing it to receive
the first impression of human tenderness, which no after-time could efface or impair.

"Did you ever hear of Jesus?"

"Yes," said Patience.

"Jesus wants you to love Him, and be His child, that He may make
you happy? Will you love Him, and try to pray to Him? If you do, He
will sure to comfort you!"

"Yes," said the still weeping child.

"I shall have to go away directly; will you not look at me, that you may
remember me? because I love you, and shall often think about you."

Patience looked up,—but the time was gone, the carriage was already
within hearing. Then despairing to comfort her, and feeling only, at that
moment, the sorrow she could not bear away, the child of rank put her
arm around the child of poverty, pressed a kiss of tenderness upon her

forehead, and putting the half-crown into her hand, turned away in answer to her nurse's knock on the half-shut door. "Oh, do be kind to her!" said the Lady Gertrude as she took leave of her nurse; and in a minute more she was driving fast away.

Mrs Clifford observed a shade of sadness on the face of her young charge, and naturally concluding that she felt leaving her nurse, immediately planned in her own mind to obtain the consent of her young visitor's father, and then send for her nurse to stay at the Hall. For far other were the thoughts of that gentle girl; her heart was lingering where she felt she had left an unsupplied want, an unsoothed sorrow—lingering with the motherless child in that bare and desolate room. She was thinking that she had done nothing, worse than nothing—had awakened the child's sorrow, and left her uncomforted. "Why," she thought, "was I so determined to speak to her! How much better if I had not attempted what I could not do!" Did she not know then how often the eye returns to look again upon the first, the only star, that has suddenly appeared to light up the gloom of a darkened lowering sky? Did she not know, how when, in all the lonely Earth no music wakes upon our ear, if suddenly the nightingale's rich melody is heard, the very heart is hushed to listen and recall the strain? Did she not know how dear—how unlike all that follow—is the first violet gathered where the sunbeam has warmed the yet wintry bank, and called forth the herald of spring? Yes, she knew that these things were so; but she knew not that her visit to the child of want and suffering had been like them; and so she passed away in sadness, and thought she had left no blessing.—How many such misgiving fears will the light of eternity, when it falls on life past, dispel for ever!

Nurse Brame watched the carriage swiftly disappearing in the dimly-lighted lane, then turned again within, and taking up her candle, slowly re-ascended the staircase. The earnest tone in which the words, "Oh do be kind to her!" had been uttered, left them impressed on the old woman's heart, the child seemed more associated with her young Lady than anything beside, and she turned into the room to speak to her.

Poor little Patience, when left alone, had ceased her tears for a minute in bewildered surprise; then raised her hand to feel where that kiss had been—to see if her forehead still felt the same; it felt the same, but she did not—she no longer felt alone in all the world! She had met the first gleam of human tenderness, and to that her shrinking spirit turned. She did not reason, but she felt; and feeling lies deeper than reason, and often in a child supplies reason's part—the lifeless chill was gone from her heart, its frozen surface thawed and left susceptible of passing impressions. Nurse Brame came in, and holding up her candle to see the child, said, in a kind voice, "Here, come along with me out of this cold place, and we will have some tea together;" Patience followed, and was soon seated on a stool by the little fire-place. Nurse Brame stirred up the dull coals into a blaze, and telling the child to make haste and get warm,—she set out the little round table with her tea-board and bread and butter, and lifting the kettle on the fire, sat down in the twilight and watched till the water boiled. The substantial slice of bread and butter, and the steaming cup of sugared tea brought a little colour to the cheek of Patience: and Nurse Brame cut the square white loaf with no sparing hand, and put more water on uncurled tea-leaves, that the poor child might be "satisfied for once!" and all the while the old nurse felt as if she were just doing her young Lady's will.

"There, now you are neither cold nor hungry at last!" said nurse Brame, "and you had better go down and go to bed, and there's no doubt you will sleep soundly enough." Patience returned to her cold dark room, and crept to the side of the heap of rags that made her bed; but she too remembered the Lady's words, and that gentle inquiry— "Will you try and pray?" led her, as by the silken bond of constraining love, to make a faint effort. Then taking from her pocket the treasured half-crown, she clasped it tight in her hand, and lying down, was soon asleep.

Nurse Brame was sitting over her decaying fire that night, her candle was out, and it was her usual early hour of rest; but she was sitting watching the fading embers, and thinking on the past events of the day—her unexpected and joyful surprise in her Lady Gerturde's visit; and then the child—but the child, the poor child, came like a shadow across the sunbeam's track! Nurse Brame had never learned the pure and simple joy of doing good; she had shewed many a little kindness to poor Patience, but it was, as she herself expressed it, because she could not bear to see so miserable a thing—not because she could not bear that silent suffering should be, if unseen! she thought that such things must be, and that it was only her call to relieve them when forced upon her notice. Suffering, when "out of sight," was "out of mind;" with old nurse Brame, therefore a gift from her was nothing more to the receiver, than the same gift picked up on the high-way side,—it came as no living witness, it left no living glow; the receiver's feeling was as shallow and transient as the feeling of the giver. But now the link between the old nurse and the poor child had changed—it was no longer the transient sight of want, but the feeling of her young Lady's interest. Nurse Brame was sitting in the dim firelight thinking upon how much it would be necessary for her to do for this unhappy and, to her, uninteresting child,—uninteresting not to her alone, but to all save the one who had so lately reached that child's buried heart! The old nurse felt she must be kind to her; she would not neglect a wish of her young Lady's for the world, but she wanted to come to a conclusion in her own mind as to what amount of kindness would be sufficient. She knew not CHARITY's indwelling influence, which, far from consisting in this or that act, is the very atmosphere in which the spirit that possesses it, lives and moves and has its being! While so pondering, nurse Brame heard a hasty knock on her door, and looking round a little startled, the woman who rented the house, letting out its rooms to lodgers, and living herself on the ground-floor, opened the door and came in. "I want you to tell me," said the woman, "what I am to do! I have just heard that pest of a man is off to escape the constables; I have not had a farthing of rent for five weeks, and what few things are in the room won't pay me a quarter of that; but such as there are, I shall make the most I can of them, and glad enough to get rid of him!—But what am I to do with the child? I can see nothing for her but the workhouse!" Now nurse Brame thought the workhouse next in disgrace to the prison itself; and the question instantly arose in her mind, What would her Lady Gertrude say, when she saw her again and asked for the child, if she found that the next day she had been carried off to the workhouse! Nurse Brame did not consider where the disgrace of the workhouse lay—whether with those who could do nothing to support themselves, or, not rather with those who suffered the young and helpless, or the old and feeble, to be carried off and nourished by the forced contributions of others. Nurse Brame considered the workhouse, in some way or other, to be a disgrace; and according to the readiest and most general custom, she associated that disgrace with the result, and not the cause of that result, and exclaimed, "Is there nothing but the WORKHOUSE?" "I can think of nothing else," replied the woman. Then suddenly within the mind of old nurse Brame rose the vision of the child, as she had been seated that evening on the stool by her fireside; the stool was still there, but the child was gone! Why might not that warm comfortable room become the child's home?—Nurse Brame might feed the worse than orphan, and yet have enough for herself—and she knew this; the child was clothed in the school; and rent of room, firing and candle, would have cost no more. All this passed before the mind of old nurse Brame; but the motive that influenced her thoughts was one of Earthly limitation, not of Heaven's boundless charity; therefore it came short of such an attainment, and she only replied, "Well, I would not be the one to send a child off to the WORKHOUSE!" The woman stood a moment considering, then said, "I have a relation in the town who wants a girl, and perhaps if I spoke for her, she would take the child, though I doubt if she would think her strong enough for the place." Now "a place" to old nurse Brame had a respectable sound; she considered it no business of her's to find out what the place of service was—it was a way, in her estimation, of earning an honest penny—little considering how often the "honest penny" of the poor is paid by dishonest hands, who have wrung three times the penny's worth from the strength that has no redress on Earth. But the day will come when the God of the poor "will plead their cause, and spoil the soul of those that spoiled them!"

And so because the name of "a place" was better than the name of "a workhouse," nurse Brame made no inquiry as to what the real thing might be, but gave her judgment in favour of the place, saying, "Well, I am sure I would try for the place, rather than send the poor thing off to the workhouse!" Meanwhile little Patience, whose fate seemed pending above, was quietly sleeping below. No rest-breaking father returned to disturb her slumber, and she did not wake till the slowly dawning light shone into her dreary room; then, hastily rising, she looked for her father—he was not there—she saw at once he had not been there; so looking again at her half-crown, and once more feeling her forehead that the lady's lips had kissed, she rose and dressed. There was no fire, no food: but the thought of spending the half-crown was not even entertained— it was the lady's gift, the sign that made the past still real and present to the child! so she put it at the bottom of her pocket, and was thinking about what time it could be, when the woman of the house came in and said, "I am sorry for you, but your father is off, no one knows where, and he has paid me no rent for these five weeks, so I must just take what he has left, and hope for a better lodger; but I don't want to be hard upon you, and if you think you would like to try service better than the workhouse, why I will go with you at once and see after a place that I know of." Poor little Patience! the avalanche of frozen words fell upon her heart, still warmed with yesterday's glow of feeling, making the chilling shock the greater. Again she hid her face and wept. "Poor thing!" said the woman in a softened tone, "I am sure none can treat you worse than your own father has done! I dare say you have not tasted food; come along with me and I will give you some breakfast, and then we will see what can be done." So taking the unresisting child by the arm, she led her down stairs, and gave her some bread and butter and cold tea; and then after awhile repeated her question, as to whether she would like best to go to service or the workhouse? Poor Patience did not know—both names were alike to her—and beginning again to cry instead of answer, she only wished in her heart that young and beautiful Lady would but come again! she felt as if then she would not be left alone in her misery. The woman seeing that words were hopeless, tied on her bonnet, and, fetching the child's bonnet and cloak, put them on her, saying, "Well, come and see what you think of the place!" and again taking her by the arm she led her through the town to a distant narrow street, stopping at the door of a high house. Patience was left in the passage while the woman went in and talked with the mistress, and then calling Patience in, the mistress of the house asked her whether she thought she could run about and do the work, for her board and a shilling a week. A shilling a week sounded like exhaustless wealth to the poor child, who knew nothing of the expense of necessary clothes, and she answered, "Yes." So the woman left the child, promising to send all that she found belonging to her; and returned well satisfied, to inform nurse Brame of the success of her attempt.

The next morning nurse Brame received a letter by the post, it was from her own young Lady. The old woman put on her spectacles, and read with astonishment and delight, that in the course of the afternoon, Mr Clifford's carriage would take her back to the Hall, to stay there during the time of her young Lady's visit. The old woman looked twice at the letter, to be quite sure, then putting on her shawl and bonnet she hurried out to buy such additions to her wardrobe as she thought necessary for so great an occasion, and then hurrying home again, began to make preparations. The sun had set when the carriage drove up to the door; the footman ran up to summon Mrs Brame, and the old woman stepped down, dressed in her neatest and best, and the footman carried her handbox behind her. Her young Lady was in the carriage alone, and when the old woman was in and the footman waiting for orders, the Lady Gertrude asked her nurse whether that poor child were at home? "Ah, no, poor thing! she went off yesterday to service!" replied Mrs Brame.

"That little girl to be a servant!" asked the young Lady Gertrude in a tone of surprise.

"Ah, yes, she is older than she has the look of, by a good bit!"

"Home," said the Lady Gertrude, and the carriage drove on: then turning, she talked with her old nurse, till, as they were about to leave the town, she suddenly, as if a thought for the first time crossed her mind, inquired, "Do you know where that little girl has gone to live?"

"Not the least in the world," replied nurse Brame, "but she is gone to service—and that's respectable! they would have sent her off to the workhouse, but I set my face against having the poor thing treated like that, and now she is once in service she must work her way as I and others have done!"

"But if she should not be happy, who will know it?" asked the young Lady Gertrude.

"You need not distress yourself," replied nurse Brame, "she has led such a wretched life, that let service be what it will, it must be better than that!"

The Lady Gertrude said no more, she felt that the child had no place in the heart of her old nurse, and from that time she never mentioned her again; and her nurse believed her satisfied, and the child a forgotten thing. In a fortnight more the young visitor and her father left the Hall; and in the spring of the same year, they quitted England again for a residence abroad.

When Miss Wilson next visited the school, she missed Patience; and when she inquired of the mistress, she heard that the child had been forsaken by her father, and was gone to service. And then the mistress told her what she had now found out about the life of misery the poor forsaken child had led in her home. Miss Wilson felt very sorry, but it was too late now to hope to do much; yet she could still go and see poor Patience in her place of service; and knowing that Patience had not earned a Bible, she directly determined to go and take her one; so she learnt from the mistress where Patience was living; then going to a shop, she bought a Bible, and went on to find poor Patience in her place of service.

It was a narrow street, and when Miss Wilson knocked at the door, a cross-looking woman opened it. Miss Wilson asked for her little scholar. The woman did not invite her in, but shouted to Patience to come down; and then went away, leaving Miss Wilson standing at the door. Patience came; just the same look over her face as when at school—as if she expected something to be said to persuade her to try and do more than she had done before. Miss Wilson would gladly now have comforted the poor desolate child—but she could only speak to her at the door of the house; she gave Patience the Bible she had brought for her; Patience took it and curtsied, but did not speak, and Miss Wilson could never forget the look of illness in the poor child's face. She went away feeling very sad about the child; she had always been kind to Patience, she had never spoken hastily or severely to her, but she had loved her less than she loved the other children, and poor Patience had wanted more love than others—not less!

Miss Wilson waited some weeks, and then she went again to see Patience in her place. The same cross-looking woman opened the door, and Miss Wilson asked if she could speak to Patience.

"Oh, she is not here," replied the woman, "she fell ill of brain-fever, and we had her carried off to the workhouse!"

Poor Patience! she had no strength for work, half-starved as she had been and miserable, her feeble limbs could stand no labour; she had toiled on till all power was gone, and now at last she was in the workhouse! We will not leave her yet, but will go and see her there. She was laid on a little bed in the sick ward of the workhouse, and nursed till the fever left her, and she was able to sit up. When she was well enough to sit up and walk about a little, she was not sent to another place of service; no, she was taken two miles away from the town, to a house in the country, where the workhouse-children were kept. It was the beginning of May; the trees were all in bud, and the hedges growing green, and the lark was singing in the clear blue sky. Patience had never been so far in the country before, she wished the drive would last very long, for she liked it very much, and she did not know what she might find at the end. It was not long, however, before they stopped at a large house that stood alone. A strong, kind-looking woman came out, and took Patience in, saying, "Never mind, my dear, you will soon get better here!" Patience heard the words, and she looked up at the workhouse matron with an expression of inquiry and wonder. But it was all true, it was the strong kind woman's heart that spoke in those first words to the timid stranger child, and Patience was to be with her. And now the cold nipping winter of the poor child's life was gone, and its bright spring-time began. Yes, its bright spring-time began in the workhouse, under the care of that strong kind woman! Patience began the next day to do a little work, but the matron saw directly that the tired look came over her face and made her leave off. Breakfast, dinner, and tea all came, with strengthening food for Patience; and now that she was no longer faint and hungry, she began to think of all that she had heard long before. And first she got her little Bible, and read to herself, and she felt happy—reading all alone and trying to remember what Miss Wilson had said at the school. After a little while, Patience thought that what made her happy would make the other children happy; so in their play-time she often persuaded them to come and sit round her; and she read out of her Bible, and taught them texts and hymns, and read to them from her other little books, and the children liked to listen.—So it was that poor Patience, who seemed at school as if she could not learn, and would never remember anything, was the first perhaps of all the children there, except little Ruth, to become a ministering child to others.

Poor Patience had never known a parent's tenderness; but she soon learned to love the strong kind matron who took care of all the work-house children; the matron moved about quickly, and spoke fast and loud, but her heart was kind, and Patience loved her, and tried to please her. When the months of May and June has passed away, and Patience was well again, there came a day of holiday in the workhouse; and the matron told Patience that she might go to the town and see her friends. Patience had no friends except Miss Wilson, and that youthful Lady far away! but she thought she should like to see Miss Wilson. Though Patience looked very small, she was older than she looked, and quite old enough to go to the town alone. She knew where Miss Wilson lived, and easily found the house. Miss Wilson was very glad to find how happy she was in the workhouse; and now Patience not only answered every question put to her, but she told how she employed her time, and how the workhouse-children came round and listened, while she read to them, and told them what she had been taught at school. Miss Wilson gave Patience some new books for her own, to carry back with her; and not being able to walk so far herself, she asked her father to go; and one day he went, and found Patience happy herself, and trying to make others happy. And there for the present we must leave her—a ministering child in the workhouse.

CHARLOTTE MARIA TUCKER (A.L.O.E.) (1821-1893)
"The Green Velvet Dress" from *Precepts in Practice; or, Stories Illustrating the Proverbs* (1858)

Born in Barnet, near Finchley, Charlotte Tucker grew up in Upper Portland Place, London, one of ten children in a boisterous family dominated by brothers, as large Victorian families usually were. After her father's death in 1851 she began a long and highly prolific career as an author—more than 150 books and booklets are credited to her—and became recognized as the leading tract writer in England. Unlike Miss Charlesworth, Charlotte Tucker—who used the pseudonym "A.L.O.E." ("A Lady of England")—was not raised in a piously Evangelical household, nor was her writing restricted to somber religious tracts. An adult convert to Evangelicalism, she was known for her practical, moral, Protestant tales. Among the most characteristic are *The Roby Family; or, Battling with the World* (1857), *Ned Franks; or, The Christian's Panoply. A Tale in Six Parts . . . illustrating the Girdle of Truth, the Breastplate of Righteousness, the Sandal of Peace, the Shield of Faith, the Helmet of Hope, the Sword of the Spirit* (1865), and *Flora; or, Self-Deception* (1878). A curiosity for Canadians is *The Lake of the Woods: A Tale Illustrative of the Twelfth Chapter of Romans* (1867), about fifteen-year-old twins, a girl and a boy, whose mother and father, a disapppointed pioneer farmer, have both died. The Canadian background, accounted for by means of a

few vague references, is obviously not the result of first-hand experience. (In the spring of 1857 Miss Tucker visited her nephew in Oakville, Canada West [Ontario].) However, the emphasis on moral rectitude and the almost maudlin piety are as strong in this book, set in "a desolate country", as in her other novels.

Miss Tucker was an exceptionally strong-minded, independent woman; at the age of fifty-four she set out—as a missionary-volunteer—for India, where she spent the rest of her life, working in the Female Normal School at Amritsar and in a school for Hindu boys at Batala, all the while writing elevating stories. She continued to write into her seventies.

Precepts in Practice offers many examples of the considerable zest Miss Tucker brought to the art of didactic storytelling. Each of the effective tales—headed by an epigraph from Proverbs and concluding with verse of her own devising—stresses common Victorian themes: the importance of family ties, the holiness of filial duty, the fitting rewards of industry and punishment of indolence, the honest pluck of the poor, and the awful burden of the rich and privileged. As in "The Green Velvet Dress", the moral pill is coated with believable talk and carefully observed detail.

THE GREEN VELVET DRESS

"Better is a dinner of herbs where love is, than a stalled ox and hatred therewith"—Prov., XV. 17.

"Wrap your cloak tight round you, my lass, for the wind's bitter cold this morning: and here—see—you wouldn't be the worse of my bit of a shawl under it."

"Oh! but, mother, remember your rheumatics."

"I'm a'most right again, Jenny, and I be n't out in the cold," said the poor woman, stirring the few glowing embers which scarcely gave even the appearance of a fire.

"And come back soon again, Jenny dear," cried a pale, bare-footed little boy, running from the corner; "I hope the grand lady won't keep you long."

"I must seek for early violets in the hedges for you, Tommy."

"No, I do n't want the violets, I want you back;" and the little thin arms were thrown round her neck, and the child's lips pressed to her cheek.

"Oh, Tommy! I wish I were a grand lady!—I wish I had plenty of money! Should n't you have meat enough, and all kinds of food, to make you strong and hearty again!"

"And new shoes!" suggested the child.

"And a blazing fire, and—"

"Hush, my children!" said the mother, gently, "and do n't let your thoughts go running after what God Almighty has not seen good to give us. We've a-many blessings in this little cot of ours, and I always say that the three prime ones, sunshine for the eyes, hope for the heart, and love in the home, are as free to the poor as to the rich."

The sharp, cutting cold of a March wind, which drove the icy sheet against her face, did not tend to make little Jenny share her mother's spirit of contentment. She hastened up the long hill, holding her bonnet to keep it on, and wishing that she had some better protection against the blast than her thin cloak or her mother's thread-bare shawl. She was to call at the house of a milliner, for whom she was accustomed to run errands, and to do little pieces of plain work, in order to carry a parcel from her to a lady who lived at the Hall about three miles distant.

Jenny arrived at the milliner's, her cheeks glowing with exercise and the cold.

"Take a seat by the fire, and warm yourself, Jenny; I've just a stitch more to put to this trimming, and the dress will be ready for you to take to Lady Grange in two minutes."

So Jenny sat down and looked on with admiring eyes, as the finishing touch was given to a dress which, to her, appeared the very perfection of beauty and splendor.

"It must be a pleasure," thought the girl, "even to touch that lovely soft green velvet; and what must it be to wear it? I could not fancy any one's ever feeling unhappy in such a dress!"

It was a very foolish thought certainly; but I have known people older than Jenny Green who have made reflections just as foolish. Those who suffer from the pressure of poverty are apt to forget that there are other and worse evils in the world; and that just as heavy a heart may, and often does, beat under a robe of velvet as beneath a thread-bare cloak.

The dress was finished, folded, wrapped up in linen, and confided to the girl, with many an injunction to carry it carefully, and not to loiter on the way; injunctions which Jenny conscientiously obeyed, being duly impressed with the importance of her errand, and the amount of confidence reposed in her. The size of her parcel occasioned her some inconvenience; she had no longer a hand free to hold on her bonnet, which, blown back on her shoulders, only hung by its faded ribbons, while the gale made sad, untidy work with her hair. Jenny's shoes were very old, and the road steep and stony—she became both foot-sore and tired; but her worst trouble was the uneasy, discontented thoughts which seemed to flow into her bosom from the parcel which she carried.

"How nice and warm and comfortable it feels. I do n't believe that the lady who will wear it ever knows what it is to be hungry or cold. She is never tired, for she has a fine coach to ride in—oh! how grand it must be to ride in a coach! And then to dress like a queen, and feast on good things every day! How very, very happy she must be! I wish that I were a lady, that I do! I'd have a velvet dress of a different color for every day in the week; and dear Tommy should have a white pony to ride on; and mother, oh! darling mother! should have everything nice that I could think of—she should never have time to wish for anything: how happy we should all be together! But there's no use thinking about it," added Jenny, sadly, as on the crest of the hill a sudden gust of wind almost carried her off her feet; "I shall never be rich, nor a lady; I shall have to work and to want all my life through."

The road now led down into the valley where the way was comparatively sheltered. Jenny felt this to be a pleasant change, though the view was not so grand or extensive as it appeared from the higher ground. She was not, however, enough of a philosopher to remark, even had she known enough of the world to perceive, that in life, as in nature, some of the sharpest blasts are felt by those who *stand on the top of the hill.*

Jenny arrived at length at the grand outer gate, and passed with a timid step through the park, where the tall trees yet stretched leafless branches, though the tiny wild flowers at their feet were already opening their blossoms to the spring. There was a beautiful garden in front of the house; and along its smooth gravel walks, wrapped up in velvet and furs, sauntered the lady who was mistress of the place.

She stopped to speak to the little messenger. Her manner was gracious and gentle; but Jenny could not help noticing how mournful was its tone; and when she ventured to raise her eyes to the face of the lady, she saw on it an expression of melancholy and care, which raised a feeling of pity as well as of surprise. Is it upon the brow of the poor alone that we see the deep lines of sorrow? is it the cheek of the poor alone that is furrowed by tears? Are the merriest faces those that look from carriage windows? can wealth shut out sorrow, sickness, bereavement, disunion, or death?

Lady Grange noticed the tired looks of Jenny, and kindly ordered the maid whom she had summoned to receive the dress, to take the girl to the kitchen, that she might have a little rest and refreshment. As Jenny, after dropping a courtesy, turned to follow the servant, her attention was arrested by the sudden clatter of horses' feet; and three young men, laughing and racing each other up the slope, dashed along to the entrance of the Hall, the hoofs tearing up the well-rolled gravel, and the loud, merry voices strangely breaking the peaceful silence which had prevailed a few minutes before. Two of the horsemen reined up at a little distance from the lady; while the third, who was mounted on a splendid white horse, approached the spot where she stood.

"Mother," said he, stroking the neck of his steed, which champed its bit and pawed on the ground, as if impatient to bound onward again; "mother, I've asked Jones and Wildrake to stop to dinner to-day."

Jenny happened to glance at Lady Grange. There was an anxious frown on the gentle face, a flush on the lately pale cheek, which gave an impression of keen suffering not unmixed with anger. What Lady Grange replied to her son, or whether she replied at all, Jenny did not know; for the lady's-maid led her towards the kitchen.

The delicious savory odor of that place, the ranges of tin pans on the shelves glittering like silver; the rows of innumerable plates and dishes—above all, the enormous joint slowly revolving before a fire larger than any that Jenny had ever dreamed of, for the moment put everything out of her head but the thought that it must be delightful to be very rich. "How proud one would be, too, to have so many servants, some of them looking themselves so very grand!" thought Jenny, as she saw various members of the household, some engaged in different occupations, some appearing as though they had nothing to do but to loiter about and gossip. An aged woman, in black bonnet and shawl, was seated at the long deal table on which the stout cook was rolling out some tempting-looking pastry. She, as Jenny soon found from the conversation going on around her, was Mrs Dale, a nurse who had attended Lady Grange in her childhood, and who had now come from some distance on a visit to that lady, whom she had not seen since her marriage.

"Well, only think!" cried the lady's-maid who had conducted Jenny into the kitchen, "only think! here's Master Philip has brought down those two companions of his whom missus cannot abide the sight of; and they're to stay dinner, and sleep here too, I'll warrant you! I wonder what master will say to it when he comes home."

"Mighty little peace there'll be in the house," observed the cook.

"Oh! as for peace, no one looks for it in this place!" observed the butler, who, with his hands behind him, was warming himself at the fire. "If you'd heard all I've heard, and seen all I've seen!" and he shook his head with an air of much meaning.

"I'm afraid my poor lady has not much comfort in her son?" said the nurse in a tone of inquiry.

"Comfort! well, I can only say that high tempers and high words— one pulling one way and another another—the father trying to bridle the son, the son kicking against the authority of the father—debts to be paid—bills to be discharged—Sir Gilbert choosing to do neither, yet having at last to do both—are not my notion of comfort!"

"Master Philip will break his mother's heart," said the lady's-maid; "you should see how she cries her eyes out when she's in her own room!"

"Master Philip's not such a bad fellow, after all," remarked the butler; "he'd have done well enough if he hadn't had the ill luck to be born heir to a large fortune!"

"Oh! he was spoilt from a baby!" cried the cook.

"'Tis n't so much that," said the moralizing butler, seating himself by the fire and leaning back on his chair. Jenny, who while taking the cold meat with which she had been provided, could not avoid hearing what was passing, listened with wonder to the easy, and, as it seemed to her, the insolent manner in which the affairs of the Hall were discussed in the kitchen. She began quite to change her mind as to the advantage of keeping many servants; her simple, honest heart, revolted from the treachery of their gossiping with any stranger about the most private concerns of the family which they served. "I'm glad we've our own little cot to ourselves," was the thought which crossed Jenny's mind; "and that we have not a set of people about us to watch every look, listen to every word, and make our troubles known to all the world!"

"You see," continued the butler, addressing himself to Mrs Dale, "here's the mischief of the thing: young master found out that he was a person of mighty importance in the house, before he was high enough to look over the table. Wasn't there fireworks on his birth-day, and his health drunk with three times three at the tenants' dinner at Christmas! I mind how he used to strut about, toss his head, and bully his nurse, and smash his toys when he got tired of them; and they never pleased him more than a day! He grew older, too old for a nurse, so mistress had a tutor for him. He didn't like a tutor—why should he, the heir to the estate, be plagued with books and study? There was no peace till the tutor was sent off! Master found the boy getting beyond all bounds, with a mighty strong will of his own—sent him to school. He didn't like school—why should the heir be tormented with schooling? He was brought back after the first half, to be a plague to himself and to every one near him! So he grew up, able to settle to nothing, never finishing anything that he began—thinking of nothing but how to kill time! He must go to London and see something of life. So to London he went; and the sharpers crowded around him as the wasps round a ripe plum. They taught him to gamble and spend money—he was apt enough at learning that! The heir to such a fortune was a bird worth the plucking: and such gentry as those that he has brought with him to-day will stick by him while there's one golden feather left! So you see the truth of what I observed," said the butler in conclusion;—"the worst luck which could have befallen young master was to be born the son of a man of fortune. If he'd had his own bread to earn, d'ye see, he'd have studied as a boy, and worked as a man, and thought of something besides pleasure; the sharpers would have left him alone; and he'd have turned out, may be, a mighty respectable member of society."

Mrs Dale nodded her head very thoughtfully. She was experienced in the management of children, and in her own nursery had always labored to maintain strict discipline, but she knew well the disadvantages which attend a rich man's son and heir. She sat for a few moments, turning over the matter in her mind, as though the expression of her opinion on the subject could influence the future of that spoilt child of fortune. Then, with the decision of one who has maturely considered a difficult question, and has come to a satisfactory conclusion, she said, "If I were Lady Grange I know what I'd do. I'd send the boy to my own old home. Her brothers are both men of sense and spirit, who would stand no nonsense; and if they did n't bring the young pickle to his senses, why I'm greatly mistaken in the matter."

"Her brothers!" exclaimed cook and lady's-maid in a breath. "Why," said the butler, "do n't you know that neither of them ever enters this house?"

Mrs Dale lifted up her hands in amazement: "Lady Grange quarrelled with her own brothers! impossible!"

"Oh! it's not mistress, but master. The worry and the distress which she has had no words can tell. Why, I do n't believe that she may so much as write to her old home!"

"Dear! dear!" exclaimed the old nurse, looking really concerned; "and they were such a happy, united family; it was quite a picture to see them! Miss Clara was the darling of the house; her brothers never thought that they could make enough of their pet. Sure it must be just a heartbreak to her to be on bad terms with them now! How could such a shocking thing have happened?"

"Why, you see," said the butler, laying the finger of his right hand on the palm of his left, and lowering his voice to a more confidential though not less audible tone, "you see it was all along of the marriage settlement. Master thought that mistress should have had more of the money—"

"Throw the money into the sea!" cried Mrs Dale indignantly; "all the gold in the world is not worth the peace, and union, and love of a family!"

"Oh!" said the butler, "one can't be much in life without seeing how very often money matters break that peace, and union, and love. The purse on one side, the heart on the other, depend on 't the purse wins the day."

"There's some truth in that," observed the cook. "My last place was with three old ladies who lived very well and comfortably together, never separated for a day, till some one died, and unluckily left them a large fortune to spend. They then began to find out that their wills could never agree. Miss Jemima liked town, Miss Jessie the country, Miss Martha was all for the sea-side. One must travel this way for health, another that way for amusement; before six months were over they were all divided, the establishment was broken up; and so I came here."

"Ah!" cried Mrs Dale, sadly, "fortune is n't always sent as a blessing; and where a bad use is made of it, it turns in the end to a curse! There are folk, I daresay, envying my poor lady, thinking, that because she has a fine house, fine estate, fine carriage, she must be a happy woman. But well I know that—unless she be much changed from what she was as a child—she would gladly give them all up to see her son a steady, sensible, God-fearing man, and to be happy with her brothers again!"

Jenny having finished her cold meat, now rose and left the house—left it with ideas how changed from those with which she entered it! The feeling of envy was changed for the feeling of pity; and the young girl, as with light step she made her way towards the home where she was sure of kind smiles and a pleasant welcome, thought how much happier was her own lot than that of the lady of fortune. Even the robe of rich green velvet had lost its attractions for Jenny—was it more beautiful than the fresh turf over which she sped with so light a heart? Her back being now turned to the wind, Jenny no longer felt its keenness; while a brilliant sun was shedding warmth and cheerfulness around. Jenny did not forget to look in the hedges for violets for her little brother. "I daresay," thought she, as she stooped to pluck one from beneath the large green leaves, "I daresay that this sweet little flower will give my Tommy as much pleasure as the rich man's son ever found in his gilded toys. How foolish was I to wish for wealth! Who knows what effect it might have upon me! Mother is right—the best blessings are as free to the poor as to the rich—sunshine for the eyes, love in the home, and a good hope of heaven for the heart! *Better is a dinner of herbs where love is, than a stalled ox and hatred therewith!*"

> N'er will I sigh for wealth,
>   Such wealth as coffers can hold:
> Contentment, union, and health,
>   Are not to be bought for gold!
> The costly treasures I prize
>   Are treasures of family love—
> A happy home here, and the hope so dear
>   Of a happier home above!
>
> Equally shines the beam
>   On palace or cottage wall,
> The golden rays that stream
>   To brighten and gladden all!
> But, oh! the sunshine I prize
>   Is the sunshine of family love—
> A happy home here, and the hope so dear
>   Of a happier home above!
>
> The poor no flatterers fear,
>   They dread no plunderer's art:
> When the voice of kindness they hear,
>   They feel it comes from the heart!
> Oh! ask the blessing from heaven,
>   The blessing of family love—
> A happy home here, and the hope so dear
>   Of a happier home above!

SARAH SMITH ("HESBA STRETTON") (1832-1911)
"Little Meg's Red Frock in Pawn" from *Little Meg's Children* (1868)

A postmaster's daughter, "Hesba Stretton" grew up in a strict Methodist family of eight children near Shrewsbury. Although qualified as a governess, she was mainly employed as a post-office clerk; from these humble lower-class beginnings she rose to become the most acclaimed and widely translated Evangelical writer of the century. Well read, sharply critical of weakness, and intolerant of folly, Hesba Stretton was so successful as a Religious Tract Society author that she acquired financial independence, eventually enjoying luxurious trips on the Continent and a well-to-do London address. As determined as A.L.O.E., but with a greater control of narrative patterning, she captured the attention of a wide audience of readers, picturing for them the labour problems of the Shropshire collieries in *Fern's Hollow* (1864), the evils of industrial Manchester in *Pilgrim Street* (1867), and the pathetic life of the slum child in *Jessica's First Prayer* (1867). Her own observation of tenement housing in London and Manchester, coupled with a crusading Methodist zeal, contributed to her stories' forcefulness and immediacy.

Little Meg's Children, one of her most popular works, was reprinted until the 1920s. It relates the difficulties of three motherless children—ten-year-old Meg, six-year-old Robin, and the unnamed baby—all living in a gloomy attic that overlooks Angel Court in London's East End, and awaiting their sailor-father's return from sea. Their existence is eerie and furtive: the mother's corpse lies in their little room for a grisly one-and-a-half days, and Meg is charged with keeping secret that a chest hidden in their garret contains a great deal of money that supposedly belongs to one of her father's mates. With her dying words Meg's mother had warned that none of the denizens of Angel Court is to be trusted. Meg is therefore cool towards the only neighbour who takes any notice of them, the young prostitute called Kitty, who lives in the back attic. As the chapter that follows shows, Kitty proves a true friend and a shrewd businesswoman. Like all the stunted children of poverty in Stretton's books, Meg is old beyond her years, wearing the "anxious air of a woman upon her face, with deep lines wrinkling her forehead, and puckering about her keen eyes". Incredible as it may seem, this ten-year-old holds the family together—with the help of Kitty and a kindly shopkeeper called Mrs Blossom (who turns out to be Kitty's long-unseen mother). A further trial is the death of the baby, which requires Meg to summon all her Christian resources. As she rationalizes falteringly. "I didn't know as baby was near going to die, and may be it's a better thing for her to go to Mother and God. Angel Court ain't a nice place to live in, and she might have growed up bad. But if people do grow up bad, . . . God can make 'em good again, if they'd only ask him" (Chap. 12). Meg's faith always buoys her confidence; furthermore, her prayers are answered. Her father returns to reveal that the safely hidden money belongs, ironically, to him; Kitty and her mother are reunited; and all five embark on a new life "across the sea". As Stretton's very powerful story makes clear, Little Meg was saved neither by money nor by formal religion. The child's close knowledge of the Bible and absolute trust in its promises ensured her survival. "It's in the Bible, and Jesus said it," Meg affirms at the end of the story. "Besides, God did everythink I asked him."

LITTLE MEG'S RED FROCK IN PAWN

Meg felt very forlorn when she opened her heavy eyelids the next morning. It was certain now that her father could not be home for some time,
it might be a long time; and how was she to buy bread for her children
and herself? She took down her mother's letter from the end of a shelf
which supplied the place of a chimney-piece, and looked at it anxiously;
but she dared not ask anybody to read it for her, lest it should contain
some mention of the money hidden in the box; and that must be taken
care of in every way, because it did not belong to her, or father even, but
to one of his mates. She had no friend to go to in all the great city. Once
she might have gone to the teacher at the school where she had learned
to read a little; but that had been in quite a different part of London, on
the other side of the river, and they had moved from it before her father
had started on his last voyage. Meg sat thinking and pondering sadly
enough, until suddenly, how she did not know, her fears were all taken
away, and her childish heart lightened. She called Robin, and bade him
kneel down beside her, and folding baby's hands together, she closed
her own eyes, and bowed her head, while she asked God for the help he
had promised to give.

"Pray God," said little Meg, "you've let mother die, and father be
took bad at the other side of the world, and there's nobody to take care
of us 'cept you; and Jesus says, if we ask you, you'll give us bread, and
everythink we want, just like father and mother. Pray God, do! I'm not a
grown-up person yet, and Robin's a very little boy, and baby can't talk

or walk at all; but there's nobody else to do anythink for us, and we'll try as hard as we can to be good. Pray God, bless father at the other side of the world, and Robbie, and baby, and me; and bless everybody, for Jesus Christ's sake. Amen."

Meg rose from her knees joyfully, feeling sure that her prayer was heard and would be answered. She went out with her children to lay out the shilling Kitty had returned to her the day before; and when they came in she and Robin sat down to a lesson in reading. The baby was making a pilgrimage of the room from chair to chair, and along the bedstead; but all of a sudden she balanced herself steadily upon her tiny feet, and with a scream of mingled dread and delight, which made Meg and Robin look up quickly, she tottered across the open floor to the place where they were sitting, and hid her face in Meg's lap, quivering with joy and wonder. Meg's gladness was full, except that there was a little feeling of sorrow that neither father nor mother was there to see it.

"Did God see baby walk?" inquired Robin.

"I should think he did!" said Meg, confidently; and her slight sorrow fled away. God could not help loving baby, she felt sure of that, nor Robin; and if he loved them, would he not take care of them himself, and show her how to take care of them, till father was at home? The day passed almost as happily as Robin's birthday; though the rain came down in torrents, and pattered through the roof, falling splash splash into the broken tub, with a sound something like the fountain in Temple Gardens.

But when Kitty's shilling was gone to the last farthing, and not a spoonful of meal remained in the bag, it was not easy to be happy. Robin and baby were both crying for food; and there was no coal to make a fire, nor any candle to give them light during the long dark evenings of November. Kitty was out all day now, and did not get home till late, so Meg had not seen her since the night she had brought the news about her father. But a bright thought came to her, and she wondered at herself for not having thought of it before. She must pawn her best clothes; her red frock and bonnet with green ribbons. There was a natural pang at parting with them, even for a time; but she comforted herself with the idea that father would get them back for her as soon as he returned. She reached them out of the box, feeling carefully, lest she should take any of Robin's or the baby's by mistake in the dark; and then she set off with her valuable bundle, wondering how many shillings she would get for them, and whether she could make the money last till her father came. The pawnbroker's shop was a small, dingy place in Rosemary Lane; and it, and the rooms above it, were as full as they could be with bundles such as poor Meg carried under her old shawl. A single gas-light was flaring away in the window, and a hard-featured, sharp-eyed man was reading a newspaper behind the counter. Meg laid down her bundle timidly, and waited till he had finished reading his paragraph; after which he opened it, spread out the half-worn frock, and held up the bonnet on his fist, regarding them both with a critical and contemptuous eye. Some one else had entered the shop, but Meg was too absorbed and too anxious to take any heed of it. The pawnbroker rolled the frock up scornfully, and gave it a push towards her.

"Tenpence for the two," he said, looking back at his newspaper.

"Oh! if you please," cried little Meg, in an agony of distress, "you must give me more than tenpence. I've got two little children, and no bread, nor coals, nor candles. I couldn't buy scarcely anythink with only tenpence. Indeed, indeed, my red frock's worth a great deal more; it's worth I don't know how many shillings."

"You go home, little Meg," said Kitty's voice behind her, "and I'll bring you three shillings for the frock, and one for the bonnet; four for the two. Mr. Sloman's an old friend o' mine, he is; and he'll oblige you for my sake. There, you run away, and I'll manage this little bit o' business for you."

Meg ran away as she was told, glad enough to leave her business with Kitty. By and by she heard her coming upstairs, and went out to meet her. Kitty placed four shillings in her hand.

"Meg," she said, "you let me do that sort o' work for you always. They'll cheat you ever so; but I wouldn't, not to save my life, if you'll only trust me. You ask me another time. Is that the way God takes care of you?"

"He does take care of me," answered Meg, with a smile; "or may be you wouldn't have come into the shop just now, and I should have got only tenpence. I suppose that's taking care of me, isn't it?"

"I don't know," said Kitty. "Only let me do that for you when you want it done again."

It was not very long before it wanted to be done again; and then Meg by daylight went through the contents of the box, choosing out those things which could best be spared, but leaving Robin's and baby's fine clothes to the last. She clung to these with a strong desire to save them, lest it should happen that her father came home too poor to redeem them. The packet of money, tied up and sealed, fell at last to the bottom of the almost empty box, and rolled noisily about whenever it was moved, but no thought of taking any of it entered into Meg's head. She was almost afraid of looking at it herself, lest the secret of it being there should get known in Angel Court; and whenever she mentioned it in her prayers, which she did every night, asking God to take care of it, she did not even whisper the words, much less speak them aloud, as she did her other requests, but she spoke inwardly only, for fear lest the very walls themselves should hear her. No one came near her attic, except Kitty, and she kept her promise faithfully. Since the four bearers had carried away her mother's coffin, and since the night Kitty came out of jail, the night of Robin's birthday, no stranger's foot had crossed the door-sill.

But November passed, and part of December, and Meg's stock of clothes, such as were of any value at the pawnshop, was almost exhausted. And at the end of the year, the term for which her father had paid rent in advance would be over, and Mr. Grigg might turn her and her children out into the streets. What was to be done? How was she to take care of Robin, and baby, and the money belonging to one of father's mates?

CATHERINE AUGUSTA WALTON (1849-1939)
"Mabel's First Lesson in Organ Grinding" from *Christie's Old Organ; or 'Home Sweet Home'* (1874)

A vicar's daughter and an Evangelical clergyman's wife, Mrs Octavius Frank Walton was a popular author whose books were published exclusively by the Religious Tract Society. Although, like Hesba Stretton, she was well paid for her efforts, she did not possess the skill of her contemporary and was much less prolific—though she did publish thirty cautionary tales. In her heart-rending depictions of loneliness (*Little Dot*, 1873; *Nobody Loves Me*, 1883), simplified cottage tales extolling the endurance of the downtrodden (*My Little Corner*, 1872; *Taken or Left*, 1885), and biblical retellings (*The King's Cup-Bearer*, 1891; *Unbeaten Paths in Sacred History*, 1906), the punishment of sin is irrevocable and virtue is rewarded in uplifting ways. Her two best stories are *A Peep Behind the Scenes* (1877), an Evangelical attack on the deceitful trumpery of the theatre, and *Christie's Old Organ*, a sentimental tale of the friendship between an orphan boy and an organ grinder, which was so popular that Mrs Walton later wrote a sequel about Christie's adult ministry, *Christie the King's Servant* (1898).

Christie's Old Organ relates how Old Treffy the organ grinder, who is given only one month to live, befriends Christie, "a little homeless wanderer", and invites the boy to share his cold attic lodging in Ivy Court. The youngster is eventually entrusted with Old Treffy's organ, is taught to play "Home Sweet Home", and while he is on the streets collecting a few pennies for their food (as the chapter reproduced here shows), he also starts to learn about gaining entry to a heavenly "home sweet home". The mission room of Mr Wilton becomes the centre of the story; there Christie hears about the necessity of being "made white for ever in the blood of the Lamb" (Chapter 10). Although Christie's understanding of this message is at first literal, the injunction—which is Mrs Walton's oft-repeated theme—becomes less frightening to the boy as the text is explained by the ever-patient clergyman. Christie relays his new-found knowledge to Old Treffy, who dies in peace. The little organ grinder's influence extends to his customers. Mabel's father is so touched by Christie's faith that, to honour his dear wife's memory, he makes provision for the boy's schooling to become "a Scripture-reader amongst the lowest class of people". The story takes Christie up to his marriage and settlement in a home close to Ivy Court, where he ministers to the poor. Although in *Christie's Old Organ* she fulfilled the Tract Society's requirements of scenes depicting repentance, conversion, and Christian death, Mrs Walton sings the praises of "home sweet home" so cloyingly that today's reader is bound to sigh with relief as the story ends.

MABEL'S FIRST LESSON IN ORGAN GRINDING

The next day Christie had to go out as usual. Old Treffy seemed no worse than before—he was able to sit up, and Christie opened the small window before he went out to let a breath of fresh air into the close attic. But there was very little fresh air anywhere that day. The atmosphere was heavy and stifling, and poor Christie's heart felt depressed and weary. He turned, he hardly knew why, to the suburban road, and stopped before the house with the pretty garden. He wanted to see those merry little faces again—perhaps they would cheer him; he felt so very dull to-day.

Christie was not disappointed this time. He had hardly turned the handle of the organ twice before Mabel and Charlie appeared at the nursery window; and after satisfying themselves that it really *was* Christie, their own organ-boy, they ran into the garden, and stood beside him as he played.

"Doesn't he turn it nicely?" whispered Charlie to his sister.

"Yes," said little Mabel; "I wish I had an organ, don't you Charlie?"

"Shall I ask papa to buy us one?" asked her brother.

"I don't know, Charlie, if mamma would like it always," said Mabel. "She has such bad headaches, you know."

"Well; but up in the nursery she would hardly hear it, I'm sure," said Charlie, regretfully.

"I *should* so like to turn it," said Mabel, shyly looking up into Christie's face.

"All right, missie; come here," said Christie.

And standing on tip-toe at his side, little Mabel took hold of the handle of the organ with her tiny white hand. Very slowly and carefully she turned it, so slowly that her mamma came to the window to see if the organ-boy had been taken ill.

It was a pretty sight which that young mother looked upon. The little fair, delicate child, in her light summer dress, turning the handle of the old, faded barrel-organ, and the organ-boy standing by, watching her with admiring eyes. Then little Mabel looked up, and saw her mother's face at the window, and smiled and nodded to her, delighted to find that she was watching. And then Mabel went on playing with a happy consciousness that mother was listening. For there was no one in the world that little Mabel loved so much as her mother.

But Mabel turned so slowly that she grew tired of the melancholy wails of "Poor Mary Ann."

"Change it, please, organ-boy," she said; "make it play 'Home, sweet Home;' mother *does* like that so."

But Christie knew that "Rule Britannia" lay between them and "Home sweet Home;" so he took the handle from Mabel, and saying brightly, "All right, missie, I'll make it come as quick as I can," he turned it round so fast, that if old Treffy had been within hearing, he would certainly have died from fright about his dear old organ before the month was over. Several people in the opposite houses came to their windows to look out; they thought the organ must be possessed with some evil spirit, so slowly did it go one minute, so quickly the next.

But they understood how it was a minute afterwards when little Mabel again began to turn, and very slowly and deliberately the first notes of "Home, sweet Home" were sounded forth. She turned the handle of the organ until "Home, sweet Home" was quite finished, and then, with a sigh of satisfaction, she gave it up to Christie.

"I like 'Home, sweet Home,' " she said; "it's such a pretty tune."

"Yes," said Christie, "it's my favourite, missie. Where is 'Home, sweet home?' " he asked suddenly, as he remembered his promise to old Treffy.

"That's *my* home," said little Mabel, nodding her head in the direction of the pretty house. "I don't know where yours is, Christie."

"I haven't much of a place to call home, missie," said Christie; "me and old Treffy, we live together in an old attic, and that won't be for long—only another month, Miss Mabel, and I shall have no home then."

"Poor organ-boy,—poor Christie!" said little Mabel, in a pitying voice.

Charlie had taken the handle of the organ now, and was rejoicing in "Poor Mary Ann;" but Mabel hardly listened to him; she was thinking of the poor boy who had no home but an attic, and who soon would have no home at all.

"There's another home somewhere," said Christie, "isn't there, missie? Isn't heaven some sort of a home?"

"Oh yes, there's heaven," said little Mabel, brightly; "you'll have a home *there*, won't you, organ-boy?"

"Where is heaven?" said Christie.

"It's up there," said little Mabel, pointing up to the sky; "up so high, Christie. The little stars live in heaven; I used to think they were the angels' eyes, but nurse says it's silly to think that."

"I like the stars," said Christie.

"Yes," said Mabel, "so do I; and you'll see them all when you go to heaven, Christie, I'm sure you will."

"What is heaven like, Miss Mabel?" asked Christie.

"Oh, it's so nice," said little Mabel; "they have white dresses on, and the streets are all gold, Christie, all gold and shining. And Jesus is there, Christie; wouldn't you like to see Jesus?" she added, in a whisper.

"I don't know," said Christie, in a bewildered tone; "I don't know much about Him."

"Don't you love Jesus, Christie?" said Mabel, with a very grave, sorrowful face, and with tears in her large, brown eyes. "Oh! organ-boy, don't you love Jesus?"

"No," said Christie; "I know so little about Him, Miss Mabel."

"But you can't go to heaven if you don't love Jesus, Christie. Oh! I'm so sorry—you won't have a home at all; what *will* you do?" and the tears ran down little Mabel's cheeks.

But just then the bell rang for dinner, and nurse's voice called the children in.

Christie walked on very thoughtfully. He was thinking of little Mabel's words, and of little Mabel's tears. "You can't go to heaven if you don't love Jesus," she had said; "and then you won't have a home at all." It was a new thought for Christie, and a very sad thought. What if he should never, never know anything of "Home, sweet Home"? And then came the remembrance of poor old Treffy, his dear old master, who had only another month to live. Did he love Jesus? He had never heard old Treffy mention His name; and what if Treffy should die, and never go to heaven at all, but go to the other place! Christie had heard of hell; he did not know much about it, and he had always fancied it was for very bad people. He must tell Treffy about Mabel's words. Perhaps, after all, his old master did love Jesus. Christie hoped very much that he did. He longed for evening to come, that he might go home and ask him.

The afternoon was still more close and sultry than the morning had been, and little Christie was very weary. The organ was heavy for him at all times, and it seemed heavier than usual to-day. He was obliged to sit down to rest for a few minutes on a door-step in one of the back streets, about half a mile from the court where old Treffy lived. As he was sitting there, with his organ resting against the wall, two women met each other just in front of the doorstep, and after asking most affectionately after each other's health, they began to talk, and Christie could not help hearing every word they said.

"What's that place?" said one of them, looking across the road at a long, low building with a board in front of it.

"Oh! that's our new mission-room, Mrs West," said the other; "it belongs to the church at the corner of Melville Street. A young man comes and preaches there every Sunday night; I like to hear him, I do," she went on, "he puts it so plain."

"Puts what plain, Mrs Smith?" said her friend.

"Oh, all about heaven, and how we're to get there, and about Jesus and what He's done for us. He's a kind man, is Mr Wilton; he came to see our Tommy when he was badly. Do you know him, Mrs West?"

"No," said Mrs West; "maybe I'll come to-morrow; what time is it?"

"It begins at seven o'clock every Sunday," said Mrs Smith; "and you needn't bother about your clothes, there's no one there but poor folks like ourselves."

"Well, I'll come, Mrs Smith. Good day;" and the two parted.

And little Christie had heard all they said, and had firmly made up his mind to be at the mission-room the next evening at seven o'clock. He must lose no time in making out what Treffy wanted to know. One day of the month was gone already.

"Master Treffy," said Christie that night, "do you love Jesus?"

"Jesus!" said the old man; "no, Christie, I can't say I do. I suppose I ought to; good folk do, don't they?"

"Master Treffy," said Christie, solemnly, "if you don't love Jesus you can't go to heaven, and you'll never have a home any more—never any more."

"Ay, ay, Christie, that's true, I'm afraid. When I was a little chap no bigger than you, I used to hear tell about these things. But I gave no heed to them then, and I've forgotten all I ever heard. I've been thinking a deal lately since I was took so bad, and some of it seems to come back to me. But I can't rightly mind what I was told. It's a bad job, Christie, a bad job."

4. DOMESTIC DELIGHTS:
THE CHILDREN'S NOVEL

We quarrelled often, but made peace as quickly,
Shed many tears, but laughed the while they fell,
Had our small woes, our childish bumps and bruises,
But Mother always "kissed and made them well".
—"Susan Coolidge", What Katy Did *(1872)*

At the same time that tract writers had discovered in fiction a means of conveying Evangelical principles, there arose a new kind of novel-writing in England and the United States, whose main purpose was to entertain the young with full-length stories of family life overflowing with domestic incident and lively characterization. They were like rich and satisying plum puddings and were consumed with as much enjoyment. The authors of the best of these books—such as Charlotte M. Yonge, Juliana Ewing, Susan Coolidge, and Edith Nesbit—lavished considerable literary gifts on novels that became an important part of children's literature in the Golden Age.

Middle-class families were usually large in the nineteenth century, and so are the families in most of these novels. Perhaps the outstanding accomplishment of their authors was the clear delineation of their large casts of characters. In *The Daisy Chain* (1856), for instance, Charlotte Yonge succeeds in making distinct individuals of the eleven motherless May children, of whom clumsy Ethel, vain Flora, and the highly intelligent Norman are most prominent. This ability was shared by Margaret Robertson, who portrayed a family of eight children in *The Bairns* (1870); by Juliana Ewing, whose heroine in *Six to Sixteen* (1875) becomes the ward in the lively vicarage home of the Arkwrights; by E. Nesbit in *Five Children and It* (1902)—and in many of their other novels. Two American equivalents of these writers of family sagas were Louisa May Alcott, the creator of the famous March family in *Little Women* (1865), and "Susan Coolidge", the author of *What Katy Did* (1872) and four more Katy books describing the adventures of the Carr family. Three other classic family novels by American writers—Mary Mapes Dodge's *Hans Brinker* (1865), Helen Hunt Jackson's *Nelly's Silver Mine* (1878), and Frances Hodgson Burnett's *Little Lord Fauntleroy* (1886)—show a similar expertise in characterization, though they are not about such large families.

The second noteworthy feature of these novels is their fullness of incident. Family members are given multifarious activities—domestic, local, sometimes foreign, and frequently covering long periods—that are not only woven into the narrative from be-ginning to end but are deftly interrelated.

The families are middle-class—the fathers are often physicians or ministers—and close family ties and mutual support are taken for granted. While they are not always overtly religious, a general piety governs their behaviour, and a gentle form of discipline is both accepted and expected. The highminded Miss Yonge was affirming a principle that contemporary novelists for children endorsed when, in a series of articles on "Children's Literature" for *Macmillan's Magazine* (July-September, 1869), she approved of "fun and playfulness", but also demanded literary entertainment that was real and uplifting: "We do not believe there can be sparkle where there is no depth."

Although to the modern reader the picture of cosy, secure, and ennobling family life in these Golden Age novels might seem to be too good to be true, their domestic atmosphere was not a fabrication. The stories would not have claimed so wide an audience if their readers had been unable to see their own lives reflected in them—to see a reality they knew and cherished.

CHARLOTTE MARY YONGE (1823-1901)
"A Scene in the Early Life of the May Family" from *The Daisy Chain; or, Aspirations. A Family Chronicle* (1856)

Born and privately educated at Otterbourne in Hants, Eng., Charlotte Yonge was a woman of extraordinary industry. As well as teaching in the Sunday School that her mother had begun in this agricultural parish, she was the author of 160 books and the editor of such magazines as *The Monthly Packet of Evening Readings for Younger Members of the English Church* (1851-94) and *The Monthly Paper of Sunday Teaching* (1860-75). Whether writing lengthy family chronicles—including novels for children such as *The Heir of Redclyffe* (1853), *The Daisy Chain* (1856), and its sequels *The Trial* (1864) and *The Pillars of the House* (1873)—or chivalric romances, in which, like her model Walter Scott, she "made history become a series of character studies", Miss Yonge imbued her stories of duty, obedience, and loyalty with her Anglican orthodoxy. She is best known as the doyenne of elevating narratives about pious middle-class families of active but generally docile youngsters. Coming herself from a family of two children, she admitted that she wrote these sagas out of her "solitude and longing for young companions" (*The Monthly Packet*, December 1894).

In her Preface Miss Yonge described *The Daisy Chain*, which had been serialized for two years in *The Monthly Packet*, as "an overgrown book of a nondescript class". The book *is* long (667 pp.), but it is far from nondescript. Set in the town of Market Stoneborough, this account of seven years in the life of the Mays—eleven motherless children and their physician father—presents a fully detailed picture of mid-Victorian family life. The boys study at Oxford and one enters the Church; their spirited sisters, tutored by a governess, are groomed as accomplished chatelaines. All, however, is not serene in the May family. In a carriage accident that killed their mother, the eldest daughter, Margaret, is severely injured; though bedridden, she presides over her siblings as the undis-

puted and revered spiritual guide. She and Richard, the ministry-bound eldest son, are the natural monitors to whom all the children defer. The family itself is a masterfully characterized and credible study in contrasts. The bookish but overconfident Norman, after capturing the Newdigate Prize for Poetry at Oxford, announces his intention of pursuing missionary work in New Zealand; wilful Flora marries fashionably, supports her husband's political ambitions, but neglects and consequently loses her infant daughter; the author's mouthpiece, Etheldred (mercifully shortened to Ethel)—awkward, untidy, and selfless—is the dutiful daughter on whom the father relies more and more. As Yonge takes pains to show in the excerpt below, Ethel does not dabble in good works but throws herself headlong into each venture. The later opening of the Cooksmoor school and the consecration of its church are major festive scenes in *The Daisy Chain*.

True to the High Church sentiments of the author, religious convictions in the May family are taken seriously: it is cause for agonizing concern when young Harry learns that because of a boyish prank his Confirmation might be delayed. Faithful to Charlotte Yonge's ideal, too, the Mays are literate as well as devout. They quote freely from Shakespeare and the Bible and busy themselves translating Horace and scanning Euripides. Academic distinction, however, is limited to the males, as Miss Yonge thought fitting; while some of the boys attend university, and are even occasionally sent down, intellectual Ethel is forced to cease her study of Latin and Greek because of what her governess perceives as ill humour. Although scenes in this Victorian family chronicle will vex the modern reader, *The Daisy Chain* has strengths that lie not only in its wealth of incident and character but in the deft handling of its grand scale.

A SCENE IN THE EARLY LIFE OF THE MAY FAMILY

'Tis not enough that Greek or Roman page
At stated hours his freakish thoughts engage,
Even in his pastimes he requires a friend
To warm and teach him safely to unbend,
O'er all his pleasures gently to preside,
Watch his emotions, and control their tide.'
—Cowper

The misfortunes of that day disheartened and disconcerted Etheldred. To do mischief where she most wished to do good, to grieve where she longed to comfort, seemed to be her fate; it was vain to attempt anything for any one's good, while all her warm feelings and high aspirations were thwarted by the awkward ungainly hands, and heedless eyes that Nature had given her. Nor did the following day, Saturday, do much for her comfort, by giving her the company of her brothers. That it was Norman's sixteenth birth-day seemed only to make it worse. Their father had apparently forgotten it, and Norman stopped Blanche, when she was going to put him in mind of it; stopped her by such a look as the child never forgot, though there was no anger in it. In reply to Ethel's inquiry what he was going to do that morning, he gave a yawn and stretch, and said, dejectedly, that he had got some Euripides to look over, and some verses to finish.

"I am sorry; this is the first time you ever have not managed so as to make a real holiday of your Saturday!"

"I could not help it, and there's nothing to do," said Norman, wearily.

"I promised to go and read to Margaret, while Flora does her music," said Ethel; "I shall come after that and do my Latin and Greek with you."

Margaret would not keep her long, saying she liked her to be with Norman, but she found him with his head sunk on his open book, fast asleep. At dinner-time, Harry and Tom, rushing in, awoke him with a violent start.

"Halloo! Norman, that was a jump!" said Harry, as his brother stretched and pinched himself. "You'll jump out of your skin some of these days, if you don't take care!"

"It's enough to startle any one to be waked up with such a noise," said Ethel.

"Then he ought to sleep at proper times," said Harry, "and not be waking me up with tumbling about, and hallooing out, and talking in his sleep half the night."

"Talking in his sleep; why, just now, you said he did not sleep," said Ethel.

"Harry knows nothing about it," said Norman.

"Don't I? well, I only know, if you slept in school, and were a junior, you would get a proper good licking for going on as you do at night."

"And I think you might chance to get a proper good licking for not holding your tongue," said Norman, which hint reduced Harry to silence.

Dr May was not come home; he had gone with Richard far into the country, and was to return to tea. He was thought to be desirous of avoiding the family dinners that used to be so delightful. Harry was impatient to depart, and when Mary and Tom ran after him, he ordered them back.

"Where can he be going?" said Mary, as she looked wistfully after him.

"I know," said Tom.

"Where? Do tell me."

"Only don't tell papa. I went down with him to the playground this morning, and there they settled it. The Andersons, and Axworthy, and he, are going to hire a gun, and shoot peewits on Cocksmoor."

"But they ought not; should they?" said Mary. "Papa would be very angry."

"Anderson said there was no harm in it, but Harry told me not to tell. Indeed, Anderson would have boxed my ears for hearing, when I could not help it."

"But Harry would not let him?"

"Aye. Harry is quite a match for Harvey Anderson, though he is so much younger; and he said he would not have me bullied."

"That's a good Harry! But I wish he would not go out shooting!" said Mary.

"Mind, you don't tell."

"And where's Hector Ernescliffe? Would not he go?"

"No. I like Hector. He did not choose to go, though Anderson teazed him, and said he was a poor Scot, and his brother didn't allow him tin enough to buy powder and shot. If Harry would have stayed at home, he would have come up here, and we might have had some fun in the garden."

"I wish he would. We never have any fun now," said Mary; "but oh! there he is:" as she spied Hector peeping over the gate which led, from the field, into the garden. It was the first time that he had been to Dr May's since his brother's departure, and he was rather shy, but the joyful welcome of Mary and Tom took off all reluctance, and they claimed him for a good game at play in the wood house. Mary ran upstairs to beg to be excused the formal walk, and, luckily for her, Miss Winter was in Margaret's room. Margaret asked if it was very wet and dirty and hearing 'not very,' gave gracious permission, and off went Mary and Blanche to construct some curious specimens of pottery, under the superintendence of Hector and Tom. There was a certain ditch where yellow mud was attainable, whereof the happy children concocted marbles and vases, which underwent a preparatory baking in the boys' pockets, that they might not crack in the nursery fire. Margaret only stipulated that her sisters should be well fenced in brown holland, and when Miss Winter looked grave, said, "Poor things, a little thorough play will do them a great deal of good."

Miss Winter could not see the good of groping in the dirt; and Margaret perceived that it would be one of her difficulties to know how to follow out her mother's views for the children, without vexing the good governess by not deferring to her.

In the meantime, Norman had disconsolately returned to his Euripides, and Ethel, who wanted to stay with him and look out his words, was ordered out by Miss Winter, because she had spent all yesterday in-doors. Miss Winter was going to stay with Margaret, and Ethel and Flora coaxed Norman to come with them, "just one mile on the turnpike road and back again; he would be much fresher for his Greek afterwards."

He came, but he did not enliven his sisters. The three plodded on, taking a diligent constitutional walk, exchanging very few words, and those chiefly between the girls. Flora gathered some hoary clematis, and red berries, and sought in the hedge-sides for some crimson 'fairy baths' to carry home; and, at the sight of the amusement Margaret derived from the placing the beauteous little Pezizas in a saucer of damp green moss, so as to hide the brown sticks on which they grew, Ethel took shame to herself for want of perception of little attentions. When she told Norman so, he answered, "There's no one who does see what is the right thing. How horrid the room looks! Everything is no how!" added he, looking round at the ornaments and things on the tables, which had lost their air of comfort and good taste. It was not disorder, and Ethel could not see what he meant. "What's wrong?" said she.

"O never mind—you can't do it. Don't try—you'll only make it worse. It will never be the same as long as we live."

"I wish you would not be so unhappy!" said Ethel.

"Never mind," again said Norman, but he put his arm round her. "Have you done your Euripides? Can I help you? Will you construe it with me, or shall I look out your words?"

"Thank you, I don't mind that. It is the verses! I want some sense!" said Norman, running his fingers through his hair till it stood on end. "Tis such a horrid subject, Coral Islands! As if there was anything to be said about them."

"Dear me, Norman, I could say ten thousand things, only I must not tell you what mine are, as yours are not done."

"No, don't," said Norman, decidedly.

"Did you read the description of them in the Quarterly? I am sure you might get some ideas there. Shall I find it for you! It is an old number."

"Well, do; thank you—"

He rested listlessly on the sofa while his sister rummaged in a chiffonniere. At last she found the article, and eagerly read him the description of the strange forms of the coral animals, and the beauties of their flower-like feelers and branching fabrics. It would once have delighted him, but his first comment was, "Nasty little brutes!" However, the next minute he thanked her, took the book, and said he could hammer something out of it, though it was too bad to give such an unclassical subject. At dusk he left off, saying he should get it done at night, his senses would come then, and he should be glad to sit up.

"Only three weeks to the holidays," said Ethel, trying to be cheerful; but his assent was depressing, and she began to fear that Christmas would only make them more sad.

Mary did not keep Tom's secret so inviolably, but that, while they were dressing for tea, she revealed to Ethel where Harry was gone. He was not yet returned, though his father and Richard were come in, and the sisters were at once in some anxiety on his account, and doubt whether they ought to let papa know of his disobedience.

Flora and Ethel, who were the first in the drawing-room, had a consultation.

"I should have told mamma directly," said Flora.

"He never did so," sighed Ethel; "things never went wrong then."

"O yes, they did; don't you remember how naughty Harry was about climbing the wall, and making faces at Mrs. Richardson's servants?"

"And how ill I behaved the first day of last Christmas holidays?"

"She knew, but I don't think she told papa."

"Not that we knew of, but I believe she did tell him everything; and I think, Flora, he ought to know everything, especially now. I never could bear the way the Mackenzies used to have of thinking their parents must be like enemies, and keeping secrets from them."

"They were always threatening each other, 'I'll tell mamma,' " said Flora, "and calling us tell-tales, because we told our own dear mamma everything. But it is not like that now—I neither like to worry papa, nor to bring Harry into disgrace—besides, Tom and Mary meant it for a secret."

"Papa would not be angry with him if we told him it was a secret," said Ethel; "I wish Harry would come in. There's the door—oh! it is only you."

"Whom did you expect?" said Richard, entering.

The sisters looked at each other, and Ethel, after an interval, explained their doubts about Harry.

"He is come in," said Richard; "I saw him running up to his own room, very muddy."

"O, I'm glad! But do you think papa ought to hear it? I don't know what's to be done. 'Tis the children's secret," said Flora.

"It will never do to have him going out with those boys continually," said Ethel—"Harvey Anderson close by all the holidays!"

"I'll try what I can do with him," said Richard. "Papa had better not hear it now, at any rate. He is very tired and sad this evening, and his arm is painful again; so we must not worry him with histories of naughtiness among the children."

"No," said Ethel, decidedly; "I am glad you were there, Ritchie. I never should have thought of one time being better than another."

"Just like Ethel," said Flora, smiling.

"Why should not you learn?" said Richard, gently.

"I can't," said Ethel, in a desponding way.

"Why not? You are much sharper than most people; and, if you tried, you would know those things as much better than I do, as you know how to learn history."

"It is quite a different sort of cleverness," said Flora. "Recollect Sir Isaac Newton, or Archimedes."

"Then you must have both sorts," said Ethel; "for you can do things nicely, and yet you learn very fast."

"Take care, Ethel, you are singeing your frock! Well, I really don't think you can help those things!" said Flora. "Your short sight is the reason of it, and it is of no use to try to mend it."

"Don't tell her so," said Richard. "It can't be all short sight—it is the not thinking. I do believe that if Ethel would think, no one would do things so well. Don't you remember the beautiful perspective drawing she made of this room, for me to take to Oxford? That was very difficult, and wanted a great deal of neatness and accuracy, so why should she not be neat and accurate in other things? And I know you can read faces Ethel—why don't you look there before you speak?"

"Ah! before instead of after, when I only see I have said something *mal-a-propos*," said Ethel.

"I must go and see about the children," said Flora; "if the tea comes while I am gone, will you make it Ritchie?"

"Flora despairs of me," said Ethel.

"I don't," said Richard. "Have you forgotten how to put in a pin yet?"

"No, I hope not."

"Well, then, see if you can't learn to make tea; and, by-the-by, Ethel, which is the next Christening Sunday?"

"The one after next, surely. The first of December is Monday—yes, tomorrow week is the next."

"Then I have thought of something; it would cost eighteen-pence to hire Joliffe's spring-cart, and we might have Mrs Taylor and the twins brought to church in it. Should you like to walk to Cocksmoor and settle it?"

"O yes, very much indeed. What a capital thought. Margaret said you would know how to manage."

"Then we will go the first fine day papa does not want me."

"I wonder if I could finish my purple frocks. But here's the tea. Now Richard, don't tell me to make it. I shall do something wrong, and Flora will never forgive you."

Richard would not let her off. He stood over her, counted her shovels-full of tea, and watched the water into the tea-pot—he superintended her warming the cups, and putting a drop in each saucer. "Ah!" said Ethel, with a concluding sigh, "it makes one hotter than double equations!"

It was all right, as Flora allowed, with a slightly superior smile. She thought Richard would never succeed in making a notable or elegant woman of Ethel, and it was best that the two sisters should take different lines. Flora knew that, though clever and with more accomplishments, she could not surpass Ethel in intellectual attainments, but she was certainly far more valuable in the house, and had been proved to have just the qualities in which her sister was most deficient. She did not relish hearing that Ethel wanted nothing but attention to be more than her equal, and she thought Richard mistaken. Flora's remembrance of their time of distress was less unmixedly wretched than it was with the others, for she knew she had done wonders.

The next day Norman told Ethel that he had got on very well with the verses, and finished them off late at night. He showed them to her before taking them to school on Monday morning, and Ethel thought they were the best he had ever written. There was too much spirit and poetical beauty, for a mere school-boy task, and she begged for the foul copy, to show it to her father. "I have not got it," said Norman. "The foul copy was not like these; but when I was writing them out quite late, it was all, I don't know how. Flora's music was in my ears, and the room seemed to get larger, and like an ocean cave; and when the candle flickered, 'twas like the green glowing light of the sun through the waves."

"As it says here," said Ethel.

"And the words all came to me of themselves in beautiful flowing Latin, just right, as if it was anybody but myself doing it, and they ran off my pen in red and blue and gold, and all sorts of colours; and fine branching zigzagging stars like what the book described, only stranger, came dancing and radiating round my pen and the candle. I could hardly believe the verses would scan by daylight, but I can't find a mistake. Do you try them again."

Ethel scanned. "I see nothing wrong," she said, "but it seems a shame to begin scanning Undine's verses, they are too pretty. I wish I could copy them. It must have been half a dream."

"I believe it was; they don't seem like my own."

"Did you dream afterwards?"

He shivered. "They had got into my head too much; my ears sang like the roaring of the sea, and I thought my feet were frozen on to an iceberg: then came darkness, and sea monsters, and drowning—it was too horrid!" and his face expressed all, and more than all, he said. "But 'tis a quarter to seven—we must go," said he, with a long yawn, and rubbing his eyes. "You are sure they are right, Ethel? Harry, come along."

Ethel thought those verses ought to make a sensation, but all that came of them was a *Quam optime*, and when she asked Norman if no special notice had been taken of them, he said, in his languid way, "No; only Dr. Hoxton said they were better than usual."

Ethel did not even have the satisfaction of hearing what Mr Wilmot, happening to meet Dr May, said to him, "Your boy has more of a poet in him than any that has come in my way. He really sometimes makes very striking verses."

Richard watched for an opportunity of speaking to Harry, which did not at once occur, as the boy spent very little of his time at home, and, as if by tacit consent, he and Norman came in later every evening. At last, on Thursday, in the additional two hours' leisure allowed to the boys, when the studious prepared their tasks, and the idle had some special diversion, Richard encountered him running up to his own room to fetch a newly-invented instrument for projecting stones.

"I'll walk back to school with you," said Richard.

"I mean to run," returned Harry.

"Is there so much hurry?" said Richard. "I am sorry for it, for I wanted to speak to you, Harry; I have something to show you."

His manner conveyed that it related to their mother, and the sobering effect was instantaneous. "Very well," said he, forgetting his haste. "I'll come into your room."

The awe-struck, shy, yet sorrowful look on his rosy face, showed preparation enough, and Richard's only preface was to say, "It is a bit of a letter that *she* was in course of writing to aunt Flora, a description of us all. The letter itself is gone, but here is a copy of it. I thought you would like to read what relates to yourself."

Richard laid before him the sheet of note-paper on which this portion of the letter was written, and left him alone with it, while he set out on the promised walk with Ethel.

They found the old woman, Granny Hall, looking like another creature, smoke-dried, and withered indeed, but all briskness and animation.

"Well! be it you, sir, and the young lady?"

"Yes; here we are come to see you again," said Richard. "I hope you are not disappointed that I've brought my sister this time instead of the Doctor."

"No, no, sir; I've done with the Doctor for this while," said the old woman, to Ethel's great amusement. "He have done me a power of good, and thank him for it heartily; but the young lady is right welcome here—but 'tis a dirty walk for her."

"Never mind that," said Ethel, a little shyly; "I came—where are your grandchildren?"

"O, somewhere out among the blocks. They gets out with the other children; I can't be always after them."

"I wanted to know if these would fit them," said Ethel, beginning to undo her basket.

"Well, 'pon my word! If ever I see! Here!" stepping out to the door, "Polly—Jenny! come in, I say, this moment! Come in, ye bad girls, or I'll give you the stick; I'll break every bone of you, that I will!" all which threats were bawled out in such a good-natured, triumphant voice, and with such a delighted air, that Richard and Ethel could not help laughing.

After a few moments, Polly and Jenny made their appearance, extremely rough and ragged, but compelled by their grandmother to duck down, by way of courtesies, and, with finger in mouth, they stood, too shy to show their delight, as the garments were unfolded; Granny talking so fast that Ethel would never have brought in the stipulation, that the frocks should be worn to school and church, if Richard, in his mild, but steady way, had not brought the old woman to listen to it. She was full of asseverations that they should go; she took them to church sometimes herself, when it was fine weather and they had clothes, and they could say their catechiz as well as anybody already; yes, they should come, that they should, and next Sunday. Ethel promised to be there to introduce them to the chief lady, the president of the committee, Mrs Ledwich, and, with a profusion of thanks, they took leave.

They found John Taylor, just come out of the hospital, looking weak and ill, as he smoked his pipe over the fire, his wife bustling about at a great rate, and one of the infants crying. It seemed to be a great relief that they were not come to complain of Lucy, and there were many looks of surprise on hearing what their business really was. Mrs Taylor thanked, and appeared not to know whether she was glad or sorry; and her husband, pipe in hand, gazed at the young gentleman as if he did not comprehend the species, since he could not be old enough to be a clergyman.

Richard hoped they would find sponsors by that time; and there Mrs Taylor gave little hope; it was a bad lot—there was no one she liked to ask to stand, she said, in a dismal voice; but there her husband put in, "I'll find some one, if that's all; my missus always thinks nobody can't do nothing."

"To be sure," said the lamentable Mrs Taylor, "all the elder ones was took to church, and I'm loth the little ones shouldn't; but you see, sir, we are poor people, and it's a long way, and they was set down in the gentleman's register book."

"But you know that is not the same, Mrs Taylor. Surely Lucy could have told you that, when she went to school."

"No, sir, 'tis not the same—I knows that; but this is a bad place to live in—"

"Always the old song, Missus!" exclaimed her husband. "Thank you kindly, sir—you have been a good friend to us, and so was Dr May, when I was up to the hospital, through the thick of his own troubles. I believe you are in the right of it, sir, and thank you. The children shall be ready, and little Jack, too, and I'll find gossips, and let 'em be christened on Sunday."

"I believe you will be glad of it," said Richard; and he went on to speak of the elder children coming to school, on Sunday, thus causing another whining from the wife about distance and bad weather, and no one else going that way. He said the little Halls were coming, but Mrs Taylor began saying she disliked their company for the children— granny let them get about so much, and they said bad words. The father again interfered. Perhaps Mr Wilmot, who acted as chaplain at the hospital, had been talking to him, for he declared at once that they should come; and Richard suggested that he might see them home when he came from church; then, turning to the boy and girl, told them they would meet their sister Lucy, and asked them if they would not like that.

On the whole, the beginning was not inauspicious, though there might be a doubt whether old Mrs Hall would keep all her promises. Ethel was so much diverted and pleased as to be convinced she would; Richard was a little doubtful as to her power over the wild girls. There could not be any doubt that John Taylor was in earnest, and had been worked upon just at the right moment; but there was danger that the impression would not last. "And his wife is such a horrible whining dawdle!" said Ethel—"there will be no good to be done if it depends on her."

Richard made no answer, and Ethel presently felt remorseful for her harsh speech about a poor ignorant woman, overwhelmed with poverty, children, and weak health.

"I have been thinking a great deal about what you said last time we took this walk," said Richard, after a considerable interval.

"O have you!" cried Ethel, eagerly; and the black peaty pond she was looking at seemed to sparkle with sunlight.

"Do you really mean it?" said Richard, deliberately.

"Yes, to be sure," she said, with some indignation.

"Because I think I see a way to make a beginning; but you must make up your mind to a great deal of trouble, and dirty walks, and you must really learn not to draggle your frock."

"Well, well; but tell me."

"This is what I was thinking. I don't think I can go back to Oxford after Christmas. It is not fit to leave you while papa is so disabled."

"O no, he could not get on at all. I heard him tell Mr Wilmot the other day that you were his right-hand."

Ethel was glad she had repeated this, for there was a deepening colour and smiling glow of pleasure on her brother's face, such as she had seldom seen on his delicate, but somewhat impassive features.

"He is very kind!" he said, warmly. "No, I am sure I cannot be spared till he is better able to use his arm, and I don't see any chance of that just yet. Then, if I stay at home, Friday is always at my own disposal, while papa is at the hospital meeting."

"Yes, yes; and we could go to Cocksmoor, and set up a school. How delightful!"

"I don't think you would find it quite as delightful as you fancy." said Richard; "the children will be very wild and ignorant, and you don't like that at the National School."

"O, but they are in such need; besides, there will be no Mrs Ledwich over me. It is just right—I shan't mind anything. You are a capital Ritchie, for having thought of it!"

"I don't think—if I am ever to be what I wish, that is, if I can get through at Oxford—I don't think it can be wrong to begin this, if Mr Ramsden does not object."

"O Mr Ramsden never objects to anything."

"And if Mr Wilmot will come and set us off. You know we cannot begin without that, or without my father's fully liking it."

"Oh! there can be no doubt of that."

"This one thing, Ethel, I must stipulate. Don't you go and tell it all out at once to him. I cannot have him worried about our concerns."

"But how?—no one can question that this is right. I am sure he won't object."

"Stop, Ethel; don't you see, it can't be done for nothing? If we undertake it, we must go on with it, and when I am away, it will fall on you and Flora. Well, then, it ought to be considered whether you are old enough and steady enough; and if it can be managed for you to go continually all this way, in this wild place. There will be expense, too."

Ethel looked wild with impatience, but could not gainsay these scruples, otherwise than by declaring they ought not to weigh against the good of Cocksmoor.

"It will worry him to have to consider all this," said Richard; "and it must not be pressed upon him."

"No," said Ethel, sorrowfully; "but you don't mean to give it up."

"You are always in extremes, Ethel. All I want is, to find a good time for proposing it."

She fidgetted, and gave a long sigh.

"Mind," said Richard, stopping short, "I'll have nothing to do with it, except on condition you are patient, and hold your tongue about it."

"I think I can, if I may talk to Margaret."

"O yes, to Margaret, of course. We could not settle anything without her help."

"And I know what she will say," said Ethel. "O I am so glad;" and she jumped over three puddles in succession.

"And, Ethel, you must learn to keep your frock out of the dirt."

"I'll do anything, if you'll help me at Cocksmoor."

MARGARET MURRAY ROBERTSON (1823-1897)
"Their First Winter in America" from *The Bairns; or, Janet's Love and Service. A Story from Canada* (1870)

The daughter of a Congregational minister from Aberdeen, Margaret Robertson came to Canada in 1832, settling in 1836 with her family in Sherbrooke, Lower Canada (Que.). She taught at a ladies' academy there and gained a considerable reputation for her stories of Canadian life, published in London, Philadelphia, and New York. In 1873 she moved to Montreal, where she lived until her death. Miss Robertson's early sagas—*Christie Redfern's Troubles* (1866) and *Shenac's Work at Home* (1868)— are set in Glengarry (eastern Ontario), and show how grit and Christian fortitude succeed in overcoming all problems. They were widely read (so popular was *Christie Redfern's Troubles* that it was offered in exchange for a kitten in the correspondence columns of the British children's periodical *Aunt Judy's Magazine*) and created a loyal following for Robertson's nine subsequent tales of Scots endurance.

The Bairns (1870) is a lengthy chronicle of about fifteen years in the lives of the motherless Elliott children who are brought up by their eternally devoted houskeeper, Janet Nasmyth, in New England and the Eastern Townships of Quebec. A widow herself, Janet makes the difficult decision to immigrate to America with the minister's

family and help him raise the bairns. This commitment means that she leaves behind in Scotland her own young son, Sandy, to be cared for by her mother. Telling Janet's story in the grand manner befitting Charlotte Yonge, Robertson focuses the narrative on two main characters: the housekeeper, or surrogate mother, and the eldest girl, Graeme, on whom a martyrizing weight of domestic duties and moral guidance falls. As the children grow up, the boys launching tremendously successful business careers, and the girls starting families of their own, the Elliotts never forget Janet and continue to revere her.

Robertson arranges some very opportune matches too. The Elliotts' new-found friend and staunch ally, Sampson Snow, eventually proposes to Janet; moreover, Janet's son marries Emily Snow. And, at long last, the destined mate for Graeme is free to marry her—after the convenient death of his wife and the passage of a suitable interval. Through the ups and downs of this family saga—with moves from rural New England to Montreal and the Eastern Townships, and many Atlantic crossings— Janet's steadfast faith and unwavering love ensure that all will turn out well for her bairns.

THEIR FIRST WINTER IN AMERICA

The next week was a busy one to all. Mr Elliott, during that time took up his residence at Judge Merle's, only making daily visits to the little brown house behind the elms where Janet and the bairns were putting things to rights. There was a great deal to be done, but it was lovely weather, and all were in excellent spirits, and each did something to help. The lads broke sticks and carried water, and Janet's mammoth washing was accomplished in an incredibly short time; and before the week was over the little brown house began to look like a home.

A great deal besides was accomplished this week. It was not all devoted to helping, by the boys. Norman caught three squirrels in a trap of his own invention, and Harry shot as many with Mr Snow's wonderful rifle. They and Marian had made the circuit of the pond, over rocks, through bushes and brambles, over brooks, or through them, as the case might be. They came home tired enough, and in a state which naturally suggested thoughts of another mammoth washing, but in high spirits with their trip, only regretting that Graeme and Janet had not been with them. It was Saturday night, after a very busy week, and Janet had her own ideas about the enjoyment of such a ramble, and was not a little put out with them for "their thoughtless ruining of their clothes and shoon." But the minister had come home, and there was but a thin partition between the room that must serve him for study and parlor, and the general room for the family, and they got off with a slight reprimand, much to their surprise and delight. For to tell the truth, Janet's patience with the bairns, exhaustless in most circumstances, was wont to give way in the presence of "torn clothes and ruined shoon."

The next week was hardly so successful. It was cold and rainy. The gold and crimson glories of the forest disappeared in a night, and the earth looked gloomy and sad under a leaden sky. The inconveniences of the little brown house became more apparent now. It had been declared, at first sight, the very worst house in Merleville, and so it was, even under a clear sky and brilliant sunshine. A wretched place it looked. The windows clattered, the chimney smoked, latches and hinges were defective, and there were a score of other evils, which Janet and the lads strove to remedy without vexing their father and Graeme. A very poor place it was, and small and inconvenient besides. But this could not be cured, and therefore must be endured. The house occupied by Mr Elliott's predecessor had been burned down, and the little brown house was the only unoccupied house in the village. When winter should be over something might be done about getting another, and in the meantime they must make the best of it.

The people were wonderfully kind. One man came to mend windows and doors, another to mend the chimney. Orrin Green spent two days in banking up the house. Deacons Fish and Slowcome sent their men to bring up wood; and apples and chickens, and pieces of beef were sent in by some of the village people.

There were some drawbacks. The wood was green, and made more smoke than heat; and Janet mortally offended Mr Green by giving him his dinner alone in the kitchen. Every latch and hinge, and pane of glass, and the driving of every nail, was charged and deducted from the half year's salary, at prices which made Janet's indignation overflow. This latter circumstance was not known, however, till the half year was done; and in the meantime it helped them all through this dreary time to find their new friends so kind.

In the course of time, things were put to rights, and the little bare place began to look wonderfully comfortable. With warm carpets on the floors, and warm curtains on the windows, with stools and sofas, and tables made out of packing boxes, disguised in various ways, it began to have a look of home to them all.

The rain and the clouds passed away, too, and the last part of November was a long and lovely Indian summer. Then the explorations of the boys were renewed with delight. Graeme and Rosie and Will went with the rest, and even Janet was beguiled into a nutting excursion one afternoon. She enjoyed it, too, and voluntarily confessed it. It was a fair view to look over the pond and the village lying so quietly in the valley, with the kirk looking down upon it from above. It was a fine country, nobody could deny; but Janet's eyes were sad enough as she gazed, and her voice shook as she said it, for the thought of home was strong at her heart.

In this month they made themselves thoroughly acquainted with the geography of the place, and with the kindly inmates of many a farmhouse besides. And a happy month it was for them all. One night they watched the sun set between red and wavering clouds, and the next day woke to behold "the beauty and mystery of the snow." Far away to the highest hill-top; down to the very verge of pond and brook; on every bush, and tree, and knoll, and over every silent valley, lay the white garment of winter. How strange! how wonderful! it seemed to their unaccustomed eyes.

"It 'minds of white grave-clothes," said Marian, with a shudder.

"Whist, Menie," said her sister. "It makes me think of how full the air will be of bonnie white angels at the resurrection-day. Just watch the flakes floating so quietly in the air."

"But, Graeme, the angels will be going up, and—"

"Well, one can hardly tell by looking at them, whether the snow-flakes are coming down or going up, they float about so silently. They mind me of beautiful and peaceful things."

"But, Graeme, it looks cold and dreary, and all the bonnie flowers are covered in the dark."

"Menie! There are no flowers to be covered now, and the earth is weary with her summer work, and will rest and sleep under the bonnie white snow. And, dear, you mustna think of dreary things when you look out upon the snow, for it will be a long time before we see the green grass and the bonnie flowers again," and Graeme sighed.

But it was with a shout of delight that the boys plunged headlong into it, rolling and tumbling and tossing it at one another in a way that was "perfect ruination to their clothes;" and yet Janet had not the heart to forbid it. It was a holiday of a new kind to them; and their enjoyment was crowned and completed when, in the afternoon, Mr Snow came down with his box-sleigh and his two handsome greys to give them a sleigh-ride. There was room for them all, and for Mr Snow's little Emily, and for half a dozen besides had they been there; so, well wrapped up with blankets and buffalo-robes, away they went. Was there ever anything so delightful, so exhilarating? Even Graeme laughed and clapped her hands, and the greys flew over the ground, and passed every sleigh and sledge on the road.

"The bonnie creatures!" she exclaimed; and Mr Snow, who loved his greys, and was proud of them, took the oft-repeated exclamation as a

compliment to himself, and drove in a way to show his favorites to the best advantage. Away they went, up hill and down, through the village and over the bridge, past the mill to the woods, where the tall hemlocks and cedars stood dressed in white "like brides." Marian had no thought of sorrowful things in her heart now. They came home again the other way, past Judge Merle's and the school-house, singing and laughing in a way that made the sober-minded boys and girls of Merleville, to whom sleigh-riding was no novelty, turn round in astonishment as they passed. The people in the store, and the people in the blacksmith's shop, and even the old ladies in their warm kitchens, opened the door and looked out to see the cause of the pleasant uproar. All were merry, and all gave voice to their mirth except Mr Snow's little Emily, and she was too full of astonishment at the others to think of saying anything herself. But none of them enjoyed the ride more than she, though it was not her first by many. None of them all remembered it so well, or spoke of it so often. It was the beginning of sleigh-riding to them, but it was the beginning of a new life to little Emily.

"Isna she a queer little creature?" whispered Harry to Graeme, as her great black eyes turned from one to another full of grave wonder.

"She's a bonnie little creature," said Graeme, caressing the little hand that had found its way to hers, "and good, too, I'm sure."

"Grandma don't think so," said the child, gravely.

"No!" exclaimed Harry. "What bad things do you do?"

"I drop stitches and look out of the window, and I hate to pick over beans."

Harry whistled.

"What an awful wee sinner! And does your grandma punish you ever? Does she whip you?"

The child's black eyes flashed.

"She dare n't. Father would n't let her. She gives me stints, and sends me to bed."

"The Turk!" exclaimed Harry. "Run away from her, and come and bide with us."

"Hush, Harry," said Graeme, softly, "grandma is Mr Snow's mother."

There was a pause. In a little Emily spoke for the first time of her own accord.

"There are no children at our house," said she.

"Poor wee lammie, and you are lonely sometimes," said Graeme.

"Yes; when father's gone and mother's sick. Then there's nobody but grandma."

"Have you a doll?" asked Menie.

"No: I have a kitten, though."

"Ah! you must come and play with my doll. She is a perfect beauty, and her name is Flora Macdonald."

Menie's doll had become much more valuable in her estimation since she had created such a sensation among the little Merleville girls.

"Will you come? Mr Snow," she said, climbing upon the front seat which Norman shared with the driver, "won't you let your little girl come and see my doll?"

"Well, yes; I guess so. If she's half as pretty as you are, she is well worth seeing."

Menie was down again in a minute.

"Yes, you may come, he says. And bring your kitten, and we'll play all day. Graeme lets us, and doesna send us to bed. Will you like to come?"

"Yes," said the child, quickly, but as gravely as ever.

They stopped at the little brown house at last, with a shout that brought their father and Janet out to see. All sprang lightly down. Little Emily staid alone in the sleigh.

"Is this your little girl, Mr Snow?" said Mr Elliott, taking the child's hand in his. Emily looked in his face as gravely and quietly as she had been looking at the children all the afternoon.

"Yes; she's your Marian's age, and looks a little like her, too. Don't you think so Mrs Nasmyth?"

Janet, thus appealed to, looked kindly at the child.

"She might, if she had any flesh on her bones," said she.

"Well, she don't look ragged, that's a fact," said her father.

The cold, which had brought the roses to the cheeks of the little Elliotts, had given Emily a blue, pinched look, which it made her father's heart ache to see.

"The bairn's cold. Let her come in and warm herself," said Janet, promptly. There was a chorus of entreaties from the children.

"Well, I don't know as I ought to wait. My horses don't like to stand much," said Mr Snow.

"Never mind waiting. If it's too far for us to take her home, you can come down for her in the evening."

Emily looked at her father wistfully.

"Would you like to stay, dear?" asked he.

"Yes, sir." And she was lifted out of the sleigh by Janet, and carried into the house, and kissed before she was set down.

"I'll be along down after dark, sometime," said Mr Snow as he drove away.

Little Emily had never heard so much noise, at least so much pleasant noise, before. Mr Elliott sat down beside the bright wood fire in the kitchen, with Marian on one knee and the little stranger on the other, and listened to the exclamations of one and all about the sleigh ride.

"And hae you nothing to say, my bonnie wee lassie?" said he pushing back the soft, brown hair from the little grave face. "What is your name, little one?"

"Emily Snow Arnold," answered she, promptly.

"Emily Arnold Snow," said Menie, laughing.

"No; Emily Snow Arnold. Grandma says I am not father's own little girl. My father is dead."

She looked grave, and so did the rest.

"But it is just the same. He loves you."

"O, yes!" There was a bright look in the eyes for once.

"O, yes."

So it was. Sampson Snow, with love enough in his heart for half a dozen children, had none of his own, and it was all lavished on this child of his wife, and she loved him dearly. But they did not have "good times" up at their house the little girl confided to Graeme.

"Mother is sick most of the time, and grandma is cross always; and, if it was n't for father, I don't know what we *should* do."

Indeed, they did not have good times. Old Mrs Snow had always been strong and healthy, altogether unconscious of "nerves," and she could have no sympathy and very little pity for his son's sickly wife. She had never liked her, even when she was a girl, and her girlhood was past, and she had been a sorrowful widow before her son brought her home as his wife. So old Mrs Snow kept her place at the head of the household, and was hard on everybody, but more especially on her son's wife and her little girl. If there had been children, she might have been different; but she almost resented her son's warm affection for his little step-daughter. At any rate she was determined that little Emily should be brought up as children used to be brought up when *she* was young, and not spoiled by over-indulgence as her mother had been; and the process was not a pleasant one to any of them, and "good times" were few and far between at their house.

Her acquaintance with the minister's children was the beginning of a new life to Emily. Her father opened his eyes with astonishment when he came into Janet's bright kitchen that night and heard his little girl laughing and clapping her hands as merrily as any of them. If anything had been needed to deepen his interest in them all, their kindness to the child would have done it; and from that day the minister and his children, and Mrs. Nasmyth, too, had a firm and true friend in Mr Snow.

SARAH CHAUNCEY WOOLSEY ("SUSAN COOLIDGE") (1835-1905)
"Kikeri" from What Katy Did: A Story (1872)

The first of five Katy books by Cleveland-born Sarah Woolsey, who wrote as "Susan Coolidge", this story introduced to eager young readers and instant fans the high-spirited and motherless brood of Carr children. Twelve-year-old Katy, an engaging hoyden, is at the centre as the narrative charts her progress from tomboy to young lady.

Coolidge individualizes each of the lively but tractable Carrs. They delight in private places, devise their own games, and fabricate exotic names for a concoction of vinegar, water, and cinnamon sticks. Their literary tastes are reflections of their time. Not only are they familiar with fairy tales and the Arabian Nights, they hope to receive for Christmas such family stories as Edgeworth's Harry and Lucy and Howitt's Strive and Thrive; Katy is overwhelmed by her gift of Warner's The Wide, Wide World.

The Carr household is competently managed, with the sternness of the housekeeper Aunt Izzie being mitigated by the sage guidance of the physician-father.

The impulsive, disobedient Katy is subdued when she falls from a swing that had been forbidden because it was unsafe. So serious is the injury to her spine that two years pass before she is able to walk again. During this period Aunt Izzie dies of typhoid fever, and Katy learns to become an effective housekeeper and a mentor for her brothers and sisters. Her model is Cousin Helen, an angelic invalid, who teaches Katy the lesson of patient acceptance. While the convalescing heroine strives to fulfil womanly duties, What Katy Did is saved from drifting into pietism by being firmly anchored in the world of rowdy and warm family fiction of the nineteenth century.

KIKERI

Monday was apt to be rather a stormy day at the Carr's. There was the big wash to be done, and Aunt Izzie always seemed a little harder to please, and the servants a good deal crosser than on common days. But I think it was also, in part, the fault of the children, who, after the quiet of Sunday, were specially frisky and uproarious, and readier than usual for all sorts of mischief.

To Clover and Elsie, Sunday seemed to begin at Saturday's bed-time, when their hair was wet, and screwed up in papers, that it might curl next day. Elsie's waved naturally, so Aunt Izzie didn't think it necessary to pin her papers very tight; but Clover's thick, straight locks required to be pinched hard before they would give even the least twirl, and to her, Saturday night was one of misery. She would lie tossing, and turning, and trying first one side of her head and then the other; but whichever way she placed herself, the hard knobs and the pins stuck out and hurt her; so when at last she fell asleep, it was face down, with her small nose buried in the pillow, which was not comfortable, and gave her bad dreams. In consequence of these sufferings Clover hated curls, and when she "made up" stories for the younger children, they always commenced: "The hair of the beautiful princess was as straight as a yardstick, and she never did it up in papers—never!"

Sunday always began with a Bible story, followed by a breakfast of baked beans, which two things were much tangled up together in Philly's mind. After breakfast the children studied their Sunday-school lessons, and then the big carryall came round, and they drove to church, which was a good mile off. It was a large, old-fashioned church, with galleries, and long pews with high red-cushioned seats. The choir sat at the end, behind a low, green curtain, which slipped from side to side on rods. When the sermon began, they would draw the curtain aside and show themselves, all ready to listen, but the rest of the time they kept it shut. Katy always guessed that they must be having good times behind the green curtain—eating orange-peel, perhaps, or reading the Sunday-school books—and she often wished she might sit up there among them.

The seat in Dr Carr's pew was so high that none of the children, except Katy, could touch the floor, even with the point of a toe. This made their feet go to sleep; and when they felt the queer little pin-pricks which drowsy feet use to rouse themselves with, they would slide off the seat, and sit on the benches to get over it. Once there, and well hidden from view, it was almost impossible not to whisper. Aunt Izzie would frown and shake her head, but it did little good, especially as Phil and Dorry were sleeping with their heads on her lap, and it took both her hands to keep them from rolling off into the bottom of the pew. When good old Dr Stone said, "Finally, my brethren," she would begin waking them up. It was hard work sometimes, but generally she succeeded, so that during the last hymn the two stood together on the seat, quite brisk and refreshed, sharing a hymn-book, and making believe to sing like the older people.

After church came Sunday-school, which the children liked very much, and then they went home to dinner, which was always the same on Sunday—cold corned-beef, baked potatoes, and rice pudding. They did not go to church in the afternoon unless they wished, but were pounced upon by Katy instead, and forced to listen to the reading of *The Sunday Visitor*, a religious paper, of which she was the editor. This paper was partly written, partly printed, on a large sheet of foolscap, and had at the top an ornamental device, in lead pencil, with "Sunday Visitor" in the middle of it. The reading part began with a dull little piece of the kind which grown people call an editorial, about "Neatness," or "Obedience," or "Punctuality." The children always fidgeted when listening to this, partly, I think, because it aggravated them to have Katy recommending on paper, as very easy, the virtues which she herself found it so hard to practise in real life. Next came anecdotes about dogs and elephants and snakes, taken from the Natural History book, and not very interesting, because the audience knew them by heart already. A hymn or two followed, or a string of original verses, and, last of all, a chapter of "Little Maria and Her Sisters," a dreadful tale, in which Katy drew so much moral, and made such personal allusions to the faults of the rest, that it was almost more than they could bear. In fact, there had just been a nursery rebellion on the subject. You must know that, for some weeks back, Katy had been too lazy to prepare any fresh *Sunday Visitors*, and so had forced the children to sit in a row and listen to the back numbers, which she read aloud from the very beginning! "Little Maria" sounded much worse when taken in these large doses, and Clover and Elsie, combining for once, made up their minds to endure it no longer. So, watching their chance, they carried off the whole edition, and poked it into the kitchen fire, where they watched it burn with a mixture of fear and delight which it was comical to witness. They dared not confess the deed, but it was impossible not to look conscious when Katy was flying about and rummaging after her lost treasure, and she suspected them, and was very irate in consequence.

The evenings of Sunday were always spent in repeating hymns to Papa and Aunt Izzie. This was fun, for they all took turns, and there was quite a scramble as to who should secure the favorites, such as "The west hath shut its gate of gold," and "Go when the morning shineth." On the whole, Sunday was a sweet and pleasant day, and the children thought so; but, from its being so much quieter than other days, they always got up on Monday full of life and mischief, and ready to fizz over at any minute, like champagne bottles with the wires just cut.

This particular Monday was rainy, so there couldn't be any out-door play, which was the usual vent for over-high spirits. The little ones, cooped up in the nursery all the afternoon, had grown perfectly riotous. Philly was not quite well, and had been taking medicine. The medicine was called *Elixir Pro*. It was a great favorite with Aunt Izzie, who kept a bottle of it always on hand. The bottle was large and black, with a paper label tied round its neck, and the children shuddered at the sight of it.

After Phil had stopped roaring and spluttering, and play had begun again, the dolls, as was only natural, were taken ill also, and so was "Pikery," John's little yellow chair, which she always pretended was a doll too. She kept an old apron tied on his back, and generally took him to bed with her—not *into* bed, that would have been troublesome; but close by, tied to the bed-post. Now, as she told the others, Pikery was very sick indeed. He must have some medicine, just like Philly.

"Give him some water," suggested Dorry.

"No," said John, decidedly, "it must be black and out of a bottle, or it won't do any good."

After thinking a moment, she trotted quietly across the passage into Aunt Izzie's room. Nobody was there, but John knew where the Elixir Pro was kept—in the closet on the third shelf. She pulled one of the drawers out a little, climbed up, and reached it down. The children were enchanted when she marched back, the bottle in one hand, the cork in the other, and proceeded to pour a liberal dose on to Pikery's wooden seat, which John called his lap.

"There!' there! my poor boy," she said, patting his shoulder—I mean his arm—"swallow it down—it'll do you good."

Just then Aunt Izzie came in, and to her dismay saw a long trickle of something dark and sticky running down on to the carpet. It was Pikery's medicine, which he had refused to swallow.

"What is that?" she asked sharply.

"My baby is sick," faltered John, displaying the guilty bottle.

Aunt Izzie rapped her over the head with a thimble, and told her that she was a very naughty child, whereupon Johnnie pouted, and cried a little. Aunt Izzie wiped up the slop, and taking away the Elixir, retired with it to her closet, saying that she "never knew anything like it—it was always so on Mondays."

What further pranks were played in the nursery that day, I cannot pretend to tell. But late in the afternoon a dreadful screaming was heard, and when people rushed from all parts of the house to see what was the matter, behold, the nursery door was locked, and nobody could get in. Aunt Izzie called through the keyhole to have it opened, but the roars were so loud that it was long before she could get an answer. At last Elsie, sobbing violently, explained that Dorry had locked the door, and now the key wouldn't turn, and they couldn't open it. *Would* they have to stay there always, and starve?

"Of course you won't, you foolish child," exclaimed Aunt Izzie. "Dear, dear, what on earth will come next? Stop crying, Elsie—do you hear me? You shall all be got out in a few minutes."

And sure enough, the next thing came a rattling at the blinds, and there was Alexander, the hired man, standing outside on a tall ladder and nodding his head at the children. The little ones forgot their fright. They flew to open the window, and frisked and jumped about Alexander as he climbed in and unlocked the door. It struck them as being such a fine thing to be let out in this way, that Dorry began to rather plume himself for fastening them in.

But Aunt Izzie didn't take this view of the case. She scolded them well, and declared they were troublesome children, who couldn't be trusted one moment out of sight, and that she was more than half sorry she had promised to go to the Lecture that evening. "How do I know," she concluded, "that before I come home you won't have set the house on fire, or killed somebody?"

"Oh, no we won't! no we won't!" whined the children, quite moved by this frightful picture. But bless you—ten minutes afterward they had forgotten all about it.

All this time Katy had been sitting on the ledge of the bookcase in the Library, poring over a book. It was called Tasso's Jerusalem Delivered. The man who wrote it was an Italian, but somebody had done the story over into English. It was rather a queer book for a little girl to take a fancy to, but somehow Katy liked it very much. It told about knights, and ladies, and giants, and battles, and made her feel hot and cold by turns as she read, and as if she must rush at something, and shout, and strike blows. Katy was naturally fond of reading. Papa encouraged it. He kept a few books locked up, and then turned her loose in the Library. She read all sorts of things: travels, and sermons, and old magazines. Nothing was so dull that she couldn't get through with it. Anything really interesting absorbed her so that she never knew what was going on about her. The little girls to whose houses she went visiting had found this out, and always hid away their storybooks when she was expected to tea. If they didn't do this, she was sure to pick one up and plunge in, and then it was no use to call her, or tug at her dress, for she neither saw nor heard anything more, till it was time to go home.

This afternoon she read the Jerusalem till it was too dark to see any more. On her way up stairs she met Aunt Izzie, with bonnet and shawl on.

"Where *have* you been?" she said. "I have been calling you for the last half-hour."

"I didn't hear you, ma'am."

"But where were you?" persisted Miss Izzie.

"In the Library, reading," replied Katy.

Her aunt gave a sort of sniff, but she knew Katy's ways, and said no more.

"I'm going out to drink tea with Mrs. Hall and attend the evening Lecture," she went on. "Be sure that Clover gets her lesson, and if Cecy comes over as usual, you must send her home early. All of you must be in bed by nine."

"Yes'm," said Katy, but I fear she was not attending much, but thinking, in her secret soul, how jolly it was to have Aunt Izzie go out for once. Miss Carr was very faithful to her duties: she seldom left the children, even for an evening; so whenever she did, they felt a certain sense of novelty and freedom, which was dangerous as well as pleasant.

Still, I am sure that on this occasion Katy meant no mischief. Like all excitable people, she seldom did *mean* to do wrong, she just did it when it came into her head. Supper passed off successfully, and all might have gone well, had it not been that after the lessons were learned, and Cecy had come in, they fell to talking about "Kikeri."

Kikeri was a game which had been very popular with them a year before. They had invented it themselves, and chosen for it this queer name out of an old fairy story. It was a sort of mixture of Blindman's Buff and Tag—only instead of any one's eyes being bandaged, they all played in the dark. One of the children would stay out in the hall, which was dimly lighted from the stairs, while the others hid themselves in the nursery. When they were all hidden, they would call out "Kikeri," as a signal for the one in the hall to come in and find them. Of course, coming from the light he could see nothing, while the others could see only dimly. It was very exciting to stand crouching up in a corner and watch the dark figure stumbling about and feeling to right and left, while every now and then somebody, just escaping his clutches, would slip past and gain the hall, which was "Freedom Castle," with a joyful shout of "Kikeri, Kikeri, Kikeri, Ki!" Whoever was caught had to take the place of the catcher. For a long time this game was the delight of the Carr children; but so many scratches and black-and-blue spots came of it, and so many of the nursery things were thrown down and broken, that at last

Aunt Izzie issued an order that it should not be played any more. This was almost a year since; but talking of it now put it into their heads to want to try it again.

"After all we didn't promise," said Cecy.

"No, and *Papa* never said a word about our not playing it," added Katy, to whom "Papa" was authority, and must always be minded, while Aunt Izzie might now and then be defied.

So they all went up stairs. Dorry and John, though half undressed, were allowed to join the game. Philly was fast asleep in another room.

It was certainly splendid fun. Once Clover climbed up on the mantle-piece and sat there, and when Katy, who was finder, groped about a little more wildly than usual, she caught hold of Clover's foot, and couldn't imagine where it came from. Dorry got a hard knock, and cried, and at another time Katy's dress caught on the bureau handle and was frightfully torn, but these were too much affairs of every day to interfere in the least with the pleasures of Kikeri. The fun and frolic seemed to grow greater the longer they played. In the excitement, time went on much faster than any of them dreamed. Suddenly, in the midst of the noise, came a sound—the sharp distinct slam of the carryall-door at the side entrance. Aunt Izzie had returned from her Lecture!

The dismay and confusion of that moment! Cecy slipped down stairs like an eel, and fled on the wings of fear along the path which led to her home. Mrs. Hall, as she bade Aunt Izzie goodnight, and shut Dr Carr's front door behind her with a bang, might have been struck with the singular fact that a distant bang came from her own front door like a sort of echo. But she was not a suspicious woman; and when she went up stairs there were Cecy's clothes neatly folded on a chair, and Cecy herself in bed, fast asleep, only with a little more color than usual in her cheeks.

Meantime, Aunt Izzie was on *her* way up stairs, and such a panic as prevailed in the nursery! Katy felt it, and basely scuttled off to her own room, where she went to bed with all possible speed. But the others found it much harder to go to bed; there were so many of them, all getting into each other's way, and with no lamp to see by. Dorry and John popped under the clothes half undressed, Elsie disappeared, and Clover, too late for either, and hearing Aunt Izzie's step in the hall, did this horrible thing—fell on her knees, with her face buried in a chair, and began to say her prayers very hard indeed.

Aunt Izzie, coming in with a candle in her hand, stood in the door-way, astonished at the spectacle. She sat down and waited for Clover to get through, while Clover, on her part, didn't dare to get through, but went on repeating "Now I lay me" over and over again, in a sort of despair. At last Aunt Izzie said very grimly: "That will do, Clover, you can get up!" and Clover rose, feeling like a culprit, which she was, for it was much naughtier to pretend to be praying than to disobey Aunt Izzie and be out of bed after ten o'clock, though I think Clover hardly understood this then.

Aunt Izzie at once began to undress her, and while doing so asked so many questions, that before long she had got at the truth of the whole matter. She gave Clover a sharp scolding, and leaving her to wash her tearful face, she went to the bed where John and Dorry lay, fast asleep, and snoring as conspicuously as they knew how. Something strange in the appearance of the bed made her look more closely: she lifted the clothes, and there, sure enough, they were—half dressed, and with their school-boots on.

Such a shake as Aunt Izzie gave the little scamps at this discovery, would have roused a couple of dormice. Much against their will, John and Dorry were forced to wake up, and be slapped and scolded, and made ready for bed, Aunt Izzie standing over them all the while, like a dragon. She had just tucked them warmly in, when for the first time she missed Elsie.

"Where is my poor little Elsie?" she exclaimed.

"In bed," said Clover, meekly.

"In bed!" repeated Aunt Izzie, much amazed. Then stooping down, she gave a vigorous pull. The trundle-bed came into view, and sure enough, there was Elsie, in full dress, shoes and all, but so fast asleep that not all Aunt Izzie's shakes, and pinches, and calls, were able to rouse her. Her clothes were taken off, her boots unlaced, her night-gown put on; but through it all Elsie slept, and she was the only one of the children who did not get the scolding she deserved that dreadful night.

Katy did not even pretend to be asleep when Aunt Izzie went to her room. Her tardy conscience had waked up, and she was lying in bed, very miserable at having drawn the others into a scrape as well as herself, and at the failure of her last set of resolutions about "setting an example to the younger ones." So unhappy was she, that Aunt Izzie's severe words were almost a relief; and though she cried herself to sleep, it was rather from the burden of her own thoughts than because she had been scolded.

She cried even harder the next day, for Dr Carr talked to her more seriously than he had ever done before. He reminded her of the time when her Mamma died, and of how she said, "Katy must be a Mamma to the little ones, when she grows up." And he asked her if she didn't think the time was come for beginning to take this dear place towards the children. Poor Katy! She sobbed as if her heart would break at this, and though she made no promises, I think she was never quite so thoughtless again, after that day. As for the rest, Papa called them together and made them distinctly understand that "Kikeri" was never to be played any more. It was so seldom that Papa forbade any games, however boisterous, that this order really made an impression on the unruly brood, and they never have played Kikeri again, from that day to this.

JULIANA HORATIA GATTY EWING (1841-1885)
"Manners and Customs" from *Six to Sixteen. A Story for Girls* (1875)

A clergyman's daughter and a British Army officer's wife, Mrs Ewing was also the author of many popular and carefully written books for the young, among them *Mrs Overtheways Remembrances* (1869), *The Brownies and Other Tales* (1870), *A Flat Iron for a Farthing* (1873), and *Jackanapes* (1879). Having entertained her brother and sisters with her first stories, Mrs Ewing continued to exercise her narrative skills as she incorporated details of her own life into her numerous books. She brought her first-hand knowledge of life in a Yorkshire vicarage and of the mindless social rounds in military outposts to *Six to Sixteen*, a story of two girls, Margaret Vandaleur and Eleanor Arkwright. It first appeared serially in *Aunt Judy's Magazine* (p. 441), a periodical edited by Mrs Ewing's mother, Margaret Gatty, but it cannot simply be termed a girls' story; mentioning it as one of his favourite childhood books, Rudyard Kipling admitted: "I knew it, as I know it still, almost by heart."

One winter two teenaged girls decide to follow the "fad" of writing autobiographies, and plan to exchange their books at the end of the season. *Six to Sixteen* is Margaret's report on her life before and after she was orphaned. Although the exchange does not take place and Margaret, coming upon her story a year later, regards it as but "a dusty relic of an old fad", Ewing's "sketch of domestic life" chronicles the eventful life of a Victorian orphan—from her childhood spent at a military camp in India to her private schooling at the home of her guardian, a Yorkshire vicar. It brings to life a whole gallery of neatly sketched characters. With accurate strokes Ewing pictures the self-appointed directress of all army wives, Mrs Minchin, a notorious gossip; Margaret's Aunt Theresa (Mrs Buller), whose foolish gadding as Minchin's protegée leads to the neglect of her own daughter; the housekeeper Keziah, whose refreshing common sense sets the tone for the welcoming Arkwright home; and the knowledgeable mistress of this home, who unconventionally performs her maternal duties while also pursuing her interests as an amateur zoologist.

When Margaret comes to live with the Arkwrights, she is educated with their only daughter, Eleanor, enjoying the brotherly affection of Jack and Clement Arkwright and thriving under the prudent influence of Eleanor's mother. So at ease does Margaret become that she even slips Yorkshire terms like "foy" into her biography, recalling Eleanor's earlier explanation that "to foy at anything is to slave—to work hard at it" (Chapter 21). Guiding her daughter and ward through that "hobbledehoy age" from girlhood to adolescence, Mrs Arkwright, as the chapter reproduced here shows, ensures that the girls do not only foy at their work but relish life besides.

MANNERS AND CUSTOMS—CLIQUE—THE LESSONS OF EXPERIENCE—OUT VISITING—HOUSE-PRIDE— DRESSMAKING

Eleanor and I were not always at home. We generally went visiting somewhere, at least once a year.

I think it was good for us. Great as were the advantages of the life I now shared over an existence wasted in a petty round of ignoble gossip and social struggle, it had the drawback of being almost too self-sufficing, perhaps—I am not certain—a little too laborious. I do think, but for me, it must, at any rate, have become the latter. I am so much less industrious, energetic, clever and good in every way than Eleanor, for one thing, that my very idleness holds us back; and I think a taste for

*Margaret Vandaleur and Eleanor Arkwright,
with pencils in their mouths.*

gaiety (I simply mean being gay, not balls and parties), and for social
pleasure, and for pretty things, and graceful "situations" runs in my
veins with my French blood, and helps to break the current of our la-
bours.

We led lives of considerable intellectual activity, constant occupation,
and engrossing interest. We were apt to "foy" at our work to the extent
of grudging meal-times and sleep. Indeed, at one time a habit obtained
with us of leaving the table in turn as we finished our respective meals.
One member of the family after another would rise, bend his or her head
for a silent "grace," and depart to the work in hand. I have known the
table gradually deserted in this fashion till Mr Arkwright was left alone.
I remember going back one day into the room, and seeing him so. My
entrance partially aroused him from a brown study. (He was at all times
very "absent.") He rose, said grace aloud for the benefit of the company—which had dispersed—and withdrew to his library. But we
abolished this uncivilized custom in conclave, and thenceforth sat our
meals out to the end.

So free were we in our isolation upon those Yorkshire moors from the
trammels of conventionality (one might almost say, civilization!), that I
think we should have come to begrudge the ordinary interchange of the
neighbourly courtesies of life, but for occasional lectures from Mrs
Arkwright, and for going out visiting from time to time.

It was not merely that a life of running in and out of other people's
houses, and chatting the same bits of news threadbare with one acquaintance after another, as at Riflebury, would have been unendurable

by us. The rare arrival of a visitor from some distant countryhouse to call at the Vicarage was the signal for every one, who could do so with decency, to escape from the unwelcome interruption. But as we grew older, Mrs Arkwright would not allow this. The boys, indeed, were hard to coerce; they "bolted" still when the door-bell rang; but domestic authority, which is apt to be magnified on "the girls," overruled Eleanor and me for our good, and her mother—who reasoned with us far more than she commanded—convinced us of how much selfishness there was in this, as in all acts of discourtesy.

But what do we not owe to her good counsels? In how many evening talks has she not warned us of the follies, affectations, or troubles to which our lives might specially be liable! Against despising interests that are not our own, or graces which we have chosen to neglect, against the danger of satire, against the love or the fear of being thought singular, and above all, against the petty pride of clique.

"I do not know which is the worst," I remember her saying, "a religious clique, an intellectual clique, a fashionable clique, a moneyed clique, or a family clique. And I have seen them all."

"Come, Mother," said Eleanor, "you cannot persuade us you would not have more sympathy with the intellectual than the moneyed clique, for instance?"

"I should have warmly declared so myself, at one time," said Mrs Arkwright, "but I have a vivid remembrance of a man belonging to an artistic clique, to whose house I once went with some friends. My friends were artists also, but their minds were enlarged, instead of being narrowed, by one chief pursuit. Their special art gave them sympathy with all others, as the high cultivation of one virtue is said to bring all the rest in its train. But this man talked the shibboleth of his craft over one's head to other members of his clique with a defiance of good manners arising more from conceit than from ignorance of the ways of society; and with a transparent intention of being overheard and admired which reminded me of the little self-conscious conceits of children before visitors. He was one of a large family with the same peculiarities, joined to a devout admiration of each other. Indeed, they combined the artistic clique and the family clique in equal proportions. From the conversation at their table you could have imagined that there was but one standard of good for poor humanity, that of one 'school' of one art, and absolutely no one who quite came up to it but the brothers, sisters, parents, cousins, or connections by marriage of your host. Now, I honestly assure you that the only other man really like this one that I ever met, was what is called a 'self-made' man in a commercial clique. Money was *his* standard, and he seemed to be as completely unembarrassed as my artist friend by the weight of any other ideas than his own, or by any feeling short of utter satisfaction with himself. Their contempt for the conventionalities of society was about equal. My artist friend had passed a sweeping criticism for my benefit now and then (there could be no conversation where no second opinion was allowed), and it was with perhaps a shade less of condescension—a shade more of friendliness—that my commercial friend once stopped some remarks of mine with the knowing observation, 'Look here, ma'am. Whenever I hear this, that, and the other bragged about a party, what I always say is this, I don't want you to tell me what he *his*, but what he *'as.'* "

Eleanor and I laughed merrily at the anecdote, even if we were not quite converted to Mrs Arkwright's views. And I must in justice add that every visit which has taken us from home—every fresh experience which has enlarged our knowledge of the world—has confirmed the truth of her sage and practical advice.

*

Certainly, seeing all sorts of people with all sorts of peculiarities is often a great help towards trying to get rid of one's own objectionable ones. But like the sketching, one sometimes gets into despair about it, and though the process of learning an art may be even pleasanter than to feel oneself a master in it, one cannot say as much for the process of discovering one's follies. I should like to get rid of *them* in a lump.

Eleanor said so one day to her mother, but Mrs Arkwright said—"We may hate ourselves, as you call it, when we come to realize failings we have not recognized before, and feel that there are probably others which we do not yet see as clearly as other people see them, but this kind of impatience for our perfection is not felt by those who love us, I am sure. It is one's greatest comfort to believe that it is not even felt by God. Just as a mother would not love her child the better for its being turned into a model of perfection by one stroke of magic, but does love it the more dearly every time it tries to be good, so I do hope and believe our Great Father does not wait for us to be good and wise to love us, but loves us, and loves to help us in the very thick of our struggles with folly and sin."

But I am becoming as discursive as ever! What I want to put down now is about our going out visiting. There is really nothing much to say about our life at home. It was very happy, but there were no great events in it, and Eleanor says it will not do for us to "go off at a tangent," and describe what happened to the boys at school and college; first, because these biographies are merely to be lives of our own selves, for nobody but us two to read when we are both old maids; and secondly, because if we put down everything we had anything to do with in these ten years, it will be so very long before our biographies are finished. We are very anxious to see them done, partly because we are getting rather tired of them, and Jack is becoming suspicious, and partly because we have got an amateur bookbinding press, and we want to bind them.

*

The neighbourhood abounded with pretty clerical and country

homes, where my cousins were intimate; each one, so it seemed to Eleanor and me, prettier than the last: sunshiny and homelike, with irregular comfortable furniture, dainty with chintz, or dark with aged oak, each room more tastefully besprinkled than the rest with old china, new books, music, sketches, needlework, and flowers.

"Do you know, Eleanor," said I, when we were dressing for dinner one evening before a toilette table that had been tastefully adorned for our use by the daughters of the house, "I wonder if Yorkshire women *are* as "house-proud" as they call themselves? I think our villagers are, in the important points of cleanliness and solid comfort, and of course we are at the vicarage as to *that*,—Keziah keeps us all like copper kettles; but don't you think we might have a little more house-pride about tasteful pretty refinements? It perhaps is rather a waste of time arranging all these vases and baskets of flowers every day, but they are *very* nice to look at, and I think it civilizes one."

"*You're* not to blame," said Eleanor decisively. "You're south-country to the backbone, and French on the top. It is we hard north-country folk, we business people, who neglect to cultivate 'the beautiful.' We're quite wrong. But I think the beautiful is revenged on us," added she, with one of her quick, bright looks, "by withdrawing itself. There's nothing comparable for ugliness to the people of a manufacturing town."

My mind was running on certain very ingenious and tasteful methods of hanging nosegays on the wall.

"Those baskets with ferns and flowers in, against the wall, were lovely, weren't they?" said I. "Do you think we shall ever be able to think of such pretty things?"

"We're not fools," said Eleanor briefly. "We shall do it when we set our minds to it. Meantime, we must make notes of whatever strikes us."

"There are plenty of jolly, old-fashioned flowers in the garden at home," said I. It was a polite way of expressing my inward regret that we had no tropical orchids or strange stove plants. And Eleanor danced round me, and improvised a song, beginning—

> "There are ferns by Ewden's waters,
> And heather on the hill."

From the better adornment of the Vicarage to the better adornment of ourselves was a short stride. Most of the young ladies in these country homes were very prettily dressed. Not *à la* Mrs. Perowne. Not in that milliner's handbook style dear to "Promenades," and places of public resort; but more daintily, and with more attention to the prettiest and most convenient of the prevailing fashions than Eleanor's and my costumes displayed.

The toilettes of one young lady in particular won our admiration; and when we learned that her pretty things were made by herself, an overwhelming ambition seized upon us to learn to do the same.

"Women ought to know about all house matters," said Eleanor, puckering her brow to a gloomy extent. "Dressmaking, cookery, and all that sort of thing; and we know nothing about any of them. I was thinking only last night, in bed, that if I were cast away on a desert island, and had to make a dress out of an old sail, I shouldn't have the ghost of an idea where to begin."

"I should," said I. "I should sew it up like a sack, make three holes for my head and arms, and tie it round my waist with ship's rope. I could manage Robinson Crusoe dresses; it's the civilized ones that will be too much for me, I'm afraid."

"I believe the sail would go twice as far if we could gore it," said Eleanor, laughing. "But there's no waste like the wastefulness of ignorance; and oh, Margery, it's the *gores* I'm afraid of! If skirts were only made the old-fashioned way, like a flannel petticoat! So many pieces all alike—run them together—hem the bottom—gather the top—and there you are, with everything straightforward but the pocket."

To our surprise we found that our new fad was a sore subject with Mrs Arkwright. She reproached herself bitterly with having given Eleanor so little training in domestic arts. But she had been brought up by a learned uncle, who considered needlework a waste of time, and she knew as little about gores as we did. She had also, unfortunately, known or heard of some excellent mother who had trained nine daughters to such perfection of domestic capabilities that it was boasted that they could never in after life employ a workwoman or domestic who would know more of her business than her employer. And this good lady was a standing trouble to poor Mrs Arkwright's conscience.

Her self-reproaches were needless. General training is perhaps quite as good (if not better than) special, even for special ends. In giving us a higher education, in teaching us to use our eyes, our wits, and our common sense, she had put all meaner arts within our grasp when need should urge, and opportunity serve.

"Aunt Theresa was always dressmaking," I said to Eleanor; "but I don't remember anything that would help us. I was so young, you know. And when one is young one is so stupid, one really resists information."

I was to have another chance, however, of gleaning hints from Aunt Theresa.

HELEN FISKE HUNT JACKSON (1831-1885)
"Rob and Nelly Go Into Business" from *Nelly's Silver Mine; A Story of Colorado Life* (1878)

Helen Maria Fiske, the daughter of a theologian turned professor at Amherst College, Conn., was a carefully educated New Englander. Her parents were close friends of Jacob Abbott, influential author of the *Rollo* series (1834 ff.), and her own widely published poetry and stories won her the comradeship of Sarah Woolsey, along with the esteem of the New England Brahmin circle of Emerson and his followers. After the deaths of her first husband, an army engineer, and her two young sons, Mrs Hunt devoted herself to writing, establishing a considerable reputation as the purveyor of Western, particularly Colorado, lore for eastern readers. In 1876 she married the Quaker businessman William Jackson and settled in Colorado Springs.

Mrs Jackson was thus uniquely qualified to describe the New England parsonage home of the twelve-year-old March twins, Nelly and Rob, and their family's arduous journey west to make a new start in the hopes of curing Mr March's asthma. *Nelly's Silver Mine* is a story of contrasts—between the genteel East and the pioneer West, the congested bustle of the city and the open, untouched country, and the angelic goodness of Nelly, who is favoured by her father, and the "bully" adventurousness of

Rob, favoured by his mother. It is also a somewhat patronizing narrative. The twins are considered superior to all the children of the mining town called Rosita, near which the Marches finally settle, and are not sent to school; they occasionally snigger at foreign accents, all clumsily stereotyped by Jackson, and at immigrant food and customs. Rob and Nelly are pragmatic survivors and, as this excerpt demonstrates, Yankee go-getters. They try to find a silver mine for their parents, and though the family does not strike it rich, the Marches are constantly reminded of the awesome goodness of Nelly, "one of the honestest little girls that ever lived". As the German assayer Herr Kleesman piously concludes, "she haf better than any silver mine in her own self. She haf such gootvill, such patient, such true, she haf always goot luck."

Though *Nelly's Silver Mine* is an idealized, sometimes saccharine depiction of pioneer life in the western U.S., its success—it was reprinted many times in the nineteenth century—lies partly in its picturesque locale and partly in its treatment of American family life that flourished even in straitened circumstances.

ROB AND NELLY GO INTO BUSINESS

The next day, Rob and Nelly set off together at six o'clock for Rosita: Rob with his trout, and Nelly with eggs and butter. They stopped a minute to speak to Lucinda and Billy, as they passed their house. Billy was not there. He had gone to work for Mr Pine, Lucinda said, and would not be at home for a week.

"You like it: don't you, Nelly?" she said.

"Yes, indeed!" said Nelly: "I think it's fun. And the people are all so kind: that Swede woman kissed me because I look so much like her little girl. I am going there again to-day. They keep boarders, you know; and she wants eggs every time I come, she said. I thought perhaps they'd take Rob's trout too."

"Oh, no! they won't," said Lucinda. "Trout is too dear eatin' for such boarders 's they keep. You take the trout right up to Miss Clapp's. She'll take 'em all, an' as many more 's you can ketch."

By the middle of the afternoon, the children were at Lucinda's door again. They both ran in shouting:—

"Lucinda! Lucinda! we've sold every thing; and we've got five dollars and seventy-five cents! Now what do you say? Won't mamma be glad? Couldn't anybody get very rich this way, if they only kept on? Isn't it splendid?"

"You dear little innocent lambs," said Lucinda: "it's much you know about gettin' rich, or bein' poor."

"Why, we are poor now; very, very poor: papa said so," interrupted Nelly. "That's the reason he lets us sell things."

"Oh, well! your pa don't know nothin' about bein' real poor," said Lucinda: "and I don't suppose he ever will; but it's a good thing you're a bringin' in somethin' this year. It's a dreadful year on everybody."

"Yes; papa said we were a real help," said Nelly: "he said so last night."

"Luce," exclaimed Rob, "what do you think Jan is going to make for us? He's taken the measure of us to-day; he showed us a picture of a man and a woman with them on. They're real nice to carry things with: you don't feel the weight a bit, he says. In his country, everybody wears them on their shoulders,—everybody that has any thing heavy to carry. They're something like our ox-yoke,—only with a straight piece, that comes out; and we can hang a basket on each end, and run along just as if we weren't carrying any thing. They're real nice folks, Jan and his wife. They're the nicest folks in Rosita."

"Oh! not so nice as Mrs Clapp, Rob," said Nelly.

"Yes, they are too; lots nicer. They don't speak so fine and mincing: but I like them lots better; they're some fun. And Luce," he continued, "they've got a picture-book full of pictures of the way people dress in their country; and they let us look at it. It was splendid. And Ulrica she keeps taking hold of Nelly's hair, and lifting up the braids and looking at them, and talking to Jan in her own language."

"It makes her cry, though," said Nelly. "I wish she wouldn't."

"But what is this Jan is going to make you?" asked Lucinda: "a real yoke, such as I've seen the men wear to bring up two water-buckets to oncet? I don't believe your pa and ma'll let you wear it."

"Why not?" said Nelly: "does it look awful on your shoulders?"

"Well, you know how the ox-yoke looks on old Starbuckle and Jim," said Rob. "It's a good deal like that: I saw one in the picture-book."

"But we're not going to be yoked together," said Nelly. "It can't look like that."

"No, no," said Lucinda, "not a bit. They're real handy things. Lots o' the men have them, to carry water-buckets up the hill with in Rosita. They just make 'em out of a bent sapling, with two hooks at each end. You'll find them a heap o' help.

"Then I shall wear it, no matter how it looks," said Nelly, resolutely.

"We needn't wear them in the streets," said Rob: "we can take them off just outside the town, and hide them among the trees."

"Now, Rob," exclaimed Nelly, "I'd be ashamed to do that! That would look as if we were too proud to be seen in them. I shall wear mine into all the houses."

"Wait till you see how it feels, Nelly," said Lucinda. "Perhaps you won't like it so well's you think."

When Nelly and Rob told their father and mother about the shoulder-yokes that the Swede Jan was going to make for them, both Mr and Mrs March laughed heartily.

"Upon my word," said Mr March, "you are going to look like little merchants in good earnest: aren't you?"

*

The next time Rob and Nelly went to Rosita, when they bade their mother good-by, they said:—

"Be on the lookout for us; mamma, this afternoon. You'll see us coming down the road with our yokes on."

So Mrs March began to watch, about three o'clock; and, sure enough, about four, there she saw them coming down the lane which led from the main road to their house. They were coming very fast, at a sort of hop-skip-and-jump pace, but keeping step with each other exactly. A sort of slender pole seemed to be growing out of each shoulder; from this hung slender rods, and on the end of each rod was fastened a basket or a pail. Rob's yoke had two pails; Nelly's had two baskets. As the children ran, they took hold of the rods with their hands, just above the baskets and pails. This steadied them, and also seemed to be a sort of support in walking. As soon as the children saw their mother, they quickened their steps, and came into the yard breathless.

"Oh, they are splendid!"

"Why, they're just as light as any thing!"

"They don't hurt your neck a bit!"

*

Ulrica had put a soft cushion of red cloth at the place where the yoke rested on the neck behind; also, on each rod just where the hands grasped them. Mrs March examined them carefully.

"This is beautiful cloth," she said: "I wonder where the woman got it."

"Oh! she has a big roll of it in a chest," said Nelly. "I saw it; and a big piece of beautiful blue, too. It was made in Sweden, she says; and she had a queer gown, which was her little girl's that is dead, all made of this red and blue cloth, with—oh!—millions of little silver buttons sewed on it, all down the front. She wanted me to try it on; but I did not like to. It was too small, too: not too short; I think it would have come down to my feet. Do little girls in Sweden wear long gowns, like grown-up ladies, mamma?"

"I don't know dear," said Mrs March.

"She has some of the little girl's hair in the same chest; and she took it out, and held it close to mine."

"Yes," said Rob: "I didn't want her to. How did we know she was clean?"

"Oh, for shame, Rob!" cried Nelly: "they're all as clean as pins; you know they are. But I didn't like her to do it, because it made her cry."

After supper they had a great time deciding where to keep the yokes. Rob wanted them hung up on the wall.

"They look just as pretty as the antlers old Mr Pine has upon the wall in his house," said Rob; "and we can't ever have any antlers, unless we shoot a deer ourselves. Mr Pine said a man offered him fifty dollars for them; but he wouldn't take it. I think our yokes look just about as pretty."

"Oh, Rob!" exclaimed Nelly, "how can you talk so? They are not pretty a bit; and you know it!"

"I don't either!" said Rob: "I do think they're pretty; honest, I do."

*

The next time Nelly and Rob went up to Rosita, they entered the town a little before nine o'clock: it was just the time when all the children were on their way to school. As soon as Rob and Nelly appeared with their little yokes on their shoulders, and a basket and pail swinging from each rod, the boys on the street set up a loud shout, and all rushed towards them.

"Hullo, bub! what kind o' harness 've you got on?"

"Did your pa cut down his ox-yoke to fit ye?"

"Oh, my! look at the gal wearin' one too," they cried; and some of the rudest of the boys pressed up close, and tried to take off the covers of the baskets and pails. In less than a second, Rob had slipped his yoke off his shoulders, and thrown it on the ground, baskets and all; and sprung in front of Nelly, doubling up his fists, and pushing the boys back, crying:—

"You let us alone, now: you'd better!"

"Hush! hush! Rob," said Nelly, who was quite white with terror. "Come right into this store: the gentleman that keeps the store won't let them touch us."

And Nelly slipped into the store, and as quick as lightning took off her yoke and put it on the floor; and, saying to the astonished storekeeper, "Please let my things stay there a minute; the boys are tormenting my brother," she ran back into the centre of the crowd, snatched up both Rob's baskets of trout, and, pushing Rob before her, came back into the store. The crowd of boys followed on, and were coming up the store steps; but the storekeeper ordered them back.

"Go away!" he said: "you ought to be ashamed of yourselves, tormenting these children so. I'd like to thrash every one of you! Go away!"

The boys shrank away, ashamed; and the storekeeper went up to Nelly, who was sitting down on a nail-keg, trembling with excitement.

"What is this thing, anyhow?" said he, taking up the yoke. "Oh! I see,—to carry your pails on."

"Yes sir," said Nelly; "and it's a great help. We have to walk so far the baskets feel real heavy before we get here. Jan, the Swede man, made them for us. It is too bad the boys won't let us wear them."

"Are you Mr March's little girl?" said the shopkeeper.

"Yes," said Nelly; "and that's my brother," pointing to Rob, who was still standing on the steps, shaking his fists at the retreating boys and calling after them.

"He'd better let 'em alone," said the shopkeeper. "The more notice ye take of 'em, the more they'll pester ye. But I reckon ye can't wear the yokes any more; I wouldn't if I was you. You tell your father that Mr Martin told you to leave 'em off. Ye can leave 'em here, if ye're a mind to. Some time when your father's a drivin' in he can stop and get 'em."

"Yes," said Nelly: "I hadn't any thought of wearing them again. All I wanted was to get in here and be safe, so they shouldn't break my eggs: I've got four dozen eggs in one pail. I think it is real cruel in the boys to plague us so." And Nelly began to cry.

"There, there, don't ye cry about it; 'taint any use. Here's a stick of candy for ye," said the kind-hearted Mr Martin. "The Rosita boys are a terrible rough set."

"We might take care not to get into town till after they're in school," said Nelly, taking the candy and breaking it in two, and handing half of it to Rob. "Thank you for the candy sir. I'm sorry I cried: I guess it was because I was so frightened. Oh! there's Ulrica now!" And she ran to the door, and called, "Ulrica! Ulrica!"

Ulrica came running as fast as possible, soon as she heard Nelly's voice. She looked surprised enough when she saw the two yokes lying on the floor, and Nelly's face all wet with tears, and Rob's deep-red with anger. When Nelly told her what the matter was, she said some very loud words in Swedish, which I am much afraid were oaths. Then she turned to Mr Martin, and said:—

"Now, is not that shame—that two children like this will not be to be let alone in these the streets? I carry the yokes myself. Come to mine house."

So saying, Ulrica lifted both the yokes up on her strong shoulders, and, taking Nelly's biggest pail in one hand, strode away with long steps.

"Come on mit me," she said; "come straight. I like to see the boy that shall dare you touch." And as she passed the boys, who had gathered sullenly in a little knot on the sidewalk, she shook her head at them, and began to say something to them in her broken English; but, finding the English come too slow, she broke into Swedish, and talked louder and faster. But the boys only laughed at her, and cried:—

"Go it, old Swedy!"

"Oh, Ulrica! don't let's speak to them," whispered Nelly. "Be quiet, Rob!" And she dragged Rob along with a firm hand.

"Now I goes mit you to the houses mineself," said Ulrica. "It shall be no more that the good-for-nothings have room that to you they one word speak."

So Ulrica put on her best gown, and a clean white handkerchief over her head, and her Sunday shoes, which had soles almost two inches thick; then she took one of the baskets and one of the pails, and, giving the others to Nelly and Rob, she set off with them to walk up to Mrs Clapp's, where the butter and trout were to be left. Mrs Clapp was astonished to see Ulrica with the children. Ulrica tried to tell her the story of the yokes; but Mrs Clapp could not understand Ulrica's English, and Nelly had to finish the story.

"It was too bad," said Mrs Clapp: "but my advice to you is, to give up the yokes. It would never be quite safe for you to wear them here: the boys in this town are a pretty lawless set."

"Oh, no, ma'am!" replied Nelly, "I haven't the least idea of wearing them again. It would be very silly. But it is a dreadful pity: they did help so much, and Jan took so much trouble to make them for us."

Rob hardly spoke. He was boiling over with rage and mortification.

"I say, Nell," he began, as soon as they got outside Mrs Clapp's gate: "you might have let me thrash that boy that spoke last, the one that called out at you. I'll die if I don't do something to him. And I'm going to wear my yoke: so there! They may's well get used to it. I'll never give up this way!"

"You'll have to, Rob," answered Nelly. "I hate it as much as you do; but there's no use going against boys,—that is, such boys as these. The Mayfield boys'd never do so. They'd run and stare, perhaps: I expected any boys would stare at our yokes; but they'd never hoot and halloo, and scare you so. We'll have to give the yokes up, Rob."

"I won't," said Rob. "I'm going to wear mine home, and ask papa. I know he'll say not to give up."

"No, he won't, Rob," persisted Nelly. I shall tell him what the kind shopkeeper said, and Mrs Clapp too. You might know better yourself than to go against them all. They know better than we do."

"I don't care," said Rob. "It's none of their business. I shall wear my yoke if I've a mind to. At any rate, I'll wear it once more, just to show them."

"Papa won't let you," said Nelly, quietly, with a tone so earnest and full of certainty that it made Rob afraid she must be right.

*

"I'm not going to think any more about it," said Nelly. "I don't care for those boys: they're too rude for any thing. I sha'n't ever look at one of them; but you wouldn't catch me wearing that yoke again, I tell you!"

"That's because you're a girl," said Rob. "If you were a boy, you'd feel just exactly as I do. Oh, goodness! don't I wish you had been a boy, Nell? If you had, we two together could thrash that whole crowd quicker 'n wink!"

"I shouldn't fight, if I were a boy," said Nelly: "I think it is beneath a boy to fight. It's just like dogs and cats: they fight with their teeth and claws; and boys fight with their fists."

"Teeth, too," said Rob, grimly.

"Do they?" cried Nelly, in a tone of horror. "Do they really? Oh, Rob! did you ever bite a boy?"

"Not many times," said Rob; "but sometimes you have to."

"Well, I'm glad I'm not a boy," said Nelly: "That's all I've got to say. The idea of biting!"

To Mrs March's great surprise, she found, when she talked the affair over with her husband, that he was inclined to sympathize with Rob's feeling.

"I don't like to have the boy give it up," said Mr March. "You don't know boys as well as I do, Sarah. They'll taunt him every time he goes through the street. I half wish Nelly hadn't hindered him from giving one of them a good, sound thrashing. He could do it."

"Why, Robert!" exclaimed Mrs March: "you don't mean to tell me that you would be willing to have your son engage in a street fight?"

"Well, no," laughed Mr March: "not exactly that; but there might be circumstances under which I should knock a man down: if he insulted you, for instance; and there might come times in a boy's life when I should think it praiseworthy in him to give another boy a thrashing, and I think this was one of them."

"Well, for mercy's sake, don't tell Rob so," said Mrs March: "he's hot-headed enough now; and, if he had a free permission beforehand from you to knock boys down, I don't know where he'd stop."

While Mr and Mrs March were talking, Billy came in. He had heard the story of the morning's adventures from a teamster who had been on the street when it happened; and Billy had walked all the way in from Pine's ranch, to—as he said in his clumsy, affectionate way—"see ef I couldn't talk the youngsters out o' their notion about them yokes."

" 'Tain't no use," he said: "an' ye won't find a man on the street but'll tell ye the same thing. 'Tain't no use flyin' in the face o' natur' with boys; and the Rosita boys, I will say for 'em, is the worst I ever did see. Their fathers is away from hum all the time, and wimmen hain't much hold on boys after they get to be long from twelve an' up'ards; an' the schools in Rosita ain't no great things, either. 'S soon's I heard about them yokes, I told Luce the children couldn't never wear 'em: the boys 'n the street'd plague their lives out on 'em. I don't know as I blame 'em so much, either,—though they might be decent enough to let a little gal alone; but them yokes is awful cur'us-lookin' things. I never see a man a haulin' water with 'em, without laughin': they make a man look like a doubled-up kind o'critter, with more arms 'n he 's any right to. You can't deny yourself, sir, thet they're queer-lookin'. Why, I've seen horses scare at 'em lots o' times."

Billy's conversation produced a strong impression on Mr March's mind. Almost as reluctantly as Rob himself, he admitted that it was the part of wisdom to give up the yokes.

"It's no giving up for Nelly," said Mrs March: "she said herself that nothing would induce her to wear it in again."

"And I think Rob would better not go in for a little while, till the boys have forgotten about it," said Mrs March.

"And not at all, unless he himself proposes it," added Mr March. "I have never wholly liked the plan, much as we have been helped by the money."

"I've got an idee in my head," said Billy, "thet I think'll help 'em more'n the yokes,—a sight more. I mean to make 'em a little light wagon. Don't tell 'em any thing about it, because it'll take me some little time yet. I've got to stay up to Pine's a week longer; an' I can't work on't there. But I'll have it ready in two weeks, or three to the farthest."

"Thank you, Billy," said Mr March: "that is very kind of you. And a wagon will be much better than the yokes were: it will save them fatigue almost as much, and not attract any attention at all. You were very good to think of it."

"Nothin' good about me," said Billy, gruffly: "never was. But I do think a heap o' your youngsters, specially Nelly, Mr March. It seems to me the Lord don't often send just sech a gal's Nelly is."

"I think so too, Billy," replied Mr March. "I have never seen a child like Nelly. I'm afraid sometimes we shall spoil her."

"No danger! no danger!" said Billy: "she ain't the kind that spoils."

"Now, you be sure an' not let on about the wagon: won't you, sir," he added, looking back over his shoulder, as he walked away fast on his great long legs; which looked almost like stilts, they were so long.

"Oh, yes! you may trust me, Billy," called Mr March. "I won't tell. Good-by!"

EDITH NESBIT (1858-1924)
"No Wings" from *Five Children and It* (1902)

The youngest child of an agricultural chemist, Edith Nesbit was born in London and grew up in a large family that frequently moved from place to place. A resilient, adaptable, and unconventional woman, she (with her first husband Hubert Bland) was a founding member of the Fabian Society and supported her own children, along with her relatively unsuccessful journalist husband, by her prolific writing. Of her more than thirty novels and collections of stories, the best liked are the sagas of the Bastable children—in *The Story of the Treasure Seekers* (1899), *The Wouldbegoods* (1901), and *The New Treasure Seekers* (1904)—and the new genre of family fantasy that she created in *Five Children and It* (1902), *The Phoenix and the Carpet* (1904), and *The Story of the Amulet* (1906). Writing under her maiden name, E. Nesbit early discovered the formula for success in family adventures. Her many stories often send well-characterized, nicely imperfect children off on magical and fantastic journeys, but also take care to return them—as ebullient and clannish as ever—to some kind of domestic centre, either to parents or to the arms of a nursemaid.

In *Five Children and It* Robert, Anthea, Jane, Cyril, and the Baby (Hilary), having been cooped up in the "prison" of London for two years, arrive at their new home "deep in the country". Although White House, to their parents' eyes, is "quite ordinary" and "rather inconvenient", the children immediately view it as "a sort of Fairy Palace set down in an Earthly Para-

dise". Conceding that "grown-up people find it very difficult to believe really wonderful things, unless they have what they call proof", Nesbit thus prepares her readers for a series of wonderful adventures involving the children and largely excluding prosaic grown-ups. With the children's discovery of the Psammead or Sand-Fairy in the gravel pit close to their home, the pretext for their adventures is established and the agent introduced.

The Psammead has the unique gift of making the four older children's wishes come true—with the proviso that the servants not notice any change in their appearance. His wish-granting spells last a single day; during these transformations the children learn about some of the drawbacks of being "beautiful as the day", "rich beyond the dreams of something or other", and blessed with "beautiful wings to fly with". In the chapter included here, the children must face the consequences of having spent a day flying about the village and ending up stranded on the church tower. The humour of this account involves the reaction of the dumbfounded and slightly fearful adults to this surprising event.

Later the Psammead grants wishes about living in a besieged castle, becoming the size of a giant, and surviving in an England overrun with scalping Red Indians. One of Nesbit's most entertaining narrative experiments is her account of the predicament that arises when one of the four children wishes, in exasperation, that the Lamb (the baby, Hilary) would "grow up". Suddenly before them appears a "very proper-looking young man in flannels and a straw hat", who pays little attention to these tiresome and grubby children, is embarrassed by their presence when he tries to converse with a charming young lady cyclist, and is positively flummoxed when Martha the nursemaid cradles him in her arms with endearing terms like "precious poppet".

It is easy to understand why C.S. Lewis called *Five Children and It* one of the favourite books of his childhood. Nesbit's skilful management of fantastic events and the minimal adult interference in her stories exerted an influence not only on the *Narnia Chronicles* but on scores of other modern fantasies written for children.

NO WINGS

Whether anyone cried or not, there was certainly an interval during which none of the party was quite itself. When they grew calmer, Anthea put her handkerchief in her pocket and her arm round Jane, and said:

"It can't be for more than one night. We can signal with our handkerchiefs in the morning. They'll be dry then. And someone will come up and let us out—"

"And find the syphon," said Cyril gloomily; "and we shall be sent to prison for stealing—"

"You said it wasn't stealing. You said you were sure it wasn't."

"I'm not sure *now*," said Cyril shortly.

"Let's throw the beastly thing slap away among the trees," said Robert, "then no one can do anything to us."

"Oh yes"—Cyril's laugh was not a lighthearted one—"and hit some chap on the head, and be murderers as well as—as the other thing."

"But we can't stay up here all night," said Jane; "and I want my tea."

"You *can't* want your tea," said Robert; "You've only just had your dinner."

"But I *do* want it," she said; "especially when you begin talking about stopping up here all night. Oh, Panther—I want to go home! I want to go home!"

"Hush, hush," Anthea said. "Don't, dear. It'll be all right, somehow. Don't, don't—"

"Let her cry," said Robert desperately; "if she howls loud enough, someone may hear and come and let us out."

"And see the soda-water thing," said Anthea swiftly. "Robert, don't be a brute. Oh, Jane, do try to be a man! It's just the same for all of us."

Jane did try to "be a man"—and reduced her howls to sniffs.

There was a pause. Then Cyril said slowly, "Look here. We must risk that syphon. I'll button it up inside my jacket—perhaps no one will notice it. You others keep well in front of me. There are lights in the clergyman's house. They've not gone to bed yet. We must just yell as loud as ever we can. Now all scream when I say three. Robert, you do the yell like the railway engine, and I'll do the coo-ee like father's. The girls can do as they please. One, two, three!"

A fourfold yell rent the silent peace of the evening, and a maid at one of the Vicarage windows paused with her hand on the blind-cord.

"One, two, three!" Another yell, piercing and complex, startled the owls and starlings to a flutter of feathers in the belfry below. The maid fled from the Vicarage window and ran down the Vicarage stairs and into the Vicarage kitchen, and fainted as soon as she had explained to the man-servant and the cook and the cook's cousin that she had seen a ghost. It was quite untrue, of course, but I suppose the girl's nerves were a little upset by the yelling.

"One, two, three!" The Vicar was on his doorstep by this time, and there was no mistaking the yell that greeted him.

"Goodness me," he said to his wife, "my dear, someone's being murdered in the church! Give me my hat and a thick stick, and tell Andrew to come after me. I expect it's the lunatic who stole the tongue."

The children had seen the flash of light when the Vicar opened his front door. They had seen his dark form on the doorstep, and they had paused for breath, and also to see what he would do.

When he turned back for his hat, Cyril said hastily:

"He thinks he only fancied he heard something. You don't half yell! Now! One, two, three!"

It was certainly a whole yell this time, and the Vicar's wife flung her arms round her husband and screamed a feeble echo of it.

"You shan't go!" she said, "not alone. Jessie!"—the maid unfainted and came out of the kitchen—"send Andrew at once. There's a dangerous lunatic in the church, and he must go immediately and catch it."

"I expect he *will* catch it too," said Jessie to herself as she went through the kitchen door. "Here, Andrew," she said, "there's someone screaming like mad in the church, and the missus says you're to go along and catch it."

"Not alone, I don't," said Andrew in low firm tones. To his master he merely said, "Yis, sir."

"You heard those screams?"

"I did think I noticed a sort of something," said Andrew.

"Well, come on, then," said the Vicar. "My dear, I *must* go!" He pushed her gently into the sitting-room, banged the door, and rushed out, dragging Andrew by the arm.

A volley of yells greeted them. As it died into silence Andrew shouted, "Hullo, you there! Did you call?"

"Yes," shouted four far-away voices.

"They seem to be in the air," said the Vicar. "Very remarkable."

"Where are you?" shouted Andrew: and Cyril replied in his deepest voice, very slow and loud:

"CHURCH! TOWER! TOP!"

"Come down, then!" said Andrew; and the same voice replied:

"Can't! Door locked!"

"My goodness!" said the Vicar. "Andrew fetch the stable lantern. Perhaps it would be as well to fetch another man from the village."

"With the rest of the gang about, very likely. No, sir; if this 'ere ain't a trap—well, may I never! There's cook's cousin at the back door now. He's a keeper, sir, and used to dealing with vicious characters. And he's got his gun, sir."

"Hullo there!" shouted Cyril from the church-tower; "come up and let us out."

"We're a-coming," said Andrew. "I'm a-going to get a policeman and a gun."

"Andrew, Andrew," said the Vicar, "that's not the truth."

"It's near enough, sir, for the likes of them."

So Andrew fetched the lantern and the cook's cousin; and the Vicar's wife begged them all to be very careful.

They went across the churchyard—it was quite dark now—and as they went they talked. The Vicar was certain a lunatic was on the church-tower—the one who had written the mad letter, and taken the cold tongue and things. Andrew thought it was a "trap"; the cook's cousin alone was calm. "Great cry, little wool," said he; "dangerous chaps is quieter." He was not at all afraid. But then he had a gun. That was why he was asked to lead the way up the worn steep dark steps of the church-tower. He did lead the way, with the lantern in one hand and the gun in the other. Andrew went next. He pretended afterwards that this was because he was braver than his master, but really it was because he thought of traps, and he did not like the idea of being behind the others for fear someone should come softly up behind him and catch hold of his legs in the dark. They went on and on, and round and round the little corkscrew staircase—then through the bell-ringers' loft, where the bell-ropes hung with soft furry ends like giant caterpillars—then up another stair into the belfry, where the big quiet bells are—and then on, up a ladder with broad steps—and then up a little stone stair. And at the top of that there was a little door. And the door was bolted on the stair side.

The cook's cousin, who was a gamekeeper, kicked at the door, and said:

"Hullo, you there!"

The children were holding on to each other on the other side of the door, and trembling with anxiousness—and very hoarse with their howls. They could hardly speak, but Cyril managed to reply huskily:

"Hullo, you there!"

"How did you get up there?"

It was no use saying "We flew up," so Cyril said:

"We got up—and then we found the door was locked and we couldn't get down. Let us out—do."

"How many of you are there?" asked the keeper.

"Only four," said Cyril.

"Are you armed?"

"Are we what?"

"I've got my gun handy—so you'd best not try any tricks," said the keeper. "If we open the door, will you promise to come quietly down, and no nonsense?"

"Yes—Oh YES!" said all the children together.

"Bless me," said the Vicar, "surely that was a female voice?"

"Shall I open the door, sir?" said the keeper. Andrew went down a few steps, "to leave room for the others" he said afterwards.

"Yes," said the Vicar, "open the door. Remember," he said through the keyhole, "we have come to release you. You will keep your promise to refrain from violence?"

"How this bolt do stick," said the keeper; "anyone 'ud think it hadn't been drawed for half a year." As a matter of fact it hadn't.

When all the bolts were drawn, the keeper spoke deep-chested words through the keyhole.

"I don't open," said he, "till you've gone over to the other side of the tower. And if one of you comes at me I fire. Now!"

"We're all over on the other side," said the voices.

The keeper felt pleased with himself, and owned himself a bold man when he threw open that door, and, stepping out into the leads, flashed the full light of the stable lantern on to the group of desperadoes standing against the parapet on the other side of the tower.

He lowered his gun, and he nearly dropped the lantern.

"So help me," he cried, "if they ain't a pack of kiddies!"

The Vicar now advanced.

"How did you come here?" he asked severely. "Tell me at once."

"Oh, take us down," said Jane, catching at his coat, "and we'll tell you anything you like. You won't believe us, but it doesn't matter. Oh, take us down?"

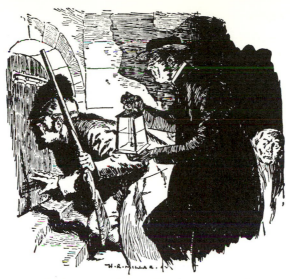

The others crowded round him, with the same entreaty. All but Cyril.
He had enough to do with the soda-water syphon, which would keep
slipping down under his jacket. It needed both hands to keep it steady
in its place.

But he said, standing as far out of the lantern light as possible:
"Please do take us down."

So they were taken down. It is no joke to go down a strange church-
tower in the dark, but the keeper helped them—only, Cyril had to be independent because of the soda-water syphon. It would keep trying to
get away. Half-way down the ladder it all but escaped. Cyril just caught
it by its spout, and as nearly as possible lost his footing. He was trembling and pale when at last they reached the bottom of the winding stair
and stepped out on to the flags of the church-porch.

Then suddenly the keeper caught Cyril and Robert each by an arm.

"You bring along the gells, sir," said he; "you and Andrew can manage them."

"Let go!" said Cyril; "we aren't running away. We haven't hurt your
old church. Leave go!"

"You just come along," said the keeper; and Cyril dared not oppose
him with violence, because just then the syphon began to slip again.

So they were all marched into the Vicarage study, and the Vicar's wife
came rushing in.

"Oh, William, *are* you safe?" she cried.

Robert hastened to allay her anxiety.

"Yes," he said, "he's quite safe. We haven't hurt him at all. And
please, we're very late, and they'll be anxious at home. Could you send
us home in your carriage?"

"Or perhaps there's a hotel near where we could get a carriage from,"
said Anthea. "Martha will be very anxious as it is."

The Vicar had sunk into a chair, overcome by emotion and amazement.

Cyril had also sat down, and was leaning forward with his elbows on his knees because of that soda-water syphon.

"But how did you come to be locked up in the church-tower?" asked the Vicar.

"We went up," said Robert slowly, "and we were tired, and we all went to sleep, and when we woke up we found the door was locked, so we yelled."

"I should think you did!" said the Vicar's wife. "Frightening everybody out of their wits like this! You ought to be ashamed of yourselves."

"We *are*," said Jane gently.

"But who locked the door?" asked the Vicar.

"I don't know at all," said Robert, with perfect truth. "Do please send us home."

"Well, really," said the Vicar, "I suppose we'd better. Andrew, put the horse to, and you can take them home."

"Not alone, I don't," said Andrew to himself.

"And," the Vicar went on, "let this be a lesson to you . . ." He went on talking, and the children listened miserably. But the keeper was not listening. He was looking at the unfortunate Cyril. He knew all about poachers of course, so he knew how people look when they're hiding something. The Vicar had just got to the part about trying to grow up to be a blessing to your parents, and not a trouble and a disgrace, when the keeper suddenly said:

"Arst him what he's got there under his jacket!; and Cyril knew that concealment was at an end. So he stood up, and squared his shoulders and tried to look noble, like the boys in books that no one can look in the face of and doubt that they come of brave and noble families and will be faithful to the death, and he pulled out the soda-water syphon and said:

"Well, there you are, then."

There was a silence. Cyril went on—there was nothing else for it:

"Yes, we took this out of your larder, and some chicken and tongue and bread. We were very hungry, and we didn't take the custard or jam. We only took bread and meat and water—and we couldn't help its being the soda kind—just the necessaries of life; and we left half-a-crown to pay for it, and we left a letter. And we're very sorry. And my father will pay a fine or anything you like, but don't send us to prison. Mother would be so vexed. You know what you said about not being a disgrace. Well, don't you go and do it to us—that's all! We're as sorry as we can be. There!"

"However did you get up to the larder window?" said Mrs Vicar.

"I can't tell you that," said Cyril firmly.

"Is this the whole truth you've been telling me?" asked the clergyman.

"No," answered Jane suddenly; "it's all true, but it's not the whole truth. We can't tell you that. It's no good asking. Oh, do forgive us and take us home!" She ran to the Vicar's wife and threw her arms round her. The Vicar's wife put her arms round Jane, and the keeper whispered behind his hand to the Vicar:

"They're all right, sir—I expect it's a pal they're standing by. Someone put 'em up to it, and they won't peach. Game little kids."

"Tell me," said the Vicar kindly, "are you screening someone else? Had anyone else anything to do with this?"

"Yes," said Anthea, thinking of the Psammead; "but it wasn't their fault."

"Very well, my dears," said the Vicar, "then let's say no more about it. Only just tell us why you wrote such an odd letter."

"I don't know," said Cyril. "You see, Anthea wrote it in such a hurry, and it really didn't seem like stealing then. But afterwards, when we found we couldn't get down off the church-tower, it seemed just exactly like it. We are all very sorry-"

"Say no more about it," said the Vicar's wife; "but another time just think before you take other people's tongues. Now—some cake and milk before you go home?"

When Andrew came to say that the horse was put to, and was he expected to be led alone into the trap that he had plainly seen from the first, he found the children eating cake and drinking milk and laughing at the Vicar's jokes. Jane was sitting on the Vicar's wife's lap.

So you see they got off better than they deserved.

The gamekeeper, who was the cook's cousin, asked leave to drive home with them, and Andrew was only too glad to have someone to protect him from the trap he was so certain of.

When the wagonette reached their own house, between the chalk-quarry and the gravel-pit, the children were very sleepy, but they felt that they and the keeper were friends for life.

Andrew dumped the children down at the iron gate without a word.

"You get along home," said the Vicarage cook's cousin, who was a gamekeeper. "I'll get me home on Shanks' mare."

So Andrew had to drive off alone, which he did not like at all, and it was the keeper that was cousin to the Vicarage cook who went with the children to the door, and, when they had been swept to bed in a whirl-wind of reproaches, remained to explain to Martha and the cook and the housemaid exactly what had happened. He explained so well that Martha was quite amiable the next morning.

After that he often used to come over and see Martha, and in the end—but that is another story, as dear Mr Kipling says.

Martha was obliged to stick to what she had said the night before about keeping the children indoors the next day for a punishment. But she wasn't at all snarky about it, and agreed to let Robert go out for half an hour to get something he particularly wanted.

This, of course, was the day's wish.

Robert rushed to the gravel-pit, found the Psammead, and presently wished for—

But that, too is another story.

5. CHILDHOOD'S PASTORAL: NURSERY FICTION

To [children] the inhabited world is composed of the two main divisions: children and upgrown people; the latter in no way superior to the former—only hopelessly different.—Kenneth Grahame, "The Finding of the Princess", The Golden Age *(1895)*

The Victorian nursery was a world unto itself, an arena of private adventures and spontaneous feelings in which the children were left, as Kenneth Grahame put it, "high and dry"—isolated from older brothers and sisters, separated from absent or negligent parents, and united in ferocious loyalty to each other. It inspired the genre of nursery fiction. The children in such Golden Age stories, far from being anxiously supervised or protected, enjoy a remarkable liberty that grants them the licence to indulge in escapades. The adult world is "out there"—hardly thought of until it materializes in the form of an exacting or reprimanding nurse, governess, or parent. As a variation on, and in a sense a liberation from, the family novel, these stories held attractions both for the imagi-native writer and for the older child who had left behind but had not forgotten the nursery.

Although authors of these stories were intimately aware of the perceptions of children, some succeeded more than others in tailoring their writing to the capacity of young readers. Mrs Molesworth was the most adept at engaging and holding children's attention. In *"Carrots": Just A Little Boy* (1876) she makes a red-headed six-year-old her hero; however, because he is misunderstood and misjudged by almost every other member of his family, readers of all ages immediately feel a kinship with him. When Geraldine, the heroine of *The Carved Lions* (1895), is separated for the first time from her parents and brother and sent to a boarding school, Molesworth's skilful use of first-person narration compels reader sympathy.

Even though they are frequently absent or preoccupied, the parents in Mrs Molesworth's stories cannot be called neglectful. But admirable adults in other Golden Age nursery fiction are rare. Setting *Castle Blair* (1878) in the picturesque surroundings of her grandfather's house near Dublin, Flora Shaw recounts the adventures of the five Blair children, whose uncaring bachelor uncle lets them do as they like. Despite the fact that they often miss meals and have never been to school, the Blairs are exceptionally intelligent, healthy, and resourceful. Rousseau would have been proud of these aristocratic ragamuffins who catch trout with their bare hands, know snatches of Shakespeare, and devise their own tribal amusements. Unhappily, the iron hand of adult justice—in the person of the vengeful land agent, Mr Plunkett—holds a fierce grip on this story, in which innocent lads are caned, a pet dog is killed, and a murder is planned. The children's antagonism to Plunkett even colours their moments of enjoyment: in Shaw's words, there is a "solemnity underlying the play". Kenneth

Grahame, equally aware of the gulf separating most adults and children, makes this sometimes humorous and sometimes melancholy reality the principal theme of *The Golden Age* (1895) and *Dream Days* (1898). He drew on memories of being raised by a succession of unsympathetic adults—a grandparent, aunts, and uncles. Unlike Mrs Molesworth, the comforting maternal observer, Grahame wrote his exquisite stories—all told by a first-person boy-narrator—from the standpoint of a philosophic and romantic adult. A surprising departure from the usual nursery-story emphasis on the chasm separating youth and age appears in Annie Keary's *Father Phim* (1879), in which a little girl is involved in sectarian violence: the divisions in this novel are drawn along religious lines.

Coloured by many moods, recalling a host of childhood memories, and subjecting the young child's world to a more intense gaze than ever before, nursery stories were probably enjoyed by the widest audience of all Golden Age fiction. They were known to adults, to older children, and, in the case of Mrs Molesworth's books, in the nursery itself.

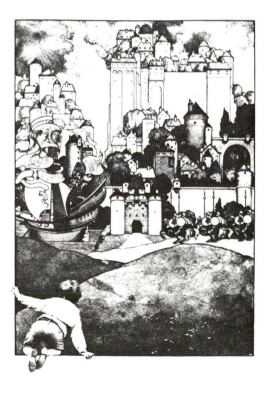

MARY LOUISA STEWART CHARLESWORTH (1842-1921)
"Carrots in Trouble" from *"Carrots": Just A Little Boy* (1876)

Mary Louisa Stewart was born in Rotterdam, Holland, but from the age of two spent her childhood in Manchester, Eng. One of six children, she often regaled her brothers and sisters with highly inventive stories that were partly based on tales of her Scottish grandmother and partly spun from her own imagination. Although her marriage, which lasted for eighteen years (1861-79), was an unhappy one (Major Molesworth had sustained a head wound in the Crimean War and was given to temperamental behaviour), Mrs Molesworth, the monarch of late Victorian nursery fiction, is nevertheless remembered for her gentle and serene domestic tales. Of her more than eighty books for children, some of the best loved are *The Cuckoo Clock* (1877), *The Tapestry Room* (1879), *The Adventures of Herr Baby* (1881), and *Little Miss Peggy* (1887). In addition to their chatty confidentiality and vivid detail, they have an amazing fidelity that allows the reader to enter—or re-enter—the child's world.

"Carrots", whose real name is Fabian, is the youngest of six Desart children. Their sailor-father is inclined to be short-tempered (a character flaw Mrs Molesworth knew only too well),while their mild but harried mother is usually preoccupied with overhauling the children's clothes and making ends meet. An honest and loving six-year-old, the curly red-haired hero has a friend, ally, and protectress in his sister Floss. Since the other members of the family are much older and intent on their school work, the two younger children form a loyal duo.

So expert is Molesworth's characterization that she makes Carrot's pristine innocence, comic ingenuousness, and willingness to please believable without making him saccharine. When he offers to tidy a drawer in which Floss keeps her many dolls, he is surprised by the discovery of a half-sovereign (a gold coin with a value of ten shillings), which he mistakes for "a yellow sixpenny". Motivated not by greed but by the desire to surprise his sister with the gift of a new doll, Carrots slips the sovereign into his own paint box. The chapter reprinted below relates the consequences, and portrays a case of misunderstanding and division in the nursery world.

CARROTS IN TROUBLE

"But bitter while they flow, are childish tears."

"Now Carrots," said Mott, when he had eaten what he considered might possibly support him for the next two hours, "now Carrots, let's have the paint-box. You needn't disturb yourself," he continued, for Carrots was preparing to descend from his high chair, "I know where you keep it; it's in your drawer, isn't it. Which is his drawer, nurse? It'll be a good opportunity for me to see if he keeps it tidy."

"No, no, let me get it myself," cried Carrots, tumbling himself off his chair anyhow in his eagerness. "Nurse, nurse, don't tell him which is mine; don't let him take my paint-box, let me get it my own self."

Nurse looked at him with some surprise; it was seldom the little boy so excited himself.

"Master Mott won't hurt your drawer, my dear," she said; "you don't mind his having your paint-box, I'm sure. But do let him get it out himself, if he wants, Master Maurice, there's a dear boy," she continued, for Maurice was by this time ferreting in Floss's drawer with great gusto,

and in another moment would have been at Carrots'! But Carrots was at
it before him. He pulled it open as far as he could, for in consequence of
Mott's investigations in the upper storey, he could not easily penetrate
to his own quarters. But he knew exactly where the paint-box lay, and
managed to slip it out, without Maurice's noticing what he was doing.
His triumph was short-lived, however; before he could open the box,
Mott was after him.

"Hi, you young sneak!" he cried, "what are you after now? Give me
the box; I believe you want to take the best paints out before you lend it
to me," and he wrenched the paint-box out of his little brother's
hands.

"I don't, I don't," sobbed Carrots, sitting down on the floor and crying bitterly; "you may have all the paints, Mott, but it's my secret, oh,
my secret!"

"What are you talking about?" said Mott roughly, pulling out the lid
as he spoke. The box had been all tumbled about in the struggle, and the
paints came rattling out, the paints and the brushes, and the little
saucers, and with them came rolling down on to the floor, children, you
know what—the "fairies' sixpenny," the little bright shining yellow
half-sovereign!

A strange change came over Mott's face.

"Nurse," he cried, "do you see that? What does that mean?"

Nurse hastened up to where he was standing; she stared for a moment in puzzled astonishment at the spot on the carpet to which the toe
of Maurice's boot was pointing, then she stooped down slowly and
picked up the coin, still without speaking.

"Well, nurse," said Maurice, impatiently, "what do you think of
that?"

"My half-sovereign," said nurse, as if hardly believing what she saw.

"Of course it's your half-sovereign," said Mott, "it's as plain as a pike-staff. But how did it come there, that's the question?"

Nurse looked at Carrots with puzzled perplexity. "He couldn't have known," she said in a low voice, too low for Carrots to hear. He was still sitting on the floor sobbing, and through his sobs was to be heard now and then the melancholy cry. "My secret, oh, my poor secret."

"You hear what he says," says Maurice; "what does his 'secret' mean but that he sneaked into your drawer and took the half-sovereign, and now doesn't like being found out. I'm ashamed to have him for my brother, that I am, the little cad!"

"But he couldn't have understood," said nurse, at a loss how otherwise to defend her little boy. "I'm not even sure that he rightly knew of my losing it, and he might have taken it, meaning no harm, not knowing what it was, indeed, very likely."

"Rubbish," said Maurice. "A child that is going without sugar to get money instead, must be old enough to understand something about what money is."

"But that was *my* plan; it wasn't Carrots that thought of it at all," said Floss, who all this time had stood by, frightened and distressed, not knowing what to say.

"Hold your tongue, Floss," said Maurice, roughly; and Floss subsided. "Carrots," he continued, turning to his brother, "leave off crying this minute, and listen to me. Who put this piece of money into your paint-box?"

"I did my own self," said Carrots.

"What for?"

"To keep it a secret for Floss," sobbed Carrots.

Maurice turned triumphantly to nurse.

"There," he said, "you see! And," he continued to Carrots again, "you took it out of nurse's drawer—out of a little paper packet?"

"No," said Carrots, "I didn't. I didn't know it was nurse's."

"You didn't know nurse had lost a half-sovereign!" exclaimed Mott, "Carrots, how dare you say so?"

"Yes," said Carrots, looking so puzzled, that for a moment or two he forgot to sob, "I did know, Floss told me."

"Then how *can* you say you didn't know this was nurse's?" said Mott.

"Oh, I don't know—I didn't know—I can't under'tand," cried Carrots, relapsing into fresh sobs.

"I wish your mamma were in, that I do," said nurse, looking ready to cry too; by this time Floss's tears were flowing freely.

"She isn't in, so it's no good wishing she were," said Maurice; "but papa is," he went on importantly, "and I'll just take Carrots to him and see what *he'll* say to all this."

"Oh, no, Master Mott, don't do that, I beg and pray of you," said nurse, all but wringing her hands in entreaty. "Your papa doesn't understand about the little ones; do wait till your mamma comes in."

"No, indeed, nurse; it's a thing papa *should* be told," said Mott, in his innermost heart half inclined to yield, but working himself up to imagine he was acting very heroically. And notwithstanding nurse's distress, and Floss's tears, off he marched his unfortunate little brother to the study.

"Papa," he said, knocking at the door, "may I come in? There's something I must speak to you about immediately."

"Come in, then," was the reply. "Well, and what's the matter now? Has Carrots hurt himself?" asked his father, naturally enough, for his red-haired little son looked pitiable in the extreme as he crept into the room after Maurice, frightened, bewildered, and, so far as his gentle disposition was capable of such a feeling, indignant also, all at once.

"No," replied Maurice, pushing Carrots forward, "he's not hurt himself; it's worse than that. Papa," he continued excitedly, "you whipped me once, when I was a little fellow, for telling a story. I am very sorry to trouble you, but I think it's right you should know; I am afraid you will have to punish Carrots more severely than you punished me, for he's done worse than tell a story." Maurice stopped to take breath, and looked at his father to see the effect of his words. Carrots had stopped crying to listen to what Maurice was saying, and there he stood, staring up with his large brown eyes, two or three tears still struggling down his cheeks, his face smeared and red and looking very miserable. Yet he did not seem to be in the least ashamed of himself, and this somehow provoked Mott and hardened him against him.

"What's he been doing?" said their father, looking at the two boys with more amusement than anxiety, and then glancing regretfully at the newspaper which he had been comfortably reading when Mott's knock came to the door.

"He's done much worse than tell a story," repeated Maurice, "though for that matter he's told two or three stories too. But, papa, you know about nurse losing a half-sovereign? Well, *Carrots* had got it all the time; he took it out of nurse's purse, and hid it away in his paint-box, without telling anybody. He can't deny it, though he tried to."

"Carrots," said his father sternly, "is this true?"

Carrots looked up in his father's face; that face, generally so kind and merry, was now all gloom and displeasure—why?—Carrots could not understand, and he was too frightened and miserable to collect his little wits together to try to do so. He just gave a sort of little tremble and began to cry again.

"Carrots," repeated his father, "is this true?"

"I don't know," sobbed Carrots.

Now Captain Desart, Carrots' father, was, as I think I have told you, a sailor. If any of you children have a sailor for your father, you must not think I mean to teach you to be disrespectful when I say that sailors *are*, there is no doubt, inclined to be hot-tempered and hasty. And I do not think on the whole that they understand much about children, though they are often very fond of them and very kind. All this was the case with Carrots' father. He had been so much away from his children while they were little, that he really hardly knew how they had been brought up or trained or anything about their childish ways—he had left them entirely to his wife, and scarcely considered them as in any way "*his* business," till they were quite big boys and girls.

But once he did begin to notice them, though very kind, he was very strict. He had most decided opinions about the only way of checking their faults whenever these were serious enough to attract his attention, and he could not and would not be troubled with arguing, or what he called "splitting hairs," about such matters. A fault was a fault; telling a falsehood was telling a falsehood; and he made no allowance for the excuses or "palliating circumstances" there might be to consider. One child, according to his ideas, was to be treated exactly like another; why the same offence should deserve severer punishment with a self-willed, self-confident, bold, matter-of-fact lad, such as Maurice, than with a timid, fanciful, baby-like creature as was his little Fabian, he could not have understood had he tried.

Nurse knew all this by long experience; no wonder, kind though she knew her master to be, that she trembled when Mott announced his intention of laying the whole affair before his father.

But poor Carrots did not know anything about it. "Papa" had never been "cross" to him before, and he was far from clearly understanding why he was "cross" to him now. So he just sobbed and said "I don't know," which was about the worst thing he could possibly have said in his own defence, though literally the truth.

"No or yes, sir," said Captain Desart, his voice growing louder and sterner—I think he really forgot that it was a poor little shrimp of six years old he was speaking to—"no nonsense of 'don't knows.' Did you or did you not take nurse's half-sovereign out of her drawer and keep it for your own?"

"No," said Carrots, "I never took nucken out of nurse's drawer. I never did, papa, and I didn't know nurse had any sovereigns."

"Didn't you know nurse had *lost* a half-sovereign? Carrots, how can you say so?" interrupted Mott.

"Yes, Floss told me," said Carrots.

"And Floss hid it away in your paint-box, I suppose?" said Mott, sarcastically.

"No, Floss didn't. I hided the sixpenny my own self," said Carrots, looking more and more puzzled.

"Hold your tongue, Maurice," said his father, angrily. "Go and fetch the money and the tom-fool paint-box thing that you say he had it in."

Mott did as he was told. He ran to the nursery and back as fast as he could; but, unobserved by him, Floss managed to run after him and crept into the study so quietly that her father never noticed her.

Maurice laid the old paint-box and the half-sovereign down on the table in front of his father; Captain Desart held up the little coin between his finger and thumb.

"Now," he said, "Carrots, look at this. Did you or did you not take this piece of money out of nurse's drawer and hide it away in your paint-box?"

Carrots stared hard at the half-sovereign.

"I did put it in my paint-box," he said, and then he stopped.

"What for?" said his father.

"I wanted to keep it for a secret," he replied. "I wanted to—to—"

"*What?*" thundered Captain Desart.

"To buy something at the toy-shop with it," sobbed Carrots.

Captain Desart sat down and looked at Mott for sympathy.

"Upon my soul," he said, "one could hardly believe it. A child that one would think scarcely knew the value of money! Where can he have learnt such cunning; you say you are sure he was told of nurse's having lost a half-sovereign?"

"Oh, yes," said Mott; "he confesses to that much himself."

"Floss told me," said Carrots.

"Then how can you pretend you didn't know this was nurse's—taking it out of her drawer, too," said his father.

"I don't know. I didn't take it out of her drawer; it was 'aside Floss's doll," said Carrots.

"He's trying to equivocate," said his father. Then he turned to the child again, looking more determined than ever.

"Carrots," he said, "I must whip you for this. Do you know that I am ashamed to think you are my son? If you were a poor boy you might be put in prison for this."

Carrots looked too bewildered to understand. "In prison," he repeated. "Would the prison-man take me?"

"What does he mean?" said Captain Desart.

Floss, who had been waiting unobserved in her corner all this time, thought this a good opportunity for coming forward.

"He means the policeman," she said. "Oh, papa," she went on, running up to her little brother and throwing her arms round him, the tears streaming down her face, "oh, papa, poor little Carrots! he *doesn't* understand."

"Where did *you* come from?" said her father, gruffly but not unkindly, for Floss was rather a favourite of his. "What do you mean about his not understanding? Did you know about this business, Floss?"

"Oh no, papa," said Floss, her face flushing; "I'm too big not to understand."

"Of course you are," said Captain Desart; "and Carrots is big enough, too, to understand the very plain rule that he is not to touch what does not belong to him. He was told, too, that nurse had lost a half-sovereign, and he might then have owned to having taken it and given it back, and then things would not have looked so bad. Take him up to my dressing-room, Maurice, and leave him there till I come."

"May I go with him, papa?" said Floss very timidly.

"No," said her father, "you may not."

So Mott led off poor weeping Carrots, and all the way upstairs he kept sobbing to himself, "I never touched nurse's sovereigns. I never did. I didn't know she had any sovereigns."

"Hold your tongue," said Mott; "what is the use of telling more stories about it?"

"I didn't tell stories. I said I hided the six-penny my own self, but I never touched nurse's sovereigns; I never did."

"I believe you're more than half an idiot," said Mott, angry and yet sorry—angry with himself, too, somehow.

Floss, left alone with her father, ventured on another appeal.

"You won't whip Carrots till mamma comes in, will you, papa?" she said softly.

"Why not? Do you think I want her to help me to whip him?" said Captain Desart.

"Oh no—but—I think perhaps mamma would understand better how it was, for, oh papa, dear, Carrots *isn't* a naughty boy; he never, never tells stories."

"Well, we'll see," replied her father; "and in the meantime it will do him no harm to think things over by himself in my dressing-room for a little."

"Oh, poor Carrots!" murmured Floss to herself; "it'll be getting dark, and he's all alone. I *wish* mamma would come in!"

FLORA LOUISA SHAW (1852-1929)
"Tribal Initiation" from *Castle Blair; A Story of Youthful Days* (1878)

Born in Dublin of a French mother and an Irish father, Flora Shaw was in many ways a "New Woman". Although she could have enjoyed a comfortable and idle existence in the family home outside Dublin, she keenly felt the need to make her life meaningful. After the death of her mother and the remarriage of her father, she left Ireland for England, where she became friendly with John Ruskin. With his assistance she set up a co-operative store for the poor at Woolwich in 1874, and during the first of many Continental tours she served meals to the soldiers of the Franco-Prussian War (1874-5). As well as writing *Castle Blair*

(1878) and serialized stories in *Aunt Judy's Magazine* beginning in 1881, Shaw developed an impressive reputation as a journalist in England, contributing regularly to *The Pall Mall Gazette* and *The Manchester Guardian*. By 1890 her facility in learning languages and her extensive travels had helped her to rise to the position of colonial editor of *The Times*. Travelling widely in Gibraltar, Morocco, South Africa, Australia, and Canada—which she crossed twice, in 1893 and again in 1898, when she ventured to the Klondike—Shaw became a respected authority on Mediterranean problems, African politics, and Imperial history. After a full career at *The Times* she married Sir Frederick Lugard, a colonial administrator, in 1902. In recognition of her pioneering contributions to journalism and her founding of the War Refugees' Commission, she was made a Dame of the British Empire (D.B.E.) in 1918.

Shaw wrote *Castle Blair*, based on memories of her Irish childhood, to raise money for one of her impoverished married sisters. It had eight printings and established its author as a storyteller of real power. Hailing *Castle Blair* as "a quite lovely little book"—a strange description of an unusually grim and intense children's story—Ruskin (who had been consulted about the plot) praised it as "good . . . and true". Although Shaw's story is frequently unlovely and distressing, it is a vivid account of childhood's ecstatic delights and deeply wounding sorrows. The five Blair children—Murtagh, Winnie, Rosie, Bobbo, and Ellie—have never been sent to school; they live with their bachelor uncle in the family's castle in Ireland, while their parents remain in India. Members of the castle's staff discreetly lament that no governess has stayed more than a few months because the children are so unruly; but John Blair's "agent" (rent-collector and manager), Mr Plunkett, has a harsher view and sets out to tame them. He sees them as cruel little criminals, and this is what they almost become where he is concerned. However, an older orphan-cousin, Adrienne—whose name the children affectionately shorten to Nessa—sees them as imaginative but sadly neglected, and they respond eagerly to her kindness. Her mollifying influence is not enough to overcome the children's very real hatred of Plunkett, whose reign of terror is fiendish. Following the ceremony on Murtagh's birthday, described below, in which the Blairs ritualistically initiate Nessa and sing patriotically of "de Shan van Vaugh" (the poor old woman, Ireland), Plunkett mercilessly canes Pat O'Toole, a local boy who has helped the children with the celebration, as well as Master Murtagh himself. When Plunkett's Red House is set ablaze, the agent blames Murtagh, although Pat is guilty. Plunkett tears down the hut where the Blairs play and shoots Royal, their dog. The children's hatred reaches its pitch when Pat and Murtagh plan to kill Plunkett. At the last moment Murtagh accidentally receives the bullet wound himself, though he is not killed by it.

This climax dissipates the feverish tensions in *Castle Blair* but also leads to a regrettable anticlimax. In the last couple of chapters Shaw makes an unconvincing effort to exonerate Plunkett by showing how concerned he has always been for the children's well-being. "I have made mistakes with you; but we must start fresh," he tells the recuperating Murtagh. For the reader, the Blairs' real hope lies in the announcement, which they greet enthusiastically, that they are to be sent to school.

TRIBAL INITIATION

At the tower the followers were eagerly expecting the return of their little chiefs. While the children had been away they had rambled about under Pat O'Toole's direction, and had each brought a beautiful branch of mountain-ash, loaded with scarlet berries, to hold in their hands, and had gathered bunches of white heather. They had added, too, to the decorations by fixing branches of mountain-ash wherever one of the festoons was looped, and they were most anxious to know whether Rosie would approve their taste. She did heartily, and the broad, good-humored faces beamed with delight at her thanks.

Plenty of hands were ready to carry the hampers from the cart to the other side of the archway, but every one was too much excited just now about the ceremony to be able to think of anything else.

A white table-cloth was hastily thrown over the hampers, and the followers were told to wash their feet and hurry on their clean pinafores, which latter had been wisely put on one side in the early part of the day. Then Rosie said, with the branches in their hands they would all look "beautifully alike." But Ellie was to be the messenger who was to summon Nessa, and her shabby little dark green frock was far from suitable to such an occasion. Rosie looked at her in despair for a moment, but only for a moment.

"Quick, quick, Winnie, the needles and thread," she said; and then, while the followers assumed their primitive uniform, she and Winnie tacked a garland of white heather round the hem of the little frock, looped it up shepherdess fashion over the short scarlet linsey petticoat, and placed bunches of white heather on the breast and shoulders with such effect that when Murtagh crowned the child's golden head with a wreath of the same white flowers, Winnie cried in delight: "Oh, Ellie, you do look like a little fairy, so you do."

"All but the boots and stockings," returned Murtagh, surveying her with more critical eyes.

"Tate 'em off," said Ellie, eagerly holding up one foot. "Ellie want to be a fairy."

"The grass'll prick," said Winnie. But Ellie, who had stood like a little statue while they decorated her dress, replied: "Me don't mind. Ellie be a fairy then, and look *so* pretty."

So they pulled off the clumsy boots, and she danced gleefully over the grass, her golden curls falling over her dimpled shoulders, her little white feet and legs twinkling in the sunlight.

" 'Deed it's like an angel right down from heaven she is!" exclaimed more than one of the followers, while Rose, with all the anxiety of a manager, said: "Take care, Ellie; don't shake off your wreath. Now you're to come with us down to there, you see where Nessa is behind the rock, and you're to tell her—What shall we say, Murtagh?"

"Tell her to come and be one of us," replied Murtagh grandiloquently, seating himself upon the throne as he spoke, and taking up his violin.

"You lead Ellie down, Rosie. All you followers follow, and as soon as Miss Nessa comes round the rock, form into two lines for her to pass through, and scatter your flowers. Now begin to sing."

He touched his violin. Winnie's clear voice rose first, then all the others joined in, and the music swelled in harmony as the little procession moved down the slope.

Notwithstanding the sunlight, the flowers, and the gay dresses of the children, there was a something almost solemn in their voices; and little Ellie looked up into Rosie's face with wide-open wondering eyes, as though not at all sure what all this meant.

"Now go," said Rosie, loosing the child's hand as the singing began gently to die away.

With flushed cheeks and the same wondering look still in her eyes Ellie sprang round the rock, and holding out her hand to Nessa she cried earnestly:

"Oor to tum and be a fairy." Then quivering all over with excitement, she added in a tone meant to be reassuring: "Ellie's not frightened. It doesn't hurt."

"No, dear," replied Nessa, taking hold of the little hot hand and keeping it firmly in her own cool fingers. "Only fun for Nessa and Ellie together."

"Yes, *only* fun," said Ellie looking up at Nessa with a sigh of relief. But she clung very closely to Nessa's hand as they came out from behind the rock and were received with a cheer ending in a burst of music.

"How very, very pretty!" exclaimed Nessa, taking in the whole scene at a glance and standing still in admiration.

Almost opposite to them rose the grassy slope with the irregular double file of followers winding down its side. Through their ranks Nessa could see Murtagh sitting, playing his violin on the rough throne they had made. Behind rose the gray ruin wreathed in flowers, and above and beyond all, clear blue sky flecked with sunny clouds spread over the purple hill-tops as far as the eye could reach.

"Tum," said Ellie, pulling her hand; and through the singing children Nessa walked slowly towards the throne. But now little Ellie was not the only one who felt solemnity underlying the play. The children as they sang could not have told how much they were in earnest; their hearts were beating fast, they scarcely knew why, and there was a tone in their voices that filled Nessa with emotion as she passed between them. No one had intended the ceremony to be solemn; it became so without their will.

When Nessa was quite close the music ceased. Murtagh descended from his seat, and with the followers pressing eagerly round to see, Nessa was with due form received into the tribe, and the green ribbon was tied about her arm. Then came the moment for her to promise to hate the "Agents." It was the interesting point, the crisis as it were of the whole ceremony; and there was an almost breathless silence while Murtagh, his voice shaking a little with excitement, said to her: "Will you promise faithfully to hate the "Agents," and to defend your tribe against them?"

There was something so curious in this request, made as it was in the midst of those intensely eager faces, that Nessa felt not the slightest inclination to laugh. She looked round the listening circle with a sort of troubled astonishment, and then turning to Murtagh she answered quite gravely:

"No. I do not like hating."

A burst of expressive lament escaped from the crowd. Murtagh looked puzzled and disappointed. He could not make up his mind.

"What shall we do?" he asked at length, turning to the followers.

"Make her princess over us anyhow, Mr Murtagh. It can't be helped," cried Pat O'Toole magnanimously, and the other followers by their acclamations seconded his request.

"Yes, do! yes, do!" cried Winnie, Bobbo, and Rosie.

Murtagh took the wreath of shamrocks and would have placed it on Nessa's head; but she drew back and said: "No; I do not think I can be your princess."

Murtagh paused with the wreath in his hands too much astonished to speak. Consternation became visible in every face; their ceremony was taking a most unexpected turn.

"Have you promised what you wanted me to promise?" asked Nessa.

"That we have; *sworn* it!" cried the children eagerly, regaining their voices.

"That was what I thought," said Nessa, beginning to unfasten the ribbon from her arm. "That is why I cannot be one of your tribe."

"Oh, stop a minute! stop a minute!" cried Rosie and the children, while Murtagh asked: "What do you want us to do?"

"I want you to undo the promise you have made, and to try never to hate any one," said Nessa resolutely, her cheeks flushing a little, and her eyes dark and bright. "Do you not feel wicked when you hate?"

There was a pause. This was very different from what they had intended, but for the moment Nessa had the little crowd in her power. Pat O'Toole was the first to speak.

"'Deed and she's right," he exclaimed. "When my paddy's up it's little I care what I do."

"Faix, and it's little good we get by hating them," remarked another of the elder followers.

But to Murtagh himself the question was a more personal one. He was thinking deeply, and seemed at first quite undecided. Then, his whole countenance opening out into a sunny smile, he turned to Nessa and said, "I'll try."

That was all that was needed.

"So will I," said Winnie; and more or less earnestly the promise was echoed by the crowd.

"Then I will be your princess if you will have me," said Nessa. "And shall I give you a *device*,—a motto for the tribe?" she added, hesitating.

"Yes, yes," cried Murtagh. "What is it?"

" 'Peace on earth, goodwill towards men.' Will you have that?"

She looked round with a gentle pleading in her eyes, and then taking off her hat she knelt down on the grass before Murtagh.

"God bless her! God bless her!" cried the followers, and Murtagh's face was white, and his hands trembling a little, as he laid the wreath upon her head.

A chorus of cheers rose from the followers' lusty throats, and in the midst of the echoing hurrahs Murtagh led her up the steps of the throne. The excitement of the children had been growing and greater from the moment that Ellie first led Nessa round the rock. During the ceremony they had been obliged to keep it down, and now it burst forth without restraint.

They danced and shouted round the throne like mad creatures, and the more they danced the wilder they grew; each seemed to try and out-rival the others in the noise. At last Murtagh, remembering his violin, struck the first notes of the "Shan van Vaugh," and every one found re-lief in spending upon that the force of their lungs. How they did sing! Their voices rang through the mountain-rocks and were echoed back again. The excitement was infectious; even little Ellie, standing on the throne beside Nessa, sang diligently all the time the only words she knew: "Says de Shan van Vaugh; says de Shan van Vaugh"; and when with a last triumphant burst came the ending lines:

> "We'll pluck the laurel tree,
> And we'll call it Liberty,
> For our country *shall* be free,
> Says the Shan van Vaugh"—

Nessa clapped her hands and cried in delight: "Oh, how pretty it is out of doors! How pretty it all is!"

Almost as she did so a strange voice exclaimed: "Well, children, are you holding a Fenian meeting?" The words were accompanied by a little laugh, but they had the effect of putting a sudden and complete stop to the children's mirth.

Nessa looked round, and standing by the low wall she perceived a lady, who at the moment was engaged in disentangling a floating gauze veil from among the bows and flowers that adorned her bonnet. By her side stood a fashionably-dressed girl of sixteen, whose face wore an ex-pression of amused contempt far from attractive. She did not seem to be aware of the elder lady's difficulties with the veil, and Nessa advanced at once to offer her assistance.

"Or have you quite given up civilized life," continued the lady, with a series of little laughs, "and resolved to live up here with your select cir-cle of friends? I thought you were to have some one to take care of you. How do you get on with the new cousin; eh, Murtagh? Oh, I'm sure I beg your pardon," she added, suddenly perceiving Nessa, and making up for her first oversight by a fixed and deliberate stare.

The color deepened in Nessa's cheeks as she bowed and asked whether she could not help to disengage the veil. But the new-comer continued none the less for that as she bent her head to Nessa's minis-trations:

"So you have a new playfellow, children. That must be very nice for you. You have good strong nerves I suppose, and don't mind noise," she added, addressing Nessa. "Well, you are quite right; it's no good having delicate ways and ideas when you have to live with a big family. Those things do well enough where there's only one or two."

At this point Murtagh seemed to think that she had monopolized the conversation long enough, for he now walked up to her, and holding out his hand said gravely:

"How do you do, Cousin Jane? How do you do, Emma?"

The three other children followed his example with automatic regularity, and no social extinguisher could have been more effective. Cousin Jane was completely silenced.

"It is no use our staying here any longer, mamma," exclaimed Emma. "We shall see them all when they are quiet and tidy in the house this evening. We could not imagine," she said, turning politely to Nessa, "what all the noise was. That is why we came up; we left the carriage in the road."

"It is a birthday," said Nessa, smiling as she glanced at the groups of followers, "and we are *en grande fête.*"

"We've got a jolly good feast for them too," said Bobbo confidentially.

"A feast, have you?" exclaimed Cousin Jane. "Oh well, there's a lot of fruit and some lollypops and cakes in the carriage. You'd like them now I daresay as well as any other time; you can make a division. Here, you little fellow," she continued, turning to one of the followers; "do you know how to eat sweeties?"

The little girl addressed put her finger sheepishly in her mouth, and Cousin Jane pulled out of her pocket a large paper of sweeties, which she proceeded good-humoredly to distribute, while Emma turning to Nessa asked if such a noise did not make her head ache?

"No!" said Nessa, "it amused me very much."

"And I daresay you've been accustomed to it," added Cousin Jane. "But I wonder what Ma'mselle would say to such lessons; eh, Emma?"

Emma laughed contemptuously, and Cousin Jane dropping her voice to a confidential tone continued: "You know I'm the only lady they have to look after them at all, so we must have some talks about them. It is quite terrible the way poor Mr Blair forgets his responsibility. It always has been the way with him; the idea of allowing them to come up here with the pack of dirty children. Nobody in the world but John would do such a thing. And just fancy not having got another governess for them yet, when their last went away more than three months ago. But he's so wrapped up in books, and stones, and pictures, he puts all his duties on one side. If it wasn't for Mr Plunkett I don't know what would become of the place; that man is the salvation of the estate."

This seemed a fruitful subject to Cousin Jane, for she continued to talk without interruption till the carriage was reached.

Nessa, quite taken aback by the sudden confidence, found nothing to say, and was only glad that the children had careered on in front. Frankie was not in the carriage; he had preferred to drive in the dog-cart with a servant; so it was the affair of a few minutes only to find the basket Cousin Jane destined for the children; and then, somewhat it must be confessed to the relief of every one, the carriage drove on towards Castle Blair.

"Wait till you see Frankie," said Murtagh, turning towards Nessa as the carriage disappeared round the corner. "*He's* not a bit like that."

"I say, Murtagh," called Bobbo from the stream at the other side of the slope where he and Winnie were already disporting themselves, "come and wash your hands, and let us see about unpacking the grub." A hatful of water flung after the invitation proved irresistible; in another minute Murtagh was taking his revenge, and water was flying in every direction.

Suddenly in the midst of the fun a splendid Newfoundland dog bounded through the hedge and over the little stream, fairly upsetting Winnie, and splashing the water over them all.

"In the name of all that's wonderful where do you come from?" exclaimed Murtagh, as Winnie, picking herself up, rushed after the dog, crying: "Oh, you beauty! come here."

A low rippling laugh made both Nessa and Murtagh look round, and in a dogcart on the other side of the hedge they saw a delicate-looking little boy sitting watching Winnie with delight.

"Frankie!" exclaimed Murtagh springing forward.

"Yes," said Frankie. "How do you do? What are you doing? Was it you making that jolly noise? Have you heard why we've come here? There is such a splendid plan. The doctors say I am to go to the seaside somewhere in the south, and some of you are to come."

Murtagh was busy climbing through the hedge and into the dog-cart, so he scarcely heard what Frankie was saying, but now took his place beside him exclaiming: "How are you, old fellow? Are you any better? Where did you get him? He is such a beauty!" The last words referred, of course, to the dog, whom Winnie had caught, and was now leading back to the stream.

The flush of excitement faded from Frankie's cheek, and he seemed to have some difficulty in getting his breath after the volley of questions he had poured out. In reply to the first part of Murtagh's inquiries he only seemed to shrink into himself, and shook his head. The servant who accompanied him began to assure Murtagh that Mr Frank was much better, and would soon be quite well now; but Frankie seemed to wish to change the subject, and said hurriedly: "Yes, isn't he splendid! He was given to me, but I've been training him for Winnie. He's no good to me, you know; if he knocks me over I don't get my breath back for a week. But I thought she'd like him. He's as quiet as a lamb unless you set him at anybody, and then he goes at them like—"

"Like an Irishman," suggested Murtagh; but though his words were meant for a joke he looked wistfully at his cousin, wishing to ask more questions about his health. He was very fond of Frankie, and it made him sorry to see the sunken cheeks and wasted hands that told even to childish eyes how ill the boy was.

Frankie nodded and sat silently looking at Winnie and the dog with a pleased smile playing round his mouth.

Winnie had not yet perceived him, and her attention was entirely absorbed by the dog. Both her arms were round its neck, and as she walked along by its side, bending down, she showered upon it every endearing epithet she could think of.

"Perhaps you're lost, and perhaps we won't be able to find your master, however hard we look, and then you'll stay with us; won't you, my beauty?" she was saying when she glanced up and saw Frankie.

Instantly the dog was forgotten, and she flew towards the road, exclaiming: "Frankie! How jolly!"

Frankie laughed again his low, pleased laugh; but having suffered for the rapid questions with which he had saluted Murtagh, he did not attempt to say more than, "Yes; here I am," as Winnie climbed up on the wheel of the dog-cart and pulled down his face to be kissed.

"We're having such fun!" she continued; "get down, and come up to the tower with us." She jumped down herself as she spoke, and threw her arms round the dog, who stood wagging his tail.

"No, I mustn't do that," replied Frankie, looking wistfully at the tower and then smiling again as his eyes fell to the dog standing by Winnie's side. "I only stopped to see what you'd think of Royal."

"You don't mean to say that this beautiful dog is yours!" exclaimed Winnie. "Oh, Frankie, you are a lucky boy!"

"Yes it is," said Murtagh.

"Your very, very own; not your mother's or anybody's?" inquired Winnie, doubtful whether it were possible for any child to possess such a treasure.

"No," said Frankie: "he isn't mine, he is yours."

"Wha—what do you mean?" asked Winnie astonished, the color deepening a little in her cheeks as the dream-like possibility flashed across her mind.

"I mean what I say," repeated Frankie, his face beaming. "He is your very own dog; I have been training him for you, and I've brought him here for you!"

Winnie did not seem able to take it in. The color spread over her cheeks and mounted to her forehead. Her big eyes grew round and bigger, but she did not dare to believe such a thing could be till Murtagh exclaimed:

"Frankie's given him to you. He's your very own, as own as own can be!"

Then a light broke over her face, and tightening the grasp of her arms round Royal's neck she half-strangled him in an embrace, while all she could say was, "Oh, Frankie!"

Frankie seemed well satisfied with her thanks.

Murtagh laughted and said: "She doesn't believe it now."

"Yes, I do," said Winnie, "only it's too good! I can't seem to know it. Oh, Frankie, I think I shall go cracky with gladness!" Suddenly finding the power of expressing her delight she tore up the hill, calling to Royal to follow, and burst upon the assembled children, exclaiming: "He's mine! He's my very own! Frankie's just given him to me!" Then she raced down again like some mad thing, and ran away at full speed over the heather with Royal at her heels. She came back in about five minutes panting and rosy, with her hand upon the dog's collar, declaring that now she could stay quiet; and her brilliant face would have been reward enough for a more selfish person than Frankie.

Frankie stayed only to display some of Royal's accomplishments and to show Winnie's name engraved upon the collar. Then he drove away, leaving their new treasure with the children.

But it was getting to be quite afternoon by this time, and nobody had had any dinner yet, so Murtagh careered up the hill, crying: "Come along now, and let's have scene number two in the entertainment. I feel as if I was quite ready for scene number two. How are you, Winnie?"

Winnie's answer was more expressive than elegant, and then they set to work to unpack the hampers. In a very few moments the white cloth was spread upon the ground and covered with Mrs Donegan's dainties. The children were in no way disappointed in the pleasure of watching the queer expressions of the followers' faces as dish after dish came out of the hampers. Poor hungry followers! they had had nothing to eat since an early hour that morning, and few of them had ever even seen such things as Mrs Donegan had prepared. So it is not to be wondered at, that when they found themselves sitting on the grass round that wonderful feast, with free leave to eat whatever they pleased, the event seemed to them really too good to be true.

*

Murtagh was the soul of the party. Nessa wondered where his words and ideas came from, they flowed out so fast. Seated in state at the head of the table she was very gay and happy. She was unusually amused by this wild, merry crew, and such spirits as theirs were infectious.

The feast over, Royal was with much mock solemnity received into the tribe, a ceremony which he disrespectfully brought to an abrupt ending by knocking over four or five of his sponsors. They then divided into parties, and played robber games among the hills, till the fading light warned them that even the pleasantest of days *will* come to an end. The remains of the feast were divided between the followers. Tommie was yoked into the cart again, and at last to his satisfaction, if to nobody else's, his willing head was turned homewards.

But even then the children were not tired. It was wonderful to see how they caracoled round the cart, and sang and laughed the whole way home; and when, finally, they drove up in state and deposited Nessa upon the hall-door steps, the last cheer they gave her was as hearty as any they had uttered that day.

ANNIE KEARY (1825-1879)
"A Watch on the Hill" from *Father Phim* (1879)

Born at Bilton Rectory, near Wetherby, Yorkshire, Annie Keary was the daughter of a clergyman who had come from County Galway, Ireland. She and her sister Eliza established a reputation for vigorous moralizing in their retellings of Scandinavian myths, *The Heroes of Asgard* (1857), and in their collection of fifteen didactic tales, *Little Wanderlin* (1865), featuring Mrs Calkill, a fairy who is ever threatening punishment with her nutcracker.

Just as it is hard for the modern reader to imagine children delighting in these impeccably moral tales, which were told by Annie Keary to her brother's three motherless children, it is equally difficult to realize that *Father Phim* (1879)—an intense story (like *Castle Blair*, set in Ireland) about hateful and bloody Catholic-Protestant feuding—was written for children, and that its heroine is only six. The youngest child of a clergyman, from a large industrial town in the north of England, Helen Neale has been sent to relatives in Galway to recuperate from smallpox. In the "large, dilapidated, untidy house" called Castle Connell, her uncle and grandfather leave their little charge "to her own devices". Helen's adored older brother Hilary used to call his once-chubby sister "Father Phelemy Phim Philip M'Quirk" as a pet name. In Ireland Helen meets her namesake, Father Phim, a jovial, rubicund, sympathetically drawn Catholic priest whom she befriends almost instinctively. His kindheartedness and ecumenical spirit are sorely needed in the County Galway described in the story. A friend of the Catholic peasants and a tolerated visitor at Castle Connell—whose Protestant bailiff, Nat O'Rhea, threatens to

dispossess the poor potato farmers on the estate—Father Phim attempts to act as a mediator between the two warring factions. When the priest is trodden under the hooves of the bailiff's horse while trying to separate shillelagh-brandishing Catholics and horse-mounted Protestants, the book's first crisis is precipitated (Chapter II).

While recovering from his near-fatal wounds, Father Phim enlists the help of his young English friend. The third and last chapter, reprinted below, shows how the plucky Helen manages to balance her loyalty to Catholic friends, like the orphaned O'More children, and her newly aroused charity for the crippled, ill-tempered daughter of the bailiff, Mary O'Rhea, and how she courageously averts a second crisis, the plotted "accidental" death of Mr O'Rhea.

Father Phim is as gripping and powerful today as it must have been for Victorian readers. It is thought that Keary did not have first-hand knowledge of Ireland; nevertheless her descriptions of the Galway countryside are accurate, and her use of dialect is believably sustained. The story is a curiosity, with its heroine, a child not yet at school, declaring that she is "too old to care for fairies now, since I have had the small-pox" and becoming involved in sectarian violence. Books as intense and unnerving as *Father Phim* (and *Castle Blair*) make today's reader wonder not only about the capacities of the children for whom such stories were intended, but about the remarkable liberty their authors enjoyed to involve young characters in such grim and serious matters as murder and religious hatred.

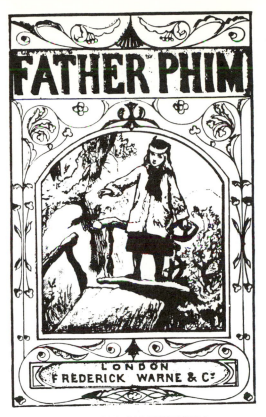

FATHER PHIM

LONDON
FREDERICK WARNE & C°

A WATCH ON THE HILL

The next day was market day at Kilseg, and not quite a common market day either. It was the day of the great annual cattle fair, which brought visitors to the town from all parts of the country, and changed the sleepy, idle little place for a few hours into a scene of great bustle and excitement. Shopkeepers smartened up their windows, and brought out their best wares; farmers, small and great, crowded in to sell their pigs and cows, and their wives followed, to spend the money their husbands received; peasants flocked from all sides to meet each other, and take part in a revel or faction-fight, as their inclination pointed; and beggars, blind pipers, wandering musicians, of every description, blocked up the narrow streets and crowded the roads that led to the town, from early morning till night.

Peace-loving people were always particularly sorry when anything occurred to excite the feelings of the peasantry about the time of the great annual gathering; and on this occasion there was such a strong feeling that disturbance was likely to arise, that grandpapa and Uncle Gerard, who were country magistrates, thought it their duty to remain in the town all day, that they might be at hand should difficulties arise. Helen saw them set out for Kilseg quite early in the morning, before she had breakfasted, Uncle Gerard driving grandpapa in the jaunting-car, and Mr O'Rhea riding by their side on Father Phim's enemy, the big-boned black horse. The other inhabitants of Castle Connell were not be-hindhand in finding reasons that proved their presence on the scene of action to be indispensable. Except Helen herself, there was hardly a per-son about the place who did not openly or secretly cherish an intention of just making his or her way out to the town some part of the day, to see what was going on. Old Mickey—as head outdoor man, and second only to the "masters" in his own opinion—took care to be the first to fol-low their example. Helen watched him drive off in style, in a very sham-bling cart, with two little pigs he intended to sell at the fair beside him; the stable-boys and helpers taking off their hats and shouting, and run-ning after him a good distance down the road. Mickey was quite in good spirits this morning with the prospect of the fair, and seemed, Helen thought, to have forgotten all about Terry and the doleful expectations he had confided to her the day before, when they were sitting on the corn-bin together.

Later on in the day, when Helen and Mrs O'Brien had had their early dinner together, the second best jaunting-car was brought round, to take Mrs O'Brien to the town. She was very sorry, she said, to leave Helen alone at home; but she durst not take her, because she did not ex-pect to be back till quite late at night, as she was to meet a married son and daughter at the fair, and spend the evening with them at a friend's house. Helen was secretly so glad to be left to her own devices, that she could hardly contain her joy; but she prudently waited till the last min-ute, when Mrs O'Brien was very much taken up in settling herself and her wraps and her parcels in the jaunting car, to whisper her petition. Might she go out for a walk this fine hot afternoon—just down to the vil-lage, to visit Father Phim? At the sound of the name Mrs O'Brien's busy face lengthened a little, and she began to blame herself vehemently for having forgotten in the bustle of the morning to send some one to in-quire after his Reverence, and carry him a mould of jelly and a bunch of grapes she had put ready in a basket. It was evidently a relief to her when Helen eagerly offered to be her messenger, and make satisfactory apologies for her negligence. Between satisfaction at having her con-science set at ease, and the bustle of departure, Mrs O'Brien quite forgot to lay any commands on Helen about taking one of the servants with her to the village and not staying out too long.

It was wonderful good luck, Helen thought, for now she was free to spend the afternoon just as she pleased. Before the jaunting-car was quite out of sight, she had her bonnet on, and had possessed herself of the basket. There were two ways of reaching the collection of cabins called Connell Town from Castle Connell. One by following the straight road to Kilseg for about half a mile, and then taking a cross road that brought you to the north end of the straggling village street. The other was a circuitous and much more varied route—across a corner of the shrubbery, through the door in the wall before described, over the stone-quarry bridge, down the Fairies' Dingle, through potato-patches and meadows, until you reached the south end of the irregular village, in which quarter of the place Father Phim resided. Any time before yes-terday Helen would have chosen the field route, as being the least public and the most interesting; but now she could not endure the thought of passing Terry's deserted cabin, and preferred the road. It was a pretty upward-sloping road, with shadows of great trees lying all across it, and making bands of light and dark to walk upon; and to-day it was very quiet, almost solemn. No voices reached Helen's ears from the fields on each side of the way, no men were to be seen leaning on their spades and looking over the hedges after her as she walked along. Everybody had gone away into Kilseg, and there was a sort of Sunday peace and stillness spread over everything. Something came over Helen that made her pause in her walk, put down her basket, and cover her eyes with her hand; she could not kneel down, but she said a little prayer in her heart—a prayer about the stillness and the Sunday-like peace, that it might not only stay spread out over the sunny country and in the bud-ding trees, but that God would put some of it in the hearts of the people who were just then crowding into the town, and keep them from grow-ing angry and hurting one another. She did not know that she was walking into any danger that day, but it was put into her heart to pray that she might be made brave, and helped to do some little thing that might make those who were hating and injuring each other, grow to be better friends.

When she took up her basket again, she walked at a pretty good pace, for she had altogether more than a mile of road to get over, besides hav-ing to walk quite through the village, which ran down one little hill and up another, before she reached Father Phim's house. He did not live in the proper priest's house near the chapel; that had been turned into an infant school since he came to the village. His cottage was the last of a row of untidy cabins, and only looked a little better cared for than its neighbours. The front entrance seemed never to be used, for there was a great hill of turf built up in the middle of the path that led to it; but Helen had not much difficulty in finding her way to the back of the house, and there the door stood wide open, and admitted her at once into a mud-floored kitchen, tenanted by three little pigs, an old sow, a flock of pi-geons, and some hens and chickens. She trod cautiously, not to disturb what seemed to be the rightful owners of the place. In a dark corner, at the end of the kitchen, was a steep flight of steps; she scrambled up, and knocked at a door at the top, and Father Phim's cheery voice bade her enter.

It was a bare, low, light room she came into; there were no curtains to the window, and the afternoon sunshine was pouring in and shining full upon a narrow settle bed that stood against the wall. Father Phim was lying there, stretched out very stiff, as if he were tied to the bed; his head was bound up with linen bandages, his eyes were shut when Helen first looked in, and there was a little frown of pain on his broad forehead; but he soon looked up, and smiled all over his face when he saw who it was standing in the doorway.

"Come in, come in, comrade," he cried, just in his usual way. "Here's a hand still for you to shake; 'you were hung at Ballytub, and I was hung at Ballytubber.'" Then, pointing to the bed, on which, to Helen's surprise, were ranged in a row a child's toy-horse, some little yellow apples, a penny trumpet, and a gilt gingerbread elephant, he added, "Come and see what a fine thing it is to be sick. Look at the illigant presents I have had this morning. Widow Rooney's children have been treated by their uncle to the fair, and what must the darlings do, the minute they get back, but bring their fairings as a present to me because I'm sick. It's little enough of pleasure they ever get, poor things; but, indeed, I could not rob them of the blessing of giving. So there my fairings lie, and I would not change them—with the warm love out of the children's hearts hanging round them—for so many heaps of gould. It's rich the children have made me this day."

Father Phim's blue eyes sparkled with pleasure, and his face seemed one great smile; but Helen could not smile in return: a hot feeling had come into her heart, and smarting painful tears into her eyes, as she looked at the disfigured face of her dear friend, and a sentence rushed to her lips that she felt she must speak out, or it would choke her.

"Father Phim, I hate—I do so hate—Mr O'Rhea! I know he did it on purpose—please don't stop me, I must say it; to see you lying there makes me feel so dreadful. I don't know how to hate Mr O'Rhea enough!"

The smile faded out of Father Phim's face, but he did not look angry, or even much surprised. "Aisy, brother, aisy! are you at that still?" he said; "just lift the water-jug from the stool there, and sit down by the bed-side, and we'll consider of it together."

Helen seated herself as he directed, and Father Phim took her little hand and spread it out on the bed, and laid his own over it; but he did not begin to talk all at once; he shut his eyes, and a frown of pain settled on his forehead.

"Well, mavourneen," he asked, after five minutes' silence, "well, what now?"

"I hate him just the same, Father," said Helen. "I hate him more and more, for he hates you; and I think he hates me a little, too, just because people say I am like you. I believe he made his horse kick you down, and that he felt glad when he saw how much you were hurt. I believe that of him, I hate him so."

"Well, darling, then that just fits in beautifully with something I am wanting to say to you. Sure, who would we do good to but them that hate us? And it's just yourself I've been counting on all day to do a kind turn for the O'Rheas."

Helen felt a little disconcerted: she knew Father Phim was right, but his precept did not fall in with her feelings at that moment.

"The O'Rheas don't want us to be kind to them," she said, discontentedly. "They have got it all their own way, they do what they please. They wanted Terry's potato-ground, and now they'll get it. They are as bad as Ahab and Jezebel. It will be like Naboth's vineyard to them. I should like to tell them so."

"Sure, I did not know you were a holy prophet, like Elijah, and could read what was in people's hearts," said Father Phim, drily.

Helen was silent for a minute, and then asked, in a humbler tone, "Father, do you know anything about Terry? Will he be taken and put in prison, do you think?"

"It's a bad business altogether, dear, and I fear we have not seen the last of it; but you may be easy about Terry himself. I have good hope that he has got clear out of the neighbourhood, among some friends of his on the other side of the bay. He has an uncle settled in America: if he gets down safe to the sea he'll do well enough; he's the boy to prosper in a new country, once he gets clear of ould ways and ould heart-burnings".

"But, O Father! are not you sorry to lose him? He always looked so bright and kind, and he knew everything about the country as no one else did—the sunny creeks by the Lough-side, and the path over the bog to where the rarest flowers grow, and the squirrels' nests in the woods, and the kingfishers' haunts by the river. No one will love them like he did, or find them out when he is gone. How can you like him to be banished, Father?"

"Well, dear, it's just breaking my heart it is, to see them go one after the other, them that I should have known how to keep together—my own children that belong to me, that are being plucked out of my hand. Helen, mavourneen, shall I tell you what is doing it?"

"I know well enough," cried Helen. "Mr O'Rhea."

"Nay, dear, he's not strong enough, nor any man. It is just that same thing you say you have got in your heart now. It is that that is turning, bit by bit, the fairest land in the world, that should be a Paradise of God, into a desert. Hatred and division, dear. One party set against another, hating and scorning, instead of being joined into one holy Church, one family of helpers. It is that that is the death of the land."

Father Phim hardly seemed to be thinking of Helen as he spoke the last sentences; his eyes closed again, and he went on murmuring words that she could not catch. She had sense enough to see that, in spite of the effort to appear cheerful he had made when she first came in, he was suffering much, and was in no state for conversation; so, after taking out the contents of the basket and giving him Mrs O'Brien's message, she rose to go. Father Phim showed her where to put the jelly—in a little recess in the wall, near the head of the bed, that had been fitted up with a shelf—"handy," Father Phim explained, for his old servant to put there all he was likely to want for the day, when she had to go out, or was too busy to think of him. He let Helen have the pleasure of washing the plate and cup and spoon that had served for his dinner, and of making his closet tidier than it had been for many a day. She was going to put the bunch of grapes beside the jelly, but Father Phim took it out of her hand, and put it back into the basket.

"It's an elegant compliment for you to take to Miss O'Rhea," he said; "for, dear, it's to her you're going after you leave me. It's there I'd be meself this minute if I could walk, and ain't you all the same as meself? That poor crippled thing is lying all alone, worrying herself, and not without rason, about her father, for fear he should never come back this night. Not a soul will come near her to speak a word to pass away the time. Judy O'More left the house the day of the fight, and has not been seen since; and none of the women from the village will come near the place because of what happened to me. It's only for you to speak a friendly word and show a kind face to her in the day of her sorrow, that I ask; and sure, Brother Phim, you'll not refuse me?"

Of course, Helen could not refuse him anything when he called her Brother Phim, and looked at her with that twinkle in his eyes, half comical and half serious. Besides, she was really sorry for Mary O'Rhea; and when, just as she was leaving the room, Father Phim put his hand on her head and said, softly, "The blessing of the holy saints and angels be about the child this night," Helen thought she could have walked a hundred miles to do his bidding.

When she reached the lower room, she was surprised to find how dark it was there; and though it was still light enough out of doors, the shadows had grown very long, and there was nothing to be seen of the sun but his last rays, spreading out like a fan behind the wooded ridge of the hills that skirted the western horizon. Father Phim had not been wrong to say *night*, for if she did not take care, night, or at all events twilight, would be upon her before she had finished her business. She did not retrace her steps. When she left Father Phim's cottage, she had only to cross a field and climb a little ridge, to gain the top of the hill that formed one side of the Fairies' Dingle. From thence her shortest road home was to descend the hill on its farther side, cross the dell, and then ascend the steep path up the opposite side of the ravine that led to O'Rhea Lodge. She determined to ask Miss O'Rhea to let her pass through their back garden, and so proceed over the stone-quarry bridge, and through the shrubbery, to the Castle. Most of the women, and not a few of the men, of Connell Town would have been afraid to cross the Fairies' Dingle just in the twilight, but Helen was not quite so silly as to dread a meeting with the "good people." She was glad to see that the last glow of the yellow fan had faded out of the western sky, and that the moon's full orb, showing faint and silvery, could be traced in the blue as she began to climb the O'Rheas' hill. She thought it would not frighten her, but delight her beyond measure, if by chance she were to spy a little wheesy green-coated man or woman sitting on a round stone or on a mushroom half-way up the steep. She was almost sorry when she reached Mr O'Rhea's door, and knocked loud on the smart brass knocker, without any adventure having befallen her. Mary O'Rhea opened the door herself. She gave a kind of frightened cry when she saw Helen standing on the step, and leant against the door-sill as if she could hardly support herself.

"What is the matter?" she asked, in a shrill, shaky voice. "Tell me at once; I had rather know at once. Father—"

"Oh! no, no," cried Helen, "nothing has happened. Please, it's only me, Helen Neale, and I've come to ask after you, and bring you a bunch of grapes."

"To ask after me! Sure it's mighty civil you're grown all at once, Miss Neale; but won't you walk in out of the mist?"

Miss O'Rhea gave a little short laugh as she finished speaking, that was almost as disagreeable as her father's sniff. It had not been one of her bad days; she had evidently been bustling about the house, doing the house-work better than all the women in Connell Town put together could have done it, for she had a great browny-white pinafore fastened about her strange figure, and a comical sort of nightcap, that stood up in a peak, on her head. As Helen followed her through the porch into the cottage parlour, she could not help thinking how like she was to the pictures of bad fairies in story-books, and how well she could imagine herself just now, the heroine of a fairy tale, in the act of being led by her angry left-out godmother to some mysterious place, where she would be shut up for a hundred years or so.

In spite of the short laugh, however, Miss O'Rhea evidently was pleased that Helen had called to see her. She made her sit down in the best parlour, and brought out a slice of dry seed-cake and a glass of cowslip wine, which she forced Helen to drink, to keep the cold out of her throat going home. She even seemed very sorry that she had nobody to send home with her, and she insisted on getting her crutches and limping down the back garden to let her out at the gate herself. As they walked down the garden she pointed out to Helen a little window at the back of the house, and a bright light burning in it. "I put it there whenever father is likely to come home after dark," she said, "to guide him across the bridge. He always leaves his horse in the Castle stables, and walks through the pleasure-grounds, and by the short cut over the bridge; and though I had a hand-rail put up, I am never quite easy about his crossing the quarry late after a market or fair dinner at Kilseg. He's as sober a man as any in Ireland not to be a teetotaller, is Mr O'Rhea, but it is not to be expected that it should be all the same with him, whether he has taken his drop of whisky after his dinner at Kilseg, or whether he is waiting for it till he gets home."

Helen quite understood that Miss O'Rhea was very anxious indeed, and that she had had a long time in which to brood over her fears, or she never would have told all this to her. It seemed to comfort her when Helen said she thought it would be a bright night, and that she felt almost certain Mr O'Rhea would come home early, though she knew she could have no reason for thinking so. It was twilight still when Helen left the garden, but the western sky was quite grey, and the silver moonlight showed on the grass-blades of the narrow strip of field Helen had still to climb before she reached the bridge. It was so pretty, she forgot to think about Terry and Judy, and their deserted garden.

Suddenly, just after she had heard Mary O'Rhea shut the door of the cottage behind, something whitish and large rose from behind a gorse-bush in front of her. It must have been waiting for her—waiting ready to spring. She stopped, and her heart beat quick and loud; she thought of Terry's tales about Leprechauns, headless witches, and other hill monsters sent to lure people into their underground prisons. She would have turned and run down the hill if there had been any spot within reach where she could have felt safe from such enemies, but the mysterious deeps of the hollow were more terrible to her than anything she could meet with on the open ground. The thing *had* a head—that was some comfort. It began to glide towards her, making wild gestures with its arms. It was only a girl after all, and before it came quite close Helen had recognized Judy O'More, but such a white-faced, wild-eyed, strange-looking Judy, that she hardly knew whether she was most frightened or most relieved at the discovery.

The instant she was within reach, Judy seized Helen's hand and began to drag her away from the edge of the quarry in a slanting direction down the hill towards Terry's garden. "It's this way you're going, Miss Helen, darlin'," she whispered in a hoarse voice; "this way, not across the bridge. I've been watching for you. Ochone! Ochone! what would have become of us at all if I had not been on the hill-side this weary night?"

Helen had presence of mind not to scream, for it occurred to her that Judy would probably not wish Mary O'Rhea to know she was so near, and that perhaps Terry himself might be waiting to speak to her in his garden. She tried to follow as quickly as she could, but she was not used to scramble along pathless hill-sides, and at last Judy fairly tucked her under her arm, and did not put her down on her feet till she had lifted her over the fence, and landed her in Terry's little enclosure.

"Oh, Judy, how you frightened me!" said Helen, as soon as she could speak.

"That'll be nothing, dear, to the fright it gave me whin I saw ye coming down the opposite hill, and comprehended it was crossing the bridge ye were maning. I shake and trimble yet wid the thoughts of it."

And indeed Judy was shaking and trembling; Helen could see, even by the moonlight, how deadly pale her cheeks were, and how her teeth chattered.

"But why should you be frightened, Judy? and why have you brought me here instead of letting me go home by the bridge?" Helen asked.

The question seemed to rouse Judy. "Shure, darlin', it's home, safe at home, I want ye to be. Ye must not stay here a minute, nor I either. There's them whose anger I dare not face, who would be bitter angry wid me for watching here this night, and knowing what I know. Spy and informer would be the best names they'd give me, but the thought of you forced me to come."

"I don't understand," said Helen.

"An' no need ye should, thin. Shure no harm's done, but just that ye've walked round the stone-quarry instead of across it. 'Twas to satisfy a bit of a shuperstition I had meself, dear. Now I'll just take ye across this plank—it's safe though there is no hand-rail to it—and then we'll climb the hill agin by these steps that'll land ye close to the shrubbery wall, beyant the quarry where the fence is low enough to climb; and when I see ye safe in the wood I'll be satisfied."

If Helen had wanted to ask any more questions, Judy did not give her time; she hurried her through the garden and up another side of the hill with such breathless speed as left Helen no inclination for talking. "Now, mavourneen, I must go and hurry away," she said, when she had helped Helen over the low wall into the pine plantation. "Run right home, and think no more of my taking the fancy to drag ye through the old potato-garden oncet more—or stay, ye are cute, Miss Helen dear, and faithful; I'll lave a word wid ye for yer own heart, Acushla, and for Father Phim. If ye hear anything tomorrow to trouble ye, be aisy; and mind what I tell ye, that neither Terry nor any of the Connell boys were in it at all. And now I'm gone."

Judy's head disappeared on the other side of the wall before Helen had sufficiently recovered her surprise to ask for an explanation of her last sentence. The race round the gravel-pit had after all taken but a few minutes. Helen could still find her way easily enough along the well-known path, though it was much darker in the wood than on the hill. She began to walk homewards, not quickly, but slowly, as if something were dragging back her steps. At first she hardly knew what it was, and then all at once she stood still. A thrill seemed to pass through her as if a flash of light had come into her mind, making a terrible thought, which she had not known to be there before, suddenly clear and certain. There was something wrong about the bridge, that was why Judy had dragged her away from it. Judy had saved her, but who would save Mr O'Rhea? Helen did not pause to think what was best to be done. The impulse was on her to go to the place of peril and watch, and drag away from it any one who came near, as Judy had dragged her. There were several paths through the wood. Mr O'Rhea was probably coming along one of them now; there was no time to be lost. She turned, and ran back to the door in the wall; the key—her key—was in the lock; she turned it, and came out on to the open hill-side again: the twilight had deepened, but the moon and the stars that studded the sky afforded a pale shimmering light. There lay the sloping strip of field before her, and the bridge looking so safe and solid, that for a minute Helen thought her alarm was all nonsense, and that she had better turn round and run quickly home. No: why had Judy trembled so? why had her face been so white? Excitement made Helen for the moment very brave; she felt that she must know the truth, and determined to look closer: she crossed the green, and stood at the head of the bridge. Then she put her hand on the rail and gave it a little push. It moved, as the bridge rail had never moved before—it seemed to be swaying backwards and forwards. She pushed again a little more strongly, she gave quite a hard push. The whole thing reeled; she could hardly believe her eyesight—was it the uncertain light that bewildered her? No: there was a loud horrible sounding crash, and a splash far below in the bottom of the pit; for a moment she could do nothing but listen to that. When the din had died in her ears, and the mist left her eyes, so that she could look steadily again, she perceived that the bridge rail was gone; it had fallen backwards into the chasm, and carried a portion of the middle of the bridge with it. The remaining parts of the severed plank were trembling and swaying, ready to follow. Some treacherous hand had sawn the plank asunder, and left it and the broken rail slightly linked together, so as to form a carefully prepared pitfall, which must precipitate the first person who attempted to cross the chasm to certain death in the water below.

Helen stood for some time staring after the rail and the plank, as if she thought they were alive, and would cry out for help from the depth beneath; then she sank down on the grass by the edge of the quarry, sick and trembling with fright, and feeling as if she never could have strength to drag herself up again. After a little while, through the tumult of her mind, two sentences came to her that seemed to stand out in letters of light, and calm and control the surging horror within her. First came the remembrance of Father Phim's farewell, "The blessing of the holy saints and angels be about the child to-night." It was very nearly night now; it seemed quite a long time since Father Phim had said that. She had been in great danger herself, and now she had to stand between some one else and danger. She could not do it alone, but she knew she was not alone. She lifted up her head; it was all still calm moonlight. Oh, if God would only open her eyes as He had opened the eyes of Elisha's servant at Dothan, and let her see her helpers! She was not even a prophet's servant to have such grace done her, but she was a Christian child. What did it matter not seeing or knowing exactly how she was to be helped? did she not know she was cared for, and that help sufficient to her utmost need was close at hand?

The second sentence that came to calm her was Judy's assurance—"Be aisy, and mind what I tell ye; neither Terry nor any of the Connell boys are in it." It was indeed a relief to be sure that the man who had done this cruel treacherous deed was not one of the people who had smiled pleasant smiles and spoken flattering words to her since she came here. Judy was very much to blame, but then she had said she was afraid. At that moment Helen felt so near being afraid herself, and knew so well what a cruel thing cowardice is, that she was less surprised at Judy's conduct than she would have been a little time before. It was only by clinging to a strength not her own that she could keep back the cold fear at her heart that might have made her cruel too.

By the time these thoughts had passed through her mind, she had recovered herself enough to get up from the grass and set herself to consider quietly what was really best to be done. Across the chasm she could see the little light that Miss O'Rhea had put to guide her father, shining clearly. It must be already past his usual hour for returning home. There would not be time for her to run to the house and try to speak to him in the stable-yard as he was dismounting from his horse; he was most likely on his way from the Castle to his own home now, and she might take a different path and miss him. Besides, even supposing there had been time for her to meet him at the Castle, she was not quite sure whether, in the absence of old Mickey and Mrs O'Brien, there was anyone among the servants she could quite trust to help her in her purpose of saving Mr O'Rhea. She was sorry to think it, but she believed that just at that moment there was no one willing to stand between that stern hard old man and danger, but just her weak frightened self, and that the best way to do it would be to stay near the place of peril, with her eyes fixed upon it, ready to warn him away. There was a round white stone—one of the stones that Judy believed the "good people" sat upon—close to the shrubbery door. Helen established herself on it with her face towards the door, so that it would be impossible for any one to pass through without her being aware of it. Would Mr O'Rhea take her for a Leprechaun, she wondered, when he first caught sight of her? For the first minute or two she was quite absorbed in watching for steps approaching from the wood. Now he was coming, now she heard his footfalls—but no; many noises came—for woods, however solitary, are not silent places—but not the sounds she was listening for. The minutes slipped away. Dark clouds began to rise from the eastern horizon, and float in thick masses up the sky, hiding the moon, and parting again to give Helen a glimpse of its silver shield. When the moon and stars were hidden, the distant landscape and even the near view of the green strip of hill-side and the broken bridge, faded from Helen's eyes into an indistinguishable dusky sea, that seemed to swallow her up. She thought of one night, now more than a year ago, when she had sat alone in Hilary's garret at home, and seen the light fade out of the little familiar room, and the darkness come in. That had been only a little strip of darkness; she wondered how she could have felt frightened then. This was the great night itself she saw, walking with solemn steps out of the distant dark woods, over the wide fields and misty lake, to wrap her in his arms. It was more awful, but then it was beautiful too—so beautiful, that Helen almost forgot to be afraid. Thicker and thicker the clusters of stars came in the clear spaces of the sky between the cloud-rifts; here a little eye of light, there a little eye of light, all looking down kindly on her, and sending out helpful rays to make the outline of the hill clear. The sky was most free from clouds just above Terry's garden, and there hung the golden wheels and horses of Charles's Wain, a friendly sign-post, pointing her way. She liked to see it, because Hilary had pointed out Charles's Wain so often from the nursery window at home. Oh, if Hilary could only come to the other side of the door now, and sing to her as he had done that other night when she had had to be brave about being alone! The wish grew so very strong in poor Helen's mind, that she had to squeeze her hand very tight over her eyes to keep herself from crying. It would never do to cry, and perhaps not be able to speak clearly and see clearly when Mr O'Rhea came. The thought of Hilary ought to make her brave, for would not he like her to be brave? She remembered how anxious she had been to think she had saved Hilary's life by not letting him come into the garret that day; and how Miss Thornton had said that perhaps the little trial of staying alone in the dark had been sent to prepare her for some more important work that might be given her to do. It seemed to have come now really and truly—the thing Helen had wished for so very much, the great honour of being permitted to help to save a person's life.

Not a person she loved, or who loved her; some one who even disliked her a little. "Who would we do good to but them that hate us?" Father Phim had said. Helen quite understood that now. Yes, it was best, it was being allowed to do it for Jesus Christ Himself. Wonder and thankfulness and joy rose so high in Helen's heart, that they left no room any longer for any touch of fear. She began to sing "Glory to Thee, my God, this night." Her voice was not nearly so strong or so sweet as Hilary's, and it was just then even rather more husky than usual; but the words sounded sweet to her through the darkness, and before she got to the end of the second verse, a night thrush on a tree near began to trill out an accompaniment to the hymn. She could not certainly have had such a fellow-songster as that in the old garret at home. The thrush stopped suddenly in the middle of a trill. Helen held her breath too. Yes, it was no mistake now,—there were steps approaching the door; uneven, stumbling steps, not like Mr O'Rhea's usual even tread. Some one fumbled at the latch of the door, twisting and turning the key as if he did not quite know how to open it. Helen jumped up from the stone, and stood ready. At last the door was pushed open, and Mr O'Rhea came out.

Helen never could remember afterwards exactly what she said and did at that moment. It was certainly Mr O'Rhea, but it was not quite the Mr O'Rhea she was used to see. She discovered that even by the moonlight. His head hung down in a strange way, and his hand, which she seized and held fast, in hers, felt hot and powerless. He listened while she spoke, without seeming quite to understand what she said, and he did not appear to be as much surprised at her being there and coming up to him as she had expected. Luckily, however, though he was too sleepy or stupid to comprehend her explanation about the bridge being unsafe to cross, he was more willing to let her lead him home than she had dared to hope he would be. He said he must get home to his poor lass, and Miss Helen might take him round by the steep side of the hill if she pleased, for he could walk quite as steadily now as when he set off in the morning. He would like his poor lass to see how steadily he could walk. Helen thought it rather fortunate that there were no windows in the cottage looking on to the steep side of the hill, for, whether it was the suddenness of the slope in that direction, or her own nervous haste in dragging him along, certainly Mr O'Rhea did not walk steadily. It was more of a roll and stumble than a walk down the hill-side. But when he fell he always managed to pick himself up again without seeming at all hurt; and Helen kept her hold on his hand and directed his steps.

The fence of Terry's garden was broken in so many places, that Helen had no difficulty in making her way through it, and coming out at last on to the smooth path at the bottom of the valley, which wound up again to the front entrance of O'Rhea Lodge. She wondered Mr O'Rhea did not ask her some questions, now they were able to walk quietly side by side along a safe path; but it was a relief to find that he was too much occupied in muttering and smiling to himself, to notice who was leading him. It was Helen who opened the little gate of the front garden at last, and lifted the smart brass knocker of the door. Miss O'Rhea again came to the door; and before she had time to speak a word or utter an exclamation of surprise, Helen had drawn Mr O'Rhea within the house, and put the hand of his she was holding into his daughter's.

She did not speak even then. She could not think of a word to say; but there was light enough in the hall for her to see Mary O'Rhea's face, and for a minute Mary and she stood in silence looking at one another. Helen could not have told anyone what it was she saw in Mary's eyes during that minute, but it was something that made her determine never again to believe that Mary O'Rhea had a black heart. A black heart could not have looked so, out of any eyes. Helen turned to go away, when she saw that Miss O'Rhea was leading her father upstairs; but before she reached the gate of the front garden, she heard limping steps behind her, and saw that Miss O'Rhea was running after her, with a great shawl in one hand, and a lighted horn lantern in the other. Even then Mary did not speak; she knelt down on the gravel walk, and wrapt the shawl well over Helen's chest, and knotted it behind; then she got up, and put the lantern into her hand; her face came quite close to Helen's as she did this—it was not a kiss, it would have been too absurd to think of Miss O'Rhea giving any one a kiss, but certainly her cheek touched Helen's, and Helen found it was all wet with tears, the tears she had been shedding during her anxious lonely watch for her father's return that night. It did not take Helen long to make her way, for the third time, across Terry's potato-ground, up the steep side of the hill, and round the stone-quarry; for just as she left the lodge gate the clouds parted again, and the moon shone so brightly, that Miss O'Rhea's lantern was of no use till she got into the wood; there it saved her from taking a wrong path, or knocking her head against the branches of the trees.

After all, the time had not been so very long. It seemed to her as if she had been watching on the hill half the night; but, in reality, the great clock in the stable-yard at the Castle was only striking ten, as she slipped back into the house by the kitchen entrance, so muffled up in Miss O'Rhea's plaid shawl, that none of the servants observed who she was, as she passed through the kitchen and up the back stairs. Mrs O'Brien had just, the moment before, driven up to the front door, after having spent a merry evening with her friends. As Helen ran across the passage to her bed-room, she heard Mrs O'Brien's voice in conversation with the parlour-maid in the entrance hall. "I suppose, Molly," Mrs O'Brien was saying, "that you gave Miss Helen the cake and preserve with her tea, that I put out for her; and that you sent her to bed at her usual hour?" Molly's answer seemed to come out rather hesitatingly, and sounded very surprising to Helen. "Sure, and I did lay her out an illigant tay, all to herself, in the little drawing-room; and where would she be but in bed at this time of night?" Molly had evidently been out pleasure-seeking, like her betters, and had forgotten all about her charge. Helen perceived that if she could only get quickly into bed, before Mrs O'Brien had taken off her wraps and come to look after her, she might avoid the necessity of answering any bewildering questions that night. She hid Miss O'Rhea's shawl and lantern in a corner of the room, undressed hurriedly, and was just laying her head on the pillow when Mrs O'Brien looked in. The kind woman, seeing that she was wide awake, came up to the bed-side to tuck her in, and gave her her nightly kiss. "I shall not tell you anything to-night about the fine fairing I have brought for you," she said, "for you ought to have been asleep long ago; and, my dear, how was it you ate so little supper? I looked into the drawing-room just now, and you have not even cut the cake I made for you; and it is your own kind of cake, Helen, the kind you like best: how was it, dear?"

Helen was glad that she could give a true answer, without saying more than she wished to say at the present.

"I forgot all about supper," she said; "but, dear Mrs O'Brien, if you would bring me the cake now, I am very hungry."

Only at Castle Connell would such a thing have been allowed, that a little girl, who had been lately ill, should sit up to eat rich cake in bed, at ten o'clock at night; but people did things at Castle Connell without taking any harm, that could not be done with impunity in any other part of the world. Helen sat on the edge of her bed, wrapped in Mrs O'Brien's cloak, and ate cake and drank wine, and heard a good deal of news about the fair, where all enjoyed themselves with great good humour; and then she lay down again, and was tucked in, and kissed, and pitied for her lonely day, by Mrs O'Brien.

She was so thoroughly wearied out, that she fell asleep quickly; but the strange events of the day were mixed up painfully in her dreams. All night long she seemed to be walking along the dizzy edge of a dark chasm, hearing noises of falling far down; or she dreamed of being prevented from clutching at hands stretched out to save her by feeling Mary O'Rhea's tear-wet face pressed so closely against hers as almost to suffocate her. The horrors of the night were far more painful than anything she had suffered during the evening; but very great joy—joy of a kind worth having—seldom comes without previous labour and pain; and in the morning a joy came to Helen that made up for all. She woke out of a nightmare struggle just as the morning was beginning to dawn, and crept out of bed, to get rid of all her uncomfortable visions by looking out of the window. The window of her sleeping-room, which was in a turret of the Castle, looked to the east, and commanded a wide view over the tops of the shrubbery trees across the dingle to the Lough, out of whose waters the sun was just rising. Helen saw the first golden streak dart up the sky, and watched how the grey mist of twilight was lifted from the joyful fields, how the trees shook themselves as if they were waking up out of sleep, into fresh, happy life, and heard the birds in the shrubbery tune their little pipes, and then burst out into a chorus of joyful welcome to the sun.

A thought came into her mind as she looked and listened, which seemed like the rising of a sun of joy which would make her heart sing for ever. The sun might rise and shine, the fields might smile, the birds did right to sing—no cruel deed had been done in their neighbourhood last night, that would have made the light and song a weariness to sorrowful eyes, a reproach to guilty ears. She had been allowed to prevent it: the glory and joy of the day seemed like a present given from God's hands to her. She knelt down at the window to thank Him. She had often thought it must have been beautiful for Daniel to say his prayers at a window, and this Castle Connell window seemed just the sort of place suitable to kneel and pray in.

She crept back to bed when her prayer was ended, and slept comfortably, without any more dreams, till Molly came to call her. At breakfast, of course, every one was talking about the wonderful escape Mr O'Rhea had had the night before, and saying what a miracle it was that he should have chosen that particular night to go home by the longest route, and thus avoided the bridge over the chasm, which, as was plainly seen by the light of morning, had been left in such a condition, that any one attempting to cross it must have been precipitated into the pit beneath, and been killed. There were different opinions expressed as to how Mr O'Rhea had avoided the danger: had he walked home through the village? or if not, what had induced him to scramble down the steep side of the hill? He had certainly not received any warning of danger—or at least, he could not recollect having had his suspicion roused in any way. Uncle Gerard, who had seen Mr O'Rhea early in the morning, said, laughingly, that he seemed to be a little confused about the events of the previous evening, and could not give a clear account of himself after he had left Kilseg. The only thing quite evident was, that he had had a miraculous escape of breaking his neck, and that the important question was, to find out and punish the villains who had planned such a horrible revenge for the grudges they fancied against him.

Helen kept silence while the conversation went on. She had made up her mind not to say anything unless she was asked, for fear of throwing suspicion on Judy; and though, as the day went on, all the household talked of the miracle of Mr ORhea's escape, it never occurred to any one that the fact of little Helen Neale having forgotten to eat her supper last night could have had anything to do with it.

Helen held to her resolution of keeping her own counsel as long as she remained at Castle Connell; but, though she never exchanged a word about the events of that memorable night with any one, she knew that there were two people in the neighbourhood who understood the true history of Mr O'Rhea's adventure, as well as she herself did.

Father Phim was one. He never once spoke on the subject to Helen: perhaps he had gained his information from a source that bound him not to reveal it; but Helen was nearly sure he was perfectly well aware of the part she had acted in saving Mr O'Rhea from the peril that threatened him. She knew that he knew, by the tone of his voice and the look on his face, when he put his hands on her head and blessed her, the first time she saw him after the Kilseg fair night; and also by a peculiar expression that would come on his face often afterwards, when, in the midst of a conversation on quite other matters, he would pause suddenly, to chuck her under the chin and say, in a half jocular, half affectionate tone, "So, Brother Phim, you hate Mr O'Rhea?"

Miss O'Rhea was the second person who understood the true state of the case, but she preserved an equally strict silence. For a little while, Helen expected every time they were alone together that she would begin to speak openly about what they both knew; but she never did. The only change it made in her was, that, after that night, she took a fancy to limp up the road, once or twice a week, to Castle Connell, and that, when she was there, she always insisted on seeing Helen. Sometimes she would sit in the old school-room, for an hour or two at a time, watching her while she wrote copies, and practised scales on the old piano. She rarely entered into any conversation, but when she did talk, it was always about her father she spoke. "Father's a very sober man not to be a teetotaller," she would often take occasion to say, "though I don't deny that it's against my will that he dines on market days before he leaves Kilseg."

She always fixed her eyes on Helen as she said this; and the look Helen had seen on that night, the look out of a sore heart, would come again into her eyes. Helen understood that it was an appeal to her not to say a word that would lower her father, in her own opinion or in that of others.

When Helen left Castle Connell almost every one about the place gave her a present. Mary O'Rhea's was a large orange and black shawl, that she had knitted herself.

Helen's brothers and sisters abused it when she got home, as the very ugliest thing they had ever seen in their lives; but she valued it more than any other of her possessions—except, perhaps, a letter that reached her two or three months after her return to England. The letter was from Judy O'More, and told how she and Terry, and two Kilseg boys, who had been accused of taking an active part in the riot on the day the police sergeant was killed, had, thanks to Father Phim, had their passage paid out to America in an emigrant ship; how they had arrived safely in their new country, and got into good work quickly, and were doing well. At the end of the letter was a postscript, that puzzled every one but Helen. It ran thus:—

P.S.—*I'll tell you the truth, Miss Helen darlin, and no lie—as why would we to you, the vein of our hearts as ye are? It was him, Murdoch Clancy—my own bachelor, the boy that is going to marry me to-morrow—that did the thing you know of on the Fairies' Hill, that May night we'll never forget, you and I. Don't go to think that it is any but the best heart in the world that is in him. 'Twas the bitter black anger for the wrong done Terry and me, that drove him mad that night. Father Phim—may it be granted to us all to see him in glory!—scoulded him into his right sinses before we sailed, and it's on our bended knees this day we thank you—he and I—for how it turned out, so that no blood-guilt will follow us, to keep us back from thriving in this new blessed country, that, they tell us, God made on purpose for the poor.''*

KENNETH GRAHAME (1859-1932)
"Exit Tyrannus" from *The Golden Age* (1895)

The son of a barrister, Kenneth Grahame was born in Edinburgh. After the death of his mother, when he was only five, he was raised—along with his brothers and a sister—by a stern grandparent and a succession of parsimonious aunts and uncles in Berkshire, Eng. At the age of eighteen, after leaving St Edward's School, Oxford, Grahame was not sent to university but instead took a position in the Bank of England. He rose quickly, becoming one of the youngest Secretaries in the Bank's history. He also found time to write a collection of personal essays called *Pagan Papers* (1893), at the back of which were tucked the first six stories—miniature pictures of childhood—that would eventually be part of *The Golden Age* (1895).

Because Grahame was gifted with a remarkable ability to recall and vivify his own pleasures and disappointments as a child, the stories in *The Golden Age* are in part an urbane sentimentalist's recollections and in part engaging tales about five small and lively individuals. Edward, Selina, Harold, Charlotte, and the boy-narrator are a family of children living under the yoke of aunts and uncles whom they call "Olympians"; they view these "dragonish" elders as merely "our betters by a trick of chance". The Olympians are an infuriating, callous, fickle lot: uncles are often the prey of inexplicable whims, while aunts are afflicted with the dreaded "antimacassar taint". Although there are some sympathetic adults—like Uncle William ("A White-washed Uncle"), a friendly doctor ("Alarums and Excursions"), a scholarly clergyman ("A Harvesting"), and an artist ("The Roman Road")—none of whom are given to Olympian palaver, most of the predicaments in all seventeen stories stress the gap between child and adult. In "Exit Tyrannus", however, there is an unexpected turn: the children suddenly evince an emotional attachment to the departing governess Miss Smedley, formerly described as the "familiar scourge" and the "cloud-compeller".

Grahame's style here, and in the eight stories of *Dream Days* (1898), is descriptively rich, witty, and elegant. Although some readers have surmised that his literary extravagance and pensive tone are of no interest to children, his powers of portraying the nuances of childhood's emotions and his well-rounded characters cannot help but engage their attention—perhaps to the exclusion of everything else.

The literary talents displayed in these two books of stories later became infused with genius when Grahame wrote *The Wind in the Willows* (1908) for the eighth birthday of his son Alastair.

EXIT TYRANNUS

The eventful day had arrived at last, the day which, when first named, had seemed—like all golden dates that promise anything definite—so immeasurably remote. When it was first announced, a fortnight before, that Miss Smedley was really going, the resultant ecstasies had occupied a full week, during which we blindly revelled in the contemplation and discussion of her past tyrannies, crimes, malignities; in recalling to each other this or that insult, dishonour, or physical assault, sullenly endured at a time when deliverance was not even a small star on the horizon: and in mapping out the shining days to come, with special new troubles of their own, no doubt—since this is but a work-a-day world!—but at least free from one familiar scourge. The time that remained had been taken up by the planning of practical expressions of the popular sentiment. Under Edward's masterly direction, arrangements had been made for a flag to be run up over the hen-house at the very moment when the fly, with Miss Smedley's boxes on top and the grim oppressor herself inside, began to move off down the drive. Three brass cannons, set on the brow of the sunk-fence, were to proclaim our deathless sentiments in the ears of the retreating foe; the dogs were to wear ribbons; and later—but this depended on our powers of evasiveness and dissimulation—there might be a small bonfire, with a cracker or two if the public funds could bear the unwonted strain.

I was awakened by Harold digging me in the ribs, and "She's going to-day!" was the morning hymn that scattered the clouds of sleep. Strange to say, it was with no corresponding jubilation of spirits that I slowly realised the momentous fact. Indeed, as I dressed, a dull disagreeable feeling that I could not define grew up in me—something like a physical bruise. Harold was evidently feeling it too, for after repeating "She's going to-day!" in a tone more befitting the Litany, he looked hard in my face for direction as to how the situation was to be taken. But I crossly bade him look sharp and say his prayers and not bother me. What could this gloom portend, that on a day of days like the present seemed to hang my heavens with black?

Down at last and out in the sun, we found Edward before us, swinging on a gate and chanting a farm-yard ditty in which all the beasts appear in due order, jargoning in their several tongues, and every verse begins with the couplet:

> "Now, my lads, come with me,
> Out in the morning early!"

The fateful exodus of the day had evidently slipped his memory entirely. I touched him on the shoulder. "She's going to-day!" I said. Edward's carol subsided like a water-tap turned off. "So she is!" he replied, and got down at once off the gate. And we returned to the house without another word.

At breakfast Miss Smedley behaved in a most mean and uncalled-for manner. The right divine of governesses to govern wrong includes no right to cry. In thus usurping the prerogative of their victims they ignore the rules of the ring, and hit below the belt. Charlotte was crying, of course; but that counted for nothing. Charlotte even cried when the pigs' noses were ringed in due season; thereby evoking the cheery contempt of the operators, who asserted they liked it, and doubtless knew. But when the cloud-compeller, her bolts laid aside, resorted to tears, mutinous humanity had a right to feel aggrieved, and think itself placed in a false and difficult position. What would the Romans have done, supposing Hannibal had cried? History has not even considered the possibility. Rules and precedents should be strictly observed on both sides. When they are violated, the other party is justified in feeling injured.

There were no lessons that morning, naturally—another grievance! The fitness of things required that we should have struggled to the last in a confused medley of moods and tenses, and parted for ever, flushed with hatred, over the dismembered corpse of the multiplication table. But this thing was not to be; and I was free to stroll by myself through the garden, and combat, as best I might, this growing feeling of depression. It was a wrong system altogether, I thought, this going of people one had got used to. Things ought always to continue as they had been. Change there must be, of course; pigs, for instance, came and went with disturbing frequency—

> "Fired their ringing shot and passed,
> Hotly charged and sank at last"—

but Nature had ordered it so, and in requital had provided for rapid successors. Did you come to love a pig, and he was taken from you, grief was quickly assuaged in the delight of selection from the new litter. But now, when it was no question of a peerless pig, but only of a governess, Nature seemed helpless, and the future held no litter of oblivion. Things might be better, or they might be worse, but they would never be the same; and the innate conservatism of youth asks neither poverty nor riches, but only immunity from change.

Edward slouched up alongside of me presently, with a hangdog look on him, as if he had been caught stealing jam. "What a lark it'll be when she's really gone!" he observed, with a swagger obviously assumed.

"Grand fun!" I replied dolorously; and conversation flagged.

We reached the hen-house, and contemplated the banner of freedom lying ready to flaunt the breezes at the supreme moment.

"Shall you run it up," I asked, "when the fly starts, or—or wait a little till it's out of sight?"

Edward gazed round him dubiously. "We're going to have some rain, I think," he said; "and—and it's a new flag. It would be a pity to spoil it. P'raps I won't run it up at all."

Harold came round the corner like a bison pursued by Indians. "I've polished up the cannons," he cried, "and they look grand! Mayn't I load 'em now?"

"You leave 'em alone," said Edward severely, "or you'll be blowing yourself up" (consideration for others was not usually Edward's strong point). "Don't touch the gunpowder till you're told, or you'll get your head smacked."

Harold fell behind, limp, squashed, obedient. "She wants me to write to her," he began presently. "Says she doesn't mind the spelling, if I'll only write. Fancy her saying that!"

"O, shut up, will you?" said Edward savagely; and once more we were silent, with only our thoughts for sorry company.

"Let's go off to the copse," I suggested timidly, feeling that something had to be done to relieve the tension, "and cut more new bows and arrows."

"She gave me a knife my last birthday," said Edward moodily, never budging. "It wasn't much of a knife—but I wish I hadn't lost it!"

"When my legs used to ache," I said, "she sat up half the night, rubbing stuff on them. I forgot all about that till this morning."

"There's the fly!" cried Harold suddenly. "I can hear it scrunching on the gravel."

Then for the first time we turned and stared each other in the face.

The fly and its contents had finally disappeared through the gate, the rumble of its wheels had died away. Yet no flag floated defiantly in the sun, no cannons proclaimed the passing of a dynasty. From out the frosted cake of our existence Fate had cut an irreplaceable segment: turn which way we would, the void was present. We sneaked off in different directions, mutually undesirous of company; and it seemed borne in upon me that I ought to go and dig my garden right over, from end to end. It didn't actually want digging; on the other hand no amount of digging could affect it, for good or for evil; so I worked steadily, strenuously, under the hot sun, stifling thought in action. At the end of an hour or so, I was joined by Edward.

"I've been chopping up wood," he explained, in a guilty sort of way, though nobody had called on him to account for his doings.

"What for?" I inquired stupidly. "There's piles and piles of it chopped up already."

"I know," said Edward, "but there's no harm in having a bit over. You never can tell what may happen. But what have you been doing all this digging for?"

"You said it was going to rain," I explained hastily. "So I thought I'd get the digging done before it came. Good gardeners always tell you that's the right thing to do."

"It did look like rain at one time," Edward admitted; "but it's passed off now. Very queer weather we're having. I suppose that's why I've felt so funny all day."

"Yes, I suppose it's the weather," I replied. "*I've* been feeling funny too."

The weather had nothing to do with it, as we well knew. But we would both have died rather than admit the real reason.

6. MANLY BOYS AND ROSY GIRLS: SCHOOL STORIES

And we all praise famous men—
Ancients of the College;
For they taught us common sense—
Tried to teach us common sense—
Truth and God's own Common Sense,
Which is more than knowledge!
—Rudyard Kipling, Stalky & Co. *(1899)*

In contrast to the liberties enjoyed by nursery-age children, middle-class Victorian students were expected to conform to rigorous codes of behaviour, both by their academic elders and by their fellow students. Furthermore, their submission to the hierarchical and monitored world of the public school in their formative years inevitably had a transforming and determining effect on their lives.

The classroom and dormitory, and school life in general, offered fiction writers an ideal platform from which to lecture on the purposes of education—and most did not neglect this opportunity—but the best school stories, like all outstanding works of Golden Age children's literature, did not preach. Instead they presented expertly de-tailed scenes of school life—portraying such basic human states as fear, suffering, joy, love, and euphoria and filled with such schoolboy ingredients as close friendships, bullies, pranks, dormitory rituals, and competitive sports—as a means of conveying certain educational principles. Always based on their authors' recollections, these stories were written by people who really believed in public schools; and while some reflected criticism of them, all strongly endorsed their value(s).

The most representative and best-known school story is *Tom Brown's Schooldays* (1857), in which Thomas Hughes fondly recalls his own school days at Rugby. Although Hughes' stress on the salutary effects of athletics would not have won Dr

Arnold's approval, his portrayal of Tom's passage from an insecure, inexperienced child to a well-rounded gentleman and leader exemplifies the objective of the school. By contrast, Frederic Farrar's Roslyn School, in *Eric; or, Little by Little* (1858), is *not* praiseworthy. In fact it is the undoing of the naive hero. Based on memories of his own early days at King William's College on the Isle of Man, Roslyn is alarmingly corrupt. In spite of the efforts of some dedicated masters, Farrar's boy-hero falls "little by little" into dissolute ways, finally leaving Roslyn in disgrace. This cautionary school story is unique for its Evangelical fervour. Though it was laughed at by schoolboys, and parodied by Rudyard Kipling (in *Stalky & Co.*), it was widely read and greatly admired by thousands of chapel-going boys, who could not attend public school, and by adults, who enjoyed its pious fantasy of school life. *Stalky & Co.* (1899), in which Kipling re-creates a hearty trio of classmates (of which he was one) at the United Services College in North Devon, was deliberately intended to ridicule the pieties of *Eric*. When Stalky receives a copy of Farrar's book from his maiden aunt, he reads passages aloud to his friends and provokes much laughter. In this secular memoir of school life Beetle, M'Turk, and Stalky collaborate as the acknowledged triumvirs of the student body; far from being crushed by their school, these three resilient boys leave their mark on it.

Although there were also schools for girls in Victorian England, stories that catered for the schoolgirl market did not appear with any regularity until the early twentieth century. As well as being more restrained and partial to more refined behaviour than most of the boys' stories, they laid particular stress on the training of young women to fill clearly defined feminine roles. Socialization, rather than educa-

tion in the strict sense, was the goal of the Welsh boarding school described in *The Third Class at Miss Kaye's* (1908) by Angela Brazil, the leading writer of schoolgirl fiction. Her central character is a selfish and demanding only child, Sylvia Lindsay, who, under the prudent guidance of Miss Kaye, and thanks to new friends, becomes a model schoolgirl. This transformation takes place amidst rivalries, tame adventures, and with the use of much schoolgirl slang—a Brazil specialty. In Jean Webster's epistolary novel, *Daddy-Long-Legs* (1912), the Massachusetts college to which the orphan Jerusha Abbott is sent by an unknown benefactor is profitable in a romantic sense. After the bleakness of the John Grier Orphan Home, Judy's college days are focused on her curiousity about, and growing attachment to, the man who has paid for the education of his future wife.

Of special Canadian interest in the school-story vein—though far removed from the conventions of the British public-school novel—is Ralph Connor's *Glengarry School Days* (1902), in which the school is a one-room log cabin in eastern Ontario and the pupils are boys *and* girls. In spite of its humble design, it—like the other schools discussed in this chapter—is a revered domain that fosters high ideals and Christian principles. Connor's book, for which he drew on his schoolboy memories with nostalgia and warmth, is still in print.

Although writers from Charles Dickens (in *Hard Times*) to Graham Greene (in *A Sort of Life*) have detailed the torments of school life, the finest school stories written for children—*Tom Brown's Schooldays*, *The Third Class at Miss Kaye's*, and *Stalky & Co.*—show instead how, in fiction at least, school could be a happy place and could improve children, moulding astute leaders, sociable women, and even radical independents.

THOMAS HUGHES (1822-1896)
"After the Match" from *Tom Brown's Schooldays* (1857)

After attending Rugby, the famous English public school, Thomas Hughes studied at Oxford; he became a barrister, served as a Liberal M.P., and was appointed a County Court judge. *Tom Brown's Schooldays*, a tribute to his school, encourages the reader to "jog on comfortably" through an account of Tom's ten-year sojourn at Rugby. His behaviour on his eventful first day, the last hours of which are described below, shows how quickly he settles in and how successfully Hughes has caught "the old boy-spirit"; having been welcomed and befriended by East and pressed into service as a goal-keeper in the football match, the boy is hailed as "a plucky youngster [who] will make a player" and tossed in a blanket by the school bully. To his credit Hughes never lets interest flag, but continually pumps his narrative full of scrapes and high jinks. Tom actually seems to learn more about foraging and fisticuffs than about Latin and Greek at Rugby.

Tom Brown's Rugby was under the reforming direction of the redoubtable Dr Thomas Arnold (father of the poet Matthew Arnold). As Brooke's tribute on Tom's first night at school makes clear, a hushed reverence always attended the mention of the Doctor's name. Arnold strove to replace the alarming violence in public schools with an emphasis on rigorous studies and sportsmanlike conduct to achieve true "manliness". The universally respected Doctor and the extremely pious younger student, George Arthur, act as tempering influences on high-spirited Tom who, by his last term at Rugby, has risen to become "a strapping figure", a praepostor, and cricket captain. Squire Brown had wanted his son to "turn out a brave, helpful, truth-telling Englishman, and a gentleman, and a Christian". Hughes' zesty narrative demonstrates how Rugby fulfilled these expectations.

Although Hughes wrote about his Oxford days as well (*Tom Brown at Oxford*, 1861), his fame today rests securely on the school story he composed to prepare his own young son for the gruelling and formative experience of Rugby.

AFTER THE MATCH

"—Some food we had."—Shakspere
*ης ποτος ἀδῦς—Theocr. Id.

As the boys scattered away from the ground, and East leaning on Tom's arm, and limping along, was beginning to consider what luxury they should go and buy for tea to celebrate that glorious victory, the two Brookes came striding by. Old Brooke caught sight of East, and stopped; put his hand kindly on his shoulder and said, "Bravo, youngster, you played famously; not much the matter, I hope?"

"No, nothing at all," said East, "only a little twist from that charge."

"Well, mind and get all right for next Saturday," and the leader passed on, leaving East better for those few words than all the opodeldoc in England would have made him, and Tom ready to give one of his ears for as much notice. Ah! light words of those whom we love and honour, what a power ye are, and how carelessly wielded by those who can use you! Surely for these things also God will ask an account.

"Tea's directly after locking-up, you see," said East, hobbling along as

---

**The drink was sweet. [Editor]

fast as he could, "so you come along down to Sally Harrowell's; that's our School-house tuck shop—she bakes such stunning murphies, we'll have a penn'orth each for tea; come along, or they'll all be gone."

Tom's new purse and money burnt in his pocket; he wondered, as they toddled through the quadrangle and along the street, whether East would be insulted if he suggested further extravagance, as he had not sufficient faith in a pennyworth of potatoes. At last he blurted out—

"I say, East, can't we get something else besides potatoes? I've got lots of money, you know."

"Bless us, yes, I forgot," said East, "you've only just come. You see all my tin's been gone this twelve weeks, it hardly ever lasts beyond the first fortnight; and our allowances were all stopped this morning for broken windows, so I haven't got a penny. I've got a tick at Sally's, of course; but then I hate running it high, you see, towards the end of the half, 'cause one has to shell out for it all directly one comes back, and that's a bore."

Tom didn't understand much of this talk, but seized on the fact that East had no money, and was denying himself some little pet luxury in consequence. "Well what shall I buy?" said he, "I'm uncommon hungry."

"I say," said East, stopping to look at him and rest his leg, "you're a trump, Brown. I'll do the same by you next half. Let's have a pound of sausages then, that's the best grub for tea I know of."

"Very well," said Tom, as pleased as possible, "where do they sell them?"

"Oh, over here, just opposite"; and they crossed the street and walked into the cleanest little front room of a small house, half parlour, half shop, and bought a pound of most particular sausages; East talking pleasantly to Mrs Porter while she put them in paper, and Tom doing the paying part.

From Porter's they adjourned to Sally Harrowell's, where they found a lot of School-house boys waiting for the roast potatoes, and relating their own exploits in the day's match at the top of their voices. The street opened at once into Sally's kitchen, a low brick-floored room, with large recess for fire, and chimney-corner seats.

East and Tom got served at last, and started back for the School-house just as the locking-up bell began to ring. The lower-school boys of the School-house, some fifteen in number, had tea in the lower-fifth school, and were presided over by the old verger or head-porter. Each boy had a quarter of a loaf of bread and pat of butter, and as much tea as he pleased, and there was scarcely one who didn't add to this some further luxury, such as baked potatoes, a herring, sprats, or something of the sort; but few, at this period of the half-year, could live up to a pound of Porter's sausages, and East was in great magnificence upon the strength of theirs. He had produced a toasting-fork from his study, and set Tom to toast the sausages, while he mounted guard over their butter and potatoes; "cause," as he explained, "you're a new boy, and they'll play you some trick and get our butter, but you can toast just as well as I." So Tom, in the midst of three or four more urchins similarly employed, toasted his face and the sausages at the same time before the huge fire, till the latter cracked; when East from his watch-tower shouted that they were done, and then the feast proceeded, and the festive cups of tea were filled and emptied, and Tom imparted of the sausages in small bits to many neighbours, and thought he had never tasted such good potatoes or seen such jolly boys. They on their parts waived all ceremony, and pegged away at the sausages and potatoes, and remembering Tom's performance in goal, voted East's new crony a brick. After tea, and while the things were being cleared away, they gathered round the fire, and the talk on the match still went on; and those who had them to show, pulled up their trousers and showed the hacks they had received in the good cause.

They were soon however all turned out of the school, and East conducted Tom up to his bedroom, that he might get on clean things and wash himself before singing.

"What's singing?" said Tom, taking his head out of his basin, where he had been plunging it in cold water.

"Well, you are jolly green," answered his friend from a neighbouring basin. "Why the last six Saturdays of every half, we sing of course; and this is the first of them. No first lesson to do, you know, and lie in bed tomorrow morning."

"But who sings?"

"Why everybody, of course; you'll see soon enough. We begin directly after supper, and sing till bed-time. It ain't such good fun now tho' as in the summer half, 'cause then we sing in the little fives' court, under the library you know. We take out tables, and the big boys sit round, and drink beer; double allowance on Saturday nights; and we cut about the quadrangle between the songs, and it looks like a lot of robbers in a cave. And the louts come and pound at the great gates, and we pound back again, and shout at them. But this half we only sing in the hall. Come along down to my study."

Their principal employment in the study was to clear out East's table, removing the drawers and ornaments and tablecloth, for he lived in the bottom passage, and his table was in requisition for the singing.

Supper came in due course at seven o'clock, consisting of bread and cheese and beer, which was all saved for the singing; and directly afterwards the fags went to work to prepare the hall. The School-house hall, as has been said, is a great long high room, with two large fires on one side, and two large iron-bound tables, one running down the middle, and the other along the wall opposite the fire-places. Around the upper fire the fags placed the tables in the form of a horse-shoe, and upon them the jugs with the Saturday night's allowance of beer. Then the big boys began to drop in and take their seats, bringing with them bottled beer and song-books; for although they all knew the songs by heart, it was the thing to have an old manuscript book descended from some departed hero, in which they were all carefully written out.

Then Warner, the head of the house, gets up and wants to speak, but he can't, for every boy knows what's coming; and the big boys who sit at the tables pound them and cheer; and the small boys who stand behind pound one another, and cheer, and rush about the hall cheering. Then silence being made, Warner reminds them of the old School-house custom of drinking the healths, on the first night of singing, of those who are going to leave at the end of the half. "He sees that they know what he is going to say already—(loud cheers)—and so won't keep them, but only ask them to treat the toast as it deserves. It is, the head of the eleven, the head of big-side football, their leader on this glorious day—Pater Brooke!"

And away goes the pounding and cheering again, becoming deafening when old Brooke gets on his legs: till, a table having broken down, and a gallon or so of beer been upset, and all throats getting dry, silence ensues, and the hero speaks, leaning his hands on the table, and bending a little forwards. No action, no tricks of oratory; plain, strong and straight, like his play.

"Gentlemen of the School-house! I am very proud of the way in which you have received my name, and I wish I could say all I should like in return. But I know I shan't. However, I'll do the best I can to say what seems to me ought to be said by a fellow who's just going to leave, and who has spent a good slice of his life here. Eight years it is, and eight such years as I can never hope to have again. So now I hope you'll all listen to me—(loud cries of 'that we will')—for I'm going to talk seriously. You're bound to listen to me, for what's the use of calling me 'pater', and all that, if you won't mind what I say? And I'm going to talk seriously, because I feel so. It's a jolly time, too, getting to the end of the half, and a goal kicked by us first day—(tremendous applause)—after one of the hardest and fiercest day's play I can remember in eight years—(frantic shoutings). The school played splendidly too, I will say, and kept it up to the last. That last charge of theirs would have carried away a house. I never thought to see anything again of old Crab there, except little pieces, when I saw him tumbled over by it—(laughter and shouting, and great slapping on the back of Jones by the boys nearest him). Well, but we beat 'em—(cheers). Aye, but why did we beat 'em? answer me that—(shouts of 'your play'). Nonsense. 'Twasn't the wind and kick-off either—that wouldn't do it. 'Twasn't because we've half-a-dozen of the best players in the school, as we have. I wouldn't change Warner, and Hedge, and Crab, and the young 'un, for any six on their side—(violent cheers). But half-a-dozen fellows can't keep it up for two hours against two hundred. Why is it, then? I'll tell you what I think. It's because we've more reliance on one another, more of a house feeling, more fellowship than the school can have. Each of us knows and can depend on his next hand man better—that's why we beat 'em today. We've union, they've division—there's the secret—(cheers). But how's this to be kept up? How's it to be improved? That's the question. For I take it, we're all in earnest about beating the school, whatever else we care about. I know I'd sooner win two School-house matches running than get the Balliol scholarship any day—(frantic cheers).

"Now, I'm as proud of the house as any one. I believe it's the best house in the school, out-and-out—(cheers). But it's a long way from what I want to see it. First, there's a deal of bullying going on. I know it well. I don't pry about and interfere; that only makes it more underhand, and encourages the small boys to come to us with their fingers in their eyes telling tales, and so we should be worse off than ever. It's very little kindness for the sixth to meddle generally—you youngsters, mind that. You'll be all the better football players for learning to stand it, and to take your own parts, and fight it through. But depend on it, there's nothing breaks up a house like bullying. Bullies are cowards, and one coward makes many; so good-bye to the School-house match if bullying gets ahead here. (Loud applause from the small boys, who look meaningly at Flashman and other boys at the tables.) Then there's fuddling about in the public-house, and drinking bad spirits, and punch, and such rot-gut stuff. That won't make good drop-kicks or chargers of you, take my word for it. You get plenty of good beer here, and that's enough for you; and drinking isn't fine or manly, whatever some of you may think of it.

"One other thing I must have a word about. A lot of you think and say, for I've heard you, "There's this new Doctor hasn't been here so long as some of us, and he's changing all the old customs. Rugby, and the School-house especially are going to the dogs. Stand up for the good old ways, and down with the Doctor!" Now I'm as fond of old Rugby customs and ways as any of you, and I've been here longer than any of you, and I'll give you a word of advice in time for I shouldn't like to see any of you getting sacked. 'Down with the Doctor's easier said than done. You'll find him pretty tight on his perch, I take it, and an awkwardish customer to handle in that line. Besides now, what customs has he put down? There was the good old custom of taking the linchpins out of the farmer's and bagmen's gigs at the fairs and a cowardly blackguard custom it was. We all know what came of it, and no wonder the Doctor objected to it. But, come now, any of you, name a custom that he has put down."

No answer.

"Well, I won't go on. Think it over for yourselves: you'll find, I believe, that he don't meddle with any one that's worth keeping. And mind now, I say again, look out for squalls, if you will go your own way, and that way ain't the Doctor's, for it'll lead to grief. You all know that I'm not the fellow to back a master through thick and thin. If I saw him stopping football, or cricket, or bathing, or sparring, I'd be as ready as any fellow to stand up about it. But he don't—he encourages them; didn't you see him out today for half-an-hour watching us? (Loud cheers for the Doctor.) And he's a strong true man, and a wise one too, and a public-school man too. (Cheers.) And so let's stick to him, and talk no more rot, and drink his health as the head of the house. (Loud cheers.) And now I've done blowing up, and very glad I am to have done. But it's a solemn thing to be thinking of leaving a place which one has lived in and loved for eight years; and if one can say a word for the good of the old house at such a time, why it should be said, whether bitter or sweet. If I hadn't been proud—I shouldn't be blowing you up. And now let's get to singing. But before I sit down I must give you a toast which I hope every one of us wherever he may go hereafter, will never fail to drink when he thinks of the brave bright days of his boyhood. It's a toast which should bind us all together, and to those who've gone before, and who'll come after us here. It is the dear old Schoolhouse—the best house of the best school in England!"

My dear boys, old and young, you who have belonged, or do belong, to other schools and other houses, don't begin throwing my poor little book about the room, and abusing me and it, and vowing you'll read no more when you get to this point. I allow you've provocation for it. But, come now—would you, any of you, give a fig for a fellow who didn't believe in, and stand up for his own house and his own school? You know you wouldn't. Then don't object to my cracking up the old Schoolhouse, Rugby. Haven't I a right to do it, when I'm taking all the trouble of writing this true history for all your benefits. If you ain't satisfied, go and write the history of your own houses in your own times, and say all you know for your own schools and houses, provided it's true, and I'll read it without abusing you.

The last few words hit the audience in their weakest place; they had been not altogether enthusiastic at several parts of old Brooke's speech; but "the best house of the best school in England" was too much for them all, and carried even the sporting and drinking interests off their legs into rapturous applause, and (it is to be hoped) resolutions to lead a new life and remember old Brooke's words; which however they didn't altogether do, as will appear hereafter.

We looked upon every trumpery little custom and habit which had obtained in the school as though it had been a law of the Medes and Persians, and regarded the infringement or variation of it as a sort of sacrilege. And the Doctor, than whom no man or boy had a stronger liking for old school customs, which were good and sensible, had, as has already been hinted, come into most decided collision with several which were neither the one or the other. And as old Brooke had said, when he came into collision with boys or customs, there was nothing for them but to give in or take themselves off; because what he said had to be done, and no mistake about it. And this was beginning to be pretty clearly understood; the boys felt that there was a strong man over them, who would have things his own way; and hadn't yet learned that he was a wise and loving man also. His personal character and influence had not had time to make itself felt, except by a very few of the bigger boys with whom he came more directly in contact; and he was looked upon with great fear and dislike by the great majority even of his own house. For he had found school, and school-house, in a state of monstrous licence and misrule, and was still employed in the necessary but unpopular work of setting up order with a strong hand.

Half-past nine struck in the middle of the performance of "Auld Lang Syne", a most obstreperous proceeding; during which there was an immense amount of standing with one foot on the table, knocking mugs together and shaking hands, without which accompaniments it seems impossible for the youth of Britain to take part in that famous old song. The under-porter of the School-house entered during the performance, bearing five or six long wooden candlesticks, with lighted dips in them, which he proceeded to stick into their holes in such part of the great tables as he could get at; and then stood outside the ring till the end of the song, when he was hailed with shouts.

"Bill, you old muff, the half-hour hasn't struck."

"Here, Bill, drink some cocktail", "Sing us a song, old boy", "Don't you wish you may get the table?" Bill drank the proffered cocktail not unwillingly, and putting down the empty glass remonstrated, "Now, gentlemen, there's only ten minutes to prayers, and we must get the hall straight."

Then the quarter to ten struck, and the prayer-bell rang. The sixth and fifth form boys ranged themselves in their school order along the wall, on either side of the great fires, the middle fifth and upper school boys round the long table in the middle of the hall, and the lower school boys round the upper part of the second long table, which ran down the side of the hall furthest from the fires. Here Tom found himself at the bottom of all, in a state of mind and body not at all fit for prayers, as he thought; and so tried hard to make himself serious, but couldn't, for the life of him, do anything but repeat in his head the choruses of some of the songs, and stare at all the boys opposite, wondering at the brilliancy of their waistcoats, and speculating what sort of fellows they were. The steps of the head-porter are heard on the stairs, and a light gleams at the door. "Hush!" from the fifth-form boys who stand there, and then in strides the Doctor, cap on head, book in one hand, and gathering up his gown in the other. He walks up the middle, and takes his post by Warner, who begins calling over the names. The Doctor takes no notice of anything, but quietly turns his book and finds the place, and then stands, cap in hand and finger in book, looking straight before his nose. He knows better than any one when to look, and when to see nothing; tonight is singing night, and there's been lots of noise and no harm done; nothing but beer drunk, and nobody the worse for it; though some of them do look hot and excited. So the Doctor sees nothing, but fascinates Tom in a horrible manner as he stands there, and reads out the Psalm in that deep, ringing, searching voice of his. Prayers are over, and Tom still stares open-mouthed after the Doctor's retiring figure, when he feels a pull at his sleeve, and turning round sees East.

"I say, were you ever tossed in a blanket?"

"No," said Tom; "why?"

"Cause there'll be tossing tonight most likely, before the sixth come up to bed. So if you funk, you just come along and hide, or else they'll catch you and toss you."

"Were you ever tossed? Does it hurt?" inquired Tom.

"Oh yes, bless you, a dozen times," said East, as he hobbled along by Tom's side upstairs. "It don't hurt unless you fall on the floor. But most fellows don't like it."

They stopped at the fireplace in the top passage, where were a crowd of small boys whispering together, and evidently unwilling to go up into the bed-rooms. In a minute, however, a study door opened and a sixth-form boy came out, and off they all scuttled up the stairs, and then noiselessly dispersed to their different rooms. Tom's heart beat rather quick as he and East reached their room, but he had made up his mind. "I shan't hide, East," said he.

"Very well, old fellow," replied East, evidently pleased; "no more shall I—they'll be here for us directly."

The room was a great big one with a dozen beds in it, but not a boy that Tom could see, except East and himself. East pulled off his coat and waistcoat, and then sat on the bottom of his bed, whistling, and pulling off his boots; Tom followed his example.

A noise and steps are heard in the passage, the door opens, and in rush four or five great fifth-form boys, headed by Flashman in his glory.

Tom and East slept in the further corner of the room, and were not seen at first.

"Gone to ground, eh?" roared Flashman; "push 'em out then, boys! took under the beds:" and he pulled up the little white curtain of the one nearest him. "Who-o-op," he roared, pulling away at the leg of a small boy, who held on tight to the leg of the bed, and sung out lustily for mercy. "Here, lend a hand, one of you, and help me pull out this young howling brute. Hold your tongue, sir, or I'll kill you."

"Oh, please, Flashman, please, Walker, don't toss me! I'll fag for you. I'll do anything, only don't toss me."

"You be hanged," said Flashman, lugging the wretched boy along. "'twon't hurt you,—you! Come along, boys, here he is."

"I say, Flashey," sung out another of the big boys, "drop that; you heard what old Pater Brooke said tonight. I'll be hanged if we'll toss any one against their will—no more bullying. Let him go, I say."

Flashman, with a oath and a kick, released his prey, who rushed headlong under his bed again, for fear they should change their minds, and crept along underneath the other beds, till he got under that of the sixth-form boy, which he knew they daren't disturb.

"There's plenty of youngsters don't care about it," said Walker. "Here, here's Scud East—you'll be tossed, won't you, young un?" Scud was East's nickname, or Black, as we called it, gained by his fleetness of foot.

"Yes," said East, "if you like, only mind my foot."

"And here's another one who didn't hide. Hullo! new boy; what's your name, sir?"

"Brown."

"Well, Whitey Brown, you don't mind being tost?"

"No," said Tom, setting his teeth.

"Come along then, boys," sung out Walker, and away they all went, carrying along Tom and East, to the intense relief of four or five other small boys, who crept out from under the beds and behind them.

"What a trump Scud is!" said one. "They won't come back here now."

"And that new boy too; he must be a good plucked one."

"Ah, wait till he's been tossed on to the floor; see how he'll like it then!"

Meantime the procession went down the passage to Number 7, the largest room, and the scene of tossing, in the middle of which was a great open space. Here they joined other parties of the bigger boys, each with a captive or two, some willing to be tossed, some sullen, and some frightened to death. At Walker's suggestion all who were afraid were let off, in honour of Brooke's speech.

Then a dozen big boys seized hold of a blanket dragged from one of the beds. "In with Scud, quick, there's no time to lose." East was chucked into the blanket. "Once, twice, thrice, and away!" up he went like a shuttlecock, but not quite up to the ceiling.

"Now, boys, with a will," cried Walker, "once, twice, thrice, and away!" This time he went clean up, and kept himself from touching the ceiling with his hand, and so again, a third time, when he was turned out, and up went another boy. And then came Tom's turn. He lay quite still by East's advice, and didn't dislike the "once, twice, thrice"; but the "away" wasn't so pleasant. They were in good wind now, and sent him slap up to the ceiling first time, against which his knees came rather sharply. But the moment's pause before descending was the rub, the feeling of utter helplessness, and of leaving his whole inside behind him sticking to the ceiling. Tom was very near shouting to be set down, when he found himself back in the blanket, but thought of East, and didn't; and so took his three tosses without a kick or a cry, and was called a young trump for his pains.

He and East, having earned it, stood now looking on. No catastrophe happened, as all the captives were cool hands, and didn't struggle. This didn't suit Flashman. What your real bully likes in tossing, is when the boys kick and struggle, or hold on to the side of the blanket, and so get pitched bodily on to the floor; it's no fun to him when no one is hurt or frightened.

"Let's toss two of them together, Walker," suggested he. "What a cursed bully you are, Flashey!" rejoined the other. "Up with another one."

And so no two boys were tossed together, the peculiar hardship of which is, that it's too much for human nature to lie still then and share troubles; and so the wretched pair of small boys struggle in the air which shall fall a-top in the descent, to the no small risk of both falling out of the blanket, and the huge delight of brutes like Flashman.

But now there's a cry that the praepostor of the room is coming; so the tossing stops, and all scatter to their different rooms; and Tom is left to turn in, with the first day's experience of a public school to meditate upon.

FREDERIC WILLIAM FARRAR (1831-1903)
" 'Dead Flies' or 'Ye Shall Be As Gods' " from *Eric; or, Little By Little* (1858)

A missionary's son, Frederic William Farrar was born in Bombay. He was educated in a series of boarding schools in England, attended Cambridge, and became a priest in 1857. As a father of ten children, a schoolmaster (who eventually became Headmaster of Marlborough), and a clergyman (who became Canon of Westminster in 1875 and Dean of Canterbury in 1895), he was completely dedicated to the twin causes of education and religion. A tireless composer of scores of uplifting books for children, Sunday School teachers, and Temperance Societies, Farrar imbued all his work with a strong sense of Christian righteousness— whether in school stories like *Eric* (1858), *Julian Home* (1859), and *St Winifred's* (1862), temperance publications like *How Working Men May Help Themselves* (1880), or exegetical studies like *The Life and Works of St Paul* (1879).

Farrar wrote *Eric* when he was employed as a schoolmaster at Harrow, and it is likely that the moral indignation of this novel was caused by the laxity and "vice" he observed around him. Roslyn, the public school attended by Eric Williams, and later by his brother Vernon, is corrupt and violent. The story of Eric—a tractable boy who, owing to the tainting influence of some schoolmates, falls "little by little" into wickedness and dishonour—was meant to be an object lesson aiming at "the vivid inculcation of inward purity and moral purpose", as the Preface explains.

A sheltered twelve-year-old, Eric spends his first day being menaced by a lazy, inso-

lent bully. Later he is caned for cribbing and flogged for writing a prompt sheet. Farrar characterizes his hero as an essentially good boy who is, however, tragically flawed by "pride and rebellion" (that is, he is not docile). As the chapter below shows, Eric becomes more and more vulnerable to the insidious atmosphere of dormitory life.

In the second part of the story his younger brother arrives at Roslyn. Although Eric has resolved to reform, his carousing with liquor and tobacco, currying of favour with the lower-school boys, and wrangling in public with the exemplary students Montagu and Owen, offer poor guidance to his brother. Only the shock of Vernon's death sobers Eric. But because Farrar insists on driving home his "moral purpose", Eric is not allowed to amend his life quietly. Instead, under threat of exposure for having, in his unregenerate past, stolen the headmaster's pigeons for a "jollification", Eric creeps from Roslyn in disgrace. After serving as a mate on a merchant ship, he returns to his aunt's home, only to receive the news from India that his mother is near death because of grief over the "scandalous" behaviour of her son. A physically weak but spiritually reformed Eric soon expires in his aunt's arms.

Because of its heavy sanctimoniousness and didacticism, both fuelled with evangelical zeal, *Eric* is a rare and extreme example of school fiction. It found a wide audience, however: it was reprinted thirty-six times in the remaining forty-five years of Farrar's life.

"DEAD FLIES," OR "YE SHALL BE AS GODS"

In the twilight, in the evening, in the black and dark night.
—Prov. vii. 9.

At Roslyn, even in summer, the hour for going to bed was half-past
nine. It was hardly likely that so many boys, overflowing with turbulent
life, should lie down quietly, and get to sleep. They never dreamt of
doing so. Very soon after the masters were gone, the sconces were often
relighted, sometimes in separate dormitories, sometimes in all of them,
and the boys amused themselves by reading novels or making a row.
They would play various games about the bed-rooms, vaulting or jumping over the beds, running races in sheets, getting through the windows
upon the roofs, to frighten the study-boys with sham ghosts, or playing
the thousand other pranks which suggested themselves to the fertile
imagination of fifteen. But the favourite amusement was a bolstering
match. One room would challenge another, and stripping the covers off
their bolsters, would meet in mortal fray. A bolster well wielded, especially when dexterously applied to the legs, is a very efficient instrument
to bring a boy to the ground; but it doesn't hurt very much, even when
the blows fall on the head. Hence these matches were excellent trials of
strength and temper, and were generally accompanied with shouts of
laughter, never ending until one side was driven back to its own room.
Many a long and tough struggle had Eric enjoyed, and his prowess was
now so universally acknowledged, that his dormitory, No. 7, was a
match for any other, and far stronger in this warfare than most of the
rest. At bolstering, Duncan was a perfect champion; his strength and activity were marvellous, and his mirth uproarious. Eric and Graham
backed him up brilliantly; while Llewellyn and Attlay, with sturdy vi-
gour, supported the skirmishers. Ball, the sixth boy in No. 7, was the
only *fainéant* among them, though he did occasionally help to keep off
the smaller fry.

Happy would it have been for all of them if Ball had never been placed
in No. 7; happier still if he had never come to Roslyn School. Backward
in work, overflowing with vanity at his supposed good looks, of mean
disposition and feeble intellect, he was the very worst specimen of a boy

that Eric had ever seen. Not even Barker so deeply excited Eric's repulsion and contempt. And yet, since the affair of Upton, Barker and Eric were declared enemies, and, much to the satisfaction of the latter, never spoke to each other; but with Ball—much as he inwardly loathed him—he was professedly and apparently on good terms. His silly love of universal popularity made him accept and tolerate the society even of this worthless boy.

Any two boys talking to each other about Ball would probably profess to like him "well enough," but if they were honest, they would generally end by allowing their contempt.

"We've got a nice set in No. 7, haven't we?" said Duncan to Eric one day.

"Capital. Old Lelewellyn's a stunner, and I like Attlay and Graham."

"Don't you like Ball, then?"

"Oh yes; pretty well."

The two boys looked each other in the face, and then, like the confidential augurs, burst out laughing.

"You know you detest him," said Duncan.

"No, I don't. He never did me any harm that I know of."

"Hm!—well, I detest him."

"Well!" answered Eric, "on coming to think of it, so do I. And yet he's popular enough in the school. I wonder how that is."

"He's not really popular. I've often noticed that fellows pretty generally despise him, yet somehow don't like to say so."

"Why do you dislike him, Duncan?"

"I don't know. Why do you?"

"I don't know either."

Neither Eric nor Duncan meant this answer to be false, and yet if they had taken the trouble to consider, they would have found out in their secret souls the reasons of their dislike.

Ball had been to school before, and of this school he often bragged as the acme of desirability and wickedness. He was always telling boys what they did at "his old school," and he quite inflamed the minds of such as fell under his influence by marvellous tales of the wild and wilful things which he and his former schoolfellows had done. Many and many a scheme of sin and mischief at Roslyn was suggested, planned, and carried out, on the model of Ball's reminiscences of his previous life.

He had tasted more largely of the tree of the knowledge of evil than any other boy, and, strange to say, this was the secret why the general odium was never expressed. He claimed his guilty experience so often as a ground of superiority, that at last the claim was silently allowed. He spoke from the platform of more advanced iniquity, and the others listened first curiously, and then eagerly to his words.

"Ye shall be as gods, knowing good and evil." Such was the temptation which assailed the other boys in dormitory No. 7; and Eric among the number. Ball was the tempter. Secretly, gradually, he dropped into their too willing ears the poison of his immorality.

In brief, this boy was cursed with a degraded and corrupting mind.

I hurry over a part of my subject inconceivably painful; I hurry over it, but if I am to perform my self-imposed duty of giving a true picture of what school life sometimes is, I must not pass it by altogether.

The first time that Eric heard indecent words in dormitory No. 7, he was shocked beyond bound or measure. Dark though it was, he felt himself blushing scarlet to the roots of his hair, and then growing pale again, while a hot dew was left upon his forehead. Ball was the speaker; but this time there was a silence, and the subject instantly dropped. The others felt that a "new boy" was in the room; they did not know how he would take it; they were unconsciously abashed.

Besides, though they had themselves joined in such conversation before, they did not love it, and, on the contrary, felt ashamed of yielding to it.

Now, Eric, now or never! Life and death, ruin and salvation, corruption and purity, are perhaps in the balance together, and the scale of your destiny may hang on a single word of yours. Speak out, boy! Tell these fellows that unseemly words wound your conscience; tell them that they are ruinous, sinful, damnable; speak out and save yourself and the rest. Virtue is strong and beautiful, Eric, and vice is downcast in her awful presence. Lose your purity of heart, Eric, and you have lost a jewel which the whole world, if it were "one entire and perfect chrysolite," cannot replace. . . .

But the sense of sin was on Eric's mind. How could he speak? was not his own language sometimes profane? How—how could he profess to reprove another boy on the ground of morality, when he himself said and did things less dangerous perhaps, but equally forbidden?

For half an hour, in an agony of struggle with himself, Eric lay silent. Since Ball's last words nobody had spoken. They were going to sleep. It was too late to speak now, Eric thought. The moment passed by forever; Eric had listened without objection to foul words, and the irreparable harm was done.

How easy it would have been to speak! With the temptation, God had provided also a way to escape. Next time it came, it was far harder to resist, and it soon became, to men, impossible.

Ah, Eric, Eric! how little we know the moments which decide the destinies of life. We live on as usual. The day is a common day, the hour a common hour. We never thought twice about the change of intention which by one of the accidents—(accidents!)—of life determined for good or for evil, for happiness or misery, the colour of our remaining years. The stroke of the pen was done in a moment which led unconsciously to our ruin; the word was uttered quite heedlessly on which turned for ever the decision of our weal or woe.

Eric lay silent. The darkness was not broken by the flashing of an angel's wing, the stillness was not syllabled by the sound of an angel's voice; but to his dying day Eric never forgot the moments which passed, until, weary and self-reproachful, he fell asleep.

Next morning he awoke, restless and feverish. He at once remembered what had passed. Ball's words haunted him; he could not forget them; they burnt within him like the flame of a moral fever. He was moody and petulant, and for a time could hardly conceal his aversion. Ah, Eric! moodiness and petulance cannot save you, but prayerfulness would; one word, Eric, at the throne of grace—one prayer before you go down among the boys, that God in His mercy would wash away, in the blood of His dear Son, your crimson stains, and keep your conscience and memory clean.

The boy knelt down for a few minutes, and repeated to himself a few formal words. Had he stayed longer on his knees, he might have given way to a burst of penitence and supplication—but he heard Ball's footstep, and getting up he ran downstairs to breakfast; so Eric did not pray. . . .

They usually walked together on Sunday. Dr Rowlands had discontinued the odious and ridiculous custom of the younger boys taking their exercise under a master's inspection. Boys are not generally fond of constitutionals, so that on the half-holidays they almost entirely confined their open-air exercise to the regular games, and many of them hardly left the playground boundaries once a week. But on Sundays they often went for walks, each with his favourite friend or companion. When Eric first came as a boarder, he invariably went with Russell on Sunday, and many a pleasant stroll they had taken together, sometimes accompanied by Duncan, Montagu, or Owen. The latter, however, had dropped even this intercourse with Eric, who for the last few weeks had more often gone with his new friend Upton.

"Come a walk, boy," said Upton, as they left the dining-room.

"Oh, excuse me to-day, Upton," said Eric, "I'm going with your cousin."

"Oh, very well," said Upton, in high dudgeon; and hoping to make Eric jealous, he went a walk with Graham, whom he had "taken up" before he knew Williams.

Russell was rather surprised when Eric came to him and said, "Come a stroll to Fort Island, Edwin—will you?"

"Oh yes," said Russell cheerfully; "why, we haven't seen each other for some time lately! I was beginning to fancy that you meant to drop me, Eric."

He spoke with a smile and in a rallying tone, but Eric hung his head; for the charge was true. Proud of his popularity among all the school, and especially at his friendship with so leading a fellow as Upton, Eric had not seen much of his friend since their last conversation about swearing. Indeed, conscious of failure, he felt sometimes uneasy in Russell's company.

He faltered, and answered humbly, "I hope you will never drop me, Edwin, whatever happens to me. But I particularly want to speak to you to-day."

In an instant Russell had twined his arm in Eric's as they turned towards Fort Island; and Eric, with an effort, was just going to begin when they heard Montagu's voice calling after them—

"I say, you fellows, where are you off to? May I come with you?"

"Oh yes, Monty, do," said Russell; "it will be quite like old times; now that my cousin Horace has got hold of Eric, we have to sing 'When shall we three meet again?' "

Russell only spoke in fun; but, unintentionally his words jarred in Eric's heart. He was silent and answered in monosyllables, so the walk was provokingly dull. At last they reached Fort Island, and sate down by the ruined chapel looking on the sea.

"Why, what's the row with you, old boy?" said Montagu, playfully shaking Eric by the shoulder; "you're as silent as Zimmerman on Solitude, and as doleful as Harvey on the Tombs. I expect you've been going through a select course of Blair's Grave, Young's Night Thoughts, and Drelincourt on Death."

To his surprise Eric's head was still bent, and, at last, he heard a deep suppressed sigh.

"My dear fellow, what is the matter with you?" said Russell, affectionately taking his hand; "surely you're not offended at my nonsense?"

Eric had not liked to speak while Montagu was by, but now he gulped down his rising emotion, and briefly told them of Ball's vile words the night before. They listened in silence.

"I knew it must come, Eric," said Russell at last, "and I am so sorry you didn't speak at the time."

"Do the fellows ever talk in that way in either of your dormitories?" asked Eric.

"No," said Russell.

"Very little," said Montagu.

A pause followed, during which all three plucked the grass and looked away.

"Let me tell you," said Russell solemnly; "my father (he is dead now, you know, Eric), when I was sent to school, warned me of this kind of thing. I had been brought up in utter ignorance of such coarse knowledge as is forced upon one here, and with my reminiscences of home, I could not bear even that much of it which it was impossible to avoid. But the very first time such talk was begun in my dormitory, I spoke out. What I said I don't know, but I felt as if I was trampling on a slimy poisonous adder, and at any rate, I showed such pain and distress that the fellows dropped it at the time. Since then I have absolutely refused to stay in the room if ever such talk is begun. So it never is now, and I do think the fellows are very glad of it themselves."

"Well," said Montagu, "I don't profess to look on it from the religious ground, you know, but I thought it blackguardly, and in bad taste, and said so. The fellow who began it threatened to kick me for a conceited little fool, but he didn't; and they hardly ever venture on that line now."

"It is more than blackguardly, it is deadly," answered Russell; "my father said it was the most fatal course which could ever become rife in a public school."

"Why do masters never give us any help or advice on these matters?" asked Eric thoughtfully.

"In sermons they do. Don't you remember Rowlands's sermon not two weeks ago on Kibroth-Hattaavah?* But I for one think them quite right not to speak to us privately on such subjects, unless we invite confidence. Besides, they cannot know that any boys talk in this way. After all, it is only a very few of the worst who ever do."

They got up and walked home, but from day to day Eric put off performing the duty which Russell had advised, viz.—a private request to Ball to abstain from his offensive communications, and an endeavour to enlist Duncan into his wishes.

One evening they were telling each other stories in No. 7. Ball's turn came, and in his story the vile element again appeared. For a while Eric said nothing, but as the strain grew worse, he made a faint remonstrance.

"Shut up there, Williams," said Attlay, "and don't spoil the story."

"Very well. It's your own fault, and I shall shut my ears."

He did for a time, but a general laugh awoke him. He pretended to be asleep, but he listened. Iniquity of this kind was utterly new to him; his curiosity was awakened; he no longer feigned indifference, and the poison of evil communication flowed deep into his veins.

Oh, young boys, if your eyes ever read these pages, pause and beware. The knowledge of evil is ruin, and the continuance in it is moral death. That little matter—that beginning of evil—it will be like the snowflake detached by the breath of air from the mountaintop, which, as it rushes down, gains size and strength and impetus, till it has swollen to the mighty and irresistible avalanche that overwhelms garden and field and village in a chaos of undistinguishable death.

Kibroth-Hattaavah!* Many and many a young Englishman has perished there! Many and many a happy English boy, the jewel of his mother's heart—brave and beautiful and strong—lies buried there. Very pale their shadows rise before us—the shadows of our young brothers who have sinned and suffered. From the sea and the sod, from foreign graves and English churchyards, they start up and throng around us in the paleness of their fall. May every schoolboy who reads this page be warned by the waving of their wasted hands, from that burning marle of passion where they found nothing but shame and ruin, polluted affections, and an early grave.

---

* Meaning "the graves of desire" in Hebrew, it designates the point in their wilderness journey where many Israelites died from eating quail (Nm. 11:34; Dt. 9:22).[Editor]

RUDYARD KIPLING (1865-1936)
"An Unsavoury Interlude" from *Stalky & Co.* (1899)

Kipling's childhood, from which he drew material for his children's books, was in many ways typically Victorian. Born in Bombay, where his father was a professor of architectural sculpture, he spent his first six years cosseted in a loving circle of family and servants before being sent to England to be schooled—until 1878, at the hands of a neglectful and malevolent guardian, and from the ages of thirteen to seventeen at the United Services College in Westward Ho!, North Devon. This school for the children of army and navy officers, and Kipling's escapades with his two special chums, L.C. Dunsterville ("your Uncle Stalky") and G.C. Beresford ("M'Turk"), provided the model for *Stalky & Co.* At seventeen he returned to India and worked for several years as a newspaper editor. He began to write full-length stories in the 1890s, during a period of extensive travelling from South Africa, to North America, and back to England. *Wee Willie Winkie* (1892), *The Jungle Books* (1894-5), *Captains Courageous* (1896), *Kim* (1901), *Just-So Stories* (1902), *Puck of Pook's Hill* (1906), and *Rewards and Fairies* (1910) all won a loyal following of young readers.

Kipling's critical reputation has undergone many fluctuations. The children who had read him faithfully often became critical adults, denouncing his imperialistic themes, manly ethic, insider's code, and swaggering righteousness. One of the most intemperate attacks on *Stalky & Co.* was made by the American critic Edmund Wilson, who declared it to be "crude in writing, trashy in feeling, implausible in a series of contrivances which resemble motion-picture 'gags' ". His severity is not merited. Far from being crude, the writing sparkles with wit and school-boy humour that operates very plausibly at the expense of the masters. Far from being trashy, the feelings are genuine and sometimes passionately expressed. *Stalky & Co.* traces the distance the school story had come from the pieties of Farrar's *Eric* (ridiculed throughout the excerpt printed here) to a situation where the triumvirate of Stalky, M'Turk, and Beetle (Kipling himself) could outmanoeuvre housemasters, who are usually characterized as pompous, imbecilic, or sarcastic. The tart criticism of one particular housemaster triggers the Pomposo Stinkadore Interlude below.

The three leaders whose exploits Kipling fondly recalled are not mindless bullies. In addition to gaining the tacit respect of the house-servant Richards, the boys are enlisted by "the Padre" (the Reverend Gillett) to deal with real bullies like Sefton and Campbell and to champion the cause of the lad they have been terrorizing—who, freed from their tyranny, becomes a normal misbehaving student. The portrayal of misbehaviour as normal and Kipling's celebration of misrule give the book a certain uproarious charm.

AN UNSAVOURY INTERLUDE

It was a maiden aunt of Stalky who sent him both books, with the inscription, "To dearest Artie, on his sixteenth birthday"; it was M'Turk who ordered their hypothecation; and it was Beetle, returned from Bideford, who flung them on the window-sill of Number Five study with news that Bastable would advance but ninepence on the two; *Eric; or, Little by Little*, being almost as great a drug as *St Winifred's*.* "An' I don't think much of your aunt. We're nearly out of cartridges, too—Artie, dear."

Whereupon Stalky rose up to grapple with him, but M'Turk sat on

---

* Another school story by F.W. Farrar. [Editor]

Stalky's head, calling him a "pure-minded boy" till peace was declared. As they were grievously in arrears with a Latin prose, as it was a glazing July afternoon, and as they ought to have been at a house cricket-match, they began to renew their acquaintance, intimate and unholy, with the volumes.

"Here we are!" said M'Turk. " 'Corporal punishment produced on Eric the worst effects. He burned *not* with remorse or regret'—make a note o' that, Beetle—'but with shame and violent indignation. He glared'—oh, naughty Eric! Let's get to where he goes in for drink."

"Hold on half a shake. Here's another sample. 'The Sixth,' he says, 'is the palladium of all public schools.' But this lot"—Stalky rapped the gilded book—"can't prevent fellows drinkin' and stealin', an' lettin' fags out of window at night, an'—an' doin' what they please. Golly, what we've missed—not goin' to St Winifred's! . . ."

"I'm sorry to see any boys of my house taking so little interest in their matches."

Mr Prout could move very silently if he pleased, though that is no merit in a boy's eyes. He had flung open the study-door without knocking—another sin—and looked at them suspiciously. "Very sorry, indeed, I am to see you frowsting in your studies."

"We've been out ever since dinner, sir," said M'Turk wearily. One house-match is just like another, and their "ploy" of that week happened to be rabbit-shooting with saloon-pistols.

"I can't see a ball when it's coming, sir," said Beatle. "I've had my gig-lamps smashed at the Nets till I got excused. I wasn't any good even as a fag, then, sir."

"Tuck is probably your form. Tuck and brewing. Why can't you three take any interest in the honour of your house?"

They had heard that phrase till they were wearied. The "honour of the house" was Prout's weak point, and they knew well how to flick him on the raw.

"If you order us to go down, sir, of course we'll go," said Stalky, with maddening politeness. But Prout knew better than that. He had tried the experiment once at a big match, when the three, self-isolated, stood to attention for half an hour in full view of all the visitors, to whom fags, subsidised for that end, pointed them out as victims of Prout's tyranny. And Prout was a sensitive man. . . .

"Must we go down, sir?" said M'Turk.

"I don't want to order you to do what a right-thinking boy should do gladly. I'm sorry." And he lurched out with some hazy impression that he had sown good seed on poor ground.

"Now what does he suppose is the use of that?" said Beetle.

"Oh, he's cracked. King jaws him in Commonroom about not keepin' us up to the mark, and Macrea burbles about 'dithcipline,' an' old Heffy sits between 'em sweatin' big drops. I heard Oke [the Common-room butler] talking to Richards [Prout's house-servant] about it down in the basement the other day when I went down to bag some bread," said Stalky. . . .

They reached the sun-blistered pavilion over against the gray Pebbleridge just before roll-call, and, asking no questions, gathered from King's voice and manner that his house was on the road to victory.

"Ah, ha!" said he, turning to show the light of his countenance. "Here we have the ornaments of the Casual House at last. You consider cricket beneath you, I believe"—the flannelled crowd sniggered—"and from what I have seen this afternoon, I fancy many others of your house hold the same view. And may I ask what you purpose to do with your noble selves till tea-time?"

"Going down to bathe, sir," said Stalky.

"And whence this sudden zeal for cleanliness? There is nothing about you that particularly suggests it. Indeed, so far as I remember—I may be at fault—but a short time ago—"

"Five years, sir," said Beetle hotly.

King scowled. "One of you was that thing called a water-funk. Yes, a water-funk. So now you wish to wash? It is well. Cleanliness never injured a boy or—a house. We will proceed to business," and he addressed himself to the call-over board.

"What the deuce did you say anything to him for, Beetle?" said M'Turk angrily, as they strolled towards the big, open sea-baths.

"'Twasn't fair—remindin' one of bein' a water-funk. My first term, too. Heaps of chaps are—when they can't swim."

"Yes, you ass; but he saw he'd fetched you. You ought never to answer King."

"But it wasn't fair, Stalky."

"My Hat! You've been here six years, and you expect fairness. Well, you *are* a dithering idiot."

A knot of King's boys, also bound for the baths, hailed them, beseeching them to wash—for the honour of their house. . . .

In a few days it became an established legend of the school that Prout's house did not wash and were therefore noisome. Mr King was pleased to smile succulently in form when one of his boys drew aside from Beetle with certain gestures. . . .

Their dormitory was a three-bed attic one, opening out of a ten-bed establishment, which, in turn, communicated with the great range of dormitories that ran practically from one end of the College to the other. Macrea's house lay next to Prout's, King's next to Macrea's, and Hartopp's beyond that again. Carefully locked doors divided house from house, but each house, in its internal arrangements—the College had originally been a terrace of twelve large houses—was a replica of the next; one straight roof covering all.

They found Stalky's bed drawn out from the wall to the left of the dormer window, and the latter end of Richards protruding from a two-foot-square cupboard in the wall.

"What's all this? I've never noticed it before. What are you tryin' to do, Fatty?"

"Fillin' basins, Muster Corkran." Richards's voice was hollow and muffled. "They've been savin' me trouble. Yiss."

"Looks like it," said M'Turk. "Hi! You'll stick if you don't take care."
Richards backed puffing.

"I can't rache un. Yiss, 'tess a stopcock, Muster M'Turk. They've took an' runned all the watter-pipes a storey higher in the houses—runned 'em all along under the 'ang of the heaves, like. Runned 'em in last holidays. *I* can't rache the stopcock."

"Let me try," said Stalky, diving into the aperture.

"Slip 'ee to the left, then, Muster Corkran. Slip 'ee to the left, an' feel in the dark."

To the left Stalky wriggled, and saw a long line of lead pipe disappearing up a triangular tunnel, whose roof was the rafters and boarding of the College roof, whose floor was sharp-edged joists, and whose side was the rough studding of the lath and plaster wall under the dormer.

"Rummy show. How far does it go?"

"Right along, Muster Corkran—right along from end to end. Her runs under the 'ang of the heaves. Have 'ee rached the stopcock yet? Mr King got un put in to save us carryin' watter from downstairs to fill the basins. No place for a lusty man like old Richards. I'm tu thickabout to go ferretin'. Thank 'ee, Muster Corkran."

The water squirted through the tap just inside the cupboard, and, having filled the basins, the grateful Richards waddled away.

The boys sat round-eyed on their beds considering the possibilities of this trove. Two floors below them they could hear the hum of the angry house; for nothing is so still as a dormitory in mid-afternoon of a mid-summer term.

"It has been papered over till now." M'Turk examined the little door. "If we'd only known before!"

"I vote we go down and explore. No one will come up this time o' day. We needn't keep *cavé*."

They crawled in, Stalky leading, drew the door behind them, and on all fours embarked on a dark and dirty road full of plaster, odd shavings, and all the raffle that builders leave in the waste room of a house. The passage was perhaps three feet wide, and, except for the straggling light round the edges of the cupboards (there was one to each dormer), almost pitchy dark.

"Here's Macrea's house," said Stalky, his eye at the crack of the third cupboard. "I can see Barnes's name on his trunk. Don't make such a row, Beetle! We can get right to the end of the Coll. Come on! . . . We're in King's house now—I can see a bit of Rattray's trunk. How these beastly boards hurt one's knees!" They heard his nails scraping on plaster. . . .

Stalky thrust an arm to the elbow between the joists.

"No good stayin' here. I vote we go back and talk it over. It's a crummy place. 'Must say I'm grateful to King for his waterworks."

They crawled out, brushed one another clean, slid the saloon-pistols down a trouser-leg, and hurried forth to a deep and solitary Devonshire lane in whose flanks a boy might sometimes slay a young rabbit. They threw themselves down under the rank elder bushes, and began to think aloud.

"You know," said Stalky at last, sighting at a distant sparrow, "we could hide our sallies in there like anything."

"Huh!" Beetle snorted, choked, and gurgled. He had been silent since they left the dormitory. "Did you ever read a book called *The History of a House* or something? I got it out of the library the other day. A French-woman wrote it—Violet somebody. But it's translated, you know; and it's very interestin'. Tells you how a house is built." . . .

"I've got a notion."

"And you'll spoil the whole show if you don't tell your Uncle Stalky. Cough it up, ducky, and we'll see what we can do. Notion, you fat impostor—I knew you had a notion when you went away! Turkey said it was a poem!"

"I've found out how houses are built. Le' me get up. The floor-joists of one room are the ceiling-joists of the room below."

"Don't be so filthy technical."

"Well, the man told me. The floor is laid on top of those joists—those boards on edge that we crawled over—but the floor stops at a partition. Well, if you get behind a partition, same as you did in the attic, don't you see that you can shove anything you please under the floor between the floor-boards and the lath and plaster of the ceiling below? Look here. I've drawn it."

He produced a rude sketch, sufficient to enlighten the allies. There is no part of the modern school curriculum that deals with architecture, and none of them had yet reflected whether floors and ceilings were hollow or solid. Outside his own immediate interests the boy is as ignorant as the savage he so admires; but he has also the savage's resource.

"I see," said Stalky. "I shoved my hand there. An' then?"

"An' then . . . They've been calling us stinkers, you know. We might shove somethin' under—sulphur, or something that stunk pretty bad—an' stink 'em out. I know it can be done somehow." Beetle's eyes turned to Stalky handling the diagrams.

"Stinks?" said Stalky interrogatively. Then his face grew luminous with delight. "By gum! I've got it. Horrid stinks! Turkey!" He leaped at the Irishman. "This afternoon—just after Beetle went away! *She's* the very thing!"

"Come to my arms, my beamish boy," carolled M'Turk, and they fell into each other's arms dancing. "Oh, frabjous day! Calloo, callay! She will! She will!"

"Hold on," said Beetle. "I don't understand."

"Dearr man! It shall, though. Oh, Artie, my pure-souled youth, let us tell our darling Reggie about Pestiferous Stinkadores."

"Not until after call-over. Come on!" . . .

Gambolling like kids at play, with bounds and side-starts, with caper-ings and curvetings, they led the almost bursting Beetle to the rabbit-lane, and from under a pile of stones drew forth the new-slain corpse of a cat. Then did Beetle see the inner meaning of what had gone before, and lifted up his voice in thanksgiving for that the world held warriors so wise as Stalky and M'Turk.

"Well-nourished old lady, ain't she?" said Stalky. "How long d'you suppose it'll take her to get a bit whiff in a confined space?"

"Bit whiff! What a coarse brute you are!" said M'Turk. "Can't a poor pussy-cat get under King's dormitory floor to die without your pursuin' her with your foul innuendoes?"

"What did she die under the floor for?" said Beetle, looking to the future.

"Oh, they won't worry about that when they find her," said Stalky.

"A cat may look at a King." M'Turk rolled down the bank at his own jest. "Pussy, you don't know how useful you're goin' to be to three pure-souled, high-minded boys."

"They'll have to take up the floor for her, same as they did in Number Nine when the rat croaked. Big medicine—heap big medicine! Phew! Oh, Lord, I wish I could stop laughin'," said Beetle.

"Stinks! Hi, stinks! Clammy ones!" M'Turk gasped as he regained his place. "And"—the exquisite humour of it brought them sliding down together in a tangle—"it's all for the honour of the house, too!"

"An' they're holdin' another meetin'—on us," Stalky panted, his knees in the ditch and his face in the long grass. "Well, let's get the bullet out of her and hurry up. The sooner she's bedded out the better."

Between them they did some grisly work with a penknife; between them (ask not who buttoned her to his bosom) they took up the corpse and hastened back, Stalky arranging their plan of action at the full trot.

The afternoon sun, lying in broad patches on the bed-rugs, saw three boys and an umbrella disappear into a dormitory wall. In five minutes they returned, brushed themselves all over, washed their hands, combed their hair, and descended.

"Are you sure you shoved her far enough under?" said M'Turk suddenly.

"Hang it, man, I shoved her the full length of my arm and Beetle's brolly. That must be about six feet. She's bung in the middle of King's big upper ten-bedder. Eligible central situation, _I_ call it. She'll stink out his chaps, and Hartopp's and Macrea's, when she really begins to fume. I swear your Uncle Stalky is a great man. Do you realise what a great man he is, Beetle?"

"Well, I had the notion first, hadn't I, only—"

"You couldn't to it without your Uncle Stalky, could you?"

"They've been calling us stinkers for a week now," said M'Turk. "Oh, won't they catch it!"

"Stinker! Yah! Stink-ah!" rang down the corridor. . . .

King was a happy man, and his house, basking in the favour of his smile, made that afternoon a long penance to the misled Prout's. And Prout himself, with a dull and lowering visage, tried to think out the rights and wrongs of it all, only plunging deeper into bewilderment. Why should his house be called "stinkers"? Truly, it was a small thing, but he had been trained to believe that straws show which way the wind blows, and that there is no smoke without fire. He approached King in Common-room with a sense of injustice, but King was pleased to be full of airy persiflage that tide, and brilliantly danced dialectical rings round Prout. . . .

That night was the first of sorrow among the jubilant King's. By some accident of under-floor draughts the cat did not vex the dormitory beneath which she lay, but the next one to the right; stealing on the air rather as a pale-blue sensation than as any poignant offence. But the mere adumbration of an odour is enough for the sensitive nose and clean tongue of youth. Decency demands that we draw several carbolised sheets over what the dormitory said to Mr King and what Mr King replied. He was genuinely proud of his house and fastidious in all that concerned their well-being. He came; he sniffed; he said things. Next morning a boy in that dormitory confided to his bosom friend, a fag of Macrea's, that there was trouble in their midst which King would fain keep secret.

But Macrea's boy had also a bosom friend in Prout's, a shock-headed fag of malignant disposition, who, when he had wormed out the secret, told—told it in a high-pitched treble that rang along the corridor like a bat's squeak.

"An'—an' they've been calling us 'stinkers' all this week. Why, Harland minor says they simply can't sleep in his dormitory for the stink. Come on!"

"With one shout and with one cry" Prout's juniors hurled themselves into the war, and through the interval between first and second lesson some fifty twelve-year-olds were embroiled on the gravel outside King's windows to a tune whose *leit-motif* was the word "stinker."

"Hark to the minute-gun at sea!" said Stalky. They were in their study collecting books for second lesson—Latin, with King. "I thought his azure brow was a bit cloudy at prayers." . . .

After dinner King took his house to bathe in the sea off the Pebbleridge. It was an old promise; but he wished he could have evaded it, for all Prout's lined up by the Five Court and cheered with intention. In his absence not less than half the school invaded the infected dormitory to draw their own conclusions. The cat had gained in the last twelve hours, but a battlefield of the fifth day could not have been so flamboyant as the spies reported.

"My word, she *is* doin' herself proud," said Stalky. "Did you ever smell anything like it? Ah, an' she isn't under White's dormitory at all yet."

"But she will be. Give her time," said Beetle. "She'll twine like a giddy honeysuckle. What howlin' Lazarites they are! No house is justified in makin' itself a stench in the nostrils of decent—"

"High-minded, pure-souled, boys. *Do* you burn with remorse and regret?" said M'Turk, as they hastened to meet the house coming up from the sea. King had deserted it, so speech was unfettered. Round its front played a crowd of skirmishers—all houses mixed—flying, re-forming, shrieking insults. On its tortured flanks marched the Hoplites, seniors hurling jests one after another—simple and primitive jests of the Stone Age. To these the three added themselves, dispassionately, with an air of aloofness, almost sadly. . . .

The wind shifted that night and wafted a carrion-reek into Macrea's dormitories; so that boys in nightgowns pounded on the locked door between the houses, entreating King's to wash. Number Five study went to second lesson with not more than half a pound of camphor apiece in their clothing; and King, too wary to ask for explanations, gibbered awhile and hurled them forth. . . .

In Common-room at lunch King discoursed acridly to Prout of boys with prurient minds, who perverted their few and baleful talents to sap discipline and corrupt their equals, to deal in foul imagery and destroy reverence.

"But you didn't seem to consider this when your house called us— ah—stinkers. If you hadn't assured me that you never interfere with another man's house, I should almost believe that it was a few casual remarks of yours that started all this nonsense."

Prout had endured much, for King always took his temper to meals.

"You spoke to Beetle yourself, didn't you? Something about not bathing, and being a water-funk?" the school chaplain put in. "I was scoring in the pavilion that day."

"I may have—jestingly. I really don't pretend to remember every remark I let fall among small boys; and full well I know the Beetle has no feelings to be hurt."

"Maybe; but he, or they—it comes to the same thing—have the fiend's own knack of discovering a man's weak place. I confess I rather go out of my way to conciliate Number Five study. It may be soft, but so far, I believe, I am the only man here whom they haven't maddened by their— well—attentions." . . .

"I don't like the boys, I own"—Prout dug viciously with his fork into the table-cloth—"and I don't pretend to be a strong man, as you know. But I confess I can't see any reason why I should take steps against Stalky and the others because King happens to be annoyed by—by—"

"Falling into the pit he has digged," said little Hartopp. "Certainly not, Prout. No one accuses you of setting one house against another through sheer idleness." . . .

The dingy den off the Common-room was never used for anything except gowns. Its windows were ground glass; one could not see out of it, but one could hear almost every word on the gravel outside. A light and wary footstep came up from Number Five.

"Rattray!" in a subdued voice—Rattray's study fronted that way. "D'you know if Mr King's anywhere about? I've got a —" M'Turk discreetly left the end of his sentence open.

"No. He's gone out," said Rattray unguardedly.

"Ah! The learned Lipsius is airing himself, is he? His Royal Highness has gone to fumigate." M'Turk climbed on the railings, where he held forth like the never-wearied rook.

"Now in all the Coll. there was no stink like the stink of King's house, for it stank vehemently and none knew what to make of it. Save King. And he washed the fags *privatim et seriatim*. In the fishpools of Heshbon washed he them, with an apron about his loins."

"Shut up, you mad Irishman!" There was the sound of a golf-ball spurting up the gravel.

"It's no good getting wrathy, Rattray. We've come to jape with you. Come on, Beetle. They're all at home. You can wind 'em."

"Where's the Pomposo Stinkadore? 'Tisn't safe for a pure-souled, high-minded boy to be seen round his house these days. Gone out, has he? Never mind. I'll do the best I can, Rattray. I'm *in loco parentis* just now."

"I have a few words to impart to you, my young friend. We will discourse together awhile." Beetle, in a strained voice, had chosen a favourite gambit of King's.

"I repeat, Master Rattray, we will confer, and the matter of our discourse shall not be stinks, for that is a loathsome and obscene word. We will, with your good leave—granted, I trust, Master Rattray, granted, I trust—study this—this scabrous upheaval of latent demoralisation. What impresses me most is not so much the blatant indecency with which you swagger abroad under your load of putrescence" (you must imagine this discourse punctuated with golf-balls, but old Rattray was ever a bad shot) "as the cynical immorality with which you revel in your abhorrent aromas. Far be it from me to interfere with another's house—"

"But to say that you stink, as certain lewd fellows of the baser sort aver, is to say nothing—less than nothing. In the absence of your beloved house-master, for whom no one has a higher regard than myself, I will, if you will allow me, explain the grossness—the unparalleled enormity—the appalling fetor of the stenches (I believe in the good old Anglo-Saxon word), stenches, sir, with which you have seen fit to infect your house. . . . Oh, bother! I've forgotten the rest, but it was very beautiful. Aren't you grateful to us for labourin' with you this way, Rattray? Lots of chaps 'ud never have taken the trouble, but we're grateful, Rattray."

"Yes, we're horrid grateful," grunted M'Turk. "We don't forget that soap. We're polite. Why ain't you polite, Rat?" . . .

"*Cave!*" in an undertone. Beetle had spied King sailing down the corridor.

"And what may you be doing here, my little friends?" the house-master began. "I had a fleeting notion—correct me if I am wrong (the listeners with one accord choked)—that if I found you outside my house I should visit you with dire pains and penalties."

"We were just goin' for a walk, sir," said Beetle.

"And you stopped to speak to Rattray *en route*?"

"Yes, sir. We've been throwing golf-balls," said Rattray, coming out of the study.

"Oh, you were sporting with them, were you? I must say I do not envy you your choice of associates. I fancied they might have been engaged in some of the prurient discourse with which they have been so disgustingly free of late. I should strongly advise you to direct your steps most carefully in the future. Pick up those golf-balls." He passed on.

*

Next day Richards, who had been a carpenter in the Navy, and to whom odd jobs were confided, was ordered to take up a dormitory floor; for Mr King held that something must have died there.

"We need not neglect all our work for a trumpery incident of this nature; though I am quite aware that little things please little minds. Yes, I have decreed the boards to be taken up after lunch under Richards' auspices. I have no doubt it will be vastly interesting to a certain type of so-called intellect; but any boy of my house or another's found on the dormitory stairs will *ipso facto* render himself liable to three hundred lines."

The boys did not collect on the stairs, but most of them waited outside King's. Richards had been bound to cry the news from the attic window, and, if possible, to exhibit the corpse.

"'Tis a cat, a dead cat!" Richards' face showed purple at the window. He had been in the chamber of death and on his knees for some time.

"Cat be blowed!" cried M'Turk. "It's a dead fag left over from last term. Three cheers for King's dead fag!"

They cheered lustily.

"Show it, show it! Let's have a squint at it!" yelled the juniors. "Give her to the Bug-hunters. [This was the Natural History Society.] The cat looked at the King—and died of it! Hoosh! Yai! Yaow! Maiow! Ftzz!" were some of the cries that followed.

Again Richards appeared.

"She've been"—he checked himself suddenly—"dead a long taime."

The school roared.

"Well, come on out for a walk." said Stalky in a well-chosen pause. "It's all very disgustin', and I do hope that the Lazar-house won't do it again."

"Do what?" a King's boy cried furiously.

"Kill a poor innocent cat every time you want to get off washing. It's awfully hard to distinguish between you as it is. I prefer the cat, I must say. She isn't quite so whiff. What are you goin' to do, Beetle?"

"*Je vais gloater. Je vais gloater tout le* blessed afternoon. *Jamais j'ai gloaté comme je gloaterai aujourd'hui. Nous bunkerons aux* bunkers."

And it seemed good to them so to do.

*

Down in the basement, where the gas flickers and the boots stand in racks, Richards, amid his blacking-brushes, held forth to Oke of the Commonroom, Gumbly of the dining-halls, and fair Lena of the laundry.

"Yiss. Her were in a shockin' staate an' condition. Her nigh made me sick, I tal 'ee. But I rowted un out, and I rowted un out, an' I made all shipshape, though her smelt like to bilges."

"Her died mousin', I rackon, poor thing," said Lena.

"Then her moused different to any made cat o' God's world, Lena. I up with the top-board, an' she were lying on her back, an' I turned un ovver with the brume-handle, an' 'twas her back was all covered with the plaster from 'twixt the lathin'. Yiss, I tal 'ee. An' under her head there lay, like, so's to say, a little pillow o' plaster druv up in front of her by raison of her slidin' along on her back. No cat niver went mousin' on her back, Lena. Some one had shoved her along right underneath, so far as they could shove un. Cats don't make theyselves pillows for to die on. Shoved along, she were, when she was settin' for to be cold, laike."

"Oh, yeou'm too clever to live, Fatty. Yeou go get wed an' taught some sense," said Lena, the affianced of Gumbly.

"Larned a little 'fore iver some maidens was born. Sarved in the Queen's Navy, I have, where yeou'm taught to use your eyes. Yeou go 'tend your own business, Lena."

"Do 'ee mean what you'm been tellin' us?" said Oke.

"Ask me no questions, I'll give 'ee no lies. Bullet-hole clane thru from side to side, an' tu heart-ribs broke like withies. I seed un when I turned un ovver. They'm clever, oh, they'm clever, but they'm not tu clever for old Richards! 'Twas on the born tip o' my tongue to tell, tu, but . . . he said us niver washed, he did. Let his dom boys call us 'stinkers,' he did. Sarved un dom well raight, I say!"

Richards spat on a fresh boot and fell to his work, chuckling.

ANGELA BRAZIL (1869-1947)
"The Secret Society" from *The Third Class at Miss Kaye's* (1908)

Born at Preston, Lancashire, Angela Brazil was educated in Manchester. Known as an elegant chatelaine and dedicated committee-woman in Coventry, where she settled, she acquired fame and fortune from her forty-nine schoolgirl novels that were beloved by two (sometimes three) generations of young girls. They created their own boarding-school slang, revered the attachment of classmates to special friends or protegées, and offered many examples of the sly behaviour that a close community can foster. Brazil's later books deteriorated into crude formula writing, but at the beginning of her career her narrative powers were appealing and strong.

Following the great success of her first schoolgirl story, *The Fortunes of Philippa* (1906), Miss Brazil's publishers, Blackie & Son, commissioned her to write another. In response to this flattering request she wrote *The Third Class at Miss Kaye's* (1908), which relates the changes in spoiled, self-

centred, ten-year-old Sylvia Lindsay after she is sent to Heathercliffe House, a girls' school judiciously run by Miss Kaye. Sylvia is assigned to be the roommate of the agreeable Linda Marshall and settles in quickly, cementing a strong friendship with Linda and competing strenuously for top place in her form with the diligent honour student, Marian Woodhouse. Brazil's story emphasizes the important socializing role of the school. Vengeful and cunning girls—like Hazel Prestbury—are tidily removed from Heathercliffe House. Sylvia learns to accept, and even begins to thrive under, the exacting pedagogy of the third-form mistress, Miss Arkwright. Despite their varied talents, the girls of the third class, as this chapter illustrates, are a tremendously loyal clan—keeping their secret from the sleuths of the second class and applauding the literary efforts of fellow "Slugs".

THE SECRET SOCIETY

School re-opened on January 18, and Sylvia found herself driving up to the well-known door with very different feelings from those she had experienced on her first arrival there. On the whole she was quite pleased to be back again, to meet all her friends, and compare notes about the holidays. There was one change in the third class which, however it might affect others, seemed to Sylvia a decided improvement. Hazel Prestbury had left. An aunt residing in Paris had offered to take her for a time to give her the opportunity of special study in French and music, and her parents had arranged for her to go at once, sending Brenda, a younger sister, to Heathercliffe House in her place. Brenda was a very different child from Hazel, and had soon sworn eternal friendship with Connie Camden, so that at last Sylvia felt she had her dear Linda absolutely and entirely to herself.

"I don't know how it is," said Nina one chilly February evening when the members of the third class were gathered round the high fireguard in the playroom, "there never seems half so much fun going on in the spring term. In the autumn we have Hallowe'en and the fifth of November and the Christmas party, and in the summer there are picnics and the shore, and the sports, and the prize-giving; but unless Miss Kaye takes us a long walk there isn't anything to look forward to now until Easter."

"And that's eleven whole weeks off," groaned Connie. "I wish it had come early this year."

"It wouldn't make any difference if it did," said Marian; "Miss Kaye keeps to the term. We should only have to spend Easter at school, and go home as usual in the middle of April."

"That would be horrid. Why should she?"

"Because it would make too long a summer term, and because she likes our holidays to be the same as those of the boys' schools."

"I hadn't thought of that. Of course it would be no fun to go home if Percy and Frank and Bertie and Godfrey weren't there. Still, I wish terms were a little shorter, or that something nice would happen." And Connie ruffled up her hair with both hands as an expression of her discontent.

"Couldn't we do something just amongst ourselves?" said Sylvia. "Not the whole school, but our class."

"There isn't anything new," said Brenda, "unless someone can invent a fresh game. We're getting tired of table croquet."

"I don't mean exactly a game. Suppose we were each to write a story, and then have a meeting to read them all out."

"Start a kind of magazine?" said Marian. "That's a good idea. We could put our tales together into an old exercise book, and perhaps paste pictures in for illustrations, and make up puzzles and competitions for the end."

"Oh yes, that would be lovely!" cried the others. "Like *Little Folks* or *The Girl's Realm*."

"But look here," said Linda. "The second class mustn't hear a word about it. They'd only make dreadful fun of us, and it will be ever so much nicer if we keep it a secret."

"Let us form a secret society, then," suggested Sylvia. "We'll pinch each others' little fingers, and vow we won't tell a soul in the school."

"How horridly inquisitive they'll be!" said Nina.

"All the more fun. We'll let them know that we're doing something, enough to make them wildly curious, but they shan't have a hint of what it is, and they'll imagine the most ridiculous things, and then we can just laugh at them and say they're quite wrong."

The girls agreed cordially with Sylvia's scheme, and the society was formed on the spot. There was a good deal of discussion as to a suitable name. Linda thought of "The Heathercliffe Magaziners," but Nina said that was tame, and that, moreover, "Magaziners" was not to be found in the dictionary of the English language. Connie considered "The 'Wouldn't you like to know?' Club" might be appropriate, but nobody approved of her title. At last Marian, who was fond of long, grand-sounding names, suggested "The Secret Society of Literary Undertakings," which was carried unanimously by the others. Marian was elected President and Sylvia Secretary, and the latter at once devoted a new notebook to writing the names of the members and the rules of the association.

"We must have rules," said Marian, "even if we don't always quite keep them. You'll have to hide the book away most carefully, Sylvia, for fear any of the second class get hold of it."

It took a long time to think of sufficiently strict and binding regulations, but at length they decided upon the following:—

1. This Society is to be called "The Secret Society of Literary Undertakings," and it can be known for short as the S.S.L.U.

2. Each member pledges herself that she will never tell a word of what goes on in it.

3. Any member who tells anything will never be spoken to again by the rest of the class.

4. There is to be a weekly magazine.

5. Every member must write something for it.

6. Even if a member says she cannot write anything, she will have to try.

7. If she does not try, she will be expelled from the society.

8. The meetings are to be held in the playroom after the fourth class has gone to bed.

9. Any member who is expelled will have to stay outside in the passage during the meetings.

10. All members are requested to write as clearly as they can.

11. The Secretary is to arrange the magazine.

12. The President is to read it out at the weekly meeting.

As Nina had prophesied, the S.S.L.U. aroused a good deal of curiosity among the second class, which, while it affected to look down upon the third, was nevertheless rather interested in what was going on there. Being permitted to know the initials, though not the full name, the elder girls promptly added a G, and christened the members "The Slugs," a title which stuck to them long after the society was abandoned. It was most difficult to preserve the secret from the little ones, who shared the playroom, but by instituting a series of private signs and signals they managed to keep up the mystery and obtain a great amount of enjoyment out of the matter. Brenda Prestbury covered herself with glory by recalling the deaf-and-dumb alphabet, the various letters of which she had learnt at home, and now taught to the others, who were soon able to talk on their fingers, a rather slow method of conversation, but delightful when they felt that nobody but a member could understand. . . .

The first grand meeting of the society was felt to be an occasion of great importance. The playroom door was carefully shut, after ascertaining that no one was in the passage, and Brenda even peeped under the table and behind the window curtains to make quite sure that none of the second class were concealed there. At last, considering themselves secure, the magazine was produced by the Secretary, and handed to the President, who, according to the rules, was to read it aloud from beginning to end. It was written on sheets of paper torn from exercise books, stitched together inside an old arithmetic cover, the back of which had been adorned with scraps and transfers and S.S.L.U. printed on a school label and gummed in the middle. The idea of illustrations had to be abandoned, because nobody had any magazines which they would spare to be cut up, neither did anybody's talent rise to the pitch of original drawings; but on the whole that did not much matter.

"It's stories we want, not pictures," said Marian, settling herself on the seat of honour with a piece of toffee handy, in case her throat grew troublesome through her arduous duties.

"The first on the list," she began, "is—

THE KNIGHT'S VENGEANCE

A Story in Two Parts

By Nina Millicent Forster

Author of 'The Baron's Secret'; 'The Mystery of the Castle'; &c. &c.

Part I

The forest was dark and gloomy as Sir Brian de Fotheringay rode along on his superb white charger, carrying his shield in one hand and his sword in the other."

"How did he manage to hold the reins?" enquired Connie Camden. "You musn't interrupt," said Marian. "Perhaps he held them bunched up with the sword. No, that would be the wrong hand, wouldn't it?"

"The horse knew its own way," explained Nina. "But if Connie's going to find fault with everything one puts—"

"She shan't!" said Marian hastily. "Nobody's to make any remarks till the end of the story. Now I'm going on.

His undaunted spirit heeded little the perils of his path, and as the moonlight flashed on his steel helmet he bade defiance to all his foes. In front of him stood the Castle, its tall towers strongly guarded by a force of armed men. The drawbridge was up, and the portcullis was down. But dangers were welcome to Sir Brian de Fotheringay, for they did but prove how much he could accomplish for the sake of his lady love. She stood at the turret window, the beautiful Lady Guinevere de Montmorency, the greatest heiress in the land. Leaving his charger on the bank, he swam the moat, and, flinging a rope ladder up to her window, he begged her to fly with him.

"Knight, for thee would I dare all!" she replied, but before she could say more, a stern figure in armour appeared in the turret behind her and seized her by her flowing golden locks. It was her angry father.

"Hence!" he cried. "Hence, Sir Brian, ere I kill thee. You, lady, will be immured in the dungeon until you have promised to wed Lord Vivian de Fitz Bracy, the suitor of my choice."

With a shriek she disappeared from the view of her despairing knight.

Part II

Determined to save his lady love from so terrible a fate, Sir Brian de Fotheringay collected all his retainers, together with a band of outlaws to whom he had rendered some services, and who had promised to assist him in time of need. Uttering his warcry, they rushed at the Castle, the portcullis gave way before their furious attack, and the archers were slain at their posts.

"Yield thee, Sir Guy de Montmorency!" cried Sir Brian, waving his invincible sword.

"Never!" shouted the Baron, but it was his last word, for Sir Brian stabbed him to the heart.

He had soon forced open the dungeon and released the beautiful Lady Guinevere. The Castle was now hers, so they were married without delay, and the King and Queen themselves came to the wedding."

"It's perfectly splendid!" cried the girls, when Marian had finished reading. "Nina, how did you manage to think of it?"

"Oh, I don't know; it just came!" said Nina, modestly. "I'm rather fond of making up tales."

"There's only one thing," said Connie. "Wasn't the lady rather sorry when her father was stabbed to the heart, even if he had shut her up in a dungeon? I should be."

"I don't think people minded in the Middle Ages," said Nina. "You see, somebody had to get killed, and she liked the knight best."

"But her own father!" objected Connie.

"I'm going to read the next one now," said Marian, who, as President, felt bound to keep the peace. "I think Nina's story's very good, and makes a capital beginning. This one seems much shorter. It's called:

MOST HASTE, LEAST SPEED

By Gwendolen Woodhouse

Matilda Jane was a girl who was always in a hurry. One day her grandmother told her to take the bucket and fetch some water from the well, but to be sure to tie her boot lace first. Now Matilda Jane wanted to be very quick, so that she might go and play, and she did not stop to tie her boot lace. As she ran out of the door, she tripped over it and fell. The bucket rolled from her hand and hit the dog; the dog howled and made the geese cackle; the geese cackling made the pigs grunt; the pigs grunting frightened the hens into the field; the hens frightened the cow, which began to run; when the horse saw the cow running, it ran too, and they both jumped over the hedge into the road; then the hens flew after the horse and the cow, and the pigs went after the hens, and the geese followed the pigs, and the dog chased the geese, and it took Matilda Jane and her grandmother the whole afternoon to drive them back, and all because she had been in too great a hurry to tie her boot lace. The moral of the tale is 'Most haste, least speed!' "

The girls laughed.

"I don't generally like stories with a moral," said Brenda, "but I don't mind this one at any rate. Go on, Marian!"

"The next is a piece of poetry," said Marian.

THE KITTENS' CHORUS

By Sylvia Lindsay

Miew! Miew! Miew! Miew!
We want to catch mice, we do, we do!
But our mother, the old white cat,
Says we are rather too young for that.

Miew! Miew! Miew! Miew!
We want to catch flies, we do, we do!

But our mother says that if we do it
We'll grow so thin that we soon shall rue it!

Miew! Miew! Miew! Miew!
We want to catch mother's tail we do!
But she says she is not such a common cat
As to let her kits be so pert as that.

Miew! Miew! Miew! Miew!
We want to be good, we do, we do!
But that's much harder to do than to say,
So we'll think about that another day.

The poem proved so popular that Marian had to read it over again. It was the first time that the class had heard any of Sylvia's effusions, and they were quite impressed.

"I'm afraid mine will seem very stupid after it," said Brenda. "I couldn't think of anything to write, but I was obliged to put something."

"The title sounds interesting," said Marian.

MY VISIT TO FRANCE

By Brenda G. Prestbury

Last summer Mother took Hazel and me with her to France, to visit Aunt Cecily, who was staying near Rouen. The first thing we saw was a funny old woman in a big white cap, like a large poke bonnet, and wooden shoes on her feet. The porters all wore baggy blue blouses something like pinafores. We were obliged to go through the Customs. A man in a uniform was looking to see if anybody had brought any tea. He took a little girl's doll away from her, and felt it to see if it had any tea inside it; then he took a lady's cushion, and because she got angry, he stuck his sword through it, and all the feathers came out over his grand coat. We were so glad! There were no carpets in the house where Aunt Cecily was living; the floors were of polished wood, and so slippery. Jean, the servant, used to rub them with beeswax every morning, but he was very cross in French when Hazel and I made slides on them. We used to have coffee and lovely little rolls at seven in the morning, and then proper breakfast at eleven, and we had quite different things to eat from what you get in England. One day Hazel and I went such a long walk that we got lost, and we couldn't remember enough French to ask our way home. A woman came along with a donkey and two big baskets on it, and when she saw us crying she gave us each an apple, and took us to the curé of the village, who could speak English. He was very kind; he showed us round his garden, and then he borrowed a cart from the farmer, and drove us home to Aunt Cecily's. This is all I can tell you about my visit to France.

"I know it's horrid!" said Brenda. "But I really can't write well, and make up tales like Nina. I don't know how she does it!"

"It's jolly!" said Marian. "We've none of us been to France, so we like to hear about it. I wish you had written more. The next one's very short indeed."

THE LADY AND THE SNAKE

By Jessie Ellis

A lady who lived in Australia one day put a great log of wood on to the fire. In a little while she was going to poke it, and she stooped to pick up what she thought was the poker, but it was really a horrible black snake, which coiled at once round her arm. She had the presence of mind not to move, but remained very still, and in a few moments it slid down on to the ground. A gentleman who was in the room killed it, and taking the log from the fire he carried it into the yard, where seven more snakes dropped out of it. The wood was hollow, and they had made a nest inside it, and gone to sleep, and the warmth of the fire had wakened them up.

"It's quite true," said Jessie. "The lady was my aunt. She told us about it in a letter."

"What a horrid thing to happen!" cried the girls.

"A nice tale, but too short," commented the President. "I'm afraid Linda hasn't written a long one either."

THE STORY OF A DOG

By Linda Acton Marshall

I have a little dog called Scamp, that follows me wherever I go. He can sit up and beg, and catch biscuits on his nose, and do all kinds of tricks. One day I was in bed with a bad cold, and Scamp came upstairs to my room. I told him I was ill, and he gave a sharp bark, and ran out. I could hear him trot up to the attic, and soon he returned with a biscuit in his mouth, and laid it on my pillow, wagging his tail, and looking very sorry for me, and very pleased at himself. He must have kept a store of biscuits in the attic. I think he is just the cleverest little dog in the world.

"My tale's true, too," said Linda. "No, I didn't make it up, Nina; he really did. There are only two stories left now, Connie's and Marian's. I wonder which comes next."

"Connie's," said Marian. "And it's in poetry, too. It's called:

THE S.S.L.U.

By Constance Mary Camden

Said the girls of the third class "All we
A Secret Society will be.
Though the second may hover
Our words to discover,
It's nothing they'll hear or they'll see.

They may listen at doors in the hall,
Or round by the keyhole may crawl,
They may search through the schools,
But they won't find our rules,
And they'll never know nothing at all."

The girls clapped, both at the sentiments expressed, and at the poetical setting.

"I know they'd listen if they could," said Connie. "They're mean enough for anything. What's that noise?"

"Why, nothing."

"I thought I heard a kind of snorting."

"I expect it was only my cold," said Nina. "Do go on, Marian; we want your story."

"But I did hear something," persisted Connie. "I believe it was outside the door, too, and I'm going to look."

She rose hastily, and, creeping softly to the door, opened it suddenly, disclosing the laughing faces of half a dozen of the second class, who had been taking it in turns to listen at the keyhole, and who jumped up in a hurry and fled from the outburst of wrath which greeted them.

"Oh! Oh!" shouted Sybil Lake. "Won't they hear or see anything? Don't make too sure!"

"I have a little dog that follows me wherever I go!" called Eileen Butler. "I think he's just the cleverest little dog in the world!"

"The slugs are crawling fast!" cried Lucy Martin. The injured third had risen in a body and pursued the intruders along the passage even to the door of their own sitting room; but, seeing Miss Barrett coming downstairs, they did not dare to carry the fight into the enemy's camp, and were obliged to return to the playroom, and hold an indignation meeting over the glasses of milk and biscuits which arrived at that moment for supper.

"We must read Marian's story to-morrow," said Sylvia. "Wasn't it horrid of them? I wonder how much they really heard? Next time we shall have to stuff up the keyhole, and keep opening the door every few minutes to see that the coast is clear. There's one good thing: they didn't discover our signs, or the password, and they'll have hard work to find the rules, because the book's hidden under the oilcloth in the corner by the piano; only be sure and don't let the little ones know, because I don't believe there's one of them that can keep a secret!"

ALICE JANE CHANDLER WEBSTER ("JEAN WEBSTER") (1876-1916)
Letters to an Unknown Benefactor from *Daddy-Long-Legs* (1912)

Alice Jane Chandler Webster was born in Fredonia, New York. Daughter of a publisher and grandniece of Mark Twain, she majored in English at Vassar and gained a considerable reputation for her many tales of campus life, the best known of which are *When Patty Went to College* (1903), *Just Patty* (1911), *Daddy-Long-Legs* (1912), and its sequel *Dear Enemy* (1914).

Unlike most Golden Age school stories, *Daddy-Long-Legs* presents a rather narrow view of school. Through a series of coy, chatty letters sent by Jerusha (or Judy) Abbott to her unknown benefactor, whom she names Daddy-Long-Legs, Webster's story tells of Judy's college days in Massachusetts; but this subject is soon displaced by her mounting interest in the unseen man whose generosity has removed her from an orphan asylum and sent her to college to study to be a writer. The letters (often enlivened with Webster's own drawings) tend to be sugary—full of girlish effusiveness and enthusiasm. The reader is not surprised when Judy eventually becomes the wife of her beloved Daddy-Long-Legs.

This sentimental romance has had a longstanding appeal for Hollywood producers. *Daddy-Long-Legs* was made into a silent picture starring Mary Pickford and Mahlon Hamilton in 1919, a talkie starring Janet Gaynor and Warner Baxter in 1930, and was transformed into a musical for Leslie Caron and Fred Astaire in 1955.

LETTERS TO AN UNKNOWN BENEFACTOR

December 19th.

Dear Daddy-Long-Legs,
You never answered my question and it was very important.

ARE YOU BALD?

I have it planned exactly what you look like—very satisfactorily—until I reach the top of your head, and then I *am* stuck. I can't decide whether you have white hair or black hair or sort of sprinkly gray hair or maybe none at all.

Here is your portrait:
But the problem is, shall I add some hair?

Would you like to know what color your eyes are? They're gray, and your eyebrows stick out like a porch roof (beetling, they're called in novels) and your mouth is a straight line with a tendency to turn down at the corners. Oh, you see, I know! Your're a snappy old thing with a temper.

(Chapel bell.)

9:45 P.M.

I have a new unbreakable rule: never, never to study at night no matter how many written reviews are coming in the morning. Instead, I read just plain books—I have to, you know, because there are eighteen blank years behind me. You wouldn't believe, Daddy, what an abyss of ignorance my mind is; I am just realizing the depths myself. The things that most girls with a properly assorted family and a home and friends and a library know by absorption, I have never heard of. For example:

I never read "Mother Goose" or "David Copperfield" or "Ivanhoe" or "Cinderella" or "Blue Beard" or "Robinson Cursoe" or "Jane Eyre" or "Alice in Wonderland" or a word of Rudyard Kipling. I didn't know that Henry the Eighth was married more than once or that Shelley was a poet. I didn't know that people used to be monkeys and that the Garden of Eden was a beautiful myth. I didn't know that R.L.S. stood for Robert Louis Stevenson or that George Eliot was a lady. I had never seen a picture of the "Mona Lisa" and (it's true but you won't believe it) I had never heard of Sherlock Holmes.

Now, I know all of these things and a lot of others besides, but you can see how much I need to catch up. And oh, but it's fun! I look forward all day to evening, and then I put an "engaged" on the door and get into my nice red bath robe and furry slippers and pile all the cushions behind me on the couch and light the brass student lamp at my elbow, and read and read and read. One book isn't enough. I have four going at once. Just now, they're Tennyson's poems and "Vanity Fair" and Kipling's "Plain Tales" and—don't laugh—"Little Women." I find that I am the only girl in college who wasn't brought up on "Little Women." I haven't told anybody though (that *would* stamp me as queer). I just quietly went and bought it with $1.12 of my last month's allowance; and the next time somebody mentions pickled limes, I'll know what she is talking about!

(Ten o'clock bell. This is a very interrupted letter.)

Saturday.

Sir,

I have the honour to report fresh explorations in the field of geometry. On Friday last we abandoned our former works in parallelopipeds and proceeded to truncated prisms. We are finding the road rough and very uphill.

Sunday.

The Christmas holidays begin next week and the trunks are up. The corridors are so cluttered that you can hardly get through, and everybody is so bubbling over with excitement that studying is getting left out. I'm going to have a beautiful time in vacation; there's another Freshman who lives in Texas staying behind, and we are planning to take long walks and—if there's any ice—learn to skate. Then there is still the whole library to be read—and three empty weeks to do it in!

Good-bye, Daddy, I hope that you are feeling as happy as I am.

Yours ever,
JUDY

P.S. Don't forget to answer my question. If you don't want the trouble of writing, have your secretary telegraph. He can just say:

Mr Smith is quite bald,

or

Mr Smith is not bald,

or

Mr Smith has white hair.

And you can deduct the twenty-five cents out of my allowance.

Good-by till January—and a merry Christmas!

Sunday.

Dearest Daddy-Long-Legs,

I have some awful, awful, awful news to tell you, but I won't begin with it; I'll try to get you in a good humor first.

Jerusha Abbott has commenced to be an author. A poem entitled, "From my Tower," appears in the February *Monthly*—on the first page, which is a very great honor for a Freshman. My English instructor stopped me on the way out from chapel last night, and said it was a charming piece of work except for the sixth line, which had too many feet. I will send you a copy in case you care to read it.

Let me see if I can't think of something else pleasant—Oh, yes! I'm learning to skate, and can glide about quite respectably all by myself. Also I've learned how to slide down a rope from the roof of the gymnasium, and I can vault a bar three feet and six inches high—I hope shortly to pull up to four feet.

We had a very inspiring sermon this morning preached by the Bishop of Alabama. His text was: "Judge not that ye be not judged." It was about the necessity of overlooking mistakes in others, and not discouraging people by harsh judgements. I wish you might have heard it.

This is the sunniest, most blinding winter afternoon, with icicles dripping from the fir trees and all the world bending under a weight of snow—except me, and I'm bending under a weight of sorrow.

Now for the news—courage, Judy!—you must tell.

Are you *surely* in a good humor? I flunked mathematics and Latin prose. I am tutoring in them, and will take another examination next month. I'm sorry if you're disappointed, but otherwise I don't care a bit because I've learned such a lot of things not mentioned in the catalogue. I've read seventeen novels and *bushels* of poetry—really necessary novels like "Vanity Fair" and "Richard Feverel" and "Alice in Wonderland." Also Emerson's "Essays" and Lockhart's "Life of Scott" and the first volume of Gibbon's "Roman Empire" and half of Benvenuto Cellini's "Life"—wasn't he entertaining? He used to saunter out and casually kill a man before breakfast.

So you see, Daddy, I'm much more intelligent than if I'd just stuck to Latin. Will you forgive me this once if I promise never to flunk again?

Yours in sackcloth,
JUDY

NEWS of the MONTH

Judy learns to skate

And to vault a bar

Also to slide down a rope

legs are very difficult

She receives two flunk notes and sheds many tears

But promises to study HARD

September 30th

Dear Daddy,

Are you still harping on that scholarship? I never knew a man so obstinate and stubborn and unreasonable, and tenacious, and bull-doggish, and unable-to-see-other-people's-points-of-view as you.

You prefer that I should not be accepting favors from strangers.

Strangers!—And what are you, pray?

Is there any one in the world that I know less? I shouldn't recognize you if I met you on the street. Now, you see, if you had been a sane, sensible person and had written nice, cheering, fatherly letters to your little Judy, and had come occasionally and patted her on the head, and had said you were glad she was such a good girl—Then, perhaps, she wouldn't have flouted you in your old age, but would have obeyed your slightest wish like the dutiful daughter she was meant to be.

Strangers indeed! You live in a glass house, Mr Smith.

And besides, this isn't a favor; it's like a prize—I earned it by hard work. If nobody had been good enough in English, the committee wouldn't have awarded the scholarship; some years they don't. Also— But what's the use of arguing with a man? You belong, Mr Smith, to a sex devoid of a sense of logic. To bring a man into line, there are just two methods: one must either coax or be disagreeable. I scorn to coax men for what I wish. Therefore, I must be disagreeable.

I refuse, sir, to give up the scholarship; and if you make any more fuss, I won't accept the monthly allowance either, but will wear myself into a nervous wreck tutoring stupid Freshmen.

That is my ultimatum!

And listen—I have a further thought. Since you are so afraid that by taking this scholarship, I am depriving some one else of an education, I know a way out. You can apply the money that you would have spent for me, toward educating some other little girl from the John Grier Home. Don't you think that's a nice idea? Only, Daddy, *educate* the new girl as much as you choose, but please don't *like* her any better than me.

I trust that your secretary won't be hurt because I pay so little attention to the suggestions offered in his letter, but I can't help it if he is. He's a spoiled child, Daddy. I've meekly given in to his whims heretofore, but this time I intend to be FIRM.

Yours,
  With a Mind,
    Completely and Irrevocably and
    World-without-End Made-up.

JERUSHA ABBOTT.

Thursday Morning.

My very dearest Master-Jervie-Daddy-Long-Legs-Pendleton-Smith,

Yesterday was the most wonderful day that could ever happen. If I live to be ninety-nine I shall never forget the tiniest detail. The girl that left Lock Willow at dawn was a very different person from the one who came back at night. Mrs Semple called me at half-past four. I started wide awake in the darkness and the first thought that popped into my head was, "I am going to see Daddy-Long-Legs!" I ate breakfast in the kitchen by candle-light, and then drove the five miles to the station through the most glorious October coloring. The sun came up on the way, and the swamp maples and dogwood glowed crimson and orange and the stone walls and cornfields sparkled with hoar frost; the air was keen and clear and full of promise. I *knew* something was going to happen. All the way in the train the rails kept singing, "You're going to see Daddy-Long-Legs." It made me feel secure. I had such faith in Daddy's ability to set things right. And I knew that somewhere another man—dearer than Daddy—was wanting to see me, and somehow I had a feeling that before the journey ended I should meet him, too. And you see!

When I came to the house on Madison Avenue it looked so big and brown and forbidding that I didn't dare go in, so I walked around the block to get up my courage. But I needn't have been a bit afraid; your butler is such a nice, fatherly old man that he made me feel at home at once. "Is this Miss Abbott?" he said to me, and I said, "Yes," so I didn't have to ask for Mr Smith after all. He told me to wait in the drawing room. It was a very somber, magnificent, man's sort of room. I sat down on the edge of a big upholstered chair and kept saying to myself:

"I'm going to see Daddy-Long-Legs! I'm going to see Daddy-Long-Legs!"

Then presently the man came back and asked me please to step up to the library. I was so excited that really and truly my feet would hardly take me up. Outside the door he turned and whispered, "He's been very ill, Miss. This is the first day he's been allowed to sit up. You'll not stay long enough to excite him?" I knew from the way he said it that he loved you—and I think he's an old dear!

Then ke knocked and said, "Miss Abbott," and I went in and the door closed behind me.

It was so dim coming from the brightly lighted hall that for a moment I could scarcely make out anything; then I saw a big easy chair before the fire and a shining tea table with a smaller chair beside it. And I realized that a man was sitting in the big chair propped up by pillows with a rug over his knees. Before I could stop him he rose—sort of shakily—and steadied himself by the back of the chair and just looked at me without a word. And then—and then—I saw it was you! But even with that I didn't understand. I thought Daddy had had you come there to meet me for a surprise.

Then you laughed and held out your hand and said, "Dear little Judy, couldn't you guess that I was Daddy-Long-Legs?"

In an instant it flashed over me. Oh, but I have been stupid! A hundred little things might have told me, if I had had any wits. I wouldn't make a very good detective, would I, Daddy?—Jervie? What must I call you? Just plain Jervie sounds disrespectful and I can't be disrespectful to you!

It was a very sweet half hour before your doctor came and sent me away. I was so dazed when I got to the station that I almost took a train for St Louis. And you were pretty dazed, too. You forgot to give me any tea. But we're both very, very happy, aren't we? I drove back to Lock Willow in the dark—but oh, how the stars were shining! And this morning I've been out with Colin visiting all the places that you and I went together, and remembering what you said and how you looked. The woods to-day are burnished bronze and the air is full of frost. It's *climbing* weather. I wish you were here to climb the hills with me. I am missing you dreadfully, Jervie dear, but it's a happy kind of missing: we'll be together soon. We belong to each other now really and truly, no make-believe. Doesn't it seem queer for me to belong to some one at last? It seems very, very sweet.

And I shall never let you be sorry for a single minute.

Yours, forever and ever,

JUDY.

P.S. This the first love letter I ever wrote. Isn't it funny that I know how?

7. TRAIL BLAZERS AND JOLLY ROVERS: STORIES OF ADVENTURE

We had on the nursery shelves a long run of Henty, and I particularly liked the dull historical parts. . . . Rider Haggard I discovered after Henty. My favourite, of course, was King Solomon's Mines.—Graham Greene, A Sort of Life (1971).

Inspired by Captain Frederick Marryat's books of adventures for boys like *Mr Midshipman Easy* (1836) and *Masterman Ready* (1841), other men of action—a soldier of fortune, a fur trader, and a sea-faring gentleman—turned their own recollections into best-selling stories that galvanized generations of boy readers. Tales like Mayne Reid's *The Rifle Rangers* (1850), R.M. Ballantyne's *Snowflakes and Sunbeams; or, The Young Fur Traders* (1856), and G.A. Henty's *Out on the Pampas* (1868) thrilled youngsters with their accounts of survival and heroic exploits in far-off lands. These in turn were followed by some of the best-known and most loved fiction of the

Golden Age: Ballantyne's *The Coral Island* (1858), Robert Louis Stevenson's *Treasure Island* (1883) and *Kidnapped* (1886), and Rider Haggard's *King Solomon's Mines* (1885).

Speaking as a writer of this fiction, Stevenson observed in a letter to W.E. Henley: "It's awful fun, boys' stories; you just indulge the pleasure of your heart, that's all; no trouble, no strain, . . . just drive along as the words come and the pen will scratch!" (25 August 1881). Adventure stories must have been "awful fun" as well for the Victorian child, raised according to so many strictures and conventions. The survival tales of boy castaways, sailors, soldiers, and hunters were more than merely sensational. They were scrupulously faithful in setting, contained very acceptable moralizing about camaraderie and resourcefulness, and imparted a cheery optimism rooted in a consciousness of the innate superiority of Britons and Britain, on whose side God was presumed to be. In addition, the narratives—all by expert storytellers—were shrewdly designed. The action never lagged, episode was piled upon episode with deft interrelation, and after many tests of fortitude the boy-hero triumphed.

Most of these Golden Age adventure stories are narrated in the first person by the young protagonist. In *The Coral Island* Ballantyne's Ralph Rover tells an action-filled story of the South Seas; in *Ran Away to Sea* (1859) Mayne Reid's narrator tells about his experiences as a teenage runaway who ends up on a slave ship bound for Africa; in *The Story of a Bad Boy* (1870) Thomas Bailey Aldrich's hero purports to be "bad" but his story proves that he is more of a prankster than a delinquent. Two of the best-known adventure storytellers, Stevenson and Rider Haggard, may have taken their cue from these forerunners. Since the boldness of Jim Hawkins leads to the final routing of the mutineers and discovery of the treasure, it is only fitting that he tell most of the story of *Treasure Island*. Similarly in *King Solomon's Mines* Allan Quatermain is one of the three white treasure-seekers who journey to Solomon's cave in search of gold and diamonds.

Much care was expended in creating realistic and intriguing locales for these adventures. Describing the rigour and intrigues aboard ship, the lushness of a coral island, or the gruelling ascent of an African mountain, Stevenson, Ballantyne, and Rider Haggard bring to life the most astonishing and exotic scenes. With a charming exactitude James DeMille, in *The "B.O.W.C."* (1869), locates the adventures of his vacationing fraternity of Acadian

schoolboys in the Minas Basin of Nova Scotia. Even though using comparatively familiar backdrops, Catharine Parr Traill in *The Canadian Crusoes* (1851) and Horatio Alger, Jr, in *Ragged Dick* (1867), are very heedful of the determining influence of milieu. Traill offers precise descriptions of the vegetation and terrain of Peterborough County, in which her young Crusoes are lost, and Alger takes pains to re-create the Bowery district of mid-nineteenth-century New York, where his bootblack-hero is growing up.

Recounting tests of mettle, most Golden Age adventure stories are unashamedly addressed to boys; girls, where they appear, are assigned decorous roles. Aldrich's "bad boy" takes time out from his usual pranks to indulge in a passing infatuation with an older female cousin. George Alfred Henty, in *With Wolfe in Canada* (1887), leaves the ever-virtuous Agnes (future wife of the heroic James Walsham) safely protected in her English home at Linthorne Hall, Sidmouth, while her courageous admirer covers himself with glory on the colonial front, winning Canada for the British. Stevenson, however, to comply with his stepson's wishes that there be "no women in the story", entirely omitted distracting females from *Treasure Island*, except the homebound widowed mother of Jim Hawkins. Norman Duncan's hardy Newfoundlander, Billy Topsail, is becomingly deferential towards his mother and old Aunt Esther, but the adventures in the book belong mainly to him and exclusively to men.

Bessie Marchant's later stories of plucky girls who are not content to sit and pine are laudable attempts to redress the balance. Her numerous tales of heroism, therefore, are—like all Golden Age adventure stories—much more than alluring escapes to other places and times. Breezily told though precisely located, they begin to reflect the wider audience for adventure stories in the twentieth century.

CATHARINE PARR TRAILL (1802-1899)
"The First Weeks in the Bush" from *The Canadian Crusoes. A Tale of the Rice Lake Plains* (1851)

Born in London, Eng., Catharine Strickland had written the popular *Little Downy; or, The History of a Field Mouse: A Moral Tale* (1822) before she married Lieutenant Traill in 1832 and immigrated with him to Upper Canada, settling in Douro Township. Her close observation of Canadian life and naturalist's curiosity formed the basis of all her subsequent works, such as *The Female Emigrant's Guide* (1854), *Rambles in the Canadian Forest* (1859), and *Canadian Wild Flowers* (1869).

Set in the Otonabee Township of Peterborough County, Canada West (Ontario), *The Canadian Crusoes* (1851) relates the survival adventures of three lost children. Hector and Catharine Maxwell, with their cousin Louis Perron, fend for themselves in the wilderness for three years. Always sustained by their prayerful faith, these junior naturalists are remarkably successful at hunting, fishing, building, sewing, and cooking. According to Mrs Traill, "to be up and doing is the maxim of a Canadian. . . . The Canadian settler . . . learns to supply all his wants by the exercise of his own energy" (Chapter X). Her Robinsonnade is designed to illustrate this theme.

At the time of the excerpt that follows, the youngsters have not been missing long. Louis now regrets having misled his cousins with the assurance that Mrs Maxwell knew of their trip to the woods, and Catharine has suffered a foot injury while trying to escape from a wolf. Yet already they have made sensible preparations about shelter, clothing, and food. Soon their number is increased; the family dog joins them and so does a wounded Mohawk girl, whom they call Indiana. They nurse her to health, and Indiana in return teaches them even more ways of surviving. Traill emphasizes the children's determination and inventiveness as they endure long winters, forest fires, and an Indian attack.

Although their parents have mounted frantic searches, the conclusion reveals the irony (amazing only to the modern reader) that during the whole three years the Crusoes were not more than seven or eight miles away from home—a considerable distance in the untracked bush. With the same accuracy of detail and keenness of observation found in Mrs Traill's famous series of letters, *The Backwoods of Canada* (1836), *The Canadian Crusoes* is both a tribute to the indomitable pioneer spirit and a catalogue of the untamed beauties of pre-Confederation Canada. As a story, however, the modern reader will find this tale very didactic and the children in it unreal paragons of adaptability, resourcefulness, and piety.

THE FIRST WEEKS IN THE BUSH

"Oh for a lodge in the vast wilderness,
The boundless contiguity of shade!"

A fortnight had now passed, and Catharine still suffered so much from pain and fever, that they were unable to continue their wanderings; all that Hector and his cousin could do, was to carry her to the bower by the lake, where she reclined whilst they caught fish. The painful longing to regain their lost home had lost nothing of its intensity; and often would the poor sufferer start from her bed of leaves and boughs, to ring her hands and weep, and call in piteous tones upon that dear father and mother, who would have given worlds, had they been at their command, to have heard but one accent of her beloved voice, to have felt one loving pressure from that fevered hand. Hope, the consoler, hovered over the path of the young wanderers long after she had ceased to whisper comfort to the desolate hearts of the mournful parents.

By the kindest and tenderest attention to all her comforts, Louis endeavoured to alleviate his cousin's sufferings, and soften her regrets; nay, he would often speak cheerfully and even gayly to her, when his own heart was heavy, and his eyes ready to overflow with tears.

"If it were not for our dear parents and the dear children at home," he would say, "we might spend our time most happily upon these charming plains; it is much more delightful here than in the dark, thick woods; see how brightly the sunbeams come down and gladden the ground, and cover the earth with fruit and flowers. It is pleasant to be able to fish and hunt, and trap the game. Yes, if they were all here, we would build us a nice log-house, and clear up these bushes on the flat near the lake. This 'Elfin Knowe,' as you call it, Kate, would be a nice spot to build upon. See these glorious old oaks; not one should be cut down, and we should have a boat and a canoe, and voyage across to yonder islands. Would it not be charming, ma belle?" and Catharine, smiling at the picture drawn so eloquently, would enter into the spirit of the project, and say,—

"Ah! Louis, that would be pleasant."

"If we had but my father's rifle now," said Hector, "and old Wolfe."

"I was thinking, Louis, that if we were doomed to remain here all our lives, we must build a house for ourselves; we could not live in the open air without shelter as we have done. The summer will soon pass, and the rainy season will come, and the bitter frosts and snows of winter will have to be provided against."

"But, Hector, do you really think there is no chance of finding our way back to Cold Springs? We know it must be behind this lake," said Louis.

"True, but whether east, west, or south, we cannot tell; and whichever way we take now is but a chance, and if once we leave the lake and get involved in the mazes of that dark forest, we should perish, for we know there is neither water nor berries, nor game to be had as there is here, and we might be soon starved to death. God was good who led us beside this fine lake, and upon these fruitful plains."

"What shall we do for clothes?" said Catharine, glancing at her homespun frock of wool and cotton plaid.

"A weighty consideration, indeed," sighed Hector; "clothes must be provided before ours are worn out, and the winter comes on."

"We must save all the skins of the woodchucks and squirrels," suggested Louis; "and fawns when we catch them."

"Yes, and fawns when we get them," added Hector; "but it is time enough to think of all these things; we must not give up all hope of home."

"I give up all hope? I shall hope on while I have life," said Catharine. "My dear, dear father, he will never forget his lost children; he will try and find us, alive or dead; he will never give up the search."

The children knew that they had been a long time absent from home, wandering hither and thither, and they fancied their journey had been as long as it had been weary. They had indeed the comfort of seeing the sun in his course from east to west, but they knew not in what direction the home they had lost lay; it was this that troubled them in their choice of the course they should take each day, and at last determined them to lose no more time so fruitlessly, where the peril was so great, but seek for some pleasant spot where they might pass their time in safety, and provide for their present and future wants.

> "The world was all before them where to choose.
> Their place of rest, and Providence their guide."[1]

Catharine declared her ankle was so much stronger than it had been since the accident, and her health so much amended, that the day after the conversation just recorded, the little party bade farewell to the valley of the "Big Stone," and ascending the steep sides of the hills bent their steps eastward, keeping the lake to their left hand. Hector led the way, loaded with their household utensils, which consisted only of the axe, which he would trust to no one but himself, the tin-pot, and the birch basket. Louis had his cousin to assist up the steep banks, like-wise some fish to carry, which had been caught early in the morning.

Our travellers, after wandering over this lovely plain, found themselves, at the close of the day, at the head of a fine ravine,[2] where they had the good fortune to perceive a spring of pure water, oozing beneath some large moss-covered blocks of black water-worn granite; the ground was thickly covered with moss about the edges of the spring, and many varieties of flowering shrubs and fruits were scattered along the valley and up the steep sides of the surrounding hills. There were whortleberries, or huckleberries, as they are more usually called, in abundance; bilberries dead ripe, and falling from the bushes at a touch. The vines that wreathed the low bushes and climbed the trees were loaded with clusters of grapes, but these were yet hard and green; dwarf filberts grew on the dry gravelly sides of the hills, yet the rough, prickly calyx that enclosed the nut, filled their fingers with minute thorns, that irritated the skin like the stings of the nettle; but as the kernel when ripe was sweet and good, they did not mind the consequences. The moist part of the valley was occupied by a large bed of May-apples,[3] the fruit of which was of unusual size, but they were not ripe, August being the month when they ripen; there were also wild plums still green, and wild cherries and blackberries ripening; there were great numbers of the woodchucks' burrows on the hills, while partridges and quails were seen under the thick covert of the blue-berried dog-wood,[4] that here

---

[1] *Paradise Lost*, Book xii, 11.646-7 [Editor].
[2] Kilvert's Ravine, above Pine-tree Point
[3] *Pedophyllum palmato*,—Mandrake, or May-apple.
[4] Cornus sericea. The blue berries of this shrub are eaten by the partridge and wild-ducks; *also* by the pigeons and other birds. There are several species of this shrub common to the Rice Lake.

grew in abundance at the mouth of the ravine where it opened to the lake. As this spot offered many advantages, our travellers halted for the night, and resolved to make it their head-quarters for a season, till they should meet with an eligible situation for building a winter shelter.

Despise not then, you, my refined young readers, the rude expedients adopted by these simple children of the forest, who knew nothing of the luxuries that were to be met with in the houses of the great and the rich. The fragrant carpet of cedar or hemlock-spruce sprigs strewn lightly over the earthen floor, was to them a luxury as great as if it had been taken from the looms of Persia or Turkey, so happy and contented were they in their ignorance. Their bed of freshly gathered grass and leaves, raised from the earth by a heap of branches carefully arranged, was to them as pleasant as beds of down, and the rude hut of bark and poles, as curtains of silk or damask.

Having collected as much of these materials as she deemed sufficient for the purpose, Catharine next gathered up dry oak branches, plenty of which lay scattered here and there, to make a watch-fire for the night, and this done, weary and warm, she sat down on a little hillock, beneath the cooling shade of a grove of young aspens, that grew near the hut; pleased with the dancing of the leaves, which fluttered above her head, and fanned her warm cheek with their incessant motion, she thought, like her cousin Louise, that the aspen was the merriest tree in the forest, for it was always dancing, dancing, dancing, even when all the rest were still.

What a state of excitement did the unexpected arrival of old Wolfe create! How many questions were put to the poor beast, as he lay with his head pillowed on the knees of his loving mistress! Catharine knew it was foolish, but she could not help talking to the dumb animal, as if he had been conversant with her own language. Ah, old Wolfe, if your homesick nurse could but have interpreted those expressive looks, those eloquent waggings of your bushy tail, as it flapped upon the grass, or waved from side to side; those gentle lickings of the hand, and mute sorrowful glances, as though he would have said, "Dear mistress, I know all your troubles. I know all you say, but I cannot answer you!" There is something touching in the silent sympathy of the dog, to which only the hard-hearted and depraved can be quite insensible.

There was no stir among the trees, the heavy rounded masses of foliage remained unmoved; the very aspen, that tremulous sensitive tree, scarcely stirred; it seemed as if the very pulses of nature were at rest. The solemn murmur that preceded the thunder-peal might have been likened to the moaning of the dying. The children felt the loneliness of the spot. Seated at the entrance of their sylvan hut, in front of which their evening fire burned brightly, they looked out upon the storm in silence and in awe. Screened by the sheltering shrubs that grew near them, they felt comparatively safe from the dangers of the storm, which now burst in terrific violence above the valley. Cloud answered to cloud, and the echoes of the hills prolonged the sound, while shattered trunks and brittle branches filled the air, and shrieked and groaned in that wild war of elements.

The storm lasted till past midnight, when it gradually subsided, and the poor wanderers were glad to see the murky clouds roll off, and the stars peep forth among their broken masses; but they were reduced to a pitiful state, the hurricane having beaten down their little hut, and their garments were drenched with rain. However, the boys made a good fire with some bark and boughs they had in store; there were a few sparks in their back log unextinguished, and this they gladly fanned up into a blaze, with which they dried their wet clothes, and warmed themselves. The air was now cool almost to chilliness, and for some days the weather remained unsettled, and the sky overcast with clouds, while the lake presented a leaden hue, crested with white mimic waves.

They soon set to work to make another hut, and found, close to the head of the ravine, a great pine uprooted, affording them large pieces of bark, which proved very serviceable in thatching the sides of the hut. The boys employed themselves in this work, while Catharine cooked the fish they had caught the night before, with a share of which old Wolfe seemed to be mightily well pleased. After they had breakfasted, they all went up towards the high tableland above the ravine, with Wolfe, to look round in hope of getting sight of their friends from Cold Springs, but though they kept an anxious look-out in every direction, they returned, towards evening, tired and hopeless. Hector had killed a red squirrel, and a partridge which Wolfe "treed,"—that is, stood barking at the foot of the tree in which it had perched,—and the supply of meat was a seasonable change. They also noticed, and marked with the axe, several trees where there were bees, intending to come in the cold weather, and cut them down. Louis's father was a great and successful bee-hunter; and Louis rather prided himself on having learned something of his father's skill in that line. Here, where flowers were so abundant and water plentiful, the wild bees seemed to be abundant also; besides, the open space between the trees, admitting the warm sunbeam freely, was favourable both for the bees and the flowers on which they fed, and Louis talked joyfully of the fine stores of honey they should collect in the fall. He had taught little Fanchon, a small French spaniel of his father's, to find out the trees where the bees hived, and also the nests of the ground-bees, and she would bark at the foot of the tree, or scratch with her feet on the ground, as the other dogs barked at the squirrels or the woodchucks; but Fanchon was far away, and Wolfe was old, and would learn no new tricks, so Louis knew he had nothing but his own observation and the axe to depend upon for procuring honey.

The boys had been unsuccessful for some days past in fishing; neither perch nor sunfish, pink roach nor mud-pouts,[5] were to be caught. However, they found water-mussels by groping in the sand, and crayfish among the gravel at the edge of the water only; the last pinched their fingers very spitefully. The mussels were not very palatable, for want of salt; but hungry folks must not be dainty, and Louis declared them very good when well roasted, covered up with hot embers.

"Catharine," said Louis, one day, "the huckleberries are now very plentiful, and I think it would be a wise thing to gather a good store of them, and dry them for the winter. See ma chere, wherever we turn our eyes, or place our feet, they are to be found; the hill sides are purple with them. We may, for aught we know, be obliged to pass the rest of our lives here; it will be well to prepare for the winter when no berries are to be found."

"It will be well, mon ami, but we must not dry them in the sun; for let me tell you, Mr Louis, that they will be quite tasteless—mere dry husks."

"Why so, ma belle?"

"I do not know the reason, but I only know the fact, for when our mothers dried the currants and raspberries in the sun, such was the case, but when they dried them on the oven floor, or on the hearth, they were quite nice."

"Well, Cath., I think I know of a flat, thin stone that will make a good hearthstone, and we can get sheets of birch bark and sew into the flat bags, to keep the dried fruit in."

They now turned all their attention to drying huckleberries (or whortleberries.)[6] Catharine and Louis (who fancied nothing could be

---

[5] All these fish are indigenous to the fresh waters of Canada.

[6] From the abundance of this fruit, the Indians have given the name of Whortleberry Plain to the lands on the south shore. During the month of July and the early part of August, large parties came to the Rice Lake Plains to gather huckleberries, which they preserve by drying, for winter use. These berries make a delicious tart or pudding, mixed with bilberries and red-currants, requiring little sugar.

contrived without help) attended to the preparing and making of the bags of birch bark; but Hector was soon tired of girl's work, as he termed it, and after gathering some berries, would wander away over the hills in search of game, and to explore the neighbouring hills and valleys, and sometimes it was sunset before he made his appearance. Hector had made an excellent strong bow, like the Indian bow, out of a tough piece of hickory wood, which he found in one of his rambles, and he made arrows with wood that he seasoned in the smoke, sharpening the heads with great care with his knife, and hardening them by exposure to strong heat, at a certain distance from the fire. The entrails of the wood-chucks, stretched, and scraped and dried, and rendered pliable by rubbing and drawing through the hands, answered for a bowstring; but afterwards, when they got the sinews and hide of the deer, they used them, properly dressed for the purpose.

While our young people seldom wanted for meat, they felt the privation of bread to which they had been accustomed very sensibly. One day, while Hector and Louis were busily engaged with their assistant, Wolfe, in unearthing a woodchuck, that had taken refuge in his burrow, on one of the gravelly hills above the lake, Catharine amused herself by looking for flowers. She had filled her lap with ripe May-apples,[7] but finding them cumbersome in climbing the steep wooded hills, she deposited them at the foot of a tree near the boys, and pursued her search; and it was not long before she perceived some pretty grassy-looking plants, with heads of bright lilac flowers, and on plucking some pulled up the root also. The root was about the size and shape of a large crocus, and, on biting it, she found it far from disagreeable, sweet, and slightly astringent; it seemed to be a favourite root with the woodchucks, for she noticed that it grew about their burrows on dry, gravelly soil, and many of the stems were bitten, and the roots eaten—a warrant in full of wholesomeness. Therefore, carrying home a parcel of the largest of the roots, she roasted them in the embers, and they proved almost as good as chestnuts, and more satisfying than the acorns of the white oak, which they had often roasted in the fire, when they were out working on the fallow, at the log heaps. Hector and Louis ate heartily of the roots, and commended Catharine for the discovery.

One fine day, Louis returned home from the lake shore in great haste, for the bows and arrows, with the interesting news that a herd of five deer were in the water, making for the Long Island.

[7] *Podophyllum pelatum*,—May-apple, or Mandrake. The fruit of the May-apple, in rich, moist soil, will attain to the size of the magnum bonum, or egg-plum which it resembles in colour and shape. It makes a delicious preserve, if seasoned with cloves or ginger; when eaten uncooked, the outer rind, which is thick and fleshy, and has a rank taste, should be thrown aside; the fine acid pulp in which the seeds are imbedded alone should be eaten. The root of the Podophyllum is used as a cathartic by the Indians. The root of this plant is reticulated, and when a large body of them are uncovered, they present a singular appearance, interlacing each other in large meshes, like an extensive network; these roots are white, as thick as a man's little finger, and fragrant, and spread horizontally along the surface. The blossom is like a small white rose.

"But, Louis, they will be gone out of sight and beyond the reach of the arrows," said Catharine, as she handed him down the bows and a sheaf of arrows, which she quickly slung round his shoulders by the belt of skin, which the young hunter had made for himself.

"No fear, ma chere; they will stop to feed on the beds of rice and lilies. We must have Wolfe. Here, Wolfe, Wolfe, Wolfe,—here, boy, here!"

Catharine caught a portion of the excitement that danced in the bright eyes of her cousin, and declaring that she too would go and witness the hunt, ran down the ravine by his side, while Wolfe, who evidently understood that they had some sport in view, trotted along by his mistress, wagging his great bushy tail, and looking in high good humour.

Hector was impatiently waiting the arrival of the bows and Wolfe. The herd of deer, consisting of a noble buck, two full-grown females, and two young half-grown males, were quietly feeding among the beds of rice and rushes, not more than fifteen or twenty yards from the shore, apparently quite unconcerned at the presence of Hector, who stood on a fallen trunk eagerly eyeing their motions; but the hurried steps of Louis and Catharine, with the deep sonorous baying of Wolfe, soon roused the timid creatures to a sense of danger, and the stag, raising his head and making, as the children thought, a signal for retreat, now struck boldly out for the nearest point of Long Island.

"We shall lose them," cried Louis, despairingly, eyeing the long bright track that cut the silvery waters, as the deer swam gallantly out.

"Hist, hist, Louis" said Hector, "all depends upon Wolfe. Turn them, Wolfe; hey, hey, seek them, boy!"

Wolfe dashed bravely into the lake.

"Head them! head them!" shouted Hector.

Wolfe knew what was meant; with the sagacity of a long-trained hunter, he made a desperate effort to gain the advantage by a circuitous route. Twice the stag turned irresolute, as if to face his foe, and Wolfe, taking the time, swam ahead, and then the race began. As soon as the boys saw the herd had turned, and that Wolfe was between them and the island, they separated, Louis making good his ambush to the right among the cedars, and Hector at the spring to the west, while Catharine was stationed at the solitary pine-tree, at the point which commanded the entrance of the ravine.

"Now, Cathy," said her brother, "when you see the herd making for the ravine, shout and clap your hands, and they will turn either to the right or to the left. Do not let them land, or we shall lose them. We must trust to Wolfe for their not escaping to the island. Wolfe is well trained— he knows what he is about."

Catharine proved a dutiful ally; she did as she was bid. She waited till the deer were within a few yards of the shore, then she shouted and clapped her hands. Frightened at the noise and clamour, the terrified creatures coasted along for some way, till within a little distance of the thicket where Hector lay concealed, the very spot from which they had emerged when they first took to the water; to this place they boldly steered.

Hector, crouched beneath the trees, waited cautiously till one of the does was within reach of his arrow, and so good and true was his aim, that it hit the animal in the throat a little above the chest. The stag now turned again, but Wolfe was behind, and pressed him forward, and again the noble animal strained every nerve for the shore. Louis now shot his arrow, but it swerved from the mark; he was too eager; it glanced harmlessly along the water; but the cool, unimpassioned hand of Hector sent another arrow between the eyes of the doe, stunning her with its force, and then, another from Louis laid her on her side, dying, and staining the water with her blood.

The boys were soon hard at work, skinning the animal, and cutting it up. This was the most valuable acquisition they had yet effected, for many uses were to be made of the deer, besides eating the flesh. It was a store of wealth in their eyes.

During the many years that their father had sojourned in the country, there had been occasional intercourse with the fur traders and trappers, and, sometimes, with friendly disposed Indians, who had called at the lodges of their white brothers for food and tobacco.

From all these men, rude as they were, some practical knowledge had been acquired, and their visits, though few and far between, had left good fruit behind them; something to think about and talk about, and turn to future advantage.

The boys had learned from the Indians how precious were the tough sinews of the deer for sewing. They knew how to prepare the skins of the deer for mocassins, which they could cut and make as neatly as the squaws themselves. They could fashion arrow-heads, and knew how best to season the wood for making both the long and cross-bow; they had seen the fish-hooks these people manufactured from bone and hard wood; they knew that strips of fresh-cut skins would make bow-strings, or the entrails of animals dried and rendered pliable. They had watched the squaws making baskets of the inner bark of the oak, elm, and bass-wood, and mats of the inner bark of the cedar, with many other ingen-ious works that they now found would prove useful to them, after a lit-tle practice had perfected their inexperienced attempts. They also knew how to dry venison as the Indians and trappers prepare it, by cutting the thick fleshy portions of the meat into strips, from four to six inches in breadth, and two or more in thickness. These strips they strung upon poles supported on forked sticks, and exposed them to the drying action of the sun and wind. Fish they split open, and removed the back and head bones, and smoked them slightly or dried them in the sun.

Their success in killing the doe greatly raised their spirits; in their joy they embraced each other, and bestowed the most affectionate caresses on Wolfe for his good conduct.

Every part of the deer seemed valuable in the eyes of the young hunt-ers; the skin they carefully stretched out upon sticks to dry gradually, and the entrails they also preserved for bow-strings. The sinews of the legs and back they drew out, and laid carefully aside for future use.

"We shall be glad enough of these strings by and by," said careful Hector; "for the summer will soon be at an end, and then we must turn our attention to making ourselves winter clothes and mocassins."

"Yes, Hec, and a good warm shanty; these huts of bark and boughs will not do when once that cold weather sets in."

"A shanty would soon be put up," said Hector; "for even Kate, wee bit lassie as she is, could give us some help in trimming up the logs."

"After all," said Hector, thoughtfully, "children can do a great many things if they only resolutely set to work, and use the wits and the strength that God has given them to work with. A few weeks ago, and we should have thought it utterly impossible to have supported ourselves in a lonely wilderness like this by our own exertions in fishing and hunting."

"If we had been lost in the forest, we must have died with hunger," said Catharine; "but let us be thankful to the good God who led us hither, and gave us health and strength to help ourselves."

ROBERT MICHAEL BALLANTYNE (1825-1894)
"An Encounter with Cannibals" from *The Coral Island; A Tale of the Pacific Ocean* (1858)

Coming from an Edinburgh family of publishers and writers, Ballantyne took his first job at the age of sixteen as a clerk for the Hudson's Bay Company. After his six-year stint in North America, where he was stationed at York Factory, Norway House, Fort Garry, and on the lower St Lawrence, he turned his journals and letters home into a vigorous and informative account of the fur trade, *Hudson's Bay; or, Every-day Life in the Wilds of North America* (1848). He followed this with his first novel for boys, *Snowflakes and Sunbeams; or, The Young Fur Traders. A Tale of the Far North* (1856). Thereafter Ballantyne launched his long and successful career as a professional writer of boys' stories, acquiring great fame with the South Seas adventures of Ralph Rover and his comrades in *The Coral Island* (1858), and keeping up a steady flow of exotic tales in novels like *Martin Rattler; or, A Boy's Adventures in the Forests of Brazil* (1858), *The Gorilla Hunters; A Tale of the Wilds of Africa* (1861), *The Pirate City; An Algerine Tale* (1874), and *The Rover of the Andes; A Tale of Adventure in South America* (1885)—as well as many stories set in North America, such as *The Dog Crusoe and His Master; A Story of Adventure in the Western Prairies* (1860). In the more than thirty boys' stories Ballantyne wrote after *The Coral Island*, he relied on the proven success of combining precise topographic detail, exceptional dangers and escapes, and manly Christian righteousness.

The *Coral Island* relates the adventures of three shipwrecked messmates: the know-ledgeable leader Jack Martin, the humorously earnest Peterkin Gay, and the narrator himself. Ballantyne's luxuriant descriptions make the boys' island refuge into an exotic paradise. In addition to praising the breathtaking natural wonders, he constantly draws attention to the concord and fraternal bond that unites the "agreeable triumvirate" of survivors—who are an idyllic contrast to Golding's more problematic trio in *The Lord of the Flies* (1954). But *The Coral Island* is not merely a picturesque tale of comradeship. It is replete with fearful adventures. Jack, Ralph, and Peterkin must fight cannibals ("incarnate fiends"); Ralph is carried off by a pirate captain and forced to witness the ruthless slaughter of scores of natives; and all three eventually end up facing the sentence of death in the prison of an island chief. Ballantyne had the knack of extricating his heroes from each of these near-fatal encounters. As the chapter reprinted here shows, Jack's courage and Peterkin's quick thinking quell the savage cannibals; miraculously even the infant tossed into the sea is saved without much ado and restored to its mother's arms.

In escaping from the pirate ship, Ralph is helped by a conscience-stricken mate. When the three reunited boys are imprisoned on account of their defence of the Samoan maiden Avatea, they are released because the chief has embraced Christianity: "amid the acclamations of the assembled thousands" he reduced "the false gods of Mango" to ashes (Chapter XXXIV).

AN ENCOUNTER WITH CANNIBALS

Shoemaking—The even tenor of our way suddenly interrupted—An unexpected visit and an appalling battle—We all become warriors, and Jack proves himself to be a hero.

For many months after this we continued to live on our island in uninterrupted harmony and happiness. Sometimes we went out a-fishing in the lagoon, and sometimes went a-hunting in the woods, or ascended to the mountain-top, by way of variety, although Peterkin always asserted that we went for the purpose of hailing any ship that might chance to heave in sight. But I am certain that none of us wished to be delivered from our captivity, for we were extremely happy, and Peterkin used to say that as we were very young we should not feel the loss of a year or two. Peterkin, as I have said before, was thirteen years of age, Jack eighteen, and I fifteen. But Jack was very tall, strong, and manly for his age, and might easily have been mistaken for twenty.

The climate was so beautiful that it seemed to be a perpetual summer and as many of the fruit-trees continued to bear fruit and blossom all the year round, we never wanted for a pentiful supply of food. The hogs, too, seemed rather to increase than diminish, although Peterkin was very frequent in his attacks on them with his spear. If at any time we failed in finding a drove, we had only to pay a visit to the plum-tree before mentioned, where we always found a large family of them asleep under its branches.

We employed ourselves very busily during this time in making various garments of cocoa-nut cloth, as those with which we had landed were beginning to be very ragged. Peterkin also succeeded in making excellent shoes out of the skin of the old hog, in the following manner: he first cut a piece of the hide, of an oblong form, a few inches longer than his foot. This he soaked in water, and while it was wet he sewed up one end of it, so as to form a rough imitation of that part of the heel of a shoe where the seam is. This done, he bored a row of holes all round the edge of the piece of skin, through which a touch line was passed. Into the sewed-up part of this shoe he thrust his heel, then drawing the string tight, the edges rose up and overlapped his foot all round. It is true there were a great many ill-looking puckers in these shoes, but we found them very serviceable notwithstanding, and Jack came at last to prefer them to his long boots. We also made various other useful articles, which added to our comfort, and once or twice spoke of building us a house; but we had so great an affection for the bower, and withal found it so serviceable, that we determined not to leave it, nor to attempt the building of a house, which, in such a climate, might turn out to be rather disagreeable than useful.

Diving in the Water Garden also continued to afford us as much pleasure as ever; and Peterkin began to be a little more expert in the water from constant practice. As for Jack and I, we began to feel as if water were our native element, and revelled in it with so much confidence and comfort that Peterkin said he feared we would turn into fish some day, and swim off and leave him; adding that he had been for a long time observing that Jack was becoming more and more like a shark every day. Whereupon Jack remarked that if he, Peterkin, were changed into a fish, he would certainly turn into nothing better or bigger than a shrimp. Poor Peterkin did not envy us our delightful excursions under water, except, indeed, when Jack would dive down to the bottom of the Water Garden, sit down on a rock and look up and make faces at him. Peterkin did feel envious then, and often said he would give anything to be able to do that. I was much amused when Peterkin said this; for if he could only have seen his own face when he happened to take a short dive, he would have seen that Jack's was far surpassed by it: the great difference being, however, that Jack made faces on purpose—Peterkin couldn't help it!

Now, while we were engaged with these occupations and amusements, an event occurred one day which was as unexpected as it was exceedingly alarming and very horrible.

Jack and I were sitting, as we were often wont to do, on the rocks at Spouting Cliff, and Peterkin was wringing the water from his garments, having recently fallen by accident into the sea—a thing he was constantly doing—when our attention was suddenly arrested by two objects which appeared on the horizon.

"What are yon, think you?" I said, addressing Jack.

"I can't imagine," answered he. "I've noticed them for some time, and fancied they were black sea-gulls, but the more I look at them the more I feel convinced they are much larger than gulls."

"They seem to be coming towards us," said I.

"Hollo! what's wrong?" inquired Peterkin, coming up.

"Look there," said Jack.

"Whales!" cried Peterkin, shading his eyes with his hand. "No—eh— *can* they be boats, Jack?"

Our hearts beat with excitement at the very thought of seeing human faces again.

"I think you are about right, Peterkin. But they seem to me to move strangely for boats," said Jack, in a low tone, as if he were talking to himself.

I noticed that a shade of anxiety crossed Jack's countenance as he gazed long and intently at the two objects, which were now nearing us fast. At last he sprang to his feet. "They are canoes, Ralph! whether war-canoes or not I cannot tell; but this I know, that all the natives of the South Sea Islands are fierce cannibals, and they have little respect for strangers. We must hide if they land here, which I earnestly hope they will not do."

I was greatly alarmed at Jack's speech, but I confess I thought less of what he said than of the earnest, anxious manner in which he said it, and it was with very uncomfortable feelings that Peterkin and I followed him quickly into the woods.

We each selected a stout club according to our several tastes, and lay down behind a rock, whence we could see the canoes approach, without ourselves being seen. At first we made an occasional remark on their appearance, but after they entered the lagoon, and drew near the beach, we ceased to speak, and gazed with intense interest at the scene before us.

We now observed that the foremost canoe was being chased by the other, and that it contained a few women and children, as well as men— perhaps forty souls altogether; while the canoe which pursued it contained only men. They seemed to be about the same in number, but were better armed, and had the appearance of being a war-party. Both crews were paddling with all their might, and it seemed as if the pursuers exerted themselves to overtake the fugitives ere they could land. In this, however, they failed. The foremost canoe made for the beach close beneath the rocks behind which we were concealed. Their short paddles flashed like meteors in the water, and sent up a constant shower of spray. The foam curled from the prow, and the eyes of the rowers glistened in their black faces as they strained every muscle of their naked bodies; nor did they relax their efforts till the canoe struck the beach with a violent shock; then, with a shout of defiance, the whole party sprang, as if by magic, from the canoe to the shore. Three women, two of whom carried infants in their arms, rushed into the woods; and the men crowded to the water's edge, with stones in their hands, spears levelled, and clubs brandished, to resist the landing of their enemies.

The distance between the two canoes had been about half a mile, and, at the great speed they were going, this was soon passed. As the pursuers neared the shore, no sign of fear or hesitation was noticeable. On they came like a wild charger—received but recked not of a shower of stones. The canoe struck, and with a yell that seemed to issue from the throats of incarnate fiends, they leaped into the water, and drove their enemies up the beach.

The battle that immediately ensued was frightful to behold. Most of the men wielded clubs of enormous size and curious shapes, with which they dashed out each other's brains. As they were almost entirely naked, and had to bound, stoop, leap, and run in their terrible hand-to-hand encounters, they looked more like demons than human beings. I felt my heart grow sick at the sight of this bloody battle, and would fain have turned away, but a species of fascination seemed to hold me down and glue my eyes upon the combatants. I observed that the attacking party was led by a most extraordinary being, who, from his size and peculiarity, I concluded was a chief. His hair was frizzed out to an enormous extent, so that it resembled a large turban. It was of a light-yellow hue, which surprised me much, for the man's body was as black as coal, and I felt convinced that the hair must have been dyed. He was tattooed from head to foot; and his face, besides being tattooed, was be-smeared with red paint, and streaked with white. Altogether, with his yellow, turban-like hair, his Herculean black frame, his glittering eyes, and white teeth, he seemed the most terrible monster I ever beheld. He was very active in the fight, and had already killed four men.

Suddenly the yellow-haired chief was attacked by a man quite as strong and large as himself. He flourished a heavy club something like an eagle's beak at the point. For a second or two these giants eyed each other warily, moving round and round, as if to catch each other at a disadvantage; but seeing that nothing was to be gained by this caution, and that the loss of time might effectually turn the tide of battle either way, they apparently made up their minds to attack at the same instant, for, with a wild shout and simultaneous spring, they swung their heavy clubs, which met with a loud report. Suddenly the yellow-haired savage tripped, his enemy sprang forward, the ponderous club was swung, but it did not descend, for at that moment the savage was felled to the ground by a stone from the hand of one who had witnessed his chief's danger. This was the turning-point in the battle. The savages who landed first turned and fled towards the bush, on seeing the fall of their chief. But not one escaped. They were all overtaken and felled to the earth. I saw, however, that they were not all killed. Indeed, their enemies, now that they were conquered, seemed anxious to take them alive; and they succeeded in securing fifteen, whom they bound hand and foot with cords, and carrying them up into the woods, laid them down among the bushes. Here they left them, for what purpose I knew not, and returned to the scene of the late battle, where the remnant of the party were bathing their wounds.

Out of the forty blacks that composed the attacking party, only twenty-eight remained alive, two of whom were sent into the bush to hunt for the women and children. Of the other party, as I have said, only fifteen survived, and these were lying bound and helpless on the grass.

Jack and Peterkin and I now looked at each other, and whispered our fears that the savages might clamber up the rocks to search for fresh water, and so discover our place of concealment; but we were so much interested in watching their movements that we agreed to remain where we were; and indeed, we could not easily have risen without exposing ourselves to detection. One of the savages now went up to the wood, and soon returned with a bundle of firewood. When the fire was kindled, two of the party went again to the woods and returned with one of the bound men. A dreadful feeling of horror crept over my heart as the thought flashed upon me that they were going to burn their enemies. As they bore him to the fire my feelings almost overpowered me. I gasped for breath, and seizing my club, endeavoured to spring to my feet; but Jack's powerful arm pinned me to the earth. Next moment one of the savages raised his club, and fractured the wretched creature's skull. He must have died instantly; and strange though it may seem, I confess to a feeling of relief when the deed was done, because I now knew that the poor savage could not be burned alive. Scarcely had his limbs ceased to quiver when the monsters cut slices of flesh from his body, and, after roasting them slightly over the fire, devoured them. Suddenly there arose a cry from the woods, and in a few seconds the two savages hastened towards the fire dragging the three women and their two infants along with them. One of those women was much younger than her companions, and we were struck with the modesty of her demeanour and the gentle expression of her face, which, although she had the flattish nose and thick lips of the others, was of a light-brown colour, and we conjectured that she must be of a different race. While we gazed with interest and some anxiety at these poor creatures, the big chief advanced to one of the elder females and laid his hand upon the child. But the mother shrank from him, and clasping the little one to her bosom, uttered a wail of fear. With a savage laugh, the chief tore the child from her arms and tossed it into the sea. A low groan burst from Jack's lips as he witnessed this atrocious act and heard the mother's shriek, as she fell insensible on the sand. The rippling waves rolled the child on the beach, as if they refused to be a party in such a foul murder, and we could observe that the little one still lived.

The young girl was now brought forward, and the chief addressed her; but although we heard his voice and even the words distinctly, of course we could not understand what he said. The girl made no answer to his fierce questions, and we saw by the way in which he pointed to the fire that he had threatened her life.

"Peterkin," said Jack, in a hoarse whisper, "Have you got your knife?"

"Yes," replied Peterkin, whose face was pale as death.

"That will do. Listen to me, and do my bidding quick. Here is the small knife, Ralph. Fly both of you through the bush, cut the cords that bind the prisoners, and set them free. There! quick, ere it be too late." Jack sprang up, and seized a heavy but short bludgeon, while his strong frame trembled with emotion, and large drops rolled down his forehead.

At this moment the man who had butchered the savage a few minutes before advanced towards the girl with his heavy club. Jack uttered a yell that rang like a death-shriek among the rocks. With one bound he leaped over a precipice full fifteen feet high, and before the savages had recovered from their surprise, was in the midst of them; while Peterkin and I dashed through the bushes towards the prisoners. With one blow of his staff Jack felled the man with the club, then turning round with a look of fury, he rushed upon the big chief with the yellow hair. Had the blow which Jack aimed at his head taken affect, the huge savage would have needed no second stroke; but he was agile as a cat, and avoided it by springing to one side, while, at the same time, he swung his ponderous club at the head of his foe. It was now Jack's turn to leap aside, and well was it for him that the first outburst of his blind fury was over, else he had become an easy prey to his gigantic antagonist; but Jack was cool now. He darted his blows rapidly and well, and the superiority of his light weapon was strikingly proved in this combat; for while he could easily evade the blows of the chief's heavy club, the chief could not so easily evade those of his light one. Nevertheless, so quick was he, and so frightfully did he fling about the mighty weapon, that although Jack struck him almost every blow, the strokes had to be delivered so quickly that they wanted force to be very effectual.

It was lucky for Jack that the other savages considered the success of their chief in this encounter to be so certain that they refrained from interfering. Had they doubted it, they would have probably ended the matter at once by felling him. But they contented themselves with awaiting the issue.

The force which the chief expended in wielding his club now began to be apparent. His movements became slower, his breath hissed through his clenched teeth, and the surprised savages drew nearer in order to render assistance. Jack observed this movement. He felt that his fate was sealed, and resolved to cast his life upon the next blow. The chief's club was again about to descend on his head. He might have evaded it easily, but instead of doing so, he suddenly shortened his grasp of his own club, rushed in under the blow, struck his adversary right between the eyes with all his force, and fell to the earth, crushed beneath the senseless body of the chief. A dozen clubs flew high in air, ready to descend, on the head of Jack; but they hesitated a moment, for the massive body of the chief completely covered him. That moment saved his life. Ere the savages could tear the chief's body away, seven of their number fell prostrate beneath the clubs of the prisoners whom Peterkin and I had set free, and two others fell under our own hand. We could never have accomplished this had not our enemies been so engrossed with the fight between Jack and their chief that they had failed to observe us until we were upon them. They still outnumbered our party by three; but we were flushed with victory, while they were taken by surprise and dispirited by the fall of their chief. Moreover, they were awestruck by the sweeping fury of Jack, who seemed to have lost his senses altogether, and had no sooner shaken himself free of the chief's body than he rushed into the midst of them, and in three blows equalised our numbers. Peterkin and I flew to the rescue, the savages followed us, and in less than ten minutes the whole of our opponents were knocked down or made prisoners, bound hand and foot, and extended side by side upon the sea-shore.

After the battle was over, the savages crowded round us and gazed at us in surprise, while they continued to pour upon us a flood of questions, which, being wholly unintelligible, of course we could not answer. However, by way of putting an end to it, Jack took the chief (who had recovered from the effects of his wound) by the hand and shook it warmly. No sooner did the blacks see that this was meant to express good-will than they shook hands with us all round. After this ceremony was gone through, Jack went up to the girl, who had never once moved from the rock where she had been left, but had continued an eager spectator of all that had passed. He made signs to her to follow him, and then, taking the chief by the hand, was about to conduct him to the bower, when his eye fell on the poor infant which had been thrown into the sea and was still lying on the shore. Dropping the chief's hand he hastened towards it, and to his great joy found it to be still alive. We also found that the mother was beginning to recover slowly.

"Here, get out o' the way," said Jack, pushing us aside, as we stooped over the poor woman and endeavoured to restore her; "I'll soon bring her round." So saying he placed the infant on her bosom and laid its warm cheek on hers. The effect was wonderful. The woman opened her eyes, felt the child, looked at it, and with a cry of joy clasped it in her arms, at the same time endeavouring to rise, for the purpose, apparently, of rushing into the woods.

"There, that's all right," said Jack, once more taking the chief by the hand. "Now, Ralph and Peterkin, make the women and these fellows follow me to the bower. We'll entertain them as hospitably as we can."

THOMAS MAYNE REID (1818-1883)
"Rescued from the Jaws of Death" from *Ran Away to Sea: An Autobiography for Boys* (1859)

Born at Ballyroney, County Down, Ireland, Mayne Reid was the son of a Presbyterian minister. He immigrated to America at the age of twenty, taking a post as a trader-adventurer in New Orleans and writing travel sketches for eastern newspapers. As a lieutenant in the American army commanding the New York Regiment of Grenadiers, Mayne Reid took part in the storming of Chapultapec Palace (1847) during the Mexican War; he was promoted to captain in 1849 and was wounded. During his recuperation he began work on his first novel, and his career as an adventure novelist was launched, upon his arrival in London, with the publication of *The Rifle Rangers; or, Adventures in Southern Mexico* (1850). This was followed by a steady stream of boys' stories, including *The Scalp Hunters; or, Romantic Adventures in Northern Mexico* (1851), *The Young Voyageurs; or, The Boy Hunters in the North* (1853), *The Boy Tar; or, A Voyage in the Dark* (1860), and *The Cliff-Climbers; or, The Lone Home in the Himalayas* (1864). He revisited the United States in 1867 and wrote for the influential American magazine *The Boys' and Girls' Weekly*. When his old war wound became infected he returned to England, where he continued to write until his death.

Always full of hair-raising escapes and death-defying exploits, Mayne Reid's books are the quintessential Golden Age adventure tales. His first-person narrator in *Ran Away to Sea* (1859) is the sixteen-year-old hero who leaves behind the protecting comforts of his family to become a seafarer to exotic places. But the unscrupulous captain who signs Will on without his parents' permission initiates the boy into the unglamorous realities of shipboard life. Only when he is on the high seas does the runaway realize that the trading barque *Pan-*

dora is actually a slaver. Will's single defender against the callous crew is his friend Ben Brace, an older mate. In every danger Will relies on Ben for rescue or safety. While the *Pandora* lies anchored on the African coast, and the two friends are out on a hunting expedition, Will and Ben scramble up a dragon tree to avoid a rampaging lion; after the animal is killed and skinned, Ben throws its fur over his body and roars in a fine baritone, thus effectively scattering yet another enemy, snout-faced baboons. Later, when the African supplier of slaves, His Majesty King Dingo Bingo, takes a liking to Will, the greedy Captain exchanges the boy for six more slaves. Will's courage is fortified when Ben suggests a plan of escape—the final stages of which are described in the excerpt that follows.

The most troubling feature of *Ran Away to Sea* is Reid's handling of the issue of slavery. Will expresses abhorrence of the fact that the ship's cargo is human and fulminates piously against slavetrading; yet the *Pandora* does carry five hundred black men, women, and children, and when she catches fire (Will releases the grating that keeps the slaves in the hold, before he leaps to safety in Ben's makeshift raft), the Blacks are left either to perish in the flames or to jump into the shark-infested water. The final explosion on the *Pandora* has a horrific theatricality: Reid compares the whole scene to "the finale of some grand-theatrical spectacle" and spends six grisly chapters describing the last hours of the ship and her cargo. The reader has an uneasy sense, finishing this and other Reid adventure novels, that the author has merely produced a series of episodes whose *raison d'être* is their sensationalism. But Reid redeems himself with his characterizations and narrative drive.

RESCUED FROM THE JAWS OF DEATH

I had gone far enough. I had reached the point where it was best for me to take to the water; and, flinging off my shoes and most of my clothing, I stepped down to the water's edge and plunged in.

The barque was not yet opposite me; but, by the rate at which she was moving, I calculated she would be so by the time I could arrive in midstream.

Brace had told me to swim for the bows,—for he would be there with his rope; while in case I should not be able to lay hold of it, another would be ready at the gangway ports with a second rope. One or other would be sure to haul me in; but it would be better if I could get aboard at the bows, as then I might not be observed either by mate or skipper, and even should his majesty come after me I could be hidden away about the forecastle. The skipper, not knowing I was aboard, would, of course, deny me with a will. I was determined, therefore, to do all I could to get aboard by the bows.

I was an excellent swimmer,—not surpassed by any of the Pandora's crew, except, perhaps, by Brace himself, who was one of the best in the world. I had practised a great deal in my school-days in rivers, freshwater lakes, and the sea itself; and I thought nothing of swimming a mile or more without rest. Crossing from the bank of the river to midstream—a distance of not over two hundred yards—was a mere bagatelle, and I had no apprehension of being able to accomplish it at my ease.

But although I had no apprehension about my powers of swimming, I was keenly sensible of danger from another source. I had not thought of it before that moment,—for the excitement of escaping, and the difficulty of making my way through the underwood, had driven every thought of danger out of my head, except that of being pursued. The peril from behind had prevented me from dwelling upon dangers ahead; and it was only after I had plunged into the stream that I became the victim of a keen apprehension. Then, and not till then, did I remember the fate of the unfortunate Dutchman!*—then, and not till then, did I think of the *crocodiles!*

A horrid sensation came over me,—a dread feeling of fear. My blood ran cold,—far colder than the water of the stream. Perhaps at that moment I was within reach of a huge man-eating crocodile,—at all events, within sight, for some of these hideous monsters were sure to be near, either by one bank or the other. Indeed, as I was about to plunge in, I saw a long dark form by the shore, some twenty yards farther down, which I had taken for a floating log. The noise made by my body striking the water had caused it to move. I thought then it was the current; but now, under my keen apprehensions, I thought differently. It was no

---

* "Dutchy" had jumped overboard to escape the inhumane crew, in Chapter xv; Will had watched his "short, sanguinary struggle" with the crocodile. [Editor].

dead log,—it was the motion of a living creature,—beyond doubt a huge crocodile!

This conjecture soon became a conviction. A floating log would scarce have settled there, against the sedgy bank, and where there was current enough to carry it onward; it was no log, it was the great lizard itself.

One glance was sufficient to make me aware of my perilous position. Merciful Heaven! my conjecture was too true!—the dead log was no log, but an enormous crocodile!—its hideous shape was plainly seen; its long cloven head and broad scaly back glittered high above the water, and its snout was elevated and turned towards me, as though it was just getting over a surprise, and coming to the knowledge of what sort of creature I was.

Its surprise, however, was soon over, and before I could stretch myself to swim on, I saw it lash the water into foam with its tail,—as if to set itself in motion,—and the next moment it parted from the bank and came rushing towards me!

Its body was now sunk below the surface, but its gaunt, haggard head, and sharp snout, were projected high above the water.

I saw all this as I turned round again; and with a feeling of cold horror upon me I swam on.

The barque was now near,—her bows were not fifty yards distant, and the crocodile was still more than a hundred behind me. But I well knew that these amphibious monsters can far outswim a man. Through the water they make progress as an otter, and with like rapidity. I felt sure I should be overtaken, and then—

The cold horror continued,—I screamed out for help,—I continued my cries as I swam on!

I heard voices from the barque, in answer to my cries. I could see forms gliding about the head, and running out upon the bumpkin-shrouds, and along the bowsprit. I could distinguish the deep voice of Brace uttering words of encouragement and direction.

I was under the bowsprit end,—I could see no rope,—I looked in vain for a rope,—none had been thrown to me. O heavens! what was I to do?

Once more I raised myself in the water, and looked back. It was an appalling sight. The black head of the crocodile glittered within ten feet of me. I could see the jaws extended,—the long, irregular tusks,—the strong, scaly limbs, as they paddled the water—

In another instant I should have felt those terrible teeth; and gripped between the hard jaws of the monster, as in a vice, would have been dragged to the bottom of the dark waters—had it been my destiny.

But it was not so written in the book of fate. Just as I had given myself up for lost, I felt a strong hand clutching my garments by the waist, and the instant after I was lifted clear out of the river, and hoisted high into the air! The crocodile made a rush forward and leaped far above the surface; but I had been raised beyond his reach, and he fell back with a plunge, and for some moments continued lashing the water with his tail. Then, seeing that his victim had escaped him, he swam off, and disappeared round the side of the vessel.

I scarce knew how I had been so miraculously saved. Despair and terror had confused my senses; and it was only after I had been passed above, and set upon my feet upon the firm deck, that I understood all.

Brace was my preserver. He had run out to the bowsprit end, and from that had slipped down the dolphin-striker, and let himself still lower by means of a looped rope. By this means he had been enabled to swing himself down, so that he could reach the surface. Fortunately, it was at that moment that I had risen in the water to face the crocodile, and had thus given Brace the opportunity of gripping me firmly and jerking me aloft.

It was a very tight fit, however; and I vowed, that, unless forced to it, I would never again bathe my limbs in the waters of an African river.

RAGGED DICK.

HORATIO ALGER, JR (1832-1899)
"The Pocket-Book" from *Ragged Dick; or, Street Life in New York With the Boot Blacks* (1867)

Born in Revere, Massachusetts, Horatio Alger, Jr, a graduate of Harvard Divinity School who earned his living for a short while as a Unitarian minister, became one of the most popular writers of juvenile fiction in the late nineteenth century with his series of rags-to-riches stories: The Ragged Dick Series (1867 ff.), The Luck and Pluck Series (1869 ff.), and The Tattered Tom Series (1871 ff.). These tales of self-made men reiterate Alger's deeply held conviction that shrewdness, hard work, self-denial, and charity to the less fortunate always pay—with monetary rewards and social advancement.

His first book to exploit this formula was *Ragged Dick* (1867), the story of an illiterate fourteen-year-old boot-black who, in the space of a year, rises to become a well-paid accounting clerk. In the Preface Alger admitted that "several characters . . . are sketched from life"—that is, they were drawn from his experience as chaplain to the Newsboys' Lodging House in New York—but that he also allowed himself considerable licence in this "unpretending

volume, which does not aspire to strict historical accuracy". A combination of realism and wonderful wish-fulfilment accounts for the appeal of *Ragged Dick*.

Dick starts out as a cocky "street kid" who calls a straw box his home; often having to work for his breakfast, he usually splurges all his earnings on an oyster stew at Tony Pastor's or a show at the Old Bowery. Although he is able to bend the truth on occasion, Dick is generous and well liked. In the chapter reprinted here he is performing the duties of a tour guide for a genteel boy, Frank, who is enroute to college in Connecticut. Dick has been clothed by Frank's Uncle William and given five dollars for his knowing guidance. With this sum he starts a new life.

Though he shrewdly detects the ploy of the confidence man, Dick admits that he is "awful ignorant". With the aplomb typical of Alger's heroes he decides to remedy the situation: he rents a room, hires and befriends a tutor (Henry Fosdick, a literate but unsuccessful boot-black), and studies in earnest every evening instead of "wast-

ing" his time at the theatre. As Alger ob-
serves, "He knew that he had only himself
to depend upon, and he determined to
make the most of himself,—a resolution
which is the secret of success in nine cases
out of ten" (Chapter xx). For Dick, the
boot-black who works so hard that he sur-
passes his teacher, prosperity is assured
when he saves a drowning boy and is
rewarded by the child's father, who happens to manage a counting house. *Ragged
Dick*—like Alger's countless other books—
is a paean to materialism and philistinism.

THE POCKET-BOOK

They had reached the junction of Broadway and of Fifth Avenue. Before
them was a beautiful park of ten acres. On the left-hand side was a large
marble building, presenting a fine appearance with its extensive white
front. This was the building at which Dick pointed.

"Is that the Fifth Avenue Hotel?" asked Frank. "I've heard of it often.
My Uncle William always stops there when he comes to New York."

"I once slept on the outside of it," said Dick. "They was very reason-
able in their charges, and told me I might come again."

"Perhaps sometime you'll be able to sleep inside," said Frank.

At that moment a gentleman passed them on the sidewalk, who
looked back at Dick, as if his face seemed familiar.

"I know that man," said Dick, after he had passed. "He's one of my
customers."

"What is his name?"

"I don't know."

"He looked back as if he thought he knew you."

"He would have knowed me at once if it hadn't been for my new
clothes," said Dick. "I don't look much like Ragged Dick now."

"I suppose your face looked familiar."

"All but the dirt," said Dick, laughing. "I don't always have the
chance of washing my face and hands in the Astor House."

"You told me," said Frank, "that there was a place where you could
get lodging for five cents. Where's that?"

"It's the News-boys' Lodgin' House, on Fulton Street," said Dick,
"up over the 'Sun' office. It's a good place. I don't know what us boys
would do without it. They give you supper for six cents, and a bed for
five cents more."

"I suppose some boys don't even have the five cents to pay,—do
they?"

"They'll trust the boys," said Dick. "But I don't like to get trusted. I'd
be ashamed to get trusted for five cents, or ten either. One night I was
comin' down Chatham Street, with fifty cents in my pocket I was going
to get a good oyster-stew, and then go to the lodgin' house; but somehow it slipped through a hole in my trowses-pocket, and I hadn't a cent
left. If it had been summer I shouldn't have cared, but it's rather tough
stayin' out winter nights."

Frank, who had always possessed a good home of his own, found it
hard to realize that the boy who was walking at his side had actually

walked the streets in the cold without a home, or money to procure the common comfort of a bed.

"What did you do?" he asked, his voice full of sympathy.

"I went to the 'Times' office. I knowed one of the pressmen, and he let me set down in a corner, where I was warm, and I soon got fast asleep."

While this conversation was going on, they had turned into Twenty-fifth Street, and had by this time reached Third Avenue.

Just before entering it, their attention was drawn to the rather singular conduct of an individual in front of them. Stopping suddenly, he appeared to pick up something from the sidewalk, and then looked about him in rather a confused way.

"I know his game," whispered Dick. "Come along and you'll see what it is."

He hurried Frank forward until they overtook the man, who had come to a stand-still.

"Have you found anything?" asked Dick.

"Yes," said the man, "I've found this."

He exhibited a wallet which seemed stuffed with bills, to judge from its plethoric appearance.

"Whew!" exclaimed Dick; "you're in luck."

"I suppose somebody has lost it," said the man, "and will offer a handsome reward."

"Which you'll get."

"Unfortunately I am obliged to take the next train to Boston. That's where I live. I haven't time to hunt up the owner."

"Then I suppose you'll take the pocket-book with you," said Dick, with assumed simplicity.

"I should like to leave it with some honest fellow who would see it returned to the owner," said the man, glancing at the boys.

"I'm honest," said Dick.

"I've no doubt of it," said the other. "Well, young man, I'll make you an offer. You take the pocket-book—"

"All right. Hand it over, then."

"Wait a minute. There must be a large sum inside. I shouldn't wonder if there might be a thousand dollars. The owner will probably give you a hundred dollars reward."

"Why don't you stay and get it?" asked Frank.

"I would, only there is sickness in my family, and I must get home as soon as possible. Just give me twenty dollars, and I'll hand you the pocket-book, and let you make whatever you can out of it. Come, that's a good offer. What do you say?"

Dick was well dressed, so that the other did not regard it as at all improbable that he might possess that sum. He was prepared, however, to let him have it for less, if necessary.

"Twenty dollars is a good deal of money," said Dick, appearing to hesitate.

"You'll get it back, and a good deal more," said the stranger, persuasively.

"I don't know but I shall. What would you do Frank.?"

"I don't know but I would," said Frank, "if you've got the money." He was not a little surprised to think that Dick had so much by him.

"I don't know but I will," said Dick, after some irresolution. "I guess I won't lose much."

"You can't lose anything," said the stranger briskly. "Only be quick, for I must be on my way to the cars. I am afraid I shall miss them now."

Dick pulled out a bill from his pocket, and handed it to the stranger, receiving the pocket-book in return. At that moment a policeman turned the corner, and the stranger, hurriedly thrusting the bill into his pocket, without looking at it, made off with rapid steps.

"What is there in the pocket-book, Dick?" asked Frank in some excitement. "I hope there's enough to pay you for the money you gave him."

Dick laughed.

"I'll risk that," said he.

"But you gave him twenty dollars. That's a good deal of money."

"If I had given him as much as that, I should deserve to be cheated out of it."

"But you did,—didn't you?"

"He thought so,"

"What was it, then?"

"It was nothing but a dry-goods circular got up to imitate a bank-bill."

Frank looked sober.

"You ought not to have cheated him, Dick," he said, reporachfully.

"Didn't he want to cheat me?"

"I don't know."

"What do you s'pose there is in that pocket-book?" asked Dick, holding it up.

Frank surveyed its ample proportions, and answered sincerely enough, "Money, and a good deal of it."

"There aint stamps enough in it to buy a oyster-stew," said Dick. "If you don't believe it, just look while I open it."

So saying he opened the pocket-book, and showed Frank that it was stuffed out with pieces of blank paper, carefully folded up in the shape of bills. Frank, who was unused to city life, and had never heard anything of the "drop-game" looked amazed at this unexpected development.

"I knowed how it was all the time," said Dick.

"I guess I got the best of him there. The wallet's worth somethin'. I shall use it to keep my stiffkit's of Erie stock in, and all my other papers what aint of no use to anybody but the owner."

"That's the kind of papers it's got in it now," said Frank, smiling.

"That's so!" said Dick.

"By hokey! he exclaimed suddenly, "if there aint the old chap comin' back ag'in. He looks as if he'd heard bad news from his sick family."

By this time the pocket-book dropper had come up.

Approaching the boys, he said in an undertone to Dick, "Give me back that pocket-book, you young rascal!"

"Beg your pardon, mister," said Dick, "but was you addressin' me?"

"Yes, I was."

"Cause you called me by the wrong name. I've knowed some rascals, but I aint the honor to belong to the family."

He looked significantly at the other as he spoke, which didn't improve the man's temper. Accustomed to swindle others, he did not fancy being practised upon in return.

"Give me back that pocket-book," he repeated in a threatening voice.

"Couldn't do it," said Dick, cooly. "I'm goin' to restore it to the owner. The contents is so valooable that most likely the loss has made him sick, and he'll be likely to come down liberal to the honest finder."

"You gave me a bogus bill," said the man.

"It's what I use myself," said Dick.

"You've swindled me."

"I thought it was the other way."

"None of your nonsense," said the man angrily. "If you don't give up that pocket-book, I'll call a policeman."

"I wish you would," said Dick, "They'll know most likely whether it's Stewart or Astor that's lost the pocket-book, and I can get 'em to return it."

The "dropper," whose object it was to recover the pocket-book, in order to try the same game on a more satisfactory customer, was irritated by Dick's refusal, and above all by the coolness he displayed. He resolved to make one more attempt.

"Do you want to pass the night in the Tombs?" he asked.

"Thank you for your very obligin' proposal," said Dick; "but it aint convenient to-day. Any other time, when you'd like to have me come and stop with you, I'm agreeable; but my two youngest children is down with the measles, and I expect I'll have to set up all night to take care of 'em. Is the Tombs, in gineral, a pleasant place of residence?"

Dick asked this question with an air of so much earnestness that Frank could scarcely forbear laughing, though it is hardly necessary to say that the dropper was by no means so inclined.

"You'll know sometime," he said, scowling.

"I'll make you a fair offer," said Dick. "If I get more'n fifty dollars as a reward for my honesty, I'll divide with you. But I say, aint it most time to go back to your sick family in Boston?"

Finding that nothing was to be made out of Dick, the man strode away with a muttered curse.

"You were too smart for him, Dick," said Frank.

"Yes," said Dick, "I aint knocked round the city streets all my life for nothin."

JAMES DE MILLE (1833-1880)
"The Fight with a Sea Monster" from The "B.O.W.C.": A Story for Boys (1869)

Born in Saint John, New Brunswick, this author of about thirty books—historical romances, international novels of manners, mystery novels, and many adventures for boys—is best remembered today for his posthumously published anti-utopian satire, *A Strange Manuscript Found in a Copper Cylinder* (1888). De Mille was an accomplished linguist; he taught classics at Acadia University and history and rhetoric at Dalhousie. He was also a regular contributor to a Boston publisher's American Boys' Series of Adventure Stories, in which his colourful and gripping Acadian stories—like *Boys of the Grand Pré School* (1870), *Lost in the Fog* (1870), and *Fire in the Woods* (1872)—first appeared.

The adventures of the Grand Pré schoolboys began with an 1869 publication, *The "B.O.W.C."* (Brethren of the Order of the White Cross), which recounts the exploits of the members of a secret society during a week's cruise around the Minas Basin in Nova Scotia. The Brethren elect themselves to impressive-sounding offices such as The Most Venerable Patriarch, The Venerable Scribe, The Right Worshipful Commander, The Grand Scholastic, and The Venerable Warden; dress in red shirts emblazoned with a huge white cross; and sport jaunty felt hats with feathers—looking, as one schoolmaster quips, "like so many juvenile Garibaldians". Their school-holiday cruise aboard a schooner—a leaky, time-worn "washtub" called the *Antelope*—allows the B.O.W.C. to demonstrate their resourcefulness and true camaraderie. Although the expedition is supervised by teachers and led by a dawdling, sentimental skipper, the resilient fraternity is often stranded; in the episode printed here Bart and his Brethren manage very capably when their boat runs aground. Never morose or despairing, the B.O.W.C. are healthy survivors—"a set of Jonahs", as one of their teachers remarks, for whom everything *does* "come out all right at last".

Once an extremely popular author of boys' novels, De Mille has been unjustly forgotten. Though his books are quite uncharacteristic of Golden Age juvenile fiction—with their rare and welcome wit, genial characters, engaging slangy dialogue, and lack of didacticism—they are still appealing today.

THE FIGHT WITH A SEA MONSTER

In Mud and Water.—A Sea Monster.—A terrific Fight.—Wonderful Pluck of the "B.O.W.C."—Swallowing a Sculpin.—The Trophy.—Waiting for Deliverance.

Finding themselves thus fixed in the mud, they looked around to see the place at which they had thus unexpectedly arrived. In front of them was a bank about sixty feet high, which extended for some miles away, commencing with the rocky headland, and covered with trees on the top; while beyond this, the country rose into hills. As far as they could see, there was no opening in the shore to indicate the presence of a cove or a harbor. From the appearance of the water, it seemed as though the mud flat extended for miles along the shore. The water was comparatively smooth, and the headland kept off the wind, so that after they had lowered the sails, the schooner remained quite still.

It was now about noon, and they knew that the tide was rising. A wide space of the mud flat lay still uncovered by the water. Their position was a safe one as yet, though not at all pleasant on many accounts.

"The tide's rising," said Phil; "isn't it, Bart?"

"Yes."

"When will it be high tide?"

"About three."

"I wonder if they'll come afer us."

"Of course they will."

"There doesn't seem to be much chance of our getting ashore."

"Well, it doesn't make much difference, for we couldn't do anything if we did get there."

"I say, boys," said Arthur, "the schooner's beginning to float again."

All stood waiting in silence, and in a few moments they felt a slight motion.

"Yes," said Bruce, "the tide has risen since we struck, and is floating us in. At high tide we shall be close up under the bank."

"And then what shall we do? We must either choose to fasten the vessel ashore if we can, or float out again and sail for it, or drift."

"I don't think we'll care about sailing again, particularly as the tide will be going out, and the night coming on."

"My idea is," said Bruce, "to fasten her to the shore if we can, and then go along the beach or the bank till we find some people and get help."

"That's about all we can do," said Bart. "We can't think of going adrift, and none of us can sail the vessel; so, if they don't come after us we had better land, and leave the vessel; or some of us can go for help, and others stay on board."

"I wonder if the vessel is safe here."

"O, safe enough—if a gale don't spring up. In that case she might get knocked on the bank."

"We don't seem to have been hurt by our knocking up there," said Arthur. "There's no water in the hold."

"O, she's all right," said Bruce; "and she's a gallant, gallant ship, as the song says."

The vessel was steadily floated nearer and nearer to the shore as the tide rose, and the boys watched her progress with close attention. At about three o'clock they could expect to be up to the bank, and then they would have to find some way to fasten her.

Suddenly Bart, who had been looking down the shore, pointed to something, and said,—

"Look, look! Do you see that?"

"What?"

"Don't you see a line—running along about a mile away?"

"What, a thin, dark line? Yes. What of it?"

"Why, it's a weir for fish. It shows that people must be living not far from here. It shows, too, that we can get something to eat at low tide, even if there are no people. So, hurrah, boys! we're all right yet."

"The fact is," said Bruce, solemnly, "I must confess that I'm starving. I've felt the pangs of hunger for the last two hours, and I can't stand it any longer. I'm going to have a regular rummage down below, for I'm bound to find something."

All the rest followed Bruce as he went below, and they began to overhaul the whole vessel. For some time they found nothing but a beggarly array of empty boxes, and loud were their murmurs and complaints.

"If it hadn't been for that miserable Sammy Ram Ram, we'd have a few turkeys and chickens here," said Bruce. "How that fellow and Johnny Blue managed to get through with them all, I can't understand."

"Pooh! those two fellows did nothing else but stuff from the time they came on board till they got to Pratt's Cove. Captain Corbet and the mate helped them, and so did Pat, too, no doubt. I haven't any hard feeling against any of them, but I must say I wouldn't be sorry if their food didn't agree with them."

"Hallo! What's this? Hurrah!" cried Tom, suddenly.

"What, Tom,—what is it?"

"See here," cried Tom, triumphantly. "Arn't we in luck? Don't ever fret again, boys. Here's a half loaf of bread that I found in the corner. It's rather stale, a little too dry, and too hard,—but I think it's about the nicest morsel I ever saw. We've got our dinner provided for us, and we needn't hanker after raw fish from the weirs any more."

Tom's joy was fully shared by all; and the half loaf of hard, stale, dried-up bread was quickly divided into five pieces, and eagerly devoured by the famished boys.

"And now," said Bruce, "I feel like a giant refreshed. I'll go on deck and have another look at the situation. My private opinion is, however, that if they're coming after us, they'd better come. The tide's getting higher every minute; and if they get here after we've fastened her to the shore, and got her high and dry, they'll have to wait for twelve good hours before they can get her to float off again,—not to speak of spring tides. Do you know, Bart, if this is spring tide?"

"I don't know, I'm sure," said Bart.

"Well, then, we'll have to trust to luck, I suppose. At the same time I've a great mind to go ashore and reconnoitre."

"I'll go too," said Bart.

"And so will I," said Arthur.

"And I," said Phil.

"I'll go too," said Tom. "But oughtn't some of us to stay on board?"

"Stay on board? What for?"

"O, to watch the vessel."

"Why, what good will that do?"

"She may drift off."

"Well, why should any of us want to drift off in her?"

"I don't believe there's any chance of her drifting off while the tide is rising," said Bruce; "and if she does drift off, I think we're all better out of her than in her. So if one of us goes ashore, we'd all better go. It's not more than three feet deep at the bows, and there's a sand-spit over there within easy distance."

"I wonder if there are any quicksands."

"O, we'll have to run the risk. There are a couple of boat-hooks there, and two of us can go ahead and try the ground with them. It's not far to the spit."

"We'll have to strip and carry our clothes with us," said Phil.

"Yes. It would be a great joke if we left our clothes behind, and the vessel drifted off with them."

The boys now proceeded to undress themselves, and prepare to go ashore. Each one tied up his clothes in a compact bundle. Bruce and Bart took each a boat-hook, which lay in the schooner; Arthur took a hand-spike, and Tom and Phil found a stout stick each. Thus equipped, they prepared for the journey.

It was about one o'clock, and the tide would not be high for two hours yet. In front of them, and between them and the bank, lay a broad expanse of mud flats, separating them from the bank by at least a quarter of a mile of distance. On their right, however, was a place which gave them a chance of a much better foothold than that which was offered by the slippery and treacherous mud. This was a long sand-spit, which stretched out from the bank, and ran down across the mud flat and into the water. It approached to within a hundred yards of the schooner, and afforded not only a good walking-place, but a much nearer chance of dry land than was possible anywhere else. Running down over the flat, it rose above it to a height of from twelve to twenty inches, and was covered with sand, gravel, and round cobblestones. It was to this place that they intended to go.

Bruce led the way. Descending carefully over the bows, he dropped into the water, which he found up to his armpits. The others followed, and found it deeper for their shorter stature. It was over the shoulders of Bart and Phil. Bart, however, took his place by Bruce's side, and prepared to walk ahead with his pole. Their first object was to get into shallower water, and so they walked in the direction of the shore until the water was not above their waists. Then they turned to the right, toward the sand-spit.

If it had not been for the bundles, they could have varied their progress by swimming; but as it was, they had to wade, and feel the way cautiously, for fear of air-holes and quicksands. The surface mud beneath their feet was very soft; but they did not sink very deeply, and with every step they acquired fresh confidence. As they neared the sand-spit, the bottom grew sensibly harder, and shoaled rapidly, till it was not much above their knees. At length it became a sandy bottom, and they walked along more rapidly, no longer feeling their way.

Suddenly they were startled by a wild shout from Arthur. He had been walking behind with Phil, and was some distance from the others, when rapidly, between him and them, darted the form of a large fish, which, in that shoal water, was as visible as if it were on land. At the cry which he gave, Bruce and the others turned, and saw Arthur with his handspike in the air, and the fish floundering and splashing close beside. For a moment the blood of all of them froze with horror; the next instant Arthur sprang forward, and dealt a tremendous blow with his heavy handspike full on the head of the fish.

The monster splashed and struggled, and moved back into deeper water for a few feet.

"Run, run!" cried Arthur. "It's a shark! Run for your lives!"

The boys all set off as fast as they could toward the sand-pit, which now was close by them.

But the fish was not to be easily escaped. In a few minutes its dark form was beside them, and soon it crossed immediately in front of Bruce and Bart. Mechanically, and in utter horror, both the boys swung up their boat-hooks, and dashed them wildly against the dark figure. Both struck home. There was a fearful splashing and writhing. Bart's boat-hook was wrenched from his hand, and the fish darted forward into shoaler water.

"Run, boys, run!" shouted Bruce, holding his boat-hook toward the fish, and slowly retreating, so as to keep the monster in sight. Away they went, Phil and Tom first, then Arthur. Bart moved forward, and then, seeing his pole floating a few feet on one side, made a rush for it and secured it. Then he kept by Bruce's side, ready to help him in guarding the retreat of the others.

The fish continued to splash and writhe about, either because he was bewildered by the shoal water, or else because he was suffering from the wounds which had been inflicted. As he did not pursue, Bruce and Bart took fresh courage.

"Let's finish him, Bruce!" cried Bart.

"Pitch in, then!" cried Bruce; and rushing at the fish, he drove his boat-hook point deep into his side, while, at the same time, Bart, raising his into the air, struck down, so that the hooked part penetrated and held.

"Hook him, Bruce!" shouted Bart. "Let's drag him ashore." Bruce raised his pole to do so; but at that instant the struggling, writhing fish turned towards them with furious energy, and moving over on its side, it tried to twist Bart's hook out of its flesh. The water was so shallow that it could not have full exercise of its strength, and Bart held on. The fish, in its struggles, opened its gasping mouth, showing wide rows of sharp, triangular teeth. At that instant Bruce lowered his pole, and drove it straight into the open mouth, forcing it deep into the throat. The monster, in its agony, closed its jaws, and held it with a death-like tenacity.

A cry of triumph burst from Bruce and Bart.

"Hurrah, boys! We've got him!" they cried. "Pull, Bruce, nearer the shore—into shoaler water."

The water was already too shoal for the fish, which had so carelessly thrown himself into it, and his resistance could not prevent the united

energies of Bruce and Bart from dragging him forward a few paces. But that was all. Rousing himself, the monster tossed, and writhed, and struggled, and lashed the water into foam. Bruce and Bart could no longer drag him. It was a struggle between them; but the boys had now got their blood up, and they would have been dragged back to the schooner rather than loose their hold.

The fish, in its fury or its agony, still kept its teeth closed on Bruce's pole, and strove to wrench it out of his grasp. His tremendous efforts were dragging them farther out. Bart's hook had already been thrown off, and he was plunging the pointed iron again and again into the fish's side.

At this instant Arthur came dashing through the foam. Raising his heavy handspike in the air, he poised it for a moment so as to take sure aim, and then, with tremendous force, the weapon descended full on the monster's head. It was a crushing blow. The struggles and writhings ceased, and changed to feeble motions and occasional convulsive vibrations. It resisted no longer. It was powerless.

They dragged it upon the dry ground of the sand-spit, and examined their conquest.

The fish was about five feet long, very broad at the head and shoulders, with a very wide mouth, armed with several rows of saw-like teeth. The nose was rounded, and the jaw was underneath. Its back was a dark slate color, and its belly white.

"It's what we call a Shovel-mouth Shark," said Bruce, as he looked at it, and admired its proportions.

"They call it a Dog Fish with us," said Bart.

"It certainly is a kind of shark," said Arthur; "and as that sound better, we'll call it by that name. Boys, we've fought and killed a shovel-mouth shark! Let the 'B.O.W.C.' remember that!"

"We must keep his jaws as a trophy," said Bruce. "Let's cut him up and get his jaws. Who's got a knife?"

"Here," said Arthur.

Thereupon, with the aid of the knife, the fish was dissected. In the stomach they found a fish quite as remarkable as the one which had swallowed it. It was a sculpin, a fish whose bony covering, and spiny back, and horny head, and wonderful voracity, make it seem like those primeval fish that swam in the waters of the world in an age when all the inhabitants thereof were formed on a similarly monstrous model.

"What a fish," cried Bart, "to swallow a sculpin! He must be a real shark, after all, for a shark could not beat that. I thought that it might have been by accident only that he met us, but it seems now as though he was ravenous enough to mean mischief. 'Pon my word, if I'd known about that sculpin, I think I would have run away instead of staying to fight."

After examining the fish, the jaws were removed, and, carrying them, they walked up the sand-spit to the shore. Then dressing themselves, they sat down and rested for a time. Then Bruce and Bart climbed to the top of the bank, and went in different directions to explore. On coming back, each had the same story. They had met with nothing but fir trees and alder bushes, and had not seen a sign of any house whatever. On this they all decided to go to the top of the bank, and wait patiently until the tide was high, then fasten the schooner as well as they could, leave a message on board to indicate their course, and set off along the coast in search of inhabitants. With this decision, they climbed the bank to a conspicuous position, and there waited.

The tide rose higher and higher. Each increase in the depth of the water allowed the schooner to approach nearer to the shore, though there was a sidelong drift, which, from time to time, changed her position, sometimes presenting her bows to the beach, at other times her side.

The water was rising higher and still higher. The mud flats extended close up to the beach below, but the beach itself was formed of sand and gravel, and rose, by a steep slope, from the mud flat to the base of the bank. By two o'clock the water had reached the edge of the gravel.

"It will take an hour more," said Bruce, "before it gets to high-water mark. One hour more, boys, and then off we must go to explore the country."

THOMAS BAILEY ALDRICH (1836-1907)
"The Snow Fort on Slatter's Hill" from *The Story of a Bad Boy* (1870)

Editor, poet, novelist, and essayist, Thomas Bailey Aldrich was born in Portsmouth, New Hampshire. After a brief career in business he worked as a magazine editor in New York, but left to become a correspondent at the Civil War front. After the war he returned to the magazine field in New York before becoming the editor of the *Atlantic Monthly* (1881-90) in Boston. Whether in short-story collections like *Marjorie Daw and Other People* (1873), poems like *Mercedes and Later Lyrics* (1884), or essays like *From Ponkapog to Pesth* (1883), his style is genteel and refined—prompting Oliver Wendell Holmes once to regret Aldrich's "tendency to vanilla-flavored adjectives and patchouli-scented participles".

The Story of a Bad Boy (1870) is a semi-autobiographical novel that introduces the reader to Tom Bailey, the narrator, who describes himself as "an amiable, impulsive lad, blessed with fine digestive powers, and no hypocrite". Tom recalls the highlights of his boyhood in Rivermouth (based on Portsmouth), where he is cared for by his maternal grandfather, his maiden grand-aunt Abigail, and their maid-of-all-work Kitty Collins. At the Temple Grammar School, Tom rapidly becomes part of the chosen group, consisting of Charley Marden, Benny Wallace, Pepper Whitcomb, Harry Blake, and Fred Langdon. Soon installed as a regular member of the R.M.C. (Rivermouth Centipedes), Tom embarks on a series of boyish pranks designed "to mystify the staid and slow-going Rivermouthians". He and his friends burn a stagecoach, rearrange street signs, and mount extensive snow-ball campaigns to defend their fort on Slatter's Hill. Although the escapades usually originate in boyish high spirits, they sometimes become serious: a full police force is needed to disperse the attackers and defenders of the snow fort, and a boating expedition actually leads to the drowning death of a beloved R.M.C. Like Aldrich himself at the time of his father's death, Tom sacrifices his opportunity to attend Harvard and takes a position in a counting house in New York instead. The story of Tom—who is far from "bad"—has a breezy superficiality. Nevertheless it is historically important as an early example of an American boys' novel—one that features an ingenuous narrator and a variety of believable misadventures.

THE SNOW FORT ON SLATTER'S HILL

The memory of man, even that of the Oldest Inhabitant, runneth not back to the time when there did not exist a feud between the North End and the South End boys of Rivermouth.

The origin of the feud is involved in mystery; it is impossible to say which party was the first aggressor in the far-off ante-revolutionary ages; but the fact remains that the youngsters of those antipodal sections entertained a mortal hatred for each other, and that this hatred had been handed down from generation to generation, like Miles Standish's punch-bowl.

I know not what laws, natural or unnatural, regulated the warmth of the quarrel; but at some seasons it raged more violently than at others. This winter both parties were unusually lively and antagonistic. Great was the wrath of the South-Enders, when they discovered that the North-Enders had thrown up a fort on the crown of Slatter's Hill.

Slatter's Hill, or No-man's-land, as it was generally called, was a rise of ground covering, perhaps, an acre and a quarter, situated on an imaginary line, marking the boundary between the two districts. An immense stratum of granite, which here and there thrust out a wrinkled boulder, prevented the site from being used for building purposes. The street ran on either side of the hill, from one part of which a quantity of rock had been removed to form the underpinning of the new jail. This excavation made the approach from that point all but impossible, especially when the ragged ledges were a-glitter with ice. You see what a spot it was for a snow-fort.

One evening twenty or thirty of the North-Enders quietly took possession of Slatter's Hill, and threw up a strong line of breastworks, something after this shape:—

The rear of the intrenchment, being protected by the quarry, was left open. The walls were four feet high, and twenty-two inches thick, strengthened at the angles by stakes driven firmly into the ground.

Fancy the rage of the South-Enders the next day, when they spied our snowy citadel, with Jack Harris's red silk pocket-handkerchief floating defiantly from the flag-staff.

In less than an hour it was known all over town, in military circles at least, that the "Puddle-dockers" and the "River-rats" (these were the derisive sub-titles bestowed on our South-End foes) intended to attack the fort that Saturday afternoon.

At two o'clock all the fighting boys of the Temple Grammar School, and as many recruits as we could muster, lay behind the walls of Fort Slatter, with three hundred compact snow-balls piled up in pyramids, awaiting the approach of the enemy. The enemy was not slow in making his approach,—fifty strong, headed by one Mat Ames. Our forces were under the command of General J. Harris.

Before the action commenced, a meeting was arranged between the rival commanders, who drew up and signed certain rules and regulations respecting the conduct of the battle. As it was impossible for the North-Enders to occupy the fort permanently, it was stipulated that the South-Enders should assault it only on Wednesday and Saturday afternoons between the hours of two and six.

The North-Enders, on the other hand, agreed to give up the fort whenever ten of the storming party succeeded in obtaining at one time a footing on the parapet, and were able to hold the same for the space of two minutes. Both sides were to abstain from putting pebbles into their snow-balls, nor was it permissible to use frozen ammunition.

These preliminaries settled, the commanders retired to their respective corps. The interview had taken place on the hillside between the opposing lines.

General Harris divided his men into two bodies; the first comprised the most skilful marksmen, or gunners; the second, the reserve force, was composed of the strongest boys, whose duty it was to repel the scaling parties, and to make occasional sallies for the purpose of capturing prisoners, who were bound by the articles of treaty to faithfully serve under our flag until they were exchanged at the close of the day.

The repellers were called light infantry; but when they carried on operations beyond the fort they became cavalry. It was also their duty, when not otherwise engaged, to manufacture snow-balls. The General's staff consisted of five Templars (I among the number, with the rank of Major), who carried the General's orders and looked after the wounded.

General Mat Ames, a veteran commander, was no less wide awake in the disposition of his army. Five companies, each numbering but six men, in order not to present too big a target to our sharpshooters, were to charge the fort from different points, their advance being covered by a heavy fire from the gunners posted in the rear. Each scaler was provided with only two rounds of ammunition, which were not to be used until he had mounted the breastwork and could deliver his shots on our heads.

The following cut represents the interior of the fort just previous to the assault. Nothing on earth could represent the state of things after the first volley.

The thrilling moment had now arrived. If I had been going into a real engagement I could not have been more deeply impressed by the importance of the occasion.

The fort opened fire first,—a single ball from the dexterous hand of General Harris taking General Ames in the very pit of his stomach. A cheer went up from Fort Slatter. In an instant the air was thick with flying missiles, in the midst of which we dimly descried the storming parties sweeping up the hill, shoulder to shoulder. The shouts of the lead-

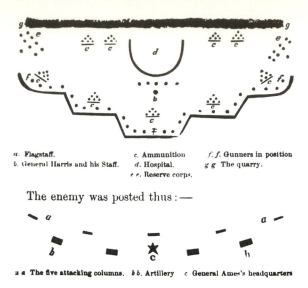

a. Flagstaff.
b. General Harris and his Staff.
c. Ammunition
d. Hospital.
e e. Reserve corps.
f. f. Gunners in position
g g. The quarry.

The enemy was posted thus : —

a a. The five attacking columns. b b. Artillery c General Ames's headquarters

ers, and the snow-balls bursting like shells about our ears, made it very lively.

Not more than a dozen of the enemy succeeded in reaching the crest of the hill; five of these clambered upon the icy walls, where they were instantly grabbed by the legs and jerked into the fort. The rest retired confused and blinded by our well-directed fire.

When General Harris (with his right eye bunged up) said, "Soldiers, I am proud of you!" my heart swelled in my bosom.

The victory, however, had not been without its price. Six North-Enders, having rushed out to harrass the discomfited enemy, were gallantly cut off by General Ames and captured. Among these were Lieutenant P. Whitcomb (who had no business to join the charge, being weak in the knees), and Captain Fred Langdon, of General Harris's staff.

But we had no time for vain regrets. The battle raged. Already there were two bad cases of black eye, and one of nose-bleed, in the hospital.

It was glorious excitement, those pell-mell onslaughts and hand-to-hand struggles. Twice we were within an ace of being driven from our stronghold, when General Harris and his staff leaped recklessly upon the ramparts and hurled the besiegers heels over head down hill.

At sunset, the garrison of Fort Slatter was still unconquered, and the South-Enders, in a solid phalanx, marched off whistling "Yankee Doodle," while we cheered and jeered them until they were out of hearing.

General Ames remained behind to effect an exchange of prisoners. We held thirteen of his men, and he eleven of ours. General Ames proposed to call it an even thing, since many of his eleven prisoners were officers, while nearly all of our thirteen captives were privates. A dispute arising on this point, the two noble generals came to fisticuffs, and in the fracas our brave commander got his remaining well eye badly damaged. This didn't prevent him from writing a general order the next day, on a slate, in which he complimented the troops on their heroic behavior.

As the winter wore on, the war-spirit waxed fiercer and fiercer. At length the provision against using heavy substances in the snow-balls was disregarded. A ball stuck full of sand-bird shot came tearing into Fort Slatter. In retaliation, General Harris ordered a broadside of shells; i.e. snow-balls containing marbles. After this, both sides never failed to freeze their ammunition.

It was no longer child's play to march up to the walls of Fort Slatter, nor was the position of the besieged less perilous. At every assault three or four boys on each side were disabled. It was not an infrequent occurrence for the combatants to hold up a flag of truce while they removed some insensible comrade.

Matters grew worse and worse. Seven North-Enders had been seriously wounded, and a dozen South-Enders were reported on the sick list. The select-men of the town awoke to the fact of what was going on, and detailed a *posse* of police to prevent further disturbance. The boys at the foot of the hill, South-Enders as it happened, finding themselves assailed in the rear and on the flank, turned round and attempted to beat off the watchmen. In this they were sustained by numerous volunteers from the fort, who looked upon the interference as tyrannical.

The watch were determined fellows, and charged the boys valiantly, driving them all into the fort, where we made common cause, fighting side by side like the best of friends. In vain the four guardians of the peace rushed up the hill, flourishing their clubs and calling upon us to surrender. They could not get within ten yards of the fort, our fire was so destructive. In one of the onsets a man named Muggridge, more valorous than his peers, threw himself upon the parapet, when he was seized by twenty pairs of hands, and dragged inside the breastwork, where fifteen boys sat down on him to keep him quiet.

Perceiving that it was impossible with their small number to dislodge us, the watch sent for reinforcements. Their call was responded to, not only by the whole constabulary force (eight men), but by a numerous body of citizens, who had become alarmed at the prospect of a riot. This formidable array brought us to our senses; we began to think that maybe discretion was the better part of valor. General Harris and General Ames, with their respective staffs, held a council of war in the hospital, and backward movement was decided on. So, after one grand farewell volley, we fled, sliding, jumping, rolling, tumbling down the quarry at the rear of the fort, and escaped without losing a man.

But we lost Fort Slatter forever. Those battle-scarred ramparts were razed to the ground, and humiliating ashes sprinkled over the historic spot, near which a solitary lynx-eyed policeman was seen prowling from time to time during the rest of the winter.

The event passed into a legend, and afterwards, when later instances of pluck and endurance were spoken of, the boys would say, "By golly! You ought to have been at the fights on Slatter's Hill!"

G. A. HENTY (1832-1902)
"The Path Down The Heights" from *With Wolfe in Canada; or, The Winning of a Continent* (1887)

Born at Trumpington, Eng., George Alfred Henty, a stockbroker's son, left Cambridge to volunteer in the Crimean War. He returned home, a decorated veteran of the Crimean hospital commissariat, to take up posts in the commissariats at Belfast and Portsmouth. He had wearied of this occupation by 1865 and decided to earn his living as a writer. Drawing on his extensive travels (to Sardinia, Austria, Abyssinia, Egypt, India, and California), Henty achieved Golden Age fame with his sober but action-packed narratives, all distinguished by the quality that he proudly referred to as "manly tone". In an article for one of the boys' magazines he edited, he disclosed that his own varied experience formed the basis of many of his plots:

I went through India with the Prince of Wales; and have traversed the United States and Canada, Russia, Egypt, and Palestine. So you see, boys, I have a very extensive store of recollections to draw upon, and have faced death in a great variety of ways and a vast number of occasions. (The Union Jack, 5 May 1881)

His first boys' adventure, *Out on the Pampas* (1868), was followed by over eighty novels, *The Young Franc-Tireurs* (1872) and *Facing Death* (1883) being among the most popular. Henty inserted a strong anglophilic bias into his boys' stories, which he produced under contract to Blackie & Son at the rate of three or four a year. In his historical narratives (like *With Clive in India*, 1884, and *With Wolfe in Canada*, 1887) he managed to create boy-heroes whose daring turns out to be crucially important.

With Wolfe in Canada was based—as Henty admits in his Preface—on one secondary and one primary source: Francis Parkman's *Montcalm and Wolfe* (1884) and John Knox's *An Historical Journal of the Campaigns in North-America* . . . (1769). The fearless hero, James Walsham, faces death several times: as aide-de-camp to Colonel Washington in Virginia (1755); as scout for General Johnson at Fort Edward on the Hudson River and at Ticonderoga on Lake Champlain; as ensign and captain under Colonel Otway after the loss of Oswego (1756); and, as the following extract shows, as the secret agent who scales the heights of the Plains of Abraham in preparation for Wolfe's victory over Montcalm (1759). For mapping the strategy of the British Conquest at Quebec, he is promoted to major—at the age of twenty-three. As soldier and patriot, son and friend, James Walsham is Henty's model of a complete hero. He is dedicated to his widowed mother and amazingly charitable towards Richard Horton, whose treasonous release of a French scout almost ruins James's mission at Quebec. So forgiving is Major Walsham that he arranges the disappearance of his now-disgraced friend so that Horton, at last humbled by his rival's understanding, can start a new life in Canada rather than face a court martial and hanging.

Henty's long novels—bulging with historical fact and incident, tirelessly but accurately descriptive, and not without emotional interest—were read and admired throughout most of the Golden Age and well into the twentieth century. A modern reader, however, requires considerable fortitude to get through them: today they are virtually unread.

THE PATH DOWN THE HEIGHTS

As the midshipman crawled away from the tent of the French general he adopted the precautions which James had suggested, and felt the ground carefully for twigs or sticks each time he moved. The still glowing embers of the campfires warned him where the Indians and Canadians were sleeping, and carefully avoiding these he made his way up beyond the limits of the camp.

He walked for about a mile, and then paused on the very edge of the sharp declivity and whistled as agreed upon.

A hundred yards further he repeated the signal. The fourth time he whistled he heard just below him the answer, and a minute later James Walsham stood beside him.

"You young scamp, what are you doing here?"

"It was not my fault, Captain Walsham—it wasn't indeed; but I should have been tomahawked if I had stayed there a moment longer."

"What do you mean by you would have been tomahawked?" James asked angrily, for he was convinced that the midshipman had made up his mind all along to accompany him.

"The pilot of the Sutherland swam ashore with the news that you had been taken prisoner on purpose and were really a spy."

"I am sorry to say, sir, that it is a case of treachery, and that one of our officers is concerned in it. The man said that an officer released him from his cell, took him to his cabin, and then lowered him by a rope through the porthole."

"Impossible!" James Walsham said.

"It sounds impossible, sir, but I am afraid it isn't, for the officer gave him a note to bring to the general telling him all about it, and the note I have got in my pocket now."

The midshipman then related the whole circumstances of his discovery.

"It is an extraordinary affair," James said. "However, you are certainly not to blame for making your escape when you did."

"I will go on if you like, sir," the boy said, "and hide somewhere else, so that if they track me they will not find you."

"No, no" James said. "I don't think there's any fear of our being tracked. Indian eyes are sharp, but they can't perform miracles. In the forest it would be hopeless to escape them, but here the grass is short and the ground dry, and without boots we cannot have left any tracks that would be followed, especially as bodies of French troops have been marching backward and forward along the edge of these heights for the last fortnight."

Cautiously they made their way down to a clump of bushes twenty feet below the edge, and there, lying down, dozed until it became light enough to see the ground.

"Is there any signature to that letter?" James asked presently.

The midshipman took the piece of paper out and looked at it.

"No, there is no signature," he said, "but I know the handwriting. I have seen it in orders over and over again."

James was silent a few minutes.

"I won't ask you who it is, though I fear I know too well. Look here, Middleton, I should like you to tear that letter up and say no more about it."

"No, sir," the boy said, putting the paper in his pocket, "I can't do that. Of course I am under your orders for this expedition, but this is not an affair in which I consider that I am bound to obey you. This concerns the honor of the officers of my ship, and I should not be doing my duty if I did not, upon my return, place this letter in the hands of the captain. A man who would betray the general's plans to the enemy would betray the ship, and I should be a traitor myself if I did not inform the captain."

The day passed quietly. That the Indians were searching for him far and wide James Walsham had no doubt, and indeed from their hiding-place he saw several parties of redskins moving along on the river bank carefully examining the ground.

Not until it was perfectly dark did they leave their hiding-place, and by the aid of the bushes worked their way up to the top of the ascent again. James had impressed on his companion that on no account was he to speak above a whisper, that he was to stop whenever he did, and should he turn off and descend the slope he was at once to follow his example. The midshipman kept close to his companion and marveled how assuredly the latter walked along, for he himself could see nothing.

Several times James stopped and listened. Presently he turned off to the right, saying "S-s-h" in the lowest possible tone, and proceeding a few paces down the slope, noiselessly lay down behind the bush. The midshipman imitated his example, though he wondered why he was so acting, for he could hear nothing. Two or three minutes later he heard a low footfall, and then the sound of men speaking in a low voice in some strange tongue. He could not see them, but held his breath as they were passing. Not till they had been gone some minutes did James rise and pursue his course.

"Two Indians," he said, "and on the search for us. One was just saying to the other he expected when they got back to camp to find that some of the other parties had overtaken us."

"I wish we could explore the inside of a farmhouse and light upon something to eat and drink," the midshipman said.

"It's no use wishing," James replied. "We can't risk anything of that sort, and probably all the farmhouses are full of troops. We have got a little bread left—that will hold us over to-morrow comfortably."

"It may hold us," Middleton said, "but it certainly won't hold me comfortably. My idea of comfort at the present time would be a round of beef and a gallon of ale."

"Ah! you are an epicure," James laughed. "If you had had three or four years of campaigning in the forest, as I have had, you would learn to content yourself on something a good deal less than that."

"I might," the boy said, "but I have my doubts about it. There's one comfort, we shall be able to sleep all day to-morrow, and so I shan't think about it. As the Indians did not find our tracks yesterday they are not likely to do so today."

They were some time before they found a hiding-place, for the descent was so steep that they had to try several times before they could get down far enough to reach a spot screened by bushes and hidden from the sight of any one passing above. At last they did so, and soon lay down to sleep after partaking of a mouthful of water each and a tiny piece of bread. They passed the day for the most part in sleep, but the midshipman woke frequently, being now really parched with thirst.

As evening approached, together they crept cautiously along the edge of the ridge until they came to a clump of some fifteen tents. As they approached they could see by the light of the fires that the encampment was one of Canadian troops. James had not intended to move forward until all were asleep, but the men were all chatting round the fires, and it did not seem to him that a sentry had as yet been placed on the edge of the descent. He therefore crept forward at once, followed closely by the midshipman, keeping as far as possible down beyond the slope of the descent. Presently he came to a path. He saw at once that this was very different from the others—it was regularly cut, sloping gradually down the face of the sharp descent and was wide enough for a cart to pass. He took his way down it, moving with the greatest caution lest a sentry should be posted some distance below. It was very dark, as in many places the trees met overhead. About halfway down he suddenly came to a stop, for in front of him rose a bank breast-high.

Here, if anywhere, a sentry should have been placed, and holding his companion's arm James listened intently for some time.

The gap cut in the path was some ten feet across and six feet deep. When with difficulty they clambered up on the other side they found the path obstructed by a number of felled trees, forming a thick abattis. They managed to climb the steep hillside and kept along it until past the obstruction; then they got on to the path again and found it unbroken to the bottom.

"So far, so good," James said. "Now do you stop here while I crawl forward to the water. The first thing to discover is whether they have a sentinel stationed anywhere near the bottom of his path."

The time seemed terribly long to Middleton before James returned, though it was really but a few minutes.

"All right!" he said as he approached him. "There is no one here, though I can hear some sentries further up the river. Now you can come forward and have a drink—fortunately the river is high."

"It won't do to hide anywhere near," James said, "for if the boat which comes to take us off were to be seen it would put them on their guard, and there would be plenty of sentries about here in future. No, we will keep along at the foot of the precipice till we are about halfway, as far as we can tell, between Samos and Sillery, and then we will climb up as high as we can get and show our signal in the morning. But you must be careful as we walk, for as I told you there are some sentries posted by the water's edge higher up."

"I will be careful—don't you fear," the midshipman said. "There is not much fear of a fellow walking about in the dark without boots not being careful. I knocked my toe against a rock just now and it was as much as I could do not to shout. I will be careful in future, I can tell you."

They climbed up until they gained a spot some fifty feet above the level of the river, and there sat down in a clump of bushes.

"As soon as it's daylight we will choose a spot where we can show a signal without the risk of its being seen from below," James said. "We mustn't go to sleep, for we must move directly the dawn commences, else those sentries below might make us out."

Presently the tide grew slacker, and half an hour later the ships were seen to hoist their sails and soon began to drop slowly up the river. When they approached James fastened his handkerchief against the trunk of a tree well open to view from the river and then stood with his eyes fixed on the approaching ships. Just as the Sutherland came abreast of the spot where they were standing the ensign was dipped. James at once removed his handkerchief.

"Now," he said, "Middleton, you can turn in and take a sleep. At twelve o'clock to-night there will be a boat below for us."

Two or three hours after darkness had fallen James and his companion made their way down the slope and crawled out to the water's edge. There was no sentry within hearing, and they sat down by the river until suddenly a light gleamed for an instant low down on the water, two or three hundred yards from the shore.

They at once stepped into the river, and wading out for some little distance struck out toward where they had seen the light. A few minutes' swimming and they saw something dark ahead, another few strokes took them alongside, and they were hauled into the boat. The slight noise attracted the attention of a sentry some little distance along the shore, and his *qui vive* came sharply across the water, followed a few seconds later by the flash of his gun.

The crew now bent to their oars, and a quarter of an hour later the boat was alongside the Sutherland, which with her consorts was slowly drifting up the stream. General Wolfe and the admiral were on deck and anxiously waiting the arrival of the boat. The former in his anxiety hailed the boat as it approached. "Is Captain James Walsham on board?"

"Yes, sir," James replied.

"Bravo! bravo!" the general cried, delighted.

"Bravo!" he repeated, seizing James Walsham's hand as he stepped on deck. "I did not expect to see you again, Captain Walsham, at least until we took Quebec. Now come to my cabin at once and tell me all about it. But perhaps you are hungry."

"I am rather hungry, general," James said quietly. "We have had nothing to eat but a crust of bread for three days."

"We? Who are we?" the general asked quickly.

"Mr Middleton and myself, sir. He escaped after I had left and joined me."

"The galley fires are out," the admiral said, "but you shall have some cold meat in my cabin instantly."

James was at once led to the cabin, where in two or three minutes food and a bottle of wine were placed before him. The general would not allow him to speak a word till his hunger was satisfied. Then when he saw him lay down his knife and fork he said:

"Now, Captain Walsham, in the first place, have you succeeded— have you found a practicable path down to the river?"

"I have found a path, sir. It is cut in one place and blocked with felled trees, but the obstacles can be passed. There are some Canadians in tents near the top of the path, but they seem to keep a very careless watch, and no sentry is placed at the bottom or on the edge of the river anywhere near."

"Admirable! admirable!" Wolfe exclaimed. "At last there is a chance of our outreaching Montcalm. And you were not seen examining the path? Nothing occurred to excite their suspicion and lead them to keep a better lookout in future?"

"No, sir," James replied, "they have had no suspicion of my presence anywhere near. The spot where I was taken off was two miles higher. I moved away in order that if we were seen swimming off to the boat no suspicion should occur that we had been reconnoitering the pathway."

"That is right," the general said. "Now tell me the whole story of what you have been doing, in your own way."

James related his adventures up to the time when he was joined by the midshipman.

"But what made Mr Middleton escape?" the admiral asked. "I

thought that his instructions were precise that he was to permit himself to be taken prisoner, and was to remain quietly in Quebec until we could either exchange him or take the place."

"That was how he understood his instructions, sir," James said, "but I would rather that you should question him yourself as to his reasons for escaping.

"I will put you in orders to-morrow for your brevet majority," he said, "and never was the rank more honorably earned."

The admiral rang a hand-bell.

"Send Mr Middleton to me."

A minute later Captain Peters entered, followed by the midshipman.

"I suppose, Peters, you have been asking young Middleton the reason why he did not carry out his instructions?"

"I have, admiral," Captain Peters said gravely, "and I was only waiting until you were disengaged to report the circumstances to you. He had better tell you, sir, his own way."

Captain Peters then took a seat at the table, while the midshipman related his story in nearly the same words in which he had told it to James.

"I am sorry to say, sir," Middleton said, "that the man gave proofs of the truth of what he was saying. The officer, he said, gave him a paper, which I heard and saw the general reading aloud. It was a warning that Captain Walsham had purposely allowed himself to be captured, and that he was, in fact, a spy. The French officer in his haste laid down the paper on the table when he rushed out, and I had just time to creep under the canvas, seize it, and make off with it. Here it is, sir. I have shown it to Captain Peters."

The admiral took the paper and read it and handed it without a word to General Wolfe.

"That is proof conclusive," he said. "Peters, do you know the handwriting?"

"Yes," Captain Peters said gravely. "I recognized it at once, as did Mr Middleton. It is the handwriting of Lieutenant Horton."

"But what on earth could be the motive of this unhappy young man?" the admiral asked.

"I imagine, sir, from what I saw on the evening before Captain Walsham set out, and indeed from what Captain Walsham said when I questioned him, that it was a case of private enmity against Captain Walsham."

"Is this so, Captain Walsham?" General Wolfe asked.

"I have no enmity against him, sir," James said, "though I own that his manner impressed me with the idea that he regarded me as an enemy. The fact is we lived near each other as boys, and had a fight. I got the best of it. He gave an account of the affair, which was not exactly correct, to his uncle, Mr Linthorne, a wealthy landowner and a magistrate. The latter had me up at the justice-room, but I brought forward witnesses who gave their account of the affair. Mr Linthorne considered that his nephew—whom he had at that time regarded as his heir—had not given a correct account, and was so angry that he sent him to sea. I would say, sir," he said earnestly, "that were it possible I should have wished this unhappy affair to be passed over."

"Impossible!" the admiral and general said together.

"I fear it is impossible now, sir," James said gravely, "but it might have been stopped before."

The admiral rang the bell.

"Tell Lieutenant Horton that I wish to speak to him, and order a corporal with a file of marines to be at the door."

The messenger found Lieutenant Horton pacing the quarter-deck with hurried steps.

"Lieutenant Horton," the admiral said, "you are accused of having assisted in the escape of the pilot who was our prisoner on board this ship. You are further accused of releasing him with the special purpose that the plans which General Wolfe had laid to obtain information might be thwarted."

"Who accuses me?" Richard Horton asked. "Captain Walsham is my enemy. He has for years intrigued against me and sought to do me harm."

"You are mistaken, Lieutenant Horton," the admiral said. "Captain Walsham is not your accuser. Nay, more: he has himself committed a grave dereliction of duty in trying to screen you and by endeavoring to destroy the principal evidence against you. Mr Middleton overheard a conversation between the Canadian pilot and the French general, and the former described how he had been liberated by an English officer, who assisted him to escape by a rope from the porthole in his cabin."

"I do not see that that is evidence against me," Richard Horton said. "In the first place, the man may have been lying; in the second place, unless he mentioned my name why am I suspected more than any other officer? And even if he did mention my name, my word is surely as good as that of a Canadian prisoner? It is probable that the man was released by one of the crew—some man, perhaps, who owed me a grudge—who told him to say that it was I who freed him, in hopes that some day this outrageous story might get about."

"Your suggestions are plausible, Mr Horton," the admiral said coldly. "Unfortunately it is not on the word of this Canadian that we have to depend. There, sir," he said, holding out the letter; "there is the chief witness against you. Captain Peters instantly recognized your handwriting, as Mr Middleton had done before him."

Richard Horton stood gazing speechlessly at the letter. So confounded was he by the unexpected production of this fatal missive that he was unable to utter a single word of explanation or excuse.

"Lay your sword on the table, sir," the admiral said, "and retire to your cabin, where you will remain under close arrest till a court-martial can be assembled."

Richard Horton unbuckled his sword and laid it on the table and left the cabin without a word.

"It would have been better to send a guard with him," Captain Peters said. "He might jump overboard or blow his brains out."

"Quite so, Peters," the admiral said; "the very thing that was in my mind when I told him to retire to his cabin—the very best thing he could do for himself and for the service. A nice scandal it would be to have to try and hang a naval officer for treachery. I am sure you agree with me, general?"

"Thoroughly," the general said. "Let him blow his brains out or desert; but you had best keep a sharp lookout that he does not desert at present. After we have once effected our landing, I should say keep as careless a watch over him as possible; but don't let him go before. It is bad enough that the French know that Captain Walsham went ashore for the purpose of discovering a landing-place, but it would be worse were they to become aware that he has rejoined the ships, and that he was taken off by a boat within a couple of miles of the spot where we mean to land."

NORMAN DUNCAN (1871-1916)
"Delivering Her Majesty's Mail" from *The Adventures of Billy Topsail* (1906)

Duncan was born in North Norwich Township, Oxford County, Ontario. After attending the University of Toronto, from which he did not graduate, he moved to the United States, where he worked as a journalist and a sometime teacher of English. In 1900 he went to Newfoundland to write articles for *McClure's Magazine*; he returned between 1901 and 1906 and again in 1910. Out of these summer visits grew his highly popular tales about Labrador and Newfoundland and the rugged, undaunted, and genial people of the outports who so impressed him. Duncan celebrated their spirit in many books, such as *Dr Luke of the Labrador* (1904), *Dr Grenfell's Parish: The Deep Sea Fisherman* (1905), and *The Cruise of the Shining Light* (1907).

The plain, brave tenacity of Newfoundlanders is the peg on which Duncan hangs the episodic tales of his Billy Topsail series

of adventure stories for boys. Billy is a typical Newfoundland boy, the son of a fisherman from Ruddy Cove, "a fishing harbour on the bleak northeast coast". Dutybound and sensible, he is a good fisherman who even catches giant squid, a successful sealer who endures near-fatal exposure to the elements, and, as the following episode from *The Adventures of Billy Topsail* illustrates, a generous community member who risks his life to deliver the mail for the injured postman. After having trudged with the mail-sack for most of a day, Billy suddenly disappears beneath "an expanse of bad ice" as this chapter opens.

Flavouring his narrative with dialect and shanties—and not above injecting it with sentimentality and melodrama—Duncan tells of Billy's resourcefulness and tight-lipped courage.

DELIVERING HER MAJESTY'S MAIL

Billy Topsail Wrings Out His Clothes and Finds Himself Cut off From Shore by Thirty Yards of Heaving Ice

Billy could swim—could swim like any Newfoundland dog bred in Green Bay. Moreover, the life he led—the rugged, venturesome calling of the shore fishermen—had inured him to sudden danger. First of all he freed himself from the cumbersome mail-bag. He would not have abandoned it had he not been in such case as when, as the Newfoundlanders say, it was "every hand for his life."

Then he made for the surface with swift, strong strokes. A few more strokes brought him to the edge of the ice. He clambered out, still gasping for breath, and turned about to account to himself for his predicament.

The drift of snow had collapsed; he observed that it had covered some part of a wide hole, and that the exposed water was almost of a colour with the ice beyond—a polished black. Hence, he did not bitterly blame himself for the false step, as he might have done when he plunged himself into obvious danger through carelessness. He did not wonder that he had been deceived.

Her Majesty's mail, so far as the boy could determine, was slowly sinking to the bottom of the bay.

There was no help in regret. To escape from the bitter wind and the dusk, now fast falling, was the present duty. He could think of all the rest when he had leisure to sit before the fire and dream. He took off his jacket and wrung it out—a matter of some difficulty, for it was already stiff with frost. His shirt followed—then his boots and his trousers. Soon he was stripped to his rosy skin. The wind, sweeping in from the open sea, stung him as it whipped past.

When the last garment was wrung out he was shivering, and his teeth were chattering so fast that he could not keep them still. Dusk soon turns to night on this coast, and the night comes early. There was left but time enough to reach the first of the goat-paths at Creepy Bluff, two miles away—not time to finish the overland tramp to Ruddy Cove—before darkness fell.

When he was about to dress, his glance chanced to pass over the water. The mail-bag—it could be nothing else—was floating twenty yards off the ice. It had been prepared with cork for such accidents, which not infrequently befall it.

" 'Tis Her Majesty's mail, b'y," Billy could hear the mailman say.

"But 'tis more than I can carry t' Ruddy Cove now," he thought.

Nevertheless, he made no move to put on his shirt. He continued to look at the mail-bag. " 'Tis the mail—gov'ment mail," he thought again. Then, after a rueful look at the water: "Sure, nobody'll know that it floated. 'Tis as much as I can do t' get myself safe t' Gull Cove. I'd freeze on the way t' Ruddy Cove."

There was no comfort in these excuses. There, before him, was the bag. It was in plain sight. It had not sunk. He would fail in his duty to the country if he left it floating there. It was an intolerable thought!

" 'Tis t' Ruddy Cove I'll take that bag this day," he muttered.

He let himself gingerly into the water, and struck out. It was bitter cold, but he persevered, with fine courage, until he had his arm safely linked through the strap of the bag. It was the country he served! In some vague form this thought sounded in his mind, repeating itself again and again, while he swam for the ice with the bag in tow.

He drew himself out with much difficulty, hauled the mail-bag after him, and proceeded to dress with all speed. His clothes were frozen stiff, and he had to beat them on the ice to soften them; but the struggle to don them sent the rich blood rushing through his body, and he was warmed to a glow.

On went the bag, and off went the boy. When he came to the firmer ice, and Creepy Bluff was within half a mile, the wind carried this cheery song up the bay:

> Lukie's boat is painted green,
> The finest boat that ever was seen;
> Lukie's boat has cotton sails,
> A juniper rudder and galvanized nails.

At Creepy Bluff, which the wind strikes with full force, the ice was breaking up inshore. The gale had risen with the coming of the night.

Great seas spent their force beneath the ice—cracking it, breaking it, slowly grinding it to pieces against the rocks.

The Bluff marks the end of the bay. No ice forms beyond. Thus the waves swept in with unbroken power, and were fast reducing the shore cakes to a mass of fragments. Billy was cut off from the shore by thirty yards of heaving ice. No bit of it would bear his weight; nor, so fine had it been ground, could he leap from place to place as he had done before.

" 'Tis sprawl I must," he thought.

The passage was no new problem. He had been in such case more than once upon his return from the offshore seal-hunt. Many fragments would together bear him up, where few would sink beneath him. He lay flat on his stomach, and, with the gaff to help support him, crawled out from the solid place, dragging the bag. His body went up and down with the ice. Now an arm was thrust through, again a leg went under water.

Progress was fearfully slow. Inch by inch he gained on the shore— crawling—crawling steadily. All the while he feared that the great pans would drift out and leave the fragments room to disperse. Once he had to spread wide his arms and legs and pause until the ice was packed closer.

"Two yards more—only two yards more!" he could say at last.

Once on the road to Ruddy Cove, which he well knew, his spirits rose; and with a cheery mood came new strength. It was a rough road, up hill and down again, through deep snowdrifts and over slippery rocks.

From the crest of Ruddy Rock he could look down on the lights of the harbour—yellow lights, lying in the shadows of the valley. There was a light in the post-office. They were waiting to send the mail on to the north. In a few minutes he could say that Her Majesty's mail had been brought safe to Ruddy Cove.

"Be the mail come?"

Billy looked up from his seat by the roaring fire in the post-office. An old woman had come in. There was a strange light in her eyes—the light of a hope which survives, spite of repeated disappointment.

"Sure, Aunt Esther; 'tis here at last."

"Be there a letter for me?"

Billy hoped that there was. He longed to see those gentle eyes shine— to see the famished look disappear.

"No, Aunt Esther; 'tis not come yet. Maybe 'twill come next—"

"Sure, I've waited these three year," she said, with a trembling lip. " 'Tis from me son—"

"Ha!" cried the postmaster. "What's this? 'Tis all blurred by the water. 'Missus E—s—B—l—g—e—l.' Sure, 'tis you, woman. 'Tis a letter for you at last!"

" 'Tis from me son!" the old woman muttered eagerly. " 'Tis t' tell me where he is, an'—an'—when he's comin' home. Thank God, the mail came safe the night."

What if Billy had left the mail-bag to soak and sink in the waters of the bay? How many other such letters might there not be in that bag for the mothers and fathers of the northern ports?

"Thank God," he thought, "that Her Majesty's mail came safe the night!"

Then he went off home, and met Bobby Lot on the way.

"Hello!" said Bobby. "Got back?"

"Hello yourself!" said Billy. "I did."

They eyed each other delightedly; they were too boyish to shake hands.

"How's the ice?" asked Bobby Lot.

"Not bad," said Billy.

BESSIE MARCHANT (1862-1941)
"Just Pluck" from *All Girls' Story Book* (1924)

Born in Petchan, Kent, England, and privately educated, Bessie Marchant, the wife of the Reverend Jabez Ambrose Comfort, has been called "the girls' Henty". Determined to reverse the pattern, usual in boys' adventure stories, that meted out passive and homebound roles to girls, she sang the praises of vigorous and resolute young women. In over 150 books—with titles like *Hilda Holds On, Di the Dauntless,* and *Harriet Goes A-Roaming,* and locales ranging from Borneo and Persia to Canada and Australia—she related the exploits of heroines like Kathleen Ellis in "Just Pluck", who single-handedly save the day. Marchant concentrated entirely on their vicissitudes, dashing off her stories with the abandon of a hasty letter-writer.

Marchant wrote many long novels about Canada, such as *A Daughter of the Ranges; A Story of Western Canada* (1906), *A Girl of the Northland* (1915), *A Heroine of the Sea; A Story of Vancouver Island* (1920), and *A Canadian Farm Mystery; or, Pam the Pioneer* (1932), in which she presented heroines

functioning competently as nurses, telegraph operators, camp cooks, restaurateurs, and—always—bold rescuers. Particularly fond of this country as a setting for her popular stories, she described it, in *Daughters of the Dominion; A Story of the Canadian Frontier* (1923), as a land of opportunity where "the needy of every nation . . . may all come . . . and find a home, if they will work to earn it." She often used the narrative formula of bringing a sheltered English girl to this vast, austere land and showing how quickly she adapts, especially in a prairie setting. Like Kitty in *Sisters of Silver Creek; A Story of Western Canada* (1907), these young women occasionally remark on "self-made colonials" and initially wonder aloud how a place called "Assiniboia" will appeal to them. Marchant's reliance on place names, rapidly paced action, and mere postcard descriptions of seasonal changes and vegetation suggest, however, that her knowledge of Canada was gleaned from atlases and photo albums alone.

JUST PLUCK

Kathleen Ellis slipped from her saddle, and letting down the bars of the south paddock, pulled the bit from the mouth of her tired horse, and sent it off to rest and feed.

She was worn to a frazzle herself, for she had been out since early breakfast, riding through the paddocks, and out on to the great sheep runs, to make sure that all was going well in the absence of her father.

Going up the steps of the back veranda, she dropped into the hammock that was slung there, content to just lie still and enjoy the coolness and the shade after her ride in the scorching sun.

Dorothy came limping out of the office, where she had been busy with station accounts. Seeing how spent Kathleen was looking, she went off to the cookhouse, to beat up a raspberry swizzle for her, and to bid Gina the black cook hurry on with lunch.

The telephone bell rang sharply, and thinking that Dorothy in the cookhouse would not hear it, Kathleen got out of the hammock and went into the office to take the message.

"Hallo! hallo!" she called. "What is it? Yes, this is the Ellis station. What do you say? Speak more slowly, please. Did you say that the new irrigation dam at Peterloo had burst, and that Blue Valley would be flooded? Have you rung up Dan Upton's place? He is nearer than we are. You can't get into touch with Dan Upton? Wire broken, and all those children at the Blue Valley schoolhouse in danger of being drowned? Hold on a minute—hallo!"

But she had been cut off. A second she waited, then hanging up the receiver, she dashed out of the office, took the veranda steps at a flying leap, and rushed along the cinder path to the cookhouse.

"Dorothy, Dorothy," she panted, "the dam has broken, and in less than an hour Blue Valley will be in flood, and all those children in the schoolhouse will be caught and drowned. We have not a man left on the place who can ride. I must be off as fast as I can go."

"Oh, Kathleen, if only I could ride! This wretched foot of mine!" cried Dorothy, with tears starting in her eyes.

"You can't, dear, so there is no sense in wailing about it," jerked out Kathleen, whose face was white and strained.

Seizing her saddle from the post of the veranda, where she had hung it when she went into the house, she ran out to the saddle pen by the water troughs, where three or four horses stood in the shade of a big pepper tree, lazily whisking their tails to dislodge the flies from their sides.

The whole business of catching the horse and saddling had taken only five minutes; then Kathleen led her horse to the mounting block, and was up and away. But it was a whole five minutes, and she had less than an hour for the work in front of her, while it was a good three miles to the Blue Valley schoolhouse, over a very rough track.

Her horse was fresh, and she had forgotten that she was tired. She had forgotten everything except that in an hour at the outside the Blue

Valley would be under water, the schoolhouse would be surrounded and cut off, and thirty children in danger of being drowned.

There was a breeze that sang in her ears as she rode, but the whistling hum of it formed into words as the big grey went forward at a swinging canter: "The water is coming; the children will drown; make haste, make haste!"

The big grey slackened a little to top the last rise, for the day was so hot, and the pace had been stiff. Kathleen was panting, perspiration was running down her face, her hat had slipped to one side, she looked a scarecrow, but she never even thought about herself as she urged her horse up the slope, where loose rocks were strewn over the scorched grass of the hillside.

They were up at last, the horse broke into a trot again to cross the level ground at the top, and Kathleen, bending forward, was peering and peering in front of her for a first sight of the schoolhouse in the valley.

Ah, there it was! And so far as she could see at present there was no sign of anything being wrong.

The trot became a canter as the horse went down the hill. A false step here, and horse and rider would have come on swift and certain disaster; but the animal was sure-footed, and Kathleen was a practised rider.

Just as she reached the place where the track turned into the level, straight for the schoolhouse, she gave a little cry of fear, for there, up the valley towards Peterloo, was visible a shimmering silvery line that reflected back the sun in glinting sparkling points of light.

"It is the water—it is coming!" she shouted to her horse as she urged it forward.

The noon spell was over, and the thirty children were at work on the first lesson of the afternoon. The midday rest was always as short as possible, because some of the children had so far to go. There were twenty-nine heads to jerk up, and as many pairs of eyes to stare at the visitor, who, thundering up to the door mounted on the big grey horse, had hurled herself from its back, and had come walking into the schoolroom without knocking or asking permission to enter. Even an inspector could not have marched in with a more assured step, and every one of the twenty-nine was eager to see what was coming next.

Straight to the desk of the mistress walked Kathleen, and bending down she whispered, "The dam has burst, and the water is coming. Can you quick march the school to Silver Ridge; it will be better, and safer than a panic run?"

The schoolmistress, a slip of a girl of twenty, had courage and tact. Summoning all her powers, she sprang to her feet, crying out, with a flourish of her hands and a radiant smile, "Come, children, all of you; we are going to quick march to Silver Ridge, and the first one to reach the top is to have the orange that I did not eat for lunch."

"Those two little ones can never run fast enough to win the orange, so they shall have a ride on my big horse," said Kathleen briskly, and

stooping, she swept a pair of tiny tots up in her arms, and following the pushing children, reached the open door of the schoolhouse.

So far there had been only curiosity and excitement, with keen pleasure at the unexpected break in lessons; but once outside the schoolhouse, Jim White, a big boy with eagle eyes, cried out in sheer horror, "The dam has given way, and the water is coming from Peterloo; we shall all be drowned!"

He bolted then in sheer panic, heading not for Silver Ridge, but straight ahead down the valley where the water would certainly overtake him.

The mistress shouted her commands; she rounded up the scared children, as a watchful sheep-dog rounds up the flock, and Kathleen, with the two mites clinging on to the saddle, was already running by the side of the big grey, shouting to the children to follow. She had to run straight across the track of the oncoming flood. At first, to the panic-stricken children, it looked as if she was running straight into it; but the mistress, urging them forward, was shouting to them that once on the ridge they would be safe. Even Jim White seemed to catch the drift of her shouting, though he must have been too far to hear the words, for he halted, looked round in an uncertain fashion, and then came tearing back to join the main body, which were plunging forward, running as only children can run. They had passed Kathleen and the horse; they were streaming ahead of the mistress, who had two of the smaller children by the hand and was helping them forward, a merry word of encouragement on her lips, while she bustled them on with never a look behind.

They had reached the rising ground, they had all slackened speed a little, for the hill was steep, and they were a good bit winded, when eight-year-old Nellie Scanes called out anxiously, "Where is Tessie? I can't see Tessie!"

"Oh, Miss Jones, I put Tessie to sleep in the hammock under the lean-to and I had quite forgotten her," cried Primrose Mayne, a big, fair-haired girl. "I must run back for her."

"No, no, you can't; here comes the water" cried Miss Jones, the mistress. "Run, children; run as straight up the hill as you can go."

"Take these," said Kathleen, in curt tones of authority, as she lifted the two small children from the saddle and thrust them into the care of Primrose Mayne. "I will ride back for Tessie. I shall be in time if I hurry. Here, you, Tommy Rentle, give me a back, will you? This horse is so high to mount."

Tommy Rentle, an urchin of ten, who had been helping on his young brother and sister, turned back, and running to the side of the big grey, crouched by the stirrup as if he was going to play leap-frog, and Kathleen, putting her foot on his back, swung herself up to her saddle and, turning the horse round, set off back to the schoolhouse once more.

The water had reached the schoolhouse. The first of the dirty brown flood was running in at the open door as she rode past to reach the other side of the building where the hammock was slung under the lean-to—a convenient place for the sleepy smaller children to take a noon rest.

There was the hammock, and there was the little fair-haired girl fast asleep; but there was the water too, getting deeper and deeper with incredible swiftness. She would have to dismount and to mount again; and her horse, wise beast, knew there was danger, and was restive accordingly.

Out of the saddle slid Kathleen, coming down plump into the water. Bah, how cold it felt! Yet the sun was shining with scorching heat. She fastened the horse to the post of the lean-to, and dashing round to the schoolhouse door, dragged out a heavy form, so that she might use it as a mounting block. Oh! she would have a tottering time of it trying to get on to that scared horse with sleepy Tessie in her arms.

"Tessie! Tessie! Wake up!" she cried in cheery tones. "I am going to take you for a ride to find Nellie. Come along, sit up, then I will lift you on to my saddle. Just see what a fine big horse I have!"

Tessie opened astonished eyes to see what manner of person it was who had come to invade her noon rest. She glimpsed a strange face; she felt the strain, the urgency there was in the manner of the unknown; and because she was frightened by what she could not understand, she lifted her small brown hands, striking out vigorously at Kathleen, and setting up a howl that made the nervous horse snort and fidget.

"Come, Tessie, Nellie wants you. Let us make haste to go and find sister Nellie," coaxed Kathleen, and she lifted the screaming child out of the hammock, and carried her towards the horse.

It was the unexpected that happened then; for Tessie, who had been

shrieking with all the force of her very vigorous lungs, dropped suddenly quiet, saying in a cooing voice, "Oh, pretty horsey; Tessie want to
go riding."

"And Tessie shall go riding," said Kathleen, gulping down a sob of
sheer thankfulness that came up in her throat and nearly choked her.
Gripping the child in her arms, she waded through the water, which
was already over her ankles. She lifted Tessie on to the saddle, where
the child clung like a limpet to a rock, and then stepping on to the form,
which she had dragged from the schoolroom, she tried to get on to the
saddle behind Tessie. But for the child this would have been easy
enough; she would have sprung on to the horse, and wriggled herself
into position while the frightened animal jumped and pranced in its fear
of the water that was surrounding it on all sides.

Holding the child with one hand, and reaching forward with the other
to hold the horse and drag it closer to the form on which she was inse-
curely perched, gave her as much occupation as she could manage, and
for some minutes she simply could not get the animal near enough. But
she was watching her chance, and just as with an extra fierce struggle it
lashed out against the form that was knocked over into the water, Kathleen jumped lightly, and just succeeded in getting across the saddle.

However, she and Tessie were safely mounted, and for the moment,
until she could get her breath, Kathleen had to leave it at that, and be
content to just cling to the neck of the horse, while she pressed Tessie's
warm little body close before her on the saddle, while the horse plunged
madly forward.

Then to her dismay she saw that the poor beast was running just where the current was deepest. And oh! how deep it was getting! The water was now right up to the body of the horse, which had broken into a gallop, snorting wildly as it sought to run away from the encompassing water.

Kathleen remembered in a flash that this horse was one of a mob driven down from a part of Queensland where there had been no rain for nearly two years. Since it had been on the Ellis station, which was in New South Wales, there had been no great rainfall, not enough to leave a puddle anywhere deep enough to wash the legs of a horse. It had plainly never had to ford a river, and so it was not wonderful that the poor thing was so badly scared.

How she wished that she had chosen another sort of mount! There was Bouncer, a steady old mare, which was afraid of nothing. Why had she not chosen Bouncer? But Bouncer, though dependable, lacked the pace of the big grey, and it was pace that she had needed in her horse when she set out to warn the school children and to get them to safety.

At the end of the valley the ground dropped into a hollow some acres in extent. This hollow was rapidly becoming a lake, and the horse was heading straight for it. Directly it was lifted off its feet they would be flung into the water, and they would be in danger of drowning.

All this went through Kathleen's mind as she made a last frantic attempt to make the big grey answer to the rein. If she could check its mad career, and turn it to the steep slope of Silver Ridge, all might yet be well; but she could not do it, and because the danger was so great she took a desperate risk, and took it boldly, knowing that the one chance of life for Tessie and herself might lie in the quickness of her action.

The horse, plunging madly forward, had to pass a solitary clump of blue gums, one of which had been broken off and showed a jagged stump sticking well above the water. Just before this was reached, Kathleen, gripping Tessie tightly, flung herself from the horse, going souse into the water.

There was a terrified shriek from Tessie, who struggled violently, hitting Kathleen in the eye with such force that she was temporarily blinded on that side. But she had calculated her fall into the water with nice accuracy, for as she scrambled on to her feet she was able to reach out and grip that upstanding stump with her hand. Good for her that she could do this, for the force with which the water was running swept her off her feet, and she and the child in her arms would have been swept onward like a pair of corks but for her desperate grip of the stump. A minute she clung, fighting hard for strength to pull herself closer to the stump, while Tessie rent the air with her shrieks, and the horse, struggling madly, was carried farther away.

"I must do it—I must!" muttered Kathleen through her clenched teeth. Then with a great effort she pulled herself in closer to the tree, and reaching up managed to perch Tessie in the fork of the jagged top.

Feeling a little more secure Tessie at once ceased from screaming, and with a wriggle of her plump legs said in great disgust, "Tessie all wet; ugh! such a nasty mess."

Kathleen had been panting and sobbing from exhaustion, and from the imminence of the danger just escaped, but at this remark she burst into a shout of hysterical laughter; for if Tessie was in a nasty mess, she herself was in a very much worse condition, being soaked to the skin and thoroughly bedraggled. But for the moment they were both safe, and they would be rescued in due course, unless indeed the water rose much higher and swept them from their precarious perch.

"What 'oo laughing at?" demanded Tessie, who did not approve of being turned into ridicule; then she burst out in plaintive tones, which showed her very near to tears, "Tessie want to go home. Tessie want Nellie."

"Tessie shall go home very soon," said Kathleen soothingly. She had dragged herself up, and by putting her foot on a convenient projection of the stump, was able to get farther up out of the water. As she stood balanced in this fashion, she could look out over the flood to Silver Ridge and the little company of school children marooned there with the plucky young teacher, who was plainly doing her best to keep their spirits up.

It was good to see them and to know they were safe. If it had not been for having to go back for Tessie, Kathleen would have been there also, and with that big horse of hers she could have taken them in twos and threes well out of reach of the flood water. She lifted her arm and waved to them. She saw the teacher waving too. Then suddenly the children drew closer round the teacher, and a minute later the sound of their voices, sweet and shrill, came to Kathleen across the flood; they were singing hymns to encourage her in holding on until help should come.

"Oh, how dear of them!" she said, her voice tremulous from emotion, her eyes hot with the tears she would not shed. Then she said to Tessie, who was wailing to be taken home, "Listen, Tessie! Can you hear Nellie singing?"

Tessie promptly stopped her wailing, she even laughed and clapped her hands as the sound of singing came to her ears, then she broke into sobs, stretching her plump arms towards that group so far away across the flood, and calling out, "Nellie, Nellie! Come quick, Tessie wants 'oo!"

"Tessie shall go to Nellie very soon now," Kathleen murmured encouragingly.

Then she shivered, and a wave of horrible depression swept over her; she literally went down before it, losing heart all at once and feeling the courage oozing from her finger-tips. The water was suddenly getting deeper; that meant that the hollow on ahead was all filled up, the narrow winding of the valley on beyond could not carry the water away fast enough, and unless help came very quickly she and Tessie would be drowned.

If it should be hours before they were rescued, could she hold out? Kathleen knew herself to be nearly at the end of her endurance; she was so hungry, and she was so tired. She would not be so tired if she could have food, but it was so many hours since she had broken her fast. A curious lethargy was stealing over her. As she clung to the stump, listening to the singing of the children on Silver Ridge, she felt herself going to sleep. Suppose she grew so drowsy that she lost consciousness and slackened her hold of Tessie. Oh, she must keep awake; she must!

Vigorously she shook herself. She said a cheery word to Tessie, who was whining and sniffing, uttering little plaints about wanting to go home. The child had sunk a little forward on her perch; she had slipped her arms round Kathleen's neck, and pressed her cheek against Kathleen's, as if the contact took some of her fear away.

A terrified shriek from Tessie, and Kathleen started broad awake to see a big black snake making for their little place of refuge. Oh, how awful! And she had no weapon at all with which to fight it off. Had she not? Suddenly she remembered her hat, which had stuck on her head through all the adventures of that strenuous afternoon. Snatching it off now, she struck out boldly at the snake, which looked as if disposed to show fight for the bit of refuge. Kathleen struck again. She felt desperate and reckless. She banged her hat full at the reptile's head; she saw its tongue darting like lightning to strike the hat. She was wondering if its next blow would light on her naked arm, when suddenly a bit of wreckage borne on the swift current punted into the creature from behind, and it was carried forward out of reach of the pair perched on the stump.

More wreckage was coming. A big chunk of timber caught Kathleen as it swept past, nearly knocking her from her roosting-place. She was awake now—the coming of the snake had dispelled her drowsiness—but she knew that she could not cling much longer.

Tessie was asleep, her arm round Kathleen's neck, and it was the desperate need of the little child that gave to Kathleen the power to keep on clinging to the stump.

The children on Silver Ridge had left off singing. Kathleen strained her ears, longing for them to begin again. Somehow her plight did not seem so awful when she could hear them singing. It was so quiet, and so fearfully lonely.

Her arms ached—ah, how they ached! The foot that balanced her on the stump felt cramped and dead; she was afraid it would slip without her having the power to prevent it, and then Tessie would be drowned.

"Boat coming! Boat coming!"

Had she dreamed it, or was it a real voice? Kathleen tried to look round, but Tessie's sleepy head blocked her view, and oh! how heavy the child seemed as she rested in blissful unconsciousness on Kathleen's shoulder.

"Boat coming! Boat coming!"

Suddenly Kathleen realized that the children were shouting to her, and then she knew that help was near. Her courage flamed up again. She could surely hold out for another five minutes if she tried.

She heard shouting in deeper voices. There were men calling to her now. Then there came to her ears the plash of oars striking the water. But her strength was going fast; there was a red mist before her eyes; Tessie's soft breathing sounded in her ears like a raging storm of wind; and the weight of the sleeping child was forcing her down, down, down.

"Well, well, you are a plucky one, and no mistake!" cried a deep voice close beside her, as a boat struck the stump, sending a quiver all through her. She was conscious that the weight of Tessie was suddenly lifted from her, and then she felt herself strongly pulled, yet could not loose her hold of the stump which had been her refuge from drowning.

"Leave go!" boomed the deep voice close in her ears, and she felt a strong arm round her; then she was dragged, and oh! it was intolerable pain, an agony so terrible, that when it ceased she lost consciousness for a brief moment.

It was only for a moment. Tessie's shrill outcries brought her back from swooning to the task of comforting the little child, and then with the strain over, she could lie in the bottom of the boat and rest.

*

It was Dorothy, left at home with the telephone, who had been ringing up every one within reach to go to the help of the Blue Valley school children. It was Dorothy who had the wit to implore Peterloo to send a boat down on the raging flood-water in case any one should have been caught and stranded somewhere, surrounded by deep water.

When grateful fathers and mothers would have overwhelmed Kathleen with thanks for her pluck in getting the children safely away from the doomed schoolhouse, Kathleen, with a happy laugh, cried out, "But it was really Dorothy who did the most, for it was she who got the boat for us in the very nick of time."

8. SCAPEGRACES AND DAREDEVILS: SHILLING SHOCKERS AND PENNY DREADFULS

And he used to think of shipping as a sea cook
And sailing to the Golden Gate
For he used to buy the yellow penny dreadfuls,
And read them where he fished for conger eels . . .
—Alfred Noyes, "Old Grey Squirrel" (1915)

The desire to entertain by spinning a good yarn assumed many forms in the Golden Age. For thousands of rambunctious schoolboys, young apprentices, and over-worked shopgirls the last half of the nine-teenth century offered a special and im-mensely popular kind of "literary" entertainment. The eight-page weekly in-stalments of the penny dreadfuls, and the longer shilling shockers, promising tales of "love, mystery, and crime" and appealing to a fascination with the macabre, gloried in presenting atrocities such as those commit-ted by Sweeney Todd, the Demon Barber of Fleet Street, Varney the Vampire, and

Sawney Beane, the Man Eater of Scotland. Treachery, violence, and bloodshed were the order of the day. The Penny Library of Fiction (1872 ff.)—with titles like *Night-Hawk Kit, The Scalp Cry*, and *The Ice Fiend*—published lurid thirty-two-page novelettes with a "commingling of passion, love, in-trigues, revenge for wrongs done, devo-tion, and truth". A different taste was satis-fied by such series as The Shilling Readable Novels (1862 ff.); Lady Lyons' *The Lover Upon Trial* and Mrs Downing's *Remem-brances of a Monthly Nurse* provided full-length sentimental romances flavoured with grisly and supernatural touches. The fans of these "shockers", "dreadfuls", and "romances" were as loyal and voracious as modern readers of the less sensational Harlequins.

The dreadfuls were intended for adults, but because of the advent of machine-produced paper their cheapness made them accessible to children, who quickly took them up. Despite scandalized protests about the damage they must surely be doing to impressionable minds, and fulminations against this "literature which has done much to people our prisons, our reformatories, and our colonies with scapegraces and ne'er-do-wells" (*Quarterly Review*, 1890), their popularity never waned throughout the Golden Age. People devoured these escapist tales about highwaymen redressing wrongs; perils avoided at the last moment; the painfully lingering deaths of the wicked; and the restored fortunes of underdogs like Sapathwa, the Blue Dwarf, Broad-Arrow Jack, and Dick Lightheart, the Scapegrace of London.

The penny dreadfuls and shilling shockers owed their success to the entrepreneurial instincts of their publishers—who were as astute as the earlier compilers of chapbooks—and to their authors' ability to concoct arresting melodramas, and to relate them in easy-to-grasp one-sentence paragraphs. The peregrinations of characters called Dashing Duval and Jack Harkaway are laughable now; but these serial heroes came into vogue before the days of comic books, radio, movie, and television melodrama, confessional tabloids, and glossy magazines—and before Young Adult sections of public libraries.

THE BLUE DWARF ESCAPING ON BLACK BESS

PERCY BOLINGBROKE ST JOHN (1821-1889)
"In the Green Wood" from *The Blue Dwarf: A Tale of Love, Mystery, and Crime, Introducing Many Startling Incidents in the Life of a Celebrated Highwayman, Dick Turpin* (1880)

Born in London, England, this journalist was a prolific author of boys' stories and popular fiction, contributing to such publications as The Castaway Series, De Witt's Ten Cent Romances, and Beadle's Dime Library, and editing such magazines as *The Mirror of Literature* (1846 ff.) and *The London Herald: A Household Journal of Literature, Art and Science* (1861 ff.). Before he began churning out the thirty-seven penny weekly numbers of *The Blue Dwarf* (1880), St John had already established a reputation as a teller of tales about haunted castles and exotic adventures—in *The King's Musketeer* (1845), *Keetsea; or, The Enchanted Rock. A Texan Tale of the Comanches* (1845), *The Arctic Crusoe. A Tale of the Polar Seas* (1854), *Quadroona; or, The Slave Mother* (1861), and *The Coral Reef* (1866).

The deformed, indigo-blotched homuncule, Sapathwa, is Dick Turpin's ally in *The Blue Dwarf*, a long-running serial that catalogues their rescues of true heirs, fair damsels, and impoverished peasants. Set in the

English countryside, the Scottish highlands, and the American prairies, their action-filled and somewhat disjointed adventures—involving all kinds of tense cliff hangers—eventually disclose the fact that the hideous Sapathwa is the rightful heir to the Mountjoye estates and Elphick Castle. The arch villain, whose "religion is vengeance", is Robert Woodstock, a supporter of the scheming usurper Brian Seymour.

The freakish Sapathwa is intended to arouse curiosity as well as sympathy, since "he was sensitive in the extreme, and shunned his fellows". Turpin, on the other hand, is an attractive rake: "one of those devil-may-care chaps, who are daunted at nothing". With the highwayman's mastery of disguise and the dwarf's eerie omnipresence, they make an impressive team. As the chapter below, in which they confound the plot of Woodstock and Seymour, makes clear, the narrative in penny dreadfuls consists of rapid, multi-layered action that always leads to another episode.

IN THE GREEN WOOD

When Dick Turpin reached the cross of St Clement, he at once rode up to the Blue Dwarf.

"I am followed by that fellow, Bob Woodstock," he said; "he is close behind."

"This way," replied the other, and at once dived into the densest part of the thicket.

As he did so he uttered a low, shrill whistle.

Ten minutes later Robert Woodstock might have been seen approaching the cross and looking about in all directions.

"Where can he have got to!" he muttered. "I believe the rascal must have spotted me."

At this moment he turned, as a sound came from behind some bushes.

As he did so two men, rough-looking fellows of the poaching persuasion, darted upon him, put a gag in his mouth, and tied his hands behind his back.

"This way, my joker," said one.

They were savage-looking men, men not to be trifled with, as might be seen by their glaring black eyes.

They were as swarthy as gipsies, with low foreheads and beetling brows, and sun-browned complexions.

Both had guns, and did not look like persons a moneyed man would care to meet on the king's highway, much less in a dark wood.

'Tis hard now to picture what this forest then was, with its huge trees and impassable enlargements of thorns and brushwood.

These gigantic solitudes were the homes of immobility and silence.

But still they were inhabited to a certain extent. Men who were outlawed, the enemies of society, poachers, gipsies, and the like abode here.

The lived in general in caves, singular underground dwellings, whose entrance was masked by coverings of branches and stones, descending at first in a sloping direction, and ending in dark chambers.

Their origin was unknown.

Tradition indicates that they were scooped out by the early Britons in the days of the Roman invasion.

It was from some such fastnesses that they emerged to harass and worry the Roman legions.

In all ages men had sought secure retreats; hence the lurking-places, like the nests of reptiles, dug out beneath the trees.

Others ascribed them to the Druids, and declared that they were as the cromlechs of the plains.

This matters little now; as, with the advancing march of civilisation, they have been filled, at all events at the mouth, and disappeared, like many other relics of our forefathers.

To one of these the terror-stricken and astounded Robert Woodstock was led; and, being placed in a dark chamber, he was loosed and left to shift for himself.

The man was aghast with terror.

What should he do? Could they mean to immure him living in a tomb?

The idea was too terrible to be seriously entertained.

He sat in a dazed way for some time, and then began to plan an escape.

On reflection, it struck him that some time should elapse before he began to move.

Doubtless his abductors would remain on the watch, but of course would not do so for any very great length of time.

While musing, he fell sound asleep.

When he awoke he could scarcely realise his position—down in the bowels of the earth in total darkness.

He mused for a moment; and then, moving slightly, he saw a faint streak of light in the distance.

He sprang to his feet in an instant, and made in the direction of the light, feeling his way along the earthy walls.

The path was level; but soon he found himself ascending a slope at the end of which was light and air.

He advanced rapidly, and soon reached an opening, which, forcing his way through, he found himself in a dark and gloomy glade of the forest, quite unknown to him.

He turned, however, to make a note of some tree or rock, by which to know the place again.

"There he goes—after him!" cried the well remembered voices of one of his captors.

His heart in his mouth, Robert Woodstock took to his heels, and made a rush for dear life.

Away! Away! for dear life he ran, neither looking to the right nor left, pursued by what seemed to him fiendish laughter.

On, on, until he found himself on the banks of a stream.

He plunged in without hesitation, being a strong and powerful swimmer, and soon reached the other bank.

There was no sign of pursuit.

He at once divined the truth. They had startled him simply to prevent his fixing the locality of the hiding-place.

Robert Woodstock laughed, and when that worthy laughed there was sure to be mischief afloat.

He determined, at any price, to discover that secret hiding-place, and thus checkmate the evil-doers of the forest.

Not from any moral motive, but from sheer envy, hatred and malice.

He now continued on his way, walking rapidly to prevent ill-effects from his involuntary bath.

It was daylight when he reached the highway.

He still kept on, and soon reached the "Horseshoe," which was open, a perfect caravan of waggons having just arrived, and all clamouring for refreshment.

Robert went in and entered the public room, where he found the waiter preparing for expected company.

He was faint from exhaustion.

"Oh, sir!" cried John, "we've been in a rare taking about you. Your friend waited up till two. Shall I tell him?"

"Time enough when I've breakfasted. I've been trapped by thieves, and had a marvellous escape. Just now I'm starving," retorted Robert.

The waiter, who knew his customer, hastened away, and soon returned with cold meat, bread, and a tankard.

Robert Woodstock said nothing, but he at once commenced eating with an appetite such as he had not known for some little time.

When he had finished, he put down his knife and fork with a deep sigh, as if he was sorry he could eat no more.

He then called for a second tankard, and swallowed it without taking it from his lips.

He then went up to announce his return to Brian Seymour.

Meanwhile, what had become of Dick Turpin and the Blue Dwarf?

In answer to the latter's whistle, the two men, whom we have already described, appeared and received their instructions in a low tone from him. He had befriended them on more than one occasion, and they were devoted to him.

"Keep him all night, and then give him a good fright," he said, "and let him go."

The men nodded assent and took their departure.

The two confederates remained alone and consulted.

Dick Turpin informed the other of all that had passed, and how he fully believed that they suspected him.

"No matter," said the Blue Dwarf; "keep your eye on them. Don't lose sight of them for four-and-twenty hours, and all will be well."

"I will do as you say," replied Dick, rising from a rude bench on which they had been sitting, in front of a hut where one of the poachers resided.

"I shall soon release you," said his temporary employers; "that is, for the present."

"I'm wholly at your orders," was the earnest reply.

And bowing not ungracefully, a habit he had acquired in the so-called polite society in which he sometimes moved, he walked away to where his horse stood patiently awaiting him.

Never did man and beast more thoroughly understand one another. Whatever his other faults, Dick Turpin was kind to his faithful steed.

He mounted gaily, took his way through paths with which he was well acquainted, and started on his new adventure.

A bold stroke!

It wanted an hour of the time, but it was best to be on the right side.

He cantered along the highway; as soon as he reached a spot that suited his purpose, he selected an ambush.

He had made minute inquiries during the day about Joe Morgan, of

Pollard Farm, and had learned that he was a well-to-do farmer, very warm, as they say, and tolerably pugnacious, and rather given to boasting.

He was a hard nut to crack, but Dick Turpin had no fear.

He was well armed, and, for this occasion, produced from the inside of his coat a short, heavy bludgeon, like that carried by Jonathan Wild, loaded at the end, and fastened to his wrist by a loop.

It was a most dangerous weapon in the hands of the unscrupulous.

Dick Turpin now retired to the side of the road, and concealed himself in the deep shadow.

He sat his horse so well, that he looked more like a Centaur than anything else.

Presently he heard, at no great distance, the trot of a horse coming along the road in the expected direction.

He felt his holsters, and assured himself that all was safe and ready.

In a moment more the farmer was close in sight, and Dick at once recognised him.

He allowed him to come within ten feet, and then suddenly darted into the middle of the road.

"Your money or your life!" he cried, clapping a pistol to his breast; "now then, shell out, you boasting braggart, or you are a dead man."

The farmer burst into a loud laugh.

"None of your fun," he said; "who's made the wager? You know I aint not nowt."

"I want that pocket-book which you showed at the market-dinner, and which was so well lined."

"I tell thee, man, there's nowt in it," was the dogged answer, as he fumbled for his pistols.

"Who be thee? what's thy name?"

"Dick Turpin," replied the other; "but touch a pistol and you are a dead man."

"You first," cried the farmer, as he clutched his pistol and fired full in the other's face.

Dick Turpin laughed.

"There were no bullets in those pistols," said the highwayman, laughing; "they were drawn while you were at supper."

And without another word he swung his heavily-loaded bludgeon, and striking Joe Morgan, of Pollard Farm, heavily on the head, he fell helpless to the ground.

The highwayman, who, when he liked could be rough enough, then alighted, searched the man's pockets, and easily found his pocket-book, his bag of gold, and other valuables, such as a family watch, which was very much bigger than it was valuable.

He then coolly remounted his horse and left the unfortunate Joe Morgan to his fate.

Twenty minutes elapsed, and then other sounds were heard coming along the road.

There were quite a dozen riders.

They were many and hilarious, and but for one sharp-sighted youth would have ridden over Joe Morgan.

"Hilloa!" said the youth, drawing up his horse until it sat on its haunches.

"What is it?" cried another.

"Summut wrong, bhoy; that's Joe Morgan's horse standing over a dead body," he shouted, while all the others drew rein and stood around him.

"And this is Joe Morgan's dead body," continued the youth, stooping. "NO," he still breathes. Brandy, some one!"

Four or five flasks were proffered him, and snatching one he poured a large quantity down the exhausted man's throat.

He heaved a heavy sigh, and then opened his eyes.

"Ah! what's all this?" he whispered.

"All right, old man; you're badly hurt," replied the youth, whose name was Warren; "but we'll take you to the 'Flower Pot' and have your wounds dressed."

Not another word was spoken. Joe Morgan was lifted on his horse, and, supported by two of his friends, was helped to the "Flower Pot," a small roadside inn, distant half a mile.

He was warmly received, and at once put to bed.

A doctor lives close handy, and soon reached the spot.

The verdict was quick and satisfactory.

Mr Joe Morgan, of Pollard, was in no way seriously injured, thanks to the thickness of his skull.

Very shortly after the departure of the doctor, Morgan sat up, and asked for something to eat.

"But," said young Warren, "how did you get this nasty knock, and have you lost any money?"

"All the money I had with me," replied the farmer; "that countrified fellow at the market-dinner was Dick Turpin.

They yelled with fury.

"And there's two hundred guineas reward for his apprehension," cried one, aghast with avarice and horror.

"That whipper-snapper Dick Turpin!" cried one of the younger farmers.

"Whipper-snapper," half chuckled Morgan. "I'd like you to try a knock on the head, such as he can give."

He now insisted on getting up, and being of the kind of stuff of which Dandie Dinmount was made, felt none the worse for his knock on the head.

He ordered a copious supper, had it put down to his account, and spent a jolly evening, untroubled by the bandages—a plaster on his head.

When he was once more put to bed he was uproariously and hopelessly drunk.

Dick Turpin returned about twelve to the "Horseshoe," but was very careful not to take either the gold or notes he had robbed the farmer of with him.

Had suspicion been excited, the money found on his person would have been enough to hang him.

A man like the highwayman had plenty of secure hiding places, which no one would possibly suspect.

He had supped at the market town, and did not go into the public room at all. He went to the bar parlour, had a drink or two, and after a chat with the landlord, went to bed.

When he went down he found both Brian and Robert in the coffee room.

"Good morning, gents," he said; "I got home so late and tired this morning, I went straight off to bed."

And he seated himself at a table.

"I see your friend has returned," he continued nodding to Brian.

"Oh yes; he seems to have lost his way," replied Brian, drily.

"Very easy thing to do about here," remarked Dick Turpin.

He then ordered his breakfast, and proceeded to attend, with his usual devotion, to his creature comforts.

While he was still engaged in his meal, the other two men rose and went out.

Dick Turpin hurried over his breakfast, first summoning the waiter.

"Have my horse saddled ready at the back of the house, out of sight. Have those gentlemen gone out?"

"No; they are in the blue room, but they have ordered their horses."

"I want to get out of the house without their seeing me. A nip of brandy," continued Dick Turpin.

The waiter went out, and returned rapidly with the brandy.

"Gentlemen just starting," he said.

Dick Turpin drank up his glass, and then, buttoning his coat, hurried out.

He caught sight of the two just turning a corner. They were going in the direction of Fairburn Castle.

If they were not, their business mattered little to him.

He however determined to find out. He knew a short cut through the forest which would bring him to a good point of observation.

In half an hour he was in sight of the castle, on the side of the road by which alone it could be reached.

He advanced still further, and posted himself so that he could have a good view of the entrance.

He here retired behind a haystack, dismounted, and concealed himself completely.

He had not long to wait, for he soon heard a cantering of horses.

Then he caught sight of the two worthies, who were rapidly lessening the distance between themselves and the castle.

The gates were open, and the entrance of the great tower was at no great distance, the park and grounds behind.

Dick Turpin could see all that passed.

Brian and his companion rode up to the gate, and alighted, throwing the bridles to a servant in attendance.

They then walked to the front entrance and rang a loud pealing bell, which Dick Turpin himself heard.

Then, after some delay, a servant came to the door, and there was some talking.

This was what happened.

"Is Mr Raymond Seymour at home?" asked Brian.

"Yes, but he is particularly engaged and cannot see you."

"Does he know that it is his cousin, Brian Seymour, who waits?" asked Brian, fiercely.

"Yes, sir. He saw you ride up, and sent for me. 'Tell the gentlemen,' he said, 'that I am particularly engaged, and cannot see them."

Brian was green with rage, and turned on his heel without a word.

Robert Woodstock smiled sardonically.

Brian's passion was so great that he could not speak.

He mounted in silence, and rode some distance without a word.

"What can it mean?" he cried, hoarsely; "how dare he inflict such an insult on me through his menials?"

"The son, I was sure at the time, suspected us," replied Woodstock; "he treated us with cool, haughty politeness, and speeded our departure very curtly."

"Curse him!" muttered Brian. "But I will be even with him yet; Brian Seymour is not to be insulted with impunity."

Woodstock shrugged his shoulders. He did not see how his friend was going to avenge his wounded susceptibilities. The old man, the family generally, had cut him dead.

At this moment a lady and gentleman came in sight, followed by two grooms.

They were cantering home after a long ride.

It was the Earl and Countess of Elphick.

Brian Seymour and Robert Woodstock drew on one side, and lifted their hats.

The earl and countess passed them without even turning their heads.

"D--n!" cried Brian; "that boy insults me too! It only makes my thirst for vengeance hotter."

And he rode back to his inn brooding moodily, and trying to plan some means of satisfying his revenge and his ambition both.

EDWIN HARCOURT BURRAGE (1839-1916)
"One" from *Broad-Arrow Jack* (1890)

Published in twenty-four instalments, *Broad-Arrow Jack* is the story of a hero's arduous return to good fortune and peace with the world after surviving shipwreck and witnessing murder. Jack Ashleigh, his father, and brother are the shipwrecked survivors of the *Esmeralda*, en route to Australia. On the unspecified coast where they are castaways, the Ashleighs are taken over by ruthless profiteers, led by "the most diabolical thing in the form of man Jack or his father had ever looked upon". The "Ogre" has no redeeming qualities; bowlegged and splayfooted, he is repulsive, cruel, and remorseless. Using a red-hot brand, he emblazons on the hero's back a broad arrow to symbolize his control over the unsubmissive "Britisher", and rechristens him with mock ceremony. When the cutthroat gang kills his father and brother, Jack vows to avenge their deaths—in the name of the Broad Arrow. A singleminded dispenser of justice, he devotes every opportunity to seeing "these hang-dog villains tortured", in which task he is assisted by a humorous but staunch peddler called "Billy Brisket" and a band of loyal retainers he collects. The chapter (XXXI) below recounts his dealings with one of the Ogre's minions. By the last chapter (CLXXXI) Jack's revenge is complete. The Ogre accidentally meets a gruesome, painful end, while the noble hero prepares to enjoy life as the master of Rockholme Castle. "He is never spoken of as Sir John Ashleigh, but Broad-Arrow Jack, and so will be until he dies."

ONE

From the hour of his capture Pedro the Spaniard had never seen the light. Placed in a cell where the faintest trace of it never came he passed many, many weary hours haunted by the words which were whispered in his ears—

"You will have but one more short look upon the light in this world—when you look upon the face of your accuser."

And who was his accuser he asked himself a thousand times—foolishly asked it, seeing that there was but one answer—

"Broad Arrow Jack."

And when he did face him—what then? Torture and death—perhaps a slow and lingering death, such as savages love to bestow upon their foes. He dare not think of it, and yet it haunted his waking and sleeping hours.

He had a gaoler, who came and went in the darkness, and gave him food. Sometimes he heard his footfall, but oft he came without a sound. But he never spoke in reply to such questions as Pedro ventured to put.

The time was long and weary, but utter despair did not take possession of him, as he lived. Every hour, every day, gave him a better chance of escape. It might be the purpose of Broad Arrow Jack to terrify him only, and after an imprisonment set him free.

Or he might relent.

Vain hope!—vain desire! And the time came at last for the terrible awakening.

He heard the door open for the twentieth time or so since his confinement, and thought it was only the usual gaoler bringing him his meal; but he thought the footstep was different, and, to his amazement, he spoke.

"Pedro, the Spaniard."

"Here," he answered.

"Advance."

He stepped forward, and immediately his arms were pinioned.

"No resistance," said the voice; "it is useless. Steady now, while I bind and blindfold you."

"Where am I going?" asked the prisoner.

"To look upon the light of day, and meet your accuser."

"Holy saints, protect me!"

"What weapon can you use best?" was next asked him.

"The rapier. I was a master of fence in Spain." he replied. "But why ask me that? What weapon can I use bound as I am?"

"You will be set free when before your accuser."

"And will he fight me fairly?"

"Yes."

"With the rapier?"

"If you wish it."

"I do," said Pedro, drawing himself up. "But if I am victorious?"

"You are free to go where you will."

"I am satisfied," said Pedro. "Let me look upon the light."

It was many years since he had handled the rapier, but in his earlier days he was renowned among his countrymen for his skill. If his right hand had not forgotten its cunning he would make short work of his Broad Arrow Jack, for what could he know of the art of fencing?

His guide took him by the arm, and led him forth through a passage into the open air. He heard a murmur of voices, and one man asked him if he should come to dig his grave.

"Silence!" said Pedro's guide, sternly. "The chief brooks no jest when serious work is on hand."

The offender apologised, and the guide led his prisoner on, leaving the murmur of voices behind him, through the stream, over broken ground, and then up, up a rough path, long and wearying.

Pedro felt the warmth of the sun and the fresh morning breeze upon his face—both grateful to him after his confinement in the close, dark cell.

"May I see now?" he asked.

"Not yet," was the reply. "Keep quiet. He who will remove the bandage will presently be here. I see he is coming. Farewell, my friend, I hope you bear me no malice."

"A curse upon you!" muttered Pedro.

"Well," said the guide, philosophically, "I suppose I must take that as there's nothing else to get. But I fancy your curse and blessing are about the same value. Adieu!"

His footsteps rapidly retreated, and Pedro was left alone a minute or so, ere he heard a steady firm footstep approaching. The bonds of his arms were severed, his bandage pulled off, and he looked upon the light, standing face to face with his accuser—Broad Arrow Jack.

Our hero had a pair of rapiers under his arm, which Pedro's appreciative eye saw were of the finest make. He took in everything before him—the tall, splendid form of Jack—the sloping mountain side—the great rent spanned by the rude bridge formed of one vast trunk of a tree—the undulating land beyond—the rising sun—all he saw, and grasped the many details of the scene in the moment which elapsed before our hero spoke.

"You know me?" he said.

"Yes," replied Pedro, with a shudder, "I do."

"And you guess why I am here?"

"You have weapons, and I suppose you mean fighting," Pedro, with assumed indifference.

"So" said Jack. "Now, make your choice, for only one of us must leave this spot alive."

In spite of his faith in his swordmanship, the heart of Pedro shrank within him. He made one last effort to turn Jack from his purpose.

"Why should you kill me?" he asked; "your life was spared."

"Is it not just you should die?" asked Jack. "Have you not, by the laws of any and every country under the sun, forfeited your life a hundred times?"

"I suppose so," said Pedro; "but there was little or no law here."

"I have established one," rejoined Jack. "I am the avenger of my own wrongs and the wrongs of others. Make your choice, and speedily, for I have work before me to-day which must be done."

"You are confident," said Pedro, scornfully.

"I am. I feel I shall conquer you."

"Perhaps you do not know I was a teacher of fence." It was Pedro's last effort to save himself by intimidating his foe, and it failed.

"I too have some knowledge of it," replied Jack, quietly. "Some years ago I took lessons from one of the first masters—Poictiers."

"He was an imposter," growled Pedro; "he knew nothing of the art."

"That shall be proved now by the performance of his pupil—are you ready."

"In a moment," replied Pedro.

He made tremendous preparations with a twofold object—to gain time, and to impress Jack with a notion of his superiority. He tried his weapon—swished it to and fro—bent it almost double—balanced it, and so on, with all the little antics of professors of fencing.

"Ready."

Their rapiers crossed, and Pedro turned cold. The first touch told him he had need of all his skill and energy to come off victor. Calm, immovable, Jack stood in an easy graceful attitude, while Pedro went through a series of assaults—well enough in their way, but feeble in their result with him. A turn of the wrist this way or that way was enough to put aside the Spaniard's weapon.

As thrust succeeded thrust without any result his heart beat quicker, and his brow grew darker. Who and what was this boy who held him so easily at bay, as man had ne'er held him before?

But it was not all skill—strength, courage, and a firm belief in being the victor helped Broad Arrow Jack in the encouter. They fenced him round and about, as it were, so securely, that if there had been two Pedros instead of one the result would have been pretty much the same.

The rapiers twirled and flashed in the sunlight as Pedro, getting hot and angry, increased the rapidity of the assault. He thrust here and there, feinted, and indulged in every trick he knew—all—all in vain.

Calm and immovable as a rock, Jack received the assault, and, gradually worked round, brought Pedro with his back to the bridge.

Then our hero pressed on.

Abandoning defence, he began to attack with great force and skill. The Spaniard, grinding his teeth with fury, had no resource but to retreat or die.

Back, step-by-step, he went, until he felt himself upon the rugged bridge. Jack pressed on furiously, and pushed him inch by inch into the centre.

"Spaniard," he cried, "prepare to die. Beneath you is your grave."

"May the light of day be—"

"Silence." cried Jack. "Blaspheme no more."

The rapier lunged forward, and entered the Spaniard's breast. He tossed up his arms, gave one short gasping groan, and fell over into the chasm five hundred feet down.

Twice his body turned, then plunged head first into a dark hollow, and disappeared.

"One," said Jack, and tossed the rapier after him. "He has a grave a king might be proud of. No foot of man has ever trodden there. Lost Leon!"

Pale and quivering, Lost Leon came out of a hiding place among some bushes, and stood before the avenger.

"Did he die in fair fight?"

"Yes," said Lost Leon.

"Was it just he should die?"

"He has had an undeserved honourable death."

"So shall all perish," said Jack, "when their time comes."

"Is that to be the grave of all your enemies?" asked Lost Leon, looking down with a shudder into the awful chasm.

"No," he replied, "I will not pollute any spot on earth with so much villainy. Each shall die a different death, and I will scatter their bones far and wide."

"I tremble as I look upon you."

"Fear not, Lost Leon," said Jack, "I will never harm you."

"Not if I give you cause?"

"But you will never give me cause. I read in your eyes that you are attached to me."

"Ay, yes," said Lost Leon, "but sometimes we sin against our will."

"If you do that I will forgive you. Now, come with me, and begin your duties as gaoler. I am going to leave a prisoner—one, Jeb Jaundice, an arrant knave—under your care for a few days, as I have something to do for a short time away from here."

"Trust me," said Lost Leon, in a low voice, "and kill me if I betray your trust."

SAMUEL BRACEBRIDGE HEMYNG (1841-1901)
"A Row at the Barn" from *Dick Lightheart, the Scapegrace of London* (1895)

Dick, the son of the Reverend Septimus Lightheart, was already known to avid readers of dreadfuls as "the scapegrace of the school" (volumes 1 and 2) and "the scapegrace at sea" (volume 3), when this fourth and final volume of his adventures appeared. With his faithful sidekick Messiter, Dick returns from sea determined to make a reputable name as an accountant, but on their first evening in London they witness a murder, hear the dying man's words about the true children of Lord Claude, and receive the daunting mission to restore the displaced heirs to their proper station. Thus Hemyng's "nice mystery" begins.

The young gentlemen rent rooms at an establishment run by the sharp-tongued Mrs Caxey, who is given to pilfering and drinking. Another lodger, Tom Cooper, soon introduces the fun-loving Dick and Messiter to the music hall known as the Barn and to his fraternity of pugnacious medical students, the Rumpumpar Boys. The fisticuffs related in the episode that follows mark the first real battle between the worldly-wise forces of good (Dick, Messiter, and Tom) and the brutal, lowbrow

forces of evil, represented by Bob Smash and Harry Wilding, the two suitably named murderers from the opening chapter. These thugs are in the hire of the malevolent usurper, Lord Borrowdale, who covets the fortune that belongs legitimately to Lord Claude's children.

Dick is not cut out for office work and loses his job, but he never despairs; he simply joins Banjo Bob as a "coloured minstrel". His father's death sobers him, however, and he is fortified by a renewed sense of filial responsibility. He not only re-enters the bosom of his family but also works very diligently to expose the plots of Borrowdale—who has "robbed the orphan and persecuted the defenceless". In the fashion typical of penny dreadfuls, the good characters are rewarded by happy betrothals, while Borrowdale suffers a lingering and painful death resulting from a freak-accident: a lighted taper touches his smock and he literally goes up in smoke, intoning "Nemesis has come at last."

In managing his large cast of characters, Hemyng shows a knowledge of street life and slangy talk comparable to that of Horatio Alger Jr.

A ROW AT THE BARN

A sign from Tosh brought up the head waiter, who touched Bob Smash on the arm.

"This won't do, sir," he said. "Must sit down. Take your seat, please."

"That's right, waiter," said Dick. "Take the low cad away."

"I'll give you low cad," cried the Caution, forgetting prudence and everything else in his passion. I'll low cad you, my boy."

He dealt a couple of open-handed blows at Dick.

The first knocked his hat off, and the second caught him a stinger on the ear.

Dick's monkey was up in an instant, and springing to his feet, he prepared to let the Caution have it.

In vain Tosh begged for silence.

"Gentlemen," he cried, "this will not do. Miss Lily Lyle is about to oblige. Gentlemen, do you hear me? Miss Lyle will appear next."

No attention was paid him.

Dick and Bob Smash were at it ding dong, and one seemed as good as the other.

Tom Cooper and Messiter were soon upon their feet.

Joe Swindles thought from this threatening attitude that they meant to fall upon his companion.

He rose also.

Miss de Vere pulled him by the sleeve.

"Sit down, Joe," she cried.

"I can't. They're going to muzzle Bob."

"Not they, he can take his own part."

"I tell you I ain't going to see a pal muzzled, and I shall slog in."

Throwing off Miss de Vere's grasp rather rudely, he stepped forward.

"You're one of them, I think," he said, addressing Tom Cooper.

"You mean you are, so mind your eye if you come too near me," answered Cooper.

Joe Swindles' reply was a straight out blow from the shoulder.

Tom dodged it and landed in return one on the nose.

"One for his conk," he cried. "Come on, my lads. Smite them hip and thigh."

The chairman and the waiters now tried to interfere between the combatants.

But the blood of all was up, and no compromise would be listened to.

Suddenly Tom Cooper fell back and said to Messiter—

"Tackle this cove for a minute for me, will you; I want to give my cry."

"Right you are," answered Messiter, who rushed in at Joe Swindles.

"Aha," said Joe, with a sort of Irish burr; "sneaking off are you."

Tom put his hands to his mouth and shouted—

"Rumpumpar Boys to the rescue!"

Instantly a dozen or more men sprang up from different parts of the hall.

They descended from galleries and climbed over partitions, all making their way to the scene of action.

Again Tom's voice was loud and clear.

"Rumpumpar Boys to the rescue!"

Tosh and the head waiter looked blankly at one another.

"Where's the governor?" asked Tosh.

"Emptied the boxes at the door and gone home," was the reply.

"Oh, lord!" said Tosh, "we're in for it. If the Rumpumpar Boys mean business, it's all up the Baltic with us."

"Shall I bring in the police?" asked the head waiter.

"Yes. Let them turn these fellows out; don't charge any one, though."

"No, sir."

"Mind there's no charge. We can't afford to have any one run in, or we shall lose our licence."

"We must keep order, you know, John, but we can't afford police cases," said Tosh.

He was in an agony of apprehension.

"And John," he cried.

"Yes, sir."

"Lower the gas, and tell the music to stop."

"Right, Mr. Tosh."

The waiter, who was an old hand and a clever man into the bargain, hurried away to carry out these orders.

Several people in the hall took the part of Bob Smash and Joe Swindles.

When they saw the medical students rushing from all parts of the hall to the attack, they came up also.

A free fight ensued.

Meanwhile, Dick was getting rather the worst of it with the Caution.

He was a stronger and bigger man.

In close contests weight will tell, and Dick was borne forcibly to the ground.

At that moment the gas was lowered, and Bob Smash got hold of Dick's throat, which he pressed in a dangerous manner.

"Hi! help!" gasped Dick.

Messiter, who was engaged in painting the eyes of a couple of young grocers' assistants who thought they ought to be in the row, heard the cry.

In a moment he threw himself on the Caution and dragged him off Dick by the back of his neck.

Hitting him under the ear, he said—

"Down you go, my dear fellow; hope you like it."

The Caution staggered and saw stars.

"Back out," he cried.

Joe Swindles was already edging towards the door.

The two ruffians joined one another, and fighting back to back, managed to make their escape.

Outside the hall they were joined by Miss de Vere.

She was in a state of great agitation.

"Are either of you hurt?" she asked.

"Banged about a bit, that's all," said Joe.

"I've got a mouse under the eye," exclaimed Bob Smash; "cuss that youngster; how he did fight!"

"We must settle his hash," replied Joe.

"I think so too, he knows too much."

"Suppose we shut him up in the old house in—"

He was interrupted by Miss de Vere.

"Are you out of your mind, Joe?" she said.

"What's up?" he asked.

"You don't know who may be listening. Don't be a fool, but call a cab."

"A Hansom?"

"Yes. I can ride bodkin, and we shall get home sooner," she said.

They hailed a cab, and getting in, were driven off, Miss de Vere sitting between the two men, partly on their knees and partly on the seat.

By dint of coaxing and pushing, the waiters had separated the combatants.

The Rumpumpar Boys meant mischief.

But Tom Cooper being appealed to by Tosh, gave them the signal to be quiet.

Consequently they sat down again, and the gas being turned up again, the performance went on.

Few of the audience remained, however, for the respectable portion had gone away at the first intimation of the riot.

Dick was not much hurt, though he and Messiter were bruised considerably.

Taking their seat at the table again, they wiped their faces.

Tom Cooper looked paternally at them.

"You're a couple of nice fellows to take out," he said. "Look at the cloud of anguish on friend Tosh's face."

"It wasn't my fault altogether," said Dick; "I think the row began in your direction."

"There's ingratitude for you. Did you hear that, Tosh?"

"Mr. Cooper," said the chairman, "if you come here for that sort of game often, you'll ruin the hall."

"What's the odds? the hall doesn't keep me," said Cooper.

"Silence, gentlemen, if you please, the original Cream of Tartar will appear in his highly characteristic Cossack of the Don feat."

"Let's cut it," said Dick.

"I'm agreeable," said Messiter.

"Don't go yet," said Tom Cooper, "we shall another lovely row on directly. I've only got one black eye at present."

"Do you want another?"

"Yes."

"I should have thought one was enough."

"Not a bit of it. If you've got two, you can say you were thrown out of a cab or were in a railway accident."

"Oh."

"One black eye is awfully low, but if you have two everybody thinks it must have been an accident, and sympathises with you accordingly."

"I'm afraid I'm in for one, said Dick, with a half smile, "and it won't look well in business.

"We must buy a raw steak here before we go," answered Tom Cooper.

"What for?"

"To tie over your eye. It will take all the inflammation down, and if the blackness won't go, I'll paint your eye for you tomorrow."

"Will you, indeed?"

"Certainly. Don't fluster your milk; I'll turn you out as bright as a new pin."

Dick thanked him for his kindness, and when the song was over they went away.

It was past twelve when they got home, and entered Mr Cooper's hospitable apartment.

"Well, I'm jiggered," said that gentleman; "I've been and gone and done it."

"What?" asked Dick.

"Left the key in my cupboard."

"Why shouldn't you?"

"Because it is a hundred to one that old Caxey has purloined my whisky."

He went to the cupboard and made an examination.

"Oh, my prophetic soul," he said, "It's all gone. Caxey must be as tight as a fly. Shall I have her up?"

"It's too late," said Dick.

"Well, perhaps it is; but if I don't get up sides with her for this, my name isn't ancient Thomas," exclaimed Tom Cooper, with a subdued howl.

"Never mind," said Dick. "I for one don't want anything."

"We will triumph, dear boy," said Tom, smiling blandly.

"How? the pubs are all closed."

"Thanks to a paternal Government, which wants to make us sober by Act of Parliament."

"And your bottle's empty. So we're licked," replied Dick.

"That's as clear as two and two make four," put in Messiter.

"Simple children," answered Tom. "I never allow any one to score over me. Did the idea of a cellar never strike you?"

"Have you one?"

"I have, and Caxey knoweth it not. There is a triumph of inventive genius for you. Remove the table."

Dick pushed the table on one side.

"Look out," exclaimed Tom.

He went to the wall, and touching a spring, similar in construction to that which moved the skeletons, a trap door flew up.

The carpet had been carefully cut to fit it, and nailed on, and being under the table, it passed unnoticed.

The door disclosed a cavity, in which were sundry bottles.

"What will you have?" inquired Tom.

The boys asked for a little claret, which was soon produced and poured out.

"This is what vexes the soul of our Caxey," remarked Tom. "She guesses I've got a cellar somewhere, but, bless her artful old heart, she can't tell where."

Dick laughed, and with a yawn expressed a wish to go to bed.

"Tired is he? Does he want to go to bye-bye?" said Tom. "So he shall but first of all here's the steak."

"The what?"

"Raw beef for the blackened peeper. I got it at the Barn. Take it up with you. Try a bit, Messiter, you're painted as well as Lightheart."

"So are you," observed Dick.

"Oh! that's nothing, I'm used to it. My friends would think there was something wrong if I didn't put one of my eyes in mourning at least once a month," said Tom.

Dick wished him good-night, and followed by Messiter, retired to his bedroom.

In the morning the bruises had assumed a milder aspect, and the boys put in an appearance as usual at Counting-house Square without exciting any remark.

THE ANIMAL STORY

9. THE ANIMAL STORY: SENTIMENTALITY AND NATURALISM

The animal story at its highest point of development is a psychological romance constructed on a framework of natural science.—
Charles G.D. Roberts, "The Animal Story" (1902)

Animals have been present in fiction for as long as folklore and literature have existed. During much of the Golden Age the animal story was restricted to moral fables, Sunday School tales, and cautionary verse for the young. Margaret Gatty and Joel Chandler Harris adapted the fable convention to a Victorian setting. In *Parables from Nature* (1855-71) Mrs Gatty used animals, both talking and mute, and humans (poor "featherless bipeds", as the council of rooks describes them in "Inferior Ani-

mals") to promote Christian principles and a caring attitude to animals. After the publication of *On the Origin of Species by Means of Natural Selection; or, The Preservation of Favoured Races in the Struggle for Life* (1859) she became an adversary of Darwin's theories and concentrated on showing the divine order in nature as well as the necessity to treat all forms of life with respect. A generation later the American Joel Chandler Harris in his *Uncle Remus* stories (1880-1907) recorded traditional Negro legends about animal tricksters who speak in a characteristic Georgia dialect.

The use of talking, percipient creatures whose words and thoughts engage the reader's sympathies was discovered by Anna Sewell, an Englishwoman, to be an effective technique to demonstrate the importance of kindness to animals; and it was adopted some years later, for similar reasons, by Marshall Saunders, a Canadian. Both *Black Beauty: The Autobiography of a Horse* (1877) and *Beautiful Joe: The Autobiography of a Dog* (1894) are about animals that had been abused—and both tend to become maudlin. As narrators Beauty and Joe are vastly different: Beauty tells his story from the standpoint of an ill-treated horse who once knew security and love and is struggling against all odds to regain them; Joe, on the other hand, is saved from a cruel master at the outset and settles comfortably into the Morris household, becoming a close-to-omniscient observer of all family activities and a tedious preacher. Sewell makes her sentimentality palatable, while Saunders goes in for cloying exaggeration. Both books have enjoyed immense popularity and even inspired many feeble imitations.

In the innovative works of two Canadians, Ernest Thompson Seton and Charles G.D. Roberts, animals were not employed for a moral purpose but instead were described knowledgeably, and with a profound understanding of their instincts. Seton's *Wild Animals I Have Known* (1898) and Roberts' *The Kindred of the Wild* (1902) mark the beginning of the realistic animal story. Both authors wrote animal biographies. Those of Seton, a naturalist, are based on fact, managing to inculcate the need for man to live in harmony with nature while making the animal figures romantic heroes. The superb animal biographies of Roberts express a passionate fidelity to exact, unglamourized, and unsentimental detail; the story in this chapter illustrates that the lessons in survival animal mothers teach their offspring are often both crucial and tragic. Another Canadian, W.A. Fraser, wrote an animal book that is a curious but effective mixture of influences. His *Mooswa and Others of the Boundaries* (1900) is a novel about a brotherhood of wild animals set in the Athabasca region of Alberta, before it became a province. Although the patriarchal moose and his animal comrades use colloquial discourse and human powers of reasoning, the novel shows the influence of Seton's compelling naturalism in its close attention to the animals' behaviour. Without trivializing the animals, or sacrificing exactness of detail, Fraser makes their fraternity, their loyalty to the Law of the Boundaries, and all their actions believable and engaging.

Two of the best-known writers of animal stories are not included in this chapter because their books are readily available, but they both made distinctive contributions to the genre. In his *Jungle Books* (1894-5) Rudyard Kipling used his knowledge of the animals of India to portray them as strong personalities and as exemplars of a highly developed jungle code; animals illustrate how things came to be in Kipling's witty *Just-So Stories* (1902). In the more than twenty books by Beatrix Potter animals inhabit a totally different world, a cosy English countryside, and are given human characteristics and dress. In both text and brilliantly executed watercolours, Potter relates their miniature dramas with great seriousness, and artlessly includes just the right amount of lovingly observed detail, with the result that the reader experiences not only a willing suspension of disbelief, but delight.

All these veins of the animal story—the sentimental and didactic, the realistic and romantic, the lovingly and seriously depicted world of humanized animals—had their definitive exponents in the Golden Age, and provided a legacy that has been drawn on to this day. The animal story has continued to be written successfully by Canadians—such as Roderick Haig-Brown, Farley Mowat, and Sheila Burnford—but an Englishman, Richard Adams, has produced the most distinguished recent work in this genre in his animal epics *Watership Down, Shardik*, and *The Plague Dogs*.

MARGARET GATTY (1809-1873)
"Purring When You're Pleased" from *Parables from Nature* (1855-71)

Daughter of Nelson's chaplain and wife of a country parson, Mrs Gatty was a bookish, perpetually curious woman who inspired reverential loyalty in all her children—the most famous of whom was Juliana Horatia Ewing. In addition to writing many short tales for the young and editing *Aunt Judy's Magazine* (see p. 441), Mrs Gatty also wrote a scientific study, *British Seaweeds* (1863). This accomplishment has led to the conjecture that the devoted mother and skilled naturalist in *Six to Sixteen* (see p. 192), Mrs Arkwright, is Ewing's tribute to her own exceptional mother.

Mrs Gatty's *Parables from Nature*, published in five series between 1855 and 1871, is a collection of stories, in most of which

animals—by means of their characteristics and their response to treatment by humans—teach lessons about Christian principles and the need to respect all life. Not every tale, however, includes humans. In "Inferior Animals" a council of rooks satirizes mankind, taking pity on human inferiority. In the foreword she contributed to the complete edition of *Parables from Nature* (1871), Ewing acknowledged her mother's love of animals and her "mental bent towards parabolic teaching, and towards the ideal rather than the actual. . . ." *Parables* was translated into German, Swedish, French, Danish, Russian, and Italian.

PURRING WHEN YOU'RE PLEASED

"Out of the abundance of the heart the mouth speaketh."—Matt. xii. 34.

They had been licked over hundreds of times by the same mother, had been brought up on the same food, lived in the same house, learnt the same lessons, heard the same advice, and yet how different they were! Never were there two kittens more thoroughly unlike than those two!

The one, with an open, loving heart, which never could contain itself in its joy, but purred it out at once to all the world; the other, who scarcely ever purred at all, and that never above its breath, let him be as happy or as fond as he would.

It was partly his mother's fault, perhaps, for she always set her children the example of reserve; rarely purring herself, and then only in a low tone. But, poor thing, there were excuses to be made for her; she had had so many troubles. Cats generally have. Their kittens are taken away from them so often, and they get so hissed about the house when people are busy, and the children pull them about so heedlessly, and make the dogs run after them—which is so irritating—that really the wonder is they ever purr at all!

Nevertheless her not feeling inclined to purr much herself was no good reason for her thinking it silly or wrong in other people to purr when they were pleased; but she did, and she and her purring daughter were always having small tiffs on the subject.

Every morning, for instance, when the nice curly-headed little boy brought the kittens a saucer of milk from his breakfast, there was sure to be a disturbance over the purring question, for, even before the saucer had reached the floor, Puss Missy was sure to be there, tail and head erect and eager, singing her loudest and best, her whole throat vibrating visibly; while Puss Master, on the contrary, took his food, but said very little about it, or, if ever tempted to express his natural delight, did it in so low a tone that nobody could hear without putting their ears close down to him to listen.

Now this was what the mother cat called keeping up one's dignity and self-respect, so it can easily be imagined how angry she used to get with the other child. "Wretched little creature!" she would say to poor Puss Missy, who, even after the meal was over, would lie purring with pleasure in front of the fire; "what in the world are you making all that noise and fuss about? Why are you to be always letting yourself down by thanking people for what they do for you, as if you did not deserve it, and had not a right to expect it? Isn't it quite right of them to feed you and keep you warm? What a shame it would be if they left you without food or fire! I am ashamed to see you make yourself so cheap, by showing gratitude for every trifle. For goodness' sake have a little proper pride, and leave off such fawning ways! Look at your brother, and see how differently *he* behaves!—takes everything as a matter of course, and has the sense to keep his feelings to himself; and people are sure to respect him all the more. It keeps up one's friends' interest when they are not too sure that one is pleased. But you, with your everlasting acknowledgments, will be seen through, and despised very soon. Have a little more esteem for your own character, I do beg! What is to become of self-respect if people are to purr whenever they are pleased?"

Puss Missy had not the least notion what would become of it in such a case, but she supposed something dreadful; so she felt quite horrified at herself for having done anything to bring such a misfortune about, and made a thousand resolutions to keep up her dignity, save self-respect from the terrible unknown fate in store, and purr no more.

But it was all in vain. As soon as ever anything happened to make her feel happy and comfortable, throb went the little throat, as naturally as flowers come out in spring, and there she was in a fresh scrape again! And the temptations were endless. The little boy's cousin, pale, and quiet, and silent as she was, would often take Puss Missy on her knee, and nurse her for half-an-hour at a time, stroking her so gently and kindly—how could any one help purring?

Or the boy would tie a string, with a cork at the end of it, to the drawer-handle of a table, so that the kittens could paw it, and pat it, and spring at it, as they pleased—how was it possible not to give vent to one's delight in the intervals of such a game, when the thing was swinging from side to side before their very eyes, inviting the next bound?

And when there was nothing else to be pleased about, there were always their own tails to run after, and the fun was surely irresistible, and well deserved a song.

Yet the brother very seldom committed himself in that way—that was the great puzzle, and Puss Missy grew more perplexed as time went on. Nay, once, when they were alone together and her spirits had quite got the better of her judgment, she boldly asked him, in as many words, "Why do you not purr when you are pleased?" as if it was quite the natural and proper thing to do. Whereat he seemed quite taken by surprise, but answered at last: "It's so weak-minded, mother says; I should be ashamed. Besides," added he, after a short pause, "to tell you the truth—but don't say anything about it—when I begin, there's something that chokes a little in my throat. Mind you don't tell—it would let me down so in mother's eyes. She likes one to keep up one's dignity, you know.

Had Mother Puss overheard these words, she might have been a little startled by such a result of her teaching; but, as it was, she remained in happy ignorance that her son was influenced by anything but her advice.

. . . Yet, strange to say, she had that choking in the throat sometimes herself! . . .

But, at last, a change came in their lives. One day their friend, the curly-headed boy, came bounding into the kitchen where Puss and her kittens were asleep, in raptures of delight, followed by a pale, quiet, silent cousin, as quiet and silent as ever. The boy rushed to the kittens at once, took up both together in his hands, laid one over the other for fun, and then said to the girl, "Cousin, now they're going to give us the kittens for our very own, just tell me which you like best, really? I'm so afraid you won't choose for yourself when they ask you, and then, if I have to chose instead, I shan't know which you would rather have! And I want you to have the one you like most—so do tell me beforehand!"

"Oh, I like them both!" answered the girl, in the same unmoved, indifferent tone, in which she generally spoke.

"So do I," replied her Cousin; "but I know which I like best for all that; and so must you, only you won't say. I wonder whether you like to have the kittens at all?" added he, looking at the pale child a little doubtfully; then whispering, as he put them both to her face to be kissed, "Cousin, dear, I wish I could see when you were pleased by your face! See! give a smile when the one you like best goes by. Do—won't you—this once—just for once?" . . .

It was in vain! he passed the kittens before her in succession, that she might see the markings of their fur, but she still only said she liked both, and, of course, was glad to have a kitten, and so on; till, at last, he was disheartened, and asked no more.

It is a great distress to some people when their friends will *not* purr when they are pleased; and as the children went back together to the drawing-room, the little boy was the sadder of the two, though he could not have explained why.

And then, just what he expected happened,—the choice between the two kittens was offered first to the girl; but, instead of accepting it as a favour, and saying "Thank you" for it, and being pleased, as she ought to have been, she would say nothing but that she liked both, and it could not matter which she had; nay, to look at her as she spoke, nobody would have thought she cared for having either at all!

How was it that she did not observe how sorrowfully her aunt was gazing at her as she spoke; aye, and with a sorrow far beyond anything the kittens could occasion?

But she did not; and presently her Aunt said, "Well, then, as she did not care, the boy should choose." On which the poor boy coloured with vexation; but when he had sought his cousin's eyes again and again in vain for some token of her feelings, he laid sudden hold on Puss Missy, and cuddled her against his cheek, exclaiming:

"Then I will have this one! I like her much the best, Mother, because she purrs when she is pleased!"

And then the little girl took up Puss Master, and kissed him very kindly, but went away without saying another word.

And so a week passed; and though the children nursed their kittens, they never discussed the question of which was liked best again, for a shyness had sprung up about it ever since the day the choice had been made.

But at the end of the week, one sunshiny morning, when the boy was riding his father's pony, and only the little girl was in the house, her aunt, coming suddenly into the school-room, discovered her kneeling by the sofa, weeping a silent rain of tears over the fur-coat of Puss Missy, who was purring loudly all the time; while her own kitten, Puss Master, was lying asleep unnoticed by the fire.

*

Now, the pale, silent little girl had been an orphan nearly two years—

father and mother having died within a few weeks of each other; and she had been ever since, till quite lately, under the care of a guardian, who, though married, had no children, and was more strict and well-intentioned than kind and comprehending; so that, between sorrow at first and fear afterwards, joined to a timid, shrinking nature, she had, without knowing anything about it, shut herself up in a sort of defensive armour of self-restraint, which, till now, neither aunt, nor uncle, nor even loving cousin, had been able to break through.

But they had gently bided their time, and the time had come at last, and Puss Missy pointed the moral; for, with her aunt's arms folded round her, and a sense of her comforting tenderness creeping into the long-lonely heart, she owned that she had fretted all the week in secret because—actually because—*it was so miserable to nurse a kitten who would not purr when he was pleased!*

*

Anybody may guess how nice it was, ten minutes afterwards, to see the little girl, with the roused colour of warm feeling on her cheeks, smiling through her tears at the thought of how like the unpurring kitten she had been herself! Anybody may guess, too, with what riotous joy the loving boy-cousin insisted on her changing kittens at once, and having Puss Missy for her very own. And how, on the other hand, he set to work himself, with a resolute heart, to make Puss Master so fond of him that purr he must, whether he would or no; and how that, now and then, by dint of delicate attentions, such as choice morsels of food and judicious rubbing under the ears, he worked the creature up to such a pitch of complacency, that the vibrations of his throat became, at any rate, visible to sight, and perceptible to touch.

Truly, they were a very happy party; for after Puss Master took Puss Missy for friend, confidante, and adviser, he grew so loving and fond, that he could not help showing his feelings in a thousand pretty, pleasant ways: and the mother-cat herself relaxed by degrees; perhaps because she found her kittens were not taken away—partly, perhaps, because Puss Missy's open-heartedness stole into her heart at last with a sense of comfort—who knows? Certainly she left off scolding and lecturing, and would not only watch their gambols, but join in them at times herself. And if neither she nor her son ever purred quite so much, or so loudly as their neighbours, the reason, no doubt, was only that tiresome choking in the throat!

Why, the pale little girl herself complained of having felt something very like it, during the sad two years before her kind aunt made her happy again! It always used to come on when she wanted to say what she felt.

And, perhaps, there is always something that chokes in the throat when people do not purr when they are pleased.

Let us hope so!

ANNA SEWELL (1820-1878)
"A Talk in the Orchard" from *Black Beauty: The Autobiography of a Horse* (1877)

Anna Sewell was born in Yarmouth, Eng., and at an early age moved with her family to Dalston; her father, a salesman, relocated his family often. From the time she was a very young child Anna was extremely fond of animals, especially of horses. When she was a schoolgirl she injured the ankles in both feet and the condition was improperly diagnosed and cared for, with the result that she was crippled for the rest of her life. She served as a literary critic and adviser to her mother, Mary Sewell, who at sixty began to publish sentimental, improving verse that became very popular (her ballad, "Mother's Last Words", sold 1,088,000 copies). Although Anna's health improved from time to time—allowing her to travel to Germany and Spain—she was never robust and spent the last seven years of her life indoors under her mother's devoted care. It was at this time that she composed *Black Beauty* (1877).

Readers in Anna Sewell's day easily accepted *Black Beauty's* convention of horses that speak in a civilized manner (the author whimsically explains on the title page that the story was "translated from the original Equine"). One reason for this is that Sewell mastered imaginatively all the feelings that might be attributed to different kinds of horses—even the sensations of having short reins, blinkers, and tightly strapped saddles. Her believable rendering of such experiences lends conviction to Beauty's sophisticated first-person narrative and to the urbane dialogue of the horses.

Beauty's ordeals and ultimate salvation, related with large doses of sentiment, provide a potent medium for Sewell's expressed desire "to induce kindness, sympathy, and an understanding treatment of horses" in her readers. *Black Beauty* has been a world-wide bestseller and has never been out of print since publication.

A TALK IN THE ORCHARD

Ginger and I were not of the regular tall carriage horse breed; we had more of the racing blood in us. We stood about fifteen and a half hands high; we were therefore just as good for riding as we were for driving, and our master used to say that he disliked either horse or man that could do but one thing; and as he did not want to show off in London parks, he preferred a more active and useful kind of horse. As for us, our greatest pleasure was when we were saddled for a riding party; the master on Ginger, the mistress on me, and the young ladies on Sir Oliver and Merrylegs. It was so cheerful to be trotting and cantering all together, that it always put us in high spirits. I had the best of it, for I always carried the mistress; her weight was little, her voice was sweet, and her hand was so light on the rein, that I was guided almost without feeling it.

Oh! if people knew what a comfort to horses a light hand is, and how it keeps a good mouth and good temper, they surely would not chuck, and drag, and pull at the rein as they often do. Our mouths are so tender, that where they have not been spoiled or hardened with bad or ignorant treatment, they feel the slightest movement of the driver's hand, and we know in an instant what is required of us. My mouth had never been spoiled, and I believe that was why the mistress preferred me to Ginger, although her paces were certainly quite as good. She used often to envy me, and said it was all the fault of breaking in, and the gag bit in London, that her mouth was not so perfect as mine; and then old Sir Oliver would say, "There, there! don't vex yourself; you have the greatest honor; a mare that can carry a tall man of our master's weight, with all your spring and sprightly action, does not need to hold her head down because she does not carry the lady; we horses must take things as they come, and always be contented and willing so long as we are kindly used."

I had often wondered how it was, that Sir Oliver had such a very short tail; it really was only six or seven inches long, with a tassel of hair hanging from it; and on one of our holidays in the orchard I ventured to ask him by what accident it was that he had lost his tail. "Accident!" he snorted with a fierce look, "it was no accident! it was a cruel, shameful, cold-blooded act! When I was young I was taken to a place where these cruel things were done; I was tied up, and made fast so that I could not stir, and then they came and cut off my long beautiful tail, through the flesh, and through the bone, and took it away."

"How dreadful!" I exclaimed.

"Dreadful! ah! it was dreadful; but it was not only the pain, though that was terrible and lasted a long time; it was not only the indignity of having my best ornament taken from me, though that was bad; but it was this, how could I ever brush the flies off my sides and my hind legs any more? You who have tails just whisk the flies without thinking about it, and you can't tell what a torment it is to have them settle upon you and sting and sting, and have nothing in the world to lash them off with. I tell you it is a lifelong wrong, and a lifelong loss; but thank Heaven! they don't do it now."

"What did they do it for then? said Ginger.

"For fashion!" said the old horse with a stamp of his foot; "for fashion! if you know what that means; there was not a well-bred young horse in my time that had not his tail docked in that shameful way, just as if the good God that made us did not know what we wanted and what looked best."

"I suppose it is fashion that makes them strap our heads up with those horrid bits that I was tortured with in London," said Ginger.

"Of course it is," said he; "to my mind, fashion is one of the wickedest things in the world. Now look, for instance, at the way they serve dogs, cutting off their tails to make them look plucky, and shearing up their pretty little ears to a point to make them look sharp, forsooth. I had a dear friend once, a brown terrier—"Skye," they called her; she was so fond of me that she never would sleep out of my stall; she made her bed under the manger, and there she had a litter of five as pretty little puppies as need be; none were drowned, for they were a valuable kind, and how pleased she was with them! and when they got their eyes open and crawled about, it was a real pretty sight; but one day the man came and took them all away; I thought he might be afraid I should tread upon them. But it was not so; in the evening poor Skye brought them back again, one by one in her mouth; not the happy little things that they were, but bleeding and crying pitifully; they had all had a piece of their tails cut off, and the soft flap of their pretty little ears was cut quite off. How their mother licked them, and how troubled she was, poor thing! I never forgot it. They healed in time, and they forgot the pain, but the nice soft flap that of course was intended to protect the delicate part of their ears from dust and injury, was gone for ever. Why don't they cut their own children's ears into points to make them look sharp? why don't they cut the end of their noses to make them look plucky? one would be just as sensible as the other. What right have they to torment and disfigure God's creatures?"

Sir Oliver, though he was so gentle, was a fiery old fellow, and what he said was all so new to me and so dreadful, that I found a bitter feeling toward men rise up in my mind that I had never had before. Of course Ginger was much excited; she flung up her head with flashing eyes, and distended nostrils, declaring that men were both brutes and block-heads.

"Who talks about blockheads?" said Merrylegs, who just came up from the old apple tree, where he had been rubbing himself against the low branch; "Who talks about blockheads? I believe that is a bad word."

"Bad words were made for bad things," said Ginger, and she told him what Sir Oliver had said. "It is all true," said Merrylegs sadly, "and I've seen that about the dogs over and over again where I lived first; but we won't talk about it here. You know that master, and John, and James are always good to us, and talking against men in such a place as this, doesn't seem fair or grateful, and you know there are good masters and good grooms besides ours, though of course ours are the best." This wise speech of good little Merrylegs, which we knew was quite true, cooled us all down, especially Sir Oliver, who was dearly fond of his master; and to turn the subject I said, "Can anyone tell me the use of blinkers?"

"No!" said Sir Oliver, shortly, "because they are no use."

"They are supposed," said Justice in his calm way, "to prevent horses from shying and starting, and getting so frightened as to cause acci-dents."

"Then what is the reason they do not put them on riding horses; espe-cially on ladies' horses?" said I.

"There is no reason at all," said he quietly, "except the fashion; they say that a horse would be so frightened to see the wheels of his own cart or carriage coming behind him, that he would be sure to run away, al-though of course when he is ridden, he sees them all about him if the streets are crowded. I admit they do sometimes come too close to be pleasant, but we don't run away; we are used to it, and understand it, and if we had never blinkers put on, we should never want them; we should see what was there, and know what was what, and be much less frightened than by only seeing bits of things, that we can't understand."

Of course there may be some nervous horses who have been hurt or frightened when they were young, and may be the better for them but as I never was nervous, I can't judge.

"I consider," said Sir Oliver, "that blinkers are dangerous things in the night; we horses can see much better in the dark than man can and many an accident would never have happened if horses might have had the full use of their eyes. Some years ago, I remember, there was a hearse with two horses returning one dark night, and just by farmer Sparrow's house, where the pond is close to the road, the wheel went too near the edge, and the hearse was overturned into the water; both the horses were drowned, and the driver hardly escaped. Of course after this account a stout white rail was put up that might be easily seen, but if those horses had not been partly blinded, they would of themselves have kept farther from the edge, and no accident would have happened. When our master's carriage was overturned, before you came here, it was said, that if the lamp on the left side had not gone out, John would have seen the great hole that the road makers had left; and so he might, but if old Colin had not had blinkers on, he would have seen it, lamp or no lamp, for he was far too knowing an old horse to run into danger. As it was, he was very much hurt, the carriage was broken, and how John escaped nobody knew."

"I should say," said Ginger, curling her nostrils, "that these men, who are so wise, and better give orders, that in future, all foals should be born with their eyes set just in the middle of their foreheads, instead of on the side; they always think they can improve upon Nature and mend what God has made."

Things were getting rather sore again, when Merrylegs held up his knowning little face and said, "I'll tell you a secret; I believe John does not approve of blinkers; I heard him talkng with master about it one day. The master said, that 'if horses had been used to them, it might be dangerous in some cases to leave them off,' and John said he thought it would be a good thing if all colts were broken in without blinkers, as was the case in some foreign countries; so let us cheer up, and have a run to the other end of the orchard; I believe the wind has blown down some apples, and we might just as well eat them as the slugs."

Merrylegs could not be resisted, so we broke off our long conversation, and got up our spirits by munching some very sweet apples which lay scattered on the grass.

JOEL CHANDLER HARRIS (1848-1908)
"The Wonderful Tar-Baby" from *Uncle Remus, His Songs and His Sayings* (1880)

Born near Eatonton, Georgia, Harris started to learn the printing trade at the age of fourteen, when he was apprenticed to the editor of the plantation newspaper *The Countryman*, of which he himself later became editor. His ear for good storytelling was always keen and he spent many hours listening to the "stories, songs, and myths of the plantation". He said in an interview that in order to preserve these stories, "dear to the Southern children", he wrote them down as told by Uncle Remus, who is a synthesis "of three or four old darkies whom I had known. I just walloped them together into one person and called him 'Uncle Remus'." For the original edition of *Uncle Remus* he supplied an introduction in which he said that in spite of its being considered a humorous book, "its intention is perfectly serious", and that his purpose had been "to preserve the legends themselves in their original simplicity, and to wed them permanently to the quaint dialect—if, indeed, it can be called a dialect. . . ." Harris's sincere convictions

about this material—expressed in relatively liberal parlance for the time—have not impressed modern liberals, who have taken exception to what they perceive as a condescending tone.

The stories feature a full cast of indefatigable tricksters, chief among them Brer Rabbit, Brer Fox, and Brer Tarrypin, and their attempts to outwit one another. (Humans are reduced to labels, like Mr Man and Miss Meadows.) Harris's genial tales—which are really brief, dramatic episodes—have a wry humour, and after the first instalments appeared in the Atlanta newspaper *The Constitution* (January 1877), Uncle Remus became firmly established as part of popular folklore. Mark Twain called the stories "bright, fine literature, and worthy to live".

The Uncle Remus stories were published with illustrations by Arthur Burdette Frost that have become permanently associated with them. Other collections followed, as well as *Uncle Remus's Magazine*, which was begun in Atlanta in 1907.

THE WONDERFUL TAR-BABY

Didn't the fox ever catch the rabbit, Uncle Remus? asked the little boy next evening.

He came mighty nigh it, honey, sho's you bawn—Brer Fox did. One day Brer Fox went ter wuk en got 'im some tar, en mix it wid some turkentime, en fix up a contraption w'at he call a Tar-Baby, en he tuck dish yer Tar-Baby en he sot 'er in de big road, en den he lay off in de bushes fer to see w'at de news wuz gwineter be. En he didn't hatter wait long, needer, kaze bimeby yer come Brer Rabbit pacin' down de road—*lippity-clippity, clippity-lippity*—des ez sassy ez a jay-bird. Brer Fox, he lay low. Brer Rabbit come prancin' 'long twel he spy the Tar-Baby, en den he fotch up on his behime legs like he wuz 'stonished. De Tar-Baby, she sot dar, she did, en Brer Fox, he lay low.

"Mawnin' " sez Brer Rabbit, sezee—"nice wedder dis mawnin'," sezee.

Tar-Baby aint sayin' nothin', en Brer Fox, he lay low.

"How does yo' sym'toms seem ter segashuate?" sez Brer Rabbit, sezee.

"Brer Fox, he wink his eye slow, en lay low, en de Tar-Baby, she aint sayin' nothin'.

"How you come on, den? Is you deaf?" sez Brer Rabbit, sezee. "Kaze if you is, I kin holler louder," sezee.

Tar-Baby stay still, en Brer Fox, he lay low.

"Youer stuck up, dat's w'at you is," sez Brer Rabbit, sezee, "en I'm gwineter kyore you, dat's w'at I'm a-gwineter do," sezee.

Brer Fox, he sorter chickle in his stomach, he did, but Tar-Baby aint sayin' nothin'.

"I'm gwineter larn you how ter talk ter 'spectable folks ef hit's de las' ack," sez Brer Rabbit, sezee. "Ef you don't take off dat hat en tell me howdy, I'm gwineter bus' you side open," sezee.

Tar-Baby stay still, en Brer Fox, he lay low.

Brer Rabbit keep on axin' 'im, en de Tar-Baby, she keep on sayin' nothin', twel present'y Brer Rabbit draw back wid his fis', he did, en *blip* he tuck 'er side er de head. Right dar's whar he broke his merlasses jug. His fis' stuck, en he can't pull loose. De tar hilt 'im. But Tar-Baby, she stay still, en Brer Fox, he lay low.

"Ef you don't lemme loose, I'll knock you agin," sez Brer Rabbit, sezee, en wid dat he fotch 'er a wipe wid de udder han', en dat stuck. Tar-Baby, she aint sayin' nothin'. She des hilt on, en den Brer Rabbit lose de use er his foots en de same way. Brer Fox, he lay low. Den Brer Rabbit squall out dat ef de Tar-Baby don't tu'n 'im loose he butt 'er cranksided. En den he butted, en his head got stuck. Den Brer Fox, he sa'ntered fort', lokin' des ez innercent ez one er yo' mammy's mockin'-birds.

"Howdy, Brer Rabbit," sez Brer Fox, sezee. "You look sorter stuck up dis mawnin'," sezee, en den he rolled on the groun', en laffed en laffed twel he couldn't laff no mo'.

MARGARET MARSHALL SAUNDERS (1861-1947)
"My New Home and a Selfish Lady" from *Beautiful Joe: The Autobiography of a Dog* (1894)

Margaret Marshall Saunders—the author of almost thirty romantic novels for adults and books for children—was born in the Annapolis Valley of Nova Scotia. She travelled a great deal, lived for several years in Maine, and in 1916 settled permanently in Toronto. In the 1880s, in Ottawa, she heard about an abused mongrel and was inspired to write a story about such an animal: *Beautiful Joe*. Saunders returned frequently to the sympathy-arousing animal story that was apparently based on fact—in *The Story of an Eskimo Dog* (1906), *My Pets; Real Happenings in My Aviary* (1908), and *Pussy Black-Face; or, The Story of a Kitten and her Friends* (1913).

Obviously influenced by the success of *Black Beauty*, which had been published in 1877, *Beautiful Joe* (1894) also became a phenomenal bestseller. Both books are "autobiographical", but Saunders' narrative is much more sentimental, digressive, and didactic than Sewell's. While Beauty's youth spent at Birtwick Park was quite serene, young Joe was maltreated by his fiendish master, the milkman Jenkins, who slaughtered Joe's brothers and sisters and cut off his ears and tail. When a minister's children rescue the bleeding animal, Joe's new

life in the genteel Morris household of Freeport, Maine, begins.

As a narrator Joe tells less about himself and more about others than Beauty does; the chapter extracted here shows him as an observer of humans and a relayer of their conversations. While Sewell's autobiography focused on the increasing degradation Beauty suffered, Saunders' narrative makes clear that after Joe's rescue by the children (Chapter III), his safety is assured: Joe's security lessens the dramatic immediacy of the narrative. Subsequent chapters, full of the awesome piety of the Morrises, provide episodic adventures involving the children's menagerie of once-maimed or neglected animals and the rewards that always follow good deeds. Despite its limitations, *Beautiful Joe* is a key book for tracing the development of the kindness-to-animals theme in children's literature. Mrs Morris is as dedicated to the instruction of her children as Mrs Benson in Trimmer's *Fabulous Histories* (1786), and the importance Saunders accords the rejected animal anticipates E.B. White's runt pig Wilbur in *Charlotte's Web* (1952), as well as Richard Adams's canine refugees, Rowf and Snitter, in *The Plague Dogs* (1977).

MY NEW HOME AND A SELFISH LADY

I don't believe that a dog could have fallen into a happier home than I did. In a week, thanks to good nursing, good food, and kind words, I was almost well. Mr Harry washed and dressed my sore ears and tail every day till he went home, and one day, he and the boys gave me a bath out in the stable. They carried out a tub of warm water and stood me in it. I had never been washed before in my life, and it felt very queer. Miss Laura stood by laughing and encouraging me not to mind the streams of water trickling all over me. I couldn't help wondering what Jenkins would have said if he could have seen me in that tub.

That reminds me to say, that two days after I arrived at the Morrises', Jack, followed by all the other boys, came running into the stable. He had a newspaper in his hand, and with a great deal of laughing and joking, read this to me:

"*Fairport Daily News*, June 3rd. In the police court this morning, James Jenkins, for cruelly torturing and mutilating a dog, fined ten dollars and costs."

Then he said, "What do you think of that, Joe? Five dollars apiece for your ears and your tail thrown in. That's all they're worth in the eyes of the law. Jenkins has had his fun and you'll go through life worth about three-quarters of a dog. I'd lash rascals like that. Tie them up and flog them till they were scarred and mutilated a little bit themselves. Just wait till I'm president. But there's some more, old fellow. Listen: 'Our reporter visited the house of the above-mentioned Jenkins and found a most deplorable state of affairs. The house, yard, and stable were indescribably filthy. His horse bears the marks of ill usage, and is in an emaciated condition. His cows are plastered up with mud and filth, and are covered with vermin. Where is our health inspector, that he does not exercise a more watchful supervision over establishments of this kind? To allow milk from an unclean place like this to be sold in the town, is endangering the health of its inhabitants. Upon inquiry, it was found that the man Jenkins bears a very bad character. Steps are being taken to have his wife and children removed from him.' "

Jack threw the paper into my box, and he and the other boys gave three cheers for the *Daily News* and then ran away. How glad I was! It did not matter so much for me, for I had escaped him, but now that it had been found out what a cruel man he was, there would be a restraint upon him, and poor Toby and the cows would have a happier time.

I was going to tell about the Morris family. There were Mr Morris, who was a clergyman and preached in a church in Fairport; Mrs Morris, his wife; Miss Laura, who was the eldest of the family; then Jack, Ned, Carl, and Willie. I think one reason why they were such a good family, was because Mrs Morris was such a good woman. She loved her husband and children, and did everything she could to make them happy.

Mr Morris was a very busy man and rarely interfered in household affairs. Mrs Morris was the one who said what was to be done and what was not to be done. Even then, when I was a young dog, I used to think that she was very wise. There was never any noise or confusion in the house, and though there was a great deal of work to be done, everything went on smoothly and pleasantly, and no one ever got angry and scolded as they did in the Jenkins family.

Mrs Morris was very particular about money matters. Whenever the boys came to her for money to get such things as candy and ice cream, expensive toys, and other things that boys often crave, she asked them why they wanted them. If it was for some selfish reason, she said, firmly: "No, my children, we are not rich people, and we must save our money for your education. I cannot buy you foolish things."

If they asked her for money for books or something to make their pet animals more comfortable, or for their outdoor games, she gave it to them willingly. Her ideas about the bringing up of children I cannot explain as clearly as she can herself, so I will give part of a conversation that she had with a lady who was calling on her shortly after I came to Washington Street.

I happened to be in the house at the time. Indeed, I used to spend the greater part of my time in the house. Jack one day looked at me, and exclaimed: "Why does that dog stalk about, first after one and then after another, looking at us with such solemn eyes?"

I wished that I could speak to tell him that I had so long been used to seeing animals kicked about and trodden upon, that I could not get used to the change. It seemed too good to be true. I could scarcely believe that dumb animals had rights; but while it lasted, and human beings were so kind to me, I wanted to be with them all the time. Miss Laura understood. She drew my head up to her lap, and put her face down to me: "You like to be with us, don't you, Joe? Stay in the house as much as you like. Jack doesn't mind, though he speaks so sharply. When you get tired of us go out in the garden and have a romp with Jim."

But I must return to the conversation I referred to. It was one fine June day, and Mrs Morris was sewing in the rocking-chair by the window. I was beside her, sitting on a hassock, so that I could look out into the street. Dogs love variety and excitement, and like to see what is going on outdoors as well as human beings. A carriage drove up to the door, and a finely dressed lady got out and came up the steps.

Mrs Morris seemed glad to see her, and called her Mrs Montague. I was pleased with her, for she had some kind of perfume about her that I liked to smell. So I went and sat on the hearth rug quite near her.

They had a little talk about things I did not understand, and then the lady's eyes fell on me. She looked at me through a bit of glass that was hanging by a chain from her neck, and pulled away her beautiful dress lest I should touch it.

I did not care any longer for the perfume, and went away and sat very straight and stiff at Mrs Morris' feet. The lady's eyes still followed me.

"I beg your pardon, Mrs Morris," she said; "but that is a very queer-looking dog you have there."

"Yes," said Mrs Morris, quietly; "he is not a handsome dog."

"And he is a new one, isn't he?" said Mrs Montague.

"Yes."

"And that makes—"

"Two dogs, a cat, fifteen or twenty rabbits, a rat, about a dozen canaries, and two dozen goldfish, I don't know how many pigeons, a few bantams, a guinea pig, and—well, I don't think there is anything more."

They both laughed, and Mrs Montague said: "You have quite a menagerie. My father would never allow one of his children to keep a pet animal. He said it would make his girls rough and noisy to romp about the house with cats, and his boys would look like rowdies if they went about with dogs at their heels."

"I have never found that it made my children more rough to play with their pets," said Mrs Morris.

"No, I should think not," said the lady, languidly. "Your boys are the most gentlemanly lads in Fairport, and as for Laura, she is a perfect little lady. I like so much to have them come and see Charlie. They wake him up, and yet don't make him naughty."

"They enjoyed their last visit very much," said Mrs Morris. "By the way, I have heard them talking about getting Charlie a dog."

"Oh," cried the lady, with a little shudder, "beg them not to. I cannot sanction that. I hate dogs."

"Why do you hate them?" asked Mrs Morris, gently.

"They are such dirty things; they always smell and have vermin on them."

"A dog," said Mrs Morris, "is something like a child. If you want it clean and pleasant, you have got to keep it so. This dog's skin is as clean as yours or mine. Hold still, Joe," and she brushed the hair on my back the wrong way, and showed Mrs Montague how pink and free from dust my skin was.

Mrs Montague looked at me more kindly, and even held out the tips of her fingers to me. I did not lick them. I only smelled them, and she drew her hand back again.

"You have never been brought in contact with the lower creation as I have," said Mrs Morris; "just let me tell you, in a few words, what a help dumb animals have been to me in the up-bringing of my children—my boys, especially. When I was a young married woman, going about the slums of New York with my husband, I used to come home and look at my two babies as they lay in their little cots, and say to him, 'What are we going to do to keep these children from selfishness—the curse of the world?' "

" 'Get them to do something for somebody outside themselves,' he always said. And I have tried to act on that principle. Laura is naturally unselfish. With her tiny, baby fingers, she would take food from her own mouth and put it into Jack's, if we did not watch her. I have never had any trouble with her. But the boys were born selfish, tiresomely, disgustingly selfish. They were good boys in many ways. As they grew older, they were respectful, obedient, they were not untidy, and not particularly rough, but their one thought was for themselves—each one for himself, and they used to quarrel with each other in regard to their rights. While we were in New York, we had only a small, back yard. When we came here, I said, 'I am going to try an experiment.' We got this house because it had a large garden, and a stable that would do for the boys to play in. Then I got them together, and had a little serious talk. I said I was not pleased with the way in which they were living. They did nothing for any one but themselves from morning to night. If I asked them to do an errand for me, it was done unwillingly. Of course, I knew they had their school for a part of the day, but they had a good deal of leisure time when they might do something for some one else. I asked them if they thought they were going to make real, manly, Christian boys at this rate, and they said no. Then I asked them what we should do about it. They all said, 'You tell us mother, and we'll do as you say.' I proposed a series of tasks. Each one to do something for somebody, outside and apart from himself, every day of his life. They all agreed to this, and told me to allot the tasks. If I could have afforded it, I would have gotten a horse and cow, and had them take charge of them; but I could not do that, so I invested in a pair of rabbits for Jack, a pair of canaries for Carl, pigeons for Ned, and bantams for Willie. I brought these creatures home, put them into their hands, and told them to provide for them. They were delighted with my choice, and it was very amusing to see them scurrying about to provide food and shelter for their pets, and hear their consultations with other boys. The end of it all is, that I am perfectly satisfied with my experiment. My boys, in caring for these dumb creatures, have become unselfish and thoughtful. They had rather go to school without their own breakfast, than have the inmates of the stable go hungry. They are getting a humane education, a heart education, added to the intellectual education of their schools. Then it keeps them at home. I used to be worried with the lingering about street corners, the dawdling around with other boys, and the idle, often worse than idle talk, indulged in. Now they have something to do, they are men of business. They are always hammering and pounding at boxes and partitions out there in the stable, or cleaning up, and if they are sent out on an errand, they do it and come right home. I don't mean to say that we have deprived them of liberty. They have their days for base ball, and foot ball, and excursions to the woods, but they have so much to do at home, that they won't go away unless for a specific purpose."

While Mrs Morris was talking, her visitor leaned forward in her chair, and listened attentively. When she finished, Mrs Montague said, quietly, "Thank you, I am glad that you told me this. I shall get Charlie a dog."

"I am glad to hear you say that," replied Mrs Morris. "It will be a good thing for your little boy. I should not wish my boys to be without a good, faithful dog. A child can learn many a lesson from a dog. This one," pointing to me, "might be held up as an example to many a human being. He is patient, quiet, and obedient. My husband says that he reminds him of three words in the Bible—'through much tribulation.' "

"Why does he say that?" asked Mrs Montague, curiously.

"Because he came to us from a very unhappy home." And Mrs Morris went on to tell her friend what she knew of my early days.

When she stopped, Mrs Montague's face was shocked and pained. "How dreadful to think that there are such creatures as that man Jenkins in the world. And you say that he has a wife and children. Mrs Morris, tell me plainly, are there many such unhappy homes in Fairport?"

Mrs Morris hesitated for a minute, then she said, earnestly: "My dear friend, if you could see all the wickedness, and cruelty, and vileness, that is practised in this little town of ours in one night, you could not rest in your bed."

Mrs Montague looked dazed. "I did not dream that it was as bad as that," she said. "Are we worse than other towns?"

"No; not worse, but bad enough. Over and over again the saying is true, one half the world does not know how the other half lives. How can all this misery touch you? You live in your lovely house out of the town. When you come in, you drive about, do your shopping, make calls, and go home again. You never visit the poorer streets. The people from them never come to you. You are rich, your people before you were rich, you live in a state of isolation."

"But that is not right," said the lady, in a wailing voice. "I have been thinking about this matter lately. I read a great deal in the papers about the misery of the lower classes, and I think we richer ones ought to do something to help them. Mrs Morris, what can I do?"

The tears came in Mrs Morris' eyes. She looked at the little, frail lady, and said, simply: "Dear Mrs Montague, I think the root of the whole matter lies in this. The Lord made us all one family. We are all brothers and sisters. The lowest woman is your sister and my sister. The man lying in the gutter is our brother. What should we do to help these members of our common family, who are not as well off as we are? We should share our last crust with them. You and I, but for God's grace in placing us in different surroundings, might be in their places. I think it is wicked neglect, criminal neglect in us to ignore this fact."

"It is, it is," said Mrs Montague, in a despairing voice. I can't help feeling it. Tell me something I can do to help some one."

Mrs Morris sank back in her chair, her face very sad, and yet with something like pleasure in her eyes as she looked at her caller. "Your washerwoman," she said, "has a drunken husband and a cripple boy. I have often seen her standing over her tub, washing your delicate muslins and laces, and dropping tears into the water."

"I will never send her anything more—she shall not be troubled," said Mrs Montague, hastily.

Mrs Morris could not help smiling. "I have not made myself clear. It is not the washing that troubles her, it is her husband who beats her, and her boy who worries her. If you and I take our work from her, she will have that much less money to depend upon, and will suffer in consequence. She is a hard-working and capable woman, and makes a fair living. I would not advise you to give her money, for her husband would find it out, and take it from her. It is sympathy that she wants. If you could visit her occasionally, and show that you are interested in her, by talking or reading to her poor foolish boy or showing him a picture-book, you have no idea how grateful she would be to you, and how it would cheer her on her dreary way."

"I will go to see her to-morrow," said Mrs Montague. "Can you think of any one else I could visit."

"A great many," said Mrs Morris, "but I don't think you had better undertake too much at once. I will give you the addresses of three or four poor families, where an occasional visit would do untold good. That is, it will do them good if you treat them as you do your richer friends. Don't give them too much money, or too many presents, till you find out what they need. Try to feel interested in them. Find out their ways of living, and what they are going to do with their children, and help them to get situations for them if you can. And be sure to remember that poverty does not always take away one's self-respect."

"I will, I will," said Mrs Montague, eagerly. "When can you give me these addresses?"

Mrs Morris smiled again, and, taking a piece of paper and a pencil from her work basket, wrote a few lines and handed them to Mrs Montague.

The lady got up to take her leave. "And in regard to the dog," said Mrs Morris, following her to the door, "if you decide to allow Charlie to have one, you had better let him come in and have a talk with my boys about it. They seem to know all the dogs that are for sale in the town."

"Thank you, I shall be most happy to do so. He shall have his dog. When can you have him?"

"To-morrow, the next day, any day at all. It makes no difference to me. Let him spend an afternoon and evening with the boys, if you do not object."

"It will give me much pleasure," and the little lady bowed and smiled, and after stooping down to pat me, tripped down the steps, and got into her carriage and drove away.

Mrs Morris stood looking after her with a beaming face, and I began to think that I should like Mrs Mongague too, if I knew her long enough. Two days later I was quite sure I should, for I had a proof that she really liked me. When her little boy Charlie came to the house, he brought something for me done up in white paper. Mrs Morris opened it, and there was a handsome, nickel-plated collar, with my name on it—*Beautiful Joe.* Wasn't I pleased! They took off the little shabby leather strap that the boys had given me when I came, and fastened on my new collar, and then Mrs Morris held me up to a glass to look at myself. I felt so happy. Up to this time I had felt a littel ashamed of my cropped ears and docked tail, but now that I had a fine new collar I could hold up my head with any dog.

"Dear old Joe," said Mrs Morris, pressing my head tightly between her hands. "You did a good thing the other day in helping me to start that little woman out of her selfish way of living."

I did not know about that, but I knew that I felt very grateful to Mrs Montague for my new collar, and ever afterward, when I met her in the street, I stopped and looked at her. Sometimes she saw me and stopped her carriage to speak to me; but I always wagged my tail, or rather my body, for I had no tail to wag, whenever I saw her, whether she saw me or not.

ERNEST THOMPSON SETON (1860-1946)
"Silverspot, The Story of a Crow" from *Wild Animals I Have Known* (1898)

Seton was born in South Shields, Eng., and came to Canada with his parents at the age of six. They first settled near Lindsay, Ontario (the setting of his famous *Two Little Savages; Being the Adventures of Two Boys Who Lived as Indians and What They Learned* (1906), and eventually moved to Toronto where, after leaving high school, Seton studied at the Ontario College of Art. Upon graduating he won a scholarship to study at the Royal Academy in London. In 1882 he moved to Manitoba, where he initiated his own exacting program of self-education as a naturalist (he published *The Birds of Manitoba* in 1891); he also received commissions as an illustrator of birds and animals from New York publishers. His first visit to New Mexico provided the basis for his most famous story, "Lobo, the King of Currumpaw", which was published in *Scribner's Magazine* (November 1894) and included in *Wild Animals I Have Known* (1898). This collection of eight stories enjoyed an immediate success and estab-

lished Seton as an author. He moved to the United States permanently in 1896 and in 1910 founded, with Lord Baden Powell and Daniel Beard, the Boy Scouts of America. He settled in Santa Fe in 1931 and that year the Seton Institute, a school for youth leaders, was begun there.

Seton published about forty collections of animal stories and books on woodcraft and nature study. His stories—unlike previous tales about animals—were closely based on his knowledge of animal behaviour. Some early stories were drawn from his observations of wildlife in Toronto's Don Valley and Rosedale Ravine. (Toronto's Ernest Thompson Seton Park in Don Mills is a tribute to his accomplishments as naturalist and artist.) Seton portrays his animal heroes with deft yet indulgently romantic strokes. Silverspot is a quickwitted leader among crows who meets a fierce predator at night, "when a crow is a fool".

SILVERSPOT
THE STORY OF A CROW

How many of us have ever got to know a wild animal? I do not mean merely to meet with one once or twice, or to have one in a cage, but to really know it for a long time while it is wild, and to get an insight into its life and history. The trouble usually is to know one creature from his fellow. One fox or crow is so much like another that we cannot be sure that it really is the same next time we meet. But once in awhile there arises an animal who is stronger or wiser than his fellow, who becomes a great leader, who is, as we would say, a genius, and if he is bigger, or has some mark by which men can know him, he soon becomes famous in his country, and shows us that the life of a wild animal may be far more interesting and exciting than that of many human beings.

Of this class were Courtant, the bob-tailed wolf that terrorized the whole city of Paris for about ten years in the beginning of the fourteenth century; Clubfoot, the lame grizzly bear that left such a terrific record in San Joaquin Valley of California; Lobo, the king-wolf of New Mexico, that killed a cow every day for five years, and the Seonee panther that in less than two years killed nearly three hundred human beings—and such also was Silverspot, whose history, so far as I could learn it, I shall now briefly tell.

Silverspot was simply a wise old crow; his name was given because of the silvery white spot that was like a nickel, stuck on his right side, between the eye and the bill, and it was owing to this spot that I was able to know him from the other crows, and put together the parts of his history that came to my knowledge.

Crows are, as you must know, our most intelligent birds—"Wise as an old crow" did not become a saying without good reason. Crows know the value of organization, and are as well drilled as soldiers—very much better than some soldiers, in fact, for crows are always on duty, always at war, and always dependent on each other for life and safety. Their leaders not only are the oldest and wisest of the band, but also the strongest and bravest, for they must be ready at any time with sheer force to put down an upstart or a rebel. The rank and file are the youngsters and the crows without special gifts.

Old Silverspot was the leader of a large band of crows that made their headquarters near Toronto, Canada, in Castle Frank, which is a pine-clad hill on the northeast edge of the city. This band numbered about two hundred, and for reasons that I never understood did not increase. In mild winters they stayed along the Niagara River; in cold winters they went much farther south. But each year in the last week of February Old Silverspot would muster his followers and boldly cross the forty miles of open water that lies between Toronto and Niagara; not, however, in a straight line would he go, but always in sight of the familiar landmark of Dundas Mountain, until the pine-clad hill itself came in view. Each year he came with his troop, and for about six weeks took up his abode on the hill. Each morning thereafter the crows set out in three bands to forage. One band went southeast to Ashbridge's Bay. One went north up the Don, and one, the largest, went northwestward up the ravine. The last Silverspot led in person. Who led the others I never found out.

On calm mornings they flew high and straight away. But when it was windy the band flew low, and followed the ravine for shelter. My windows overlooked the ravine, and it was thus that in 1885 I first noticed this old crow. I was a new-comer in the neighborhood, but an old resident said to me then "that there old crow has been a-flying up and down this ravine for more than twenty years." My chances to watch were in the ravine, and Silverspot doggedly clinging to the old route, though now it was edged with houses and spanned by bridges, became a very familiar acquaintance. Twice each day in March and part of April, then again in the late summer and the fall, he passed and repassed, and gave me chances to see his movements, and hear his orders to his bands, and so, little by little, opened my eyes to the fact that the crows, though a little people, are of great wit, a race of birds with a language and a social system that is wonderfully human in many of its chief points, and in some is better carried out than our own.

One windy day I stood on the high bridge across the ravine, as the old crow, heading his long, straggling troop, came flying down homeward. Half a mile away I could hear the contented *"All's well, come right along!"*

as we should say, or as he put it, and as also his lieutenant echoed it at the rear of the band. They were flying very low to be out of the wind, and would have to rise a little to clear the bridge on which I was. Silverspot saw me standing there, and as I was closely watching him he didn't like it. He checked his flight and called one, *"Be on your guard,"* or

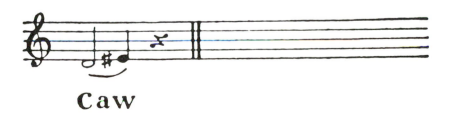

and rose much higher in the air. Then seeing that I was not armed he flew over my head about twenty feet, and his followers in turn did the same, dipping again to the old level when past the bridge.

Next day I was at the same place, and as the crows came near I raised my walking stick and pointed it at them. The old fellow at once cried out *"Danger,"* and rose fifty feet higher

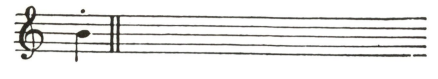

Ca

than before. Seeing that is was not a gun, he ventured to fly over. But on the third day I took with me a gun, and at once he cried out, *"Great danger—a gun."*

ca ca ca ca   Caw

His lieutenant repeated the cry, and every crow in the troop began to tower and scatter from the rest, till they were far above gun shot, and so passed safely over, coming down again to the shelter of the valley when well beyond reach. Another time, as the long, straggling troop came down the valley, a red-tailed hawk alighted on a tree close by their intended route. The leader cried out, *"Hawk, hawk,"* and stayed

Caw   Caw

his flight, as did each crow on nearing him, until all were massed in a solid body. Then, no longer fearing the hawk, they passed on. But a quarter of a mile farther on a man with a gun appeared below, and the cry, *"Great Danger—a gun, a gun; scatter for your lives"*, at once caused them to scatter widely

ca ca ca ca   Caw

and tower till far beyond range. Many others of his words of command I learned in the course of my long acquaintance, and found that sometimes a very little difference in the sound makes a very great difference in meaning. Thus while No. 5 means hawk, or any large, dangerous bird, this *"wheel around,"* evidently a

combination of No. 5, whose root idea is danger, and of No. 4, whose root idea is retreat, and this again is a mere *"good day,"* to a far away comrade.

This is usually addressed to the ranks and means *"attention."*

Early in April there began to be great doings among the crows. Some new cause of excitement seemed to have come on them. They spent half the day among the pines, instead of foraging from dawn till dark. Pairs and trios might be seen chasing each other, and from time to time they showed off in various feats of flight. A favorite sport was to dart down suddenly from a great height toward some perching crow, and just before touching it to turn at a hairbreadth and rebound in the air so fast that the wings of the swooper whirred with a sound like distant thunder. Sometimes one crow would lower his head, raise every feather, and coming close to another would gurgle out a long note like

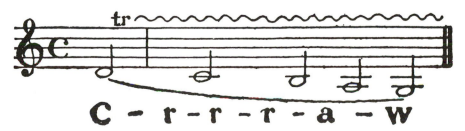

What did it all mean? I soon learned. They were making love and pairing off. The males were showing off their wing powers and their voices to the lady crows. And they must have been highly appreciated, for by the middle of April all had mated and had scattered over the country for their honeymoon, leaving the sombre old pines of Castle Frank deserted and silent.

II

The Sugar Loaf hill stands alone in the Don Valley. It is still covered with woods that join with those of Castle Frank, a quarter of a mile off. In the woods, between the two hills, is a pine-tree in whose top is a deserted hawk's nest. Every Toronto school-boy knows the nest, and, excepting that I had once shot a black squirrel on its edge, no one had ever seen a sign of life about it. There it was year after year, ragged and old, and falling to pieces. Yet, strange to tell, in all that time it never did drop to pieces, like other old nests.

One morning in May I was out at gray dawn, and stealing gently through the woods, whose dead leaves were so wet that no rustle was made. I chanced to pass under the old nest, and was surprised to see a black tail sticking over the edge. I struck the tree a smart blow, off flew a crow, and the secret was out. I had long suspected that a pair of crows nested each year about the pines, but now I realized that it was Silverspot and his wife. The old nest was theirs, and they were too wise to give it an air of spring-cleaning and housekeeping each year. Here they had nested for long, though guns in the hands of men and boys hungry to shoot crows were carried under their home every day. I never surprised the old fellow again, though I several times saw him through my telescope.

One day while watching I saw a crow crossing the Don Valley with something white in his beak. He flew to the mouth of the Rosedale Brook, then took a short flight to the Beaver Elm. There he dropped the white object, and looking about gave me a chance to recognize my old friend Silverspot. After a minute he picked up the white thing—a shell—and walked over past the spring, and here, among the docks and the skunk-cabbages, he unearthed a pile of shells and other white, shiny things. He spread them out in the sun, turned them over, lifted them one by one in his beak, dropped them, nestled on them as though they were eggs, toyed with them and gloated over them like a miser. This was his hobby, his weakness. He could not have explained *why* he enjoyed them, any more than a boy can explain why he collects postage-stamps, or a girl why she prefers pearls to rubies; but his pleasure in them was very real, and after half an hour he covered them all, including the new one, with earth and leaves, and flew off. I went at once to the spot and examined the hoard; there was about a hatful in all, chiefly white pebbles, clam-shells, and some bits of tin, but there was also the handle of a china cup, which must have been the gem of the collection. That was the last time I saw them. Silverspot knew that I had found his treasures, and he removed them at once; where I never knew.

Silverspot was a crow of the world. He was truly a successful crow. He lived in a region that, though full of dangers, abounded with food. In the old, unrepaired nest he raised a brood each year with his wife, whom, by the way, I never could distinguish, and when the crows again gathered together he was their acknowledged chief.

The reassembling takes place about the end of June—the young crows with their bob-tails, soft wings, and falsetto voices are brought by their parents, whom they nearly equal in size, and introduced to society at the old pine woods, a woods that is at once their fortress and college. Here they find security in numbers and in lofty yet sheltered perches, and here they begin their schooling and are taught all the secrets of success in crow life, and in crow life the least failure does not simply mean begin again. It means *death*.

The first week or two after their arrival is spent by the young ones in getting acquainted, for each crow must know personally all the others in the band. Their parents meanwhile have time to rest a little after the work of raising them, for now the youngsters are able to feed themselves and roost on a branch in a row, just like big folks.

In a week or two the moulting season comes. At this time the old crows are usually irritable and nervous, but it does not stop them from beginning to drill the youngsters, who, of course, do not much enjoy the punishment and nagging they get so soon after they have been mamma's own darlings. But it is all for their good, as the old lady said when she skinned the eels, and old Silverspot is an excellent teacher. Sometimes he seems to make a speech to them. What he says I cannot guess, but, judging by the way they receive it, it must be extremely witty. Each morning there is a company drill, for the young ones naturally drop into two or three squads according to their age and strength. The rest of the day they forage with their parents.

When at length September comes we find a great change. The rabble of silly little crows have begun to learn sense. The delicate blue iris of their eyes, the sign of a fool-crow, has given place to the dark brown eye of the old stager. They know their drill now and have learned sentry duty. They have been taught guns and traps and taken a special course in wire-worms and greencorn. They know that a fat old farmer's wife is much less dangerous, though so much larger, than her fifteen-year-old son, and they can tell the boy from his sister. They know that an umbrella is not a gun, and they can count up to six, which is fair for young crows, though Silverspot can go up nearly to thirty. They know the smell of gunpowder and the south side of a hemlock-tree, and begin to plume themselves upon being crows of the world. They always fold their wings three times after alighting, to be sure that it is neatly done. They know how to worry a fox into giving up half his dinner, and also that when the kingbird or the purple martin assails them they must dash into a bush, for it is as impossible to fight the little pests as it is for the fat apple-woman to catch the small boys who have raided her basket. All these things do the young crows know; but they have taken no lessons in egg-hunting yet, for it is not the season. They are unacquainted with clams, and have never tasted horses' eyes, or seen sprouted corn, and they don't know a thing about travel, the greatest educator of all. They did not think of that two months ago, and since then they have thought of it, but have learned to wait till their betters are ready.

September sees a great change in the old crows, too. Their moulting is over. They are now in full feather again and proud of the handsome coats. Their health is again good, and with it their tempers are improved. Even old Silverspot, the strict teacher, becomes quite jolly, and the youngsters, who have long ago learned to respect him, begin really to love him.

He has hammered away at drill, teaching them all the signals and words of command in use, and now it is a pleasure to see them in the early morning.

"*Company I!*" the old chieftain would cry in crow, and Company I would answer with a great clamor.

"*Fly!*" and himself leading them, they would all fly straight forward.

"*Mount!*" and straight upward they turned in a moment.

"*Bunch!*" and they all massed into a dense black flock.

"*Scatter!*" and they spread out like leaves before the wind.

"*Form line!*" and they strung out into the long line of ordinary flight.

"*Descend!*" and they all dropped nearly to the ground.

"*Forage!*" and they alighted and scattered about to feed, while two of the permanent sentries mounted duty—one on a tree to the right, the other on a mound to the far left. A minute or two later Silverspot would cry out, "*A man with a gun!*" The sentries repeated the cry and the company flew at once in open order as quickly as possible toward the tree. Once behind these, they formed line again in safety and returned to the home pines.

Sentry duty is not taken in turn by all the crows, but a certain number whose watchfulness has been often proved are the perpetual sentries, and are expected to watch and forage at the same time. Rather hard on them it seems to us, but it works well and the crow organization is admitted by all birds to be the very best is existence.

Finally, each November sees the troop sail away southward to learn new modes of life, new landmarks and new kinds of food, under the guidance of the ever-wise Silverspot.

III

There is only one time when a crow is a fool, and that is at night. There is only one bird that terrifies the crow, and that is the owl. When, therefore, these come together it is a woeful thing for the sable birds. The distant hoot of an owl after dark is enough to make them withdraw their heads from under their wings, and sit trembling and miserable till morning. In very cold weather the exposure of their faces thus has often resulted in a crow having one or both of his eyes frozen, so that blindness followed and therefore death. There are no hospitals for sick crows.

But with the morning their courage comes again, and arousing themselves they ransack the woods for a mile around till they find that owl, and if they do not kill him they at least worry him half to death and drive him twenty miles away.

In 1893 the crows had come as usual to Castle Frank. I was walking in these woods a few days afterward when I chanced upon the track of a rabbit that had been running at full speed over the snow and dodging about among the trees as though pursued. Strange to tell, I could see no track of the pursuer. I followed the trail and presently saw a drop of blood on the snow, and a little farther on found the partly devoured remains of a little brown bunny. What had killed him was a mystery until a careful search showed in the snow a great double-toed track and a beautiful pencilled brown feather. Then all was clear—*a horned owl*. Half an hour later, in passing again by the place, there, in a tree, within ten feet of the bones of his victim, was the fierce-eyed owl himself. The murderer still hung about the scene of his crime. For once circumstantial evidence had not lied. At my approach he gave a guttural *"grr-oo"* and flew off with low flagging flight to haunt the distant sombre woods.

Two days afterward, at dawn, there was a great uproar among the crows. I went out early to see, and found some black feathers drifting over the snow. I followed up the wind in the direction from which they came and soon saw the bloody remains of a crow and the great double-toed track which again told me that the murderer was the owl. All around were signs of the struggle, but the fell destroyer was too strong. The poor crow had been dragged from his perch at night, when the darkness had put him at a hopeless disadvantage.

I turned over the remains, and by chance unburied the head—then started with an exclamation of sorrow. Alas! It was the head of old Silverspot. His long life of usefulness to his tribe was over—slain at last by the owl that he had taught so many hundreds of young crows to beware of.

The old nest on the Sugar Loaf is abandoned now. The crows still come in spring-time to Castle Frank but without their famous leader their numbers are dwindling, and soon they will be seen no more about the old pine-grove in which they and their forefathers had lived and learned for ages.

W. A. FRASER (1857-1933)
"The Law of the Boundaries" from *Mooswa and Others of the Boundaries* (1900)

William Alexander Fraser was born in River John, Nova Scotia, and educated in the United States. He had prospected in India and the Canadian Northwest before starting his career as a writer of popular, frequently exotic fiction. After a period in the United States, he settled in Georgetown, Ontario, and spent his final years in Toronto. His stories, in which he incorporated the sights and lore gleaned from extensive travelling, were well liked in their day. Among his most popular books were *The Eye of a God and Other Tales of the East and West* (1899), *Mooswa and Others of the Boundaries* (1900), *The Sa'zada Tales* (1905), and *Thoroughbreds* (1920).

As he states in the introduction to *Mooswa*, the tale is based on his experiences as a hunter-adventurer "on the Athabasca and Saskatchewan Rivers in the far North-West of Canada". Fraser calls his novel "simple" and "light", but to modern eyes it is a naturalist's *tour de force*. He manages a large cast of vividly individualized animal characters, who not only formulate their own laws and discipline recalcitrant brethren (the murdering lynx Pisew is hanged and left as carrion), but, without

straining credibility, rescue the injured son of the Hudson's Bay Company factor, "the Man-Cub". Nor does the animals' ability to converse in an intelligent and colloquial manner lessen credibility, an overall verisimilitude being achieved through their plausible actions and the careful descriptions of the natural environment. In its account of the mystical bonding of noble wild animals and caring humans and in the firmly upheld Law of the Boundaries, *Mooswa* recalls Rudyard Kipling's *Jungle Books* (1894-5). The Bible is also suggested by the sovereignty of the tribe and its wanderings; the figure of the patriarchal moose; the Law, which is as important as an Old Testament covenant; and the diction, which often has a biblical ring.

Mooswa was complemented by the romantically realistic illustrations of the Canadian artist Arthur Heming (1870-1940), which were considered so saleable by the New York publisher, Scribner's, that they recovered Heming's fee by selling the originals from their Fifth Avenue shop window. Heming illustrated three more books by Fraser: *The Outcasts* (1901), *The Sa'zada Tales*, and *The Three Sapphires* (1918).

THE LAW OF THE BOUNDARIES

THE DWELLERS OF THE BOUNDARIES AND
THEIR NAMES IN THE CREE
INDIAN LANGUAGE

MOOSWA, *the Moose*. Protector of The Boy.

MUSKWA, *the Bear*.

BLACK FOX, *King of the Boundaries*.

THE RED WIDOW, *Black Fox's Mother*.

CROSS-STRIPES, *Black Fox's Baby Brother*.

ROF, *the Blue Wolf*. Leader of the Gray Wolf Pack.

CARCAJOU, *the Wolverine*. Lieutenant to Black King. and known as the "Devil of the Woods".

PISEW, *the Lynx*. Possessed of a cat-like treachery.

UMISK, *the Beaver*. Known for his honest industry.

WAPOOS, *the Rabbit* (really a Hare). The meat food for Man and Beast in the Boundaries.

WAPISTAN, *the Marten*. With fur like the Sable

NEKIK, *the Otter*. An eater of Fish.

SAKWASEW, *the Mink*. Would sell his Mother for a Fish.

WUCHUSK, *the Muskrat*. A houseless vagabond who admired Umisk, the Beaver.

SIKAK, *the Skunk*. A chap to be avoided, and who broke up the party at Nekik's slide.

WENUSK, *the Badger*.

WUCHAK, *the Fisher*.

WHISKY-JACK, *the Canada Jay*. A sharp-tongued Gossip.

COUGAR, EAGLE, BUFFALO, ANT, and CARIBOU.

WIE-SAH-KE-CHACK. Legendary God of the Indians, who could change himself into an animal at will.

FRANÇOIS, *French Half-breed Trapper*.

NICHEMOUS, *Half-breed hunter who tried to kill Muskwa*.

TRAPPERS, HALF-BREEDS, and TRAIN DOGS.

ROD, *The Boy*. Son of Donald MacGregor, formerly Factor to Hudson's Bay Company at Fort Resolution.

When Rod was a little chap, Mooswa had been brought into Fort Resolution as a calf, his mother having been killed, and they became playmates. Then MacGregor was moved to Edmonton, and Rod was brought up in civilization until he was fourteen, when he got permission to go back to the Athabasca for a Winter's trapping with François, who was an old servant of the Factor's. This story is of that Winter. Mooswa had been turned loose in the forest by Factor MacGregor when leaving the Fort.

THE BOUNDARIES. The greet Spruce forests and Muskeg lands lying between the Saskatchewan River, the Arctic Ocean, and the Rocky Mountains—being the home of the fur-bearing animals.

*   *   *

Three days later, as had been spoken in the Council, Black King, accompanied by three Fox Brothers, and his Mother the Red Widow, crept cautiously into the open space that was fringed by a tangle of Red and Gray Willows, inside of which grew a second frieze of Raspberry Bushes, sat on his haunches and peered discontentedly, furtively about. There was nobody, nothing in sight—nothing but the dilapidated old Hudson's Bay Company's Log Shack that had been a Trading Post, and against which Time had leaned so heavily that the rotted logs were sent sprawling in a disconsolate heap.

"This does not look overmuch like our Council Court, does it, Dame?" he asked of the Red Widow. "I, the King, am first to arrive—ah, here is Rof!" as Blue Wolf slouched into the open, his froth-lined jaws swinging low in suspicious watchfulness.

"I'm late," he growled, sniffing at each bush and stump as he made the circuit of the Court. "What! only Your Majesty and the Red Widow here as yet. It's bad form for our Comrades to keep the King waiting."

While Blue Wolf was still speaking the Willows were thrust open as though a tree had crashed through them, and Mooswa's massive head protruded, just for all the world as if hanging from a wall in the hall of some great house. His Chinese-shaped eyes blinked at the light. "May I be knock-kneed," he wheezed plaintively, "if it didn't take me longer to do those thirty miles this morning than I thought it would—the going was so soft. I should have been here on time, though, if I hadn't struck just the loveliest patch of my favourite weed at Little Rapids—where the fire swept last year, you know."

"That's what the Men call Fire-weed," cried Carcajou, pushing his strong body through the fringe of berry bushes.

"That's because they don't know," retorted Mooswa; "and because it always grows in good soil after the Fire has passed, I suppose."

"Where does the seed come from, Mooswa?" asked Lynx, who had come up while they were talking. "Does the Fire bring it?"

"I don't know," answered the Bull Moose.

"It is not written in Man's books, either," affirmed Carcajou.

"Can the King, who is so wise, tell us?" pleaded Fisher, who had arrived.

"Manitou sends it!" Black Fox asserted decisively.

"The King answers worthily," declared Wolverine. "If Mooswa can stand in the Fire-flower until it tops his back, and eat of the juice-filled stalk without straining his short neck until his belly is like the gorge of a Sturgeon, what matters how it has come. Let the Men, who are silly creatures, bother over that. Manitou has sent it, and it is good; that is enough for Mooswa."

"You are late, Nekik," said the King, severely; "and you, too, Sakwasu."

"I am lame!" pleaded Otter.

"My ear is bleeding!" said Mink.

"Who got the Fish?" queried Carcajou. They both tried to look very innocent.

"What Fish?" asked Black Fox.

"My Fish," replied Mink.

"Mine!" claimed Otter, in the same breath.

Wolverine winked solemnly at the Red Widow.

"Yap! that won't do—been fighting!" came from the King.

"It was a Doré, Your Majesty," pleaded Sakwasu, "and I caught him first."

"Just as I dove for him," declared Otter, "Sakwasu followed after and tried to take him from me—a great big Fish it was. I've been fishing for four years, but this was the biggest Doré I ever saw—why, he was the length of Pisew."

"A Fisherman's lie," quoth the Red Widow.

"Who got the Doré? That's the main question," demanded Carcajou.

"He escaped," replied Nekik, sorrowfully; "and we have come to the Meeting without any breakfast."

"Bah! Bah! Bah!" laughed Blue Wolf; "that's rich! Hey, Muskwa, you heard the end of the story—isn't it good?"

"I, too, have had no breakfast," declared Muskwa, "so I don't see the point—it's not a bit funny. Seven hard-baked Ant Hills have I torn up in the grass-flat down by the river, and not a single dweller in one of them. My arms ache, for the clay was hard; and the dust has choked up my lungs. Wuf-f-f! I could hardly get my breath coming up the hill, and I have more mortar in my lungs than Ants in my stomach."

"Are there no Berries to be had, then, Muskwa?" asked Wapistan.

"Oh, yes; there are Berries hereabouts, but they're all hard and bitter. The white Dogberries, and the pink Buffalo-berries, and the Wolf-willow berries—what are they! Perhaps not to be despised in this Year of Famine, for they pucker up one's stomach until a Cub's ration fills it; but the Saskatoons are now dry on the Bush, and I miss them sorely. Gluck! they're the berries—full of oil, not vinegar; a feed of them is like eating a little Sucking Pig."

"What's a Sucking Pig?" queried Lynx; "I never saw one growing."

"I know," declared Carcajou. "The Priest over at Wapiscaw had six little white fellows in a small corral. They had voices like Pallas, the Black Eagle. I could always tell when they were being fed, their wondrous song reached a good three miles."

"That's where I got mine," remarked Muskwa, looking cautiously about to see that there were no eavesdroppers; "I had three, and the Priest keeps three. But talking of food, one Summer I crossed the great up-hills that Men call Rockies, and along the rivers of that land grows just the loveliest Berry any poor Bear ever ate."

"Saskatoons?" queried Carcajou.

"No, the Salmon Berry—great, yellow, juicy chaps, the size of Mooswa's nose."

"Fat Birds! what a sized Berry!" ejaculated the Widow, dubiously.

"Well, almost as big," modified Muskwa; "and sweet and nippy. Ugh! ugh! It was like eating a handful of the fattest black Ants you ever tasted."

"I don't eat Ants," declared the Red Widow.

"Neither did I this morning, I'm sorry to say," added Bear, hungrily.

"Weren't they hairy little Beggars, Muskwa?" asked Blue Wolf, harking back longingly to the meat food.

"What, the Salmon Berries?"

"No; the Padre's little Pigs at Wapiscaw."

"Yes, somewhat; I had bristles in my teeth for a week—awfully coarse fur they wore. But they were noisy little rats—the screeching gave me an earache. Huf, huf, huh! You should have seen the Factor, who is a fat, pot-bellied little Chap, built like Carcajou, come running with his short Otter-shaped legs when he heard me among the Pigs."

"What did you do, Muskwa—weren't you afraid?" asked the Red Widow.

"I threw a little Pig out of the corral and he took to the Forest. The Factor in his excitement ran after him, and I laughed so much to see this that I really couldn't eat a fourth Pig."

"But you did well," cried Black King; "there's nothing like a good laugh at meal-time to aid digestion."

"I thought they would eat like that, Muskwa," continued Blue Wolf. "You remember the thick, white-furred animals they once brought to the Mission at Lac La Biche?"

"Sheep," interposed Mooswa, "I remember them; stupid creatures they were—always frightened by something; and always bunching up together like the Plain Buffalo, so that a Killer had more slaying than running to do amongst them."

"That was the worst of it," declared Blue Wolf. "My Pack acted as foolishly as Man did with the Buffalo—killed them all off in a single season, for that very reason."

"And for that trick Man put the blood-bounty on your scalp," cried Carcajou.

"Oh, the bounty doesn't matter so long as I keep the scalp on my own head. But, as I was going to say, the queer fur they had got into my teeth, and made me fair furious. Where one Sheep would have sufficed for my supper, I killed three—though I'm generally of an even temper. The Priest did much good in this country—"

"Bringing in the Sheep, eh?" interrupted Carcajou.

"Perhaps, perhaps; each one according as his interests are affected."

"The Priests are a benefit," asserted Marten. "The Father at Little Slave Lake had a corral full of the loveliest tame Grouse—Chickens, they called them. They were like the Sheep, silly enough to please the laziest Hunter."

"Did you join the Mission, Brother?" asked Carcajou, licking his chops hungrily.

"For three nights," answered Wapistan, "then I left it, carrying a scar on my hip from the snap of a white bob-tailed Dog they call a Fox-terrier. A busy, meddlesome, yelping little cur, lacking the composure of a Dweller in the Boundaries. I became disgusted at his clatter and cleared out."

"A Fox *what?*" asked the Red Widow. "He was not of our tribe to interfere with a Comrade's Kill."

"It must have been great hunting," remarked Black King, his mouth watering at the idea of a corral full of Chickens.

"It was!" asserted Wapistan. "All in a row they sat, shoulder to shoulder—it was night, you know. They simply blinked at me with their glassy eyes, and exclaimed, "Peek! Peek!" until I cut their throats. Yes, the Mission is a good thing."

"It is," concurred Black King—"they should establish more of them. But where in the world is Chatterbox, the Jay?"

"Gabbler the Fool must have trailed in with a party of Men going down the river," suggested Carcajou. "Nothing but eating would keep him away from a party of talkers."

"Well, Comrades," said Black King, "shall the Boundaries be the same as last year? Are there any changes to be made?"

"I roam everywhere; is that not so, King?" asked Muskwa.

"Yes; but not eat everywhere. There is truce for the young Beaver, because workmen are not free to the Kill."

"I have not eaten of Trowel Tail's Children," declared Muskwa, proudly. "I have kept the Law of the Boundaries."

"And yet he has lost two sons," said Black Fox, looking sternly about.

A tear trickled down the sandy beard of Beaver and glistened on his black nose.

"Two sturdy Sons, Your Majesty, a year old. Next year, or the year after, they would have gone out and built lodges of their own. Such plasterers I never saw in my life. Why, their work was as smooth as the inner bark of the Poplar; and no two Beavers on the whole length of Pelican River could cut down a tree with them."

"Oh, never mind their virtues, Trowel Tail," interrupted Carcajou, heartlessly; "they are dead—that is the main thing; and who killed them, the question. Who broke the Boundary Law is what we want to know."

"Whisky-Jack should be here during the inquiry," grumbled the King. "He's our detective—Jack sees everything, tells everything, and finds out everything. Shouldn't wonder but he knows—strange that he's not with us."

"Must have struck some Men friends, Your Majesty," said the Bull Moose. "As I drank at the river, twenty miles up, one of those floating houses the Traders use passed with two Men in it. There was the smell of hot Meat came to me, and if Jack was within a Bird's scent of the river, which is a long distance, he also would know of the food."

"Very likely, Mooswa," rejoined Black King. "A cooked pork rind would coax Jay from his duty any time. We must go on with the enquiry without him. Who broke the Law of the Boundaries and killed Umisk's two Sons?" he demanded sternly.

"I didn't," wheezed Mooswa, rubbing his big, soft nose caressingly down Beaver's back, as the latter sat on one of the old stumps. "I have kept the law. Like Muskwa I roam from lake to lake, and from river to river; but I kill no one—that is, with one exception."

"That was within the law," asserted the King. "for we kill in our own defence."

"I think it was Pisew," whispered the Red Widow. "See the Sneak's eye. Call him up, O Son, and command him to look straight into your Royal Face and say if he has kept the law."

"Pisew," commanded Black Fox, "come closer!"

Lynx started guiltily at the call of his name. There was something soft and unpleasant in the slipping sound of his big muffled feet as he walked toward the King.

"Has Pisew kept the Law of the Boundaries?" asked Black King, sternly, looking full in the mustached face of the slim-bodied cat.

Lynx turned his head sideways, and his eyes sought to avoid those of the questioner.

"Your Majesty, I roam from the Pelican on one side, to Fish Creek on the other; and the law is that therein I, who eat flesh, may kill Wapoos the Rabbit. This year it has been hard living, Your Majesty—hard living. Because of the fire, Wapoos fled beyond the waters of the creeks, and I have eaten of the things that could not fly the Boundaries—Mice, and Frogs, and Slugs: a diet that is horrible to think of. Look, Your Majesty, at my gaunt sides—am I not like one that is already skinned by the Trappers?"

"He is making much talk," whispered the Red Widow, "to the end that you forget the murder of Trowel Tail's Sons."

"Didst like Beaver Meat?" queried Black King, abruptly.

"I am not the slayer of Umisk's children," denied Lynx. "It was Wapoos, or Whisky-Jack; they are mischief makers, and ready for any evil."

"Oh, you silly liar!" cried Carcajou, in derision. "Wapoos the Rabbit kill a Beaver? Why not say the Moon came down and ate them up. Thou hast a sharp nose and a full appetite, but little brain."

"He is a poor liar!" remarked the Red Widow.

"I have kept the law," whined Lynx. "I have eaten so little that I am starved."

"What shall we do, Brothers, about the murdered Sons of Umisk? Beaver is the worker of our lands. But for him, and the dams he builds, the Muskegs would soon dry up, the fires would burn the Forests, and we should have no place to live. If we kill the Sons, presently there will be no workers—nobody but ourselves who are Killers." Black Fox thus put the case wisely to the others.

"Gr-a-a-h-wuh! let me speak," cried Blue Wolf. "Pisew has done this thing. If any in my Pack make a kill and I come to speak of it, do I not know from their eyes that grow tired, which it is?"

Said the Lieutenant, Carcajou: "I think you are right, Rof; but you can't hang a Comrade because he has weak eyes. No one has seen Pisew make the kill. We must have a new law, Your Majesty. That if again Kit-Beaver, or Cub-Fox, or Babe-Wapoos, or Young-Anyone is slain for eating, we shall all, sitting in Council, decide who is to pay the penalty. I think that will stop this murderous poaching."

"It will," whispered the Red Widow. "Lynx will never touch one of them again. He knows what Carcajou means."

"That is a new law, then," cried the King. "If any of Umisk's children are killed by one of us, sitting in Council we shall decide who is to be executed for the crime."

"Please, Your Majesty," squeaked Rabbit, "I keep the Boundary Law, but others do not. From Beaver's dam to the Pelican, straighter than a Man's trail, are my three Run-ways. My Cousin's family has three more; and in the Muskeg our streets run clear to view. Beyond our Run-ways we do not go. Nor do we build houses in violation of the law—only roads are we allowed, and these we have made. In the Muskeg parks, the nice open places Beaver has formed by damming back the waters, we labor.

"When the young Spruce are growing, and would choke up the park, we strip the bark off and they die, and the open is still with us. Neither do we kill any Animal, nor make trouble for them—keeping well within the law. Are we not ourselves food for all the Animal Kingdom? Lynx lives off us, and Marten lives off us, and Fox lives off us, and Wolf and Bear sometimes. Neither I nor my Tribe complains, because that law is older than the laws we make ourselves.

"But have we not certain rights which are known to the Council? For one hour in the morning, and one hour in the evening, just when the Sun and the Stars change their season of toil, are we not to be free from the Hunting?"

"Yes, it is written," replied Black King, "that no one shall kill Wapoos at the hour of dusk and the hour of dawn. Has anyone done so?"

"If they have, it's a shame!" cried Carcajou. "I do not eat Wapoos; but if everything else fails—if the Fish fail, if there are no Berries, if the Nuts and the Seeds are dried in the heart before they ripen, we still have Wapoos to carry us over. The Indians know this—it is of their history; and many a time has Wapoos, the Rabbit, our Little Brother, saved them from starvation."

"Who has slain Wapoos at the forbidden hour?" thundered Black King.

Again there was denial all around the circle; and again everybody felt convinced that Lynx was the breaker of the law. Said Black Fox: "It is well because of the new ruling we have passed, I think. If again Wapoos is killed or hunted at the forbidden hours, we shall decide in Council who must die."

"Also, O King," still pleaded Rabbit, "for all time have we claimed another protection. You know our way of life. For seven years we go on peopling the streets of our Muskeg Cities, growing more plentiful all the time, until there is a great population. Then comes the sickness on The Seventh Year, and we die off like Flies."

"It has been so for sixty years", assented Mooswa. "My father, who is sixty, has always known of this thing."

"For a hundred times sixty, Brother," quoth Carcajou; "it is so written in the legends of the Indians."

"It is a queer sickness," continued Wapoos. "The lumps come in our throats, and under our arms, and it kills. Your Majesty knows the Law of the Seventh Season."

"Yes, it is that no one shall eat Wapoos that year, or next."

"Most wise ruling!" concurred Carcajou. "The Rabbits with the lumps in their necks are poisonous. Besides, when there are so few of them, if they were eaten, the food supply of the Boundaries would be forever gone. A most wise rule."

"Has any one violated this protection-right?" asked the King.

"Yes, Your Majesty. This is the Seventh Year, is it not?" said Rabbit.

"Bless me! so it is," exclaimed Mooswa, thoughtfully. "I, who do not eat Rabbits, have paid no attention to the calendar. I wondered what made the woods so silent and dreary; that's just it. No pudgy little Wapooses darting across one's path. Why, now I remember, last year, The Year of the Plenty, when I laid down for a rest they'd be all about me. Actually sat up on my side many a time."

"Yes, it's the Seventh Year," whined Lynx; "look how thin I am. Perhaps miles and miles of river bank, and not even a Frog to be had."

"Alas! it's the Plague-year," declared Wapoos; "and my whole family were stricken with the sickness. They died off one—by—one—" Here he stopped, and covered his big, sympathetic eyes with soft, fur-ruffled hands. His tender heart choked.

Mooswa sniffed through his big nose, and browsed absent-mindedly off the Gray-willows. My! but they were bitter—he never ate them at any time; but one must do something when a Father is talking about his dead Children.

"Did they all die, Wapoos? asked Otter; and in his black snake-like eyes there actually glistened a tear of sympathy.

"Yes; and our whole city was almost depopulated."

"Dreadful!" cried Carcajou.

"The nearest neighbor left me was a Widow on the third main Runway—two cross-paths from my lane. All her family died off, even the Husband. We were a great help to each other in the way of consolation, and became fast friends. Yesterday morning, when I called to talk over our affliction, there was nothing left of her but a beautiful, white, fluffy tail."

"Horrible! oh, the Wretch!" screamed Black Fox's Mother; "to treat a Widow that way—eat her!"

"If I knew who did it," growled Muskwa, savagely, "I would break his neck with one stroke of my fist. Poor little Wapoos! come over here. Eat these Black Currants that I've just picked—I don't want them."

"That is a most criminal breach of the law," said the King, with emphasis. "If Wapoos can prove who did it, we'll give the culprit quick justice."

"Flif—fluf, flif—fluf," came the sound of wings at this juncture, and with an erratic swoop Whisky-Jack shot into the circle.

He was trembling with excitement—something of tremendous importance had occurred; every blue-gray feather of his coat vibrated with it. He strutted about to catch his breath, and his walk was the walk of one who feels his superiority.

"Good-morning, Glib-tongue!" greeted Carcajou.

"Welcome, Clerk!" said the King, graciously.

"Hop up on my antler," murmured Mooswa, condescendingly; "you'll get your throat full of dust down there."

Whisky-Jack swished up on the big platter-like leaf that was the first spread of Mooswa's lordly crown. He picked a remnant of meat food from his beak with his big toe, coughed three times impressively, and commenced:—

"Comrades, who do you suppose has come within our Boundaries?"

"Is it Cougar, the Slayer? asked Black King, apprehensively."

"Is it Death Song, the Rattler, he who glides?" cried Marten, his little legs trembling with fear.

"Has my cousin, Ookistutoowan the Grizzly, come down from his home in the up-hills to dispute with me the way of the road?" queried Black Bear, Muskwa. "I am ready for him!" he declared, shaking his back like a huge St. Bernard.

"Didst see Train Dogs, bearer of ill news?" demanded Wolf. "Ur-r-r! I fear not!" and he bared his great yellow fangs viciously.

"Worse, worse still!" piped Whisky-Jack, spreading his wings out, and sloping his small round head down toward them. "Worse than any you have mentioned—some one to make you all tremble."

"Tell us, tell us!" cried Carcajou. "One would think Wiesahkechack had come back from his Spirit Home where the Northern Lights grow."

"*François has come!*" declared the Jay, in an even, dramatic voice.

The silence of consternation settled over the group.

"François and *The Boy!*" added Jack.

"What's a Boy?" asked Lynx.

"I know," asserted Mooswa. "When I was a calf in the Company's corral at Fort Resolution, I played with a Boy, the Factor's Man-Cub. Great Horns! he was nice. Many a time he gave me to eat the queer grass things that grew in the Factor's garden."

"Where is François?" queried the King.

"At Red Stone Brook—he and The Boy. I had breakfast with them."

"Renegade!" sneered Carcajou.

"And François says they will stay here all Winter and kill fur. There are three big Bear Traps in the outfit—I saw them, Muskwa; what think you? Great steel jaws to them, with hungry teeth. They would crack the leg of a Moose, even a Buffalo; and there are Number Four Traps for Umisk and Nekik; and smaller ones for you, Mister Marten—many of them. Oh, my! but it's nice to have an eight-dollar coat. All the Thief-trappers in the land covet it.

"And François has an Ironstick, and The Boy has an Ironstick, and there will be great sport here all Winter. That's what François said, and I think it is true—not that a Halfbreed sticks to the truth over-close."

The Hunt-fear settled over the gathering. No one had heart even to check the spiteful gibes of their feathered Clerk. The Law of the Bound-aries, and the suspicious evidence of its violation that pointed to Lynx, were forgotten—which was, perhaps, a good thing for that unprincipled poacher.

Black King was first to break the fear-silence.

"Subjects, draw close, for already it has come to us that we have need of all our wisdom, and all our loyalty one to another, and the full strength of our laws."

Silently they bunched up; then he proceeded:—

"François is a great Hunter. He has the cunning of Wolverine, the strength of Muskwa, the speed of mine own people, and the endurance of Mooswa. Besides, there are the Traps, and the Ironstick; and Snares made from Deer-sinew and Cod-line. The soft strong cord which Man weaves. Also will this Evil Slayer, who is but a vile Halfbreed, have the White Powder of Death in a tiny bottle—such a small bottle, and yet holding enough Devil-medicine to slay every Dweller in the Bound-aries."

"That it will, Your Majesty," confirmed Jack; "and it kills while you breathe thrice—so, If-f-h, if-f-h, if-f-h! and you fall—your legs kick out stiff, and you are dead. I've seen it do its terrible work."

"Just so," assented Black King. "The use of that is against Man's law, even; but François cares not, so be it the Red-coats know not of its use. Now must we take an oath to help one the other, if we prefer not to have our coats nailed on the Hunt-Man's Shack walls, or stretched on the wedge-boards he uses for the hides of Otter, and Mink, and Fisher, and myself. Even Muskrat and Pisew go on a wedgeboard when they are skinned. You, Beaver, and Muskwa, and Mooswa have your skins stretched by iron thorns on the side of a Shack.

"Now take we the oath?" he asked, looking from one to the other.

A murmur of eager assent started with the deep bass of Blue Wolf and died away in the plaintive treble of Wapoos.

"Then, listen and repeat with me," he commanded.

THE OATH OF THE BOUNDARIES

" 'We, Dwellers within the Boundaries, swear by the Spirit of Wiesah-kechack, who is God of the Indians and all Animals, that, come Trap, come Ironstick, come White-powdered Bait, come Snare, come Arrow, come what soe'er may, we will help each other, and warn each other, and keep ward for each other; in the Star-time and the Sun-time, in the Flower-time and the Snow-time; that the call of one for help shall be the call of all; and the fight of one shall be the fight of all; and the enemy of one shall be the enemy of all.

" 'By the Mark that is on the tail of each of us, we swear this. By the White Tip that is on the tail of Fox; by the Black Gloss that is on the tail of Marten; by the Perfume that is on the tail of Sikak; by the great, bushy tail of Blue Wolf, and the short tail of Bear; the broad, hairless tail of Beaver, and the strong tapered tail of Otter; by the Kink that is in the tail of Mink; by the much-haired tail of Fisher; the white Cotton-tail of Rabbit, the fawn-coloured tail of Mooswa, and the Bob-tail of Lynx; by the feathered tail of Whisky-Jack: and all others according to their Tail-mark, we swear it.'

"Now," said Black King, "François will have his work cut out, for we are many against one."

"You forget The Boy, Your Majesty," interrupted Carcajou.

"Oh, he doesn't count," cried Jack, disdainfully. "He's a Moneas—which means a greenhorn. He's new to the Forest—has lived where the paths of Man are more plentiful than the Run-ways in Wapoos's Muskeg.

"Of course, personally, I don't mind their coming—like it; it means free food without far flying. Oh, but The Boy is a wasteful greenhorn. When he fried the white fat-meat, which is from the animal that dwells with Man, the Hog, he poured the juice out on the leaves, and the cold turned it into food like butter—white butter. Such rich living will make my voice soft. The Man-cub has a voice like mine—full of rich, sweet notes. Did any of you ever hear a Man or Man-cub sing 'Down upon the Suwanee River'? That's what The Boy sang this morning. But I don't know that river—it's not about here; and in my time I have flown far and wide over more broad streams than I have toes to my feet."

"Be still, empty-head!" cried the King, angrily. "You chatter as though the saving of our lives were good fun. Brother Carcajou, François needs no help. For five years he has followed me for my Black Coat—for five Winters I have eluded his Traps, and his Baits, and the cough of his Ironstick. But one never knows when the evil day is to come. Last Winter François trapped on Hay River. I was there; as you know, it is a great place for Black Currants."

"Do you eat the bitter, sour Berries, Your Majesty?" queried Marten.

"No, Silly; except for the flavour of them that is in the flesh of Gay Cock, the Pheasant. But it is in every child's book of the Fox tribe, that where Berries are thick, the Birds are many."

"How comes François here to the Pelican this year, then?" growled Blue Wolf.

"Because of the thing Men call Fate," answered Black King, learnedly; "though they do not understand the shape of it. We call it the Whisper of Wiesahkechack. Wiesahke whispered to me that because of the fire there were no Berries at Hay River, that the Birds had all come to the Pelican; and I have no doubt that He, who is the King of evil Mischief Makers, has also talked in thought-words to François, that here is much fur to be had for the killing."

"I should like to see François," exclaimed Nekik, the Otter.

"And The Boy!" suggested Mooswa. "It's years since I saw a Man-cub."

"W-h-e-u-f-f-!" ejaculated Muskwa. "I saw a Man once—Nichemous. Did I tell you about—"

"Save me from Owls!" interrupted Whisky-Jack; "that's your stock-story, old Squeaky Nose. I've heard it fifty times in the last two years."

The Bear stood rocking his big body back and forth while the saucy bird chattered.

"But I should like to see more of Man," he continued, when Jay had finished. "Tell me, Jack, do they always walk on their hind-legs—or only when they are going to kill or fight—as I do? I think we must be cousins," he went on, meditatively.

"You ought to be ashamed of it, then!" snapped the Bird.

"They leave a trail just like mine," proceeded Muskwa, paying no attention to the Jay. "I once saw a Man's track on the mud bank of the river; I could have sworn it was one of my family had passed—a long foot-print with a heel."

"Perhaps it was your own track—you are so terribly stupid at times," suggested Jack.

"*You* might have made that mistake," retorted Muskwa, "for you can't scent; but when I investigated with my nose, I knew that it was Man. There was the same horrible smell that came to me once as two of these creatures passed down the river in a canoe, whilst I was eating Berries by the water's edge. But you spend most of your time begging a living from these Men, Jack—tell me if they generally walk as I do, on all fours?"

"Long ago they did, Muskwa; when their brains were small, like yours. Then they developed, and got more sense, and learned to balance themselves on their hind-legs."

"What's the use of having four legs and only using two?" grunted Bear, with a dissatisfied air.

"You'll find out, my Fat Friend, if you come within range of the Iron-stick—what did Nichemous try to do? After that you won't ask silly questions, for François will take your skin, dry it in the sun, and put your brainless head on a tree as a Medicine Offering to the Hunt Spirit; and he'll take your big carcass home, and The Boy will help him eat it. Don't bother me about Man—if you want to know his ways, come and see for yourself."

"I'd like to, Clerk," answered Bear, humbly.

"They're going to build a house," asserted Whisky-Jack.

"A lodge!" exclaimed Beaver. "Oh, I must see that."

"What say you, Black King?" queried Carcajou. "May we all go tomorrow, and see this Trapper and The Boy—think you it's safe?"

"Better now than when the Traps are set and Firestick loaded."

So they arranged amongst themselves to go at dawn the next day, and watch from the bush François and Roderick.

Then the meeting broke up.

CHARLES G.D. ROBERTS (1860-1945)
"Wild Motherhood" from *The Kindred of the Wild* (1902)

Born in Douglas, New Brunswick, Roberts was the first Canadian man of letters and achieved an international reputation with over sixty books—collections of verse, light historical romances, nature stories, travel books, and histories. Following his graduation from the University of New Brunswick, he published a notable collection of poems, *Orion* (1880). He taught English literature at King's College in Windsor, Nova Scotia, from 1885 to 1895, after which he lived chiefly in New York (1897-1907) and on the Continent (1907-25), supporting himself by writing prose. He returned to Canada in 1925 and spent the rest of his life in Toronto. He was knighted in 1935.

Roberts' first collection of sportsmen and animal tales, *Earth's Enigmas: A Book of Animal and Nature Life*, appeared in 1896. When a demand for stories about animals developed after the publication two years later of Seton's *Wild Animals I have Known* (1898), Roberts soon explored the vein of the realistic animal story discovered by his contemporary. In *The Kindred of the Wild* (1902) he showed himself to be a master storyteller who attempted exact descriptions of animal behaviour while also producing narratives that are artistically and dramatically satisfying. In a short period he wrote several other classics in the genre: *The Watchers of the Trails* (1904), *Red Fox* (1905), and *The Haunters of the Silences* (1907). He was a fine apologist for this kind of writing, prefacing *The Kindred of the Wild* with an essay called "The Animal Story", in which he recognized that "in one form or another [it]is as old as the beginnings of literature". Roberts concludes: "It leads us back to the old kinship of earth without asking us to relinquish by way of toll any part of the wisdom of the ages."

In "Wild Motherhood" Roberts leads his readers back to this old kinship by showing how the desire to protect and provide is shared by animals and humans. Because his animals function both instinctively and rationally, Roberts was charged with anthropomorphism; his firm answer to this was that in his view animals are governed not only by instinct but by a form of reason.

WILD MOTHERHOOD

The deep snow in the moose-yard was trodden down to the moss, and darkly soiled with many days of occupancy. The young spruce and birch trees which lined the trodden paths were cropped of all but their toughest and coarsest branches; and the wall of loftier growth which fenced the yard was stripped of its tenderer twigs to the utmost height of the tall bull's neck. The available provender was all but gone, and the herd was in that restlessness which precedes a move to new pastures.

The herd of moose was a small one—three gaunt, rusty-brown, slouching cows, two ungainly calves of a lighter hue, and one huge, high-shouldered bull, whose sweep of palmated antlers bristled like a forest. Compared with the towering bulk of his forequarters, the massive depth of his roughmaned neck, the weight of the formidable antlers, the length and thickness of his clumsy, hooked muzzle with its prehensile upper lip, his lean and frayed hindquarters looked grotesquely diminutive. Surprised by three days of blinding snowfall, the great bull-moose had been forced to establish the yard for his herd in an unfavourable neighbourhood; and now he found himself confronted by the necessity of a long march through snow of such softness and depth as would make swift movement impossible and fetter him in the face of his enemies. In deep snow the moose can neither flee nor fight, at both of which he is adept under fair conditions; and deep snow, as he knew, is the opportunity of the wolf and the hunter. But in this case the herd had no choice. It was simply take the risk or starve.

That same night, when the moon was rising round and white behind the fir-tops, the tall bull breasted and trod down the snowy barriers, and led his herd off northward between the hemlock trunks and the jutting granite boulders. He moved slowly, his immense muzzle stretched straight out before him, the bony array of his antlers laid back level to avoid the hindrance of clinging boughs. Here and there a hollow under the level surface would set him plunging and wallowing for a moment, but in the main his giant strength enabled him to forage his way ahead with a steady majesty of might. Behind him, in dutiful line, came the three cows; and behind these, again, the calves followed at ease in a clear trail, their muzzles not outstretched like that of the leader, but drooping almost to the snow, their high shoulders working awkwardly at every stride. In utter silence, like dark, monstrous spectres, the line of strange shapes moved on; and down the bewildering, ever-rearranging forest corridors the ominous fingers of long moonlight felt curiously after them. When they had journeyed for some hours the herd came out upon a high and somewhat bare plateau, dotted sparsely with clumps of aspen, stunted yellow birch, and spruce. From this table-land the streaming northwest winds had swept the snow almost clean, carrying it off to fill the neighbouring valleys. The big bull, who knew where he was going and had no will to linger on the way, halted only for a few minutes' browsing, and then started forward on a long, swinging trot. At every stride his loose-hung, wild-cleft, spreading hoofs came sharply together with a flat, clacking noise. The rest of the line swept dutifully into place, and the herd was off.

But not all the herd. One of the calves, tempted a little aside by a thicket of special juiciness and savour, took alarm, and thought he was going to be left behind. He sprang forward, a powerful but clumsy stride, careless of his footing. A treacherous screen of snow-crusted scrub gave way, and he slid sprawling to the bottom of a little narrow gully or crevice, a natural pitfall. His mother, looking solicitously backward, saw him disappear. With a heave of her shoulders, a sweep of her long, hornless head, an anxious flick of her little naked tail, she swung out of the line and trotted swiftly to the rescue.

There was nothing she could do. The crevice was some ten or twelve feet long and five or six in width, with sides almost perpendicular. The calf could just reach its bushy edges with his upstretched muzzle, but he could get no foothold by which to clamber out. On every side he essayed it, falling back with a hoarse bleat from each frightened effort; while the mother, with head down and piteous eyes staring upon him, ran round and round the rim of the trap. At last, when he stopped and stood with palpitating sides and wide nostrils of terror, she, too, halted. Dropping awkwardly upon her knees in the snowy bushes, with loud, blowing breaths, she reached down her head to nose and comfort him with her sensitive muzzle. The calf leaned up as close as possible to her caresses. Under their tenderness the tremblings of his gaunt, pathetic knees presently ceased. And in this position the two remained almost motionless for an hour, under the white, unfriendly moon. The herd had gone on without them.

II

In the wolf's cave in the great blue and white wall of plaster-rock, miles back beside the rushing of the river, there was famine. The she-wolf, heavy and near her time, lay agonising in the darkest corner of the cave, licking in grim silence the raw stump of her right foreleg. Caught in a steel trap, she had gnawed off her own paw as the price of freedom. She could not hunt; and the hunting was bad that winter in the forest by the blue and white wall. The wapiti deer had migrated to safer ranges, and her gray mate, hunting alone, was hard put to it to keep starvation from the cave.

The gray wolf trotted briskly down the broken face of the plaster-rock, in the full glare of the moon, and stood for a moment to sniff the air that came blowing lightly but keenly over the stiff tops of the forest. The wind was clean. It gave him no tidings of a quarry. Descending hurriedly the last fifty yards of the slope, he plunged into the darkness of the fir woods. Soft as was the snow in those quiet recesses, it was yet sufficiently packed to support him as he trotted, noiseless and alert, on the broad-spreading pads of his paws. Furtive and fierce, he slipped through the shadow like a ghost. Across the open glades he fleeted more swiftly, a bright and sinister shape, his head swinging a little from side to side, every sense upon the watch. His direction was pretty steadily to the west of north.

He had travelled long, till the direction of the moon-shadows had taken a different angle to his path, when suddenly there came a scent upon the wind. He stopped, one foot up, arrested in his stride. The gray, cloudy brush of his tail stiffened out. His nostrils, held high to catch every waft of the new scent, dilated; and the edges of his upper lip came down over the white fangs, from which they had been snarlingly withdrawn. His pause was but for a breath or two. Yes, there was no mistaking it. The scene was moose—very far off, but moose, without question. He darted forward at a gallop, but with his muzzle still held high, following that scent up the wind.

Presently he struck the trail of the herd. An instant's scrutiny told his trained sense that there were calves and young cows, one or another of which he might hope to stampede by his cunning. The same instant's scrutiny revealed to him that the herd had passed nearly an hour ahead of him. Up went the gray cloud of his tail and down went his nose; and then he straightened himself to his top speed, compared to which the pace wherewith he had followed the scent up the wind was a mere casual sauntering.

When he emerged upon the open plateau and reached the spot where the herd had scattered to browse, he slackened his pace and went warily, peering from side to side. The cow-moose, lying down in the bushes to fondle her imprisoned young, was hidden from his sight for a moment; and so it chanced that before he discovered her he came between her and the wind. That scent—it was the taint of death to her. It went

through her frame like an electric shock. With a snort of fear and fury she heaved to her feet and stood, wide-eyed and with lowered brow, facing the menace.

The wolf heard that snorting challenge, and saw the awkward bulk of her shoulders as she rose above the scrub. His jaws wrinkled back tightly, baring the full length of his keen white fangs, and a greenish phosphorescent film seemed to pass suddenly across his narrowed eye-balls. But he did not spring at once to the attack. He was surprised. Moreover, he inferred the calf, from the presence of the cow apart from the rest of the herd. And a full-grown cow-moose, with the mother fury in her heart, he knew to be a dangerous adversary. Though she was hornless, he knew the force of her battering front, the swift, sharp stroke of her hoof, the dauntless intrepidity of her courage. Further, though his own courage and the avid urge of his hunger might have led him under other circumstances to attack forthwith, to-night he knew that he must take no chances. The cave in the blue and white rocks was depending on his success. His mate, wounded and heavy with young—if he let himself get disabled in this hunting she must perish miserably. With prudent tactics, therefore, he circled at a safe distance around the hidden pit; and around its rim circled the wary mother, presenting to him ceaseless the defiance of her huge and sullen front. By this means he easily concluded that the calf was a prisoner in the pit. This being the case, he knew that with patience and his experienced craft the game was safely his. He drew off some half-dozen paces, and sat upon his haunches contemplatively to weigh the situation. Everything had turned out most fortunately for his hunting, and food would no longer be scarce in the cave of the painted rocks.

III

That same night, in a cabin of unutterable loneliness some miles to the west of the trail from the moose-yard, a sallow-faced, lean backwoodsman was awakened by the moonlight streaming into his face through the small square window. He glanced at the embers of the open hearth, and knew that for the white maple logs to have so burned down he must have been sleeping a good six hours. And he had turned in soon after the early winter sunset. Rising on his elbow, he threw down the gaudy patchwork quilt of red, yellow, blue, and mottled squares, which draped the bunk in its corner against the rough log walls. He looked long at the thin face of his wife, whose pale brown hair lay over the bare arm crooked beneath her cheek. Her lips looked pathetically white in the decolourising rays which streamed through the window. His mouth, stubbled with a week's growth of dark beard, twitched curiously as he looked. Then he got up, very noiselessly. Stepping across the bare, hard room, whose austerity the moon made more austere, he gazed into a trundle-bed where a yellow-haired round-faced boy slept, with the chubby sprawling legs and arms of perfect security. The lad's face looked pale to his troubled eyes.

"It's fresh meat they want, the both of 'em," he muttered to himself. "They can't live and thrive on pork an' molasses, nohow!"

His big fingers, clumsily gentle, played for a moment with the child's yellow curls. Then he pulled a thick, gray homespun hunting-shirt over his head, hitched his heavy trousers up under his belt, clothed his feet in three pairs of home-knit socks and heavy cowhide moccasins, took down his rifle, cartridge-pouch, and snowshoes from their nails on the moss-chinked wall, cast one tender look on the sleepers' faces, and slipped out of the cabin door as silently as a shadow.

"I'll have fresh meat for them before next sundown," he vowed to himself.

Outside, amid the chips of his chopping, with a rough well-sweep on one hand and a rougher barn on the other, he knelt to put on his snowshoes. The cabin stood, a desolate, silver-gray dot in the waste of snow, naked to the steely skies of winter. With the curious improvidence of the backwoodsman, he had cut down every tree in the neighbourhood of the cabin, and the thick woods which might so well have sheltered him stood acres distant on every side. When he had settled the thongs of his snowshoes over his moccasins quite to his satisfaction, he straightened himself with a deep breath, pulled his cap well down over his ears, slung his rifle over his shoulder, and started out with the white moon in his face.

In the ancient forest, among the silent wilderness folk, things happen with the slow inexorableness of time. For days, for weeks, nothing may befall. Hour may tread noiselessly on hour, apparently working no change; yet all the time the forces are assembling, and at last doom strikes. The violence is swift, and soon done. And then the great, still world looks inscrutable, unhurried, changeless as before.

So, after long tranquillity, the forces of fate were assembling about that high plateau in the wilderness. The backwoodsman could no longer endure to see the woman and boy pining for the tonic, vitalizing juices of fresh meat. He was not a professional hunter. Absorbed in the clearing and securing of a farm in the free forest, he cared not to kill for the killing's sake. For his own part, he was well content with his salt pork, beans and molasses, and corn-meal mush; but when occasion called, he could handle a rifle as backwoodsmen should. On this night, he was all hunter, and his quiet, wide-open eye, alert for every woodland sign, had a fire in it that would have looked strange to the wife and child.

His long strides carried him swiftly through the glimmering glades. Journeying to the north of east, as the gray wolf had to the north of west, he too, before long, struck the trail of the moose, but at a point far beyond that at which the wolf had come upon it. So trampled and confused a trail it was, however, that for a time he took no note of the light wolf track among the heavy footprints of the moose. Suddenly it caught his eyes—one print on a smooth spread of snow, emphasised in a pour of unobstructed radiance. He stopped, scrutinised the trail minutely to assure himself he had but a single wolf to deal with, then resumed his march with new zest and springier pace. Hunting was not without its relish for him when it admitted some savour of the combat.

The cabin stood in the valley lands just back of the high plateau, and so it chanced that the backwoodsman had not far to travel that night. Where the trail broke into the open, he stopped, and reconnoitred cautiously through a screen of hemlock boughs. He saw the big gray wolf sitting straight up on his haunches, his tongue hanging out, contemplating securely his intended prey. He saw the dark shape of the cowmoose, obstinately confronting her foe, her hindquarters backed close up to the edge of the gully. He caught the fierce and anxious gleam of her eyes, as she rolled them backward for an instant's reassuring glance at her young one. And, though he could not see the calf in its prisoning pit, he understood the whole situation.

Well, there was a bounty on wolf-snouts, and this fellow's pelt was worth considering. As for the moose, he knew that not a broadside of cannon would scare her away from that hole in the rocks so long as the calf was in it. He took careful aim from his covert. At the report the wolf shot into the air, straightened out, and fell upon the snow, kicking dumbly, a bullet through his neck. As the light faded from his fierce eyes, with it faded out a vision of the cave in the painted rocks. In half a minute he lay still; and the cow-moose, startled by his convulsive leaps more than by the rifle-shot, blew and snorted, eyeing him with new suspicion. Her spacious flank was toward the hunter. He, with cool but hasty fingers, slipped a fresh cartridge into the breech, and aimed with care at the spot low down behind the fore-shoulder.

Again rang out the thin, vicious report, slapping the great silences in the face. The woodsman's aim was true. With a cough the moose fell forward on her knees. Then, with a mighty, shuddering effort, she got up, turned about, and fell again with her head over the edge of the crevice. Her awkward muzzle touched and twitched against the neck of the frightened calf, and with a heavy sigh she lay still.

The settler stepped out from his hiding-place and examined with deep satisfaction the results of his night's hunting. Already he saw the colour coming back into the pale cheeks of the woman and the child. The wolf's pelt and snout, too, he thought to himself, would get them both some little things they'd like, from the cross-roads store, next time he went in for corn-meal. Then, there was the calf—no meat like moose-veal, after all. He drew his knife from its sheath. But, no; he hated butchering. He slipped the knife back, reloaded his rifle, stepped to the side of the pit, and stood looking down at the baby captive, where it leaned nosing in piteous bewilderment at the head of its dead mother.

Again the woodsman changed his mind. He bit off a chew of black tobacco, and for some moments stood deliberating, stubbly chin in hand. "I'll save him for the boy to play with and bring up," he at last decided.

The Kindred of the Wild
A Book of Animal Life

10. STORIES, GAMES, AND PICTURES: CHILDREN'S PERIODICALS

Doubtless a great deal of instruction and good moral teaching may be inculcated in the pages of a magazine; but it must be by hints dropped incidentally here and there; by a few brisk, hearty statements of the difference between right and wrong; a sharp, clean thrust at falsehood, a sunny recognition of truth, a gracious application of politeness, an unwilling glimpse of the odious doings of the uncharitable and base.—Mary Mapes Dodge, "Children's Magazines", Scribner's Monthly (July 1873)

Magazines addressed specifically to boys or girls flourished in both England and the United States throughout the Golden Age. Entertaining and stultifying examples existed side by side, and were often bought by or for the same youngsters. Scores of magazines were intended to instil piety. *The Child's Own Magazine* (1852-?), emanating from the London Sunday School Union, tried hard to be engaging as well as pithy; but later periodicals of an uplifting moral character, like *Chatterbox* (1866-1943) and *Little Wide-Awake* (1875-92), were so pious and didactic that they had to rely on an excessive number of line drawings to hold their readers' attention while improving and admonishing them. On the other hand, the *Boy's Own* volumes, begun by the Beeton publishing firm in London in the 1850s, offered an impressive sampling of adventure stories and precise scientific accounts by some leading writers of the day. The two outstanding magazines that escaped any kind of narrowness—such as catering for boys or girls alone—had consistently fine literary content. The editor of *Aunt Judy's Magazine* (1886-85), Mrs Alfred Gatty (see p. 385), herself a widely published storyteller, used talented members of her family (including Mrs Ewing) as contributors to assist in maintaining an editorial policy that featured a pleasing array of well-told illustrated stories, natural history lessons, songs, and reviews. In New York, Scribner's offered Mary Mapes Dodge the editorship of its new children's monthly *St Nicholas* (1873-1940), and she turned out to be an equally discriminating and successful editor. She was an acclaimed novelist who had had five years' experience as an associate editor of *Hearth and Home*, and so brought to *St. Nicholas* not only an artistic sensibility and business acumen but an extensive network of literary acquaintances who could be asked to contribute. Under her leadership *St. Nicholas* prospered as the organ of middle-class culture for "young folks".

By the time mass-produced weeklies like *Chums: A Paper for Boys* (1892-1934), and quarterlies like *The Girl's Own Paper* (1880-1927; 1928-50), began flooding the market, the literary content sadly declined—with the emphasis falling on the racy exploits of boy patriots and the domestic pursuits of homebound girls.

From *The Boy's Own Volume of Facts, Fiction, History, and Adventure* (1863)

In their original *Boy's Own Magazine* (1855-62), which became *The Boy's Own Volume* (1863-74; 1880-90) and *The Boy's Penny Magazine*, the London publishing firm of S.O. Beeton clearly knew how to attract and please young male readers and their monitoring parents. As well as employing adventure authors of the calibre of W.H.G. Kingston and Mayne Reid, they offered a healthy assortment of factual and fictional entertainment, and literary contests with alluring prizes like watches and pencil cases. The Christmas 1863 issue of *The Boy's*

Own Volume had instalments of serialized tales like *The Adventures of Reuben Davidger: Seventeen Years and Four Months a Captive Among the Dyaks of Borneo* and descriptions by the naturalist J.G. Woods of different animals housed in the Zoological Gardens; it also offered its well-heeled readers a glimpse of a peculiar Victorian phenomenon, "Street Arabs", in Tom Hood's condescending observations of London street boys (reprinted below), plus several pages of literary puzzles suited to its bookish clientele.

LONDON STREET BOYS

Being a Word About Arabia Anglicana

At the mention of Arabia, the idea of the vast sandy desert at once rises before the mind's eye. And then follows a picture of some oasis in that sterile tract—most probably (for I am sure my readers have perused Sir Walter Scott) that one described in "The Talisman"—shaded with feathery palms, green with emerald turf, and with the "Diamond of the Desert" bubbling clear, cool, delicious, in its midst. A lovely picture—an enchanting imagination.

But it is precisely the opposite of an oasis that is conjured up at the thought of *Street* Arabia. Of no little speck of verdure in a wide ocean of barrenness is that suggestive, but of one dark blot upon a prosperous country—one little cloud of poverty and destitution, mental and bodily, in the broad sunshine of a nation's well-doing—one dark and ineffaceable stain upon the purple robe of an empire city.

We will talk this anomaly over, if you please; for, if the evil is ever to be remedied, it must be discussed and debated, and the very heart of it laid bare beneath the dissecting-knife. How else shall the root and workings of the disease be discovered?

Street Arabia is a wild and unwholesome country—a country of scanty meals, and those poor ones; of lax morals, and even those few; and land shoeless and shirtless, and very ragged. Its roofs are of two sorts: a lofty and spacious one—none other than heaven's canopy—and a low, damp, dirty one—the roof of a cellar, or some chamber no better than that. Within its boundaries combs are unknown, and its only brushes are for boots. Washing is known certainly, but rather as a thing to be avoided than practised; and cleanliness not being held desirable, that to which it is reputed next akin is, I fear, sadly neglected likewise. An improvident country it is, and on that account a happy one after its own fashion; a land that revels in dirt and rejoices in rags is easily made happy. And, chief reason of all for its happiness, it is young. Young and improvident! How happy, therefore, as long as its capital lasts—as long as youth remains, and care for the morrow is absent!

Where the real Street Arabia is I cannot tell; but I am quite certain that somewhere—perhaps near the place where Aladdin plucked the golden and jewelled fruit, or close to the palace which Kubla Khan decreed in Xanadu, or along the shores of the lake whose fish jumped up and conversed in the frying-pan, or beyond the Talking River, or across the Mountains of the Moon, or on the further side of the Enchanted Forest—there exists Street Arabia proper, from which colonies are sent out. For whether those colonies establish themselves in London or in Paris, adopting to some extent the customs of those cities, they everywhere retain a common likeness and common traditions which point to one origin.

The colonists in Paris call themselves *gamins*; those in London are contented with the title of Street Arabs, or street-boys, with various species underlying the genus—for instance, to classify them in scientific fashion, the *homunculus ocreatergens*, or shoeblack; the *homunculus triviatergens*, or crossing-sweeper; and the *puerulus rotifer*, or tumbling Arab, which last is fully established as a separate species, although the practice from which it takes its name is in use among the previously mentioned varieties.

It is a very strange feature of great cities that their streets should teem with a class so peculiar, and at the same time so young. What becomes of the street-children? Superficial philosophers, who found a similar question, "Whence do waiters come?" afloat in the world, extemporised a wild theory that the street-boy, on attaining a certain age, became a chrysalis, burying himself in cellars, from which he emerged a full-blown waiter. Beyond the fact that little is known certainly of the ultimate development of the one and the early origin of the other, there is nothing to lend countenance to so wild a scheme. That the staid, quiet man in a white tie and black suit should ever have been a shoeless, hatless vagabond is impossible! It is more—it is ridiculous! I would sooner believe that the street-boy becomes full-blown in a London sparrow, as some sages aver, and that the waiter springs full-armed, like Minerva, from the brain of a prosperous publican.

The capital of British Arabia Petraea is, I take it, the flight of steps in front of St. Martin's Church. There the boys lounge, like veritable lazzaroni; there they eat, when they do eat, which they are not often doing; and there they plan schemes against society, which they are always doing.

Just about Trafalgar-square there are lots of crossings, and well-frequented ones. The West-End goes to the City over them, and returns homeward over them, so that they are the main arteries of wealth, little droppings of which overflow, and are picked up by the Street Arab.

Trafalgar-square itself is a fine playground for the boys. There is water, which is always a delight—to play with. And the water is dirty, which removes the only objection—a suspicion of cleanliness—which could attach to it as a plaything.

There are low parapets and high walls to be leapt and vaulted over, or "dropped." And, O delightful! the police set their countenances against these gymnastics. Wherefore the young Arab, as he flies over the boundaries, experiences a threefold pleasure. First, in the sense of freedom and the poetry of motion inseparable from such rapid action in the air. Second, in the knowledge that the proceeding is obnoxious to people of weak nerves (and only respectable people possess those luxuries) and to the police. Third, in the certainty that the policeman in his tight blue suit cannot pursue him through his saltatory exercises, or that if he does an inevitable disruption of his uniform in various places must ensue.

In the neighbourhood of Trafalgar-square, about the Opera Colonnade, is also the place where the street-boy is enabled to earn money after dark (when crossings are undistinguishable, and the polish of boots is disregarded) by cart-wheels, catherine-wheels, or flip-flaps.

Yes, beyond a doubt, the steps of St. Martin's Church form the headquarters of the Arab camp in the metropolis.

The amusements of the street-boy are not numerous. Pitch-halfpenny, chuck-farthing, and buttons are the chief ones. But he extemporises a game readily, and from very unpromising materials.

Our young friends in the illustration* attached to this paper have done something of this sort. With no better material than an old hat, ragged beyond repair, and dirty beyond redemption, they have started a game which may pass for foot-ball in its wild state. How they kick it! How they shout with laughter, and wave their shreds of head-gear!

Splendid fun! "Its last day" has come, and its end is not peaceful. By implication they are kicking respectability about; for, possibly, that beaver once wandered, glossy and faultless, down Pall-Mall and Bond-street. Now they have got it down to their own level, and are kicking the supercilious swell, who once wore it, by proxy.

I have no wish to injure the trade of the Street Arab, but, my gentle reader, if, on your way to see your charmer, a chance mud-spot or drop of water defile the purity of your upper-leathers, stop not to have the

* See p. 434.

nuisance abolished where two or three shoeblacks are assembled. Pass on until you find a solitary polisher. If you find him not, prefer to appear before Angelina with the blemish to enduring a polishing under the inspection of those young persons. I once myself, near London-bridge Station, went through the painful operation. My personal appearance, my dress, my means, my probable rank in life, and my profession or trade were freely canvassed in a lofty but satirical manner. It is true the language was slang, but not a very unintelligible form of that dialect. I am not ashamed to confess that I had a wild idea of rushing away after my first boot was finished. To have done so would have been fatal. I was like a man facing half-a-dozen rats in a cellar. It was only by showing a bold front that I could escape. At length the deed was done, and I was released. But the tortures I suffered! Had I been all one corn from head to sole I could scarcely have felt more uncomfortable under the polishing.

But my article is approaching its appointed limits.

There remains one more point to discuss. What is to become of the Street Arab?

You, my young friend, who read this Magazine, and you, my good lady, who read it too, these unkempt, dirty, godless little creatures were innocent babes once—just like little baby in the crib there, looking so rosy and sleeping so sweetly—pure as that child once, with immortal souls. We inhabitants of this great city shall be held responsible for these lost lambs. It is our fault that the Divine gift of childhood is smirched and blurred out of all recognition. Can we mend this? Victor Hugo has hit at the root of the evil when he declares that the race of the *gamin* is sprung of the hatred the old aristocracy of France bore for anything like the education of the people.

"Or l'enfant errant est le corollaire de l'enfant ignorant." (The vagabond child is a necessary consequence of the untaught child.) That is the blot, and now how shall we efface it?

The English in this age are not opposed to the education of the people. But, unfortunately, though approving it in theory, they throw obstacles in the way of it in practice. The form in which the religious element is to be combined with education is the great difficulty before which philanthropists have been compelled to stand powerless. Extremes meet. The widest liberty may become a close servitude, and religious freedom fetters action in this instance. Where so many sects are joined to form a people, it is impossible to fix on any method of education which shall include religious instruction, and yet offend no prejudices.

The question stands thus.

Well-intentioned, earnest people, and otherwise practical philanthropists, are devoting precious time in attempts to solve the problem.

In the meantime, generation after generation of Street Arabs passes away—whither? From a black, bottomless pit of ignorance and degradation—for these children are not as pearly pure as Victor Hugo would have us think, so those who have scrutinised their life in low lodging-houses have discovered—from an abyss of sin and shame—whither?

A serious question, and one it behoves us to answer to ourselves.

There are a few generally accounted sensible people who say something after this fashion:—"We have an old saw which places cleanliness next to godliness. We are divided as to the best means of inculcating the latter. We are unanimous as to the easy mode of teaching the former. Perhaps, while the difficult question is under discussion, we might adopt a course that requires no debating. Let us teach the urchins to live cleanly. It will be doing what all our mere discussions as to how to make them live godly will never do—it will bring them nearer to godliness. If a little learning be a dangerous thing, it is the little learning they have got—the mere step above the intelligence of the brute—and more learning would be anything but a dangerous thing." What shall we say to these people? I, for my part, say "God speed" to them. I have a recollection of a parable which I have met with somewhere—perhaps in my own brain. It told how the servants of a great king had to conduct certain guests to him at night. There was a discussion among them how they should carry the light: one was for a bronze lamp, one for a torch, one for a silver candlestick. Meanwhile, a poor scullion, hearing the guests stumble, rose and took a little farthing candle, and showed them to the front door. Once there, each took such a light from the hall as suited him. I forget how the tale goes on, but I know they all reached the great king.

I have a great belief in the importation of farthing candles into the outer darkness of Arabia Anglicana. I think a joint-stock company would accumulate a large capital by so doing—but not in any earthly bank.   T. HOOD

ANSWERS TO THE PUZZLES OVERLEAF

115. The curfew tolls the knell of parting day. To be read—THE curfew TOLLS—THE Nell—OF parting DAY.

116. A creek.

117. Door-jamb.

118. Because they presided over a Jewry.

119. Because leeks often spring in them.

120. Forty bushels; because where there's a will there's a *wey*.

121. By his sighs.

122. Because it shows its peak against all England.

123. Because it's an axey-dent.

124. Because then they are *bawl'd* about the streets.

125. Because it's "no end of a cell."

126. He turns it into a Rhone.

127. Dun.

128. Too many cooks spoil the broth. To be read—Two men-E cooks—spoil—the B wrath.

129. Artemisium.

115.—A LINE FROM GRAY.

CONUNDRUMS.

116. What is the smallest sound made by the sea?

117. What is the only jam a schoolboy will not eat?

118. Why were the early rulers of Israel called judges?

119. Why is it unsafe to sail in a Welsh vessel?

120. What does a testamentary disposition measure?

121. How would you measure your lover's sincerity?

122. Why is Derbyshire an ill-natured county?

123. Why is a chop with a hatchet always fortuitous?

124. Why do hares lose all their fur directly they come in season?

125. Why is a nun invariably disappointed with her mode of life?

126. If an inhabitant of Lyons waters his horse at the river, what colour does it become?

127. What is the best colour for a good action?

128.—ILLUSTRATED PROVERB.

129.—TRANSPOSITION.

MMHIREATSU.—A naval engagement fought on the same day that the Spartans unsuccessfully defended the pass of Thermopylæ.

From *Aunt Judy's Magazine For Young People* (1866)

In the first of the twenty-two volumes of *Aunt Judy's Magazine* (1866-85) Mrs Alfred Gatty (see p. 385) prepared her young readers for varied literary fare, while assuring them that excellence would always be her overriding criterion: "our honest endeavour and wish have been to provide the best of mental food for all ages of young people." Into the "monthly cauldron" of *Aunt Judy's Magazine* Mrs Gatty tossed useful anecdotes, moral fables, specially arranged songs and hymns, and reviews of current books for the young. One of the reviews in the 1866 volume welcomed *Alice's Adventures in Wonderland* (1865) as an "exquisitely wild, fantastic, impossible, yet most natural history". The periodical was a real family enterprise—with Mrs Gatty's clergyman husband providing the arrangements for many hymns and her gifted daughter, Juliana Horatia Ewing, publishing stories like *Mrs Overtheway's Remembrances* and *Six to Sixteen* in serial form. *Aunt Judy's Magazine* paid particular attention to accounts of "natural history", befitting the scientific bent of its editor.

AHMEEK THE BEAVER

The facts as to these undoubtedly wonderful animals are as follows:—It is generally in June or July that they assemble in companies varying greatly in number, but sometimes of 200 or 300 at a time, on the borders of lakes, ponds, rivers, or creeks connecting lakes, for the purpose of choosing a spot suitable for the island homes which it is their peculiar nature to construct. And in this choice they have several things to consider. First, they require such a depth of water as is certain not to be frozen to the bottom by the frosts of winter; secondly, they prefer running water to still, on account of the use they make of the current above in conveying wood and other necessaries to their dwelling-places. Hearne adds, "and because houses built in streams are less easily taken than those in standing water." That they secure a current when the place suits in other respects is certain, unless their population be so large for the neighbourhood that some must take to the lakes and ponds. With regard to the depth of water, where they cannot get it exactly to their mind, or have reason to fear that the water in the stream above may freeze or fail, and so leave their habitations dry, they provide against any possible accident in the following ingenious manner: At a convenient distance below their building-place they throw a dam right across the stream, just as we should do ourselves for a similar purpose, and by this means insure round their dwellings a sufficient quantity of water at all seasons to keep their entrance doors below the surface—that being their great object; while to prevent an excess which might submerge the whole habitation, they leave an opening in the embankment to let the water out when it rises above a certain level!

This dam or embankment, which is of very frequent occurrence—though never made when rendered unnecessary by natural depth of water—is the first building operation of the beavers, and the whole company join in executing it. But *how* is the question; for these dams are strong masses of wood, mud, and stones so intermixed as to secure so-

lidity, and they are of considerable extent where a river is wide as well as shallow. Where are the beaver's tools, for such a work? Where do they get their hatchets, their pickaxes, their spades, their wheelbarrows?

Nay! they have not to look beyond themselves for tools. If they do not find driftwood sufficient, and want a tree or two besides, say ten inches in diameter, for instance—a party of three or four of them sit round it on their haunches, and gnaw it down with their four huge front teeth or "incisors," which, having chisel-like edges, and being very powerful, accomplish the work with very little trouble. Long ago the American Indians discovered the value of these natural tools, and stuck them in wooden handles to make use of in carving their bone weapons.

Here it is to be observed that our intelligent little friends collect driftwood and cut down trees only in the upper part of the stream in which they are going to build, and thus, as before hinted, save themselves the trouble of conveyance. For which purpose they cut through the trunk in such a manner that it shall fall towards the water; but whenever personal labour is necessary, it is their *teeth* they make use of to drag the logs from one place to another, as well as to cut off branches and make them portable. After being dropped into the current, the trees and branches so obtained are of course carried safely down to the building place, and there detained, and laid sideways across the stream, being kept in their place by stones and mud. For all the old stories about piled foundations to these dams are delusions of the imagination. Both dams and houses are masses of wood of all sizes, commonly placed crosswise, and intermingled with mud and stones in such proportion as to secure solidity and firmness; but certainly not built up on stakes, as was once supposed. They so thoroughly answer their purpose, however, that old embankments, after frequent repairs (for they are kept regularly repaired), will resist almost any amount of water and ice. Moreover, they are sometimes so well wooded that birds build their nests in the trees which have rooted and sprung up from the green willow, birch, and poplar branches, originally thrown in with the heavier wood. There is another curious peculiarity. They are differently shaped, according to the nature of the stream. Where the current is very strong, they are formed with a considerable curve, the convex side to the stream, while in quieter water they are thrown across nearly in a straight line. The conveyance of the mud and stones, which form so important a part of the solid mass of their embankments and houses, is another proof of beaver ingenuity. They carry these materials between their little forepaws and chins, and, Hearne tells us, are so expeditious in their work, that he has seen thousands of these tiny handfuls of mud so conveyed during one night—night being always, be it observed, the worktime of beavers.

With respect to the beaver houses or lodges themselves we sadly need more exact information. Still, all accounts agree in describing them as dome-shaped, and closed in so that no enemy can get into them from the land, the only entrances being from the water and, there is little doubt, always below it. Also they are built of the same materials as their dams, and in the same way with the wood held down by stones and mud; and their one object in raising them above the water seems to be that they like to have a dry place to lie on; for, being amphibious animals, they do not care to be under water for a very long time together, and need therefore a dry place of retreat for sleeping, or occasionally eating; but such a thing as a separate set of eating and sleeping apartments in unknown.

Beavers choose their building grounds and cut their wood chiefly in the summer, and at the same season lay up stores of provisions for the winter, by collecting bark and the green boughs and branches of trees, and sinking them near the door of their habitations by stones laid on the heap; the bark of trees and the root of a kind of water lily (*Nuphar luteum*), which grows in the water, being their chief food during winter. In summer, when most of the beavers go about on shore, they eat several kinds of herbage, and the berries of shrubs. The actual building of a new *lodge*, or common house, seldom begins before the middle of August, and is never completed till the cold weather sets in; and the builder's last act is to put on a final coat of mud, which, being accomplished in the late autumn, freezes hard when winter comes on. This being done year by year, the walls, especially the roofs of the lodges, become exceedingly strong, sometimes six or seven feet in thickness. Hearne speaks of these annual late autumnal mud coverings as "a great piece of policy," for by the roofs freezing, in consequence as hard as stones, their enemy the "wolverine," or "glutton" (*Gulo luscus*), is kept out. He also mentions, as no doubt the origin of the idea that beavers used their tails for trowels, their habit of flapping them occasionally as they walk over their work, and always when they plunge into the water; a custom they retain even when domesticated—for, be it observed, beavers are easily tamed, and make very pleasant, docile indoor companions, learning to answer to their names, and following those they are accustomed to like a dog;

and quite as much pleased as any domestic animal at being fondled.

But, after all, M. Bonnet's philosophy, if not his facts, is correct. They do not reason. Mr Wood, in his "Sketches and Anecdotes of Animal Life," quotes the account of a tame beaver, kept by Mr Broderip, in which the building propensity, as an unreasoning instinct, was carefully observed. The creature built purposeless dams across the corners of the room with anything it could lay hold of, and the family took care to leave a variety of materials in its way. A sweeping-brush and a warming-pan were among the large things he chose, and, after laying these crosswise, he filled up the area between the ends with rush-baskets, books, sticks, cloths, dried turf, or anything portable! Another curious fact Mr Broderip mentions is, that after the animal had built his house, and carried in cotton and hay to make a nest, he sat up and combed his fur with the nails of his hind feet. He was also very fond of dipping his tail in water, and when it was kept moist he never seemed to care to drink. Strange to say, bread and milk and sugar were the pet beaver's favourite food; a curious change from the green bark of trees, his natural food; but, it must be owned, he also liked succulent fruits and roots. He was a most entertaining creature, Mr Broderip said; and his account is enough to tempt any one, who had the power, to follow his example, and bring one of these animals home to be placed among the domestic pets of an English household.

The scientific name of the common American beaver is *Castor fiber*. Length of head and body about three feet and a half; of the tail or "caudal paddle," about a foot. It is three years in attaining its full size; its fur varies from glossy brown to almost black, and was, till lately, in great request for gentlemen's hats and ladies' bonnets. Its tail is used as a rudder in diving or ascending, and is flat, scaled, and oar-like. Its hind paws are webbed.

In conclusion, we must allow the beaver to be one of the most gifted of the lower animals, but still the limits of its powers are fixed. The beavers of to-day have made no advance from the beavers of generations ago, and they are born from age to age, with neither more nor less of ability. In other words, the race of Ahmeek does not *progress*.

We are happy in being able to illustrate our beavers from real life. The woodcut, by M Grisét, which accompanies this paper, was drawn from the lodge built by the beavers in the Zoological Gardens, Regent's Park. Some time ago they burrowed their way from their enclosure in the gardens to the canal, as offering them a larger field for their operations. They were, of course, reclaimed, and measures were adopted for keeping them more safely enclosed.

The Burial of the Linnet.

Words by J. H. G.

Music by Alfred Scott Gatty.

Andantino.

1. Found in the gar-den—dead in his beau-ty. Ah! that a lin-net should
2. Bu - ry him kind-ly— up in the cor-ner; Bird, beast, and gold-fish are

die in the Spring! Bu - ry him, com-rades, in pi - ti - ful
se - pulchred there. Bid the black kit - ten march as chief

du - ty, Muf - fle the din - ner bell, So - lemn - ly ring.
mourn - er, Wav - ing her tail like a plume in the air.

3. Bury him nobly—next to the donkey;
   Fetch the old banner, and wave it about:
   Bury him deeply—think of the monkey,
   Shallow his grave, and the dogs got him out.

From *The Child's Own Magazine* (1875)

In its assortment of hymns, improving vignettes, and pious verse, *The Child's Own Magazine* (1852-71; 1872-?) dinned the message of prayerful obedience. Pocket-sized and attractively illustrated, several volumes of this half-penny monthly were sometimes bound together as gift books for diligent Sunday scholars.

LUCY LINTWHITE

The branch that shows the sharpest thorn
    Oft bears the sweetest rose;
And oft mid toil and sorrow born
    The loveliest flow'ret grows.

Dear Lucy Lintwhite, such art thou—
    The mansion halls of pride
No brighter face, or purer brow
    Behind their portals hide.

From them perchance a child might roam,
    And others fill its place;
But what were Lucy's cottage-home
    Except for Lucy's face?

Each household task she blithely shares,
    She guards each younger child,
And hears them say their little prayers
    To "Jesus meek and mild."

To her her mother, when her arms
    Are weary of their load,
Entrusts her baby brother's charms,
    And knows him well bestowed.

And she it is that daily trips
    So lightly o'er the fields,
And carries to her father's lips
    The best their cupboard yields.

Sweet Lucy, in a simple round
    Of duties like thy own,
That peace of heart and mind is found,
    To great ones rarely known.

The wisest man may search in vain
    The world's pretentious lore,
But till he is a child again
    He dwells with peace no more.
A. HUME

NEVER SULK.

NEVER SULK

By Austin Q. Hagerman

Don't sulk, it is neither pretty nor wise. It makes one look ugly and act foolishly. I knew about a boy who once took a sulky notion to refuse his dinner because something or other didn't quite suit him.

He waited; no one coaxed him to eat; they just let him alone. Soon he grew tired of his notion, and was quite vexed and almost troubled about this severe "letting alone."

By and by he said pettishly, "You wouldn't *make* me eat if I starved to death."

You see, he seemed to want the family to make a kind of "fuss" over his refusal to eat. Then he could have shown them how stubborn he could be.

And the little girl in the picture she is sulky too, she is sucking a corner of her pinafore. Poor child, how unhappy she looks, shut up in her bed-room by her mamma until she is cured!

Ah! 'Tis a foolish, poor business to sulk. It doesn't pay. It is wrong. See that you never do it.

From *St Nicholas: An Illustrated Magazine For Young Folks* (1881)

St Nicholas (1873-1940) was the best-known American juvenile periodical in the late nineteenth century. Published in New York by Scribner's, and then by The Century Co., this monthly flourished in its first thirty-two years mainly because of the capable editorship of Mary Mapes Dodge, the famous author of *Hans Brinker; or, The Silver Skates* (1865). *Scribner's Monthly* (November 1873) announced the new venture with this confident proclamation: "Wherever SCRIBNER goes, ST NICHOLAS ought to go. They be harmonious companions in the family, and the helpers of each other in the work of instruction, culture and entertainment." Mrs Dodge promoted such work energetically, devising a well-rounded stable format with regular "departments" to instruct and entertain her young middle-class readers, and assembling an impressive coterie of paid professional contributors. With its articles ranging from geography and history to natural science, and serialized stories by authors like Frances Hodgson Burnett, Frank Stockton, Susan Coolidge, Rudyard Kipling, and L. Frank Baum, *St Nicholas*—especially while Mrs Dodge was at the helm—was a genuine reflection of the informed and cultured side of American life. In addition to her rigorous inspection of each feature, Mrs Dodge herself wrote one of the columns, "Jack-in-the-Pulpit", an example of which appears below.

St Nicholas successfully absorbed other magazines, among them *Our Young Folks* in 1874 and *Wide-Awake* in 1893. Mrs Dodge's successor, William Fayal Clarke, kept the periodical on a steady course; but the influences of cheaper competitors, inconsistent editorial policies, and a change of ownership in the 1930s contributed to the sad decline of this once-prestigious magazine.

There was a small servant called Kate,
Who sat on the stairs very late;
When asked how she fared,
She said she was scared,
But was otherwise doing first rate.

UP

By George H. Hebard

Poor old Mr *Preface* was tired,—not that he had been particularly busy,—no, that was the pity of it. Time had been when every caller at Dictionary Mansion had, first of all, paid their respects to him; in return, he imparted to each new visitor such little hints and general information as its founder, Mr. Webster, had thought they might need to aid them in their researches.

But, alas! those days were of the past! In the rush and hurry of modern American life, people could not wait to confer with him. There were constant callers at the mansion with whom he had never interchanged a word,—people who rushed through the halls, found the room of the Word they desired to consult, made their inquiries, and then bolted unceremoniously. All this worried Mr *Preface* very much, for was he not an old and faithful servant? Mr Webster himself had given him the position of janitor when Dictionary Mansion was first completed. It was comparatively a small house then; and through all its changes to the present enormous structure, with its numberless lodgers, he had remained faithfully at his post.

These were a few of the sad thoughts occupying his attention one night as he sat restlessly in his arm-chair, wearied with enforced idleness. It was rather late for him, too. He usually closed the doors early in the evening; but, that night, Orator Puff was to speak at the Town Hall, and had engaged many of the biggest Words to assist him, and Mr *Preface* was awaiting their return.

Meanwhile, the poor old fellow was slowly going over his sorrowful thoughts, when he was suddenly startled by a scream. It evidently came from a distant part of the building. Going into the hall, he found it rapidly filling with excited Words, anxious to know the cause of the alarm. As the commotion appeared greatest in the corridor of the "U's," he hurried there, and soon found himself at the room of little Mr *Up*. Crowding past *Curiosity*, who stood vacantly staring through the door, he saw the body of the little lodger lying prostrate on the floor. Bending over him were *Pity* and *Sympathy*, vainly trying to bring him to consciousness.

Miss *Upas*, the lady who lived in the adjoining chamber, gave this explanation: Her neighbor had come home unusually late that evening. After hearing him close his door, she felt the jar of some one falling. Hurrying to his room, she discovered him lying on the floor, apparently dead, and, in her terror, she gave the piercing scream which alarmed the house. Mr *Aid* was the first to appear on the scene, and was doing all he could to revive the sufferer.

When *Up* had sufficiently recovered, he told his story, as follows:

"Mine is simply a case of nervous and bodily exhaustion, caused by constant overwork. There has not been a night for the last two years that

I have not come home so utterly fagged out that it seemed as if I never could begin my endless labor again. Ever since the Jones family came to this town, my services have been in constant demand from early dawn till late night. It appears there is hardly an idea in their heads but they think my presence necessary for its expression. For instance, there is Father Jones. At first cock-crow, he 'wakes up'; then 'gets up' and 'makes up' the fire; 'does up' his chores; 'blacks up' his boots; 'goes up' to the store; 'figures up' the cash account; 'buys up' more goods; 'marks up' the prices; 'fills up' the orders; 'foots up' the profits; 'shuts up' the store; 'dresses up' for dinner; 'sits up' awhile afterward, calling for my assistance continually, until he 'locks up' the house for the night and 'shuts up' his eyes in slumber.

"At the same time Miss Fanny 'dresses up'; 'does up' her hair; 'takes up' her book; 'gets herself up' in her lesson; 'hunts up' her bonnet; 'hurries up' to school; 'catches up' with a school-mate; 'stands up' to recite; 'passes up' to the head of the class; 'flushes up' at the praise of her teacher; 'divides up' her luncheon at recess; and, as she 'rides up' home in the horse-car, 'makes up' her mind to 'be up' at the head of the school ere the term is 'up.'

"Tommy Jones 'runs up' to the store on an errand; 'trips up' over a stick; cries out that he is all 'bruised up,' until his mother 'bandages up' his knee, and 'hugs him up' a dozen times, and tells him to 'keep up' good courage, and try to 'cheer up.'

"And so it is the long, long, weary day. I go from one to the other until I can scarcely totter. Nor would I complain even now if I thought my help was really needed. But there is the Brown family living next door; they are certainly quite as active as the Joneses, and, as they seldom require my services, I can only think that my presence on every occasion (for it can not fairly be called assistance) is not indispensable, as the Joneses seem to imagine."

"Shameful, shameful!" was the indignant comment of the group of listeners, as *Up* finished his story.

Said *Incomprehensibility:* "I scarcely can believe the Joneses to be so cruel as to abuse such a little man as *Up* like that. Just think of it—only two letters high! And here am I, a very giant among Words, and yet have only been called out once for a month! Then it was for spelling at a public school, and I was immediately dismissed. Why could not the work be more evenly distributed among us?"

"You have spoken my sentiments exactly," said *Procrastination.* "We ought to labor according to our size. My only work this week was in serving for an hour as writing-copy for Tommy Jones. I was very glad to be put to use, although the teacher did say I was a "thief of time.""

"Let us hold an indignation meeting," suggested another. "We can at least protest against such barbaric cruelty and injustice."

The idea met with favor, and the fast-increasing assemblage adjourned without delay to the main hall of the building, whither all the other inmates were soon summoned. *Arbiter* was chosen moderator, in acknowledgment of his wisdom, and because of his reputation as a settler of disputes. Vice-presidents were selected from Scripture proper names, abbreviations, and noted names of fiction, and *Record* elected secretary. The meeting being duly organized, the chairman announced the business to come before it, giving a brief but spirited account of *Up's* history and sufferings.

He was followed by *Argument*, an old and experienced debater who had spent much time in court, and was noted chiefly for always being on the contrary side. For this once, however, he happily agreed with the prevailing opinion. Said he:

"No doubt the Americans are a well-meaning race. But they are extremely careless and seldom think. And no doubt the Joneses are, at this very moment, serenely sleeping in utter unconsciousness of the pain and misery which their dullness has inflicted upon poor little *Up*. Of course they mean to do right, and would not knowingly injure any one. But that is a poor excuse. Now these same Americans have a society for the prevention of cruelty to animals. They seem to be in greater need of a society for the prevention of cruelty to the English language, a society whose rigid laws should be strictly enforced. Perhaps my words seem strong, but, my friends, *Up's* case is not an unusual one. I see before me even now two Words, *You* and *Know*, who have had an equally bitter experience. Whenever some people summon us to the aid of their ideas, *You* and *Know* are hitched in with the other Words. Sometimes they trot before and sometimes behind. In either case, while they do not help the expressions, but are rather a hindrance, they become quite as fatigued as if doing regular and proper work. Now, if Mr Jones, for instance, should see a pair of horses used in the same way, he would at once set down their driver as an idiot, if not something worse. But the two cases are not unlike, although our unthinking friends seem not to perceive this."

Another speaker thought that, "As the Joneses and others have probably never looked at the subject in that light, it might be that if it were so presented to them they would see the justice of the complaint and offend no more. I should, therefore, move, Mr Chairman, that our friend *Preface* should be appointed a committee of one to call their attention to the matter, and urge a reform."

At this point, Mr *Preface* arose and addressed the meeting in a sorrowful manner. He thought the appeal should be spread far and wide by some able and influential advocate. Reminding his hearers of his own neglected position and waning powers, he moved to amend by having an account of the whole affair sent to the ST NICHOLAS for publication.

The amendment being accepted, the resolution as amended was passed by a unanimous vote, after which the meeting adjourned.

JACK-IN-THE-PULPIT.

JACK-IN-THE-PULPIT

"April showers bring May flowers," and May flowers bring happy hours,—that is, in the country,—and what can an honest Jack-in-the-Pulpit know about the city, excepting by hearsay? The Little School-ma'am says that in New York, and a few other brick-and-stone con-glomerations, the inhabitants have a way of swapping houses with one another on the first day of May, and, in consequence, the streets are filled with carts carrying household goods and chattles to and fro, hither and thither, till the city is nearly distracted. Then in the houses, she tells me, the broom-spirit has full sway; wives rule the home-universe, and husbands and fathers stand aside and weep. Busy times, I should say!

Well, and are not *my* people busy, too? Birds with their cradles and housekeeping; early spiders with their shiny little hammocks and awn-ings; ants with their apartment-houses, and, above all, dear, rosy, noisy *bipeds* (known by learned naturalists as *boysandgirlses semiwildses*), run-ning about in the fields and woods, and having the best kind of a busy time. Bless them! They make me think of bees, humming with health and cheerfulness, and storing up sweets and flower-wealth for all to share who will.

Talking of busy times and hours, packed full of simple enjoyment, my hearers, consider this bit of true history about

POOR FRITZ

How would you like to have such a bringing-up as befell Fritz, son of Frederick William the Second, King of Prussia? Let me tell you about it.

When the child was in his tenth year, the father wrote out directions to the three tutors as to Fritz's mode of life. The boy was to be called at six o'clock, and the tutors were to stand by to see that he did not loiter nor turn in bed; he must get up at once. As soon as he had put on his slippers, he was to kneel at his bedside and pray aloud a prayer, so that all in the room might hear. Then, as rapidly as possible, he was to put on his shoes and spatterdashes, vigorously and briskly wash himself, get into his clothes, and have his hair powdered and combed. During the hair-dressing, he was at the same time to take a breakfast of tea, so that both jobs should go on at once, in order to save time; and all this, from the calling to the end of the breakfast, was to be done in fifteen minutes!

At half-past nine in the evening he was to bid his father good-night, go directly to his room, very rapidly take off his clothes, wash, and hear a prayer on his knees. Then a hymn was to be sung, and Fritz was to hop instantly into bed.

Poor Fritz! No room for bed-time stories nor pillow-fights!

But, not so fast. "Poor Fritz" afterward became Frederick the Great.

A PLEASANT CHILD!

By Isabel Francis Bellows.

The idea of making believe it is true
That if you are good, you 'll be happy, too!
They always are writing it down in books;
I think they might know how silly it looks.

There 's nothing under the sun could be worse
Than to have to be washed and dressed by nurse;
And another thing I perfectly hate,
Is to go to bed exactly at eight.

I 'm crazy to cut my hair in a bang,
And frizzle the ends, and let them hang.
All the stylish girls in our school do that,
But they make me wear mine perfectly flat.

A girl in our class, named Matilda Chase,
Has a lovely pink overskirt trimmed with lace,
And, of course, I wanted to have one, too,
But they said I must make my old one do.

I hate to do sums, and I hate to spell,
And don't like geography very well;
In music they bother about my touch,
And they make me practice the scales too much.

I was reading a splendid book last night,
Called "A Nun's Revenge, or The Hidden Blight,"
And I wanted to read the rest to-day,
But when they saw it, they took it away.

Well, I know you 'd think it was horrid, too,
If you did the things that they make me do;
And I guess *you* 'd worry, and whine, and tease,
If you never once could do as you please.

When I 'm grown up, I 'll do as I please,
And then I sha' n't have to worry and tease.
Then I 'll be good and pleasant all day,
For all I want is to have my own way.

From *Little Wide-Awake; An Illustrated Magazine For Good Children* (1882)

Little Wide-Awake's editor, Mrs Sale Barker (1841-92), provided most of the literary matter for this handsomely designed compendium of edifying stories. She was an instructress for whom the words of Isaac Watts's Divine Song, "Against Idleness and Mischief"—the first stanza of which is the epigraph to the story reprinted here— were models of good behaviour. In addition to writing for and managing *Little Wide-Awake* (1875-92), Mrs Barker supplied the verses for Kate Greenaway's *Birthday Book for Children* (1880), and published picture-stories about prissy heroines with names like Little Golden Locks and Little Ruby Lips.

LAURA JANE LAZENBY,

What She Did, And What She Didn't; And What Came Of It.

> *"How doth the little busy bee*
> *Improve each shining hour,*
> *And gather honey all the day*
> *From every opening flower."*

And that is what you should do, my children. I do not mean gather honey exactly, because that is the bees' business, and you would not understand it; but do something, or learn something, every day, to be useful to yourself or others. Don't sit and wonder how to begin, or what to do next. Don't waste your time over a foolish story book, but set about something in earnest at once.

Above all things, don't lie in bed in the morning half asleep and half awake, instead of getting up as soon as you are called, and making the day as long as you possibly can.

I say nothing about the grown-up people. It is too late for them to become active and industrious, I fear, if unfortunately they did not acquire the habit in their childhood, or early youth, but for you, my darlings, my little ones, who have "the world before you where to choose," and what to choose, take my advice, as an experienced old person, and learn betimes to be active, and orderly, and industrious.

And now, if you like, I will tell you a story.

Once upon a time, a time not very long ago, there lived a little girl named Laura Jane Lazenby. You see she had several names, though she was always called by only one of them, and she had also several brothers and sisters, and a papa and mamma like everybody else.

A very good papa and mamma they were too, and yet when I say good, perhaps I should not, I should rather say kind, for they were too indulgent to her; in fact, I am sorry to say they completely spoiled her. They allowed her to do as she liked, and what do you think she liked to do? why, just nothing at all! But she was their eldest daughter, and they thought a great deal of her.

Look at this picture. There she is, dressing herself in the morning. After washing herself, very slowly, and putting on some of her clothes, not her stockings and shoes—that would be too much trouble—she holds up her frock, and looks at it, and thinks how much pleasanter it would be to get into bed again, and have her sleep out, and sometimes she does.

Then when she gets down to breakfast, it is nearly over, and she has cold tea, and hard toast, and if she complains, her brothers say, "Serve her right." She is too lazy to be cross, so she listens quietly, and wishes she had no lessons to do, and she is so slow about them, that she is just beginning when the others have all finished, and have run away to play. When she plays it is in a sleepy kind of way. If she has a doll she takes so little care of its clothes, that it is soon spoilt and dirty, and if it is given to her undressed, the poor thing never gets any clothes at all!

But now I must get to the pith of my story, and by the way, if you don't know what pith is, you must ask somebody who can tell you, for I have no time just now, as I am going to relate to you all that befell Laura Lazenby on a fine spring day, entirely in consequence of her bad habits.

One afternoon, Aunt Katherine—Aunt Kate as they always called her—kindly came to see them.

Now she was the very best of aunts, who often gave treats to her nephews and nieces, and having no children of her own, it was surely the very best thing she could do. I do not see much use in aunts and uncles, when they are not papas or mammas also, except to give treats to their nephews and nieces; but then I consider that it is the duty of children to behave prettily to their uncles and aunts, and to mind what they say.

Upon this occasion, Aunt Kate sat down upon the sofa in the drawing-room, and calling the children round her, said to them: "My dears, I intend to take you all to-morrow to the Crystal Palace. It is a very large house, made entirely of glass, just like the houses in fairy land, where all day long the most amusing and delightful things are continually going on. You will hear the most beautiful music, and see the prettiest pictures. Some actors will perform a play, and a conjuror will do some wonderful tricks which will astonish you greatly; and what perhaps you will like best of all, there is a splendid toy shop, full of the most beautiful toys imaginable, and if you are all good children, and mind what I say, I promise to give to each of you whichever toy you may set your heart on.

"We will dine there, and have for dinner everything that we all like best, and then, after taking a nice little turn about the Palace, will come home in good time, before papa and mamma have begun to say, 'Is it not time those children should be here?' Nurse shall go with us, partly to take care of us, and partly because poor nurse will perhaps also like to see these beautiful sights. Let's see, there are four of you; nurse shall take Grace and Tommy under her wing, and I will look after Frederick and Laura, and show them all that is to be seen, and do all I can to make them happy.

"But now, my dears, as we shall go down by the railway, you must not keep me waiting a moment when I come to fetch you. I shall be here at half-past eight o'clock precisely, and if any of you are not ready I shall start without you, for we must be at the station at the right time. You know, my dears, according to the old proverb, a little improved, 'Time, tide, and railway trains wait neither for man, woman, nor child.' "

Then she went away, after many good-byes and kisses to dear Aunt Kate, and a little shower of thanks as you may guess. Frederick and Laura decided that they never were so happy before, and could scarcely eat their supper for thinking of the pleasure before them, while the two little ones fairly jumped for joy, and a very pretty little performance that was I can assure you.

But the night came, as it always will, whether we are pleased or sorry, and it was time to go to bed.

Frederick dreamed all night long of Aunt Kate—but she was not a common Aunt Kate in a bonnet, and mantle, and gown, like everybody else. In Frederick's dream she had shining wings on her shoulders, and a crown of stars on her head exactly like the Queen of the Fairies, and she had a golden key in her hand with which to open the gates of her palace; and the two little ones went to sleep thinking of the toys promised them, and hesitating which they should choose. Grace thought of a nice little work box, with scissors and thimble in it, or a pretty little fancy basket; then it suddenly occurred to her why should the poor dolls be forgotten, why not buy something for them, chairs and a table, or even a carriage for them to take their daily drive in; and Tommy went to sleep with drums and trumpets sounding in his ears, and hoops and balls bounding before his closed eyes.

But as for Laura, she was too indolent to be excited about anything; she thought it would be very nice to go to the Crystal Palace, and that Aunt Kate was very good, but that it was better to go to sleep now. It was indeed a great drawback to the pleasure that she would have to get up so early the next morning.

Well, it was a fine May morning as ever was seen. The sun shone his very best, and a nice little soft breeze just ruffled the tops of the trees in the square.

Long before seven o'clock Frederick, and Grace, and Tommy were "alive and kicking," as the old saying is; they were up, and ready to be washed and dressed, and running about in their bed-rooms in the meantime, till nurse should come to call them.

They certainly did not want much calling.

But when nurse went in to Laura, there she was, fast asleep. Nurse said, "Come. Miss Laura, get up directly, your aunt will be here in an hour to take us to the beautiful Crystal Palace. Get up at once. I will come again in half an hour to finish dressing you, and then we will all go down to breakfast, and be ready for your aunt at half-past eight." Laura said she would get up, and away went nurse; but no sooner was she gone than Laura said to herself, "An hour is more than I want to dress in, and bed is so comfortable:" and so she turned over on the other side, and in three minutes was as sound asleep as ever.

At a little past eight in came nurse. "Why, Miss Laura, asleep! Miss Kindly will be here in twenty minutes. I have been expecting to hear you ring, now I must send some one else in to you, for I must go and put on my own bonnet, and get my breakfast with your sister and brothers. I am sorry for you, but you know it is your own fault."

Then did not Laura get up quickly for once! Jane the nursemaid came to help her, but in their hurry everything went wrong, as it always does on those occasions. The soap was not to be found, the clean towels were not on the horse. Then her pretty best frock was torn out of the gathers behind, and buttons came off her boots.

In short, she was not half dressed when Aunt Kate's carriage drove up to the door, and the three other children, with nurse, got in in high spirits.

"Where is Laura?"

The nursemaid came down. "Oh Ma'am, Miss Laura is not ready, but if you will wait a quarter of an hour, she will have finished dressing, and have her breakfast."

"And be too late for the train," said Aunt Kate, "and have to go by a much later one, and spoil the day's pleasure for the others. No. Coachman, drive on," and away they went.

Poor Laura looked out of her bed-room window, and saw them go, and then sat down, and cried fit to break her heart.

Now perhaps some people may think this cruel, but I do not. Her papa and mamma, who spoiled her, would no doubt have waited, and so spoiled everything else; but Aunt Kate knew better. She said, it will be a lesson to her, and so it was. She thought of it all day, and she said to herself, "I will get up early to-morrow morning," and she did; and gradually from that time she became more active and energetic, and is now just as brisk and bonny as other children of her age, which I hope you will be glad to hear.

But before I end this true story I must tell you that the day at the Crystal Palace was the happiest that ever was spent, and kind Aunt Kate brought home a very pretty present for Laura, to console her.

Good-bye, my dears, mind you get up when you are called to-morrow morning.

A.E.B.

Chatterbox

EDITED BY J. ERSKINE CLARKE, M.A.

BOSTON: ESTES AND LAURIAT, 301 WASHINGTON STREET.

From *Chatterbox* (1895)

Begun by the Reverend J. Erskine Clarke (1827-1920) of Derby, Eng., as an alternative to the "blood and thunder" of the penny dreadfuls, this half-penny weekly set out to inculcate Christian principles. Clarke, who later became a London vicar and the honorary Canon of Rochester, was a tireless composer of scripture parables, church stories, and "simple sermons for the children of working people" before he founded *Chatterbox* (1866-1943). Informative and often pietistic, it enjoyed a remarkable longevity on both sides of the Atlantic. However, whether retelling classics such as Dickens' novels, or relating historical events, the narrative style was prosaic and sentimental, and the magazine's profuse line drawings at times approached greeting-card coyness.

THE CRUEL DONKEY-DRIVER

"Young man, don't beat that poor donkey so hard!" said a lady one day to a rough man who was thrashing a lean, over-loaded donkey with all his strength.

"He's mine," growled the man, "and I've a right to do what I like with him."

"No man has any right to be cruel to any of God's creatures," rejoined the lady; "but what will you take for your donkey?"

"Two pounds," replied the man.

"Two pounds is a large sum to give for a donkey which looks so worn-out and so sick as yours," said the lady; "but I will give it to you for the sake of getting the poor creature out of your hands."

"As you like," muttered the bad man, with a sneer.

So this lady bought the poor donkey, which was soon relieved of its load and led to her door.

"Oh, a donkey! a donkey! Won't it be nice to ride on?" cried rosy-faced Alice, the lady's little daughter.

"That's only the skeleton of a donkey," shouted Neddie, a jolly-looking boy of twelve. "He's a regular Barebones. I think, if he was to run a race with a snail, the snail would beat. I wouldn't give my black puppy-dog for that dying donkey."

This was meant to be funny talk, but I think it was rude and not respectful to their mother. The lady felt it to be so. With a grave countenance she said—

"I bought that donkey for two reasons. First, I wanted to take it from the hands of a cruel man; and I thought that, if treated kindly and fed well, it would soon be strong, and then my fat little Alice and sickly little Mollie could ride side by side."

"Oh! thank you so much, mother dear," said pale-faced Mollie, who had crept from the sofa to the window-seat to look at the donkey. "I think the donkey will soon get fat in our meadow, and then we will have fine times riding him."

The lady kissed Mollie, and told Neddie to tell John to rub down the donkey and then to put him in the meadow. Neddie went out to the stable and said to the servant man: "John, go to the front door and lead Barebones round here."

"Who's Barebones?" asked John.

"You'll see," replied Neddie, laughing.

John soon returned with the poor donkey. "Yes Master Neddie," said he, "his bones are bare enough, but he's a good donkey for all that. The creature has been starved, whipped, and overworked by some brute of a man who isn't fit to own a dog. I'll soon bring him round so that you will be proud to ride him."

"Maybe I shall and maybe I shan't," said Neddie, as John began combing and brushing the donkey.

John was as good as his word. The poor donkey soon began to improve. His hair became glossy, his ribs were covered with flesh, his eyes grew bright, and in two months there was not a handsomer donkey in the neighbourhood. Alice named him Johnny Plump, and even Neddie confessed that it wouldn't do to call him Barebones any more.

Thus you see what kindness did for a donkey. Oh, there is nothing like kindness! It is good for children as well as for animals. I have seen boys treat cats and dogs, and even ponies and donkeys, with cruelty; but I never knew any boy who was cruel to a dumb animal to be kind to his brothers, sisters, or companions. Did you?

I think you never did, because cruelty hardens the heart. It freezes up all gentle and loving feelings.

Don't be unkind, then, my children, even to a fly or a worm. Never take pleasure in seeing any creature, however mean, suffer pain. If you must kill noxious insects or animals, do it quickly. Never torment anything. On the contrary, be kind to everything—to birds, to animals, and especially to each other. Never give pain, either by word or act, to any one if you can help it. Treat all your friends gently. Then you will grow lovely, loving, and beloved.

WASN'T WANTED THERE

She was a little old woman, very plainly dressed in black bombazine which had seen much careful wear, her bonnet was very old-fashioned, and people stared at her as she tottered up the aisle of the grand church, evidently bent on getting a good seat. A great man was to preach on that day, and the church was filled with splendidly dressed people who had heard of the fame of the preacher, and had come to hear him. Some of those who were there early saw the old woman. They thought that she must be in her dotage, for she picked out the pew of the richest and proudest member of the church and took a seat. The three ladies who were seated there beckoned to the verger, who bent over the intruder and whispered something, but she was hard of hearing, and smiled a little withered smile, as she said gently, "Oh, I'm quite comfortable here, quite comfortable here."

"But you are not wanted here," said the verger, pompously. "There is not room. Come with me, my good woman; I will see that you have a seat."

"Not room!" said the old woman. "Why, I'm not crowded a bit. I rode ten miles to hear the sermon to-day, because—

But the verger took her by the arm, and shook her roughly in a polite, underhand way, and she took the hint. Her faded old eyes filled with tears, her chin quivered, but she rose meekly and left the pew. Turning quietly to the ladies, who were spreading their rich dresses over the seat which she left vacant she said gently, "I hope, my dears, there will be room in Heaven for us all."

Then she followed the pompous verger to the rear of the church, where, in the last pew, she was seated between a threadbare girl and a shabby old man.

"She must be crazy," said one of the ladies in the pew which she had at first occupied. "How can an ignorant old woman like her wish to hear Dr. Blank preach? She would not be able to understand a word he said."

"Those people are so persistent. The idea of her forcing herself into our pew! There's Dr. Blank coming out of the vestry. "Isn't he grand?"

"Splendid! What a stately man! You know he has promised to dine with us while he is here."

He was a commanding-looking man, and as the organ voluntary stopped and he looked over the vast crowd of worshippers gathered in the great church, he seemed to scan every face. Suddenly he leaned over the reading-desk and beckoned to the verger, who mounted the steps to receive his bidding. Then the three ladies in the grand pew were amazed to see the verger take his way the whole length of the church, to return with the old woman, whom he placed in the front pew of all, its occupants making willing room for her. The great preacher looked at her with a smile of recognition, and then the service went on, and he preached a sermon which struck fire from every heart.

"Who was she?" asked the ladies who could not make room for her, as they passed the verger at the door.

"*The preacher's mother*," replied the verger, in an injured tone, remembering how they had led him to act.

How few remember that "while man looketh on the outward appearance, the Lord looketh on the heart."

11. "WORDS IN TUNEFUL ORDER": CHILDREN'S POETRY

The world is so full of a number of things,
I'm sure we should all be as happy as kings.
—Robert Louis Stevenson, "Happy Thought" (1885)

After Lewis Carroll's Humpty Dumpty finishes one of his uproariously pedantic explications, he admits: "When I make a word do a lot of work like that, I always pay it extra." The poets sampled here would have come close to bankruptcy if they had had to reimburse their "words in tuneful order" (Wordsworth) for all of their expressive, captivating lyricism. Employing a remarkable variety of techniques and voices, they created a rich body of poems that are songs of play—touching on play's frivolous and ecstatic limits. Indeed, the works of poets best symbolize the richness and artistry of the Golden Age of children's literature.

For the sheer beauty and poignancy of their lines—their deft melodies and tenderness—certain children's poets must stand apart. Christina Rossetti's singing "high" and "low", as she puts it at the opening of *A Nursery Rhyme Book* (1872), lovingly enfolds the reader. The graceful prosody and artless simplicity of Robert Louis Stevenson and Walter de la Mare are without equal. In *A Child's Garden of Verses* (1885) the metrical dexterity of "My Shadow" and "The Land of Counterpane" ensures that they will continue to enchant and amuse—and be recited. Similarly the "inward melody" to which de la Mare's "slim Sophia" paces, in

"Reverie", haunts readers with its elegant suggestiveness.

Many poets strove to capture the essence of everyday talk and events in their work. James Whitcomb Riley recreates a quaint Hoosier dialect, and Eugene Field composes gentle lullabies from simple childhood fantasies. In pieces like "Eletelephony" and "The Orang-Outang" another American, Laura Richards (1850-1943), celebrates the fun of transposed language with a zest that forecasts the word-play of Ogden Nash. The English man of letters and humorist Hilaire Belloc is warmly remembered for his mock cautionary verses about what happens to children who chew string, slam doors, or tell lies.

The two greatest poetic wits of the Golden Age were of course Lewis Carroll and Edward Lear, the grand masters whose works best display Victorian excellence. No Golden Age parodist matches the brilliance of Carroll when he submits well-loved works by Watts, Taylor, and Southey to witty burlesque. Lear was the champion of another form of mimicry in nonsense lyrics, botanies, and alphabets whose newly coined words and absurd story lines parodied conventions; his world of luminous Dongs, runcible spoons, and Crumpetty trees makes its own peculiar sense.

CHARLES LUTWIDGE DODGSON ("LEWIS CARROLL") (1832-1898)

From *Alice's Adventures in Wonderland* (1865) and *Through the Looking-Glass and What Alice Found There* (1872)

Charles Lutwidge Dodgson, a cantankerous don of mathematics at Christ Church, Oxford, and the author of such academic tomes as *An Elementary Treatise on Determinants* (1867) and *Curiosa Mathematica* (1888), numbered among his enthusiasms an adoration—always properly though extravagantly expressed—for little girls. One golden July afternoon he took Alice Liddell and her two sisters, the daughters of Dean Liddell, on a rowing expedition up the Thames and on that outing he recited extemporaneously the beginning of *Alice's Adventures in Wonderland*, which was published three years later. The narrative describing Alice's curious experiences is punctuated by verse that parodies Isaac Watts, Robert Southey, and Jane Taylor. "The Crocodile Song" drains the piety from Isaac Watts's Divine Song "Against Idleness and Mischief", just as his nonsense masterpiece "Father William" cleverly extracts all the sententiousness from Robert Southey's "The Old Man's Comforts and How He Gained Them". The Mad Hatter's "Twinkle, twinkle, little bat" superimposes a farcical absurdity on Jane Taylor's beloved "Twinkle, twinkle, little star". "Jabberwocky", from *Through the Looking-Glass*, displays Carroll's brilliant skill at making neologisms, portmanteau words, and sound and rhythm, rather than meaning, adumbrate the tale of a heroic deed.

From *Alice's Adventures in Wonderland*

THE CROCODILE SONG

How doth the little crocodile
Improve his shining tail,
And pours the waters of the Nile
On every golden scale!

How cheerfully he seems to grin,
How neatly spreads his claws,
And welcomes little fishes in
With gently smiling jaws!

TWINKLE, TWINKLE, LITTLE BAT

Twinkle, twinkle, little bat:
How I wonder what you're at?
Up above the world you fly,
Like a treatray in the sky.
Twinkle, twinkle—

YOU ARE OLD, FATHER WILLIAM

"You are old, Father William," the young man said,
    "And your hair has become very white;
And yet you incessantly stand on hour head—
    Do you think at your age, it is right?"

"In my youth," Father William replied to his son,
    "I feared it might injure the brain;
But, now that I'm perfectly sure I have none,
    Why, I do it again and again."

"You are old," said the youth, "as I mentioned before,
    And have grown most uncommonly fat;
Yet you turned a back-somersault in at the door—
    Pray, what is the reason for that?"

"In my youth," said the sage, as he shook his grey locks,
    "I kept all my limbs very supple
By the use of this ointment—one shilling the box—
    Allow me to sell you a couple?"

"You are old," said the youth, "and your jaws are too weak
    For anything tougher than suet;
Yet you finished the goose, with the bones and the beak—
    Pray, how did you manage to do it?

"In my youth," said his father, "I took to the law,
    And argued each case with my wife;
And the muscular strength, which it gave to my jaw,
    Has lasted the rest of my life."

"You are old," said the youth, "one would hardly suppose
    That your eye was as steady as ever;
Yet you balanced an eel on the end of your nose—
    What made you so awfully clever?"

"I have answered three questions, and that is enough,"
    Said his father. "Don't give yourself airs!
Do you think I can listen all day to such stuff?
    Be off, or I'll kick you downstairs!"

From *Through the Looking-Glass and What Alice Found There*

JABBERWOCKY

"Twas brillig, and the slithy toves
   Did gyre and gimble in the wabe:
All mimsy were the borogoves,
   And the mome raths outgrabe.

"Beware the Jabberwock, my son!
   The jaws that bite, the claws that catch!
Beware the Jubjub bird, and shun
   The frumious Bandersnatch!"

He took his vorpal sword in hand:
   Long time the manxome foe he sought—
So rested he by the Tumtum tree,
   And stood awhile in thought.

And as in uffish thought he stood,
   The Jabberwock, with eyes of flame,
Came whiffling through the tulgey wood,
   And burbled as it came!

One, two! One, two! And through and through
   The vorpal blade went snicker-snack!
He left it dead, and with its head
   He went galumphing back.

"And hast thou slain the Jabberwock?
   Come to my arms, my beamish boy!
O frabjous day! Callooh! Callay!"
   He chortled in his joy.

'Twas brillig, and the slithy toves
   Did gyre and gimble in the wabe:
All mimsy were the borogoves,
   And the mome raths outgrabe.

CHRISTINA GEORGINA ROSSETTI (1830-1894)
From *Sing-Song. A Nursery Rhyme Book* (1872)

The youngest in a gifted family, Christina Rossetti was educated by her Anglo-Italian mother, the accomplished Frances Polidori. The Rossettis, who lived mainly in London, were all passionately devoted to their mother; their indulgent Neapolitan father, Gabriele, was less favourably treated and remembered by his offspring. Christina was a precocious child, writing poems at the age of twelve and having a collection of them privately published when she was only sixteen. Among her mature collections, the best known are *Goblin Market* (1862), *The Prince's Progress* (1866), and *Sing-Song* (1872), a collection for children. Known for her beauty as well as her poetry, she moved with ease in the avant-garde circle of Pre-Raphaelites that congregated around her brother, the poet Dante Gabriel Rossetti. Although accepted by the Pre-Raphaelites, however, Christina often demonstrated an astonishing prudery and clung to love of God.

The themes of longing, privation, and sorrow that appear so frequently in *Sing-Song* (1872) had real equivalents in Christina's own life at the time. Suffering from Graves disease (characterized by a disfiguring exophthalmic goiter and general sallowness) that ruined her beauty, she was also witnessing, with extreme anguish, the progressive deterioration of her beloved brother. Later, following Dante Gabriel's temporary recovery, she grieved deeply over the death of her sister Maria, an Anglican nun. The wonderful lyricism of her poems for children is always tempered by an awareness of pain and tragedy. Christina's expressive text, a blending of joy and sorrow, is gracefully complemented by Arthur Hughes' illustrations which, the poet acknowledged, "deserve to sell the volume".

Love me,—I love you,
Love me, my baby;
Sing it high, sing it low,
Sing it as may be.

Mother's arms under you,
Her eyes above you
Sing it high, sing it low,
Love me,—I love you.

Your brother has a falcon,
   Your sister has a flower;
But what is left for mannikin,
   Born within an hour?

I'll nurse you on my knee, my knee,
   My own little son;
I'll rock you, rock you, in my arms,
   My least little one.

Growing in the vale
   By the uplands hilly,
Growing straight and frail,
   Lady Daffadowndilly.

In a golden crown,
And a scant green gown
   While the spring blows chilly,
Lady Daffadown,
   Sweet Daffadowndilly.

My baby has a mottled fist,
  My baby has a neck in creases;
My baby kisses and is kissed,
  For he's the very thing for kisses.

Who has seen the wind?
  Neither I nor you:
But when the leaves hang trembling
  The wind is passing thro'.

Who has seen the wind?
  Neither you nor I:
But when the trees bow down their heads
  The wind is passing by.

Boats sail on the rivers,
  And ships sail on the seas;
But clouds that sail across the sky
  Are prettier far than these.

There are bridges on the rivers,
  As pretty as you please;
But the bow that bridges heaven,
  And overtops the trees,
And builds a road from earth to sky,
  Is prettier far than these.

A frisky lamb
And a frisky child
Playing their pranks
  In a cowslip meadow:
The sky all blue
And the air all mild
And the fields all sun
  And the lanes half shadow.

I planted a hand
  And there came up a palm,
I planted a heart
  And there came up balm.

Then I planted a wish,
  But there sprang a thorn,
While heaven frowned with thunder
  And earth sighed forlorn.

   Lullaby, oh, lullaby!
Flowers are closed and lambs are sleeping;
   Lullaby, oh, lullaby!
Stars are up, the moon is peeping;
   Lullaby, oh, lullaby!
While the birds are silence keeping,
   (Lullaby, oh, lullaby!)
Sleep, my baby, fall a-sleeping,
   Lullaby, oh, lullaby!

EDWARD LEAR (1812-1888)
From *Laughable Lyrics: A Fourth Book of Nonsense Poems, Songs, Botany, Music, &.* (1877)

Although he was a landscape painter, ornithological draughtsman, and travel essayist in his day, Lear is most remembered for his nonsense verse—lyrics, botanies, and alphabets—that invariably combine the absurd and the exotic. Despite the vivacity of their bouncing rhymes and freshly coined words, however, many of Lear's "laughable" ditties are tinged with melancholy. An old bachelor who was convinced of his own unattractiveness, he often added elements of self-deprecating humour to his songs about strange or unhappy creatures, such as the rejected "Yonghy-Bonghy-Bo" and the freakish "Dong with the Luminous Nose".

THE COURTSHIP OF THE YONGHY-BONGHY-BÒ

I

On the Coast of Coromandel
  Where the early pumpkins blow,
    In the middle of the woods
Lived the Yonghy-Bonghy-Bò.
Two old chairs, and half a candle,—
One old jug without a handle,—
    These were all his worldly goods:
    In the middle of the woods,
    These were all the worldly goods,
  Of the Yonghy-Bonghy-Bò,
  Of the Yonghy-Bonghy-Bò.

II

Once, among the Bong-trees walking
  Where the early pumpkins blow,
    To a little heap of stones
Came the Yonghy-Bonghy-Bò.
There he heard a Lady talking,
To some milk-white Hens of Dorking,—
    " 'Tis the Lady Jingly Jones!
    "On that little heap of stones
    "Sits the Lady Jingly Jones!"
Said the Yonghy-Bonghy-Bò,
Said the Yonghy-Bonghy-Bò.

III

"Lady Jingly! Lady Jingly!
  "Sitting where the pumpkins blow,
    "Will you come and be my wife?"
Said the Yonghy-Bonghy-Bò.
"I am tired of living singly,—
"On this coast so wild and shingly,—
    "I'm a-weary of my life;
    "If you'll come and be my wife,
    "Quite serene would be my life!"—
Said the Yonghy-Bonghy-Bò,
Said the Yonghy-Bonghy-Bò.

IV

"On this Coast of Coromandel,
  "Shrimps and watercresses grow,
    "Prawns are plentiful and cheap,"
Said the Yonghy-Bonghy-Bò.
"You shall have my chairs and candle,
"And my jug without a handle!—
    "Gaze upon the rolling deep
    ("Fish is plentiful and cheap;)
    "As the sea, my love is deep!"
Said the Yonghy-Bonghy-Bò,
Said the Yonghy-Bonghy-Bò.

V

Lady Jingly answered sadly,
And her tears began to flow,—
"Your proposal comes too late,
"Mr Yonghy-Bonghy-Bò!
"I would be your wife most gladly!"
(Here she twirled her fingers madly,)
"But in England I've a mate!
"Yes! you've asked me far too late,
"For in England I've a mate,
"Mr Yonghy-Bonghy-Bò!
"Mr Yonghy-Bonghy-Bò!"

VI

"Mr Jones—(his name is Handel,—
"Handel Jones, Esquire, & Co.)
"Dorking fowls delights to send,
"Mr Yonghy-Bonghy-Bò!
"Keep, oh! keep your chairs and candle,
And your jug without a handle,—
"I can merely be your friend!
"—Should my Jones more Dorkings send,
"I will give you three, my friend!
"Mr Yonghy-Bonghy-Bò!
"Mr Yonghy-Bonghy-Bò!

VII

"Though you've such a tiny body,
"And your head so large doth grow,—
"Though your hat may blow away,
"Mr Yonghy-Bonghy-Bò!
"Though you're such a Hoddy Doddy—
"Yet I wish that I could modi-
"fy the words I needs must say!
"Will you please to go away?
"That is all I have to say—
"Mr Yonghy-Bonghy-Bò!
"Mr Yonghy-Bonghy-Bò!"

VIII

Down the slippery slopes of Myrtle,
　Where the early pumpkins blow,
　　To the calm and silent sea
　Fled the Yonghy-Bonghy-Bò.
There, beyond the Bay of Gurtle,
Lay a large and lively Turtle;—
　　　"You're the Cove," he said, "for me
　　　"On your back beyond the sea,
　　　"Turtle, you shall carry me!"
　Said the Yonghy-Bonghy-Bò,
　Said the Yonghy-Bonghy-Bò.

IX

Through the silent-roaring ocean
　Did the Turtle swiftly go;
　　Holding fast upon his shell
　Rode the Yonghy-Bonghy-Bò.
With a sad primaeval motion
Towards the sunset isles of Boshen
　　　Still the Turtle bore him well.
　　　Holding fast upon his shell,
　　　"Lady Jingle Jones, farewell!"
　Sang the Yonghy-Bonghy-Bò,
　Sang the Yonghy-Bonghy-Bò.

X

From the Coast of Coromandel,
　Did that Lady never go;
　　On that heap of stones she mourns
　For the Yonghy-Bonghy-Bò.
On that Coast of Coromandel,
In his jug without a handle
　　　Still she weeps, and daily moans;
　　　On that little heap of stones
　　　To her Dorking Hens she moans,
　For the Yonghy-Bonghy-Bò,
　For the Yonghy-Bonghy-Bò.

THE QUANGLE WANGLE'S HAT

I

On the top of the Crumpetty Tree
   The Quangle Wangle sat,
    But his face you could not see,
   On account of his Beaver Hat.
For his Hat was a hundred and two feet wide,
With ribbons and bibbons on every side
And bells, and buttons, and loops, and lace,
So that nobody ever could see the face
      Of the Quangle Wangle Quee.

II

The Quangle Wangle said
   To himself on the Crumpetty Tree,—
"Jam; and jelly; and bread;
   "Are the best of food for me!
"But the longer I live on this Crumpetty Tree
"The plainer than ever it seems to me
"That very few people come this way
"And that life on the whole is far from gay!"
      Said the Quangle Wangle Quee.

III

But there came to the Crumpetty Tree,
   Mr and Mrs Canary;
And they said,—"Did ever you see
   "Any spot so charmingly airy?
"May we build a nest on your lovely Hat?
"Mr Quangle Wangle, grant us that!
"O please let us come and build a nest
"Of whatever material suits you best,
       "Mr Quangle Wangle Quee!"

IV

And besides, to the Crumpetty Tree
   Came the Stork, the Duck, and the Owl;
The Snail, and the Bumble-Bee,
   The Frog, and the Fimble Fowl;
(The Fimble Fowl, with a Corkscrew leg;)
And all of them said,—"We humbly beg,
"We may build our homes on your lovely Hat,—
"Mr Quangle Wangle, grant us that!
      "Mr Quangle Wangle Quee!"

V

And the Golden Grouse came there,
   And the Pobble who has no toes,—
And the small Olympian bear,—
   And the Dong with a luminous nose.
And the Blue Baboon, who played the flute,—
And the Orient Calf from the Land of Tute,—
And the Attery Squash, and the Bisky Bat,—
All came and built on the lovely Hat
      Of the Quangle Wangle Quee.

VI

And the Quangle Wangle said
   To himself on the Crumpetty Tree,—
"When all these creatures move
   "What a wonderful noise there'll be!"
And at night by the light of the Mulberry moon
They danced to the Flute of the Blue Baboon,
On the broad green leaves of the Crumpetty Tree,
And all were as happy as happy could be,
      With the Quangle Wangle Quee.

NONSENSE ALPHABET, NO. 6.

A   tumbled down, and hurt his Arm, against a bit of wood.
B   said, "My Boy, O! do not cry; it cannot do you good!"
C   said, "A Cup of Coffee hot can't do you any harm."
D   said, "A Doctor should be fetched, and he would cure the arm."
E   said, "An Egg beat up with milk would quickly make him well,"
F   said, "A Fish, if broiled, might cure, if only by the smell."
G   said, "Green Gooseberry fool, the best of cures I hold."
H   said, "His Hat should be kept on, to keep him from the cold."
I   said, "Some Ice upon his head will make him better soon."
J   said, "Some Jam, if spread on bread, or given in a spoon!"
K   said, "A Kangaroo is here,—this picture let him see."
L   said, "A Lamp pray keep alight, to make some barley tea."
M   said, "A Mulberry or two might give him satisfaction."
N   said, "Some Nuts, if rolled about, might be a slight attraction."
O   said, "An Owl might make him laugh, if only it would wink."
P   said, "Some Poetry might be read aloud, to make him think."
Q   said, "A Quince I recommend,—a Quince, or else a Quail."
R   said, "Some Rats might make him move, if fastened by their tail."
S   said, "A Song should now be sung, in hopes to make him laugh!"
T   said, "A Turnip might avail, if sliced or cut in half!"
U   said, "An Urn, with water hot, place underneath his chin!"
V   said, "I'll stand upon a chair, and play a Violin!"
W   said, "Some Whisky-Whizzgigs fetch, some marbles and a ball!"
X   said, "Some double XX ale would be the best of all!"
Y   said, "Some Yeast mixed up with salt would make a perfect
        plaster!"
Z   said, "Here is a box of Zinc! Get in, my little master!
     "We'll shut you up! We'll nail you down! We will, my little master!
     "We think we've all heard quite enough of this your sad disaster!"

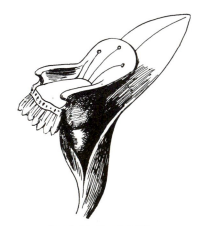

Armchairia Comfortabilis.

Smalltoothcombia Domestica.

Manypeeplia Upsidownia

HOWARD PYLE (1853-1911)
From *Pepper & Salt; or, Seasoning for Young Folk* (1885)

Born in Wilmington, Delaware, of Quaker parents, Howard Pyle studied art and received his first professional assignment to illustrate and write for *St Nicholas* in the 1870s. His work as an illustrator, for which he is best remembered today, was immensely innovative and influential in late nineteenth-century American illustration. By bringing to bear exactly-detailed historical knowledge and an expert—at times decorative—craftsmanship, he always succeeded in capturing the spirit of the tale and identifying himself with the folk in it. The art classes he taught at the Drexel Institute of Arts and Sciences in Philadelphia, beginning in 1894, and at Chadds Ford, Delaware, impressed his realistic yet romantic style on students like Maxfield Parrish (see p. 250) and Jessie Wilcox Smith (see p. 481).

In his handsomely illustrated prose works, which were mainly retellings, Pyle revealed again and again his admiration of heroic men of action, as can be seen in *The Merry Adventures of Robin Hood of Great Renown in Nottinghamshire* (1883) and *The Story of King Arthur and His Knights* (1903). *Pepper & Salt* (1885) is a collection of his prose and poetry, also illustrated in his charmingly archaic style. The jog-trot metrics of his poetry show Pyle's mastery of delightful caricature.

THE·FORCE·OF·NEED·

"Hey, Robin! ho, Robin!
Singing on the tree,
I will give you white bread,
If you will come to me."

"Oh! the little breeze is singing
To the nodding daisies white;
And the tender grass is springing,
And the sun is warm and bright;
And my little mate is waiting
In the budding hedge for me;
So, on the whole, I'll not accept
Your kindly courtesy."

"Hey, Robin! ho, Robin!
Now the north winds blow;
Wherefore do you come here,
In the ice and snow?"

"The wind is raw, the flowers are dead,
The frost is on the thorn,
So I'll gladly take a crust of bread,
And come where it is warm."

Oh, Children! little Children!
Have *you* ever chanced to see
One beg for crust that sneered at crumb
In bright prosperity?

· HP ·

FANCY·AND·FACT

O! a shepherd and a shepherdess,
   They dwelt in Arcadee,
And they were dressed in Watteau dress,
   Most charming for to see.

They sat upon the dewy grass,
   With buds and blossoms set,
And the shepherd played unto the lass,
   Upon a flageolet.

It seemed to me as though it was
   A very pleasant thing;
Particularly so because
   The time of year was Spring.

But, O! the ground was damp, and so,
   At least, I have been told,
The shepherd caught the lumbago,
   The shepherdess, a cold.

My darling Child! the fact is
   That the Poets often sing
Of those joys which in the practice
   Are another sort of thing.

Superficial Culture

I'll tell of a certain old dame;
        The same
Had a beautiful piggy, whose name
    Was Jame-
    -s; and whose beauty and worth,
From the day of his birth,
Were matters of popular fame,
        And his claim
To gentility no one could blame.

So, seeing his promise, she thought
        She ought
To have him sufficiently taught
        The art
Of deportment, to go
Into company; so
A master of dancing she brought,
        Who was fraught
With a style which the piggiwig caught.

So his company manners were rare.
    His care
Of social observances there
        Would bear
The closest inspection,
And not a reflection
Could rest on his actions, howe'er
    You might care
To examine 'em down to a hair.

Now, things went beau-ti-ful-ly,
        Till he
Fell in love with a dame of degree;
        Pardie!
When he tried for to speak,
    But could only say, "O-w-e-e-k!"
For, whatever his polish might be,
        Why, dear me!
He was pig at the bottom, you see.

H. PYLE.

ROBERT LOUIS STEVENSON (1850-1894)
From *A Child's Garden of Verses* (1885)

Although he studied engineering and prepared for a legal career, the Scottish-born Robert Louis Stevenson was attracted to the bohemian and artistic life. Essayist, poet, short-story writer, novelist, and dramatist, he travelled widely—on the Continent and in America—and finally settled on the island of Samoa in the South Seas, where he died of a cerebral haemorrhage at the age of forty-four. A master storyteller, he contributed a keen and mysterious realism to his tales of adventure and romance—in such famous works as *Treasure Island* (1883), *The Strange Case of Dr Jekyll and Mr Hyde* (1886), *Kidnapped* (1886), and *The*

Black Arrow (1888)—that are still enjoyed by young and old alike.

A Child's Garden of Verses (1885) has had an unrivalled popularity. Stevenson has made his garden and the child who inhabits it (himself, "far, far away . . .") very real and substantial. The poems are metrically pure re-creations of his quiet delights as a bookish and sickly boy—pictured in "The Unseen Playmate" as "happy and lonely and good"—who has a rich imaginative life. For such a child stairs become a ship, a washbasket converts to a ranging pirate galleon, and picture books are passports to exotic lands.

BED IN SUMMER

In winter I get up at night
    And dress by yellow candle-light.
In summer, quite the other way,
    I have to go to bed by day.

I have to go to bed and see
    The birds still hopping on the tree,
Or hear the grown-up people's feet
    Still going past me in the street.

And does it not seem hard to you,
    When all the sky is clear and blue,
And I should like so much to play,
    To have to go to bed by day?

WHOLE DUTY OF CHILDREN

A child should always say what's true
    And speak when he is spoken to,
And behave mannerly at table;
    At least as far as he is able.

THE LAND OF COUNTERPANE

When I was sick and lay a-bed,
  I had two pillows at my head,
  And all my toys beside me lay
  To keep me happy all the day.

And sometimes for an hour or so
I watched my leaden soldiers go,
With different uniforms and drills,
Among the bed-clothes, through the hills;

And sometimes sent my ships in fleets
All up and down among the sheets;
Or brought my trees and houses out,
And planted cities all about.

I was the giant great and still
That sits upon the pillow-hill,
And sees before him, dale and plain,
The pleasant land of counterpane.

MY SHADOW

I have a little shadow that goes in and out with me,
And what can be the use of him is more than I can see.
He is very, very like me from the heels up to the head;
And I see him jump before me, when I jump into my bed.

The funniest thing about him is the way he likes to grow—
Not at all like proper children, which is always very slow;
For he sometimes shoots up taller like an india-rubber ball,
And he sometimes gets so little that there's none of him at all.

He hasn't got a notion of how children ought to play,
And can only make a fool of me in every sort of way.
He stays so close beside me, he's a coward you can see;
I'd think shame to stick to Nursie as that shadow sticks to me!

One morning, very early, before the sun was up,
I rose and found the shining dew on every buttercup;
But my lazy little shadow, like an arrant sleepy-head,
Had stayed at home behind me and was fast asleep in bed.

THE UNSEEN PLAYMATE

When children are playing alone on the green,
In comes the playmate that never was seen.
When children are happy and lonely and good,
The Friend of the Children comes out of the wood.

Nobody heard him and nobody saw,
His is a picture you never could draw,
But he's sure to be present, abroad or at home,
When children are happy and playing alone.

He lies in the laurels, he runs on the grass,
He sings when you tinkle the musical glass;
Whene'er you are happy and cannot tell why,
The Friend of the Children is sure to be by!

He loves to be little, he hates to be big,
'Tis he that inhabits the caves that you dig;
'Tis he when you play with your soldiers of tin
That sides with the Frenchmen and never can win.

'Tis he, when at night you go off to your bed,
Bids you go to your sleep and not trouble your head;
For wherever they're lying, in cupboard or shelf,
'Tis he will take care of your playthings himself!

HILAIRE BELLOC (1870-1953)
From *The Bad Child's Book of Beasts* (1896) and *Cautionary Tales for Children* (1907)

Novelist, essayist, biographer, and critic, Hilaire Belloc scored his first literary success with the publication of *The Bad Child's Book of Beasts* (1896). *More Beasts for Worse Children* (1897) followed, as the poet's wry interest in bizarre misbehaviour grew. His *Cautionary Tales* (1907), like the more grisly admonitions in Heinrich Hoffmann's *Struwwelpeter* or *Shock-headed Peter* (1848), describe the usually fatal results of wrong-doing or disobedience, but do so with a jovial metre and rhyme and a comic hyperbole that is very English.

From *The Bad Child's Book of Beasts*

THE HIPPOPOTAMUS

I shoot the Hippopotamus with bullets made of platinum,
Because if I use leaden ones his hide is sure to flatten 'em.

THE FROG

Be kind and tender to the Frog,
  And do not call him names,
As "Slimy skin", or "Polly-wog",
  Or likewise "Ugly James",
Or "Gap-a-grin", or "Toad-gone-wrong",
  Or "Billy Bandy-knees":
The Frog is justly sensitive
  To epithets like these.
No animal will more repay
  A treatment kind and fair;
At least so lonely people say
Who keep a frog (and, by the way,
They are extremely rare).

From *Cautionary Tales for Children*

HENRY KING

*Who Chewed Bits of String, and Was Early
Cut Off in Dreadful Agonies*

The Chief Defect of Henry King
Was chewing little bits of String.
At last he swallowed some which tied
Itself in ugly Knots inside.
Physicians of the Utmost Fame
Were called at once; but when they came
They answered, as they took their Fees,
"There is no Cure for this Disease.
Henry will very soon be dead."

His parents stood about his Bed
Lamenting his Untimely Death,
When Henry, with his Latest Breath,
Cried—"Oh, my Friends, be warned by me,
That Breakfast, Dinner, Lunch and Tea
Are all the Human Frame requires . . ."
With that the Wretched Child expires.

MATILDA

Who Told Lies, and Was Burned to Death

Matilda told such Dreadful Lies,
It made one Gasp and Stretch one's Eyes;
Her Aunt, who, from her Earliest Youth,
Had kept a Strict Regard for Truth,
Attempted to Believe Matilda:
The effort very nearly killed her,
And would have done so, had not She
Discovered this Infirmity.
For once, towards the Close of Day,
Matilda, growing tired of play,
And finding she was left alone,
Went tiptoe to the Telephone
And summoned the Immediate Aid
Of London's Noble Fire-Brigade.
Within an hour the Gallant Band
Were pouring in on every hand,
From Putney, Hackney Downs and Bow,

With Courage high and Hearts a-glow
They galloped, roaring through the Town,
"Matilda's House is Burning Down!"
Inspired by British Cheers and Loud
Proceeding from the Frenzied Crowd,
They ran their ladders through a score
Of windows on the Ball Room Floor;
And took Peculiar Pains to Souse
The Pictures up and down the House
Until Matilda's Aunt succeeded
In showing them they were not needed
And even then she had to pay
To get the Men to go away!

*

It happened that a few Weeks later
Her Aunt was off to the Theatre
To see that Interesting Play
The Second Mrs Tanqueray.
She had refused to take her Niece
To hear this Entertaining Piece:
A Deprivation Just and Wise
To Punish her for Telling Lies.
That Night a Fire *did* break out—
You should have heard Matilda Shout!
You should have heard her Scream and Bawl,
And throw the window up and call
To People passing in the Street—
(The rapidly increasing Heat
Encouraging her to obtain
Their confidence)—but all in vain!
For every time She shouted "Fire!"
They only answered "Little Liar!"
And therefore when her Aunt returned,
Matilda, and the House, were Burned.

REBECCA

*Who Slammed Doors for Fun and Perished
Miserably*

A Trick that everyone abhors
In Little Girls is slamming Doors.
A Wealthy Banker's Little Daughter
Who Lived in Palace Green, Bayswater
(By name Rebecca Offendort),
Was given to this Furious Sport.

She would deliberately go
And Slam the door like Billy-Ho!
To make her Uncle Jacob start.
She was not really bad at heart,
But only rather rude and wild:
She was an aggravating child. . . .

It happened that a Marble Bust
Of Abraham was standing just
Above the Door this little Lamb
Had carefully prepared to Slam,
And Down it came! It knocked her flat!
It laid her out! She looked like that.

Her funeral Sermon (which was long
And followed by a Sacred Song)
Mentioned her Virtues, it is true,
But dwelt upon her Vices too,
And showed the Dreadful End of One
Who goes and slams the door for Fun.

The children who were brought to hear
The awful Tale from far and near
Were much impressed and inly swore
They never more would slam the Door.
—As often they had done before.

WALTER JOHN DE LA MARE (1873-1956)
From *Songs of Childhood* (1902)

In addition to his many publications for adults, this poet, storyteller, and anthologist made a sizeable and distinctive contribution to children's literature. *Songs of Childhood* (1902) was his first collection of poems; it was followed in 1913 by the famous *Peacock Pie: A Book of Rhymes*. Combining rare fancy and uncommon vowel melodies, de la Mare's poetry impresses young and old readers alike with its simplicity and naturalness, which of course are the result of painstaking care and verbal mastery. These books—and his phantasmagoric stories, like *The Three Mulla-Mulgars* of 1910, an allegory about the adventures of three monkeys; deft retellings in *Stories from the Bible* (1929); and rich anthologies of poems for the young, especially *Come Hither* (1923) and *Tom Tiddler's Ground* (1931)—have earned for de la Mare a respected place in the Golden Age and beyond.

REVERIE

When slim Sophia mounts her horse
    And paces down the avenue,
It seems an inward melody
    She paces to.

Each narrow hoof is lifted high
    Beneath the dark enclust'ring pines,
A silver ray within his bit
    And bridle shines.

His eye burns deep, his tail is arched,
    And streams upon the shadowy air,
The daylight sleeks his jetty flanks,
    His mistress' hair.

Her habit flows in darkness down,
    Upon the stirrup rests her foot,
Her brow is lifted, as if earth
    She heeded not.

'Tis silent in the avenue,
    The sombre pines are mute of song,
The blue is dark, there moves no breeze
    The boughs among.

When slim Sophia mounts her horse
    And paces down the avenue,
It seems an inward melody
    She paces to.

TARTARY

If I were Lord of Tartary,
  Myself and me alone,
My bed should be of ivory,
  Of beaten gold my throne;
And in my court should peacocks flaunt,
And in my forests tigers haunt,
And in my pools great fishes slant
  Their fins athwart the sun.

If I were Lord of Tartary,
  Trumpeters every day
To all my meals should summon me,
  And in my courtyards bray;
And in the evenings lamps should shine,
Yellow as honey, red as wine,
While harp, and flute, and mandoline,
  Made music sweet and gay.

If I were Lord of Tartary,
  I'd wear a robe of beads,
White, and gold, and green they'd be—
  And small, and thick as seeds;
And ere should wane the morning-star,
I'd don my robe and scimitar,
And zebras seven should draw my car
  Through Tartary's dark glades.

Lord of the fruits of Tartary,
  Her rivers silver-pale!
Lord of the hills of Tartary,
  Glen, thicket, wood, and dale!
Her flashing stars, her scented breeze,
Her trembling lakes, like foamless seas,
Her bird-delighting citron-trees
  In every purple vale!

I MET AT EVE

I met at even the Prince of Sleep,
His was a still and lovely face,
He wandered through a valley steep
   Lovely in a lonely place.

His garb was grey of lavender,
About his brows a poppy-wreath
Burned like dim coals, and everywhere
   The air was sweeter for his breath.

His twilight feet no sandals wore,
His eyes shone faint in their own flame,
Fair moths that gloomed his steps before
   Seemed letters of his lovely name.

His house is in the mountain ways,
A phantom house of misty walls,
Whose golden flocks at evening graze,
   And witch the moon with muffled calls.

Updwelling from his shadowy springs
Sweet waters shake a trembling sound,
There flit the hoot-owl's silent wings,
   There hath his web the silkworm wound.

Dark in his pools clear visions lurk,
And rosy, as with morning buds,
Along his dales of broom and birk
   Dreams haunt his solitary woods.

I met at eve the Prince of Sleep,
His was a still and lovely face,
He wandered through a valley steep,
   Lovely in a lonely place.

JAMES WHITCOMB RILEY (1849-1916)
From *The Book of Joyous Children* (1902)

Born in Greenfield, Indiana, James Whitcomb Riley was a journalist and versifier. To the Canadian poet Bliss Carman, who wrote an essay commemorating him, he was "a whimsical pure poet and a constant lovely friend". Called affectionately "the children's poet", he is best remembered for his use of a quaint Hoosier dialect.

Riley's genially sentimental poems are all rooted in the things, people, and places of his childhood. His memories of a curious fifteen-year-old girl who worked for a time at the Riley house when he was a child inspired "Little Orphant Annie", with its famous refrain: "the Gobble-uns'll git you ef you don't watch out!"

LITTLE DICK AND THE CLOCK

When Dicky was sick
  In the night, and the clock,
As he listened, said "Tick-
  Atty—tick-atty—tock!"
He said that *it* said,
  Every time it said "Tick,"
It said "Sick," instead,
  And he *heard* it say "Sick!"
And when it said "Tick-
  Atty—tick-atty—tock,"
He said it said "Sick-
  Atty—sick-atty—sock!"
And he tried to *see* then,
  But the light was too dim,
Yet he *heard* it again—
  And 't was *talking* to him!

And then it said "Sick-
  Atty-—sick-atty—sick!
You poor little Dick-
  Atty—Dick-atty—Dick!—
Have you got the hick-
  Atties? Hi! send for Doc
To hurry up quick-
  Atty—quick-atty—quock,
And heat a hot brick-
  Atty—brick-atty—brock,
And rikle-ty wrap it
And clickle-ty clap it
  Against his cold feet-
    Al-ty—weep-aty—eepaty—
There he goes, slapit-
  Ty—slippaty—sleepaty!"

THE RAGGEDY MAN

O THE RAGGEDY MAN! He works fer Pa;
 An' he's the goodest man ever you saw!
He comes to our house every day,
An' waters the horses, an' feeds 'em hay;
An' he opens the shed—an' we all ist laugh
When he drives out our little old wobble-ly calf;
An' nen—ef our hired girl says he can—
He milks the cow fer 'Lizabuth Ann.—
 Ain't he a' awful good Raggedy Man?
  Raggedy! Raggedy! Raggedy Man!

W'y, The Raggedy Man—he's ist so good
He splits the kindlin' an' chops the wood;
An' nen he spades in our garden, too,
An' does most things 'at *boys* can't do!—
He clumbed clean up in our big tree
An' shooked a' apple down fer me—
An' nother'n', too, fer 'Lizabuth Ann—
An' nother'n', too, fer The Raggedy Man.—
 Ain't he a' awful kind Raggedy Man?
  Raggedy! Raggedy! Raggedy Man!

An' The Raggedy Man, he knows most rhymes
An' tells 'em, ef I be good sometimes:
Knows 'bout Giunts, an' Griffuns, an' Elves,
An' the Squidgicum-Squees 'at swallers therselves!
An', wite by the pump in our pasture-lot,
He showed me the hole 'at the Wunks is got,
'At lives 'way deep in the ground, an' can
Turn into me, er 'Lizabuth Ann,
Er Ma er Pa er The Raggedy Man!
 Ain't he a funny old Raggedy Man?
  Raggedy! Raggedy! Raggedy Man!

The Raggedy Man—one time when he
Wuz makin' a little bow-'n'-orry fer me,
Says "When *you're* big like your Pa is,
Air *you* go' to keep a fine store like his—
An' be a rich merchunt—an' wear fine clothes?—
Er what *air* you go' to be, goodness knows!"
An' nen he laughed at 'Lizabuth Ann,
An' I says " 'M go' to be a Raggedy Man!—
 I'm ist go' to be a nice Raggedy Man!"
  Raggedy! Raggedy! Raggedy Man!
(1890)

LITTLE ORPHANT ANNIE

LITTLE Orphant Annie's come to our house to stay,
An' wash the cups an' saucers up, an' bresh the crumbs away,
An' shoo the chickens off the porch, an' dust the hearth, an' sweep,
An' make the fire, an' bake the bread, an' earn her board-an'-keep;
An' all us other children, when the supper-things is done,
We set around the kitchen fire an' has the mostest fun
A-list'nin' to the witch-tales 'at Annie tells about,
An' the Gobble-uns 'at gits you
    Ef you
      Don't
        Watch
        Out!

Onc't they was a little boy wouldn't say his prayers,—
So when he went to bed at night, away up stairs,
His Mammy heerd him holler, an' his Daddy heerd
    him bawl,
An' when they turn't the kivvers down, he wasn't there at all!
An' they seeked him in the rafter-room, an' cubby hole, an' press,
An' seeked him up the chimbly-flue, an' ever'wheres, I guess;
But all they ever found was thist his pants an' round about:—
An' the Gobble-uns'll git you
    Ef you
      Don't
        Watch
        Out!

An' one time a little girl 'ud allus laugh an' grin,
An make fun of ever'one, an' all her blood an' kin;
An' onc't, when they was "company," an' ole folks was there,
She mocked 'em an' shocked 'em, an' said she didn't care!
An' thist as she kicked her heels, an' turn't to run an' hide,
They was two great big Black Things a-standin' by her side,
An' they snatched her through the ceilin' 'fore she knowed what she's
about!
An' the Gobble-uns'll git you
    Ef you
      Don't
        Watch
        Out!

An' little Orphant Annie says when the blaze is blue,
An' the lamp-wick sputters, an' the wind goes *woo-oo*!
An' you hear the crickets quit, an' the moon is gray,
An' the lightnin'-bugs in dew is all squenched away,—
You better mind yer parunts an' yer teachers fond an' dear,
An' churish them 'at loves you, an' dry the orphant's tear,

An' he'p the pore un' needy ones 'at clusters all about,
Er the Gobble-uns'll git you

  Ef you
   Don't
    Watch
     Out!

(1890)

EUGENE FIELD (1850-1895)
From *Poems of Childhood* (1904)

The American humorist and Chicago journalist Eugene Field attempted to recreate the perceptions of childhood in many ways, some more successful than others. Laboured ethnic dialects and maudlin veneration of children's innocence afflicted much of his poetry, along with ponderous diction like "sapient people", "mournful requiem", and "dolorous monotone". Field was capable, however, of writing some very enjoyable, lilting verse, such as "Wynken, Blynken, and Nod".

THE SUGAR-PLUM TREE

Have you ever heard of the Sugar-Plum Tree?
 'Tis a marvel of great renown!
It blooms on the shore of the Lollipop sea
 In the garden of Shut-Eye Town;
The fruit that it bears is so wondrously sweet
 (As those who have tasted it say)
That good little children have only to eat
 Of that fruit to be happy next day.

When you've got to the tree, you would have a hard time
 To capture the fruit which I sing;
The tree is so tall that no person could climb
 To the boughs where the sugar-plums swing!
But up in that tree sits a chocolate cat,
 And a gingerbread dog prowls below—
And this is the way you contrive to get at
 Those sugar-plums tempting you so:

You say but the word to that gingerbread dog
    And he barks with such terrible zest
That the chocolate cat is at once all agog,
    As her swelling proportions attest.
And the chocolate cat goes cavorting around
    From this leafy limb unto that,
And the sugar-plums tumble, of course to the ground—
    Hurrah for that chocolate cat!

There are marshamallows, gumdrops, and peppermint canes,
    With stripings of scarlet or gold,
And you carry away of the treasure that rains
    As much as your apron can hold!
So come, little child, cuddle closer to me
    In your dainty white nightcap and gown,
And I'll rock you away to that Sugar-Plum Tree
    In the garden of Shut-Eye Town.

WYNKEN, BLYNKEN, AND NOD

Wynken, Blynken, and Nod one night
    Sailed off in a wooden shoe—
Sailed on a river of crystal light,
    Into a sea of dew.
"Where are you going, and what do you wish?"
    The old moon asked the three.
"We have come to fish for the herring fish
    That live in this beautiful sea;
Nets of silver and gold have we!"
        Said Wynken
        Blynken,
        And Nod.

The old moon laughed and sang a song,
    As they rocked in the wooden shoe,
And the wind that sped them all night long
    Ruffled the waves of dew.
The little stars were the herring fish
    That lived in that beautiful sea—
"Now cast your nets wherever you wish—
    Never afeard are we":
So cried the stars to the fishermen three:
        Wynken,
        Blynken,
        And Nod.

All night long their nets they threw
　To the stars in the twinkling foam—
Then down from the skies came the wooden shoe,
　Bringing the fishermen home;
'Twas all so pretty a sail it seemed
　As if it could not be,
And some folks thought 'twas a dream they'd dreamed
　Of sailing that beautiful sea—
But I shall name you the fishermen three:
　　　Wynken,
　　　Blynken,
　　　And Nod.

Wynken and Blynken are two little eyes,
　And Nod is a little head;
And the wooden shoe that sailed the skies
　Is a wee one's trundle-bed.
So shut your eyes while mother sings
　Of wonderful sights that be,
And you shall see the beautiful things
　As you rock in the misty sea,
　Where the old shoe rocked the fishermen three:
　　　Wynken,
　　　Blynken
　　　and Nod.

BIBLIOGRAPHY

CRITICAL AND HISTORICAL STUDIES

Avery, Gillian and Angela Bull. *Nineteenth Century Children; Heroes and Heroines in English Children's Stories 1780-1900*. London: Hodder and Stoughton, 1965.

Avery, Gillian. *Childhood's Pattern; A Study of the Heroes and Heroines of Children's Fiction 1770-1950*. London: Hodder and Stoughton, 1975.

_____. *Victorian People: in Life and Literature*. New York: Holt, Rinehart and Winston, 1970.

Barry, Florence V. *A Century of Children's Books*. London: Methuen, 1922; 1968.

Bratton, Jacqueline S. *The Impact of Victorian Children's Fiction*. London: Croom Helm Ltd., 1981.

Cadogan, Mary and Patricia Craig. *You're A Brick, Angela!; A New Look at Girls' Fiction from 1839 to 1975*. London: Victor Gollancz Ltd., 1975.

Darton, F.J. Harvey. *Children's Books in England; Five Centuries of Social Life*. Third Edition. Revised by Brian Alderson. Cambridge: Cambridge University Press, 1982.

Egoff, Sheila. *The Republic of Childhood: A Critical Guide to Canadian Children's Literature in English*. Section Edition. Toronto: Oxford University Press, 1975.

Green, Roger Lancelyn. *Tellers of Tales: Children's Books and Their Authors from 1800 to 1968*. London: Kaye & Ward Ltd., 1969.

Macleod, Anne Scott. *A Moral Tale: Children's Fiction and American Culture, 1829-1860*. Hamden: The Shoe String Press, 1975.

Meigs, Cornelia, A. Eaton, E. Nesbitt, R.G. Viguers. *A Critical History of Children's Literature in English from Earliest Times to the Present*. New York: Macmillan, 1953.

Muir, Percy. *English Children's Books 1600 to 1900*. New York: Frederick A. Praeger, 1954.

Pickering, Samuel F., Jr. *John Locke and Children's Books in Eighteenth-Century England*. Knoxville: University of Tennessee Press, 1981.

Smith, Lillian H. *The Unreluctant Years; A Critical Approach to Children's Literature*. New York: The Viking Press, 1953.

Thwaite, Mary F. *From Primer to Pleasure in Reading: An Introduction to the History of Children's Books in England from the Invention of Printing to 1914 with an outline of some developments in other countries*. Boston: The Horn Book, 1972.

Townsend, John Rowe. *Written for Children: An Outline of English Children's Literature*. London: Garnet Miller, 1965.

Whalley, Joyce Irene. *Cobwebs to Catch Flies: Illustrated Books for the Nursery and Schoolroom 1700-1900*. London: Elek Books, 1974.

ANTHOLOGIES, CATALOGUES, AND REPRINTS

Arnold, Arnold. *Pictures and Stories from Forgotten Children's Books*. New York: Dover Publications, 1969.

Brand, Christiana, ed. *Naughty Children*. London: Victor Gollancz, 1962.

de Vries, Leonard, ed. *Flowers of Delight culled from the Osborne Collection of Early Children's Books: An Agreeable Garland of Prose and Poetry for the instruction and amusement of little masters and misses and their distinguished parents*. London: Dennis Dobson, 1965.

_____. *Little Wide-Awake: An Anthology from Victorian Children's Books and Periodicals in the Collection of Anne and Fernand G. Renier*. London: Arthur Barker Ltd., 1967.

Early Children's Books and Their Illustration. The Pierpont Morgan Library, New York. With a Preface by Charles Ryskamp. Boston: David R. Godine, 1975.

John W. Griffith and C.H. Frey, ed. *Classics of Children's Literature*. New York: Macmillan Publishing Co., Inc., 1981.

Haviland, Virginia. *Yankee Doodle's Literary Sampler of Prose, Poetry, Pictures Being an anthology of diverse works published for the edification and/or entertainment of young readers in America before 1900 selected from Rare Book Collections of the Library of Congress*. Washington: Library of Congress, 1974.

Lurie, Alison and J.G. Schiller, ed. *Classics of Children's Literature; A collection of 117 titles reprinted in photo-facsimile in 73 volumes*. New York & London: Garland Publishing, Inc., 1976-79.

Opie, Iona and Peter. *A Nursery Companion*. London: Oxford University Press, 1980.

Seymour-Smith, Martin, ed. *A Cupful of Tears: Sixteen Victorian Novelettes*. London: Wolfe Publishing, 1965.

St. John, Judith, ed. *The Osborne Collection of Early Children's Books 1566-1910 A Catalogue Volume I and The Osborne Collection of Early Children's Books 1476-1910 A Catalogue Volume II*. Toronto: University of Toronto Press, 1958; 1966; 1975.

Temple, Nigel. *Seen and Not Heard: A Garland of Fancies for Victorian Children*. London: Hutchinson, 1970.

Tuer, Andrew W. *Forgotten Children's Books*. New York: Benjamin Blom, 1898.
_____. *Stories from Old-fashioned Children's Books*. London: Leadenhall Press, 1899-1900.

THE FAIRY TALE

Bettelheim, Bruno. *The Uses of Enchantment; the Meaning and Importance of Fairy Tales*. New York: Alfred A. Knopf, Inc., 1976.

Browne, Frances. *Granny's Wonderful Chair, and Its Tales of Fairy Times*, illus. K. Meadows. London: Griffith and Farran, 1857. (Osborne Collection)

Clifford, Mrs. W.K. *Anyhow Stories for Children*, illus. D. Tennant. London: Macmillan, 1885. (Osborne Collection)

Cook, Elizabeth. *The Ordinary and the Fabulous: An Introduction to Myths, Legends, and Fairy Tales for Teachers and Storytellers*. London: Cambridge University Press, 1969.

Cott, Jonathan, ed. *Beyond the Looking Glass: Extraordinary Works of Fairy Tale and Fantasy*. New York: R.R. Bowker Company, 1973.

Dickens, Charles. *The Magic Fishbone*, illus. F.D. Bedford. London: Frederick Warne & Co. Ltd., 1922.

Farrow, G.E. *The Little Panjandrum's Dodo*, illus. A. Wright. London: Skiffington & Son, Piccadilly, 1899. (Osborne Collection)

_____. *Professor Philanderpan*. London: C. Arthur Pearson Ltd., 1904.

_____. *The Wallypug of Why*. London: Hutchinson, 1895. (Osborne Collection)

Filstrup, Jane Merrill. "Thirst for Enchanted Views in Ruskin's *The King of the Golden River*", *Children's Literature*, 8 (1980), 68-79.

Hood, Tom. *Petsetilla's Posy*, illus. F. Barnard. London: George Routledge & Sons, 1870.

Ingelow, Jean. *Mopsa the Fairy*. London & Toronto: J.M. Dent & Sons, Ltd., 1912.

Keary, A. and E. *Little Wanderlin, and Other Fairy Tales*. London: Macmillan and Co., 1865.

Knatchbull-Hugessen, E.H. *Puss-Cat Mew, and Other Stories for My Children*. New York: Harper & Brothers, 1871. (Library Science Collection, University of Alberta)

Lagerlof, Selma. *The Wonderful Adventures of Nils*, trans. V.S. Howard. Decorations by Harold Heartt. New York: Doubleday, Page & Company, 1912. (Library Science Collection, University of Alberta)

Lüthi, Max. *Once Upon a Time; On the Nature of Fairy Tales*, trans. L. Chadeayne & P. Gottwald. Bloomington: Indiana University Press, 1976.

Opie, Iona and Peter, ed. *The Classic Fairy Tales*. London: Oxford University Press, 1974.

Rossetti, Christina. *Speaking Likenesses*, illus. A. Hughes. London: Macmillan and Co., 1874.

Ruskin, John. *The King of the Golden River or the Black Brothers. A Legend of Stiria*, illus. R. Doyle. Boston: Mayhew & Baker, 1860. (Library Science Collection, University of Alberta)

Sale, Roger. *Fairy Tales and After; From Snow White to E.B. White*. Cambridge, Mass.: Harvard University Press, 1978.

Wilde, Oscar. *The Happy Prince and Other Tales*, illus. W. Crane and J. Hood. London: David Nutt, 1888. (Osborne Collection)

Zipes, Jack. *Breaking the Magic Spell; Radical Theories of Folk and Fairy Tales*. London: Heinemann, 1979.

THE ALLEGORICAL NARRATIVE

Barrie, J.M. *Peter and Wendy*, illus. F.D. Bedford. London: Hodder & Stoughton, 1911. (Osborne Collection)

Burnett, Frances Hodgson. *The Secret Garden*. New York: Charles Scribner's Sons, 1911.

Fletcher, Angus. *Allegory; The Theory of a Symbolic Mode*. Ithaca: Cornell University Press, 1964.

Frye, Northrop. *Anatomy of Criticism; Four Essays*. Princeton: Princeton University Press, 1957.

Green, Martin. "The Charm of Peter Pan", *Children's Literature*, 9 (1981), 19-27.

Kingsley, Charles. *The Water-Babies: A Fairy Tale for a Land-Baby*, illus. J. Noel Patton. London and Cambridge: Macmillan and Co., 1863. (Osborne Collection)

Koppes, Phyllis Bixler. "Tradition and the Individual Talent of Frances Hodgson Burnett: A Generic Analysis of *Little Lord Fauntleroy*, *A Little Princess*, and *The Secret Garden*", *Children's Literature*, 7 (1978), 191-207.

MacDonald, George. *At the Back of the North Wind*. London: Strahan & Co., 1871. (Osborne Collection)

————. *The Princess and Curdie*. London: Chatto & Windus, 1883. (Osborne Collection)

Macleod, Rev. Donald. *Memoir of Norman Macleod, D.D.* Toronto: Belford Brothers, 1876.

Macleod, Rev. Norman. *The Gold Thread. A Story for the Young*, illus. J.D. Watson. Edinburgh: Alex Strahan & Co., 1861. (Osborne Collection)

Mulock, Miss. *The Little Lame Prince and His Traveling Cloak. A Parable for Old and Young*. New York; Grosset & Dunlap, n.d.

Wolff, Robert Lee. *The Golden Key: A Study of the Fiction of George MacDonald*. New Haven: Yale University Press, 1961.

EVANGELICAL WRITING

A.L.O.E. *The Lake of the Woods: A Tale Illustrative of the Twelfth Chapter of Romans*. London: Gall & Inglis, 1867. (Osborne Collection)

————. *Precepts in Practice; or, Stories Illustrating the Proverbs*. New York: Hurst & Company, 1893.

Bready, John. *Dr. Barnardo: Physician, Pioneer, Prophet*. London: George Allen & Unwin, 1932.

Charlesworth, Maria Louisa. *Ministering Children: A Tale*. London: Seeley, Jackson and Halliday, 1857. (Osborne Collection)

Christie's Old Organ; or, "Home Sweet Home". London: The Religious Tract Society, 1875. (Osborne Collection)

Cutt, Margaret Nancy. *Ministering Angels; A Study of Nineteenth-Century Evangelical Writing for Children*. Wormley: Five Owls Press Ltd., 1979.

Giberne, Agnes. *A Lady of England; The Life and Letters of Charlotte Maria Tucker*. London: Hodder and Stoughton, 1895.

Little Meg's Children. London: The Religious Tract Society, 1868. (Osborne Collection)

THE CHILDREN'S NOVEL

The Bairns; or, Janet's Love and Service. A Story from Canada. London: Hodder and Stoughton, 1883.

Battiscombe, Georgina and Marghanita Laski, ed. *A Chaplet for Charlotte Yonge*. London: The Cresset Press, 1965.

Bell, Anthea. *E. Nesbit. A Bodley Head Monograph*. London: The Bodley Head, 1960.

Burnett, Frances Hodgson. *Little Lord Fauntleroy*. New York: Charles Scribner's Sons, 1886. (Library Science Collection, University of Alberta)

Coleridge, Christabel. *Charlotte Mary Yonge; Her Life and Letters*. London: Macmillan, 1903.

Coolidge, Susan. *What Katy Did. A Story*, illus. A. Ledyard. Boston: Roberts Brothers, 1886. (Library Science Collection, University of Alberta)

The Daisy Chain; or, Aspirations. A Family Chronicle. London: John W. Parker & Son, 1856. (Osborne Collection)

Dodge, Mary Mapes. *Hans Brinker; or, the Silver Skates. A Story of Life in Holland*. New York: Scribner, Armstrong and Company, 1876. (Library Science Collection, University of Alberta)

Ewing, Juliana Horatia. *The Ewing Omnibus*. London: Oxford University Press, 1935.

————. *Six to Sixteen. A Story for Girls*, illus. Helen Paterson. Boston: Roberts Brothers, 1886. (Library Science Collection, University of Alberta)

H.H. *Nelly's Silver Mine. A Story of Colorado Life*. Boston: Little, Brown, & Company, 1906.

Laski, Marghanita. *Mrs. Ewing, Mrs. Molesworth and Mrs. Hodgson Burnett*. London: Arthur Barker, Ltd., 1958.

————, ed. *Victorian Tales for Girls*. London: The Pilot Press, 1947.

Nesbit, E. *Five Children and It*. London: T. Fisher Unwin, 1902. (Osborne Collection)

Odell, Ruth. *Helen Hunt Jackson*. New York: D. Appleton-Century Company, 1939.

Romanes, Ethel. *Charlotte Mary Yonge. An Appreciation*. London: A.R. Mowbray, 1908.

Thwaite, Ann. *Waiting for the Party; the Life of Frances Hodgson Burnett 1849-1924*. New York: Charles Scribner's Sons, 1974.

Wright, Catherine Morris. *Lady of the Silver Skates*. Jamestown, R.I.: Clingstone Press, 1979.

NURSERY FICTION

Bell, Enid Moberly. *Flora Shaw*. London: Constable, 1947.

Grahame, Kenneth. *Dream Days*, illus. Maxfield Parrish. London: John Lane, The Bodley Head, 1902. (Library Science Collection, University of Alberta)

————. *The Golden Age*, illus. Maxfield Parrish. London: John Lane, The Bodley Head, 1900. (Library Science Collection, University of Alberta)

Green, Roger Lancelyn. *Mrs Molesworth*. A Bodley Head Monograph. London: The Bodley Head, 1961.

Keary, Annie. *Father Phim*. London: Frederick Warne & Co, 1879. (Osborne Collection)

Molesworth, Mrs *"Carrots": Just A Little Boy And Other Stories*, illus. Walter Crane. New York: Macmillan, 1899. (Library Science Collection, University of Alberta)

Shaw, Flora I. *Castle Blair: A Story of Youthful Days*. Boston: Roberts Brothers, 1879. (Library Science Collection, University of Alberta)

SCHOOL STORIES

Beresford, G.C. *Schooldays with Kipling*. New York: G.P. Putnam's Sons, 1936.

Brazil, Angela. "How Kathsie Scored" in *The Rose Book for Girls*, ed. Mrs Herbert Strang. London: Hodder & Stoughton, 1915.

————. *The Third Class at Miss Kaye's: A School Story*, illus. Arthur Dixon. London: Blackie and Son Limited, 1909. (Library Science Collection, University of Alberta)

Connor, Ralph. *Glengarry School Days; A Story of Early Days in Glengarry*. Toronto: The Westminster Co, Limited, 1902.

Croft-Cooke, Rupert. *Rudyard Kipling*. London: Home & Van Thal Ltd, 1948.

Farrar, Frederick W. *Eric; or, Little by Little. A Tale of Roslyn School*, illus. Gordon Browne. Chicago: A.C. McClurg & Co, 1901. (Library Science Collection, University of Alberta)

————. *General Aims of the Teacher*. London: Pitt Press, 1883.

Freeman, Gillian. *The Schoolgirl Ethic; The Life and Work of Angela Brazil*. London: Allen Lane, 1976.

Greene, Graham. *A Sort of Life*. London: The Bodley Head, 1971.

Kipling, Rudyard. *Stalky & Co* London: Macmillan, 1899. (Osborne Collection)

Kipling, Rudyard. *Stalky & Co* London: Macmillan, 1899. (Osborne Collection)

Mangan, J.A. *Athleticism in the Victorian and Edwardian Public School; The Emergence and Consolidation of an Educational Ideology*. Cambridge: Cambridge University Press, 1981.

Newsome, David. *Godliness and Good Learning; Four Studies on a Victorian Ideal*. London: John Murray, 1961.

Page, Norman. "Kipling's World of Men", *Ariel*, 10 (1979), 81-93.

Tom Brown's School Days by an Old Boy, illus. A. Hughes and S. Prior Hall. London: Macmillan, 1869. (Osborne Collection)

Webster, Jean. *Daddy-Long-Legs*. New York: The Century Co, 1912.

Wilson, Edmund. "The Kipling That Nobody Read" in *Kipling's Mind and Art*, ed. A. Rutherford. Edinburgh: Oliver & Boyd, 1964.

STORIES OF ADVENTURE

Aldrich, Thomas Bailey. *The Story of a Bad Boy.* Boston and New York: Houghton Mifflin and Company, 1900. (Library Science Collection, University of Alberta)

Alger, Horatio Jr *Ragged Dick; or, Street Life in New York With the Boot-Blacks.* Philadelphia: The John C. Winston Co, n.d. (Library Science Collection, University of Alberta)

Ballantyne, R.M. *The Coral Island; A Tale of the Pacific Ocean.* London: Blackie & Son, 1902. (Library Science Collection, University of Alberta)

———. *The Dog Crusoe and His Master; A Story of Adventure in the Western Prairies.* London: Blackie and Son Limited, n.d.

Colvin, Sidney, ed. *The Letters of Robert Louis Stevenson To His Family and Friends.* London: Methuen and Co, 1909.

Dartt, Captain Robert L. *G.A. Henty. A Bibliography.* Cedar Grove, N.J.: Dar-Web, Inc, 1971.

DeMille, James. *The "B.O.W.C."; A Book for Boys.* Boston: Lee and Shepard Publishers, 1869. (Thomas Fisher Rare Book Collection, University of Toronto)

Duncan, Norman. *The Adventures of Billy Topsail.* New York: Fleming H. Revell Co, 1906.

Haggard, H. Rider. *King Solomon's Mines.* London: Cassell & Company Ltd, 1885. (Osborne Collection)

Henty, G.A. *With Wolfe in Canada; or, The Winning of a Continent,* illus. Gordon Browne. New York: Scribner and Welford, n.d. (Library Science Collection, University of Alberta)

Marchant, Bessie. "Just Pluck" in *All Girls' Story Book.* London: Thomas Nelson and Sons, Ltd, 1924.

Reid, Elizabeth. *Captain Mayne Reid, His Life and Adventures.* London: Greening & Co, Ltd, 1900.

Reid, Captain Mayne. *Ran Away to Sea; An Autobiography for Boys.* A new edition with a memoir by R.H. Stoddard. New York: John W. Lovell Company, 1885. (Library Science Collection, University of Alberta)

Stevenson, Robert Louis. *Treasure Island,* illus. Wal Paget. New York: Charles Scribner's Sons, 1920. (Library Science Collection, University of Alberta)

Traill, Catharine Parr. *Canadian Crusoes. A Tale of the Rice Lake Plains.* Illustrated by Harvey, New York: C.S. Francis & Co, 1853.

Young, Egerton R. *Winter Adventures of Three Boys In the Great Lone Land.* New York: Eaton & Mains, 1899.

SHILLING SHOCKERS AND PENNY DREADFULS

Birkhead, Edith. *The Tale of Terror; A Study of the Gothic Romance.* London: Constable & Co, 1921.

Broad-Arrow Jack. London: "Best for Boys" Publishing Co, *c.* 1890. (Osborne Collection)

Dick Lightheart, the Scapegrace of London. Beautifully illustrated. London: Harkaway House, *c.* 1895. (Osborne Collection)

Haining, Peter, ed. *The Shilling Shockers; Stories of Terror from the Gothic Bluebooks.* London: Victor Gollancz, 1978.

James, Louis. *Fiction for the Working Man 1830-1850; A Study of the Literature Produced for the Working Classes in Early Victorian Urban England.* London: Oxford University Press, 1963.

Orczy, Baroness Emmuska. *Lady Molly of Scotland Yard.* London: Cassell and Company, Ltd, 1926.

———. *Links in the Chain of Life.* London: Hutchinson, 1947.

The Penny Library. London: F. Farrah, 1872.

The Shilling Readable Novels. London: C.H. Clarke, 1862.

St. John, Percy Bolingbroke. *The Blue Dwarf; A Tale of Love, Mystery, and Crime.* London: Hogarth House, Bouverie Street, *c.* 1880. (Osborne Collection)

Slung, Michele B., ed. *Crime on her Mind; Fifteen Stories of Female Sleuths from the Victorian Era to the Forties.* New York: Pantheon Books, 1975.

Summers, Montague. *The Gothic Quest; A History of the Gothic Novel.* New York: Russell & Russell, Inc, 1938; rpt. 1964.

Turner, E.S. *Boys will be Boys.* London: Michael Joseph, 1948.

Wells, H.G. *Ann Veronica; A Modern Love Story.* New York: Boni and Liveright, n.d.

THE ANIMAL STORY

Blount, Margaret. *Animal Land; The Creatures of Children's Fiction*. London: Hutchinson & Co, 1974.

Chitty, Susan. *The Woman Who Wrote Black Beauty: A Life of Anna Sewell*. London: Hodder and Stoughton, 1971.

Ford, Mary. "The Wolf as Victim", *Canadian Children's Literature*, (1977), 5-15.

Fraser, W.A. *Mooswa and Others of the Boundaries*, illus. Arthur Heming. Toronto: W. Briggs, 1900.

Gatty, Margaret. *Parables from Nature*. With a memoir by her daughter, Juliana Horatia Ewing. London: George Bell and Sons, 1891. (Library Science Collection, University of Alberta)

Harris, Joel Chandler. *Uncle Remus, His Songs and His Sayings*, illus. A.B. Frost. New York: D. Appleton and Company, 1896. (Library Science Collection, University of Alberta)

Harris, Julia Collier. *The Life and Letters of Joel Chandler Harris*. Boston: Houghton Mifflin Company, 1918.

Morley, Patricia, ed. *Selected Stories of Ernest Thompson Seton*. Ottawa: University of Ottawa Press, 1977.

Roberts, Charles G.D. *The Kindred of the Wild; A Book of Animal Life*, illus. C.L. Bull. Boston: L.C. Page & Company, 1902.

Saunders, Marshall. *Beautiful Joe; The Autobiography of a Dog*. London: Jarrold & Sons, 1894.

Sewell, Anna. *Black Beauty His Grooms and Companions. The Autobiography of a Horse. Translated from the Original Equine*. London: Jarrold and Sons, 1877. (Osborne Collection)

Seton, Ernest Thompson. *Wild Animals I have Known*. Toronto: Morang, 1900.

Whitaker, Muriel, "Tales of the Wilderness: The Canadian Animal Story", *Canadian Children's Literature*, 1 (1975), 38-46.

CHILDREN'S PERIODICALS

Barker, Mrs Sale, ed. *Little Wide-Awake. An Illustrated Magazine for Good Children*. London: George Routledge and Sons, 1882. (Library Science Collection, University of Alberta)

The Boy's Own Volume of Fact, Fiction, History, and Adventure. Edited by the Publisher. London: S.O. Beeton, 1863. (Library Science Collection, University of Alberta)

The Child's Own Magazine. London: Sunday School Union, 1875. (Library Science Collection, University of Alberta)

Chums. London: Cassell & Company, 1918. (Library Science Collection, University of Alberta)

Clarke, J. Erskine, ed. *Chatterbox*. Boston: Estes and Lauriat, 1883, 1895. (Library Science Collection, University of Alberta)

Dodge, Mary Mapes, ed. *St Nicholas: An Illustrated Magazine for Young Folks*. New York: The Century Co, 1881. (Library Science Collection, University of Alberta)

Egoff, Sheila. *Children's Periodicals of the Nineteenth Century: A Survey and Bibliography*. London: Library Association, 1951.

Gatty, Mrs Alfred, ed. *Aunt Judy's Magazine For Young People*. London: Bell and Daldy, 1866. (Library Science Collection, University of Alberta)

Howard, Alice B. *Mary Mapes Dodge of St Nicholas*. New York: Julian Messner, Inc, 1943.

Klickmann, Flora, ed. *The Girl's Own Annual*. London: 4 Bouverie Street, Fleet Street, 1923. (Library Science Collection, University of Alberta)

CHILDREN'S POETRY

Battiscombe, Georgina. *Christina Rossetti; A Divided Life*. London: Constable, 1981.

Belloc, Hilaire. *The Bad Child's Book of Beasts*. London: Gerald Duckworth & Co, Ltd, 1896.

————. *Cautionary Tales for Children. Designed for the Admonition of Children between the Ages of Eight and Fourteen Years*. Pictures by B.T.B. (Lord Ian B.G.T. Blackwood). London: Eveleigh Nash, 1908. (Osborne Collection)

Carman, Bliss. *James Whitcomb Riley. An Essay*. New York: Privately printed for George D. Smith, 1922.

Carroll, Lewis. *Alice's Adventures in Wonderland*. With 42 illustrations by John Tenniel. London: Macmillan and Co, 1866. (Osborne Collection)

———. *Through the Looking-Glass, and What Alice Found There*. With 50 illustrations by John Tenniel. London: Macmillan & Co, 1873. (Osborne Collection)

Clark, Leonard. *Walter de la Mare*. A Bodley Head Monograph. London: The Bodley Head, 1960.

Cooper, Lettice. *Robert Louis Stevenson*. London: Arthur Barker Limited, 1947.

de la Mare, Walter, ed. *Come Hither; A Collection of Rhymes and Poems for the Young of All Ages*. New York: Alfred A. Knopf, 1923.

———. *Peacock Pie: A Book of Rhymes*. With embellishments by C. Lovat Fraser. London: Constable & Company, Ltd, 1924. (Osborne Collection)

———, ed. *Tom Tiddler's Ground; A Book of Poetry for Children*. London: The Bodley Head, 1931.

Farjeon, Eleanor. *More Nursery Rhymes of London Town*, illus. Macdonald Gill. London: Duckworth & Co, 1917.

———. *Nursery Rhymes of London Town*, illus. Macdonald Gill. London: Gerald Duckworth & Co, 1916.

Field, Eugene. *Poems of Childhood*, illus. Maxfield Parrish. New York: Charles Scribner's Sons, 1904.

Fyleman, Rose. *The Fairy Green*. London: Methuen & Co Ltd, 1919.

An Illustrated Comic Alphabet. Designed by Amelia Frances Howard-Gibbon. 1859. MS. (Osborne Collection)

Lear, Edward. *Laughable Lyrics: A Fourth Book of Nonsense Poems, Songs, Botany, Music &.* London: Robert John Bush, 1877.

Milne, Alan Alexander. *It's Too Late Now: The Autobiography of a Writer*. London: Methuen, 1939.

———. *When We Were Very Young*. New York: E.P. Dutton & Co, 1924.

Mitchell, Minnie Bell. *Hoosier Boy: James Whitcomb Riley*. Indianapolis: The Bobbs-Merrill Co, 1942.

Nesbitt, Elizabeth. *Howard Pyle*. A Bodley Head Monograph. London: The Bodley Head, 1966.

Opie, Iona and Peter, ed. *The Oxford Book of Children's Verse*. Oxford: Clarendon Press, 1973.

Packer, Lona Mosk. *Christina Rossetti*. Berkeley: University of California Press, 1963.

Pyle, Howard. *Pepper & Salt; or, Seasoning for Young Folk*. New York: Harper and Brothers, 1886. (Library Science Collection, University of Alberta)

Ramal, Walter. *Songs of Childhood*. London: Longmans, Green, and Co, 1902. (Osborne Collection)

Richards, Laura E. *Tirra Lirra: Rhymes Old and New*. Boston & Toronto: Little, Brown, and Company, 1955.

Riley, James Whitcomb. *The Best Loved Poems of J.W. Riley*. New York: Blue Ribbon Books, n.d.

———. *The Book of Joyous Children*, illus. J.W. Vawter. New York: Charles Scribner's Sons, 1902. (Library Science Collection, University of Alberta)

Rossetti, Christina. *Sing-Song. A Nursery Rhyme Book*, illus. A. Hughes. London: George Routledge & Sons, 1872. (Osborne Collection)

Stevenson, Robert Louis. *A Child's Garden of Verses*, illus. Jessie Wilcox Smith. New York: Charles Scribner's Sons, 1905. (Library Science Collection, University of Alberta)

INDEX